Teaching Singing in the

Landscapes: the Arts, Aesthetics, and Education

SCOPE

This series aims to provide conceptual and empirical research in arts education, (including music, visual arts, drama, dance, media, and poetry), in a variety of areas related to the post-modern paradigm shift. The changing cultural, historical, and political contexts of arts education are recognized to be central to learning, experience, and knowledge. The books in this series present theories and methodological approaches used in arts education research as well as related disciplines – including philosophy, sociology, anthropology and psychology of arts education.

For further volumes:
http://www.springer.com/series/6199

Scott D. Harrison • Jessica O'Bryan
Editors

Teaching Singing in the 21st Century

🐎 Springer

Editors
Scott D. Harrison
Jessica O'Bryan
Queensland Conservatorium
Griffith University
South Brisbane
QLD, Australia

ISSN 1573-4528   ISSN 2214-0069 (electronic)
ISBN 978-94-024-0638-2   ISBN 978-94-017-8851-9 (eBook)
DOI 10.1007/978-94-017-8851-9
Springer Dordrecht Heidelberg New York London

Springer is part of Springer Science+Business Media (www.springer.com)

Contents

1 Prelude: Positioning Singing Pedagogy
   in the Twenty-First Century... 1
   Jessica O'Bryan and Scott D. Harrison

Part I Overview

2 Singing Pedagogy in the Twenty-First Century:
   A Look Toward the Future... 13
   Scott McCoy

3 Habits of the Mind, Hand and Heart: Approaches
   to Classical Singing Training... 21
   Jessica O'Bryan

4 Teaching Popular Music Styles 35
   Kim Chandler

5 A Brief Overview of Approaches to Teaching
   the Music Theatre Song... 53
   Jeannette L. LoVetri, Mary Saunders-Barton, and Edrie Means Weekly

Part II Singing, the Body and the Mind

6 Vocal Health and Singing Pedagogy:
   Considerations from Biology and Motor Learning 69
   Douglas F. Roth and Katherine Verdolini Abbott

7 The Role of the Speech and Language Therapist – Speech
   Pathologist – In the Modern Singing Studio...................................... 91
   Ron Morris

8 The Extra-Normal Voice: EVT in Singing 109
   Michael Edward Edgerton

9   Registers Defined Through Visual Feedback... 133
    Donald Gray Miller

10 Body Mapping: Enhancing Voice Performance
    Through Somatic Pedagogy 143
    Heather J. Buchanan

11 Vocal Pedagogy and the Feldenkrais Method..................................... 175
    Stephen J. Grant

12 Perception, Evaluation and Communication of Singing Voices.......... 187
    Helen F. Mitchell

13 The Teacher-Student Relationship in One-to-One
    Singing Lessons: An Investigation of Personality
    and Adult Attachment... 201
    Sofia Serra-Dawa

14 Negotiating an 'Opera Singer Identity' 221
    Jane Oakland

Part III   Approaches to Style

15 Style and Ornamentation in Classical and Bel Canto Arias 237
    Martha Elliott

16 Handel and the Voice Practitioner: Perspectives
    on Performance Practice and Higher Education Pedagogy 263
    Paul McMahon

17 Contemporary Vocal Artistry in Popular Culture Musics:
    Perceptions, Observations and Lived Experiences 287
    Diane Hughes

18 Pathways for Teaching Vocal Jazz Improvisation 303
    Wendy Hargreaves

19 Voice in Worship: The Contemporary Worship Singer....................... 319
    Daniel K. Robinson

20 Take My Hand: Teaching the Gospel Singer
    in the Applied Voice Studio.. 335
    Trineice Robinson-Martin

Part IV   The Training Ground

21 The Conservatorium Environment: Reflections
    on the Tertiary Vocal Setting Past and Present 353
    Margaret Schindler

**22 More than Just Style: A Profile of Professional
     Contemporary Gig Singers** 367
     Irene Bartlett

23 Developing a Tertiary Course in Music Theatre 383
     Paul Sabey

24 Training the Singing Researcher 399
     Scott D. Harrison

25 Postlude: The Future of Singing Pedagogy 411
     Scott D. Harrison and Jessica O'Bryan

Author Details and Affiliations

Irene Bartlett Queensland Conservatorium, Griffith University, Brisbane, QLD, Australia

Heather J. Buchanan John J. Cali School of Music, Montclair State University, Upper Montclair, NJ, USA

Kim Chandler Popular Music Pathway, Leeds College of Music, Leeds, UK

Michael Edward Edgerton The Cultural Centre, Department of Music, University of Malaya, Kuala Lumpur, Malaysia

Martha Elliott Department of Music, Princeton University, Princeton, NJ, USA

Stephen J. Grant Vocal Department, Melbourne Conservatorium of Music, University of Melbourne, Melbourne, VIC, Australia

Wendy Hargreaves Queensland Conservatorium, Griffith University, Brisbane, QLD, Australia

Scott D. Harrison Queensland Conservatorium, Griffith University, South Brisbane, QLD, Australia

Diane Hughes Media, Music, Communication and Cultural Studies, Macquarie University, Sydney, NSW, Australia

Jeannette L. LoVetri The Voice Workshop, New York, NY, USA

Scott McCoy Swank Voice Research Laboratory, School of Music, The Ohio State University, Columbus, OH, USA

Paul McMahon School of Music, Research School of Humanities and the Arts, College of Arts and Social Sciences, Australian National University, Canberra, ACT, Australia

Donald Gray Miller Groningen Voice Research, Groningen, The Netherlands

Helen F. Mitchell Sydney Conservatorium of Music, University of Sydney, Sydney, NSW, Australia

Ron Morris The Brisbane Speech and Hearing Clinic, Brisbane, QLD, Australia

Queensland Conservatorium Griffith University, Brisbane, QLD, Australia

Jane Oakland Psychology Department, Glasgow Caledonian University, Glasgow, Scotland, UK

Jessica O'Bryan Queensland Conservatorium, Griffith University, South Brisbane, QLD, Australia

Daniel K. Robinson Academic Department, Djarts Contemporary Voice Studio, Brisbane, QLD, Australia

Trineice Robinson-Martin Academic/Education Division, Soul Ingredients® Voice Studio, Lawrenceville, NJ, USA

Douglas F. Roth Voice and Swallowing Center, Department of Otolaryngology, Tufts Medical Center, Boston, MA, USA

School of Medicine, Tufts University, Boston, MA, USA

Paul Sabey Queensland Conservatorium, Griffith University, Brisbane, QLD, Australia

Mary Saunders-Barton Departments of Music and Theatre, Pennsylvania State University, University Park, PA, USA

Margaret Schindler Queensland Conservatorium, Griffith University, Brisbane, QLD, Australia

Sofia Serra-Dawa Escola das Artes, Research Center for Science and Technology in Art, Portuguese Catholic University, Porto, Portugal

Katherine Verdolini Abbott Department of Communication Science and Disorders, Otolaryngology, McGowan Institute for Regenerative Medicine, University of Pittsburgh, Pittsburgh, PA, USA

Center for the Neural Basis of Cognition, Carnegie-Mellon University and University of Pittsburgh, Pittsburgh, PA, USA

Edrie Means Weekly Shenandoah Conservatory, CCM Vocal Pedagogy Institute, Winchester, VA, USA

Biographies

Editors

Scott D. Harrison is Professor and Director of the Queensland Conservatorium, Griffith University. A graduate of Queensland Conservatorium and the University of Queensland, Professor Harrison has experience in teaching singing and music in primary, secondary, and tertiary environments. His performance interests and experience include opera and music theatre as both singer and musical director. Over the past 25 years, he has performed in more than 30 productions. His teaching areas focus on teacher education, research design, and gender. His major research areas are music and wellbeing, vocal education, music teacher education, and masculinities and music. He has published extensively in these fields and is author or editor of *Research and Research Education in Music Performance and Pedagogy* (2013), *Perspectives on Males and Singing* (2012), *Perspectives on Teaching Singing* (2010), *Male Voices: Stories of Boys Learning through Making Music* (2009), and *Masculinities and Music* (2008). Scott Harrison is a past President of the Australian National Association of Teachers of Singing and an Australian National Teaching Fellow.

Jessica O'Bryan, soprano, teaches singing in the Musical Theatre program at the Queensland Conservatorium Griffith University and runs a busy private practice teaching crossover singing in musical theatre, classical, jazz, and pop. She lectures on research methods, music history, vocal health, and audition techniques, and is a Senior Research Assistant at the Queensland Conservatorium. Currently completing doctoral studies exploring participant values, beliefs, and practices of tertiary classical voice training at the University of Queensland, she has published in the field of singing pedagogy and artistic practice. She is past Vice President of ANATS Queensland Chapter; past Editor of the ANATS national newsletter *Voice of ANATS*; was previously President of aMuse, and was for 6 years Head of Voice at Wesley College. A graduate of The University of Melbourne and Monash University, Jessica O'Bryan is the recipient of a number of awards and scholarships, including the Mona McCaughey Award, the Dame Nellie Melba Award, and three-time recipient of the Dame Mabel Kent Scholarship from Melbourne University. She has sung in jazz and rock bands and has appeared as a principal artist with Victorian Opera and Opera Queensland.

Contributing Authors

Irene Bartlett Ph.D., is Coordinator of Jazz/Contemporary Vocal Studies and Lecturer in Vocal Pedagogy at the Queensland Conservatorium, Griffith University, where her teaching and research centres on the development of technique, vocal health, and performance longevity for singers of contemporary vocal styles. She is in demand for conference and symposia and is a past Australian Master Teacher for the Australian National Association of Teachers of Singing. In both national and international contexts, Irene's students work as professional contemporary gig singers in the popular music industry and in nationally touring music theatre productions; many are recipients of prestigious industry and academic awards. In addition to her pedagogical work, Irene Bartlett has an enduring career as a professional contemporary vocalist and is in demand for both corporate, private, and concert performances.

Heather J. Buchanan is Professor of Music and Director of Choral Activities at Montclair State University, New Jersey, USA. A licensed Andover Educator, Heather Buchanan has specialized in the teaching of body mapping (BMG) and somatic pedagogy to musicians for over a decade. Her BMG research was also the first published in this field. Dr. Buchanan holds degrees from the Queensland Conservatorium, Griffith University (Australia), Westminster Choir College of Rider University (USA), and a Ph.D. from the University of New England (Australia). Her publications include the DVD Evoking Sound: Body Mapping & Gesture Fundamentals, octavos in the Evoking Sound Choral Series (GIA), and co-editing the landmark GIA choral series *Teaching Music through Performance in Choir*. A vibrant teacher, dynamic performer, and passionate musicians' health advocate, Heather Buchanan is in demand as a guest conductor and clinician in the USA and abroad.

Kim Chandler is one of the UK's leading session singers and contemporary vocal coaches. She runs a busy private studio in West London where she coaches an elite clientele of professional singers, established artists, artists in development and other vocal coaches. She also runs a successful recording studio with her producer husband, working with a team of the UK's top session singers (www.virtualvocals.com). Kim has coached many high-profile artists and regularly presents at national and international voice conferences. She became a Director of the British Voice Association in 2008 and President from 2012 to 2013. Kim is a Principal Lecturer at Leeds College of Music and was also a Senior Lecturer at the London College of Music; the institution from where she also holds a master's degree in Performance. She was also the Academic Head of the UK's leading contemporary vocal college

('Vocaltech') for 3 years. Kim Chandler's pioneering "Funky 'n Fun" vocal training series is a favourite of many music institutions and singing teachers and is a popular seller internationally (www.funkynfun.com).

Michael Edward Edgerton is a composer, singer, and teacher. In the last 10 years he became increasingly interested in experimental complex systems and the application of physical and perceptual models. His compositions have received international recognition, including the important German award, the Kompositionspreis der Landeshauptstadt Stuttgart. Michael's music has been performed by Stefan Östersjö, Kairos String Quartet, Ensemble Ars Nova, Matthias Bauer, Stockholm Saxophone Quartet, Gary Verkade, Angela Rademacher, Timo Kinnunen, Works-in-Progress Ensemble, Chatschatur Kanajan, Quartet New Generation, Jeffrey Burns. His research into voice and psychoacoustics is internationally known through performances, journal publications, and a book, *The 21st Century Voice*.

Martha Elliott, author of *Singing in Style: A Guide to Vocal Performance Practices* (Yale: 2006) has been teaching at Princeton University since 1985. Her book has been enthusiastically received throughout the USA and the UK. She has presented talks, workshops, and master classes for NATS, NEMA in the UK, at Brown University, Smith College, and elsewhere around the USA. As a singer, she has performed avant-garde contemporary music, opera, chamber music, and Baroque music with period instruments, and around the world with the New York New Music ensemble Continuum. Recent performances include appearances with the Odessa Philharmonic in the Ukraine, and with the Brentano String Quartet in Princeton. She holds degrees from Princeton University and Juilliard.

Stephen J. Grant holds the positions of Convenor of Voice and Convenor of Early Music at the Melbourne Conservatorium of Music, University of Melbourne. He has taught voice, chamber music, and Feldenkrais both in Australia and abroad for the last 15 years and is currently undertaking research on German Baroque performance practices.

Wendy Hargreaves began her career as a singer touring fulltime in a rock band for 2 years. She then returned to study and completed a degree in music, a graduate diploma of education in music, and a Master of Music at QUT. For the past 20 years she has worked as a singer, composer, and music teacher in Brisbane, Australia. Wendy Hargreaves obtained her doctoral studies at the Queensland Conservatorium Griffith University, investigating the learning needs of improvising jazz vocalists as distinguished from instrumentalists. She is currently undertaking post-doctoral studies at Griffith University.

Diane Hughes is Senior Lecturer in Vocal Studies at Macquarie University, and is the Director of Learning and Teaching for the Department of Media, Music, Communication and Cultural Studies. In 2013, Diane Hughes received a Vice Chancellor's Citation for an outstanding contribution to facilitating student engagement and learning through the design of contemporary and innovative music curricula. She has an extensive background in contemporary popular singing pedagogy, and has been an invited speaker at conferences and seminars. Her work within the industry has involved artist development and recording and her research interests include vocal artistry, vocal pedagogy, vocal recording, vocal performance, and singing in schools; current research projects include career pathways in the new music industries, emotion and voice, and collaborative producing in recording. Research on singing in schools led her to become an advocate for the development of cross-curricula voice studies in school education. Diane Hughes is currently the President of the Australian National Association of Teachers of Singing (ANATS).

Jeannette L. LoVetri is a music theatre expert in New York City. Her students have appeared recently on Broadway as the leads in Shrek, Sunday in the Park With George (both Tony nominees), Jersey Boys and How To Succeed... as well as many other Broadway shows, national tours, and regional productions. Jeannette LoVetri has taught on four continents about the Contemporary Commercial Music styles that are now found in music theatre worldwide including jazz, rock, pop, gospel, rap, and country and traditional "legit". She is Director of The Voice Workshop and teaches Somatic Voicework™, her method, at four universities in the USA. www.thevoiceworkshop.com, www.somaticvoicework.com.

Scott McCoy is Professor of Voice and Pedagogy at The Ohio State University where he is co-director of the Helen Swank Voice Teaching and Research Lab. He has been Professor of Voice and Pedagogy, Director of the Presser Music Center Voice Laboratory, and the Director of Graduate Studies at Westminster Choir College of Rider University. His multimedia voice science and pedagogy textbook, *Your Voice, An Inside View*, is used extensively by colleges and universities throughout the United States and abroad. He is immediate past president and director of the National Intern Program of the National Association of Teachers of Singing (NATS), associate director of the *Journal of Singing* for voice pedagogy, and has also served NATS as Vice President for Workshops, Program Chair for the 2006 and 2008 National Conferences, chair of the Voice Science Advisory Committee, and master teacher for the national Intern Program. Deeply committed to teacher education, Scott McCoy is a founding faculty member in the NYSTA Professional Development Program, teaching classes in voice anatomy and physiology and acoustics and voice analysis. He is a member of the distinguished American Academy of Teachers of Singing.

Enjoying a multi-faceted career incorporating music research, performance, and pedagogy, Dr. **Paul McMahon** is a graduate of Queensland Conservatorium Griffith University (Ph.D. and Graduate Diploma of Music). In 2002, he was awarded a Churchill Fellowship for intensive study of Baroque repertory under Marius van Altena at the Royal Conservatoire, The Hague. Performing regularly as a soloist with symphony orchestras, chamber music groups, and choirs throughout the Asia-Pacific region, Paul McMahon's career highlights include Bach's *Matthäus-Passion* under Roy Goodman, Haydn's *Die Schöpfung* under the late Richard Hickox, Mozart's Great Mass in C Minor under Masaaki Suzuki, and Mozart's Requiem under Manfred Honeck. His extensive discography includes recordings of Renaissance lute-songs, and several significant works of the Baroque and Classical periods, including Handel's *Messiah*, Monteverdi's *L'Orfeo* and Mozart's Requiem. Paul McMahon's research interests include historical performance practice, the role of *affekt* and emotion in music of the Baroque period, and aspects of vocal pedagogy. He is currently a Lecturer in Music at The Australian National University, Canberra.

Operatic bass-baritone **Donald Gray Miller** was professor at the Syracuse University School of Music when he began research on the acoustics and physiology of the singing voice with Harm Schutte in Groningen, The Netherlands. Later in that decade, he settled in Groningen full time, where he and Professor Schutte published a number of articles, earning him a Ph.D. with the publication of Registers in Singing in the year 2000. A product of that research has been the software program VoceVista, providing digital feedback for singing instruction from spectrum analysis and the electroglottograph (EGG). In 2008, he published *Resonance in Singing*, concisely describing the application of the system to analysis of the recorded literature, as well as to live instruction in the voice studio.

Originally from Scotland, **Helen F. Mitchell** graduated from the University of Oxford with an Honours degree in music in 2000. After winning the Northcote Graduate Scholarship, she moved to Australia in 2001 to undertake doctoral studies at the University of Sydney. She completed her Ph.D. in 2005 and subsequently won an Australian Postdoctoral Fellowship at Sydney Conservatorium of Music (SCM), where her research tracked the impact of singing training on the development of the singing voice. She is currently Senior Lecturer at the Sydney Conservatorium of Music, University of Sydney. Her research focuses on music perception, performance and pedagogy, and her current work investigates audiences' perceptions and descriptions of individual performers, by sound alone and through an audio-visual fusion of sensory information.

Ron Morris, speech therapist, audiologist, and counter tenor, graduated from the University of Queensland in 1985 with an honours degree in Speech Therapy and Audiology. It was during that time that he commenced singing studies at the Queensland Conservatorium of Music. He holds a Performer's Certificate from Trinity College, London, and completed a Master of Musical Studies (Vocal Performance). His recently completed Ph.D. evaluated the Accent Method of Breathing in young classical singers, and he is a visiting research fellow and lecturer at the Guildhall School of Music and Drama, London. Ron Morris lectures in vocal pedagogy and vocal health at Queensland Conservatorium Griffith University. He continues to work as a speech therapist and audiologist, working in private practice and in a head and neck surgery unit in a large private hospital in Brisbane. He sings professionally as a soloist, as a member of Queensland Opera Chorus and in St John's Cathedral Choir. Ron Morris is in demand worldwide as a memorably entertaining presenter of lectures and workshops on vocal anatomy and physiology, respiration, and most commonly articulation and tongue function.

Jane Oakland is an experienced professional singer with a special interest in the social psychology of music. Her Ph.D. thesis "'Giving Voice': Exploring Enforced Occupational Change in Opera Choristers" investigated the implications of redundancy on a musical identity for professional opera choristers. Current research interests are the careers of professional musicians. She is a visiting researcher with Royal Northern College of Music in Manchester, UK and Glasgow Caledonian University, Scotland.

Daniel K. Robinson is a freelance artist and educator. In 2011 he completed his Doctor of Musical Arts degree at the Queensland Conservatorium Griffith University. He has served as National Vice President (2009–2011) and National Secretary for the Australian National Association of Teachers of Singing (2006–2011). Daniel Robinson is the principal Singing Voice Specialist for Djarts (www.djarts.com.au) and presents workshops and seminars to church singers across Australia and abroad.

Trineice Robinson-Martin completed her doctorate at Teachers College Columbia University. She holds master degrees in music education and jazz studies from Teachers College and Indiana University-Bloomington, respectively, and a B.A. from San Jose State University. Based on her graduate research, Trineice Robinson-Martin designed Soul Ingredients®, a teaching methodology for developing a singer's musical style/interpretation in African-American folk based music styles (i.e., jazz, gospel, R&B, blues, etc.). As an accomplished performer, teacher, and scholar, Trieneice Robinson-Martin has travelled and taught students from all over the world and lectures worldwide on a variety of Soul Ingredients® topics. She authored and produced "Soul Ingredients®: Gospel Music, Voice Training for the Gospel Soloist," a book and CD, which encompasses her complete method and experience of training, about which more information can be found at www.trineicerobinson.com.

Douglas F. Roth is a tenor, teacher of singing, speech-language pathologist and singing voice specialist. He holds degrees in vocal performance from the University of Cincinnati College-Conservatory of Music and Arizona State University and a master's degree in Speech-Language Pathology from Indiana University. He is a voice clinician and singing voice specialist at the University of Pittsburgh UPMC Voice Center, where he has guided the vocal rehabilitation of amateur and professional singers in various genres ranging from classical, musical theater and jazz to hard rock. Douglas Roth is currently completing his Ph.D. at the University of Pittsburgh under the direction of Professor Katherine Verdolini Abbott, with an emphasis on the cognitive aspects of vocal skill acquisition.

For 23 years **Paul Sabey** was the Director of the Musical Theatre Programme at Mountview Academy of Theatre Arts, London (one of the premiere courses for Musical Theatre training in the world). Whilst studying, his musical 'First Time' was published by Samuel French Ltd and he made his European conducting debut – conducting 'Dido and Aeneas' – at the Nantes Opera House, France, with the European Chamber Orchestra and members from the English National Opera. Paul is in constant demand as a musical director, vocal coach, vocal arranger and regularly gives master classes in Musical Theatre. His work has taken him around the world working with singers, musicians, as an academic and artistic programme advisor and as a musical director, including: Thailand, America, New Zealand, Denmark, Sweden, Amsterdam, Singapore, France, Germany, Malaysia, Italy and Russia. As a musical director, he has directed and vocally arranged over 60 London West End Showcases, countless shows and produced and conducted eight annual Christmas Concerts at St. Pauls, Covent Garden, London. Paul Sabey is Head of Musical Theatre at the Queensland Conservatorium, Griffith University, where his current research interest is examining approaches to assessment in music theatre.

Mary Saunders-Barton Is Head of Voice for Musical Theatre and Voice Pedagogy for Musical Theatre at Penn State University. Mary also maintains a professional voice studio in New York City. Her students have been seen on Broadway in *West Side Story, Hair, Follies, Kinky Boots, Mamma Mia, Wicked, Book of Mormon, Newsies* and *Beautiful*, among others. Mary is frequently invited to present her workshop *Bel Canto/Can Belto* in the USA and Europe. Her DVD tutorial, *Teaching Women to Sing Musical Theatre*, was released in 2007. A second installment, *"What about the Boys?"*, followed in 2014. Mary is a member of the American Academy of Teachers of Singing (AATS).

Margaret Schindler studied at the Queensland Conservatorium before travelling to Belgium, the UK and the USA, where she studied with renowned voice teacher Marlena Malas. She has appeared as soloist with many major orchestras and performing organisations throughout Australia, New Zealand, and Germany in opera, concert, song recital and oratorio. Margaret Schindler is an outstanding interpreter of new music and has premiered and recorded numerous Australian works. She is a member of acclaimed chamber ensemble and Queensland Performing Arts Centre Artists-in-Residence, Southern Cross Soloists, who have a national and international profile. Senior Lecturer in Voice and Head of Vocal Studies at Queensland Conservatorium Griffith University, Margaret Schindler enjoys the creative nexus of teaching and performing: many of her students have enjoyed success in national competitions and are forging singing careers within Australia and abroad. Her soon to be completed doctoral studies focus on the role of the singer-teacher in the tertiary environment. She is a board member of the Australian Voice Association, promoting multidisciplinary activity and research in voice.

Sofia Serra-Dawa is a lecturer and coordinator of Music Education's Masters in the Music Department of the Catholic Portuguese University. She is a member of the Editorial Board of CITAR Journal and researcher at Research Center for Science and Technology in Art (RCSTA) and Research Center in Human Development (RCHD). Sofia graduated from ESMAE, obtaining a Master of Music degree and doctorate on Music Psychology/Singing at the University of Sheffield. She completed a performance master's degree at the Guildhall School of Music and Drama. She has performed roles in opera, oratorio and Lied, winning 2nd prize in the 2005 Tracey Chadwell singing competition and the Jovens Empreendedores XXI.

Katherine Verdolini Abbott is a former singer and teacher of singing, as well as speech-language pathologist specializing in vocal fold injury and recovery. Prior academic appointments were on the faculty in the Department of Speech and Hearing and the Department of Music, The University of Iowa; and in the Department of Otolaryngology, Harvard Medical School. She is currently Professor in the Department of Communication Science and Disorders at the University of Pittsburgh. She also has ties with the National Center for Voice and Speech, directed by Professor Ingo Titze. She has obtained extensive federal funds from the National Institutes of Health for projects relating to vocal health. She has trained numerous masters and doctoral students in clinical voice and voice science.

Edrie Means Weekly, "rock star of vocal crossover", is an active professional singer and recognized expert in training singers in all vocal styles. Her students appear in films, on Broadway, television, tours, *American Idol*, *Kidz Star USA*, on recordings, concerts and opera. Edrie helped create the NATS National Music Theatre Competition. Edrie was Master Teacher for the National Association of Teachers of Singing (NATS) Intern Program in 2013 and is Co-Founder of the Contemporary Commercial Music Vocal Pedagogy Institute at Shenandoah University. Edrie originated roles in works by Glass, Argento and Wallace/Korie (*Kaballah*, Koch Records). She had principal roles with the Kennedy Center, Houston Grand Opera, Washington Opera (*La Rondine*, Decca DVD), Wolf Trap Opera, and Opera of Cairo, to name a few. Her performances are broadcast internationally on NPR/PBS. A leading researcher in functional/healthy vocal production, Edrie has publications in *The Journal of Voice* on teaching the Broadway voice.

Chapter 1
Prelude: Positioning Singing Pedagogy in the Twenty-First Century

Jessica O'Bryan and Scott D. Harrison

Abstract Singing is ubiquitous throughout nearly all world cultures, for many reasons and in a variety of settings. We sing alone and together for joy, love, enlightenment or entertainment; out of grief, or hate, or for emotional and spiritual succour in a musical manifestation of the human spirit. For some singers, training in singing is an inevitable outcome of the desire to represent these sung emotions in the most sublime and flawless manner possible. In European cultures from Christianity onward there exists a documented culture of church singing, stemming from even earlier worship singing of the Jewish faith and other cultures. These cultures undoubtedly had an oral transmission of singing training in the ancient master/apprentice tradition. From the time singing became more public, professional and highly regarded, the need for singing training arose in response to the desire for greater excellence in the performative art. Those cultures in which the history of singing training is written down bring much to bear in the processes of training the modern singer. The aim of this book is not to provide a history of singing training throughout every world culture: it would be disingenuous of us to even try. Instead this volume celebrates the art of singing teaching today across a range of musical styles and cultures, through inquiry in such areas as scientific investigation, cultural research and practitioner expertise. Although we will not be documenting the full history of singing training, the purpose of this chapter is to contextualise the chapters to follow, and therefore a declaration of the 'state of play' is necessary before launching into the volume overall. We begin with an acknowledgement of the medieval European Guilds and the European conservatoire environment before we examine the most relevant and recent documentation regarding singing training. We then conclude the chapter by introducing our contributors.

J. O'Bryan (✉) • S.D. Harrison
Queensland Conservatorium, Griffith University, 140 Grey St,
South Brisbane, 4101 QLD, Australia
e-mail: jessica.obryan@gmail.com; scott.harrison@griffith.edu.au

S.D. Harrison and J. O'Bryan (eds.), *Teaching Singing in the 21st Century*,
Landscapes: the Arts, Aesthetics, and Education 14, DOI 10.1007/978-94-017-8851-9_1,
© Springer Science+Business Media Dordrecht 2014

Keywords Singing pedagogy • Voice science • Conservatoire • Performer/teacher • Master/apprentice

1.1 Where Have We Come From?

1.1.1 The Master-Apprentice Model

The master-apprentice learning and teaching model of predominantly European canonic vocal training developed from the formation of the European Guilds of the late middle ages. These guilds set down strict rules and 'principles for the work of the musician, to cultivate a professional ethic and to provide social relief for infirm members and the families of deceased colleagues' (Brainerd Slocum 1995, 258). From the middle ages until the late nineteenth century, it was normal educational practice for young singers to be apprenticed for up to 12 years to a singing teacher who was responsible for not only their musical and vocal education, but also their moral and physical development. The master was the conduit through which all music knowledge, experience and know-how passed to the student. This musical knowledge included the development of skills in music theory, musicianship and history, stagecraft and performance practice. The master may also have been responsible for the teaching of languages, literacy and numeracy in the young apprentice.

1.1.2 The Conservatoire

As music training developed throughout Europe other types of learning and teaching models emerged, particularly in the Ospedali environments of Naples and Venice in the late sixteenth century, where class and group training became commonplace. Despite this addition to learning and teaching models and a change of environment, the master was still regarded as the preeminent educator for emerging artists. The modern day conservatoire can be said to have emerged from these environments, although it was not until the twentieth century that conservatoires were considered training grounds for adult musicians. The modern conservatoire has taken over much of the role of the master teacher, with studies in musicianship, music literature, aural studies and other classes sitting alongside practical music making courses. At the beginning of the twenty-first century, however, the one-to-one lesson between a master and student is still the primary mode of learning singing for most developing singers in the European canonic tradition, and the conservatoire is normally the environment in which this learning takes place.

1.1.3   A New Pedagogy?

Of course, this tradition does not take into account the proliferation in the twentieth century of a range of musical cultures, styles and techniques, which has forced a rethink of European canonic approaches to singing pedagogy. Each new style–or musical content–requires a unique pedagogy. Singing is now learnt in a variety of environments, and expert singing training is no longer the sole province of the conservatoire. Singers learn to sing at gigs; in recording studios; through imitation of their favourite singers; in church; in group-singing activities; through peer interaction; and in online tutorial environments. The way we teach singing has had to radically change to meet the demands of our students. Nevertheless, the transmission of knowledge remains one that follows the master apprentice tradition. Students of singing seek knowledge from experts in the field, and, arguably, expert singing is still most efficiently learned in a one-to-one environment, regardless of whether it is in a conservatoire, private teaching studio, or on the job with a professional coach.

1.1.4   Performers as Teachers

Singing pedagogy is traditionally and commonly the province of singers with performing experience (Callaghan 2000; Welch et al. 2005). Typical pedagogical strategies employed by singing teachers include the use of visual imagery through verbal instruction, imitation of vocal models and gestural instructions. According to Callinan-Robertson, Mitchell and Kenny,

> Historical singing texts play a critical role in the transmission of pedagogy but it is not always clear how the terminology or singing techniques they describe are interpreted or transmitted to students. In both the singing literature and in practice, singers and pedagogues elicit vocal gestures using figurative language to describe vocal quality and to communicate technical instructions. (2006, 1)

Welch et al. take this premise one step further: 'Singing teachers draw on their personal experiences within an essentially hegemonic oral culture (Callaghan 2000; Potter 1998). Such experiences dominate and differentiate the language of singing pedagogy literature from that found in texts on the science of singing' (Welch et al. 2005, 226).

This language differentiation between singing pedagogy and voice science is an important factor in determining approaches to singing training. Beginning less than 100 years after Gutenberg, some 1,240 treatises and teaching manuals were written between 1517 and 1992 (Singing: A Bibliography 2013), most of which prior to 1855 were based on practitioner experience. An early writer of note was Tosi (c. 1653–1732), a castrato and singing teacher who wrote *Opinioni de'cantori antichi e moderni* (1723) which was translated to English by John Galliard in 1743. In this seminal work, he codified important aesthetic principles, gave practical directions for singers, defended ancient style against the moderns and recommended practices still in use today. For example, he advocated the use of the mirror as a teaching tool: 'let him sometimes sing before a looking glass, not to be enamoured with his own person but to avoid those convulsive motions of the body or face...' (1987, 40). In Tosi's time, the emerging florid musical style, the prevalence of the castrati and the size of the opera houses and orchestras determined the qualities most admired in the human voice. His era admired high voices capable of virtuosic agile florid movement and excellent breath management. Such voices did not carry huge weight or volume, but these characteristics were not necessary in an age where there were few large opera houses or orchestras.

By the early nineteenth century, as large opera houses and orchestras became commonplace, voices needed to carry sound further, to be larger in size and louder in volume. This change in size and weight of the voice reduced the singer's capacity to make florid vocal embellishments. Singing techniques and pedagogy thus changed in response to the change in musical and societal demands (see Potter 1998, 2000), and from the early nineteenth century observable changes to singing pedagogy are evident in the literature.

1.1.5   Voice Science – A Revolution?

The advent of research in voice physiology and acoustics has revolutionised singing pedagogy, and the greatest shift in the understanding and teaching of singing technique has occurred in the last 30 years, although Manuel Garcia began the revolution in 1840. Garcia (1805–1906), after much experimentation, invented the laryngoscope (1855) and published a number of works about the vocal mechanism, which paved the way for a more scientifically rigorous approach to singing pedagogy.

Research in singing, voice physiology and acoustics has substantially increased our knowledge about how the human voice is shaped by improving our knowledge of physiology; increasing our understanding of acoustical properties affecting vocal tone and resonance; and developing electronic teaching aids, real-time feedback systems, computer programs and so on to assist in the voice teaching studio. The research in voice sciences can identify biological and acoustical attributes of the vocal mechanism but it still cannot tell one how to teach. As Fields noted in 1947, 'the laboratory research worker is often far removed in his thinking from the teaching practices of the classroom or studio. Conversely, the singing teacher must often handle unpredictable personality problems with intuitive insight and improvised instructional techniques that are not readily amenable to experimental analysis' (1947, 15). Nevertheless, of the many twentieth century landmark voice science researchers, William Vennard, author of *Singing: The mechanism and the technic* (1967) was a pioneer in voice science and singing pedagogy. He was instrumental in fostering collaborative efforts between singers, physicists, psychologists and voice scientists, paving the way for today's landmark voice science researchers who include Ingo Titze (1994), Johann Sundberg (1987), Robert Sataloff (2005), Leon Thurmann and Graham Welch (2000), and many others. Voice science research has even extended into the neurological sciences, where investigators are examining the effects of singing on physical and neurological development.

Knowledge about singing pedagogy and physiology has grown exponentially as our capacity to investigate the vocal mechanism has improved. Landmark practitioner researchers include: Oren Brown (1997), Cornelius Reid (1975), Richard Miller (1983, 1996, 2004), Scott McCoy (2004), Elizabeth Blades-Zeller (2003), Meribeth Bunch (1995), and Jean Callaghan (2000), whose research and writings cover topics from the scientific explanations of vocal function to the description of pedagogical techniques designed to assist singing teachers in their craft. In these works these researcher-practitioners take the findings from rigorous scientific investigation and applies them to pedagogical approaches to singing teaching. A recent addition to the literature in classical singing was Janice Chapman's volume *Singing and Teaching Singing* (2006, revised 2011). In addition to the usual anatomical and acoustical chapters, Chapman discusses her philosophy of teaching, and explores a range of teaching and learning concepts, offering chapters on the multi-disciplinary nature of teaching singing. Her teaching philosophy combines three main approaches under the following headings: holistic, physiological and incremental. She points out that 'all good teaching has a philosophy that underpins its practice' (2) and that 'teaching is a creative process, never static, and must be fed constantly by the teacher/student interaction and growth' (14). What makes Chapman's treatise distinct from many others is her in-depth exploration of the learning and teaching relationship between singer and teacher, and her strong belief that singing teachers need to be 'open to the continual growth of their knowledge base to ensure that their teaching remains creative' (14). As Vennard warns, the scientist cannot be present in the singing studio, and a positive learning and teaching relationship between student and teacher remains arguably the most important factor in the creation of a successful singer.

1.2 Where Are We Now?

The physiology of the singing voice has not changed since those first treatises 500 years ago, although musical styles have markedly changed. Musicological theories and 'even those which are genuinely scientific cannot tell us exactly how, when and why singing began, and still less what it was and what it sounded like' (Potter and Sorrell 2012, 33). Similarly, we are not aware of the precise sound of the singing voice resulting from the use of these early teaching methods. Research in voice science has allowed us to measure the voice in increasing detail from the mirror to the stroboscope, yet what has remained largely undocumented are the environment, the culture, and the society in which vocal and musical preferences exist, and the bearing these influences have on the sound qualities of the voice and the techniques used to develop them.

Singing teaching approaches have been entrenched in centuries old practices that are somewhat resistant to change, yet change is the only means by which knowledge and practices are improved. It is therefore exciting to note that it is in volumes such as this where we find robust discussion, research and investigation in singing pedagogy, where we find practitioners and researchers valuing diverse musical styles and cultures and embracing an attitude of discovery. While we value and honour the great tradition of the European canon and the many artist-practitioners who have documented their teaching practices in centuries past, we are, in the twenty-first century making great strides in the improving the knowledge, understanding and appreciation of diverse music styles from a range of cultures, and applying new pedagogical knowledge for the benefit of our students. We are no longer stuck in a rut of complacency and assumption that one way to learn singing is the best way. We research new approaches to pedagogy designed for many musical styles. We base our knowledge on more than a century of scientific inquiry of the vocal mechanism. And we value the age-old art of apprenticeship: learning by showing, doing, and becoming.

1.3   What Does the Future Hold?

This volume brings together leading researchers in voice science and singing pedagogy alongside the innovative work of emerging academics and expert practitioners, in one publication. The volume opens with approaches to singing teaching research up to this point, and ends with implications for training singing researchers of the future. Aligned with the work of the Eighth International Congress of Voice Teachers, held in Brisbane, Australia in 2013 the initial chapters explore approaches to three styles: Classical, Musical Theatre and Contemporary Commercial Music, though some contributors question the use of the latter term. The closing chapters return to these three broad styles, but with a more practical viewpoint for training, and should be viewed as a manual for use in the studio rather than a reference book in the library. The remaining chapters follow the tradition of other teaching manuals of recent times, dealing with matters of Breathing and Support; the Vocal Mechanism, Resonance; Registration; and Articulation. There is an emphasis on the whole body with chapters on Feldenkrais and Body-mapping. Questions of identity, perception and personality are also addressed. Perhaps unusually, the chapters at the centre of the volume deal with a vast array of stylistic approaches. These styles are typically separated out into stand-alone volumes in other publications. The singing teacher of the twenty-first century has to be adaptable: it is increasingly rare that singers and singing teachers specialise. Diversity is the buzzword of the century and the volume does not need to be slavishly read from cover to cover – a linear reading will not provide any more illumination than dipping into the collection like a box of liquorish all-sorts, selecting those chapters that are pertinent for the readers' context. While the intended readership is singing teachers, there is much here for classroom music teachers, choral directors, singing researchers, research students – even singers themselves.

The contributors represent a range of authors who have worked or studied singing training across a variety of fields: in Contemporary Commercial Music; in Gospel; in Opera and classical voice; in Musical Theatre; in Jazz; in Religious Worship; and in extended vocal techniques commonly found in contemporary classical music. There are speech pathologists and body specialists, and authors include scientists, singers, researchers and teacher practitioners of vast experience. Most of the contributions are from Australia, the UK, Europe and the United States of America and there is, with few exceptions, an acknowledged bias towards those cultures in which pedagogical practices are communicated through text. Thus, the emphasis leans towards practices of Western music, or at least music styles that have been subsumed within western culture in the recent past.

Part I of the volume begins with an overview of singing pedagogy. McCoy brings a breadth of understanding to the topic and positions the thinking for the remainder of the volume. The following three chapters explore, in turn, the domains of classical, contemporary and musical theatre singing. The values and beliefs of teachers largely influence the outcomes for students. In O'Bryan's chapter, the classical studio is laid bare as teachers speak of this often secret space in which tacit and enculturated transactions take place between participants. Chandler unpacks the processes for teaching contemporary singing while LoVetri shares the approaches of teachers who have worked (and continue to work) on Broadway, revealing the issues they believe to be important in the preparation and maintenance of singing up to eight shows a week.

In Part II, the volume heads into the territory of body, mind and voice. Given that the instrument is housed in the body for singers, this section begins with a discussion of the issues of vocal health as they pertain to singing pedagogy deftly described by Roth and Verdolini-Abbott. Next, Morris – a singing speech pathologist who is best known for his work in breathing and articulation, unveils the role of the speech therapist. This chapter emphasises the collaborative ways in which singing teachers and medical practitioners can work together, with a focus on Morris' work on the articulators. The chapter that follows could not be further from these practices, as Edgerton provides ways in which the extra-normal voice might be taught, based on discoveries in voice physiology. These unusual techniques will be confronting for some readers, but the emphasis here is on decoding the practices of extra-normal singing and discovering ways in which they may be taught safely. Miller then revisits the processes of registration–an under-explored and vital aspect of the singing teachers' work. The next two chapters, from Buchanan and Grant respectively, address two ways in which the body overall contributes to the act of singing. It is acknowledged that there are many different approaches to bodywork and singing. These two chapters put forward aspects of body mapping and Feldenkrais, each independent yet complementary ways of viewing body use for singing. The final section of Part II draws on aspects of the mind as it interplays with the singing voice. It is frequently acknowledged that, like athletes, if all other aspects of a singer's armoury are in order it is the mind that ultimately makes the difference between those that succeed and those that don't. Mitchell explores the perception of the singing voice, while aspects of attachment and personality from the bulk of Serra's chapter. Oakland concludes this section with new research on the nature of the opera singer, and the ways in which identity plays a role in the construction of these singers, often revered as iconic pinnacles of achievement in the European canonic music tradition.

In the third part of the volume, approaches to the teaching of European canonic music are juxtaposed with training for other styles of music. Elliott's chapter continues the focus on European canonic music, with her contribution on the teaching of classical and romantic repertoire. In McMahon's chapter, the focus on sacred music is also present as he posits the ways in which the teaching of baroque repertoire might be approached. McMahon brings the perspective of teacher-performer to this research, and contextualises it within an institutional setting. The final four chapters in this section deal with what Hughes terms 'Popular Culture Musics.' This chapter further explores Hughes' claiming of this term, originally raised in her earlier work (see Hughes 2010). The area of contemporary singing pedagogy has struggled for identity, and Hughes' chapter seeks to explore this, and provide alternate ways of thinking about this domain. Hargreaves' ground-breaking work in the area of jazz pedagogy, particularly the teaching of improvisation to singers, forms the core of the next chapter. The next chapter discusses worship singing in the now ubiquitous contemporary worship environment. Robinson's recent research in this domain illuminates the constructs of the worship environment, and provides the reader with ways in which new pedagogies can be introduced to the church setting. The section is completed with Robinson-Martin's revelations about Gospel singing, adding to an as-yet little explored area of singing practice and pedagogy.

The fourth and final part seeks to bring together institutional perspectives on singing training. These chapters are largely practitioner reflections, and the section bookends the volume by providing an insight into the practices of conservatoires in training the singer in classical, musical theatre and contemporary genres. Schindler describes the changes in the conservatoire setting in relation to classical singing teaching with a focus on the impact of music schools' amalgamation with universities in the last 20 years. The chapter on musical theatre illuminates the structures and pedagogies behind a 3-year musical theatre degree from an expert practitioner in the field; one in which students are gradually given independence and ownership over their learning. Sabey's writing on this topic draws on 26 years of training students for the West End, and this complements the earlier chapter from LoVetri on the Broadway experience. Similarly, Bartlett's chapter draws on more than 40 years of singing and teaching contemporary styles, and explains why existing modes of teaching are not always applicable across styles.

Finally, Harrison's chapter talks through the ways in which research into the teaching of singing can be perpetuated through the training of singing researchers. The chapter draws on both the aspects of existing research, as they are manifest in the preceding chapters, and on the institutional practices of preparing the next generation of singing researchers. As such, the final chapter represents both a summation of the volume as well as a jumping off point for new and innovative ways of exploring singing research and practice.

References

Blades-Zeller, E. (2003). *A spectrum of voices*. Lanham: Scarecrow Press.

Brainerd Slocum, K. (1995). Confrerie, Bruderschaft and Guild: The formation of musicians' fraternal organisations in thirteenth and fourteenth century Europe. *Early Music History, 14*, 257–274.

Brown, O. L. (1997). *Discover your voice*. San Diego: Singular Publishing.

Bunch, M. A. (1995). *Dynamics of the singing voice* (3rd ed.). Wien: Springer.

Callaghan, J. (2000). *Singing and voice science*. San Diego: Singular Publishing Group.

Callinan-Robertson, J., Mitchell, H. F., & Kenny, D. T. (2006). Effect of pedagogical imagery of 'halo' on vocal quality in young classical female singers. *Australian Voice, 12*, 39–52.

Chapman, J. (2006). *Singing and teaching singing: A holistic approach to classical voice*. San Diego: Plural.

Fields, V. (1947). *Training the singing voice*. New York: Kings Crown Press.

Garcia, M. (1855). Observations on the human voice. *Proceedings of the Royal Society of London, 7*(1854–1855), 399–410.

Hughes, D. (2010). Popular culture musics. In S. Harrison (Ed.), *Perspectives on teaching singing: Australian vocal pedagogues sing their stories*. Brisbane: Australian Academic Press.

McCoy, S. (2004). *Your voice: An inside view*. Princeton: Inside View Press.

Miller, R. (1983). *The structure of singing: System and art in vocal technique*. New York: Schirmer Books.

Miller, R. (1996). *On the art of singing*. New York: Oxford University Press.

Miller, R. (2004). *Solutions for singers*. New York: Oxford University Press.

Potter, J. (1998). *Vocal authority*. New York: Cambridge University Press.

Potter, J. (Ed.). (2000). *The Cambridge handbook of singing*. New York: Cambridge University Press.

Potter, J., & Sorrell, N. (2012). *A history of singing*. Cambridge: Cambridge University Press.

Reid, C. (1975). *Voice, psyche and soma*. New York: Joseph Patelson Music House.

Sataloff, R. T. (2005). *Voice science*. San Diego: Plural Publishing.

'Singing: A Bibliography.' (2013). *The new Grove dictionary of opera. Grove Music Online. Oxford Music Online*. Oxford University Press. http://www.oxfordmusiconline.com/subscriber/article/grove/music/O904501. Accessed 10 Mar 2013.

Sundberg, J. (1987). *The science of the singing voice*. Dekalb: North Illinois University Press.

Thurman, L., & Welch, G. (2000). *Bodymind and voice: Foundations of voice education* (Rev. ed.). Minneapolis: The VoiceCare Network.

Titze, I. (1994). *Principles of voice production*. Englewood Cliffs: Prentice-Hall.

Tosi, P. F. (1987). *Observations on the florid song* (J. E. Galliard, Trans.). London: Stainer and Bell. (Original work published 1743)

Vennard, W. (1967). *Singing: The mechanism and the technic*. New York: Carl Fischer.

Welch, G., Howard, D., Himonides, E., & Brereton, J. (2005). Real time feedback in the singing studio: An innovatory action-research project using new voice technology. *Music Education Research, 7*(2), 225–249.

Part I
Overview

Chapter 2
Singing Pedagogy in the Twenty-First Century: A Look Toward the Future

Scott McCoy

Abstract This article evaluates the current state of singing pedagogy, and explores some of the directions the profession might take as time moves forward. Primary focus is on three areas: the role of voice science and technology, the burgeoning field of the singing health specialist, and specialized training programs in singing pedagogy. In many ways, contemporary voice science has revolutionized understanding of the human voice, leading to new methods for training the singing voice. These advances are particularly apparent in the application of acoustic voice analysis in teacher education and as biofeedback in singer training. Singing Health Specialists, sometimes called *vocologists*, are increasingly in demand as liaisons between the medical and artistic communities. Efforts are underway to establish qualifications for this profession, along with criteria and curricula for training and certifying practitioners. Historically, the most important qualification expected of singing teachers was a successful career as a performer: it was assumed that if you could sing, you also could teach. Practical experience often demonstrated the fallacy of this assumption. Teacher training programs are increasingly common in the academy, focusing on the educational needs of singers for whom teaching is the primary career goal, and for professional singers who seek to move from the stage to the teaching studio.

Keywords Voice training • Singing health • Voice pedagogy • Voice teacher training • Vocology • Voice analysis

S. McCoy (✉)
Swank Voice Research Laboratory, School of Music,
The Ohio State University, Columbus, OH, USA
e-mail: mccoy.479@osu.edu

S.D. Harrison and J. O'Bryan (eds.), *Teaching Singing in the 21st Century*,
Landscapes: the Arts, Aesthetics, and Education 14, DOI 10.1007/978-94-017-8851-9_2,
© Springer Science+Business Media Dordrecht 2014

All around the world, people sing spontaneously in expressions of joy, sorrow, and for the simple pleasure of making music. A much smaller subset of people avidly pursue singing as a profession or avocation. For this diverse group, which ranges from volunteer choristers to stars of the Metropolitan Opera and the Grand ole Opry, spontaneity is insufficient: training is required. This training begins with the simple songs that accompany our early childhood, which teach us first to follow general melodic direction (up and down), and then to match pitches with increasing accuracy. Eventually, we become more independent, able to sustain our part in a simple cannon, partner song, or harmonization. As we grow, we might join a choir, perform in a school musical, or join with friends in a band that celebrates the current flavor of commercial music. Throughout this journey, our skills improve as we practice our art and emulate our vocal role models. Some will take their learning to a higher level and engage in formal studies with an experienced mentor.

But how did these mentors learn their craft? Time-honored traditions favor a direct path from a performing career to the teaching studio; unfortunately, not all great singers are equally gifted as teachers. In recent years, a new path to teaching has been established in the form of specialized training in the field of singing pedagogy. Coursework and advanced degrees in pedagogy augment traditional performance focused education with practical information on how to teach. Increasingly, pedagogy curricula are expanded to include the scientific foundations of voice production, including study of anatomy, physiology, acoustics, learning theory, and voice disorders. Some students are stimulated by this objective information to pursue new career paths in voice research, speech pathology, or singing voice health. Others use it in service to the art, using their new-found knowledge to help students become more beautiful, expressive, and commercially viable singers. The remainder of this article will explore some of the recent trends in pedagogy and their possible trajectory toward the future.

2.1 Technology

Those of us who predate the digital age often fail to understand the extent to which technology is ubiquitous in the lives of our younger students. Often described as *digital natives*, they can compile new applications for their cell phones or create videos for posting on the Internet as easily as we resolved dominant seventh chords for our music theory assignments. In my position as director of the Voice Research Laboratory at The Ohio State University, I am humbled by my students who instinctively understand the inner workings of advanced voice analysis software; they seem to have instant facility in tasks that took me months, if not years to master. In the digital world, I speak with an accent and an adolescent vocabulary, but that is sufficient for me to see the value of technology as an aid to teaching. Nowhere is this more important than in acoustic analysis and the insights it permits into the workings of the voice.

I taught my first college course in singing pedagogy in 1991 at the University of Iowa. Ingo Titze, one the most respected authorities on the voice in world, was my colleague (I had taken his course *Principles of Voice Production* several years earlier, which was the source of my fascination with voice science). Dr. Titze ran a state-of-the-art voice laboratory, filled with the latest gadgets and whiz-bang gizmos for understanding and quantifying the acoustic properties of the human voice. While some of my students found their way to his lab to participate in experiments and 'see' their voices, most had to settle for a visit with the musicologist down the hall who was studying harpsichord acoustics. Using his rudimentary oscilloscope, we were able to view soundwaves and power spectrums. The image was tiny and the resolution terrible, but those weaknesses made the impact no less astounding. Here was concrete visual evidence that the abstract theories we'd studied about voice acoustics and formants actually were true.

Jump forward 20 years. I now find myself teaching the voice science component of a comprehensive pedagogy curriculum in courses at two major universities, online, and as a guest in lectures around the world. My indispensable travel companion is a laptop computer, fully equipped with the latest generation of voice-specific acoustic analysis software and sound acquisition hardware, which always is available for real time demonstrations of the principles under discussion. What once required a large, dedicated space and an investment of tens to hundreds of thousands of dollars is now portable and affordable—even on the salary of a voice teacher or choral conductor. In fact, if you don't need all the bells and whistles, you can accomplish a great deal with the computer you already you own and inexpensive or free software readily available for download. The catalog of available analysis programs is constantly changing as new titles become available and old friends become incompatible with the latest generation of operating systems and computer hardware. Therefore, I am not going to endorse specific programs, but will speak to the features and capabilities I find most important.

Enter the term *spectrum analyzer* into an Internet search engine and over a million results will be returned. Few of these are specific to the human voice—especially the free ones—but most can provide useful information. As a minimum, you need something that is able to produce power spectrums (amplitude + frequency) and spectrograms (amplitude + frequency + time). Many, but far from all programs include the option for displays in real time, which is imperative if you intend to use the technology as visual feedback in the studio or rehearsal room. Spectrograms will provide information about vowel and consonant integrity, legato, timbre, onset and release of tones, and vibrato. Visualization of these events requires the spectrogram to be configured in *narrow band* mode with a frequency range of at least 0–5,000 Hz. Ideally, there should be user adjustable settings for sampling rate, analysis size, amplitude range, display colors, and scrolling rate. If the previous sentence appeared to be in a foreign language, you might want to review one of the excellent books that deal with acoustic voice analysis, including *Voice Tradition and Technology: A State-of-the-Art Studio* (Nair et al. 1999), *Resonance in Singing: Voice Building through Acoustic*

Feedback (Miller 2008), *Clinical Measurement of Voice and Speech* (Baken and Orlikoff 2000), *Your Voice: An Inside View* (McCoy 2012).

To get beyond the basics, we must venture into software written (or adapted) specifically to look at the voice. These programs will add features, including automated routines to measure the rate and extent of vibrato (*VoceVista*), real time display of pitch accuracy and timbre (*Sing & See*), phonetic transcription in IPA (*Praat*), formant estimation and vowel matching (*CSL* or *Multi-Speech*), vocal tract configuration (*WinSingAd*), and multiple, simultaneous analysis windows for both acoustic and electroglottograph data (*VoceVista Professional*). These types of programs vary in price over a wide range; start with something minimal and move up as your budget and understanding increase.

At the current time, most of the better voice analysis programs are specific and exclusive to the Windows operating system; musicians, however, tend to prefer computers running Apple's OS-X. This mismatch is explained by the fact that these programs are written for research scientists and clinicians who live in a world that is strongly dominated by PC's. Fortunately, newer Apple computers use an Intel processor that can run Windows and OS-X on the same system, enabling access to programs like *VoceVista* and *Multi-Speech* on a Mac.

Colleagues in the academy frequently contact me for recommendations on setting up a voice lab, including what kind of computer and microphone to buy. My advice always begins with a question: what do you hope to achieve? A lab designed to conduct research will be configured very differently from one that is primarily used to provide feedback for voice students and demonstrations for pedagogy courses. The former requires a significant investment in sound acquisition hardware with ultra clean specifications and uniform frequency response (if you intend to publish the results of research, you must be certain your data are reliable); for the latter, a basic analysis program running on a laptop with its built-in microphone might be sufficient. Top tier collegiate voice labs currently might also include instruments to measure nasality, vocal fold movement and closed/open quotients, breath capacity, airflow rates and phonation pressure, physical movements of respiration, activity in specific muscles, and visualization of the larynx (stroboscopy). Of course, some of these instruments can only be used by appropriately licensed professionals and medical doctors who would participate as members of the research team.

One can only imagine what the future might hold in terms of analysis options. Researchers are starting to look at voice acoustics as a *nonlinear*, rather than linear system. The ramifications of this new perspective remain to be seen, but could result in a complete revision of our understanding of formants. Eventually, new analysis paradigms might be required to take advantage of this information.

As voice analysis, in service to understanding vocal function, becomes more widespread in our teacher training programs—something that very clearly is happening in the academy—we can expect future generations of singing teachers to have a high level of comfort and expertise with the technology. To them, using a spectrogram in a voice lesson will be no more unusual than referring a student to a mirror, using an exercise ball, or making an audio or video recording of the lesson.

It simply will be another tool in their pedagogical repertoire. Given the exponential advancement of computer technology, one can envision a time when every voice teacher and conductor has a miniature device that provides three-dimensional imaging of the vocal tract, monitoring of breath support, and a full complement of acoustic data, all projected as a hologram with concise instructions for improvement. Smart phones already have spectrogram apps; can the rest of this be far behind? Of course, the best technology in the world can only help to improve *the sound* a singer produces. People, including singers, voice teachers, and conductors, always will be responsible for turning that sound into expressive, beautiful music.

Technology impacts singing in many ways beyond voice analysis. Aspiring singers make extensive use of Internet resources for self-promotion and career development, including social networks and personal websites. Setting up a group on Facebook is often the most efficient and effective way for teachers and conductors to communicate with their studio or ensemble. As bandwidth increases, more and more singing teachers are giving lessons over the Internet by video-conference. I find it hard to imagine a choir whose singers are dispersed around the world, connected only by computer networks. But if it doesn't already exist, it will soon.

2.2 Singing Health Specialist

One of the more important trends in singing pedagogy is the creation of a new area of study that integrates science, medicine, and voice therapy, with the artistry of singing and teaching. Practitioners in the field are referred to as *Singing Health Specialists* or *Vocologists*, and are expected to be excellent singers and teachers of singing. The training regimen generally includes specialized coursework in voice disorders and therapy, instrumentation for voice analysis, and training of the speaking voice for actors and other non-singing voice professionals. The curriculum is also likely to include extensive clinical and surgical observations in a practice that specializes in clients who are professional voice users. At the conclusion of this training, the Singing Voice Specialist is qualified to work as a member of a therapeutic team that includes a laryngologist, voice pathologist/therapist, and possibly a neurologist and psychologist.

At this point, there are no formal curricular standards for training in this new field, nor is there an accrediting body to oversee and approve certification for recipients of the training. Discussions are underway, however, among the invested parties, including the National Association of Teachers of Singing (NATS), the Voice and Speech Trainers Association (VASTA), the American Speech and Hearing Association (ASHA), the National Center for Voice and Speech (NCVS), and the Voice Foundation. We should expect to see progress toward standardization of this profession and requirements for certification within the next several years.

In the meanwhile, advanced training is available in the field from at least two sources. The Summer Vocology Institute operates under the joint auspices of The National Center for Voice and Speech (which recently moved from Denver to Salt

Lake City), the University of Iowa, and the University of Utah. This pioneering program is staffed by some of the most important researchers and clinicians in field. Courses are offered every summer, leading to a non-accredited certificate of completion. The Ohio State University offers a similar curriculum through its Singing Health Specialist program. Offered as a multi-disciplinary course of study jointly by the School of Music, the department of Speech and Hearing Science, and the Laryngology department within the College of Medicine, the SHS curriculum is an add-on to graduate study in music or speech science. At this point, enrollment is only open to OSU students who already are matriculated in one of the previously listed programs, but plans are underway to offer it as a stand-alone curriculum.

2.3   Singing Voice Pedagogy Degree Programs

As I stated earlier in this article, the traditional path to the teaching studio begins on the opera stage. This is still a viable and important trajectory, albeit one that is complicated by the demands of the academy. Increasingly, candidates for permanent, fulltime positions on the faculties of colleges and universities are required to possess an earned doctorate by the time of review for promotion and tenure. Jobs exist for people with significant performing experience and a master's degree, but they are relatively few and far between, especially for positions beyond the adjunct level. Performers who began their fulltime singing careers prior to completion of a master's degree are pretty much out of the running. At least two schools have established programs to help. The University of Houston and Westminster Choir College both offer master's programs in singing pedagogy that are specifically geared to the needs of professional singers who are ready to move from the stage to the studio. These working singers have no need for traditional academic programs that focus on applied study, performance oriented courses, and solo recitals. They do, however, need assistance to become the best possible teachers, grounded in contemporary pedagogic thought and practice. Many also will need to expand their knowledge of repertoire, including art song and operatic literature for voice types other than their own. The Westminster and Houston programs are structured to fill in these gaps while providing academic credentials that can lead to greater employability.

A new path to the teaching studio is increasingly prominent in the academy: graduate degrees in pedagogy combined with performance. This trend might be traced to the Doctor of Musical Arts degree, which often carries the designation DMA in Performance *and* Pedagogy. All too frequently, however, the pedagogic component in these programs consisted of little more than teaching non-majors with little or no supervision. In recent years, the number of schools offering significant training in singing pedagogy has skyrocketed, both at the master's and doctoral levels. Curricula have expanded, often including core courses in voice science, teaching methods, and literature. Most programs also include a formal practicum experience with pedagogy students teaching under direct supervision of an experienced faculty member.

Under the best circumstances, this new system produces artists who are equally well prepared for successful careers as singers and teachers. But it doesn't always turn out that way. With so many programs available, it is inevitable that some people will fall through the cracks, completing their training in pedagogy without every really learning to sing at a professional level. I see evidence of this phenomenon almost every time I review applications for teaching positions and professional training programs. Inevitably, there will be a number of submissions from people who completed their doctoral degrees and secured fulltime university positions without ever performing at a significant level outside the academy. Some of these young professionals are gifted singers who elected to pursue teaching instead of performing because of a true passion for the art. Others, however, have more modest vocal gifts, and might even have significant unresolved vocal issues. Unfortunately, I have evaluated far too many audition recordings by people in this group whose performances are musically inaccurate, display inconsistent vocalism and incorrect diction, and include music that is ill-suited or completely inappropriate to their voice type. But they have earned their doctorate, been hired in the academy, and are now teaching the future generation of singers. We can only hope that this does not become a closed loop, with future generations of singers who are only prepared for academic positions.

Looking toward the future, we must work harder to ensure that singers who are admitted to pedagogy programs possess the desire to teach and the skill to perform in nearly equal portion. If vocal music is to survive, we must have teachers who truly know the art and what it means to sing; therefore, we must help administrations and accrediting agencies understand that for musicians, professional experience can be a job qualification equal to, or surpassing a terminal degree.

2.4 Toward a Common Pedagogic Language

One of the most important contributions of the current wave of pedagogic interest is the development of a common point of reference, based on physiologic and acoustic reality. Generations of singers and their teachers have succeeded in spite of incomplete or erroneous understanding of how the human body functions as a biomechanical, acoustic instrument. We still hear of teachers who instruct singers to lift their palates by inhaling through the nose (a mutually incompatible action), produce vowels in the larynx without ever moving the tongue, jaw, or lips (a physical and acoustic impossibility), and to articulate rapid notes in coloratura passages through diaphragmatic pulses (which actually are hiccups). We now have a rich tradition of pedagogy texts, written by performing singers, steeped in fact, not fiction and intuition. My own text, *Your Voice: An Inside View* (2012), only was possible because of the prior contributions of William Vennard (1967), Ralph Appleman (1986), Barbara Doscher (1994), Richard Miller (1986), Clifton Ware (1997), and many, many others. The pure science, so elegantly explained by giants in the field including Ingo Titze (1994) and Johann Sundberg (1987, 1991) illuminates our work, often explaining *why* a traditional pedagogic practice is effective.

Pedagogy based on reality does not mean we must speak to our students in the language of formant frequencies, phonation threshold pressures, closed quotients, and decibel levels. But as pedagogues become increasingly conversant with this language and these concepts, teaching efficiency and creativity should improve. By understanding their underlying cause, problems with vocal technique are diagnosed more quickly and accurately, and better solutions can be offered for improvements. Teachers will still rely on imagery, sensation, and misdirection, but they will know the difference between imagination and reality. In the end, all the vested participants in this endeavor, including singing teachers, vocal coaches, conductors, impresarios, and audiences, want the same thing: beautiful, expressive singing. The pedagogic tools toward this end are at our disposal and become better all the time. We don't know for sure what the future will bring, but it certainly will include great singing!

References

Appleman, R. (1986). *The science of vocal pedagogy: Theory and application.* Bloomington: Indiana University Press.

Baken, R. J., & Orlikof, R. F. (2000). *Clinical measurement of speech and voice* (2nd ed.). San Diego: Singular.

Doscher, B. (1994). *The functional unity of the singing voice.* Lanham: Scarecrow Press.

McCoy, S. J. (2012). *Your voice: An inside view* (2nd ed.). Columbus: Inside View Press.

Miller, R. (1986). *The structure of singing: System and art in vocal technique.* New York: Schirmer.

Miller, D. G. (2008). *Resonance in singing: Voice building through acoustic feedback.* Princeton: Inside View Press.

Nair, G., Miller, D. G., & Nair, R. (1999). *Voice tradition and technology: A state-of-the-art studio.* San Diego: Singular.

Sundberg, J. (1987). *The science of the singing voice.* DeKalb: Northern Illinois University Press.

Sundberg, J. (1991). *The science of musical sounds.* San Diego: Academic.

Titze, I. R. (1994). *Principles of voice production.* Englewood Cliffs: Prentice Hall.

Vennard, W. (1967). *Singing: The mechanism and the technic* [sic]. New York: Carl Fischer Music.

Ware, C. (1997). *The basics of vocal pedagogy.* Columbus: McGraw Hill.

Chapter 3
Habits of the Mind, Hand and Heart: Approaches to Classical Singing Training

Jessica O'Bryan

Abstract This chapter explores three classical singing teachers' values and beliefs about singing teaching and learning, informed by 400 years of singing pedagogy traditions. Employing Shulman's theory of Signature Pedagogy, (Daedalus: Am Acad Art Sci 134(3):52–59, 2005), I explore how the time-honoured tradition of one-on-one classical singing teaching forms 'habits of the mind, hand and heart'. Through an examination of three case studies of classical singing teaching, I investigate how the life experiences of three eminent teachers have shaped their own practices and how implicit cultural values and beliefs about classical singing have likewise shaped their approaches in the one-on-one lesson. Within classical singing pedagogy and the history of singing, 'singing teachers draw on their personal experiences within an essentially hegemonic oral culture' (Welch et al, Music Educ Res 7(2):225–249, 2005). This chapter illuminates this oral tradition and offers an alternative insight into approaches to singing teaching and learning.

Keywords Singing pedagogy • Signature pedagogy • Classical singing training • Enculturation • Tertiary singing • One-to-one music lessons

3.1 Context

'From the first lesson to the last, let the master remember that he is answerable for any omission in his instructions, and for the errors he did not correct' (Tosi 1987, 3).

One-to-one teaching is claimed to be the oldest form of education. It can be seen in interactions between a mother and her young child. Bruner calls this the 'interactional tenet', where 'it is principally through interacting with others that children

J. O'Bryan (✉)
Queensland Conservatorium, Griffith University, 140 Grey St,
South Brisbane, 4101 QLD, Australia
e-mail: jessica.obryan@gmail.com

S.D. Harrison and J. O'Bryan (eds.), *Teaching Singing in the 21st Century*,   21
Landscapes: the Arts, Aesthetics, and Education 14, DOI 10.1007/978-94-017-8851-9_3,
© Springer Science+Business Media Dordrecht 2014

find out what the culture is about and how it conceives of the world...' (Bruner 1996, 20). The one-to-one singing lesson might be defined at its simplest as the transmission of music skills from an expert singer to a novice learner so that the learner eventually develops those same skills. But, as Bruner states, it is through this interaction that a shared culture of learning emerges.

The Tosi quote comes from a time when the master and apprentice mode of singing training was the primary model of instruction. More recently, knowledge about singing pedagogy has been expanded with the myriad research available on 'vocal physiology and acoustics, on cognition, neurobiology, and teaching and learning' (Callaghan et al. 2012, 559). Singing teachers now have access to various approaches in pedagogy; they can view YouTube clips that show the workings of the larynx; and access to professional development in singing teaching and learning has improved.

Despite these advances, Johnson claims, 'most educational institutions in the developed world still teach the older classical skills and conventions exclusively and in isolation from almost anything else' (2009, 18). Also apparently common to conservatoire communities are 'cult-like teaching methods' and the adherence to a particular teacher and 'pedigree' (ibid.), which may influence student perceptions about music learning, and perhaps their professional attitudes and dispositions within the music profession. Perceptions of singing teaching are shaped by its history and from the embodied nature of the singing voice (see Chapman 2006). Nevertheless, it is apparent that there are singing teachers who are mindful of not repeating the omissions in their own practice of the teaching they experienced, within a highly competitive artistic culture.

This chapter focuses on the case studies of three singing teachers and their current approaches to teaching classical singing, examined through the lens of Shulman's theory of 'Signature Pedagogy' (2005). I discuss how implicit cultural values and beliefs about classical singing, the environment in which they teach, and their experiences with singing and learning singing have shaped their approaches in the one-to-one classical singing lesson.

3.2 Signature Pedagogy

Shulman originally conceived of 'signature pedagogies' as those learning and teaching approaches unique to professions such as Medicine and Law. According to Shulman, 'these are types of teaching that organize the fundamental ways in which future practitioners are educated for their new professions' (2005, 52), and which form 'habits of the mind, habits of the heart and habits of the hand' (ibid.). He claims signature pedagogies prepare their future practitioners in 'critical aspects of the three fundamental dimensions of professional work: to think, to perform, and to act with integrity' (ibid.). Arguably, training musicians for their careers can be characterised as 'signature pedagogy', as indeed can any profession or trade where the traits of that training are identifiable over a long time span. Classical singing training within the European canonic context is a tradition spanning more than 400 years and classical singers are arguably being trained to perform and to think in ways that prepare them for that profession.

Shulman identifies four dimensions to signature pedagogy. The first is the *surface structure*, which consists of the 'concrete, operational acts of teaching and learning, of showing and demonstrating, of questioning and answering' (54–55). There is the *deep structure*, which is the 'set of assumptions about how best to impart a certain body of knowledge and know-how', and then there is the *implicit structure*, which Shulman claims is a moral dimension that 'comprises a set of beliefs about professional attitudes, values and dispositions'. He notes finally that a signature pedagogy can 'be characterized by what it is not–by the way it is shaped by what it does not impart or exemplify' (ibid.).

3.3   Surface Structure

In classical singing training, its surface structure of singing pedagogy can be characterized at its simplest by how it is taught in conservatoires. Until the late nineteenth century, it was common for singing students to be 'apprenticed' to a singer or singing teacher for the duration of their long education, even being housed by the teacher, who then took a percentage of the student's takings as a professional for payment of their training. Once conservatoires in Britain and Europe took hold, however, a new delivery mode of vocal education emerged, although still tied to the Master/Apprentice mode of vocal instruction, which persists today. Conservatoire training is widely considered to be the most appropriate place to teach young singers. Singers will have usually three to four years of undergraduate training and the normal approach is through regular one-to-one singing lessons with an assigned singing teacher.

Across most conservatoires in Europe, the U.S., the U.K. and Australia, students typically attend private singing lessons of between 45 min and an hour per week for the duration of the semester, and may attend a range of other classes spanning acting, stagecraft, pedagogy and performance, although specifics will change with each institution. The institution defines the number of private lessons per student per semester; in certain European conservatoires, students often have private lessons in groups, their lessons freely observable by the other students of the teacher (Ritterman 2010.).

3.4   Deep Structure

Deep structure assumes a body of knowledge about how best to teach classical singing. Shulman's deep structure, or 'assumptions about the best way to impart certain knowledge and know-how' (55) may apply to an individual teacher's experience of learning and teaching singing pedagogy. Research indicates singing lessons typically take a tri-partite form, where greetings and a chat about the week's work often precedes vocal warm ups and diagnosis of faults, followed by work on repertoire (Gaunt 2008).

In singing teaching, image-based instruction remains common, and vocal development of motor skills remains frequently a product of aural modelling and imitation. According to a study by Burwell (2006), in the typical singing lesson 'singers place more emphasis on technique, and less on interpretation, than do instrumental teachers, and... they also employ affective language and metaphor, appealing to the student's imagination, more' (331).

Teachers of singing may perpetuate the approaches taken by their previous teachers, whether or not these approaches were successful. Teachers of singing have been most commonly employed on the basis of their performance history, subsequently drawing on 'their personal experiences within an essentially hegemonic oral culture' (Welch et al. 2005, 226). This experience-based approach strongly mirrors the master/apprentice model. Of research into one-on-one lessons, Gaunt's 2008 article found that conservatoire teachers 'had learned to teach on the job, drawing heavily on their own experiences as learners' (6), and Davidson and Jordan noted that 'teachers tend to approach teaching with strategies that make them feel safe, whether these are effective or not' (2007, 734).

3.5 Implicit Structure

There is more to the singing lesson than the transmission of a domain skill. Teachers subconsciously influence their students in the way they perceive the industry, their approaches to teaching and learning, approaches to musical style and repertoire, and they may model their expectations of demeanour, behaviour and industry knowledge. This forms the 'implicit structure' of Shulman's Signature Pedagogy, for which there is little available research other than anecdotal accounts of how one learnt. Implicit structure 'comprises a set of beliefs about professional attitudes, values and dispositions' (55). In singing education this structure comprises attitudes about how to teach, what to teach and for what purpose.

This chapter therefore focuses on the following three questions: How have experiences of teaching and learning singing influenced the three teachers' current pedagogical approaches to their students in the conservatorium studio? How may the environment in which a teacher works influence their teaching approach? What are some of the implicit assumptions about singing that each teacher is imparting to their student?

3.6 Method

As part of a larger project, three teachers in Australian institutions took part in a collective case study examining participant values, beliefs and practices of classical singing lessons. Ninety-minute interviews with teachers were held about their values, beliefs, experiences and practices of singing teaching, prior to a series of video-recorded lessons with one student over the course of a semester. A final interview was held 1 year later, where the teachers viewed several excerpts from the lessons and discussed their approaches to vocal pedagogy. Analysis of the data was through Narrative Inquiry methods, which is a methodological approach that stories data. Clandinin and Caine note that 'each story told and lived is situated and understood within larger cultural, social and institutional narratives' (2008, 541), and which aims at 'understanding and making meaning of experience through conversations, dialogue and participation in the ongoing lives of research participants' (ibid.). Not all stories have happy endings, therefore one of the stories in this chapter reports a problematic learning and teaching relationship. All names and places have been de-identified. Each participant read through their narrative drafts prior to publication and was able to request alterations and deletions where they felt appropriate, and to comment on the content and shape of the draft. The following accounts are in part rewritten from data contained in the case studies. Each account contains teacher stories about their own learning and teaching experiences, their current approach to teaching, a short excerpt from one of their singing lessons with their student and a brief discussion on some of the tacit and enculturated learning taking place.

3.7 Case Studies

3.7.1 Norah

Norah has been talking to me about how she came to be a singer, which she explains she 'stumbled into very late'. While Norah has had a full and interesting career as a singer on both the operatic and concert stages, her main focus is now the teaching of tertiary singing students. Her path to teaching was not altogether a smooth one. While her early education as a musician was profound and rich, she considers her early singing training was not as successful. She does not blame her singing teachers for this, saying, 'the way I was taught was still very much a sort of empirical method, based largely on imitation, and on mental imagery, and of course as we know that has its limits'. Norah suffered a vocal health issue during her early career, culminating in what she terms a 'vocal crisis', which momentarily halted her performance career. She was later 'rescued' by a forward thinking singing teacher who had herself suffered a vocal crisis. This rescue teacher's approach to singing training was a motor-learned approach. Norah learned how to breathe and how to approach singing in its physical act, embodied and connected to an artistic output. She explains that this has become her approach to teaching singing:

> To teach that aspect of the craft needs to be understood and be able to be unpacked, because you can say to someone 'there will be a big physical awareness, you need to feel that' but if they don't know how to get to that stage of what that feels like then it's enormously frustrating.

Through various experiences with her teachers, Norah's approach to pedagogy incorporates not just the physical act of teaching singing through a motor-learned approach, but gentle instruction in the culture of opera, incorporated throughout the lessons in the guise of mentor. Norah acknowledges that singing is an extremely personal art. Personal and psychological characterisations of teacher and students can determine success of the learning and teaching relationship over and above pedagogical approaches. Norah makes use of a network of professionals she has developed over the last 15 years, which includes speech pathologists, doctors, other singing teachers, accompanists and opera industry experts. She claims,

> that's how the outside world works, that's how the professional world works: a professional singer needs to take instruction and a variety of ideas from a variety of people, like their coach and their language tutor, and the prompt in the box and the conductor, and the director.

We discuss a session with a student, Jennifer, who Norah has been teaching for nearly 3 years. Jennifer's voice has gone through radical changes in that time. They have been discussing Jennifer's results from a large singing competition she entered a little earlier in the year. Jennifer has gotten through to the final round. Below is an edited transcript of the conversation between teacher and student. This conversation takes place before any singing occurs.

> *'I got through to the final!' Jennifer says to Norah. They talk about her results in the competition and whether Jennifer's place in the final was justified. Norah says, 'You got there by true merit!'*
> *'Well! It's very exciting!' Norah smiles at Jennifer.*
> *'Oh! I also have to ask you about this other competition' says Jennifer. 'I need four contrasting arias.'*
> *Norah nods her head.*
> *'So I chose He Israel, Il est Doux,'*
> *'You'll just do four operatic ones?' interrupts Norah.*
> *'It said it could be from oratorio or whatever and some of mine were a little samey. They were all Romantic' explains Jennifer.*
> *'Oh, ok.'*
> *'So that's why I chose the Mendelssohn, the Massenet, um, and then I ...' Jennifer's voice dribbles off.*
> *'But you've got four contrasted ones!', smiles Norah, encouragingly. 'You've got Per Pieta',*
> *'I was waiting for that!' mutters Jennifer.*
> *'You've got Il est doux, In Quelle and Steal Me!'*
> *'Do I have to put the Mozart in?' Jennifer mutters again.*
> *Norah laughs.*
> *Jennifer continues, 'So that's right, I did Mendelssohn, Massenet, Steal Me, and then I wanted to ask what you think was better, In Quelle or Io Son, which do you think was better for the Italian?'*
> *'Oh, I love the way you sing In Quelle, but I'm just wondering if with an orchestra, oh, I don't know.'*
> *'I honestly couldn't choose', says Jennifer.*
> *'No, I'm just wondering what is better for a competition', muses Norah.*
> *'That's all I'm wondering', agrees Jennifer, 'is whether because it would be last, so I didn't know whether after three quite substantial arias whether it was a nice little...*

*because I mean Io Son is beautiful, but I didn't know whether it was as well known.'
Jennifer's confusion is evident.*

'Oh, it is beautiful, and the ending is quite dramatic, isn't it?' enthuses Norah.

'So I just thought I'd check with you before I put that in', Jennifer finishes.

Norah confesses, 'I'm not much help, I can't decide – they're both beautiful. Maybe we should sing Io Son now... You're moving into a stage where there's going to be quite a few comps – are you going to Roseberry Creek Eisteddfods?'

'Yeah, I want to do that' agrees Jennifer.

'That's good, and there'll be others as well. Next year we'll put you in the MacDonald's Aria', predicts Norah, thoughtfully.

They continue chatting about other concerns for quite a while, then, as they begin to discuss a production of Troilus and Cressida, Norah says suddenly, 'that's an aria we might explore for you, next year, but your voice might be a bit beautiful for that. It's a great aria, you'd love it. 'How shall I sleep', or something. It's Walton. It's a great Aria, and it has this big – Norah sings a dramatic phrase, accompanying herself with the vocal line on the piano – that's the final phrase, goes to a top C, it's great! We should look at that maybe'.

'Okay! Maybe as my final recital aria. Pencil that in now!' laughs Jennifer.

'Get everyone to back up a few rows!' Norah chuckles.

They talk for a while longer about exam repertoire and then Jennifer begins to sing.

In this excerpt, Norah's complimentary attitude towards Jennifer's voice shows that she thinks it beautiful and large. Norah has encouraged Jennifer to become fully autonomous by stepping back from imposing repertoire constraints on the singer. Norah gives casual encouragement to Jennifer about her future, the goal setting for future competitions, songs and exams, getting Jennifer to think to the years ahead, and mentoring her through the space between student and professional. Norah believes Jennifer has the talent and ambition to compete in competitions, and her deeply mentoring approach is readily observable in this excerpt.

Norah's 'habits of the hand': her approaches to singing teaching, have been informed by her personal experience as a learner, her professional experiences as a singer, and her ongoing experience as a teacher. These experiences have shaped her teaching approach, shaped her thinking and will inform her students about how they learn, live and teach singing. As she says, 'I teach in a reaction to the way I was taught, in a bid to give students those elements that were not offered to me'. Norah is breaking with traditional 'habits of the mind, heart and hand' while acknowledging the traditions and rigors of the profession and seeking ways for her students to meet those challenges.

3.7.2 Lukas

Lukas appears highly motivated and self-reliant, and his successful performance career is testimony to his drive and determination. Lukas made use of networks and contacts as he built his performing career in his chosen musical style, but acknowledges it's his own perseverance that has enabled his success.

You have to have the drive, you have to push yourself forward, you know, singing is not something that people without a thick skin can survive in, because critics and other musicians

and conductors and artistic directors can be very confronting. And even dealing with your
own individual psyche, you have to have a very thick skin, to survive as a singer.

Alongside his performing, Lukas has had 20 years experience in singing teaching.
He is vehemently opposed to the notion of the guru teacher, because he feels it promotes unhealthy reliance on and loyalty to one teacher. His own experience of singing lessons was wide ranging and he has made use of many learning experiences.
He states,

> I studied in various places with a whole lot of people... and there'd be lots of influences on
> my development that have led me to the point where I am now. If I think just back to my
> training, there's no one teacher that has led me to where I am now.

For Lukas, he believes that students should go to another teacher after 3 years, saying 'it's time for them to broaden their horizons and go and seek out somebody
else'. This belief shapes his approach to teaching, which mirrors much of his own
performance practice. He is methodical; he sets goals; he values autonomy and
independence in learning and he believes that students need to be prepared, warmed
up and self-directing; however, he believes his own students are frequently not of
this mould. Lukas feels that his students are the products of a poor school education
system. They lack basic musicianship skills and have poor vocal readiness, which
affects how he can teach them. He asks, wryly, 'what is going on with the standard
of entry, the cut-off point? Because it's often been said here, 'well, if you don't have
a certain number of students then you'll be out of a job'. Lukas regularly sets goals
for his students, as he finds 'with most students that's absolutely crucial. Because
they simply do not have the music reading skills, and, in some cases, the initiative
to keep moving forward.'

For Lukas, the relational experience between student and teacher is not predi-
cated on the initial ability of the student, rather, on the work ethic of the student and
their ability to progress, which parallels his own learning experiences, and the
approach he takes to his professional career. He admits to being frustrated by the
poor self-motivation shown by some of his students, but acknowledges he's not
allowed to send them away from the lesson if they don't know their music. Instead,
he says, 'I try and take the line, of 'I'll give you these resources to help you learn the
music, and it's in your best interests to learn it, not as quickly as possible, but to
learn it correctly'.

For Lukas, his attempts to teach his students the value of self-motivation and
hard work, essential requirements in the profession, are made more difficult by his
students' poor musicianship, lack of motivation and low singing standard. The following excerpt shows a brief example of the problems faced by both teacher and
student as they struggle to reconcile their responsibilities in learning and teaching.

This lesson excerpt takes place some ten days before Marilyn's final exam, and
it is her penultimate lesson for the semester. Marilyn, a second year undergraduate, has just entered the studio and is putting her music on the stand as Lukas
adjusts the video.

> *Lukas asks Marilyn, 'what's on the agenda today? Or do you just want to get through every-
> thing [for your exam]?'*

'Pretty much', agrees Marilyn.

'Um, the order, you could do the exercises first or at the end.' Lukas muses.

'Um, I was thinking first, because then I'll know that I'm definitely warmed up!' she laughs.

'So the exercises first, then Concone, and the three pieces', confirms Lukas.

'Two pieces', corrects Marilyn. 'Because we discovered I only needed to do two pieces'.

'Well, let's do it kind of in reverse. The pieces first. Which one?' asks Lukas.

'Doesn't bother me: whichever one you pick'.

Lukas gets out his copy of the music from the cupboard, and asks: 'have you done any singing today?'

Marilyn replies, 'no because I've been composing', as she fidgets with the music stand.

'Ok, well, let's do a little warming up'. Lukas plays a chord on the piano. 'Um, some humming. Bright vowel behind the mm.'

They begin a warm up routine. Marilyn sticks her neck and head forward when she opens her mouth to sing. She holds onto the stand and fusses with it throughout. Her vocal sound is awkward and tight. Lukas says: 'good, try and keep your head still! And now, on an aah.' Marilyn nods. She sings the arpeggio on an aah, which changes colour on each note. 'Good, a bit more sob'. They continue to an E flat arpeggio. Marilyn's voice sounds harsh and uneven and she is unable to negotiate between her lower and middle registers. There is no vibrato in the sound.

As she continues the warm up Marilyn's voice cracks noticeably and she aspirates her top notes. She coughs drily, and says, apologetically, 'my throat can get a little scratchy'. Lukas murmurs, 'yeah', as he begins the first phrases of the chosen song.

As they discuss the tempo, Marilyn asks, 'do you know when my recital is perchance?'

Lukas trumpets a sardonic laugh. 'No!' He replies, with an upward inflection at the end.

'It would be good to know, wouldn't it!' jokes Lukas.

'It would be handy', laughs Marilyn.

'No, unfortunately I can say that the construction of the exam timetable has not been put in my line of work. So, one would expect that it would have been out by now', says Lukas.

'At least before my exam, would be nice!' Replies Marilyn. They both laugh. The lesson continues.

Marilyn has not warmed up prior to entering the studio and seems unwilling to take responsibility for song choice or order of rehearsal. Lukas asks for input from Marilyn but does not comment on her lack of direction, although he structures the lesson to include a warm-up session. They share a complicit understanding of the lack of institutional organisation preventing them from finalising exam plans.

For Lukas, Marilyn's lack of self-direction and poor practice regime has been a constant source of frustration, and the excerpt indicates Mark's quiet annoyance at her lack of exam readiness only a few days out. The pedagogy Lukas employs is designed to help develop autonomy in his students, however, due to the culture in which he teaches, he feels he may not chastise his students for their lack of effort. His 'habits of the head' and 'habits of the hand' are being challenged by underperforming students, and setting up less than ideal expectations about the role of the student in the learning and teaching transaction, and possibly unrealistic expectations about the capacity of the singing teacher to help their students with the fundamentals of music education. The inability for Lukas to move beyond a basic approach to singing training with this particular student is apparent and the deep and implicit structures of singing to which he subscribes cannot even be countenanced in such an environment.

3.7.3   Laurel

Laurel makes no bones about what she thought of her early singing education. As an undergraduate Laurel didn't understand the rudiments of vocal technique, nor were they explained to her. She recalls,

> The people here just spoke a language that meant nothing to me, even though they were intelligent people...but nobody said anything that I could...really understand! And as in, grab hold of. Ok you might get a result in a lesson, but the point of getting a result in a lesson is so that you can reproduce it at home and you have to have a means of doing that, and for me, that just didn't work.

Laurel was being taught in a way that mirrors the experiences of many in the operatic profession – through imagery and imitation and with little or no basis in vocal physiology. Laurel's personality also was at odds with the 'template singer-learner' she was expected to be, as she refused to 'kow-tow or forelock-tug' to the guru-teacher personalities prevalent at the time. Laurel's frustrations with her vocal education eventually took her overseas, where she finally learned to manage her breath and support, and where she learned about vocal physiology. She comments,

> I was beginning to do my reading for my studies, and it was just a revelation...And I think more than anything it was reading the voice science that did it. And it was the visual side of things, it was being able to actually visualise what was going on in there, and getting a pretty broad view... So I just read and read and read and read, and finally it started to dawn on me: the physiology started to make sense, and I went: 'ok'!

Her studies provided Laurel with a visual template of the human body and gave her pedagogical clues as to how to approach vocal physiology. She says, recounting a challenging but rewarding experience with her final teacher:

> I learned how to speak nicely to myself for the first time in my life. I really stopped and calmed myself down... And stopped literally saying, 'you stupid girl' you know, 'you can't do this' and started kind of parenting myself, started saying 'it's ok, you'll be alright, you're doing well. Just be calm, and just try it again. Calmly.' I teach that way, to this day, and I talk to my students about how to speak to themselves.

Laurel's pedagogic experiences have shaped her approach to teaching, partly in response to the frustration she felt as a young learner, but also through continual reflection about what she can offer as a teacher. Laurel feels she has a responsibility to the students who enter her studio to provide a safe learning environment.

> I see it very much as my responsibility now, to find a way of allowing the little person who walks in my door, who has talent, or who might have talent, to be in that world and feel comfortable, and to feel accepted. And to feel valued, while they are in the process of learning, because otherwise, frankly, I don't think they will learn.

Her own unsatisfactory learning experiences have taught her to be ever mindful of the intensity of the one-to-one lesson mode, and to value the learning and teaching processes taking place. She believes the work she does with the student is one of a mentor and she shapes her practice to provide mentoring and networking opportunities.

Despite Laurel's impressive post-graduate training and experience, her teaching involves constant reflection, an ongoing quest to ensure singers understand the pedagogy and vocal embodiment necessary for quality singing. As she says, wryly,

> You have to have a bit of courage of your convictions sometimes. And be damned sure you keep reassessing your convictions, what's more. Instead of just going, 'you can't do it, what I've given you to do'. It is our job to find other ways in for them, but sometimes it is hard.

In the following lesson excerpt, second-year undergraduate Phoebe has been learning a Mozart aria and grappling with the embodied sensations of the singing voice. Phoebe has just finished singing the aria.

> *Laurel finishes the end phrase and asks, 'Good! How did you think you did with Mozart's style that time?'*
>
> *Phoebe replies, 'a bit better! I think it's just for me, finding – and this is just part of the style I guess – for me, finding, um, the different place where it sits for Mozart, and – it's kind of like …that place, but then I've kind of got to make sure my vowels don't kind of morph as you said, then it's easy to sing the high phrases when it's just in that little sweet place, but then I have to make sure I go like this and then have the nice vowels happening.' While Phoebe speaks, she looks at Laurel off camera and makes intricate shapes with her hands near her head, shaping her fingers into beaks and ovals and creating circular patterns in the air. She is externalising the sensation of what is happening inside her head with her hands.*
>
> *Laurel agrees, saying 'yes, yes. And I think you've seen me dancing around there. I mean, the point of my doing that is to give you a sense of how I feel the impetus of the phrase. And as I've said to you before it comes from the harmony. And the text, but he always makes the two of them go together.' Laurel sings 'tension, release' in accurate time and pitch and then says, 'it's always to do with tension and release – it just draws you across the phrase like I'm drawing you across the room.'*
>
> *Phoebe draws big circles in the air with her hands and exclaims, 'and it's so true! It's such a body thing! It's such a –'*
>
> *Laurel finishes, 'absolutely, it's a body thing.'*
>
> *Phoebe continues, 'It's such a…how does everything in your body respond? How does what you are doing, make you respond, and how does the way you're responding make you do something different?'*
>
> *Laurel agrees, remarking 'yeah, I do try to actually communicate that through the piano part as well, so that you feel me coming with you, and, and given that there will be a time when you have a pianist that doesn't give you that much, you have to take responsibility for that yourself, too.'*
>
> *Phoebe jumps in and exclaims, 'and that's what I think, I guess I'm saying that it's a thing that my head is going 'oh now I understand that" – she draws a spiral by her temple with her right hand – 'and then transferring it to the body so the body can then also transfer that to the head – gotcha!, you know!' Phoebe gives the thumbs up and smiles at Laurel.*
>
> *Laurel adds, 'absolutely, that's true and then the two will feed each other, I think, and it will become natural. I was thinking in those few cases where I corrected your vowels: Mozart is almost like dressing like Audrey Hepburn. Absolutely clear and absolutely classic, and no frou frous. You know, singing nineteenth century stuff is full of frou frous, you know, burbles and…all sort of hair everywhere…*
>
> *'That's what we call it 'classic' for – clean lines and it feels clean, and you pursue a line in that way. It's really quite a different thing; a wonderful thing. Good. I think that no matter what kind of a voice you end up with, honey, you will go through a period where Mozart will be your bread and butter, literally. It will be what you will earn your living doing. So to do it well… Mozart's not a matter of little voice or big voice, it's a matter of understanding, I think – it's a matter of… really good technique, and understanding the style. If you don't have really good technique you won't do it.'*

Phoebe grins and says, 'wunderbar!'
Laurel pauses and looks at her watch. 'Beautiful. I think we've done extremely well –
look at the time by golly! It's time we stopped!'

In this excerpt Laurel is giving Phoebe permission to verbally articulate sensation. Laurel also supports and validates Phoebe's experiences, by agreeing with her and then proffering alternative suggestions that extends Phoebe's concepts about singing technique and music. She provides Phoebe with emerging ideas about Mozart's style, gently inculcating her in ways that will not necessarily be understood at the time, but which may be explored in future. Laurel's mentoring is evident also, through comments about future performance preparation and career. Also evident is the deep engagement of the two in the learning and teaching process, so much so that the passing of time goes unobserved until after the end of the hour.

The moments in this exchange that are the 'implicit structure' of Shulman's signature pedagogy may be considered the typical, throw away lines of a singing teacher explaining concepts about Mozart and accompaniment, tension and release, couched within a profound understanding of the rigours of the profession. Laurel is shaping Phoebe's mental concepts about Mozart and about vocal technique. By asking Phoebe how she understood Mozart style, she is ensuring Phoebe will be able to replicate the sensation during home practice, a skill Laurel was not taught as a student. Laurel's teaching approach is a deliberate reaction to how she was taught, both good and bad. Laurel seems determined not to repeat obsolete traditions, but instead is attempting to forge a new pedagogic path for her students.

3.8   Discussion and Conclusion

This chapter focussed on the following three questions: How have experiences of teaching and learning singing influenced the three teachers' current pedagogical approaches to their students in the conservatorium studio? How may the environment in which a teacher works influence their teaching approach? What are some of the implicit assumptions about singing that each teacher is imparting to their student?

As was illustrated by the three singing teachers and their experiences, singing teachers are imparting more than mere technical skill development. Shulman's 'habits of the mind, heart and hand' are well in evidence in these three examples, where tacit and enculturated knowledge about the operatic community are embedded within seemingly casual conversation, and where the implicit structure of this signature pedagogy shapes ways to approach teaching and learning and much of current attitudes towards the operatic profession.

Norah's mentor-like approach reveals her desire that her student develop autonomy and independence in preparation for a life in opera. Her casual praise of her student's voice indicates how well she knows the need to be encouraging and supportive and her long teaching experience helps guide the student through the maze of repertoire choices available.

Lukas's approach to his student, attempting to guide her through the rigours of planning, practice and self-awareness, has been shaped in part by the student's low ability and commitment, which he claims is the product of a low entrance standard and lackadaisical institutional organisation. This has prevented him from successfully imparting what he feels are implicit essentials for the operatic profession: hard work, preparation and commitment.

Laurel's approach to vocal pedagogy incorporates not just the physical act of vocal pedagogy, but as was seen in the excerpt, many comments about Mozart style and the connection between musical style and technique. Her teaching style in this excerpt allows for open discussion and contemplation, as she carefully guides her student towards correct singing technique by ensuring it comes back to the music.

The role of the singing teacher has at once expanded and contracted. Expanded, as Callaghan, Emmons and Popeil claim, because the master/apprentice mode of teaching, based within a

> continuous tradition has become fragmented, since teachers now confront a genre and style proliferation encompassing a wide time span and geographic spread. Teachers must be time efficient, must work with students of all voice types, and must work with a wide repertoire. (2012, 559)

Contracted, because the time spent with each student has reduced from perhaps several hours per week, to, in many cases, less than 1 h per week, usually because of the financial constraints of conservatoires unable to offer more than a bare bones education for their undergraduates.

It is the singing teacher who perhaps bears the brunt of much of this stripping back of what is essentially an apprenticeship path, becoming coach, mentor, advisor and technician, all within the space of perhaps an hour a week. Arguably, teachers are vital conduits of information for students, providing mentor-like assistance for competitions, and enabling acceptance into the profession. A student's tertiary singing teacher may even be the only person with whom the singer has any point of reference about how the operatic world works, from repertoire choices, to performance attire, to networking opportunities and the international stage.

As was seen in the above excerpts, teachers impart implicit knowledge, domain skills and professional attitudes throughout even the smallest transactions. Enculturation into the operatic profession is an ongoing process, and experienced, expert singing teachers are themselves important conduits to enabling students to realise their operatic ambitions, in more areas than skill acquisition. Of the singing teachers in this chapter, and of their students, they are indeed forming helping form habits of the mind, heart and hand.

References

Bruner, J. (1996). *The culture of education*. Cambridge, MA: Harvard University Press.

Burwell, K. (2006). On musicians and singers. An investigation of different approaches taken by vocal and instrumental teachers in higher education. *Music Education Research, 8*(3), 331–347.

Callaghan, J., Emmons, S., & Popeil, L. (2012). Solo voice pedagogy. In G. E. McPherson & G. F. Welch (Eds.), *The Oxford handbook of music education* (Vol. 1, pp. 559–580). New York: Oxford University Press.

Chapman, J. (2006). *Singing and teaching singing: A holistic approach to classical voice*. San Diego: Plural.

Clandinin, J., & Caine, V. (2008). Narrative inquiry. In *The Sage encyclopedia of qualitative research methods* (Vol. 2, pp. 514–544). Thousand Oaks: Sage Publications.

Davidson, J., & Jordan, N. (2007). Private teaching, private learning: An exploration of music instrument learning in the private studio, Junior and Senior Conservatories. In L. Bresler (Ed.), *International handbook of research in arts education* (pp. 729–744). Dordrecht, The Netherlands: Springer.

Gaunt, H. (2008). One-to-one tuition in a conservatoire: The perceptions of instrumental and vocal teachers. *Psychology of Music, 36*, 215–245.

Johnson, R. (2009). Critically reflective musicianship. In T. A. Regelski & J. T. Gates (Eds.), *Music education for changing times* (Landscapes: The arts, aesthetics, and education 7) (pp. 17–28). Dordrecht, The Netherlands: Springer.

Ritterman, J. (2010). Conservatories 5: English speaking countries. *Grove Music Online*. Retrieved from http://www.oxfordmusiconline.com:80/subscriber/article/grove/music/41225

Shulman, L. (2005). Signature pedagogies in the professions. *Daedalus: American Academy of Arts and Sciences, 134*(3), 52–59.

Tosi, F. (1743/1987). *Observations on the florid song* (J. E. Galliard, Trans.). London: Stainer and Bell. (Original work published 1743)

Welch, G., Himonides, E., & Brereton, J. (2005). Real time feedback in the singing studio: An innovatory action-research project using new voice technology. *Music Education Research, 7*(2), 225–249.

Chapter 4
Teaching Popular Music Styles

Kim Chandler

Abstract As the newest of the singing styles to be taught in music institutions and private studios, the pedagogy for teaching popular singing is in its early days relative to other styles of singing, i.e. classical, jazz and musical theatre. Nonetheless, given that there are now pop stars celebrating career lengths of over 50 years, pop singing has been in existence sufficiently long that, for teaching purposes, a cohesive picture of the desired 'pop voice' is emerging. While contemporary singing shares commonalities with other singing styles, the specifics are distinctive and non-generic, requiring a level of specialized knowledge, training and competence by the people teaching it. Though not intended to be exhaustive, a broad overview of the main requirements for teaching contemporary singers is the purpose of this chapter, presented under three main headings: Technique, Musicianship and Interpretation.

Keywords Contemporary singing technique • Modern vocal pedagogy • Popular music • Voice • Vocal • Vocalist • Singing • Singer • Contemporary pedagogy • Teaching

Popular music has been an important part of contemporary society since the advent of Rock and Roll in the 1950s. It has grown and developed into a plethora of styles, such as Rock, Soul, Dance, R&B, Funk, Reggae, Indie, Country, Folk, and Metal, by having combined various elements of American Folk and African-American music. Vocally, it is identified by a speech-like or naturalistic sound. Individuality is highly prized, and its directness in performance evidently appeals to the largest music market in the world.

For the purposes of this chapter, the definition of pop singing shall be limited to the mainstream vocal styles pioneered by pop artists in the 1960s, whose innovations

K. Chandler (✉)
Popular Music Pathway, Leeds College of Music, Leeds, UK
e-mail: kim@kimchandler.com

S.D. Harrison and J. O'Bryan (eds.), *Teaching Singing in the 21st Century*,
Landscapes: the Arts, Aesthetics, and Education 14, DOI 10.1007/978-94-017-8851-9_4,
© Springer Science+Business Media Dordrecht 2014

continue to develop to the present day. In comparison to Classical, Jazz and Musical Theatre singing, there is less established tradition to rely upon. Nonetheless, given that there are now pop stars celebrating career lengths of over 50 years, it has been in existence sufficiently long that, for teaching purposes, a cohesive picture of the desired 'pop voice' is emerging.

Because Classical singing is the oldest and most established form of singing in the Western world, it is arguably the prevailing teaching model. Many singing teachers are classically trained and oriented. Classical teaching methods were designed for singing Classical repertoire so aspects of it do not automatically apply to non-Classical styles of singing. There are many fundamental differences between Classical and Contemporary singing as the Table 4.1 outlines.

Although contemporary singing is routinely taught in music institutions and private studios throughout the world, the pedagogy for teaching it is still in its early days relative to other styles of singing. While pop singing certainly shares commonalities with other singing styles, the specifics are distinctive and non-generic, requiring specialized knowledge, training and competence on behalf of those teaching it. Though not intended to be exhaustive, a broad overview of the main requirements for teaching contemporary singers is the purpose of this chapter. This topic shall be presented in three parts: Technique, Musicianship and Interpretation.

4.1 Technique

4.1.1 Posture and Alignment

Contemporary singers generally move to the beat when they perform, so a dynamic, flexible posture is required. Apart from the obvious benefits of regular cardiovascular exercise, the practice of exercise systems such as Yoga, Pilates, the Alexander Technique and Feldenkrais can help singers gain core strength and a balanced posture, as evidenced by an efficient alignment of the head, neck, shoulders, chest. Posture also has implications for vocal efficiency, as American pedagogue Meribeth Dayme (Bunch) claims: 'resolution of problems of alignment and posture can evoke startling improvement in voice production' (2000, 5). Technical benefits aside, efficient posture also looks strong and confident.

A significant number of pop performers sing and accompany themselves on instruments. Keyboard players and guitarists (including bass players) are prone to jutting their jaw forward and drummers lifting their chins up in an effort to reach the microphone to sing. This can compromise vocal efficiency, as Australian pedagogue Janice Chapman outlines: '…asymmetric singers may be distorting their resonating tube as well as affecting laryngeal efficiency' (2006, 31).

Due to habit, they can continue to sing with these undesirable postures even when singing without their instruments. Therefore, the microphone and stand used in rehearsal and performance should always be placed in the best possible position for efficient singing alignment, whether singers are accompanying themselves or not.

Table 4.1 Fundamental differences between classical and contemporary singing

Issue	Classical	Contemporary
1. Posture	Static/dramatic action (opera)	Dynamic/movement to beat
2. Breathing	Long, legato phrases	Shorter phrases (conversational)
3. Onsets	Simultaneous, balanced, coordinated	Glottal, aspirate, 'scoops', 'creak', 'cry'
4. Larynx position	Neutral/lowered	Neutral/raised
5. Sung tone	Pure, 'trained' tone (Women) use of 'head' voice 'Sob'/'Cry' quality 'Covered' tone	'Naturalistic' tone 'Chest' voice (for both genders) 'Mix' & 'Belt' quality Sometimes 'twangy' (or strident)
6. Diction	Italianate vowels All consonants pronounced	Americanised vowels Initial consonants are emphasized, ending consonants de-emphasized
7. Sung Accent	English (R.P.) or various European accents	Generic, Americanised slang or vernacular
8. Rhythm	Unsyncopated ('straight'), rubato	Syncopated, specific to 'groove'
9. Vibrato	Heavy	Light
10. Pitch (scales used in vocal melodies)	Traditional diatonic scales used, Chromatic	Hexatonic scales such as the Blues, Pentatonic scales, Modes
11. Vocal harmony	Reading parts SATB voicings, specific harmonic rules	Intuitive parts, i.e. 'by ear' Triadic, added-note chords
12. Range	Italian voice classifications	Generic male and female ranges
13. Agility	Diatonic/chromatic coloratura	Pentatonic/hexatonic melismas
14. Musicianship	Classical theory	Popular Music theory
15. Improvisation	Cadenzas, avant-garde music	'Ad libs', 'riffs', 'runs' are improvised
16. Paralinguistic Vocal 'effects'	Only generally found in extended vocal techniques (avant-garde)	Vocal distortion, growls, grunts, moans, aspirate endings, etc. can be used
17. Visual	Formal attire, costumes (opera)	Informal, smart casual dress
18. Performance Venue	Formal, early evening performances	Informal, late evening performances
19. Amplification	Technique designed for unamplified singing	Performances always amplified. Microphone technique important
20. Vocal Health Issues	Competing with live orchestral accompaniment. Loud, acoustic singing practice in small practice rooms	Loud, amplified singing in competition with loud, amplified instruments, bad monitoring, hearing damage, lifestyle issues

Sentinal Ltd. Reproduced with permission

4.1.2   Breathing and Support

While in classical singing long, legato phrases are commonplace, in popular music vocal phrases are generally delivered in a more conversational way, as befits the vernacular lyric. American rock specialist Mark Baxter explains: 'the singer breathes as if it was speech with a natural exchange of air' (1989, 57). Nonetheless, the breathing requirements are still over and above that of the relatively shallow, tidal breathing of everyday life and therefore benefits from being exercised and optimized.

It is my experience that breathing for singing generally needs to be explained to untrained singers because there is often a tendency to gasp in a shallow, clavicular (chest) breath that can lead to a reverse abdominal breathing pattern. A silent, low, effective, reflexive 'catch' breath or 'recoil' breath, taken in through the mouth, is the most appropriate type of in-breath for singing this repertoire. While breathing through the nose is desirable in terms of warming and humidifying the air, it is too slow for practical usage, except perhaps in a slow tempo song, like a ballad.

There can also be a tendency towards overfilling with air in the mistaken belief that 'more is better', especially as preparation for high intensity singing. This myth needs dispelling straight away, as American teacher Seth Riggs asserts: 'you can have a tremendous supply of air and still not sing well. The more air you send them, the tighter your cords have to get to hold it back' (1994, 146, 22).

The support system, like posture, needs to be flexible and dynamic for this music. The support strategy I find most effective is similar to that which one can feel happening in natural responses such as laughter, i.e. a gentle inward/upward movement of the lower abdominal wall on voicing. This movement should happen at the onset of each sung phrase and adjust reflexively depending on the intensity of the singing. For example, the authors of *Rock Singing Techniques* advise that 'steady support from the strong muscles of the lower abdomen is essential to achieving a healthy belting style' (Farnum Surmani and Mitchell 1997, 41).

Danish professor Svend Smith's 'Accent Method' approach is particularly appropriate for pop singers given that the exercises are accompanied by a drum (as is most pop music) and feature call and response – a musical device that harks back to the African roots of pop music (Thyme-Frokjaer et al. 2001).

4.1.3   Tone

There are many terms in current use for describing different voice qualities, settings and registers. Each sector of the vocal community, i.e. the classical community, musical theatre community, contemporary community, medical community, voice science community and even certain vocal methods, use an array of different terms that I advocate teachers to be aware of. However, I personally favour the use of the more traditional terms 'chest voice', 'head voice' and 'falsetto', because they are the terms in use in the music industry. In addition, I use other terms familiar to the contemporary vocal community such as 'mix voice' and 'belt'.

Establishing an efficient, sustainable, balanced, free, clear tone and a smoothly connected vocal range is the goal of all healthy singing. Nonetheless, certain commercial repertoire also requires the tonal extremes of breathy singing through to belting, and even deliberate register breaks or 'flips'.

Breathy singing – the 'stock-in-trade' sound of boy bands, sultry soul, Pop R&B voices, folk singers etc., only became possible with the advent of the microphone. Technically it's quite inefficient and puts a deal of pressure on the breathing mechanism; it is inherently unstable and can tend to dry the voice out. Artistically, however, it can be very emotive. Sometimes untrained singers present with this quality as the only one they can produce, due to inefficient cord closure, so it is a priority to work on developing an air-efficient tone first. Later, once the cord closure has improved, breathy tone can be reinstated as a conscious artistic tonal choice.

At times pop repertoire requires singers to take a heavy vocal setting above the main passaggio. Singing at the intensity level of yelling or calling is known as 'belting' and its various forms feature in genres such as Rock, Gospel, Soul, Dance, Metal and so forth. Finding safe and sustainable ways of belting is possible, so it is necessary for teachers to learn these strategies if they wish to teach it.

American voice teacher Anne Peckham sensibly advises: 'Healthy belting can be achieved only if singers are careful to maintain their vocal health, avoid overuse, and use common sense when singing' (2000, 55). American pedagogue Jo Estill, one of the first teachers to legitimize belting, and Danish pedagogue Cathrine Sadolin[1] are amongst those who have forged effective, research-based methods for teaching belting.

There are times when it's desirable to be able to effect a controlled register break for stylistic purposes, e.g. the characteristic 'flip' heard in country, folk, indie pop/rock and in pop R&B. While beginning singers can be prone to flipping unceremoniously into falsetto at higher pitches due to insufficient technical control, the essential difference here is that this break is being utilised as an artistic, interpretative choice by the singer and isn't a technical fault.

Apart from the extremes of breathy tone and belt, a quintessentially 'pop' quality, particularly for female singers, is their 'mix' voice.[2] The definition I use is the continuation of a 'chest'-like tone above the main passaggio but with more 'Twang' and 'Cry' added.[3] There is no sensation of a 'gear change' and, with practice and training, most singers can take this setting up quite high in the range (with repertoire these days requiring this quality up to around an F5). It's a medium-intensity setting that is qualitatively different to both head voice and belt (other settings that share this higher range).

For female singers, head voice and falsetto are rarely featured in pop repertoire. Nonetheless, routine practice of vocal exercises that extend up into the head

---

[1] Sadolin has changed her use of the term 'Belting' in her model to 'Edge'.
[2] Known variously as 'mixed' voice and 'blended' voice.
[3] See Sect. 4.1.4 for definitions of these terms.

voice range are important for vocal health and flexibility, and for the occasional times that this quality is used in repertoire. For male singers however, these qualities can be heard more often, for example in Soul and R&B. For all singers though, checking the accessibility of lighter qualities such as head voice is a reliable test of vocal health.

The practice of onsets is suggested, e.g. glottal onsets, 'simultaneous' or 'glide' onsets, 'aspirate' (or breathy) onsets (Estill 1997a, 46–51), 'creak' onsets, 'cry' onsets etc., as they have implications for technique, tone and style. The glottal onset, variously known as the glottal 'stroke', 'stop', 'attack', 'plosive' and 'shock', has been viewed with suspicion in the past, as the following statement by esteemed American pedagogue William Vennard represents: 'The glottal plosive is really a slight cough…[and]…laryngologists agree [it] is damaging…' (1968, 43).

However, due to the vernacular language used in pop songs, a light glottal onset is wholly appropriate. It also has technical benefits for improving inefficient vocal cord closure (as does the simultaneous onset). Breathy onsets are stylistic and can also assist in helping singers presenting with pressed phonation. Creak onsets, cry onsets in addition to scooping up to and even down onto notes are stylistic onsets only. There are many offsets used too that should be included in training, such as aspirate, creak and cry offsets.

4.1.4   Tonal Additions

In addition to the main tonal settings described previously, there are other sounds that can be added for effect, e.g. twang, various vocal distortions etc.

'Twang' (Estill 1997a, 158) or 'Pharyngeal Voice' (Buescher and Sims 2011, 23) are the terms used to describe the bright, nasally resonant sound that is heard to a greater or lesser extent in many mainstream pop styles. Because it boosts the higher frequencies in the acoustic spectrum, it is projective but requires little physical effort. As a result, it's a particularly effective strategy for pacing oneself through the rigors of live performance. Estill has devised a whole technique for isolating and controlling this quality that pop singers may benefit from exploring (1997a, 158–163 and 1997b, 29–36). 'Cry', achieved according to Estill via the thyroid cartilage tilting forward (1997a, 84), is also a useful quality '…making pop music easier to sing at any part of the range, but especially in the upper frequencies' (1997a, 85).

Vocal distortion and 'grit' are heard mostly in Rock and Metal, but they can also be heard at times in other styles such as Gospel, Soul, Disco and Funk. Although sometimes associated with vocal pathology, there are singers who naturally sing with a raspy, gritty texture and present no problems with vocal reliability and stamina, as American voice teacher Jeffrey Allen observes: 'They can sing for hours this way and not feel any discomfort' (1994, 302).

While there are a handful of coaches tackling the teaching of vocal grit and distortion, Sadolin in particular has devised a lexicon of terms and robust technique for teaching these extreme, high intensity, somewhat controversial sounds in sustainable, achievable ways. The terms used in this method are Growl, Rattle, Scream, Distortion and Grunt, each formed by various supraglottic structures in the vocal tract, thereby not directly interfering with the free vibratory pattern of the vocal folds (2008, 177).

4.1.5 Larynx Position

Altering the larynx position is volitional and can elicit distinct changes in the resulting vocal sound by lengthening or shortening the vocal tract. Unlike in Classical singing, using a lowered larynx isn't generally found in many contemporary singers. The resultant darker quality doesn't feature much except in rare cases, such as Cher or Heather Small from 'M People'.

The preferred larynx position for singing commercial music is either neutral (speech-like) or slightly raised to help achieve the brighter, 'twangier' effect discussed previously. A raised larynx position can cause concern to classically trained teachers, as is evidenced in the following statement by American pedagogue Richard Miller: 'A high larynx causes [laryngeal] hypertension…' (1996, 83). On the other hand, Oren Brown, another well-respected American classical singing teacher, adopted a more moderate view by considering the laryngeal position for singing to be a matter of choice and taste: 'The high larynx position produces the quality used by many popular singers…There seems to be no harm done to the vocal folds' (1998, 84).

4.1.6 Diction

Due to pop music's conversational style, the use of slang and a speech-like pronunciation is most appropriate. The primary articulators: the tongue and lips, are worked hardest in styles such as Pop R&B, Funk and particularly Rap, where consonants are used for their percussive effect and rhythmic energy. Musically relevant articulation exercises are recommended, such as taking segments of pop songs to use for this purpose. An example would be the iconic 2-part vocal hook featured in the Coda section of Michael Jackson's hit song *Wanna Be Starting Something* (Epic 1983).[4]

A delicate balance between over and under articulation is required. My general suggestion is that the initial consonants of lyrically and rhythmically significant words be emphasized in order to create drive and intensity. Conversely, the consonants at the ends of words are generally de-emphasized. Fortunately, the right amount of consonant pressure is also technically efficient.

---

[4]This sung Coda section has been reused in other more recent pop songs such as Rihanna's hit *Don't Stop The Music* (Def Jam 2007).

In classical singing it is necessary to sing in an authentic accent in languages such as Italian, French, German, Russian and suchlike. It is often necessary to modify one's own native speaking accent for singing, as Howard explains: 'a singing technique constrains vowel sounds, because all singers have to be able to produce similar sounds for the particular style, whereas in speech the range of accents is limitless' (in Comins 2001, 29).

Because America has been the foundation and epicenter of popular music, it comes as no surprise that the vast majority of contemporary repertoire is sung with an American accent. Even for non-American singers, there is an Americanization of the sung vowels, in most cases, in order to achieve an authentic delivery. It creates a more homogenized sung accent, thereby making it difficult to tell the nationality of the singer, as Gibson states:

> Singers draw on their memories of popular music when they sing. Their use of American pronunciation in singing is therefore the result of the fact that a majority of their memories of pop singing involve American-influenced phonetic forms (2010).

Exceptions to this are groups like the Beatles, The Proclaimers, The Cranberries, and Catatonia where their British regional accents are fully embraced, constituting their signature sound.

4.1.7   Vibrato

A controlled, natural vibrato is an asset to any singer, as Allen notes: 'a smooth, even vibrato appears…when the secrets of singing are mastered and well-integrated' (1994, 194). A balanced vocal instrument doesn't display a shaking jaw, pulsating tongue, wobble, bleat, tremolo or uneven modulation. Vibrato also ought not be too wide, too slow, too fast, or completely non-existent, except where it's an artistic choice.

Pop music requires the subtlest use of vibrato in comparison to other styles of singing. In fact, there are pop artists with highly successful, well-established careers who sing with a relatively straight tone, for example, Chris Martin from Coldplay, Liam Gallagher from Oasis, Sting and Sade. However, the general vibrato setting for contemporary singers is light and even. It should vary slightly in speed depending upon the type of song being sung, that is, faster for an energetic song and slower for ballad. Howard elucidates:

> Vibrato is one aspect which varies with singing style for even a single performer. Thus it is not simply physiologically based, but it must derive in part from characteristics of other aspects of the music itself such as style, culture, and performance practice. (2010, 88)

There are various terms used to describe different types of vibrato. For example, Swedish contemporary coach Daniel Zangger-Borch identifies two types of vibrato: 'Natural Vibrato' based on pitch variation and 'Pop Vibrato' based on intensity fluctuation (2005, 51). Sadolin also identifies two similar types but calls them 'Laryngeal Vibrato' and 'Hammer Vibrato' respectively (2008, 209). In my experience a subtle pitch-modulation vibrato is the usual option for contemporary singers, in most cases.

4.1.8 Range

In broad terms, pop melodies for female singers are written within a G3 to a D5 range (i.e. standard Alto range) and between a C3 to a G4 (i.e. standard Tenor range) for male singers. The Italian voice classifications associated with classical music (i.e. Soprano, Alto, Tenor, Bass) are not appropriate descriptions for pop singers' range types. Pop singers are generally described firstly by their gender and then by the style they sing, e.g. a 'male soul singer' or a 'female rock singer'.

Nevertheless, in keeping with the ideals of individuality, there are artists who sing outside of the 'normal' ranges. For example, rock singer Robert Plant from Led Zeppelin can sing in full voice in female range and folk-rock singer Tracy Chapman can sing comfortably in male range. Soul singer Barry White made his career on his unusually low voice and Pop R&B singer Mariah Carey often made a feature of her ability to sing to excessively high in 'whistle tone'.

In training, singers should vocalize over their whole range for the sake of vocal efficiency. The various 'sirens', or semi-occluded pitch-glide/portamento exercises, are particularly suitable for this purpose in smoothing out the passaggi and for stretching out and optimizing the vocal range. Arpeggios of different types are also useful for developing the range and the ear, when based on the various chords used in contemporary repertoire (see Sect. 4.2.2 for more detail).

Borch claims that 'a vocal range of around two octaves is quite common and generally considered a pre-requisite for working as a professional singer' (2005, 39). This is an ideal 'working range' that will cover the span of notes likely to be encountered in most pop melodies. However, I would also advocate that singers work towards establishing at least a three-octave 'exercising range' in order to maintain optimal vocal flexibility.

4.1.9 Agility

Like coloratura and fioratura in Classical music, African-American pop styles also feature melismatic runs. Known as 'licks' or 'riffs', I have observed through analysis that they tend to be based on the Major and Minor Pentatonic scales and the Minor Hexatonic Scale,[5] so routine practice of these scales is advisable. Licks can be quite

---

[5] See Sect. 4.2.2 for a definition of this scale.

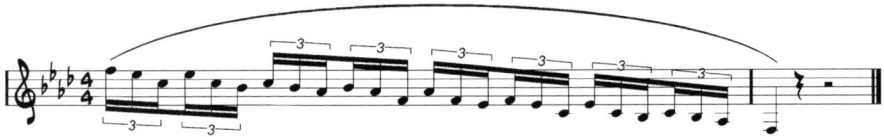

Fig. 4.1 Two-octave 'lick' exercise based on the Minor Pentatonic scale

short, i.e. only 3–4 notes long, or quite extended, as the following 2-octave exercise I created here, based on the Minor Pentatonic scale, demonstrates (Fig. 4.1).

It has been my experience that singers with limited control in this area tend to slide from note to note, creating an indistinct execution of the notes in the run. Therefore, singers should only practice agility exercises at a tempo where the pitch is accurate, incrementally increasing the speed over time (with a metronome) as more skill develops.

Singers and teachers can create their own agility exercises from repertoire. For example, one can practice the embellishments encountered in recorded pop material by isolating one run at a time, learning it and then repeating it in the semitonal (or half-step) key changes of standard vocal exercises. Not only does this work on vocal agility, but also develops the ability to aurally distinguish the notes involved – a useful pursuit in itself. In addition, using repertoire examples ensures an endless supply of directly relevant, up-to-date vocal exercises.

4.2 Musicianship

'*Be first a musician and second a singer*' – Richard Miller

The commercial music industry doesn't expect or require artists and musicians to be formally trained. Nevertheless, it is arguable that every serious musician, including singers, should understand the fundamentals of their craft, i.e. music theory, ear training, analyzing, reading and even transcribing music. Musical training brings immeasurable insight to all aspects of performing and writing music. Pop singers are recognizing the need to be trained these days as evidenced by the surge in popular music courses in institutions around the world and an increased interest in having private tuition.

The basis for theoretical training should be popular music theory rather than classical theory as it's specific to the idiom, placing '… more emphasis on the practical application of knowledge with regard to improvisation and the particular harmonic structures, modes, etc. prevalent in popular music genres' (London College of Music grades syllabus 2011, 12). The vast majority of pop work requires singers to operate 'by ear' and therefore aural training directly related to the repertoire is indispensable.

doon-t-t-ka-t-t-doon-t-t-ka-t-t...

Fig. 4.2 doon: voiced low, imitating a kick drum, t: unvoiced, imitating a high-hat cymbal, ka: voiced higher, imitating a snare drum*

4.2.1   Rhythm

Pop singers need a strong sense of 'pulse' (ground beat) and a highly refined sense of syncopation, as this is one of the main musical elements of the repertoire. All 'grooves' in pop music can be reduced to specific pulse beats of 8ths (also known as 'quavers'), 16ths (also known as 'semiquavers') or triplets. 'Feels' are used to describe how these subdivisions are to be interpreted, e.g. straight, swing, half-time, double-time, etc. However, stylistic labels such as 'rock' can be further sub-categorised into pop-rock, funk-rock, hard-rock, soft-rock, and others (Stoloff 1999, 120).

To be an effective part of a musical team, singers need to be conversant with the subtle differences of rhythmic phrasing specific to each sub-genre of pop they perform. As British teacher Tona de Brett explains: 'rhythm is supple and elastic…understand the difference between what you do, with the underlying beat of the music' (1996, 16). I also suggest that pop singers practice rhythmic co-ordination exercises, such as learning to imitate basic drum patterns with the voice that's known as 'beatboxing' (Fig. 4.2).

This not only helps internalize the sense of groove that a singer's rhythmic phrasing is dependent upon, but also serves as a useful form of articulation exercise.

4.2.2   Melody

Singers need to be knowledgeable about the musical 'alphabet' used in the melodies they sing. The routine practice of standard vocal exercises built around major[6] and natural minor[7] scales is valuable, as most pop melodies are built on these scales. However, other scales and modes that feature prominently in pop melodies are the Blues scale, Minor Hexatonic scale,[8] Pentatonic scales and the

---

*This is inspired by the work of Bob Stoloff who has many & varied beatboxing exercises in his book Scat (see References for details)

[6] Or Ionian mode.

[7] Or Aeolian mode.

[8] Minor Hexatonic scale: 1-2-b3-4-5-b7. This scale came out as the third most-used scale in pop vocal melodies (after the Natural Minor scale and Major scale respectively) in a recent analysis of many charting pop songs conducted by this author.

Fig. 4.3 Major – Lydian – Major exercise

modes of the Major Scale,[9] thereby necessitating vocal exercises to be based on these patterns also.

To serve as an example, Fig. 4.3 is a vocal exercise I created that is a variation of a standard 5-note scale exercise based on the more familiar major scale and less familiar Lydian mode.

I also advocate routine practice of all the intervals, to at least an octave, and arpeggios based on a variety of the different chords types found in contemporary music:

- Triads: Major, Minor, Augmented, Diminished, Sus2 and Sus4
- 4-note chords: Major 6ths, Minor 6ths, Dominant 7ths, Major 7ths, Minor 7ths, Half-Diminished, Diminished 7ths
- 5-note chords: Dominant 9th, Major 9ths, Minor 9ths etc.

In espousing the benefits of this knowledge for helping develop harmonization skills, American teachers Mike Campbell and Tracee Lewis state, 'learning to read notes, recognize intervals, and sing scales and chords will be a tremendous help…' (2001, 22). It's also important that the musical examples used to learn these patterns are sourced from contemporary repertoire so that vocalists can see the direct relevance of music theory to the songs they sing.

4.2.3 Harmony

While reading SATB scores is common practice in traditional choral training, vocal harmonies in pop are mostly constructed instinctively 'by ear', as befits the cultural roots of the music. To be more widely employable in the pop music industry, it is my opinion that singers should not only be competent lead vocalists, but also be proficient backing (background) vocalists.

Being a backing vocalist requires a singer to work as part of a team with other singers. It is a support role to the lead vocalist, demanding uniform breathing, blending tone and vibrato, pitch accuracy, confidence in holding one's own harmony part, matching rhythmic feel, phrasing, diction and dynamics of the song; all in addition to coordinated movement. Backing vocals are a vital ingredient of many pop performances in both recording and live performance.

---

[9] Being the Dorian, Phrygian, Lydian, Mixolydian and Locrian modes.

In outlining the educational value of vocal harmonization, de Brett claims 'you will learn more about music in a few hours than a dozen books could teach you...' (1996, 16). As a backing vocal specialist myself, it is my opinion that an intuitive rather than theoretical approach is the best strategy for working out harmonies. Students can practice singing spontaneous harmony lines to any song to help develop this area. In contrast to classical 4-part harmonies, pop singers need to master basic triadic harmony, moving onto more complex harmonies when more proficiency is developed.

It has been my observation that learning a chordal instrument, such as the keyboard or guitar, seems to provide an advantage to singers as regards their ability to harmonize by ear, perhaps due to the internalization of chord structure that takes place. It also provides many other benefits such as the discipline of practice, the learning of musical fundamentals, the basis of accompaniment and creative invention and the development of reading skills that can be further extended into sight singing.

4.2.4 Improvisation

Vocal improvisation is a common feature of popular music, most especially in that of African-American origin or influence, providing singers with the opportunity to create spontaneous melody that is fresh and exciting for the both the performer and audience. I encourage singers to experiment with melodic variation (having learnt the original melody first), adding embellishment and experimenting with the spontaneous improvisation of melodies known as 'ad-libbing', 'raving' or 'riffing'.

Part of the exhilaration of singing results from improvisatory elements being incorporated into the music, but what is the thrill of risk for some may be crippling fear of the unknown to others. For those who are apprehensive about improvising, it is advisable to work to a simple chord sequence, giving the student song lyrics to use and encouraging them to spontaneously invent a new melody. As contemporary teacher Donna Soto-Morettini observes: 'In order to improvise well, a singer must be very comfortable with the harmonic structure of a song' (2006, 66). The practice of improvisation can constitute a regular part of a vocal practice regime for those who need it.

4.2.5 Notation

There are occasions, such as in some studio sessions and live performances, where vocalists are required to read music. This reduces rehearsal time where the material would be too long to memorize. Sight singing should ideally form part of a pop singer's training, as Campbell advises: 'learning to read music is not very difficult if you organize your time and practice the exercises every day ... one of the most important keys to sight-singing is simply reading through lots of material' (1998, 4). Musical literacy in singers is desirable because the music industry is becoming increasingly more competitive and therefore singers will benefit from being musically educated and multi-skilled.

4.3   Interpretation

4.3.1   Historical Context

Knowing the basic history of music in general, and the roots of popular music specifically is useful background knowledge. It informs who the key artists are in the genre and outlines stylistic movements and trends over the decades, since its inception to the present day.

4.3.2   Repertoire

Teachers should have a wide knowledge of popular repertoire from the more 'classic' material through to the current. This will help them make informed decisions about the appropriateness of repertoire choice for students and provide awareness of the issues related to the performance of specific songs.

4.3.3   Musical Styles

It is desirable that teachers know the stylistic differences between the various genres of contemporary music. Even a little research into each genre will further reveal sub-genres, cross genres, derivative genres and 'sibling' genres. To be aware of at least the basic differences is necessary so as to pass on accurate advice about how to achieve an authentic vocal delivery in each style. In Table 4.2 is a summary of some broad generalizations I've made regarding the variation in vocal requirements across some of the main styles.

4.3.4   Live Performance

As distinct from recordings, in live performance the audience watches and listens to a singer, as Australian teacher Pat Wilson explains: 'it is elementary courtesy as well as good business to ensure that your customers are visually entertained' (1997, 59). Therefore, it's important that students are given advice regarding the visual side of

Table 4.2 Broad generalizations of stylistic variation

Rock: This is a strong, direct vocal style delivered with high intensity. It can be heard using clean tone, but vocal grit and distortion are more usual. It favors vocal power and size over vocal embellishment and flourish

Soul: Having come straight out of the Black Gospel church, this vocal style favours emotionality delivered via a wide dynamic range, legato phrases and some melodic embellishment

Funk: Though having grown directly out of Soul music, Funk differs by being more punctuated, energetic, rhythmically percussive and less embellished. The melody lines are often like horn (brass) parts and the rhythmic phrasing pushed

R&B: Early R&B was synonymous with Soul & Funk, whereas the more recent Pop R&B often fuses with Hip Hop and Rap. It's characterized by a relatively light vocal delivery with heavy use of embellishment, melisma and fast vibrato

Dance: This is a wide genre vocally if one considers the fact that it covers everything from the often dreamy, light vocals of Trip Hop, through the Funk/Pop singers of Funky House to the belty Soul 'divas' of the charting Dance Anthems

Reggae: Given its Jamaican roots, the accent that Reggae is sung in is highly distinctive. It's generally sung at a medium level of intensity and features minimal vibrato. It's often back phrased

Folk: This style arguably requires the lightest vocal delivery because of the acoustic instruments used in the accompaniment. The lyrics and the story-telling elements of the song are paramount. Singing in regional accents is also embraced

Country: Due to its musical roots, this twangy vocal style is delivered in a strong 'Southern' accent and often features stylistic flips (similar to yodeling) and little 'cries'. It's mostly at a medium intensity and can feature some melodic embellishment

Indie: Is for all intents and purposes a Pop/Rock fusion vocally, but is generally characterized by a rawness & edginess in the vocal delivery and by minimal use of vibrato. An element of quirkiness in the vocals is embraced in this genre

Metal: Having come out of Heavy Rock, this is the most extreme vocal style and requires the highest intensity levels. It features highly expressive, aggressive vocal sounds not heard much in other genres (see Sect. 4.1.4) and is physically very demanding

their performing life. They need to be aware of appropriate attire, grooming, movement, gestures, facial expressions, eye contact, use of stage space and audience psychology. Capturing performances on video is a useful teaching tool, providing invaluable, direct feedback to the student.

As a style that pre-dates the invention of electricity, traditional opera technique is designed to develop voices that can be heard clearly, unamplified, over an orchestral accompaniment. Conversely, pop singers never perform unamplified and this stark contrast has implications for teaching. There is a partnership arrangement between the singer and the microphone, as Wilson explains: 'as a pop vocalist, your instrument is actually a two-part one–body plus microphone' (1997, 59). Therefore, singers should be encouraged to invest in a reliable, industry-standard microphone and be given advice about efficient use, e.g. angle, grip, cable-holding etiquette, avoidance of microphone 'drift' and monitor feedback, and proximity issues, such as avoiding 'popping' on plosive consonants such as 'p' and 'b'.

4.4 Conclusion

With a topic of such magnitude it is inevitable that no one area presented could be investigated fully. It is evident that there are distinct differences between classical and popular singing, as Brown eloquently states (1996, 136): 'popular and classical singers live in different worlds. They have instruments that are physically different and they use different vocal techniques.' A customized teaching methodology is desirable, and I would argue mandatory, for teaching pop singers. Just as there are specialist teachers in the other genres of singing, the time has come to become cognisant of the specific requirements of the pop idiom in order to contribute valuably to the training of the future generations of singers who wish to perform this highly rewarding, exciting, ever-evolving genre.

References

Allen, J. (1994). *Secrets of singing*. Miami: Belwin-Mills.

Baxter, M. (1989). *The rock-n-roll singer's survival manual*. Milwaukee: Hal Leonard.

Brown, O. L. (1996). *Discover your voice*. San Diego: Singular.

Buescher, R., & Sims, S. (2011). The female pharyngeal voice and theories of low vocal fold damping. *Journal of Singing, 68*(1), 23–28.

Bunch, M. (2000). *A handbook of the singing voice*. London: M Bunch.

Campbell, M. (1998). *Sightsinging: The complete method for singers*. Milwaukee: Hal Leonard Corp.

Campbell, M., & Lewis, T. (2001). *Harmony vocals: The essential guide*. Milwaukee: Hal Leonard Corp.

Chandler, K. (2001). *A methodology for singers of popular music*. Masters dissertation, London College of Music, London.

Chapman, J. L. (2006). *Singing and teaching singing: A holistic approach to classical voice*. San Diego: Plural.

Comins, J. (2001). The Pygmalion factor. *The Singer* (June/July ed.).

De Brett, T. (1996). *Discover your voice: Learn to sing from rock to classic*. London: Schott.

Estill, J. (1997a). *Level one: Primer of basic figures*. Santa Rosa: Estill Voice Training Systems.

Estill, J. (1997b). *Level two: Six basic voice qualities*. Santa Rosa: Estill Voice Training Systems.

Farnum Surmani, K., & Mitchell, K. M. (1997). *Rock singing techniques*. Van Nuys: Alfred.

Gibson, A. (2010). *Production and perception of vowels in New Zealand Popular Music*. Masters thesis abstract. http://aut.researchgateway.ac.nz/handle/10292/962. Accessed 14 Apr 2012.

Howard, D. M. (2010). Electrolaryngographically revealed aspects of the voice source in singing. *Logopedics, Phoniatrics, Vocology, 35*, 81–89.

London College of Music. (2011). http://www.popularmusictheory.org/music_theory-syllabus_2011.pdf. Accessed 17 Apr 2012.

Miller, R. (1996). *On the art of singing*. New York: Oxford University Press.

Peckham, A. (2000). *The contemporary singer: Elements of vocal technique*. Boston: Berklee Press.

Riggs, S. (1994). *Singing for the stars*. Van Nuys: Alfred.

Sadolin, C. (2008). *Complete vocal technique*. Copenhagen: CVI.

Soto-Morettini, D. (2006). *Popular singing: A practical guide to: Pop, jazz, blues, rock, country and gospel*. London: A & C Black.

Stoloff, B. (1999). *Scat! Vocal improvisation techniques*. Brooklyn: Gerard and Sarzin.

Thyme-Frokjaer, K., & Frokjaer-Jensen, B. (2001). *The accent method: A rational voice therapy in theory & practice*. Bicester: Speechmark.

Vennard, W. (1968). *Singing: The mechanism and the technic*. New York: Carl Fischer.

Wilson, P. (1997). *The singing voice: An owner's manual*. Paddington/London: Currency Press Ltd/Nick Hern Books.

Zangger Borch, D. (2005). *Ultimate vocal voyage: The definitive method for unleashing the rock, pop or soul singer within you*. Bromma: Notfabriken Music.

Chapter 5
A Brief Overview of Approaches to Teaching the Music Theatre Song

Jeannette L. LoVetri, Mary Saunders-Barton, and Edrie Means Weekly

Abstract As music theatre becomes more important throughout the world, it is being taught in universities and conservatories, often as part of a degree curriculum. While the form has been around for approximately 100 years, in New York and London particularly, there are no universally accepted criteria for teaching it. Performers with music theatre life experience have been asked to become teachers and, over the past several decades, have contributed their approaches as to which ingredients must be conveyed to singers and teachers of singing in order to be effective. This chapter represents the opinions of three women who are college professors who have life experience in professional music theatre at the highest levels. Each of these experts presents their unique viewpoint on how to successfully approach learning a music theatre song, understanding how it should be taught both from a vocal health and vocal production viewpoint, but with an eye and ear towards the expectations of the professional demands of the song itself. Their broad experience as music theatre performers and as teachers, instructing both students and working professionals, offers a close-up overview of twenty-first century expectations for singers in professional music theatre who need to understand how to address today's very challenging repertoire.

Keywords Vocal stylisms • Laryngeal flexibility • Song authenticity • Rock musicals • Vocal endurance • Eight-show weeks • Legit • Belt • Mix • Contemporary Commercial Music

J.L. LoVetri (✉)
The Voice Workshop, New York, NY, USA
e-mail: lovetri@thevoiceworkshop.com

M. Saunders-Barton
Departments of Music and Theatre, Pennsylvania State University,
University Park, PA, USA

E.M. Weekly
Shenandoah Conservatory, CCM Vocal Pedagogy Institute,
Winchester, VA, USA

S.D. Harrison and J. O'Bryan (eds.), *Teaching Singing in the 21st Century*,
Landscapes: the Arts, Aesthetics, and Education 14, DOI 10.1007/978-94-017-8851-9_5,
© Springer Science+Business Media Dordrecht 2014

5.1   How to Begin

There are many ways to approach teaching a music theatre song.

The first requisite is that the teacher be familiar with music theatre. Here in the USA we are faced with a situation in which colleges that heretofore were teaching only classical vocal production and repertoire are now adding music theatre emphasis or degrees to their programs. In most cases the teachers are the same people and find themselves suddenly asked to teach the new repertoire even though they may have neither training to do so nor professional experience in music theatre (LoVetri and Weekly 2003). This being the case, sometimes people teaching music theatre are *not* familiar with it. This is a less than agreeable situation.

Nevertheless, there are many resources available that did not exist even a decade ago to help teachers. Most music from mainstream shows is available online in some form or other, whether it be on YouTube, on iTunes, or on other internet-based sites. Further, the music publisher Hal Leonard has compiled an entire library of songs that are separated into vocal categories, as well as settings for duets and for belters. Sheet music can be purchased online so even those who are isolated in a small town or university, can access music resources for both the ear and eye that will help make it easier to be knowledgeable about the repertoire.

The second requisite is being clear about vocal quality. This goes along with having an educated ear. *If one does not recognize the qualities of sound found in music theatre repertoire it will not be possible to teach them effectively.* Singing teachers and coaches worldwide must become conversant with these vocal qualities and the words used to describe them because using them in a different way is counterproductive.

5.2   The Big Three

The three most important terms to understand are 'legit', 'belt' and 'mix'. There are others, but these three have been used for many decades, particularly here in the USA on Broadway, and have very specific auditory criteria that teachers or coaches should understand when approaching songs.

A 'legit' sound is a classical sound. The term comes from 'legitimate' and in the early days of theatre, prior to electronic amplification, there were only two kinds of vocalists who could fill a theatre with the sound of their voices without help. One group was the classically trained singers – the 'legitimate' ones. The other group was the 'belters'. These people were shouting, in a way, and their sound was clear and trumpet-like. The origin of the term is uncertain, but in the early days of jazz, particularly in New Orleans, singers such as Bessie Smith and Ma Rainey were able to 'shout out' the music over the instruments. In the early 30s a young Ethel Merman burst upon the scene. Her voice was powerful, bright and accurate with both pitches and lyrics. Both Cole Porter, who wrote 'Anything Goes' and Irving Berlin who wrote 'Annie Get Your Gun' for her were thrilled with her singing. Al Jolson, too, was able to sing with power and strong emotion long before amplification. He was the most celebrated performer of his time and sang for decades with his signature sound. All of these people were 'belters' who seemed to be singing the notes by 'hitting them hard' (the dictionary definition of 'belt').

The origin of the term 'mix' on Broadway is unknown. It came to mean a vocal quality that was not quite belt and not quite legit but somewhere in between. Generally, it has leanings more towards a belt sound because it is closely aligned with speech production, but it can also flow easily over into a sound that is lighter on higher notes as well. It generally does not involve 'modified' vowels as would be found in classical singing and varies greatly from song to song and voice to voice.

There are many variables of these terms, mostly created by casting directors as they attempt to describe in words the kinds of sounds they want singers to use in particular songs or roles. Teachers of singing, also, who have developed their own methods or approaches, often come up with their own descriptors, thinking they have found something new and different. This serves to make the terminology involved with singing music theatre songs very confusing.

It's best when the verbal description is coupled to a simultaneous vocalization. Then the label for the sound and the sound itself are inextricably connected. Writing about singing, using words to describe vocal sound, isn't particularly useful. Without a way to replicate the sound consistently and know what to call it, it is difficult to develop a reliable way to depend upon it in music. Therefore, those who wish to teach a music theatre song must understand that having access to a reliable technique to produce the desired or required vocal quality sounds is a necessity. Those sounds, too, should always been connected to current-moment market standards as measured in only two places – Broadway and/or the West End in London.

5.3   Ingredients in a Song and How to Break Them Down

In approaching a music theatre song there are many things to consider prior to doing it and as it is being learned. Here is a partial list.

The three first things are

1. the lyrics
2. the rhythm
3. the melodic line

After that we must consider

4. the key
5. the tempo
6. the overall tessitura
7. the vocal quality
8. the nature of the accompaniment

Then, we must address

 9. the character who is singing
10. the motivations of that character
11. the nature of the show from which the song is taken

Then, there are also other considerations:

12. what do we know about this composer?
13. what do we know about this style of music?
14. what do we know about the period of time this was done originally?
15. if the song is new, what do the composer and the lyricist want?

It is also important to know:

16. what are the characteristics of the singer's voice?
17. what age is the person singing supposed to be?
18. how does the song match up with the singer in terms of range, volume, stamina and vocal quality?
19. how much vocal training does the singer have?
20. how much vocal ability does the singer have?

   In taking a look at these and other particulars, finding more detailed ways to look at some of the ingredients on the list above, we present here two experts who will discuss their own approaches to learning a music theatre song. The following segments are written by two of America's most well-known teachers of music theatre styles. Both experts teach children, college students and working professionals. Both of them have considerable professional music theatre experience at the highest levels and long years of teaching music theatre in all its forms. Here are their individual perspectives on how to work with learning a music theatre song.

5.4   Making the Song Authentic: It's a Matter of Style

5.4.1   By Edrie Means Weekly

The desire and goal is for the singer to sing a musical theatre song authentically. It is more than singing the notes and lyrics in the written score; acting cannot be left out of the voice. Authenticity includes the style, expression, emotion and storytelling used so that the audience is invited into the character's world through song. The story line is expressed vocally through the choice of style such as country, jazz, pop, rap, Rhythm and Blues (R&B) and rock with variations in vocal quality ranging from legit, to mix and belt.

   The demand today is for singers to be trained in a variety of music styles. It is important to understand that current musical theatre productions may encompass blues, country, jazz, rock and even rap all in one show. Frequently in twenty-first century musical theatre, one character is required to sing equally well in multiple styles within the same show. Tony® award winner Norbert Leo Butz sings rap, Broadway legit, character voice and pop/rock. Song titles: rap ('Great Big Stuff'), Broadway legit ('Nothing Is Too Wonderful To Be True'), character voice ('All About Ruprecht') and pop/rock ('Love Is My Legs') in the Broadway production of *Dirty Rotten Scoundrels* (Butz 2000). As a credit to his extraordinary vocal ability, each style is authentic and stands alone.

On a technical level, in order for the singer to be successful in contemporary musical theatre productions, he or she will need to cross-train the vocal production muscles to create laryngeal flexibility. The singer can switch back and forth between registers and styles by making different interior shapes to allow changes in the resonance to serve the style. Good musical theatre singers greatly vary their tone quality by altering the shape of the vocal tract, which extends from the vocal folds to the mouth opening, and adding 'vocal stylisms' to support the various styles. For example, the tongue will intentionally retract for certain words in blues, country, rock, R&B, or in some accents such as 'Cockney' English. The singer is in control of these physiological and acoustical changes involving movement of the jaw, tongue and soft palate.

Some exercises to gain laryngeal flexibility may include the following in a comfortable range:

1. Y[ae]: Tonic to 8va. Tonic in Chest Register – 8va in Head Register (Yodel or without)
2. [ae]: Start in chest and stay on note, change to head. First as Yodel transition and then non-yodel transition
3. With a bright Y[ae]: 3, 2, 1 (mi, re, do) good for 'tails' or 'scream'
4. Whoa: Pentatonic scale (C-D-E-G-A) in reverse with an added ½ step above; A-Bb-A-Bb-A-G-E-D-C. Use up and down the vocal range as feels comfortable in head, mix and chest as well as different dynamics. This scale is common in rock music.
5. Blues Scale: C, Eb, F, F#, G, Bb, C. Use ascending and descending with various melodies made up from the scale. Use up and down the vocal range as feels comfortable in head, mix and chest as well as different dynamics. This is great for learning to improvise. The blues scale is prevalent in the blues, R&B, Gospel and rock.

Authenticity is more than technical craft. Great singers connect with their audiences through vocal emotion and expression. To connect on an emotional plane, a singer should take some time to read the story and get to know the character. Doing so gives the performer a better understanding of how to communicate the character, acting through song.

Most songs will evolve emotionally throughout the duration of the song. Although essential for singers to connect emotionally, it can be challenging for a singer to express or connect to a song if he or she has not personally gone through certain life experiences. This is where researching literature, personal imagination and empathy come into play. In order to understand how to connect and how the character should feel, it is useful to break down each line of a song. This allows the singer to identify the emotion and then physically feel the emotion in the body.

Some common questions to consider about any character and song:

1. Can the student describe their character in detail, age, personality, physical characteristics, etc.
2. Does the music describe the character?
3. How does the character fit into the book?
4. Has the singer experienced any of the character's scenarios?
5. Is the singer able to connect with the character or imagine what that emotion feels like?
6. Where does song come in the show?
7. What is the emotional state of the character as the song begins?
8. How do the dynamic changes affect the vocal quality? Does it cause the singer to sing in chest register, head or mixy?
9. Are there emotions behind the dynamic changes? What is the character's subtext?
10. How does tempo change affect the mood of the character and the singer's voice?
11. Are there any repeats of phrases? Words? If so, how is the singer going to express these repeats?
12. Has the singer spoken their song as a monologue without sounding 'poetic'?

Unlike opera, musical scores aren't normally well annotated. However, Broadway musicals have existed almost completely in an age where productions could be recorded. Recordings by the original cast of a show are often available, even of older shows. For original Broadway productions, the composers and lyricists were typically in a room with the cast influencing the way they want the songs sung. While listening to cast recordings, make note of how the singers use slides, word painting, consonants, tone color, 'bend' notes and 'swing' the rhythm to mimic the orchestration for expression.

For some shows, there are DVDs of the making of the cast recording. These have a wealth of information and may include the composer or music director telling cast members about how a particular word or passage is pronounced or sung. The internet site YouTube is another valuable asset to a singer's research, although many times videos may be removed. The website http://www.bluegobo.com/ is a fabulous place to find a plethora of original and revival videos of songs within a show. At this site the singer may find interviews of cast members providing more insight to their character or how they approached learning the score.

The original cast recording may not be infallible however. The song 'Swing' in the original Broadway production of *Wonderful Town* (Russell 1953), co-star Jordan Bentley stated Leonard Bernstein had asked for certain stylistic choices and sounds, but Rosalind Russell was unable to produce what he wanted (Bentley 2007). It took the revival, 50 years later, for Donna Murphy to bring the desired expression to 'swing' (Murphy 2003) the way Leonard Bernstein wanted it. On the other hand, the revival's rendition of 'Pass the Football' (McLeod 2003), is boring when compared to Jordan Bentley's rendition in the original, with his growl accenting 'pass' (Bentley 1953). It was the difference between passing butter at a family dinner and passing a winning touchdown in a rambunctious college game.

Emotion and expression is created vocally by varying the dynamic, coloring the tone and adding 'vocal stylisms'. Singing styles found in musical theatre such as blues, country, jazz, pop, R&B, rock, etc. have their own various expressive 'vocal stylisms'.

Common stylisms include:

1. Slides: steady slide upward, End Slide-ups, Fry slide
2. Fall-Offs: one note sliding down to the next note
3. Bending: a slide from 1/2 note below
4. Pop Appoggiatura: accented grace note from below (1/2 step), often quick
5. Cry: a grace note from above that sounds like a whine. Used in blues, country, gospel, pop, R&B and torch songs
6. Swinging the note: dotted eighth notes followed by sixteenth notes. Used in blues, country and jazz styles
7. Growls: low, guttural sound. Used for character roles, country, pop and rock
8. Screams: higher pitch sound with extreme intensity. Used in pop, and rock
9. Onsets: hard glottal, soft glottal click, breathy onset
10. Shadow Vowel: follows final vowel or consonant sound, e.g. 'you-uh'
11. Tails: 3 and 5 note descending patterns with decrescendo
12. Licks, Wails, or Riffs: Brief improvisation–a distinctive few notes or short phrase in pop music or jazz, often improvised. Most improvisations can be traced back to Baroque ornaments.

As with all new songs, it is wise for the vocalist to learn the song as written, both the rhythms and the melody, so they can later include authentic stylistic choices. Establish the original tune before adding any improvisational items from the jazz and pop recipe. 'Aquarius' from *Hair* provides a good example (White 2005). The first time through is the basic melody. At the end of the B section Lilias White adds an 'acciaccatura' and 'turn' on the word 'Aquarius' leading into the repeat of 'when the moon is in the seventh house'. Returning to the line a second time, she adds an additional 'turn' when she sings the word 'moon'.

In 'And I Am Telling You', from the Broadway production of *Dreamgirls,* written and sung in R&B style, Jennifer Holliday gives a clear example of a shadow vowel. She adds 'uh' on the word 'you' making it 'you-uh'. She also adds extra articulated 'ees' to the end of the word 'free' in 'I'm not livin' without you, I don't wanna be free-ee-ee' (Holliday 1982). Note all the slides, fry slides, growls, screams, fall-offs and glottals. A singer must use caution and always aim for healthy functional singing while using these vocal stylisms.

Another useful vocal stylism is the 'cry'. It is most often used in blues, country, Gospel, pop, R&B and torch songs. In a country twang Robin Baxter produces cries, yodels, bends, improvisational turns and good use of blues notes in her licks, in 'Let's Make Believe We're In Love' from the Broadway production of *Footloose* (Baxter 1999).

Orchestration is an important tool in developing the character's emotions and personality. Who isn't familiar with Sergei Prokofiev's narrated symphony *Peter and the Wolf*? All the characters in the story have a unique musical theme played by a specific instrument. In vocal music, often the orchestration will provide the opportunity for the vocalist to mimic a sound not written in the vocal line. This can convey or enhance a specific expression or emotion. It could be as simple as a giggle on a flute trill. In a written out scat, Emily Skinner does a fine job of mimicking the instruments in the orchestra as she sings 'Life With Harold' from *The Full Monty* (Skinner 2000). She adjusts her tone color and dynamics for the different instruments she is mimicking.

Emotion and expression is also created vocally by varying the dynamics, coloring the tone, varying the use of vowels and consonants, using alliterations (repetitions of a particular sound), and by using 'vocal stylisms' such as bending the pitch (sliding into it from above or below), sliding from one pitch to another, crying, growling, and using vocal fry or a kind of 'creaky' sound. The singer can also shorten the vowel and emphasize a particular consonant or use 'word painting' to color lyrics by creatively singing onomatopoetic words such as *chirp*, *drip*, *bang*, *knock*, zip, and *click*, as if to make them sound like the things the words represent. On words such as *fall* and *drool,* it's also possible to seem to 'fall off' the pitch by gliding down to the next note, which adds more color and emphasis to the meaning of the words.

Carol Burnett in 'Living a lie' in the song 'Shy' from *Once Upon A Mattress* (Burnett 1959) lengthens the consonant 'L' causing emphasis and back phrasing for expression. Consider exploding the consonants 'b', 'c' and 't' in the lyrics 'He vas a **b**ully und a **br**u**t**e, he vas as **c**razy as a **c**oo**t**, still I didn't give a hoo**t**, he vas my boyfriend!' in the song 'He Vas My Boyfriend' from the Broadway production *Young Frankenstein* (Martin 2007). In 'Hello Little Girl' from *Into The Woods*, the singer expresses the wolf's desire for Red with salivating sounds by elongating the 'sh' on the words 'flesh', 'fresh', 'lush', and 'delicious' (Westernberg 1988).

Composer Stephen Sondheim writes a rap singing style in the middle of the 'Prologue: Into The Woods' to better articulate the alliterations and consonants, in communicating the witch's story. Bernadette Peters clearly speaks/sings the rhyming lyrics 'robbing me, raping me, rooting through my rutabaga, raiding my arugula and ripping up my rampion' (Peters 1988) in a rhythmic rap beat. Twenty years later composer Lin-Manuel Miranda would open his musical *In The Heights* (Miranda 2008) with a rap as well.

Consonants for expression are primarily used for character songs or dramatic legit songs. If the singer over enunciates the consonants, they may sound operatic, particularly when coupled with round pure vowels or sound too dramatic or too 'charactery' for the style of the song. Broadway composer Stephen Sondheim is a stickler for consonants. If a vocalist sings for him, he or she will get pages of notes!

Song authenticity comes by knowing the composer's intended style and understanding the emotional state of the character. Cross training vocal production muscles and knowing how to alter the shape of the vocal tract provides the ability to perform the correct style authentically. The singer's ability to produce vocal stylisms provides expression. Song authenticity and expression makes the character come alive for the singer and the audience.

5.5   Yes, But Can You Do That Eight Shows a Week?

5.5.1   By Mary Saunders-Barton

The arrival of Duncan Sheik's 'Spring Awakening' in 2007 created excitement because it seemed to bring with it the possibility of a new 'relevance' for the musical and the promise of a younger, hipper audience. Whether this trend is actually borne out in ticket-purchases over the long term remains to be seen but the rock genre is the style of choice for many young composers today.

Jon Pareles, music critic for The New York Times, wrote an excellent analysis of the rock musical in 2010, concluding that 'Broadway may be the final place in America, if not the known universe, where rock still registers as rebellious.' Whether that is true, it is apparent that rock music seems somehow more 'dangerous' in a traditional theatre setting. Nevertheless, it doesn't approach the excitement of the real thing. Pareles went on to say,

> Two nights after the official opening of [the Broadway show] *American Idiot*, Green Day [the band who had written the score and was on stage as part of the show] itself played an unannounced encore. The show had poured on its razzle-dazzle. .... but Green Day set off pandemonium. ... Green Day's members may not be able to act or execute choreography … but they also hold rock's wild card: the potential, realized or not, for spontaneity. (Pareles 2010)

Rock singing challenges most musical theatre voice teachers precisely because of the qualities that make it so exciting. The great appeal of rock singing is its gritty, edgy, spontaneous and above all, youthful abandon; in a word, its 'untrained' quality. We've heard Randy Jackson, judge on the American TV show *American Idol*, bemoan a sound that's 'too Broadway.' The clarity and freedom of the well-trained musical theatre singer seems to be at odds with this aesthetic, and voice teachers concerned for the longevity of young voices under unpredictable circumstances, are understandably befuddled.

The Tony® Awards are given on Broadway each year for various categories of Broadway shows and performers. In 2010, all four Tony® contenders for 'Best Musical of the Year' were rock musicals. The genre will offer for the foreseeable future the promise of considerable employment for young performers. It is critical for voice teachers to understand the vocal requirements of these shows and how to guide singers constructively so that when they finish the *American Idiot* tour, they will be in good shape to go out with *Oklahoma!*

Musical theatre performers today are vocal and physical athletes. Everybody sings, dances and acts. The sheer punishment of Elphaba's 'No Good Deed', from

Wicked, which requires racing around a raked stage and up through a trap, screaming and ranting while metamorphosing into evil incarnate, is a huge physical and emotional challenge for a young singer regardless of talent and skill. To do this eight times a week seems almost impossible.

Our main responsibility as voice teachers is the healthy function of the voice, whatever the style. Young professionals today should not feel threatened by extreme use of the voice provided they understand what they are doing physically. Access to a fully integrated and balanced speaking voice is critical to singing musical theatre. Speech pathologists warn of the three 'L's': 'too long, too low, too loud.' This is an issue of balance. Like any muscles, the vocal muscles need to be exercised completely. If a woman is performing in a show that requires intense and extended use of her belt and chest quality she will want to re-balance by vocalizing her treble range. The same applies to a male singer.

It is regrettable that producers do not routinely provide voice teachers and physical therapists 'on call' to monitor singers and dancers on Broadway, particularly in shows with extreme physical and vocal demands. The Public Theatre's original founder, Joseph Papp, provided a voice teacher for all of his shows and I have known of numerous producers providing this service for their stars as part of their contract. It is hard to imagine a college football team or the National Football League without trainers and medical staff for the players.

In working with a young woman who came to the studio as a classical soprano with excellent acting and dancing skills, the task was to integrate speech into her middle voice to eliminate the register break and make it possible for her to audition successfully for belt roles and contemporary rock and pop-rock shows. The studio work has involved a careful and conscious knitting together of the middle range, between D4 and D5 so that the speech quality (chest dominant quality) has a train track to run on from the lowest to the highest note. The so-called 'high belt' in women, which creates such excitement (between E flat 5 and A flat 5 or higher), is easier for most young women than the transitional notes between C5 and E flat 5 where they feel a natural impulse to move to head voice/soprano. The trick is to help develop optional balancings in registration so that the transitional ranges become effortless but maintain the desired color. Eventually this young woman found the flexibility to belt in all ranges, notably as Mimi in *Rent*, without sacrificing the bloom in her soprano sound. For a recent *American Idiot* audition, she chose *Don't Stop Me Now* by Queen. She was able to sing it with power and energy, and ended up booking the tour. Maintaining a straight tone to the point of release was new for her. I can encounter occasional difficulty helping singers achieve a straight tone quality without pushing the voice, which can lead to problems reinstating it and returning to flow phonation. Pitch sometimes suffers. My only advice is to keep balancing back and forth, straight-tone to vibrato. The appearance of effort is part of a rock style but the production must be energized, not effortful.

What this young woman has achieved is what I would hope for with any singer moving into the contemporary world of musical theatre. Being afraid of an unfamiliar use of the voice can be as much of a problem as having no concept of the possibility of harm.

We need to encourage our students to know their limits but not limit themselves. I have a young hugely talented student who came to me with the opposite issue from the girl mentioned above. He had a powerful chest voice, baritone to F, then pushed above that with no mixed quality, i.e. not enough treble. The repertoire today kills a male voice that does not make the transition above F4 easily. The belt quality can occur above that, bright and strong, if the register balance is correct. The first thing I address is the mixed or classical quality to bring treble into the upper tones. Mixing ensures range and flexibility and overall health of the instrument. This young man succeeded in developing his upper range and has recently been cast in *Book of Mormon.*

The popular 'reinforced falsetto' or pop falsetto (as in *Jersey Boys*) is comparable to the woman's head-dominant or soprano mix. I encourage all of these qualities in male singers just as I would in women, so that no matter what style they are singing in, they have somewhere reliable to be vocally. However, it is important that any type of falsetto use be kept as a special stylistic spice in male voices and not encroach upon the chest dominant sound as a 'substitute.' The countertenor and the pop falsettist are very special types. For musical theatre, there is limited work for this voice quality although men love to use it because it because it feels so easy.

No singer is immune to vocal trouble. All of us in the trenches working with musical theatre voices are responsible for understanding the requirements and the technical demands of the shows currently being cast. We can't be frightened ourselves or we will convey that anxiety and get nowhere. We need to encourage singers to monitor themselves, especially when they are away on tour. Young performers want to please. They might be inclined to do anything they are asked without checking in with their self-monitor. This might not be a problem at an audition (musical directors can ask for some crazy things) but if they are cast, it will be important for them to understand how they will survive a long run and still come out swinging.

5.6   The Biggest Challenges

5.6.1   By Jeannette LoVetri

'Wicked' opened on Broadway in 2003 and won many awards. It is still running and can be found in productions all over world. It continues to be one of the top grossing shows every week in New York and is particularly popular with young fans. The 'show stopper' piece in 'Wicked' has always been 'Defying Gravity' sung by the character Elphaba. The song ends on a loud, climactic Db5 that is belted or sung in a very strong mix that is a borderline belt. It encompasses many of the biggest challenges of twenty-first century music theatre songs.

That high note cannot be sung in a classical head register dominant 'legit' sound. In whatever manner the vocalist can manage, the sound must resemble loud speech or it won't serve the energy of the character or the intention of the song.

It starts out in a rather quiet manner in the key of Db major on a Db4, dropping to an Ab3. The first high pitch is Db5, sung in a light heady quality on an /u/ in the word *rules*. This is followed just three measures later with a Gb3 on the syllable *guess* in the word *guessing,* thus making the full span of the song a half step less than two octaves.

Shortly thereafter, the melodic theme of the piece is introduced as the title words are sung. 'It's time to try defying gravity' which starts on Ab4, rises to Eb5 on the word *to* and settles on the Db5 on the word *try.* This musical pattern returns repeatedly in the song and it is the apex of the music as it builds to the dramatic end. The last 18 bars of the song encapsulate the entire piece. As Elphaba sings 'I'm flying high defying gravity, and soon I'll match them in renown. And nobody in all of Oz, no Wizard that there is or was, is ever gonna bring me down!! Ah!' she is encompassing F, another sustained loud Eb5 and a very long, loud Db5, followed by a 'riff' of several ornamented notes touching on F5, centering around Eb5 (pitch references from Titze 2000). The singing here is labeled 'with determination' and is meant to be impassioned and strong.

The pitches in this song matter because this vocal quality, that of high chest/mix, is something that was rarely found on Broadway just three decades ago. It was considered nearly impossible. It was also thought to be aesthetically unpleasant and therefore, unacceptable, for most people's musical ears. This quality, that of a 'high belt' or 'high belt mix' is now found in many pieces, for both men and woman, and is more frequently than ever considered 'standard' vocal production for rock or pop vocalists. The pitch range, typically for women to a F5 or G5 or an A4, B4 or even a C5 for men, is meant to be strong, open and 'edgy'.

The quality is often more dramatic in women because it requires a definite balance of power or strength with freedom in pitches which lie well above the typical pitch range of speech for women. It is always produced with the mouth of the vocalist very wide open, with the jaw dropped very far down. The vocal production requires this because of the position of the larynx and the degree to which the system is being pressured in terms of the breath. Optimally, the neck muscles should be relaxed, the head should remain over, not in front of the torso, and the breath pressure from the abdominal muscles should be strong.

The vowels in the song and their placement in the words are quite random. There is no particular pattern to be found in all the high pitches such that one could say they were all open vowels or all closed. Rather, it is as if the composer set the words (which he wrote) in order to convey a certain message rather than accommodate any specific type of vocal production that would be easier for a singer to manage. Since there have now been many Elphaba's both on Broadway and on stages throughout the world and since many of them have survived singing in the show for multiple performances, it can be concluded that a good many woman have cultivated a way of singing the role that is both professionally viable and vocally healthy. It is a point of argument whether or not the musical writing itself promotes vocal health or provokes vocal illness, but it is a fact that the writing makes the song very challenging to sing well repeatedly.

As we can see in this piece, and from comments by both Professors, Saunders-Barton and Means Weekly, music theatre at the highest professional levels is very challenging and asks that singers be very versatile. It requires that they know their throats and bodies very well and that they learn to get as much from them as possible while remaining healthy. Young performers are generally at greater risk than older ones simply because life experience is really the only way one can learn to pace the output necessary to keep everything in balance and intact.

5.7   Classical Training

Good classical training helps with vocal production if it is aligned with functional principles. A voice that encompasses two or more evenly balanced octaves that is deliberately coordinated with aligned posture, deep and controlled inhalation and managed exhalation, and which is both strong and flexible should move into music theatre repertoire easily, especially when guided by an experienced teacher. Training which focuses exclusively on resonance and breath support, however, could be inadequate. Those whose classical training does not follow a functional direction that incorporates a deliberate use of vocal register development, could find that their typical mode of singing won't flow into today's music theatre styles without retraining. As Professor Saunders-Barton points out, much of the present moment music theatre is rock driven and the vocal production needed in the music of Mozart or Bellini is very far away from that which would be necessary in shows like *Rent* or *Jesus Christ Superstar*.

5.8   Everybody Needs to Sing Everything

As Professor Means-Weekly has mentioned, the need for performers to be well versed in many styles in just one show is not uncommon. Approaching a song from 'Dirty Rotten Scoundrels' would require both the performer and the teacher to understand which style was being used in the song, since it was not predominantly one single style in the show itself. Other shows, such as 'Grease' are written as if from another, typically earlier, era. The music from 'Grease' is meant to sound like it was from the 50s, just as the music in 'Thoroughly Modern Millie' is meant to sound like it was from the 20s, even though neither show was from the decades referenced. The printed sheet music from either show would not indicate these distinctions, therefore the performers would have to do research first to avoid learning to sing them with incorrect style.

5.9   In Conclusion

Music theatre is a vast world. As long as stylistic integrity is maintained, vocal health is always a requisite and individuality is brought forth in the song, there are many avenues open to performers who wish to enter into this exciting profession. Excellent training leading to solid professional skills helps make success much more likely. Singers are encouraged to gather their dreams and take their places in auditions all over the world!

References

Baxter, R. (1999). Let's Make Believe We're In Love. *Footloose the Musical – Original Broadway Cast*. Tom Snow, Dean Pitchford. Q. Records.

Bentley, J. (1953). Pass The Football, Wonderful Town - *Original Broadway Cast*, Leonard Bernstein, Betty Comden, Adolph Green, Decca.

Bentley, J. (2007). Interview during a Musical Theatre Styles Class at the Contemporary Commercial Music Vocal Pedagogy Institute, Shenandoah University.

Burnett, C. (1959). Shy. *Once Upon A Mattress – Original Cast Recording*. Mary Rodgers, Marshall Barer, Decca U.S.

Butz, N. L. (2000). Great Big Stuff, Nothing Is Too Wonderful To Be True, All About Ruprecht, Love Is My Legs. Dirty Rotten Scoundrels – *Original Broadway Cast Recording*. David Yazbek, Ghostlight Record.

Holliday, J. (1982). And I Am Telling You. *Dreamgirls – Original Broadway Cast*. Henry Krieger, Tom Eyen, Decca U.S.

LoVetri, J., & Weekly, E. M. (2003). Contemporary Commercial Music (CCM) survey: Who's teaching what in non-classical vocal music. *Journal of Voice, 17*(2), 207–216.

Martin, A. (2007). He Vas My Boyfriend. *Young Frankenstein – Original Broadway Cast*. Mel Brooks, Decca Broadway.

McLeod, R. J. (2003). Pass The Football. *Wonderful Town New Broadway Cast Recording (Featuring Donna Murphy)*. Leonard Bernstein, Betty Comden, Adolph Green, DRG Records.

Miranda, Lin-Manuel & Company. (2008). In The Heights. *In The Heights – Original Broadway Cast*. Lin-Manuel Miranda, Ghostlight.

Murphy, D. (2003). Swing. *Wonderful Town New Broadway Cast Recording (Featuring Donna Murphy)*. Leonard Bernstein, Betty Comden, Adolph Green, DRG Records.

Pareles, J. (2010). Broadway rocks. Get over it. *New York Times*.

Peters, B. (1988). Prologue: Into The Woods. *Into The Woods – Original Broadway Cast*. Stephen Sondheim, RCA Victor Broadway.

Russell, R. (1953). Swing. *Wonderful Town – Original Broadway Cast*. Leonard Bernstein, Betty Comden, Adolph Green, Decca.

Skinner, E. (2000). Life With Harold. *The Full Monty – Original Broadway Cast*. David Yazbek, RCA Victor Broadway, 2000.

Titze, I. R. (2000). *Principles of voice production*. Iowa City: National Center for Voice and Speech.

Westenberg, R. (1988). Hello Little Girl. *Into The Woods – Original Broadway Cast*. Stephen Sondheim, RCA Victor Broadway.

White, L. (2005). Aquarius. *Hair – Actors' Fund of America Benefit Recording*. Galt MacDermot, James Rado, Gerome Ragni, Ghostlight.

Part II
Singing, the Body and the Mind

Chapter 6
Vocal Health and Singing Pedagogy: Considerations from Biology and Motor Learning

Douglas F. Roth and Katherine Verdolini Abbott

Abstract It is clear that vocal health is influenced by numerous factors, involving physiological, mechanical, and psychological mechanisms. This chapter provides an overview of such issues, emphasizing the role of the voice teacher in fostering vocal health and identifying early signs of physiological vocal changes. A particular focus will be two issues of recent interest within the clinical voice science community: (1) approaches to recovery from acute vocal fold injury and (2) approaches to voice training in general. Novel biological data indicate the counter-intuitive possibility that some forms of light classical singing may not only not exacerbate injury, but may actually help to reverse it in some cases. Regarding training, this question has been the target of intensive investigation in the general motor learning literature for the past decade. Again counter-intuitively, recent literature strongly indicates the typical practice of training learners verbally, analytically and biomechanically may actually interfere with both immediate performance and long-term motor learning. Data instead suggest that experiential learning in which learners' attention is directed to performance outcomes rather than biomechanics enhances performance and learning over traditional verbal-analytical approaches. Data and implications for singing pedagogy will be discussed with practical examples.

Keywords Singing • Health • Vocal • Otolaryngology • Vocal health

D.F. Roth (✉)
Voice and Swallowing Center, Department of Otolaryngology,
Tufts Medical Center, Boston, MA, USA

School of Medicine, Tufts University, Boston, MA, USA
e-mail: droth@tuftsmedicalcenter.org

K. Verdolini Abbott
Department of Communication Science and Disorders, Otolaryngology,
McGowan Institute for Regenerative Medicine,
University of Pittsburgh, Pittsburgh, PA, USA

Center for the Neural Basis of Cognition, Carnegie-Mellon University
and University of Pittsburgh, Pittsburgh, PA, USA

S.D. Harrison and J. O'Bryan (eds.), *Teaching Singing in the 21st Century*,
Landscapes: the Arts, Aesthetics, and Education 14, DOI 10.1007/978-94-017-8851-9_6,
© Springer Science+Business Media Dordrecht 2014

6.1   Introduction

Vocal pedagogy as we understand it today is a conglomeration of stylistic, philosophical and national traditions passed down from teacher to student over hundreds of years. Common to most approaches to singing is an emphasis on vocally healthy technique that meets the technical and artistic demands of singing. Clearly, singing teachers are strongly invested in promoting students' vocal health. Without the foundation of a healthy vocal mechanism, attempts to train students for the extraordinary vocal athleticism and artistry required for any singing style would be futile, at best. For hundreds of years, teachers of singing have relied on their own training, intuition, anecdotal observation and personal experience to guide their methods of instruction and foster vocal health in their students. These are valuable tools that, over the centuries, have formed the foundation of modern vocal pedagogy.

However, contemporary voice teachers now have new tools at their disposal with which to further refine and build upon centuries of knowledge and tradition. Modern science has provided us with a much deeper understanding than previously available around the physiology of vocal function, biological aspects of vocal health, mechanisms of vocal injury and recovery and cognitive aspects of motor skill learning. This new knowledge provides empirical support for many traditional approaches to vocal health and vocal pedagogy while at the same time introducing findings that are counterintuitive, challenging some of our current methods in the studio.

We start our chapter with a brief overview of critical physiological, mechanical and psychological factors involved in vocal health. Important in this discussion will be practical approaches singing teachers can use in their 'front line' function as early identifiers of emerging vocal pathology. The chapter then turns to two issues of recent interest within the clinical voice science community relevant to vocal pedagogy: (1) approaches to treatment and recovery from acute vocal fold injury and (2) approaches to structuring exercises and practice, regardless of the specific singing technique or singing style.

6.2   Vocal Health

Numerous factors contribute to vocal health. Subtle deviations, unnoticed by most individuals, can have meaningful consequences for a singer. To prevent the demands of singing from producing negative effects on the vocal mechanism, voice teachers spend a great deal of time honing their students' vocal technique. Although a healthy vocal technique is necessary to prevent voice problems, good technique alone will not guarantee vocal health. As such, singing voice teachers have a responsibility to teach their students about factors that can negatively and positively affect vocal health. The following paragraphs provide an overview of several critical issues.

6.2.1   *Phonotrauma*

The obvious first step to vocal health is to prevent any process that undermines vocal well-being. Phonotrauma – that is, vocal fold injury due to phonation – is one of the primary factors that over time contribute to the development of benign vocal fold lesions such as nodules, cysts and polyps. Pathophysiologically, the primary catalyst of phonotrauma is believed to be the perpendicular impact stress on the tissues when the vocal folds collide. Singing voice teachers have traditionally discouraged singers from engaging in voicing patterns thought to be vocally harmful such as extensive talking on the phone, cheerleading and singing rock music. However, a number of factors including duration and the manner of voice production will modulate impact stress and contribute to the accumulated vocal dose[1] (Titze et al. 2003). Just as important, individual differences among singers, such as physiology and genetics, determine susceptibility to injury and will influence each singer's maximum safe vocal dose. For example, we now know that singing rock music is not intrinsically any more harmful than singing Wagner. However, a singer's range, tessitura, vocal weight, etc., should all be considered in selecting repertoire for any style of music. Asking a skilled leggiero tenor such as Luigi Alva to sing a Heldentenor role would be just as questionable as asking Art Garfunkel to attempt Bohemian Rhapsody by Queen. Individual differences in susceptibility to injury can be seen in the contrast between talented, young singers with excellent training who are unable to vocally endure the performance schedule of a high school musical, and singers such as James Hetfield from Metallica who have limited vocal training but enjoy long careers despite demanding performance schedules singing aggressive styles of music. Unfortunately, currently no test exists to determine an individual's susceptibility to injury before the fact. The limits of each singer's voice can only be determined over time.

However, a number of tools can be used to determine a singer's vocal 'boundaries.' The teacher's ear is certainly one tool. However, the student's perception of feeling 'vocally tired' or 'fatigued' is one of the best indicators. Even if voice quality remains unaffected, if a singer feels fatigued in a period of time shorter than would be expected for the vocal demands imposed, it is a good idea to have the student examined by a laryngologist.[2] The student can also be asked to create a brief log of daily voice use including rehearsals, practice, phone talking, talking in background noise together with periodic self-ratings of perceived fatigue, effort and vocal quality. Logs can provide valuable information about certain activities that may be contributing to any voice problem and potential modifications that may need to be made. The primary pattern that should be discouraged is outright screaming. The exception is a singer who has had and implements specialized training by a

---

[1] Overall vocal dose is determined by (1) distance dose, which is the cumulative distance traveled by the vocal tissues over a given period of time, (2) time dose, which is the cumulative amount of phonation time within a given time frame, and (3) energy dissipation dose, which is the cumulative heat dissipation and can be loosely associated with the amount of rest between phonation events.

[2] Evaluation by a specialized laryngologist is preferred over evaluation by a general otolaryngologist because of the former's additional training and experience with voice problems.

theatre professional with expertise in healthy stage screaming, which is thought to involve the use of high-pitched falsetto, overlaying noise from a non-glottal source such as the false vocal folds or epiglottis (Ufema and Montequin 2001).

6.2.2   Factors Influencing Vocal Health

Hydration

Hydration is crucial for good vocal function. Dehydration can cause a reduction in the vocal fold tissues both internally and externally (Titze and Verdolini 2012; Jiang et al. 2000). As a result, tissue viscosity (resistance to flow) increases. Two effects may ensue. First, the lung pressures required to initiate and sustain vocal fold oscillation may be increased, thus increasing both physiological and perceived effort to phonate. In contrast, lung pressures are reduced, and phonation may feel 'easier' when the system is well hydrated, especially at high pitches (Verdolini et al. 1994, 2002; Verdolini-Marston et al. 1990; Titze 1988). Second, dehydrated, viscous vocal fold tissues may be more susceptible to injury than moist ones, and conversely, well-hydrated tissue may help to reduce the severity of vocal fold injury where it already exists (Titze 1981; Verdolini-Marston et al. 1994).

Unfortunately, dosage information is lacking about the amount of daily fluids and ambient humidity needed to support vocal health. Some clinicians recommend the consumption of about 64 oz. of water daily (water is, in absolute, the best fluid for hydration). However, this amount may not be adequate for all individuals. For people who engage in rigorous physical exercise, more water will be needed to replace fluid lost from perspiration. Also, oral breathing associated with strenuous cardiovascular exercise can dry the vocal fold surfaces and should be avoided prior to singing. Caffeine and alcohol have diuretic properties and any quantities consumed should be offset by increasing water intake by an equivalent amount, or even double. Similarly, antihistamines, psychoactive medications for anxiety and depression, and diuretics used to manage high blood pressure and certain heart conditions are drying to vocal fold tissue, and singers should use them judiciously. When used, fluids should be replaced by drinking more water or using steam inhalations (typically twice daily for 5 min), assuming medical clearance. The singing voice teacher can certainly counsel the student regarding alcohol and caffeine consumption, and adequate hydration. However, suspected voice problems related to medications or medical fluid restrictions should only be modified by the student's physician.

Laryngopharyngeal Reflux

A number of vocal pathologies can be associated with acid reflux that spills from the esophagus into the laryngeal vestibule. Acid reflux has been brought to public attention by advertisements for antacids and anti-reflux medications.

However, laryngopharyngeal reflux (LPR), which affects voice, differs from classic gastroesophageal reflux disease (GERD) that is most often described commercially. Many people with LPR do not experience heartburn and are unaware they suffer from reflux. More common symptoms of LPR are morning hoarseness, recurring sore throats, sensation of excessive mucous, throat clearing, chronic cough, asthma and globus (i.e. feeling of a 'lump' in the throat) (Koufman et al. 1996). Although these symptoms alone can be disruptive to voice, LPR can have broader implications for vocal health. Irritation from stomach acid can cause vocal edema, granuloma, exacerbate other vocal pathologies and can be a contributing factor in esophageal and laryngeal cancer (Qadeer et al. 2006). The clinical signs of LPR include diffuse laryngeal edema, vocal fold edema, thick, viscous mucous and vocal fold redness (Koufman 1991; Koufman et al. 1996).

Reflux occurs when the lower esophageal sphincter (LES) allows stomach contents to escape upwards into the esophagus. Although certain medications can reduce the acidity of reflux, they do little to improve LES tonicity or restrain reflux events themselves. In fact, acid in reflux contents is not the only source of inflammation to the esophagus and, in the case of LPR, to the upper airway. Other noxious contents in non-acid reflux can include bile and pepsin (Johnston et al. 2006; Koufman 1991). Therefore, the first, most important element of LPR treatment involves diet modification and lifestyle adjustments, which may affect either LES tonicity or acidity (Kessing et al. 2011; Tsunoda et al. 2007). Such modifications include avoiding spicy and acid-producing foods such as tomato based foods, fatty foods, peppers, citrus, and also caffeine and alcohol. Importantly, singers with LPR should also avoid exercise, laying down or singing within a couple of hours of eating as these activities increase abdominal pressure and the probability of a reflux event. Singers who chronically experience an increased sense of phlegm while singing should consider being evaluated for possible LPR. It should be noted that signs and symptoms of LPR overlap to a large degree with those of environmental allergies and are not always easy to differentiate without targeted testing (Roth and Ferguson 2010; Randhawa et al. 2010; Garrett and Cohen 2008).

Allergies

Allergies are an overreaction by the body's immune system to various antigens such as pollens, molds, and danders. The impact of environmental allergies can vary widely among individuals and depends on a number of factors including the perennial or seasonal nature of allergic triggers and the degree of allergic sensitivity. Similar to LPR, allergic symptoms include chronic hoarseness, recurring sore throats, sensations of 'mucous' in the throat, throat clearing, chronic cough, asthma and globus sensation (Roth and Ferguson 2010). Some but not all individuals may experience itchy eyes, which does not occur with LPR. Several laryngeal signs of allergic responses also overlap with those for LPR and include diffuse laryngeal edema, vocal fold edema, and thick viscous mucous. The large degree of overlap across the signs and symptoms of LPR versus allergies presents a challenge in distinguishing the two conditions, and diagnosis is often accomplished only after a series of diagnostic tests and therapeutic trials of LPR and allergy medications.

The current treatment approach for singers with allergies can differ slightly from approaches used with the general population. As previously discussed, medications such as antihistamines can have a drying effect on the vocal folds. Singers with minimal allergies may do well to attempt to prevent the initial allergic response, if possible, rather than treating it once it has occurred. The most obvious approach is to avoid allergen exposure. However, in more severe cases, avoidance is impractical and the benefits of antihistamines may outweigh negative effects caused by drying. This trade-off should be discussed with the physician, as many of the newer antihistamines are much less drying than the older ones. Often, the preferred approach involves allergy injections to gradually reduce the body's response to allergens. However, it can take 6 months to a year before noticeable changes are observed. This approach is not always practical for travelling singers because injections are required 1–2 times weekly for up to 5 years. In addition, serums used for immunosuppression therapy only include local allergens and will not protect the singer from allergens in other regions. A third treatment approach for singers with allergies involves the use of nasal steroids to minimize the localized allergic response in the nose. According to clinical wisdom, this approach is based on the idea that negative effects of allergies on voice are caused by postnasal drip, subsequent throat clearing, and oral breathing (Chadwick 2003). However, recent evidence indicates that a primary allergic response may occur directly in the larynx (Roth et al. 2014). Thus, treatments of allergic symptoms with nasal treatments alone may be incomplete at best, particularly for singers.

6.3 Treatment and Recovery from Acute Vocal Fold Injury

6.3.1 Vocal Exercise and Recovery

So, when a singer becomes injured, how do we go about the rehabilitation process? First, all of the factors impacting vocal health described above need to be examined in detail and any contributing factors addressed. For some individuals, eliminating sources of dehydration and inflammation may be sufficient to restore to voice to a state that meets the singer's demands. However, despite our best efforts, even conscientious singers with healthy vocal habits and good voice training can become injured. Regardless of whether surgery is a component of the treatment process, as rarely occurs, the injured singer will most likely need some form of speaking voice therapy, singing voice therapy or both. These therapies are designed to identify and train vocal modifications that match the student's vocal needs with the student's current abilities. In some individuals such intervention may involve eliminating patterns that contributed to the voice problem in the first place. For individuals whose vocal technique is not thought to be a contributing factor, vocal adjustments will still need to be made because anatomical and physiological changes associated with the injury will require a corresponding change in the muscle coordination used to produce voice. The timing for the onset of active therapy is non-trivial and can have a significant impact on outcomes. In cases of haemorrhage, therapy should not begin until bleeding has subsided. On the other hand, a delay in the onset of therapy for most injury risks missing an optimal window to positively influence tissue recovery. Some intriguing new data indicate that engaging in some form of resonant voice exercises during the healing process may improve recovery in cases of acute vocal fold injury in particular (Verdolini Abbott et al. 2012).

Voice Rest vs. Tissue Mobilization

Voice rest or reduced voice use continue to be standard care for the treatment of vocal haemorrhage, acute vocal fold injury, and chronic benign vocal lesions such as nodules, cysts and polyps (Colton and Casper 1996; Boone and McFarlane 1994). Although voice rest remains a sound approach in minimizing the severity of acute vocal haemorrhage, recent data have suggested a possible benefit from resonant voice exercises in the treatment of acute inflammation that may ultimately progress to chronic lesions such as nodules, polyps, and cysts (Verdolini Abbott et al. 2012).

The logic behind the current use of voice rest makes sense considering benign phonotraumatic vocal fold lesions are caused by collision forces of the vocal folds (Gray 1997; Gunter 2004; Titze 1994). Thus, if vocal fold collisions caused the problem, it is sensible to think of treating it by avoiding collision altogether as with voice rest. However, in other domains, such as physical therapy and sports medicine, current data indicate rest is not always the ideal approach for treating soft tissue injuries. In fact, emerging evidence in other domains indicates that mobilizing tissues early after injury may actually reduce inflammation and maximize long-term recovery (Ferretti et al. 2006). For example, in physical therapy, the current standard of care for ankle inversion sprains has transitioned from joint immobilization to therapeutic approaches involving tissue mobilization (Green et al. 2001). As a result, patients have experienced improved outcomes with increased range of motion. In sports medicine, tissue mobilization has resulted in reduced scar formation following surgical injury of the patellar tendon (Kamps et al. 1994). These types of findings have served as a context in which to re-examine current treatment methods for phonotraumatic injury and investigate the potential applicability of tissue mobilization in the vocal folds as a means to improve outcomes following acute vocal fold injury.

Wound Healing

To understand why tissue mobilization holds promise for vocal rehabilitation, we need to understand some rudimentary aspects of wound healing. Following injury of any source, a fairly consistent cascade of overlapping biological events ensues.

The initial stage, called the inflammatory phase, lasts only a few days. Inflammatory processes control blood flow into the injury site, recruit inflammatory cells and produce mediators that regulate subsequent events in healing. The inflammatory phase is critical, because its characteristics appear to influence the long-term outcome of healing. Specifically, final tissue architecture and function generally appear optimized by limiting the magnitude of the initial inflammatory response (Verdolini Abbott et al. 2012). The next stage of healing involves the generation of new proteins in the tissue. This protein synthesis phase lasts about 2 weeks. The final stage of healing, called the remodeling phase, involves the re-organization of proteins which become realigned based on the forces applied to the tissue during healing. Ideally, the remodeling phase serves to minimize scar and optimize long term tissue function (Branski et al. 2006).

To date, attempts to abate the initial inflammatory response in the vocal folds have been limited to either voice rest or the use of systemic or injected steroids (Mishra et al. 2000; Mortensen and Woo 2006). Unfortunately, steroids cannot be used repeatedly or for prolonged periods due to numerous negative medical effects which paradoxically can include hoarseness (Schwartz et al. 2009). A novel, recently emerging paradigm regards the utility of selected forms of vocal fold tissue mobilization in lieu of voice rest post-traumatically. Specifically, data from *in vitro*[3] (Branski et al. 2007), *in vivo*[4] (Verdolini Abbott et al. 2012), and *in silico*[5] (Li et al. 2008, 2011) studies point to the value of vocal fold tissue mobilization after injury, in particular 'resonant voice exercises' in comparison to results from spontaneous speech or voice rest, for some individuals with acute vocal fold injury. Resonant voice exercises are heavily derived from traditional methods in singing training. In brief, the exercises involve humming, through the pitch range, with attention directed to easy anterior oral vibrations during voicing (see Verdolini et al. in press for details).

Critical for resonant voice's potential therapeutic properties are two aspects of this voice pattern's physiology, which involves relatively large-amplitude, low-impact vocal fold oscillations. Consistent with findings in other domains, the large-amplitude feature of resonant voice is thought to induce healing processes, among other things by recruiting anti-inflammatory mediators to the tissue. The low-impact feature of resonant voice may help to prevent an aggravation of injury, allowing for natural healing mechanisms to kick in, in a manner similar to voice rest (Verdolini Abbott et al. 2012).

---

[3] *In vitro* refers to research conducted on isolated tissues in a lab. This approach avoids risks to human subjects and allows greater experiment control than is possible with human subjects. However, findings do not always translate back to the living organic system.

[4] *In vivo* refers to research conducted with living subjects. This approach has the advantage of observing effects within the context of the entire organic system and has greater power for clinical applicability. However, experimental controls with human subjects may be poorer than for *in vitro* studies or *in vivo* animal studies.

[5] *In silico* refers to computer modeling of biologic systems. This approach allows for faster than real-time observations of a biologic process. However, these types of simulations are limited in their ability to fully model and predict the behavior of an entire system.

A caveat is that wide variability exists in biological responses to injury and treatment. Thus, although the initial data provide grounds for optimism regarding the utility of resonant voice exercises in acute injury, conclusions are thus far preliminary.

6.3.2 Collaboration with the Medical Team

Teachers of singing are in a unique position to identify the early signs of potential voice problems. Their intimate familiarity with their students' voices allows them to detect subtle changes in vocal quality, stability, flexibility, range or endurance that might indicate a voice problem. Good singing voice teachers tend to have a 'low threshold' in referring students for evaluation when problems are suspected or vocal progress becomes limited for no identifiable reason. In fact, some music schools require baseline laryngeal examinations of all incoming students. Such an evaluation can identify any unknown voice problems or serve as a valuable benchmark from which to compare future examinations should a voice problem arise.

The 'core' medial team at a voice center will usually include a laryngologist, a speech-language pathologist and a singing voice specialist. A laryngologist is an otolaryngologist who has received 1–2 additional years of training beyond medical residency in the diagnosis, treatment and pharmaceutical and surgical treatments for voice problems. Typically, the laryngologist coordinates the entire team through the evaluation and treatment process, manages medical aspects of the patient's care such as LPR, and performs any surgical procedures if necessary. The speech-language pathologist in the team will have received specialized training in the evaluation of voice disorders and the therapeutic techniques used for voice problems. The laryngologist will usually work closely with other team members during the initial evaluation and consult with the team at various points during the rehabilitation process. The third member of the team, the singing voice specialist, may not be present during the initial appointment but may be consulted to provide input to the evaluation and recommendations for treatment. There is currently no professional organization that certifies singing voice specialists but those affiliated with larger voice centers are usually experienced teachers of singing with a degree in vocal performance or musical theatre, professional performance experience, and specialized training in voice disorders and rehabilitation. In addition to having musical background, many singing voice specialists are also certified speech-language pathologists. Depending on the factors contributing to the voice problem, the team may also include a number of other professionals including a gastroenterologist, neurologist, allergist, physical therapist or psychologist with whom the primary voice team has formed a close relationship.

The team member with whom the teacher of singing may work most closely is the singing voice specialist (SVS). A SVS is first and foremost a skilled singing teacher. He will also have additional training in the anatomy and physiology of the normal and disordered voice, diagnostic procedures, basic knowledge of medications, surgical interventions and the behavioral rehabilitation of disordered voices. As the team member with training in the medical aspects of voice disorders and vocal pedagogy, the SVS can be a valuable resource for the voice teacher, in understanding the student's medical diagnosis, implications for immediate and long term singing training, and a possible timeline for a return to unrestricted singing. Communication between the singing voice teacher and SVS during the evaluation process can be helpful in developing the overall treatment plan. Some singers with anatomic or physiologic laryngeal changes are able to make healthy, compensatory modifications to their vocal technique and do so in a manner that meets the aesthetic and technical demands of their singing style. If a singer is able to do so, surgery can often be avoided. For those singers with a medical condition requiring surgery, post-surgical rehabilitation is often necessary. The SVS will work with the singer to ensure a healthy return to singing and to modify any deleterious voicing patterns established as a result of the vocal injury.

Although techniques used in singing voice therapy are often similar to those used in normal singing voice training, differences may also exist. For example, singers with vocal fold lesions often unknowingly compensate for breathiness associated with a glottal gap by increasing glottal adduction. However, a narrower glottal width increases impact stress at the site of the lesions and will further exacerbate the injury. Therefore, the singer may need to be trained to temporarily allow some degree of breathy quality to minimize impact stress and assist with lesion reduction. As another example, singers with vocal scar often benefit from a semi-occluded vocal tract to facilitate voice. For example, the singer with scar may need to use a more closed vowel or smaller mouth opening than a singer without scar. During rehabilitation, the singing voice specialist's role is to use her knowledge of and experience rehabilitating disordered voices to identify techniques and approaches appropriate for the singer's medical condition. Once established, the singing voice specialist will work with the singer during the initial recovery process to help the singer establish a foundation with the new techniques. A typical duration for work with the singing voice teacher varies, but often involves four to eight sessions. At that point, if the singer has a voice teacher, the voice teacher will typically assume the primary role in training. The transition can vary depending on the singing voice teacher's comfort level working with singers with voice disorders. The SVS may continue some level of involvement at the request of the voice teacher.

6.4   Voice Training Rooted in Understanding of Motor Learning

As singing teachers, we have an exceptional ability to identify a student's strengths and weaknesses. Based on the student's current skill set we can identify the next logical skills to be targeted and appropriate vocalizes and repertoire with which to train those skills. However, knowing what to address and what materials to use in training is not sufficient. We also need to know how to go about addressing our targets in a way that will make a long-term change in the student's skills. Stated differently, it is helpful to know something about how people acquire new motor skills and override old ones.

The optimal structure for training, as well as instruction and feedback modalities for lessons and practice are often counterintuitive. In particular, we need to discriminate learning from performance and understand the cognitive processes that influence each. We now consider these issues, in turn.

6.4.1 Cognitive Aspects of Motor Learning

Two Types of Learning

The manner in which the people process information is not a unitary phenomenon. A distinction has been observed between declarative learning which is roughly equivalent to what some scholars call explicit learning and procedural learning which is similar to implicit learning (Graf and Schacter 1985; Squire 1986). Declarative learning encompasses knowledge of facts and events, and procedural learning encompasses knowledge for processes or procedures. Declarative learning is assessed by verbal report about what an individual knows (e.g. the capitals of the 50 states, how to make a pizza, what to expect at the symphony, etc.). Evidence for procedural learning is demonstrated by assessment of changes in performance following exposure or practice rather than by verbal report. An important aspect of the distinction between learning and memory types is that declarative and explicit learning are generally verbally mediated and occur with an awareness of what has been learned. Conversely, procedural learning occurs as a result of prior exposure and can occur outside of awareness. A lack of awareness for what specifically has been learned can even extend to a having no knowledge of the prior exposures that contributed to the learning process, as occurs for example with individuals with amnesia Motor skill learning, such as learning to sing, falls under the domain of procedural learning. Strong evidence for the distinction between these two memory systems comes from observations of individuals with anterograde amnesia, which involves damage to parts of the brain called the hippocampus and amygdala. These brain regions are integrally involved in the encoding and retrieval of facts and conscious memories of events. Interestingly, although individuals with anterograde amnesia have an impaired ability to learn new information or memories of events (declarative learning), they retain the ability to acquire new skills (procedural learning). Intuitively we tend to think all learning occurs within our awareness and that any learning can be influenced by our conscious verbal processing. Although anterograde amnesia demonstrates that awareness of 'how' to do something is not required for learning, one should not infer that procedural learning takes place passively. Learning requires active attention. So, how does the fact that motor learning is procedural impact our approach to singing instruction?

Perceptual vs. Verbal Processing

First, the fact that motor learning is procedural and not declarative means that the learning process for motor skills is perceptual and not verbal. In addition to sensory perceptions (e.g. vibratory sensations that occur on the bony and cartilage structures 'in the mask,' acoustic features of the sound, etc.), singing training has traditionally also included the use of metaphoric images (e.g. 'Make your voice like a ping pong ball suspended on a column of air,' 'white tone,' 'velvety voice,' 'like a wave,' etc.). Teachers often use sensory and metaphoric images in tandem and as the student improves it is easy to infer that the metaphoric images contributed to the learning process. Although the use of sensory images has been shown to be beneficial for motor learning (Toussaint and Blandin 2010, Verdolini et al. 2006), a benefit of metaphoric images has yet to be demonstrated (Verdolini-Marston and Balota 1994). Additionally, the associational nature of metaphoric images may invoke a declarative mode of processing that is largely incompatible with skill learning (Verdolini-Marston and Balota 1994). Based on the evidence, training should emphasize attention to and processing of acoustic and kinesthetic sensory targets. Furthermore, any spontaneous post-hoc analysis by the student regarding the biomechanics (I released my jaw, I dropped my larynx, etc.) involved in producing the perceptual targets should be actively discouraged. If sensory images were able to elicit the target initially then knowledge of the biomechanics behind their production was not necessary to produce it. Not only is knowledge of the biomechanics unnecessary for motor learning, experimental studies have unequivocally demonstrated that such biomechanical introspection is disruptive to the learning process[6] (Liao and Masters 2002; Singer et al. 1994; Wulf et al. 1998; Wulf and Weigelt 1997).

Consciousness

This leads directly to the second factor related to the procedural nature of motor learning which has a direct impact on singing instruction; motor learning occurs without conscious awareness of what has been learned. Often in the course of a lesson I will provide a sensory cue that elicits the target production (your goal is for the sensation you feel on your hard palate to be further forward than last time, double the sensations you are feeling in 'the mask,' etc.) to which I will often hear, 'I don't know what I *did* to make the change!' My response to the student is that, 'you don't need to know what you *did* (muscle adjustments, etc.), you just need to know what you want to *have happen* (which in these examples were clear sensory target

---

[6]This is *not* to imply the teacher should shy away from *internally* analyzing and considering biomechanical information, as such knowledge informs how the teacher will guide the student to the desired target. Ultimately, the student will need to know this information for the time when he will teach but during skill acquisition, attention to such information is known to impair the rate and depth of learning.

changes on the hard palate or in the 'mask' that related in some tangible way to what they had experienced on the prior production). It is not possible for the student to be aware of the multitude of respiratory, phonatory and articulatory muscle adjustments in general, let alone how they may subtly differ from production to production. Attempting to do so is incompatible with the procedural nature of motor learning and would exceed the resources available for the slow, serial processing involved with declarative learning. Short-term memory of the human brain is limited to processing about 7 ± 2 items within a given, brief time span (Miller 1956). Speculatively, phone numbers were designed to be seven digits for this very reason. If the student were to employ an explicit, declarative process during practice and actively bring the biomechanics of singing into 'consciousness' the student would be unable to monitor more than seven 'elements' involved in the production of sound (not to mention stylistic interpretation, translation, diction, etc.). The number of respiratory and phonatory muscles alone would exceed the seven-item capacity of short-term memory. Conscious intervention would interfere with the procedural processing necessary for normal motor control and would constrain the system to no more than seven degrees of freedom[7] (McNevin et al. 2003; Wulf et al. 2001a; Freedman et al. 2007). In essence, the student is no longer able to employ the full complement of rapid adjustments normally involved in singing as a result of the muscular tension required to 'freeze' the degrees of freedom to only those most essential (Vereijken et al. 1992). With this background in mind a clear definition of motor learning can be better understood.

6.4.2   Basic Motor Learning Concepts

Motor Learning Definition

Schmidt and Lee (2005) operationally define motor learning as 'a set of processes associated with practice or experience leading to relatively permanent changes in the capability for movement' (Schmidt and Lee 2005). Let us examine the component parts of the definition in greater detail with reference to singing, (1) the processes refer to the prior exposure or practice that culminated in skill acquisition. There are many singers who become quite skilled at singing through their participation in choirs, jazz ensembles, etc. without formal instruction. Even among formally trained singers, the majority of 'prior exposure' occurs during practice and rehearsal rather than the voice studio. (2) The acquired capability for movement refers to a change in the internal habit or 'motor memory' for the desired coordinative pattern of muscle activation. Although this capability may not always manifest in observed

---

[7] The degrees of freedom refer to the large number of independent states that could be employed to produce an action. The number independent states are derived from each of the independent joint movements that could be activated in concert and each of the many muscles that could be employed for those joint movements.

behavior the capability for the motor skill is still present. For example, a skilled singer may come down with a cold that negatively impacts her passaggio but this does not mean she does not still possess the ability to make a smooth transition between her middle and head registers. (3) If motor learning causes changes that are relatively permanent then the change in capability is not momentary. The skill will be relatively resistant to external distractions and will manifest even in the absence of external influences such as the presence of the voice teacher, increased motivation, context, location or feedback.

This leads to a very important distinction in the understanding of motor learning and that is the difference between performance and learning. A multitude of factors have the capability to momentarily improve observed performance on a skill but once that factor is removed the performance gain is lost. For example, in the early stages of learning a song, a singer may be able to vocally navigate the notes of their vocal line when provided the harmonic support of the piano but if asked to sing a cappella he is no longer able sing the correct notes. Another example is the case where a singer is able to consistently achieve the desired resonance target in the studio with constant feedback from the teacher but is unable to consistently produce the same target on their own in the practice room. In these two cases once the piano or the teacher's feedback were removed the student's performance returned to the prior capability. The final component of the definition highlights an important distinction which is made between performance and learning.

Performance vs. Learning

Performance refers to the momentary observation of an action (Schmidt and Lee 2005). In the two examples above the students appeared to be doing well based on their performance during the lessons but the capability was not retained. Performance is not a reflection of a learned skill. To demonstrate learning, the ability to produce an action must endure outside the conditions involved in training and practice. *Skill or learning* refers to an underlying change in the capability to perform an action and is a result of prior experience or exposure (Schmidt and Lee 2005). There are two methods traditionally used to evaluate learning; retention and transfer tests. Retention refers to the degree a skill is retained after practice. For example, a student who has retained the ability to produce a forward, 'in the mask' placement of/i/without a gesture cue from the teacher has demonstrated skill learning. The same can be said for a student who has retained the ability to maintain abdominal breathing without need of visual feedback from a mirror to monitor clavicular breathing. Transfer refers to the skill level demonstrated in a new variation of a practiced skill. In the first example above, transfer would be shown if the student were able to transfer the forward, 'in the mask' placement trained on the/i/vowel to additional vowels not addressed during the lesson. Transfer could also refer to a vocal technique practiced during vocalizes (e.g. 9-note coloratura scales) transferring to repertoire without specific training on the target work (e.g. coloratura in a Purcell song) or even from small live environment indicative of studios and practice rooms to performance halls.

In general, the amount of transfer that can be expected is quite limited and depends on the similarity between the desired target and what was practiced (Schmidt and Young 1987). For singing training, the amount of transfer from studio to stage or even from verse to verse may be limited. Think of the student working on a strophic song who has no difficulty with the high note in a phrase when the sustained vowel is/a/but struggles on the same note in the second verse when the vowel is/i/. The notes and dynamics are the same but the simple change of vowel may necessitate training each verse without the expectation that the skills learned from work on the first verse will transfer to the second. As another example of the limits of transfer, many a voice teacher can relate to having a student with impeccable vocal technique but finds that these same skills do not transfer into her speaking voice.

Given the fact that most teachers only have an hour a week with their students, the ideal pedagogic approach is one which engenders independent learning in the student and does not require constant feedback from the teacher. As such, this approach favors long-term skill learning over momentary performance gains only possible with the teacher no matter how virtuosic. Intuitively, it seems logical that observed improvements in vocal technique displayed during a lesson would be positively related with permanent skill acquisition. However, motor learning research has identified some counterintuitive generalities related to instructions, feedback and the conditions of practice. In general, factors that positively affect in-the-moment performance during lessons or practice impede long-term skill learning. Conversely, factors that disturb observed performance during lessons or practice contribute to the development of long-term skill learning. Those factors that present a greater challenge to the student will disrupt momentary performance but they also require greater sensory processing and cognitive engagement during the learning process which contributes to permanent skill acquisition. However, factors that improve and even sustain *momentary performance* increases while practicing or during a lesson are in essence 'guiding' the student through the process. This reduces the amount of sensory processing and cognitive engagement required of the student. When the student is 'in the groove' less sensory processing and cognitive engagement are required to maintain the same level of performance. As a result, subsequent repetitions contribute little to reinforcing the cognitive representation (muscle memory) essential for current performance levels to become a permanent skill. So, how can our approach to teaching be structured to avoid the instant gratification associated with increased performance during lessons and foster long-term skill learning? Scientifically informed methods for maximizing skill learning are provided in the next sections regarding the structure of lessons and practice, the nature of feedback and the approach to verbal instruction.

6.4.3 Conditions of Practice

The conditions of practice refer to the ways in which the structure of lessons and practice affect performance and learning. The order in which vocalises are presented, the selection of target vowels and scale degrees within a vocalise and the manner in which repertoire is addressed are but a few factors that can be implemented in a way to maximize sensory and cognitive processing by the student and positively impact learning.

Practice Distribution

Practice distribution refers to the schedule of practice or the order of tasks during lessons. Traditional approaches to singing instruction use a *massed practice*. A lesson might start with descending lip trills, progress in sequential order from scales on single vowels, to five-note arpeggios, on various vowels, nine-note coloratura scales and messa di voce. Each exercise is completed before progressing to the next. Although this approach immediately benefits and sustains performance and imparts a sense of progress for the teacher, it does not provide the greatest benefit for learning (Shea and Morgan 1979; Verdolini et al. 2006). *Distributed practice* randomly orders single or small sets from a variety of exercises. In this way, only a few examples of a given exercise are completed before moving on to a new vocalise. In this approach, trials of slow five-note scales, nine-note coloratura scales and messa di voce exercise might be intermingled in a random order.[8] The benefits for random over blocked practice have been demonstrated for a voice task in which voice patients were trained in the use of resonant voice therapy (Verdolini et al. 2006). The random ordering of tasks produces a *contextual interference effect* by which the student is never able to 'get in the groove' with a single exercise before having to shift to a new exercise with different task goals and sensory targets. With consecutive repetitions of the same exercise the student is able to use information from the prior trial for the next. However, when returning to the first exercise following separate, intervening exercises there is no immediate reference from which the student can draw. Thus, a sort of 'forgetting' and 're-discovering' takes place requiring a depth of cognitive and sensory processing similar to that engaged the first time. It is this depth of processing that activates the entirety of the neural activation involved in forming 'muscle memory'.

Practice Variability

Practice variability has to do with the degree to which a given task is varied from trial to trial. Although traditional approaches of instruction vary the scale degree from trial to trial by a semi-tone, a broad portion of the students range may be traversed on a single vowel before returning to the starting point using a new vowel. This would be considered *non-variable* practice and has a distinct benefit on performance since few variables change from trial to trial. However, similar to practice distribution, minimizing the variation from trial to trial also reduces the amount of

---

[8] This of course assumes the student has been adequately warmed-up before engaging in exercises that present a technical challenge.

cognitive effort required of the student. *Variable practice* would employ a variety of vowels in non-sequential order or could vary by differing intervals from trial to trial rather than progressing by half-steps. Variability of practice not only has been shown to benefit learning (Verdolini et al. 2006; Shea and Kohl 1991) but it can contribute to the generalization of trained techniques to novel conditions (McCracken and Stelmach 1977). When a single target is practiced (e.g. singing a leap of a 5th from an/u/to an/i/vowel) a specific neural pathway is repeatedly activated and a highly specific 'motor memory' is formed for traversing from an/u/to an/i/. However, if practice trials vary among the use of an/u/to an**/i/**and an/u/to an**/e/**the similarity between of the two front vowels combined with the same intervallic approach would activate proximal or possibly overlapping neural pathways. Now, how might this benefit the production of singing the leap of a 5th from an/u/to an**/I/**which lies between/i/and/e/on the vowel quadrilateral? Using a schema theory (Schmidt 1975) viewpoint, the relationship between the initial performance conditions (body position, lung volume), the motor program parameters issued and the sensory outcome of the movements (sound, sensations 'in the mask') used in producing the/i/ and the/e/during prior practice could be used to 'triangulate' the motor program parameters required for singing a leap of a 5th from an/u/to an/I/. When practice is less varied, the 'motor memory' representations may become highly specific to the practiced conditions. However, when practice variability is increased, the 'motor memory' representations are more abstract and can be used in relational processes (of movements and their related sensory consequences) to interpolate the parameters required for generalization to non-practiced conditions.

6.4.4   Verbal Information

Although we have stressed the fact that the procedural nature of motor learning means that the learning process is perceptual and not verbal, this does not mean we as teachers need to learn to teach without speaking! The conflict arises when an associational, explicit mode of processing is induced through the use of metaphoric images. If the student is not being asked to associate verbal imagery to their kinesthetic experience, verbal information, such as instructions and feedback, can be powerful tools for learning when it increases the processing of sensory information by the student.

So how can instructions and feedback be provided to the student without inducing an explicit/declarative mode of processing? On the surface, what we're describing initially seems foreign to our traditional approach but in our experience most teachers with whom we interact are already providing instructions and feedback related to sensory information. An experienced teacher is able to ascertain the range of potential kinesthetic sensations a singer might have experienced based on the sound of the tone. In addition, he is able to direct the student's attention through instruction and feedback in a way that increases the likelihood that the desired production will occur. The real challenge for some comes in eliminating the simultaneous use of metaphor or biomechanical instructions and feedback. The benefit for directing attention to the sensory effects of the biomechanics is unequivocal (McNevin et al. 2003; Shea and Wulf 1999; Wulf et al. 2000, 2002; Wulf and Prinz 2001; Freedman et al. 2007), has even been demonstrated in conjunction with the oral articulation (Freedman et al. 2007) and is robust to individual differences (Wulf et al. 2001b). Likewise, the negative consequences of directing attention toward biomechanical adjustments are equally robust (Singer et al. 1991, 1993, 1994; Wulf et al. 1998; Wulf and McNevin 2003; Liao and Masters 2002; Beilock et al. 2002). The increasing knowledge base of information related to attention and motor learning provides the opportunity to advance students' skills at a faster rate and with a higher degree of retention. This can be accomplished by expanding the use of instructions and feedback related to kinesthetic and acoustic sensory processing, eliminating biomechanical instructions and actively discouraging students' post facto attempts to analyze the biomechanics involved with successful vocal productions. The reward will be that the 'three steps forward' gained from effects oriented instructions and feedback will not only *not* be partially negated by the subsequent 'two steps back' cost associated with metaphoric images or biomechanical instructions but replaced by 'four steps forward' and 'no steps backward.'

6.5 Conclusion

The convergence of scientific research with vocal pedagogy provides the modern voice teacher with a wealth evidence based knowledge from which to base their approach to teaching. When that evidence supports anecdotal experience it allows the teacher to proceed with added confidence. When that evidence is counterintuitive and contrary to perceived experience it allow the teacher to eliminate approaches that deceptively appear beneficial and replace them with methods with demonstrated results. This also means that the modern voice teacher needs to be more informed that his predecessors. Although a good ear and introspective problem solving are still necessary skills for the teacher of singing, they cannot be fully realized without a strong knowledge base of the cognitive aspects of motor learning, vocal physiology and the variety of factors involved with vocal health. Fortunately, the interdisciplinary nature of voice research means that the modern voice teacher does not have to navigate the breadth of this knowledge alone but can recruit the expertise and assistance of other professionals to advance his own skills as a teacher of singing.

References

Beilock, S. L., Carr, T. H., MacMahon, C., & Starkes, J. L. (2002). When paying attention becomes counterproductive: Impact of divided versus skill-focused attention on novice and experienced performance of sensorimotor skills. *Journal of Experimental Psychology. Applied, 8*(1), 6–16.
Boone, D. R., & McFarlane, S. C. (1994). *The voice and voice therapy* (5th Aufl.). Englewood Cliffs: Prentice-Hall, Inc.

Branski, R. C., Verdolini, K., Sandulache, V., Rosen, C. A., & Hebda, P. A. (2006). Vocal fold wound healing: A review for clinicians. *Journal of Voice, 20*(3), 432–442. doi:S0892-1997(05)00097-4 [pii] 10.1016/j.jvoice.2005.08.005.

Branski, R. C., Perera, P., Verdolini, K., Rosen, C. A., Hebda, P. A. & Agarwal, S (2007). Dynamic biomechanical strain inhibits IL-1beta-induced inflammation in vocal fold fibroblasts. *Journal of Voice, 21*(6), 651–660. doi:S0892-1997(06)00083-X [pii] 10.1016/j.jvoice.2006.06.005.

Chadwick, S. J. (2003). Allergy and the contemporary laryngologist. *Otolaryngologic Clinics of North America, 36*(5), 957–988.

Colton, R., & Casper, J. K. (1996). *Understanding voice problems: A physiological perspective for diagnosis and treatment* (2nd Aufl.). Baltimore: Williams & Wilkins.

Ferretti, M., Gassner, R., Wang, Z., Perera, P., Deschner, J., Sowa, G., Salter, R. B., & Agarwal, S. (2006). Biomechanical signals suppress proinflammatory responses in cartilage: Early events in experimental antigen-induced arthritis. *Journal of Immunology, 177*(12), 8757–8766. doi:177/12/8757 [pii].

Freedman, S. E., Maas, E., Caligiuri, M. P, Wulf, G., & Robin, D. A. (2007). Internal versus external: Oral-motor performance as a function of attentional focus. *Journal of Speech, Language, and Hearing Research, 50*(1), 131–136. doi:50/1/131 [pii] 10.1044/1092-4388(2007/011).

Garrett, C. G., & Cohen, S. M. (2008). Otolaryngological perspective on patients with throat symptoms and laryngeal irritation. *Current Gastroenterology Reports, 10*(3), 195–199.

Graf, P., & Schacter, D. L. (1985). Implicit and explicit memory for new associations in normal and amnesic subjects. *Journal of Experimental Psychology. Learning, Memory, and Cognition, 11*(3), 501–518.

Gray, S. D. (1997). Benign pathologic responses of the larynx. *NCVS Status and Progress Report, 11*, 135–148.

Green, T., Refshauge, K., Crosbie, J., & Adams, R. (2001). A randomized controlled trial of a passive accessory joint mobilization on acute ankle inversion sprains. *Physical Therapy, 81*(4), 984–994.

Gunter, H. E. (2004). Modeling mechanical stresses as a factor in the etiology of benign vocal fold lesions. *Journal of Biomechanics, 37*(7), 1119–1124. doi:10.1016/j.jbiomech.2003.11.007/S0021929003004202 [pii].

Jiang, J., Verdolini, K., Aquino, B., Ng, J., & Hanson, D. (2000). Effects of dehydration on phonation in excised canine larynges. *Annals of Otology, Rhinology and Laryngology, 109*(6), 568–575.

Johnston, N., Dettmar, P. W., Lively, M. O., Postma, G. N., Belafsky, P. C., Birchall, M., & Koufman, J. A. (2006). Effect of pepsin on laryngeal stress protein (Sep70, Sep53, and Hsp70) response: Role in laryngopharyngeal reflux disease. *Annals of Otology, Rhinology and Laryngology, 115*(1), 47–58.

Kamps, B. S., Linder, L. H., DeCamp, C. E., & Haut, R. C. (1994). The influence of immobilization versus exercise on scar formation in the rabbit patellar tendon after excision of the central third. *American Journal of Sports Medicine, 22*(6), 803–811.

Kessing, B. F., Conchillo, J. M., Bredenoord, A. J., Smout, A. J., & Masclee, A. A. (2011). Review article: The clinical relevance of transient lower oesophageal sphincter relaxations in gastro-oesophageal reflux disease. *Alimentary Pharmacology and Therapeutics, 33*(6), 650–661. doi:10.1111/j.1365-2036.2010.04565.x.

Koufman, J. A. (1991). The otolaryngologic manifestations of gastroesophageal reflux disease (GERD): A clinical investigation of 225 patients using ambulatory 24-hour pH monitoring and an experimental investigation of the role of acid and pepsin in the development of laryngeal injury. *Laryngoscope, 101*(4 Pt 2 Suppl 53), 1–78.

Koufman, J., Sataloff, R. T., & Toohill, R. (1996). Laryngopharyngeal reflux: Consensus conference report. *Journal of Voice, 10*(3), 215–216. doi:S0892-1997(96)80001-4 [pii].

Li, N. Y., Verdolini, K., Clermont, G., Mi, Q., Rubinstein, E. N., Hebda, P. A., & Vodovotz, Y. (2008). A patient-specific in silico model of inflammation and healing tested in acute vocal fold injury. *PLoS One, 3*(7), e2789. doi:10.1371/journal.pone.0002789.

Li, N. Y., Vodovotz, Y., Kim, K. H., Mi, Q., Hebda, P. A., & Abbott, K. V. (2011). Biosimulation of acute phonotrauma: An extended model. *Laryngoscope, 121*(11), 2418–2428. doi:10.1002/lary.22226.

Liao, C. M., & Masters, R. S. W. (2002). Self-focused attention and performance failure under psychological stress. *Journal of Sport & Exercise Psychology, 24,* 289–305.

McCracken, H. D., & Stelmach, G. E. (1977). A test of the schema theory of discrete motor learning. *Journal of Motor Behavior, 9,* 193–201.

McNevin, N. H., Shea, C. H., & Wulf, G. (2003). Increasing the distance of an external focus of attention enhances learning. *Psychological Research, 67*(1), 22–29.

Miller, G. A. (1956). The magical number seven plus or minus two: some limits on our capacity for processing information. *Psychology Review, 63*(2), 81–97.

Mishra, S., Rosen, C. A., & Murry, T. (2000). Acute management of the performing voice. *Otolaryngologic Clinics of North America, 33*(5), 957–966.

Mortensen, M., & Woo, P. (2006). Office steroid injections of the larynx. *Laryngoscope, 116*(10), 1735–1739. doi:10.1097/01.mlg.0000231455.19183.8c.

Qadeer, M. A., Colabianchi, N., Strome, M., & Vaezi, M. F. (2006). Gastroesophageal reflux and laryngeal cancer: Causation or association? A critical review. *American Journal of Otolaryngology, 27* (2), 119–128. doi:S0196-0709(05)00139-0 [pii] 10.1016/j.amjoto.2005.07.010.

Randhawa, P. S., Mansuri, S., & Rubin, J. S. (2010). Is dysphonia due to allergic laryngitis being misdiagnosed as laryngopharyngeal reflux? *Logopedics Phoniatrics Vocology, 35*(1), 1–5. doi:912651419 [pii] 10.1080/14015430903002262.

Roth, D. F., & Ferguson, B. J. (2010). Vocal allergy: Recent advances in understanding the role of allergy in dysphonia. *Current Opinion in Otolaryngology & Head and Neck Surgery, 18*(3), 176–181. doi:10.1097/MOO.0b013e32833952af.

Roth, D. F., Verdolini Abbott, K., Carroll, T. L., & Ferguson, B. J. (2014). Evidence for primary laryngeal inhalant allergy: A randomized, double-blinded cross-over study. *International Forum of Allergy and Rhinology, 3*(1), 10–18.

Schmidt, R. (1975). A schema theory of discrete motor skill learning. *Psychological Review, 82,* 225–260.

Schmidt, R. A., & Lee, T. D. (2005). *Motor control and learning: A behavioral emphasis* (4th Aufl.). Champaign: Human Kinetics.

Schmidt, R. A., & Young, D. E. (1987). Transfer of movement control in learning. In S. M. Cormier & J. D. Hagman (Eds.), *Transfer of learning.* Orlando: Academic.

Schwartz, S. R., Cohen, S. M., Dailey, S. H., Rosenfeld, R. M., Deutsch, E. S., Gillespie, M. B., & Granieri, E. et al. (2009). Clinical practice guideline: Hoarseness (dysphonia). *Otolaryngol Head Neck Surgery, 141*(3 Suppl 2), S1–S31. doi:S0194-5998(09)01193-0 [pii] 10.1016/j.otohns.2009.06.744.

Shea, C. H., & Kohl, R. M. (1991). Composition of practice: Influence on the retention of motor skills. *Research Quarterly for Exercise and Sport, 62*(2), 187–195.

Shea, J. B., & Morgan, R. L. (1979). Contextual interference effects on the acquisition, retention, and transfer of a motor skill. *Journal of Experimental Psychology: Human Learning and Memory, 5,* 179–187.

Shea, C., & Wulf, G. (1999). Enhancing motor learning through external-focus instructions and feedback. *Human Movement Science, 18*(4), 553–571.

Singer, R. N., Cauraugh, J. H., Keith Tennant, L., Murphey, M., Chen, D., & Lidor, R. (1991). Attention and distractors: Considerations for enhancing sport performances. *International Journal of Sport Psychology, 22,* 95–114.

Singer, R. N., Lidor, R., & Cauraugh, J. H. (1993). To be aware or not aware: What to think about while learning and performing a motor skill. *The Sport Psychologist, 7,* 19–30.

Singer, R. N., Lidor, R., & Cauraugh, J. H. (1994). Focus of attention during motor skill performance. *Journal of Sport Sciences, 12,* 335–340.

Squire, L. R. (1986). Mechanisms of memory. *Science, 232,* 1612–1619.

Titze, I. R. (1981). Heat generation in the vocal folds and its possible effect on vocal endurance. In V. L. Lawrence (Ed.), *Transcripts of the tenth symposium: Care of the professional voice. Part 1: Instrumentation in voice research* (pp. 52–65). New York: The Voice Foundation.

Titze, I. R. (1988). The physics of small-amplitude oscillation of the vocal folds. *Journal of the Acoustical Society of America, 83*(4), 1536–1552.

Titze, I. R. (1994). Mechanical stress in phonation. *Journal of Voice, 8*(2), 99–105. doi:S0892-1997(05)80302-9 [pii].

Titze, M. R., & Verdolini, K. (2012). *Vocology*. Salt Lake City: National Center for Voice and Speech.

Titze, I. R., Svec, J. G., & Popolo, P. S. (2003). Vocal dose measures: Quantifying accumulated vibration exposure in vocal fold tissues. *Journal of Speech, Language, and Hearing Research, 46*(4), 919–932.

Toussaint, L., & Blandin, Y. (2010). On the role of imagery modalities on motor learning. *Journal of Sports Science, 28*(5), 497–504. doi:920977912 [pii] 10.1080/02640410903555855.

Tsunoda, K., Ishimoto, S., Suzuki, M., Hara, M., Yamaguchi, H., Sugimoto, M., & Takeuchi, S. et al. (2007). An effective management regimen for laryngeal granuloma caused by gastro-esophageal reflux: Combination therapy with suggestions for lifestyle modifications. *Acta Oto-Laryngologica, 127*(1), 88–92. doi:769780783 [pii] 10.1080/00016480600606665.

Ufema, K., & Montequin, D. (2001). The performance scream: vocal use or abuse? In R. Dal Vera (Ed.), *The voice in violence and other contemporary issues in professional voice and speech training* (pp. 74–86). Cincinnati: Voice and Speech Trainer Association, Inc.

Verdolini, K., Titze, I. R., & Fennell, A. (1994). Dependence of phonatory effort on hydration level. *Journal of Speech and Hearing Research, 37*(5), 1001–1007.

Verdolini, K., Min, Y., Titze, I. R., Lemke, J., Brown, K., van Mersbergen, M., Jiang, J., & Fisher, K. (2002). Biological mechanisms underlying voice changes due to dehydration. *Journal of Speech, Language, and Hearing Research, 45*(2), 268–281.

Verdolini, K., Rosen, C. A., Dietrich, M., Branski, R., Hersan, R., Li, N., & Scheffel, L. (2006). *The influence of training instructions and therapy structure on item-specific and generalized learning in voice therapy.* Paper presented at the 35th annual symposium: Care of the professional voice, Philadelphia, PA.

Verdolini Abbott, K., Li, N. Y. K., Branski, R. C., Rosen, C. A., Grillo, E., Steinhauer, K., & Hebda, P. A. (2012). Vocal exercise may attenuate acute vocal fold inflammation. *Journal of Voice, 26*(6), e1–e13.

Verdolini-Marston, K., & Balota, D. A. (1994). Role of elaborative and perceptual integrative processes in perceptual-motor performance. *Journal of Experimental Psychology: Learning, Memory, and Cognition, 20*(3), 739–749.

Verdolini-Marston, K., Titze, M. R., & Druker, D. G. (1990). Changes in phonation threshold pressure with induced conditions of hydration. *Journal of Voice, 4*(2), 142–151.

Verdolini-Marston, K., Sandage, M., & Titze, I. R. (1994). Effect of hydration treatments on laryngeal nodules and polyps and related voice measures. *Journal of Voice, 8*(1), 30–47. doi:S0892-1997(05)80317-0 [pii].

Vereijken, B., van Emmerik, R. E. A., Whiting, H. T. A., & Newell, K. M. (1992). Free(z)ing degrees of freedom in skill acquisition. *Journal of Motor Behavior, 24*, 133–142.

Wulf, G., & McNevin, N. H. (2003). Simply distracting learners is not enough: More evidence for the learning benefits of an external focus of attention. *European Journal of Sport Science, 3*(5), 1–13.

Wulf, G., & Prinz, W. (2001). Directing attention to movement effects enhances learning: A review. *Psychonomic Bulletin & Review, 8*(4), 648–660.

Wulf, G., & Weigelt, C. (1997). Instructions about physical principles in learning a complex motor skill: To tell or not to tell. *Research Quarterly for Exercise and Sport, 68*(4), 362–367.

Wulf, G., Höß, M., & Prinz, W. (1998). Instructions for motor learning: Differential effects of internal versus external focus of attention. *Journal of Motor Behavior, 30*(2), 169–179.

Wulf, G., McNevin, N. H., Fuchs, T., Ritter, F., & Toole, T. (2000). Attentional focus in complex skill learning. *Research Quarterly for Exercise and Sport, 71*(3), 229–239.

Wulf, G., McNevin, N., & Shea, C. H. (2001a). The automaticity of complex motor skill learning as a function of attentional focus. *The Quarterly Journal of Experimental Psychology, A, 54*(4), 1143–1154.

Wulf, G., Shea, C., & Park, J. H. (2001b). Attention and motor performance: Preferences for and advantages of an external focus. *Research Quarterly for Exercise and Sport, 72*(4), 335–344.

Wulf, G., McConnel, N., Gartner, M., & Schwarz, A. (2002). Enhancing the learning of sport skills through external-focus feedback. *Journal of Motor Behavior, 34*(2), 171–182.

Chapter 7
The Role of the Speech and Language Therapist – Speech Pathologist – In the Modern Singing Studio

Ron Morris

Abstract Speech and Language therapists are holders of a large body of knowledge that can assist the singing pedagogue. They are usually part of the multidisciplinary team that assist in the remediation and rehabilitation of singers suffering from vocal pathologies, working directly on respiration, phonation, resonance and articulation. Speech and Language therapists can also be integral to the development of a solid vocal technique in students who do not have any form of vocal pathology. Assistance can be rendered to the singing teacher and student in many ways but this chapter will focus on the development of breathing and support using the Accent Method of Breathing and on the identification and remediation of faults and inefficiencies within the articulation system.

Keywords Accent Method • Breathing for singing • Articulation

There have been a large number of changes in the vocal studio in the last 50 years with much of the pedagogy now influenced by science rather than by the teacher's own experience and sensations alone. The interaction of the vocal pedagogue with other professionals such as physicians, voice scientists and therapists has changed the way in which voice teachers think about voices and has also influenced approaches to teaching. This multidisciplinary approach to vocal pedagogy is now seen as the norm in many institutions as well as in many private vocal studios. Current publications on vocal pedagogy such as Janice Chapman's book *Singing and Teaching Singing: A Holistic Approach to Classical Voice* (2012) are champions of the multidisciplinary approach, using specialist input from other professionals to support, clarify and expand on the vocal pedagogy espoused.

R. Morris (✉)
The Brisbane Speech and Hearing Clinic, Brisbane, QLD, Australia

Queensland Conservatorium, Griffith University, Brisbane, QLD, Australia
e-mail: rmor8605@bigpond.net.au

S.D. Harrison and J. O'Bryan (eds.), *Teaching Singing in the 21st Century*,
Landscapes: the Arts, Aesthetics, and Education 14, DOI 10.1007/978-94-017-8851-9_7,
© Springer Science+Business Media Dordrecht 2014

The speech and language therapist is a key member of the multidisciplinary team, though often called upon when the vocal instrument is not functioning as well as it can (the speech and language therapist is vital in the remediation of voice disorders or vocal inefficiencies). The speech and language therapist is also the holder of body of knowledge that can assist the vocal pedagogue in the development of voices and the training of singers even where no specific vocal deficit is identified. The speech and language therapist has an intimate knowledge of the anatomy and physiology of the vocal tract as well as an in-depth understanding of its function and use. They also have access to a body of knowledge about communication and the systems used in communication that is unique. These systems include language; its structure, function and use and speech sounds; their development, production and use. The speech and language therapist also has knowledge about swallowing and the anatomy and physiology of deglutition that can assist the understanding of the relationships amongst the muscles of the mouth, pharynx and larynx. This understanding of muscular and structural interactions in the vocal tract allows the speech and language therapist to work with articulation, resonance, voice and swallowing in a way that few other professions can.

There are many areas in which the speech and language therapist can assist the vocal pedagogue but the two areas in which my personal experience lies is in the development of breathing and support and in the identification and correction of articulatory inefficiencies.

7.1 Breathing and Support

The development of appropriate breathing and breath support for singing continues to be an area that many students find difficult to understand and to master. Chapman states,

> This (breathing and support) is an area of vocal pedagogy that has always occupied the singing world. Great controversy still exists over the issues surrounding breathing and support, and students invariably find this the most difficult area of their training. (2012, 41)

The main reason for the difficulties that the students face is a lack of understanding about breathing and support on the part of their teachers. Many vocal pedagogues use language and imagery that is not completely founded in scientific fact or is in some way a distortion of the true anatomy and physiology of breath. This lack of understanding of breathing and support is not limited to the student. Many professional singers, even today, have only a very hazy idea about what they are doing when they breathe and support. Hixon, in a now classic study from 1985, highlighted this fact perfectly. Hixon used six professional singers in his study; prior to the collection of data (respiratory kinematics and lung volumes) he asked the singers to describe how they believed they managed their breath for singing. These statements were then compared to the actual data recorded. He assumed that highly trained and successful singers would be 'in touch' with their respiratory apparatus whilst singing; his conclusion however was quite different: '...singers who are highly trained, and in some cases have been recognized through success in competitions, generally do not have accurate knowledge of the mechanisms associated with their singing performance' (Hixon and Collaborators 1987, 369). Interestingly Hixon did not believe that the lack of correspondence between perception and reality was due to knowledge of respiratory anatomy but rather from the test subjects' lack of understanding of the function and interaction of some of the respiratory system components (1987, 369).

Many students and singers of today have a good understanding of the anatomy of the respiratory system as it is routinely taught in pedagogy, teaching skills or vocal mechanics classes the world over, the link between the actual anatomy and the function of the respiratory system components still appears to missing for many however which is the prime cause for the confusion that still exists.

There are a myriad of texts that carefully and adequately explain the anatomy and the physiology of the respiratory system, some of which are Hixon and Collaborators (1987), Bunch (1997), Thyme-Frøkjær and Frøkjær-Jensen (2001), Hixon (2006) and Chapman (2012).

The most important thing to be remembered about the function of the respiratory system in singing, and vital to the whole notion of 'support' for singing is that the respiratory system must provide a steady stream of air, at the correct pressure throughout the sung phrase so that the vocal folds may vibrate and the vocal tract resonate appropriately. This balance of pressure and flow is regulated by an interaction of the abdominal muscles (responsible for raising the intra-abdominal pressure, which in turn raises the intra-thoracic pressure) and the rib cage wall and diaphragm. The diaphragm acts as a releasing brake when lung volumes are high and the rib cage with its muscular system is adept at managing pressure and flow. The chest wall is liberally supplied with mechano-pressure receptors that send signals to the respiratory centre in the brainstem which in turn regulates the actions of the diaphragm and rib cage. When active expiration is required i.e. for singing, the increase in the intra-abdominal pressure caused by the abdominal muscles raises the intra-thoracic pressure stimulating the mechano-pressure receptors and triggering the action of the diaphragm and ribs. The actions of the large muscles in the abdomen, particularly the Transverse Abdominus and the Internal and External Obliques can be easily felt with the fingers giving an explicit sensation of muscular support.

These interactions can be easily identified when reflexive or primal sounds are emitted. The cough, laugh, groan or scream usually recruit the correct muscular interactions to support the voice, what Pam Davis calls 'the vocal component of the emotional motor system' (Davis in Chapman 2012, 229). Singers need to be able to access this support at will, which must become the core of a breathing and support technique for singing.

It is a commonly held belief that breathing and support is central to a good vocal technique and based on our understanding of the respiratory system and the demands placed on it by singing it is possible to outline the requirements of a breath management system.

There must be voluntary control of breathing. The singer must be able to initiate the breathing cycle quickly and efficiently as well as being able to control the outward flow of breath for the requirements of the singing. Secondary to this is that the singer should be able to use supported airflow at will. The singer must have adequate control of the voluntary components of the respiratory system, in particular the abdominal musculature, as support is dependent on appropriate muscular activity. Ideally this control should become almost unconscious, being driven by the emotional connection to the music and text. The control of the respiratory system must become so trained and bound to the production of voice that the correct muscles are recruited with the act of singing itself as well as with the emotional intent to sing.

There must be efficient and flexible use of the respiratory physiology. Support is not tension (as is so wrongly thought by many a student!), it is dynamic, flexible and ever changing to meet the demands of the music, text and emotion. Support must respond to the demands placed on the respiratory system by phrase length, pitch, dynamics and articulation. The maintenance of good postural alignment is also vital for a breathing and support system for singing. Good postural alignment assists the management of breath itself as well as providing an appropriate muscular framework for the voice. Resonance, timbre and pitching can also be affected by posture and alignment so a breath management system must not impinge on the alignment of the vocal instrument.

Any breathing and support system must follow the natural functions and actions of both the inspiratory and expiratory muscles. The expiratory muscles are much more under the singer's voluntary control than the inspiratory ones so care must be taken that any breathing system employed follows the dictates of natural function. Using the expiratory muscles to assist the in-breath (often seen in forced deep inspiration) when the muscles of the abdominal girdle (especially the flanks) are used to breathe in, tend to make it difficult for the singer to use appropriate air flow. This is a case where there is active muscular support but the timing is not appropriate (breathing out muscles are on too early) which affects the balance of pressure and flow, which can have a detrimental effect on the voice, particularly over time.

Finally the respiratory muscles must be trained in terms of strength, coordination and endurance. Singers are vocal athletes and as such require careful muscular development to ensure longevity and efficacy. The muscles of the respiratory system are in use every day to keep us alive but the demands of singing are so much greater. Lung volumes are higher, singers often use air from their reserve capacity, inspirations are quicker and deeper, expirations are longer and more controlled and there is a repetitive use of these 'super' functions that requires a marked endurance.

Vocal pedagogues have developed many systems over the past 400 years in an attempt to fulfill all of these requirements. Unfortunately many of the systems fall down on at least one of the points raised, most commonly on the requirement that the natural functions of the respiratory system should be followed. Typical examples of this are Rib Reserve breathing where the singer is actively encouraged to hold the rib cage out and open, and Belly Out breathing where the singer is told to breathe in then push the belly wall out and down to support the voice. The action of the rib cage is vital to a good breathing and support strategy, but the intercostal muscles respond to lung volumes and pressures through the pressure receptors in the rib cage wall and not to conscious control, so singers often use other secondary muscles in the shoulders and neck in their attempt to keep the rib cage out and open which often leads to excessive tension in the vocal tract. Belly out breathing does activate the muscles of the abdominal girdle and does alter intra-abdominal pressure which is correct, but the action is more consistent with defecation than breathing and the front of the abdominal wall is also locked which tends to impede the easy flow of air through the system. This down and out motion (pardon the pun) also tends to close the glottis and often encourages excessive tongue root tension as the singer struggles to adjust the airflow for voicing. Over the years many successful singers have claimed to use methods such as these so there must be some allowance for individual differences, but it is also important to recall Hixon's experiment (1987) where the singers' description of how they breathed did not match the physiological facts.

Many pedagogues have developed methods of teaching breathing and support that do fulfill all the requirements outlined above, but in an effort to develop a cohesive and completely scientific approach to the development of breathing and support, speech and language therapists are able to assist by using one of the tools developed within their profession for the treatment of voice and fluency disorders. Accent Method (breathing) was developed in the 1930s by Professor Svend Smith, a voice scientist and speech and language therapist. Professor Smith was particularly interested in patients with voice and fluency problems; at that time speech and language therapy was still in its infancy and most of the work carried out with voice and fluency patients centered on exercises for singing or for non-disordered voices. Professor Smith developed a breathing method that was based firmly in the anatomical and physiological knowledge of his time (subsequently validated by more recent understanding of respiratory anatomy and physiology) that aimed to normalize respiratory and vocal function by the use of abdomino-diaphragmatic breathing taught through a series of graduated exercises. 'The main goal of the Accent Method is to resolve pathological symptoms by optimizing normal functions, and to do this by achieving the best possible coordination between breathing, voicing, articulation, body movement and language for each individual' (Thyme-Frøkjær and Frøkjær-Jenson 2001, 7). Accent Method fulfills all of the requirements of a breath management system for singers, although initially designed for use with pathological voices, Accent Method because of its desire to optimize normal functions translates well to use for singing pedagogy.

Some slight modifications to classical Accent Method have been found to increase its efficacy with singers as the demands for abdominal support are greater than for speech but overall the traditional Accent Method paradigm is followed. Accent Method has been taught to all of the classical voice students the Queensland Conservatorium Griffith University (QCGU) since 2004 with anecdotal reports from both the students and teaching staff being favorable. A PhD study into the efficacy of the Accent Method approach taught at QCGU has recently been completed and some of the research findings are detailed within this chapter.

7.2   Overview of the Accent Method as Taught at QCGU

The students are initially given a simple explanation of the anatomy and physiology of breathing. This consists of use of correct anatomical terms, the identification of the components of the respiratory system and a summary of the actions of the muscles of respiration. Students are also introduced to the functions of the main respiratory muscles and an understanding of the interactions between the structure and function of the muscles is encouraged.

The students are placed on the floor in the Alexander Technique's semi-supine position so that 'Tidal Breathing' can be experienced and explained. This floor position assists postural alignment for breathing and provides a mechanical advantage for the diaphragm as the rib cage is pre-elevated and shoulder and neck involvement is minimized. In this position inspiration is carried out mainly by the diaphragm and expiration occurs though simple elastic recoil of the system. It is also possible to demonstrate that actions of the abdominal muscles are under the singer's voluntary control whilst those of the rib cage are breath dependent. Singers can also feel the natural expansion of the ribs that occurs when the diaphragms descends for the in-breath. Voluntary control of breathing is commenced with an emphasis on the actions of the abdominal muscles. Voiceless/ʃ, s, f, and θ/and voiced fricatives/ʒ, z, v, ð and ʍ/and the close vowel/ɣ/are used to promote airflow and freedom within the vocal tract.

Once tidal breathing is well established and the students have an understanding of the functions of the respiratory system the position is changed from semi-supine to side lying. In this position there is less advantage for the diaphragm but it is easier for the students to feel the action of the abdominal muscles on the out-breath. Students are also taught to 'waste the air', to use a vigorous abdominal movement to expel the air as quickly as possible. This is a deviation from the classic approach to Accent Method but it assists the student to activate the abdominal girdle which is required for supported singing (Chapman 2012, 59). The side lying position is also used to teach Chapman's SPLAT in-breath.

> Diaphragmatic/belly release inhalation or *Singers Please Loosen Abdominal Tension*, here-after referred to as SPLAT, … does not recruit any respiratory muscles during the in-breath but relies on a flexible abdominal wall, which allows the diaphragm to descend quickly, fully and efficiently. (Chapman 2012, 43)

Once this SPLAT in-breath and vigorous supported out-breath are established the student is then moved from the floor to sitting and standing positions.

The next stage of Accent Method is again taught on the floor, in side lying position. This is the first accent bounce, which consists of a small initial out-breath followed by a release of the abdominal wall before the re-application of the muscles of expiration for a larger out-breath. This is the first accentuation and forms the basis for all of the later patterns. Ideally the air continues to flow between the accentuations, meaning that the pelvic floor and the lower abdominals continue to operate even though the front of the tummy is releasing. This appears to be important in the singing of legato phrases and must be trained carefully at this point before more complex rhythms are taught. This first accent bounce is practised in sitting and standing positions. Movement is used, swaying side-by-side and face-to-face to accompany this pattern. The movement is helpful in releasing tension and to ensure a flexible and dynamic abdominal wall. At this point students are also encouraged to identify the support junctions described by Janice Chapman, namely the xyphoid region, the lower abdominal pubic synthesis, the sides of the waistbands and the back of the waistbands (the waistbands are thought to be the transverse abdominus and the internal and external obliques) (Chapman 2012, 47).

Classic Accent Method is then followed with the introduction of the Largo patterns. The use of the rhythmic patterns encourages motor learning and helps develop the strength, flexibility and coordination required for singing. Once these patterns are well established some additional movement involving both the arms and the legs is added and the student is encouraged to vocalize using both consonant and vowels. At this point exercises to help connect the breath to the singing voice can be commenced. These consist of simple glides and scale patterns over a fifth in a comfortable vocal range with the emphasis being on the correct use of respiratory physiology and the identification of appropriate abdominal support.

Patterns in Andante and Allegro tempi are also added with body movements such as marching. These levels require a large amount of practice and the increased number of patterns again encourages motor learning and the development of strength, flexibility and coordination. Patterns are practised with the fricative sounds, syllable babble and even words and phrases to ensure carry-over of the new breathing patterns into all types of vocalization. More time is spent in each session on singing exercises with use of semi-occluded vocal tract exercises, especially rolled 'r' and the voiced fricatives used in Accent Method instruction. The connection exercises described by Janice Chapman are also used here (2012, 276). It is vitally important that during this practice phase the student is monitored to ensure that postural alignment is correct, that the respiratory muscles are engaged appropriately and that the instrument is free from tension.

At QCGU Accent Method classes take place once a week for an hour over the duration of a single semester. Singing teachers also monitor, encourage, correct and practise breathing and support during the student's individual singing lesson. Students are also required to diarize their Accent Method classes so that they have a record of the exercises and explanations for future reference. This is extremely important as at the current time there is no longer a readily available printed source for students to refer to that describes the whole method in detail.

Accent Method has been used therapeutically since its creation in the 1930s and there is now a large body of evidence that confirms its efficacy with disordered voices. Thyme-Frøkjær and Frøkjær-Jenson (2001) reports that Accent Method improves airflow, normalizes vocal fold closure and has an impact on many of the acoustic and perceptual features of disordered voices. She also has a large set of data from speech and language therapists and speech and language therapy students that show increased duration of phonation, normalized air flow rates and improved dynamic ranges after training with Accent Method even though these test subjects had normal voices (Thyme-Frøkjær and Frøkjær-Jenson 2001, 144–153). Anecdotal evidence from QCGU appeared to confirm this with both the students and singing teachers reporting good improvements in breath management and dynamic range after Accent Method training.

A study has been recently completed that aimed to evaluate the efficacy of Accent Method in the development of young classical voice students. The subjects were 30 first and second year singers from the Guildhall School of Music and Drama in London. At this institution Accent Method was only taught by a limited number of teachers so it was possible to obtain a study group that had not been exposed to the method in any form. The students were randomly assigned into either the experimental group who underwent Accent Method instruction as out lined above, or the control group who received sight reading instruction for the same amount of time and sessions. An effort was made to balance males and females and first and second year students in each group. Measurements were taken pre and post training that consisted of: Maximum Phonation Time (MPT) of the vowels /a and i/, Mean Flow Rates (MFR) at modal pitch and one octave above modal pitch for the vowels /a and i/ and a Phonetogram (dynamic range profile) where the student was asked to phonate as softly and as loudly as possible on every pitch in their vocal range. In addition, the students were recorded singing *Caro Mio Ben* by Giordani in a key chosen by their teacher, pre and post training.

Statistical analysis indicated that there were no significant differences between the two groups on the pre training assessment apart from a slightly longer MPT of the /i/ vowel for the control group. This suggested that the two groups were appropriately randomized and equivalent prior to training. At the post training assessment there were no significant differences between or within groups on measures of MPT and MFR though some significant morphological differences were identified within the MFR tracings. There were however statistically significant differences between the two groups on the Phonetograms at the post training assessment and the experimental group had also shown a statistically significant change from the pre training phonetograms. Trained judges (singing teachers in Australia who did not know the voices and had no preconceived ideas about them) also preferred the post training recordings of the experimental group more frequently than those of the control group which suggested a significant change in the sound of the voices post training. Some of these results are detail in Fig. 7.1.

This phonetogram (Fig. 7.1) shows the average dynamic range for the subjects from the control group pre and post intervention. Male and Female data has been combined. This phonetogram indicates that whilst there was some change in the dynamic ranges for the singers in the control group, these changes were not statistically significant. They do however show some ability to sing more softly at the post-intervention assessment than was possible initially ($t = -1.843$, $df = 13$ and $p = .088$).

Figure 7.2's phonetogram shows a clear difference between the Pre and Post recordings. There was a very highly significant difference seen in the average dynamic range measures ($t = -4.757$, $df = 14$ and $p = .000$.) with the subjects in the Experimental group improving in their ability to sing both softly and loudly. The total number of semitones sung was also significantly greater ($t = -3.437$, $df = 14$,

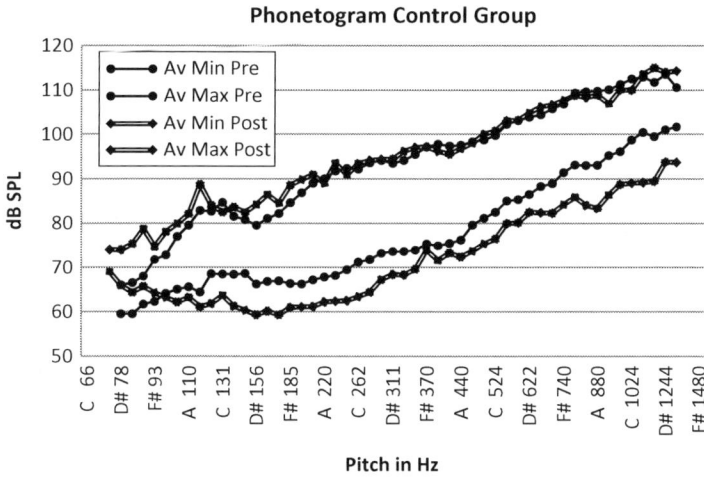

Fig. 7.1 Phonetogram for the Control group pre and post intervention

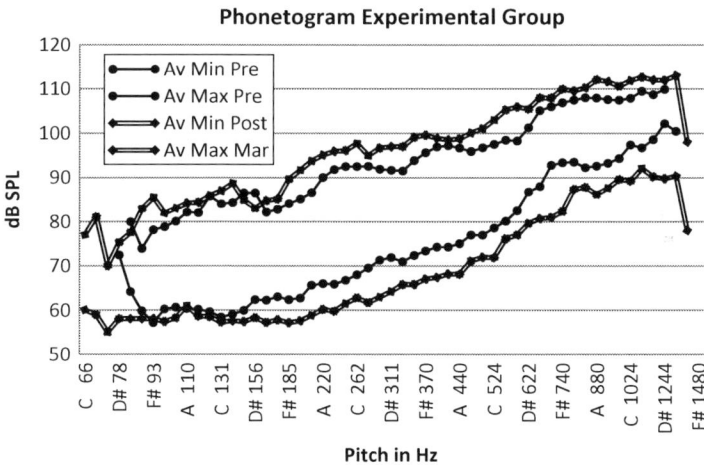

Fig. 7.2 Phonetogram for the Experimental group pre and post intervention with Accent Method

$p = .004$). This result suggests that Accent Method was effective in increasing the dynamic range of the singers in this group over the course of the study (1 h sessions weekly for 10 weeks).

This phonetogram (Fig. 7.3) shows both the control and experimental group post training. The phonetogram for the experimental group is larger overall with both soft and loud tones showing an advantage. The difference between the two groups' mean dynamic ranges were statistically significant ($t = -2.768$, $df = 27$

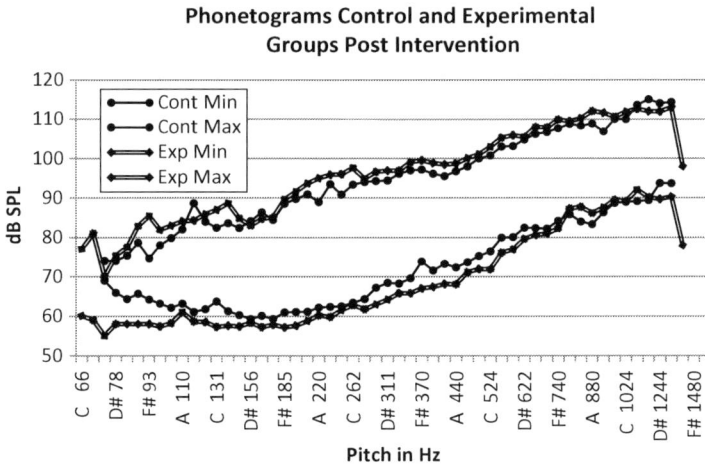

Phonetograms Control and Experimental Groups Post Intervention

Fig. 7.3 Comparison of the Control and Experimental group phonetograms post intervention

and $p = .010$) confirming that the experimental group showed a larger dynamic range than the control group post training, this is despite the group phonetograms being not statistically significantly different pre training (phonetogram not shown).

These phonetograms indicated that the group that received Accent Method instruction had significantly improved dynamic ranges and there was also some evidence that the pitch range also increased for this group. Some individual singers from the experimental group showed very large changes whilst others showed no significant change. Overall the group showed highly significant change with the possibility of the change being due to chance less than 0.001 %. Mean air flow rates did not change significantly for either group, though it is interesting to note that the mean flow rates (MFR) through steady state vowels were significantly higher than the norms reported by Thyme-Frøkjær, but there were marked differences in the morphology of the airflow traces following Accent Method instruction. At the pre intervention testing session two distinct patterns of airflow trace were identified: the typical pattern reported in the literature, and a second atypical one where there were rapid regular perturbations in the airflow trace. It became obvious that the atypical patterns were obtained from students who were actively being taught or who had been taught a 'belly out' or 'hold the position of inspiration' method of support. Further evidence was obtained when there were additional students in the control group with this pattern in the post intervention stage but many fewer in the experimental group post intervention with Accent Method. A typical morphology is shown in Fig. 7.4 and an atypical morphology is shown in Fig. 7.5. Steady airflow and steady volume (the SPL trace) can be easily seen.

These atypical morphologies were present with the vowel sounds phonated at modal pitch but it was more obvious when the vowels were phonated one octave above modal pitch. In some examples of this atypical morphology there was a corresponding perturbation in the SPL trace, which may become audible over time sounding

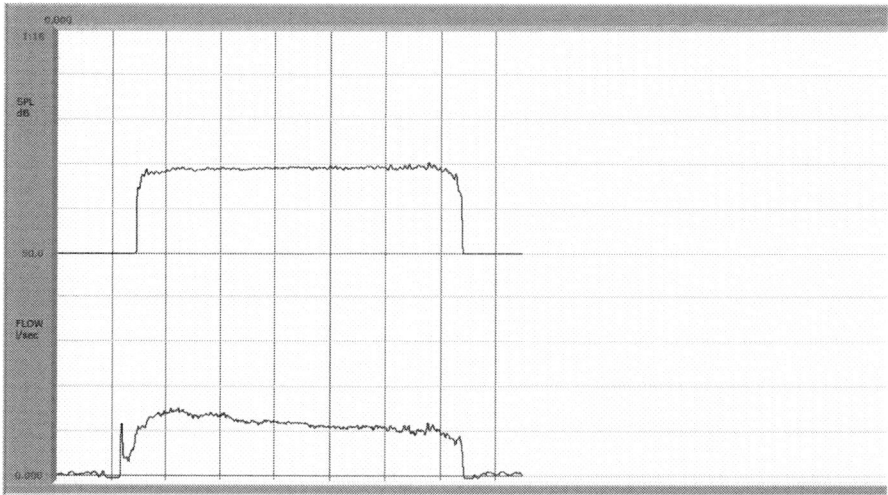

Fig. 7.4 MFR tracing /a/ 8va from a female subject showing typical morphology

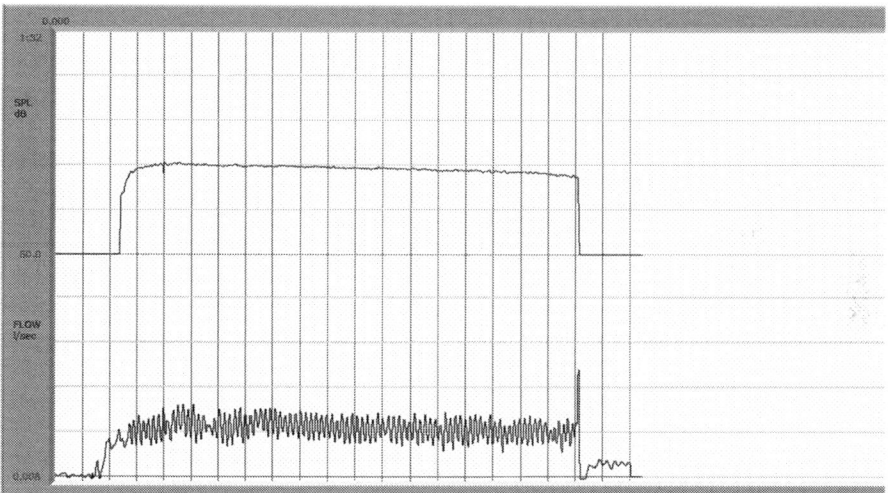

Fig. 7.5 MRF tracing /a/ 8va from a female subject showing atypical morphology

like unstable vibrato or a 'wobble'. It can only be postulated as to the cause of this perturbation but it is most likely that the incorrect use of the respiratory physiology is at fault (Fig. 7.6).

In Example 6 the perturbation of the SPL trace can clearly be seen pre intervention but this is eradicated in the post intervention trace as is the marked perturbation in the airflow. Female examples have been given here but there were a number of similar examples in the male subjects. Accent Method through its focus on

a

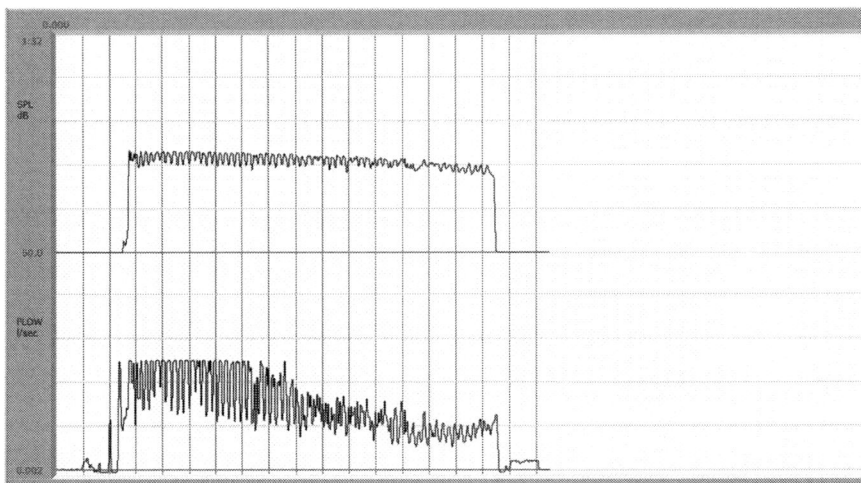

b

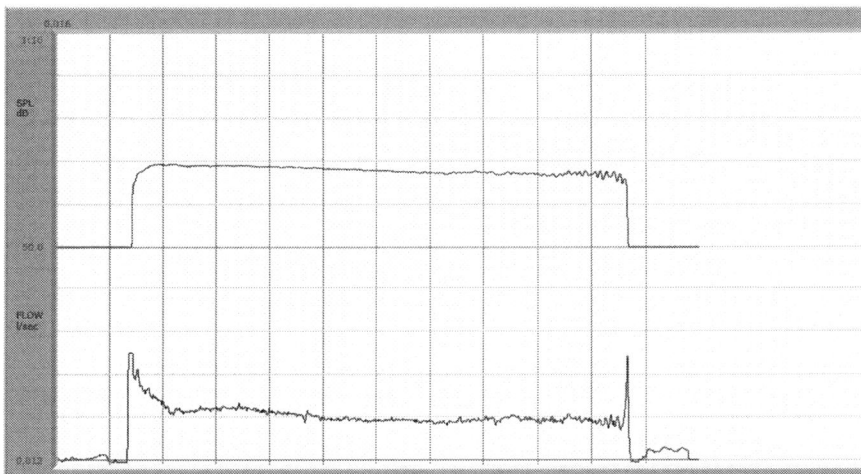

Fig. 7.6 Tracings of a female subject showing normalization of the morphology pre (**a**) and post (**b**) intervention with Accent Method

abdomino-diaphragmatic breathing, and the correct use of the respiratory physiology appears to be effective in not only increasing dynamic and pitch ranges but in remediating abnormal airflow tracing morphology.

Instruction in Accent Method is an area in which the speech and language therapist has much to offer the singing pedagogue. As a general rule speech and language therapists are not skilled or are reluctant to work on the development of a singer's vocal technique, so a team approach with speech and language therapist and the singing teacher working together is often the most effective.

7.3   Articulation

Vocal pedagogues have long been interested in articulation but it is usually only seen as important in the transmission of clear and intelligible text. Singers are the only musicians that have the burden of text to add to the production of pitch, timing, dynamic range and timbre, so it is natural that exercises to ensure the clarity of the text have been fundamental to the development of a good vocal technique. Speech and language therapists also have a desire for articulation to be clear and intelligible as it is through oral communication, spoken language, that most of the world's population communicates. The speech and language therapist also works with those who have disordered articulation and aims to normalize the speech sound usage so that the spoken communication is clear and intelligible. In working with a number of speech-disordered populations (especially the deaf) it has become apparent that there is a closer link between voice quality and timbre and the articulation system than was first thought. This can be easily seen in the speech of the profoundly deaf where tongue height on vowel sounds often affects vocal register and pitch. These patients demonstrate a lack of independence between the tongue and larynx height. High vowels such as /i/ or /u/ are produced with one pitch whilst low vowels such as /a/ or /ɔ/ are produced with a much lower one. In extreme examples of this phenomenon the vocal register may also be changed by the tongue height. This of course occurs as the profoundly deaf speaker does not have the same access to auditory feedback that allows easy monitoring of the voice.

In my own work with the profoundly deaf it was also obvious that our way of examining and working with vowel sounds was not adequate for teaching these sounds when the ability for auditory feedback was limited. It is possible to teach the consonant sounds using the International Phonetic Alphabet classification system based on manner of articulation, place of articulation and voicing even when auditory feedback is very limited (this has been well documented and clearly explained in Ling 2002) but the vowel classification system based on tongue height and lip rounding is not adequate for the task. When teaching vowel sounds to the profoundly deaf it is vital that every tiny amount of residual hearing is exploited if the vowels are to be well articulated. This suggests that something other than tongue height and lip rounding are operating. Tongue height has been known to be much more powerful in vowel articulation than lip rounding but even this cannot explain all the difficulties. Work in artificial speech production in the areas of computer generated speech also assisted the understanding of vowel articulation but it is actually the quite old research of Wood (1979) which holds the key to clear vowel sounds, especially for singers!

Wood used radiographic studies of the whole vocal tract during vowel production; by looking below the mouth he was able to identify points of constriction within the pharynx that he felt important in vowel articulation. Tongue height was seen as differentiating between the vowels that had that point of constriction. The tongue is the most important modifier of pharyngeal shape, though larynx height also plays a significant role and this can explain why lip rounding is really of only secondary importance in vowel articulation.

Wood identified four points of constriction that appear to drive vowel articulation:

- Palatal
- Velar
- Upper Pharyngeal (uvular)
- Lower Pharyngeal (pharyngeal)

The palatal vowels are the highest in the vocal tract and are the most oral of all the vowels. Tongue height and to a much lesser extent lip rounding differentiates between: /I, i, ɛ and e/. The larynx tends to be at the highest setting for these vowels, which probably accounts for their designation by many pedagogues as the 'bright' vowels.

The velar vowels are made with the point of constriction towards the back of the mouth, tongue height is used to differentiate /u and ʊ/. Larynx position for these vowels, especially the /u/, is low and indeed these are the vowels which have the lowest larynx setting. The point of constriction at the back of the mouth allows a high back tongue position which in turn allows the larynx to drop giving a long pharynx.

The upper pharyngeal vowels are /ɔ and o/ with tongue height again the main differentiator between them. Larynx height is again low but is not as low as for the /u/ vowel.

The lower pharyngeal vowels are: /a, æ and ʌ/ with tongue and larynx height much more important than lip rounding to differentiate between them. /a/ is a somewhat problematical vowel for many singers as it has the lowest tongue height of all the vowels but this is combined with only a middle laryngeal height. Old fashioned singing pedagogies that encouraged a low flat tongue for /a/, some even requested a groove in the tongue, often resulted in a depressed larynx and the development of significant tongue root tension.

This knowledge about the pharyngeal targets for vowel sounds is very powerful for the singing pedagogue. It is much easier to match the resonance characteristics of the various vowels if the pharyngeal target position is correct and once the vowel resonances are better matched this leads to an immediate improvement in vowel intelligibility and in evenness of vocal tone across the vowels.

Mastering the pharyngeal targets is best done by ear with the caveat that the less done with the lips and even with the tongue body, the easier the correct pharyngeal target will be to achieve. The over produced or over mouthed vowels that many teachers strive for, in an effort to obtain vowel clarity, is actually detrimental to the acquisition of correct pharyngeal targets. The over use of the lips, too much rounding or spreading will change the vowel shape but because it is occurring at the end of the vocal tract it will be difficult to match vowel resonances and vocal tone. Over opening of the jaw also makes it difficult to maintain the correct pharyngeal length and depth and again matching of vowel resonances is much more difficult when the jaw is over open. This can be demonstrated by choosing a pitch in the upper middle range of the voice and then attempting to sing the five Italian vowels with as little mouth movement as possible. If the mouth is essentially immobilized (and the tongue root is not engaged) the larynx can be felt to slightly lower as the sequence runs from /i/ through /e, a and ɔ/ to /u/. Once this is achieved try the sequence again but purposely over mouth the vowels and notice how the larynx descends less and how the vowels do not resonate so evenly. This phenomenon can be made more obvious by singing down a five note scale as the descent in pitch encourages a descent in the larynx (as long as there is no tongue root constriction!).

Training of the pharynx to assist in the production of the vowels needs to be systematic and does take some time. Janice Chapman has an exercise entitled 'Dial-a-Vowel', which serves this purpose well (2012, 284–285). This is an exercise originally designed to assist singers whose mother tongue was not Italian to develop the correct articulatory setting for that language, however careful palpation of the larynx height confirms that by placing the tongue in that high Italianate position the correct pharyngeal target for the vowels is also achieved. Fundamental to the success of this exercise is appropriate tongue height with minimal to no activity of the lips and jaw so that the singer's and teacher's ear may guide the correct vowel acoustically.

The concept of tongue root tension has already been mentioned and it is one of the main misuses of the articulatory physiology that can impact on the singing voice through the vowel sounds in particular. Tongue, jaw and larynx interdependence is another of the more vowel driven misuses. Tongue root tension (TRT) is perhaps the most common and is unfortunately very insidious. TRT is a misuse of the articulatory physiology and tends to occur when some of the swallowing mechanism is recruited in the act of singing. When we swallow the tongue propels the food or liquid backwards into the pharynx and then the tongue root is activated to press down on the epiglottis so that the epiglottis acts like a lid when the larynx rises during the swallow. This prevents food or liquid entering into the larynx and thus into the airway. How this mechanism can be recruited into singing appears nonsensical but unfortunately the activation of the tongue root has a number of sequellae that seem helpful for singing.

When TRT is engaged the downward pressure can act as a false depressor of the larynx. In classical singing a lower larynx setting is usually desired to increase the pharyngeal depth and width to promote the best possible resonance. If this lowering is brought about by the tongue root however, resonance is hampered rather than enhanced, leading to a dark or bottled voice quality. Engagement of TRT also changes the singer's perception of their own voice as it removes many of the upper partials in the sound making it sound darker, heavier or more mature to themselves but less good to the listener who can perceive this as too dark, bottled or woolly! TRT also seems to aid the singer hear themselves over other singers or instruments, so it tends to occur more in singers who are constantly sight singing and thus need to check for intonation. TRT also gives the singer a greater sense of control over the voice, and in this respect it is like the deaf person who uses tongue retraction and tension to improve the kinesthetic feedback of their articulators. Related to this sense of increased control is the fact that the tongue root is perhaps one of the strongest muscles in the vocal tract and will also attempt to assist support the singing voice if abdominal breath support is reduced or inadequate. Dealing with TRT therefore requires the teacher to identify the reasons for the presence of the TRT, dealing with those as much as possible and then tackling the TRT directly. Chapman (2012) has a wealth of exercises for addressing TRT contained in both chapter 7 (Articulatory options) and in the exercise chapter (appendix 1).

Tongue, jaw and larynx interdependence is a case where marked TRT is combined with jaw tension, through the connections of the hyoid bone the larynx can also become enmeshed in this inappropriate link. Larynx height becomes influenced by both jaw and tongue position and in fact it may be impossible to separate the tongue and jaw functioning during articulation. Often the tongue and jaw can be seen choreographing pitch changes, the jaw becomes over involved in consonant production and vibrato or tremolo can be detected in the jaw, floor of the mouth or tongue.

Articulatory clarity is often affected by this interdependence, as the jaw will attempt to perform some of the functions of the tongue tip when consonant sounds are produced. This leads to 'chewy' over mouthed text and there can be weakness in some of the consonant sounds. Vowel clarity is also affected and it can be very difficult to use the correct pharyngeal targets for the vowel sounds, which will often affect vowel resonances and vowel matching. Teacher requests for clearer text usually make the problem worse since the over-activity of the jaw is increased by attempts to make the text clearer! If larynx height is also influenced by the tongue or jaw position difficulties with intonation can occur and there can be unusual intonation problems with specific vowels at certain parts of the pitch range (problems usually occur in the upper range of the voice).

Intervention requires that the vocal structures regain their independence so the acquisition of a divorce is required. Initially a divorce of the tongue and jaw is in order with then further action taken to separate the larynx from the tongue and the jaw if it is still too dependent. In most cases returning freedom to the tongue and jaw allows the larynx to resume its free and unconstricted state. The marked TRT that usually accompanies this type of inefficiency must also be tackled. It is important to note that attempts to separate out these vocal structures will not be successful if there is inadequate airflow or insufficient abdominal support so intervention will often need to occur at the level of airflow and support first. Chapman (2012) has a set of exercises in Chapter 7 that can assist in developing more freedom for these vocal structures.

Consonant sounds can also impact on voice quality and vocal tone. Singing teachers have an excellent ear for articulation and are usually very astute in identifying consonant articulation deficits. Students with frank errors of articulation such as /f/ for /θ/, /w/ for /r/, lisps or weak /r/ sounds should be referred to the speech and language therapist for standard speech sound therapy. These articulation errors respond well to patient treatment and if the student is motivated 3 or 4 months should be sufficient to see their eradication in both speaking and singing. Speech sounds that appear correct to the ear but are produced with compensation can create more difficulties. Tongue blade articulation is the most common of these and it can have a marked effect on the voice. Tongue blade users produce some or all of the tongue-tip sounds with the blade of the tongue rather than with the tip. These consonants sound normal in most cases but they are often produced with a forward movement of the jaw, which compensates for the use of the blade of the tongue. Tongue blade articulation is usually of no consequence in the general population as the speech sounds normal, but for the singer the forward compensation of the jaw can affect vowel resonances. Once again the text can sound 'chewed' or muffled (especially in fast passages) if the jaw compensation is not quick enough to ensure good consonant articulation. If the jaw compensation forward is significant enough problems with intonation or even with achieving higher pitches can occur.

Most singers who have tongue blade articulation are good aural musicians and as children have fine-tuned their speech to sound normal despite an inefficient articulatory pattern. The central fricatives and affricates /ʃ, ʒ, tʃ and ʤ/ tend to be the most affected by the forward movement of the jaw but any of the tongue tip alveolar sounds /s, z, t, d, n or l/ can also be effected. It is important to note that the possible error sounds contain the most common sounds of English giving many opportunities for the jaw compensation to act and the voice and vocal tone be affected. Diagnosis of tongue blade articulation must be done by eye as well as by ear as most of the sounds produced do sound normal! The forward displacement of the jaw during consonant articulation is the most important diagnostic sign. A description of the characteristics of tongue blade articulation can be found in Chapman (2012, 127, 128).

Intervention for tongue blade articulation centers on the use of the tongue tip for articulation. Simple exercises to strengthen the tongue tip and improve its flexibility are important. The consonant sounds must be taught with clear cues on tongue-tip placement as the use of aural modeling is usually ineffective in these cases. The central fricatives and affricates should be tackled first as they tend to have the greatest jaw compensation and therefore the greatest impact on the voice. /s and z/ are perhaps more common sounds but for many tongue blade users the jaw compensation on these sounds is less and they can be treated later. Once the speech sounds are correctly evoked they must be used in a traditional articulation paradigm, single syllables, syllable babble, words, phrases and sentences before carry over into normal speaking and singing. Once again Chapman (2012) has some exercises to assist the carry over into singing.

The modern vocal pedagogue has access a vast amount of information on vocal and respiratory anatomy and physiology to inform and drive their teaching. The use of the interdisciplinary team can assist in the acquisition and use of this ever-expanding knowledge base. The speech and language therapist is in a unique position to assist in some very specific as well as more general ways. Certainly the vocal pedagogue can call on the speech and language therapist not only when the student's voice is in crisis but to help with the development of the core components of technique such as breathing and support and articulation.

References

Bunch, M. A. (1997). *Dynamics of the singing voice* (4th ed.). New York: Springer.

Chapman, J. C. (2012). *Singing and teaching singing – a holistic approach to classical voice* (2nd ed.). San Diego/Oxford/Brisbane: Plural.

Hixon, T. J. (2006). *Respiratory function in singing. A primer for singers and singing teachers*. Tucson: Redington Brown.

Hixon, T.J., & Collaborators. (1987). *Respiratory function in speech and song*. Boston: College-Hill Press.

Ling, D. (2002). *Speech and the hearing impaired child: Theory and practice* (2nd ed.). Washington, DC: Alexander Graham Bell Association for the Deaf.

Thyme-Frøkjær, K., & Frøkjær-Jenson, B. (2001). *The Accent Method: A rational voice therapy in theory and practice*. Bicester: Speechmark.

Wood, S. (1979). A radiographic analysis of constriction locations for vowels. *Journal of Phonetics, 7*, 25–43.

Chapter 8
The Extra-Normal Voice: EVT in Singing

Michael Edward Edgerton

Abstract The human voice is a remarkable instrument that encompasses enormous bio-acoustic diversity. Whether singing in folk, world, popular, classical, contemporary, experimental or improvisatory settings these practices may involve widely varying methods of sound production and aesthetic. However, across all of these traditions it is important to note that humans (without disease or anomaly) have the same anatomical parts, but just utilize them in different ways. This chapter will discuss the pedagogy of the extra-normal voice by first presenting key concepts of voice production within the framework of voice science, followed by examples of ethnic and experimental vocal practice. Then in an attempt to communicate the idea that what was known as extended vocal techniques (EVTs) may be developed to a far greater degree using systematic methods, and not dissimilar to the bel canto voice, a series of exercises were designed to explore the structure, production and mentality of EVT in singing.

Keywords Extended vocal techniques • Extra-normal voice • Singing exercises • Experimental • Ethnic

The human voice is a remarkable instrument that encompasses enormous bio-acoustic diversity. Whether singing in folk, world, popular, classical, contemporary, experimental or improvisatory settings these practices may involve widely varying methods of sound production and aesthetic (Edgerton 2005). However, across all of these traditions it is important to note that humans (without disease or anomaly) have the same anatomical parts, but just utilize them in different ways (Levin and Edgerton 1999).

In this chapter I will discuss the pedagogy of the extra-normal voice by presenting examples of ethnic and experimental vocal practice followed by exercises designed to explore the production and mentality of EVT in singing.

M.E. Edgerton (✉)
The Cultural Centre, Department of Music, University of Malaya, Kuala Lumpur, Malaysia
e-mail: edgertonmichael@hotmail.com

S.D. Harrison and J. O'Bryan (eds.), *Teaching Singing in the 21st Century*,
Landscapes: the Arts, Aesthetics, and Education 14, DOI 10.1007/978-94-017-8851-9_8,
© Springer Science+Business Media Dordrecht 2014

8.1   Key Concepts

The classical theory of speech production suggests that voiced sounds are produced by a wave-like motion of the vocal folds that disturb airflow resulting in a series of air pulsations. These pulses carry an acoustically complex tone with a fundamental frequency and associated harmonic spectrum. For more than 50 years this theory, developed for speech acoustics, has described an independent relationship between the sound source and resonator (Sundberg 1977). However, recent research has shown that nonlinear interactions between the source and resonator feed off each other, sometimes to such an extent that nonlinear phenomena may appear (Titze 2008, Neubauer et al. 2004). Such extra-complex sonorities result from two interdependent components: (1) that all sounds are produced by a multidimensional network of physical elements, and; (2) when one of more of those elements are desynchronized from normal then changes to a sound identity may range from slight timbre change leading towards dramatic bifurcations of distantly removed attractor states (Edgerton et al. 2003).

In normal speech and song, the sound source is a disturbance to an outgoing airflow which is filtered by the upper vocal tract before propagating into the external environment. The movement of the lips, jaw, tongue, etc. articulate and shape an outward moving airflow. This filtering action imposes a passive frequency curve consisting of a series of amplitude peaks and valleys on the composite source tone. Normally speech science considers the first three or four resonant amplitude peaks (formants) as the most perceptually relevant (Hall 2002).

8.1.1   Air

Air drives speech and song. For egressive phonation (expiration), air volume in the lungs decreases as air passes through the upper vocal tract. Beginning subglottally, air pressure increases until a threshold is reached and air passes through the glottis. As the glottis rapidly opens and closes a difference of air pressure effects subglottal and supraglottal cavities. In speech, this variation is too small to have much of an effect, but in singing becomes more important that may even affect pitch, such as singing out of tune (Titze 1994). Regarding the extra-normal voice, air may be used to include not only expiration, but also inspiration; lunged or unlunged volume; air as an inharmonic sonority.

8.1.2   Source

A sound source refers to some acoustic disturbance within a resonant environment, such as the movement of the lips against the cup of a tuba mouthpiece, or the oscillation of paired vocal folds. Humans feature a relatively wide extent of pitch (fundamental frequency), each with many harmonics that are dependent upon both length and tension. The loudness of a tone is dependent on the efficiency of the transfer of power between sub-glottal pressure and voice source. The mode of phonation effects both timbre and register of the voice source that are heavily influenced by the closing phase of the average glottal cycle. For example, a longer closing phase results in a reduction of amplitude that appears as pressed or tense; and when increased further such sounds may become strained or strangled. Alternatively, a reduction of the closing phase may even fail to close the glottis, resulting in a breathy phonation. Somewhere in the middle is a mode known as flow phonation, which is features a strong fundamental frequency whose spectrum consists of a gently descending amplitude slope (Sundberg 1987). Regarding the extra-normal voice, the source may be desynchronized from *ordinario* to produce extra-normal voice via: laryngeal manipulation, un- to barely-voiced, voiced, on- to offset, breathiness, vocal fry, low damped phonation, open to close ratio manipulation, pressed to loose, wide vibrato/tremolo, asymmetries, glottal whistle, supraglottal, subglottal and esophageal phonation, register oscillation, color (timbre), unusual tessitura, emphasis of shifting mechanism and glissandi.

8.1.3   Articulation/Resonance

Articulation refers to movement of the tongue, lips, jaw, soft palate, etc., during speech and song. Resonance refers to the acoustic properties of the vocal tract. When moving the articulators around in the vocal tract, we are manipulating the regions of high and low acoustic pressure that are better known as formant (resonant) frequencies. The length of the vocal tract influences resonances such that a longer tract will feature lower formant frequencies, which affects the perception of voice quality (Sataloff 1992). Regarding the extra-normal voice, resonance & articulation may be desynchronized from *ordinario* to produce extra-normal voice via: oral Modification, IPA/linguistic emphasis, two-stage combinatorial principle, Edgerton Model of Articulation (Edgerton 2005), timbral changes, reinforced harmonics, external filters, turbulent approximants, frications and stops (see Fig. 8.1).

8.1.4   Heightened Potentials

Heightened potentials refer to expanded potentials of voice – often using combinatorial principles that involve: (1) voiced and voiced; (2) voiced and unvoiced; (3) unvoiced and unvoiced; (4) three or more sources (Edgerton 2005) (see Table 8.1).

8.1.5   Examples of EVT

Reinforced harmonics (in Tuva known as throat singing; in the west as overtone singing) is a remarkable vocal phenomenon in which one person is able to sculpt out

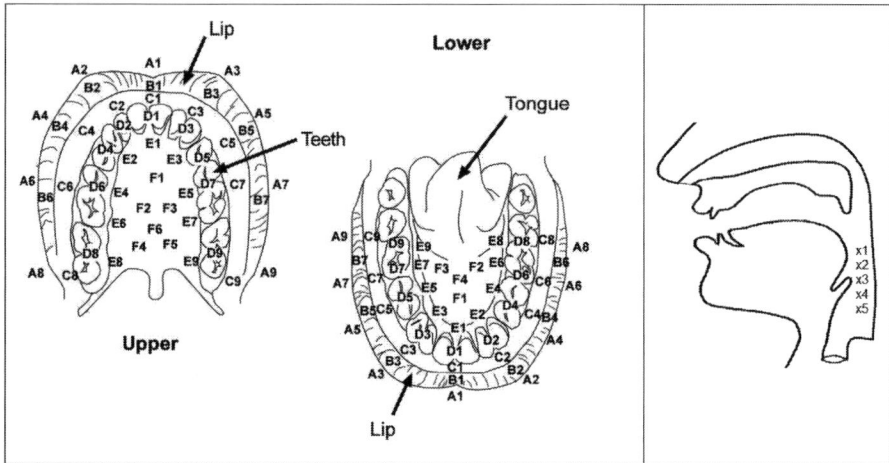

Fig. 8.1 Edgerton model of articulation – here showing only points of articulation (Edgerton 2005)

of a fundamental frequency and associated spectra, a melody built entirely on the harmonics. In Fig. 8.2, a single voice produces a drone with melody based on harmonics 8, 9, 10 and 12. Additionally this melody features frequent upper neighbor grace notes that most often return to the pitch of departure. Note that the singer produces a strong resonant band at approximately 3.1 kHz (Mongush 1990).

Figure 8.3 presents another example of diverse ethnic voice – this time from Korea. In this example, Kim, So-Hee produces rapid and wide pitch changes that often involve what appears to be a shift in register as well as changing the extent of vibrato from moderate to large (Kim 1988).

Figure 8.4 presents an aggressive high oscillation which changes from a narrow to a wide oscillation. This production seems to use a series of rapid glottal stops that may assist the perception of pitch change. The production may involve mixed nasality (Namtchylak 1999).

The next example by Fatimah Miranda features a classic example in the presentation of nonlinear phenomena (Neubauer et al. 2004). At the outset of this example, Miranda produces a periodic (Limit Cycle Attractor) tone which is followed by a subharmonic (Period-Doubling Attractor) at one-half. This subharmonic leads directly into a subharmonic at one-fourth which is then succeeded by a laryngeally produced inharmonic tone (Chaotic Attractor) (see Fig. 8.5) (Miranda 1992).

Figure 8.6 presents biphonation in the male voice, produced by Demetrio Stratos (1978). This example features two independent frequency contours over time which additionally produces voice crossings at 3.25″, 5.7″ and 6.5″ s. Both voices are produced by the glottal whistle (M4) and notated as f(t) for the lower voice and g(t) for the higher voice.

Table 8.1 Combinatorial principles – voiced-voiced; voiced-unvoiced; unvoiced-unvoiced; three or more

Combinatorial, multiphonic framework	
Voiced and voiced	*Voiced and unvoiced*
1. Chant and variants (falsetto with 'fry' + ingressive glottal pitch with ingressive 'fry')	1. Glottal pitch with lip buzz
2. Asymmetrical vocal fold vibration	2. Glottal pitch with whistle (lateral or rounded)
3. Sub- or supraglottis oscillation with voice	3. Glottal pitch with pharyngeal articulation
4. Esophageal speech with other	4. Glottal pitch with articulation in the oral cavity
	5. Glottal pitch with nasal articulation
	6. Glottal pitch with salival articulation
	7. Glottal pitch with air
	8. Glottal pitch with lingualabial
	9. Glottal pitch with tongue flutter or frication
	10. Glottal pitch with velar articulation
	11. Glottal pitch with uvula
	12. Glottal pitch with externally produced sources
	13. Vocal fry with air
	14. Vocal fry with bilabial
Unvoiced and unvoiced	*Three or more*
1. Pharyngeal articulation with lip buzz	1. Chant mode with lingual
2. Pharyngeal articulation with oral cavity frication	2. Chant mode with whistle
3. Whistle with lip vibration	3. Chant [asymmetrical mode] with pharyngeal articulation
4. Whistle with sustained oral cavity fricative, approximation	4. Glottal pitch, lingual fric. and salival fric. between cheek and gum
5. Whistle with pharyngeal articulation	5. Glottal pitch, pharyngeal articulation, tongue vibration
6. Whistle with egressive nasal fricatives or approximations	6. Glottal pitch, tongue vib. (front, mid, rear), lip vib. (buzz or fric.)
7. 2-part whistle	7. Glottal pitch, rear tongue vibration, front tongue vibration
8. Double bilabial	8. Glottal pitch, tongue vibration, labialdental frication
9. Cheek with lip	9. Glottal pitch, mid-to-rear tongue vibration, linguadental frication
10. Double tongue vibration	10. Glottal pitch, tongue, whistle
11. Tongue with cheek	11. Glottal pitch, cheek, lip
12. Tongue with labial flutter	12. Glottal pitch, saliva, uvula
13. Tongue with oral cavity frication	13. Three-part laryngeal source
14. Salival frication – dental	14. Ingressive dental, salival fric. w/egressive nasal fric./approx..
15. Salival frication – cheek	15. Ingressive bilabial, salival fric. w/egressive nasal fric./approx..
16. Salival frication – bilabial	
17. Salival articulation with percussive dental articulations	
18. Egressive nasal frication or approximation with percussive dental	
19. Egressive nasal frication or approx.. with bilabial articulation	

(continued)

Table 8.1 (continued)

Combinatorial, multiphonic framework	
20. Egressive nasal fric. or approx.. with percussive lingual-alveolar	16. Salival fricative, nasal and mouth air
21. Egress. nasal fric. or approx.. w sustained alveolar/palatal fric.	17. Dual lip vibration with cheek
	18. Dual lip vibration with glottal pitch
22. Egressive nasal frication or approximation with lip buzz	19. Dual lip vibration, glottal pitch, saliva
	20. 2-part asymmetry with air
23. Egressive nasal frication or approx.. with ingressive lip buzz	21. 2-part asymmetry, air, saliva

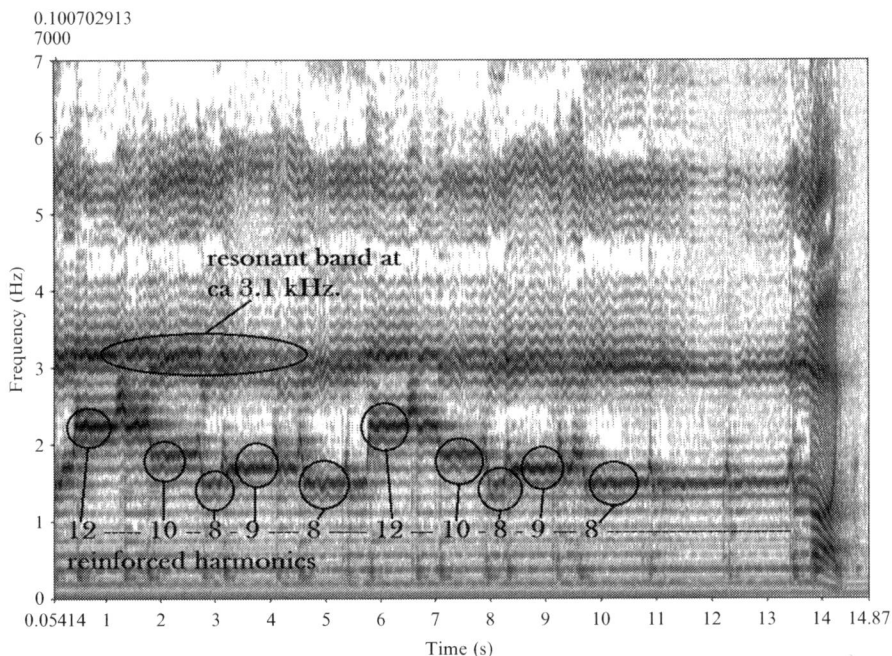

Fig. 8.2 Reinforced harmonics (Mongush 1990)

Figure 8.7 presents the only reported example of a singer who was able to reproduce on demand biphonic contours in similar, oblique and contrary motion (Ward et al. 1969, 1970). In the example the singer produces two stable voiced tones moving in contrary motion.

Figure 8.8 combines two pitch contours each produced with a separate mode, as the lower voice f(t) is produced in the whistle register (M3) while the upper tone is produced with the glottal whistle (M4). Note how f(t) and g(t) are detuned

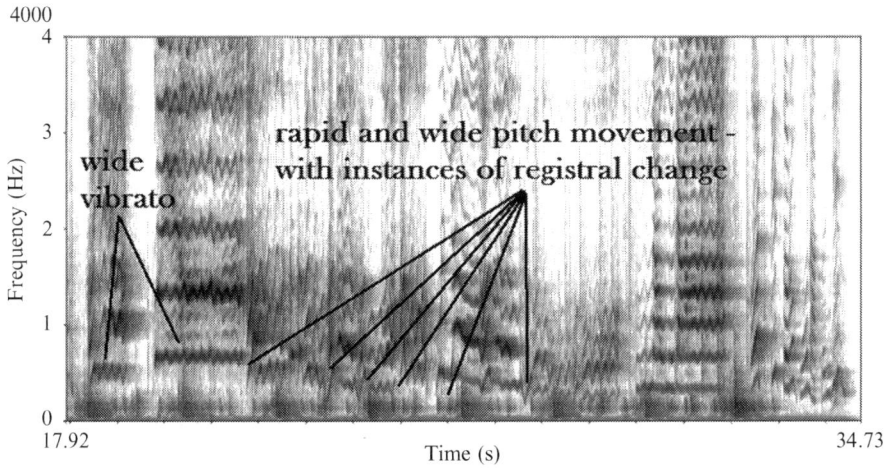

Fig. 8.3 P'ansori tradition, scene from Heung Boo-Ga, song 'Pahk Taryeung' (Kim 1988)

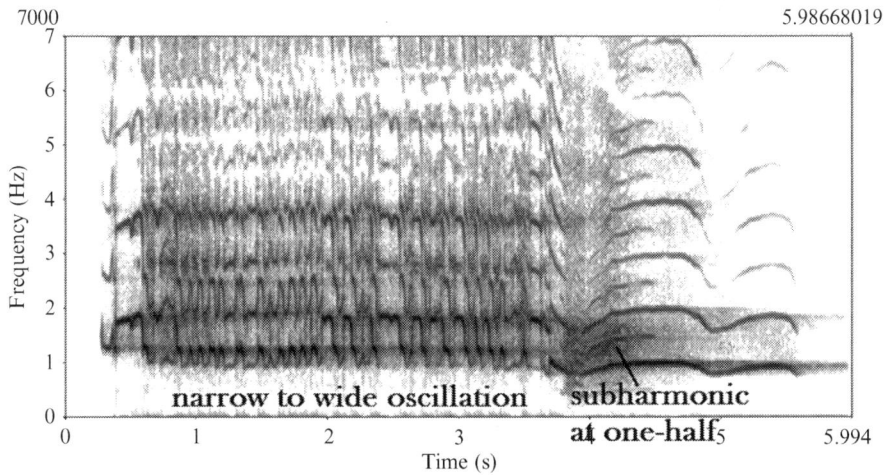

Fig. 8.4 High oscillation (Namtchylak 1999)

until about approximately 3.5 s – at which point 2f and g(t) are coupled (Wingerath 2004).

8.2   Exercises for the Extra-Normal Voice

The remainder of this chapter will present exercises designed for singers who primarily wish to explore voice outside of the western classical tradition, though to be sure there may be limited applications within the historical canon, such as with the use of vocal

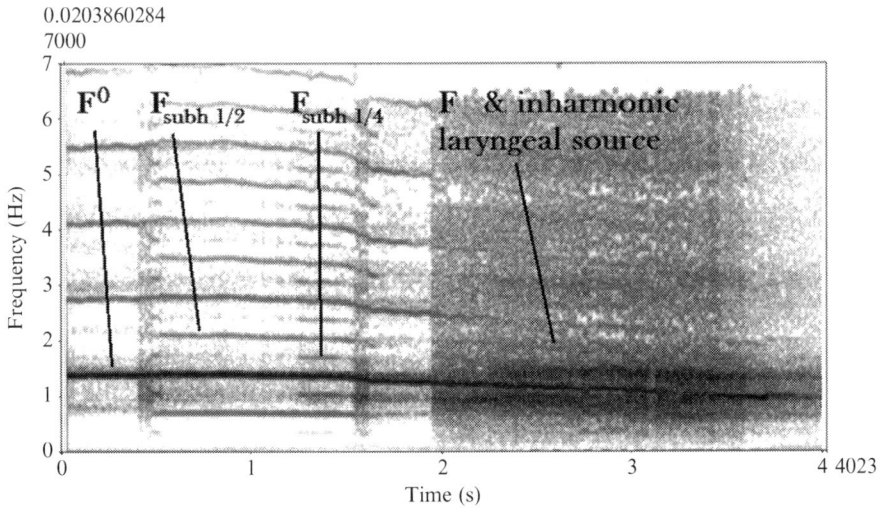

Fig. 8.5 Limit cycle to subharmonic at ½ to subharmonic at ¼ to inharmonic source (chaos) (Miranda 1992)

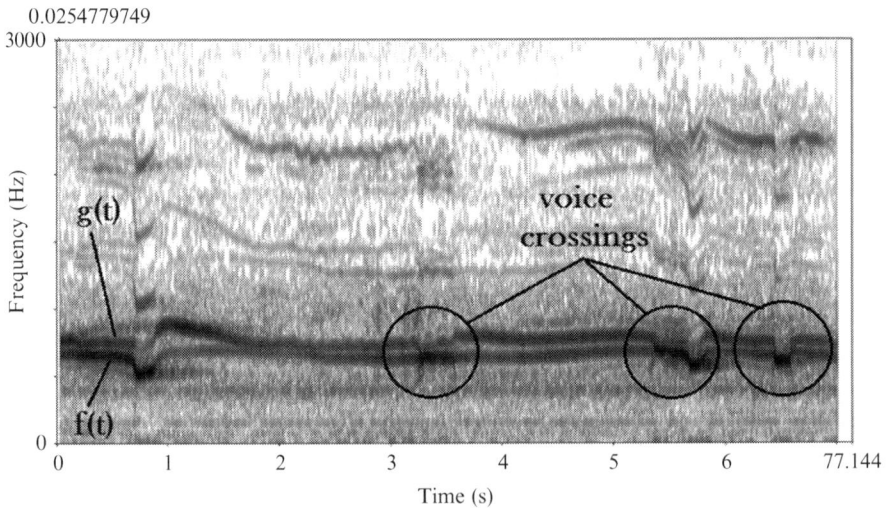

Fig. 8.6 Biphonation in male voice by Demetrio Stratos using glottal whistle (M4) (Stratos 1978)

fry to accentuate a particularly sorrowful theatrical moment. It will be clear that these exercises do not consist of a graded series, but rather they present snapshots of different aspects from the extra-normal voice. As might be expected the enormous quantity of biological diversity prohibits such an approach in a single chapter.

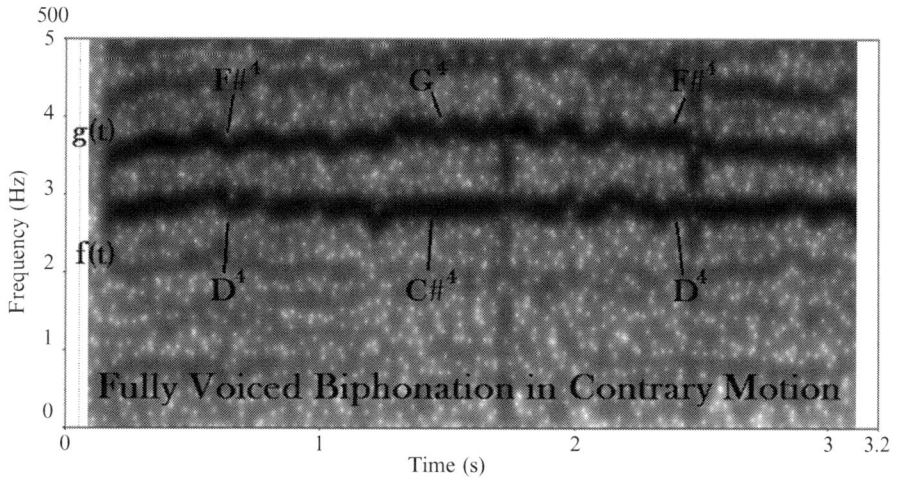

Fig. 8.7 Fully voiced biphonation in female voice (Ward et al. 1969, 1970)

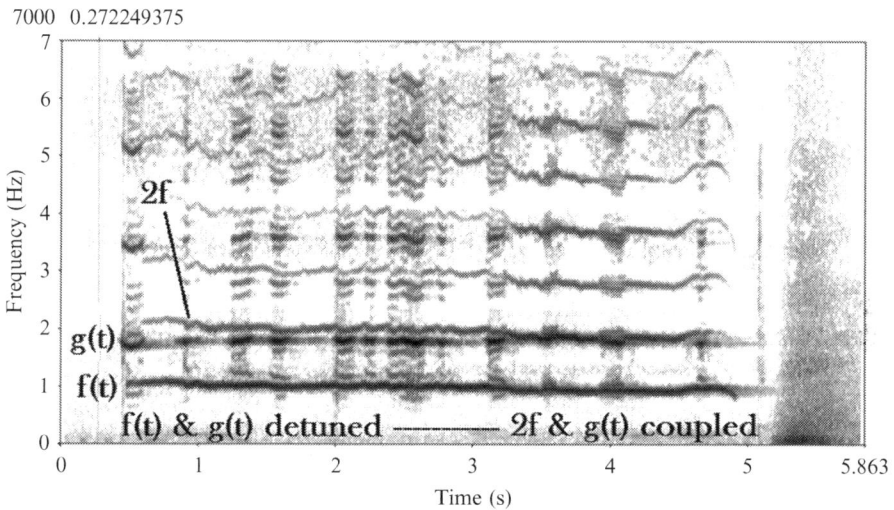

Fig. 8.8 Combination of M4 & M3 (Wingerath 2004)

8.2.1   Air

Breath is the basis of all voice. During the inspiratory-expiratory cycle it is paramount to maximize the efficient transfer of power (air) driving the source. In performance a singer needs physical flexibility, stamina and strength relative to phonation which is assisted by an effective alignment and stability of the torso. In order to sustain phrases longer than normally used in speech, it is important that the singer

Ex. 8.1 Sternum on exhalation (abdomen in vs. abdomen out)

resist the natural diaphragmatic release of air by slowing the rate of exhalation while keeping the rib cage and solar plexus moderately high. Although a singer's posture needs to be well supported, one should never feel overinflated. Voice production is complex that begins with respiration while involving the entire body. During inspiration the torso should be moderately high with widely suspended ribs. The singer should have the feeling that action occurs below the ribs by moving the abdominals inward and outward (Miller 1986).

Exercise 8.1 does not specifically focus on training the extra-normal voice, but rather to assist the stamina and strength needed to support all vocal production. This exercise is in two parts with both focusing on exhalation; the first pulling the abdominals inward on exhalation, with the second pushing the abdominals outward on exhalation.

Exercise 8.2 extends the idea of using both abdominal contraction & expansion on expiration; however this exercise is intended to begin our journey into the extra-normal voice by suggesting the use of dynamic expansion and contraction during both inspiration and expiration. Such dynamic abdominal use has enormous potential to support the production of a wide variety of nonharmonic and multiphonic sonorities.

As with all the preceding exercises it is important to train intelligently and efficiently; therefore a basic principle I will suggest is to focus on an appropriate form, rather than a loose expressionistic approximation. Additionally, as with all voice it is important to do no harm, which for the extra-normal voice means if tightness, pain or laryngeal dryness occurs, then a singer should refine the underlying technique or to refrain from such behavior (McCoy 2004).

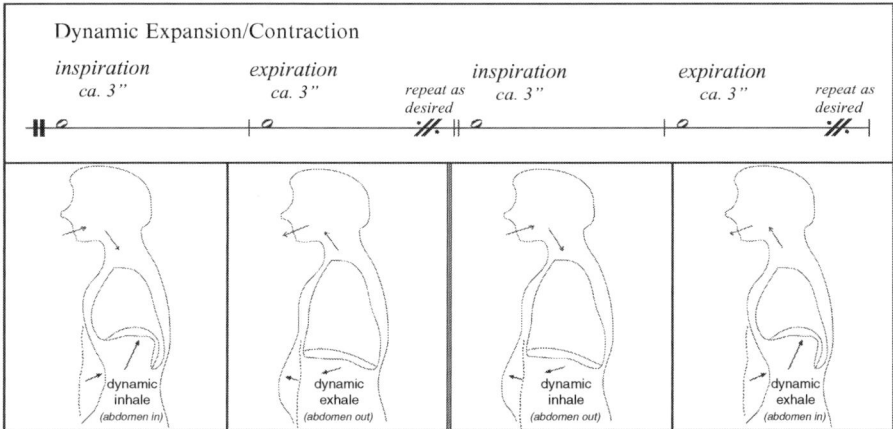

Ex. 8.2   Sternum on exhalation (dynamic movement)

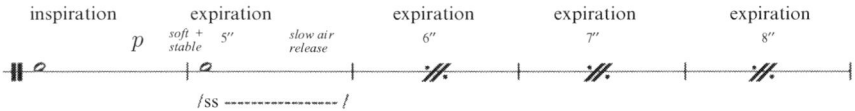

Ex. 8.3   /s/ to strengthen your support muscles

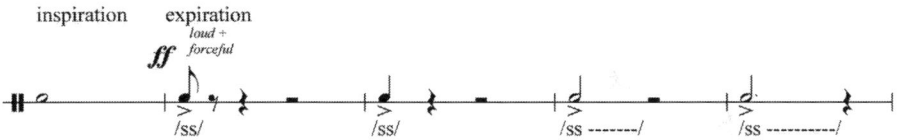

Ex. 8.4   Increase dynamic power

Exercise 8.3 is designed to increase stamina of airflow. After inspiration, the singer will make a soft /s/ sibilant in order to slowly release air through a very small aperture. As the sequence continues to involve longer durations it is important to focus on keeping the sound stable and the volume uniform.

Exercise 8.4 is focused on increasing dynamic power by producing /s/ as loudly and forcefully as possible. Naturally it will not be possible to sustain this for too long, but the point of the exercise is to develop a strong dynamic response of diaphragmatic air control to an increased load – in this case a heightened air pressure and velocity.

Exercise 8.5 is designed to increase flexibility by training a series of light & quick bursts using an /s/ sibilant. Try to make each burst as even as possible. This action will transfer to all manner of articulatory behavior – even to quickly articulated glottal stops!

Exercise 8.6 continues to build a strong foundation of air control by training support in a cycle involving inhalation, suspension and exhalation of breath.

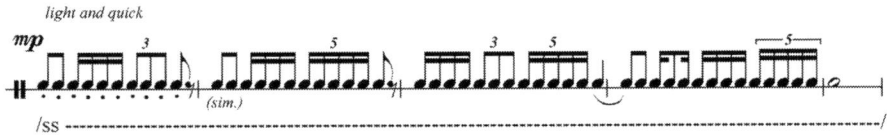

Ex. 8.5 Increase flexibility

Inhale	Suspend	Exhale
1 2 3 4 5	1 2 3 4 5	1 2 3 4 5
1 2 3 4 5 6	1 2 3 4 5 6	1 2 3 4 5 6
1 2 3 4 5 6 7	1 2 3 4 5 6 7	1 2 3 4 5 6 7
1 2 3 4 5 6 7 8	1 2 3 4 5 6 7 8	1 2 3 4 5 6 7 8
1 2 3 4 5 6 7 8 9	1 2 3 4 5 6 7 8 9	1 2 3 4 5 6 7 8 9

Ex. 8.6 Support

Ex. 8.7 Ordinario to breathy sound

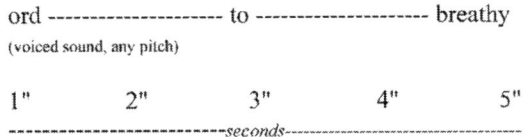

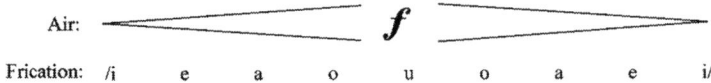

Ex. 8.8 Air as sound source

As durations increase in succeeding strata, try to focus on keeping the ribs broadly expanded.

Exercise 8.7 begins with an *ordinario* tone of any pitch and vowel, to which air is added to produce a breathy tone. The exercise indicates a duration of 5 s, but any duration will work.

Exercise 8.8 is designed to train the production of airflow over a robust duration involving a sequence of vowel-based fricatives. Try to develop a consistent crescendo/decrescendo of airflow. Such exercises provide the added benefit of increasing what is considered legitimate vocal expression.

Exercise 8.9 is designed to train our ability to recognize finely tuned differences of airflow volume in conjunction with inner oral cavity vowels. In this sequence airflow is scaled between 1 (low flow) and 5 (high flow). The melody may be heard as following the principle of good continuation based on flow volume or the frequencies of a dominant resonant peak of the unvoiced vowels – or both. Note that the lips are tuned to an /u/, while the inner oral cavity will attempt to produce the notated vowels – allow the instrument to struggle against homogeneity and thus allowing a counterpoint to occur between the strata of flow (quantity) versus vowel change (frequency contours).

Airflow "melody" exercise, volume (amount)

	1	2	3	4	5		1	3	2	4	3	5		5	3	4	2	3	1
aperture (lips):	u	-----------------					-------------------------							-------------------------					
inner oral cavity:	u	o	a	e	i		u	a	o	e	a	i		i	a	e	o	a	u

all unvoiced

Ex. 8.9 Airflow melodies

Ex. 8.10 Airflow using consonant /ʃ/

Ex. 8.11 Lunged/unlunged & ingressive/egressive

(any combination of vowels)

1. glottal stops	gl		gl		gl		gl	gl		gl	gl
2. diaphragm pulse	dp		dp		dp		dp	dp		dp	dp
3. gl. stop with	2	-	3	-	4	-	5	6		7	8
dphrm. plse	-	2	-	3	-	4	-	3		-	2

Ex. 8.12 Diaphragm pulsing vs. glottal pulsing of airflow

Exercise 8.10 continues to train dynamic flexibility of air, in this case driving an unvoiced fricative. The scaling of airflow is between 0 (very low) and 5 (high).

Expired air may be driven from the lungs (lunged) or from above a closed glottis (unlunged). Exercise 8.11 trains two elements: lunged versus unlunged power combined with egressive versus ingressive flow, all using an unvoiced /t/.

Generally airflow is shaped into the elements of speech or song using the articulators of the upper vocal tract. However, two lessor used methods that shape expiration include an accented glottal closure (glottal stops), and subglottal pulsations driven by diaphragmatic and abdominal activity (diaphragm pulses). Exercise 8.12 presents a

voiced: /i/
unvoiced: /s/

Ex. 8.13 Simple combination of sustained unvoiced sound with voiced

tuning, detuning, tuning
voice 1:
voice 2:

Ex. 8.14 Tuning between two voices

phrase to be repeated in three stanzas; the first using an articulation of glottal stops, the second articulating diaphragm pulses, the third combining both. For verses one and two the integers above the notes indicate how many articulations are to be produced on each note, while for verse three the integers indicate position and quantity.

8.2.2 Source

The efficient and robust oscillation of the vocal folds is central to singing. With contemporary and ethnic voice the modes of oscillation will feature differences to the duration and velocity of the opening and closing phases (Schutte and Miller 1993, Roubeau et al. 1987, Titze 1994, Sundberg 1987). Additionally we have evidence that the mucosal wave seen in normal speech and song is considerably altered, such as during the production of voiced biphonic sequences (see Fig. 8.7). However, whatever the behavior, each singer must take care to avoid prolonged exposure to maneuvers that create excess laryngeal tension. Exercise 8.13 is designed to combine voiced and unvoiced sounds, with each retaining a separate identity. Here a voiced /i/ is sustained on any pitch while an unvoiced sibilant /s/ is brought in and out of the texture.

An issue with much contemporary music is to place the voice within the threshold of what is normally considered a dissonant sonority, which has been reported to have the extent of a small minor third (Roederer 1979). The issue of tuning is presented here as the difference tones that are generated with closely spaced tones tend to feel as physical phenomena to which a singer must respond. Therefore it is beneficial to practice tuning (Ex. 8.14).

Vibrato is a naturally occurring phenomenon for most singers. The elements of vibrato include pitch extent, temporal rate, amplitude and regularity profile. As is expected the extra-normal voice may focus on the desynchronization of any of these elements in performance. Exercise 8.15 offers four sequences each focused on one element.

Vocal fry is a nearly periodic tone with a 'crackly' quality, sounding somewhat like the embers of a decaying fire. This may be produced on either an egressive or

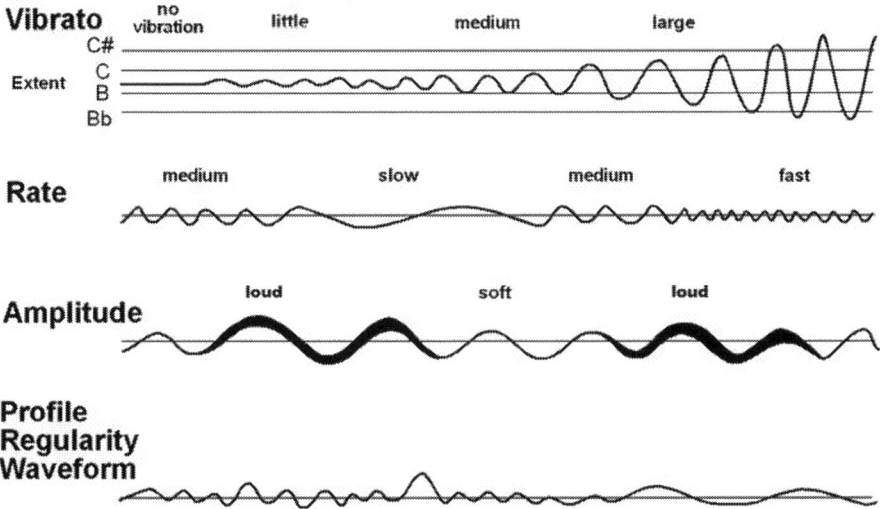

Ex. 8.15 Vibrato scaled

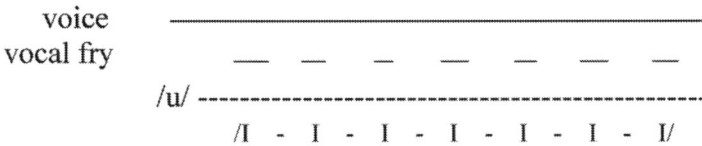

Ex. 8.16 Vocal folds in combination

ingressive airflow that seems to involve asymmetry of oscillation. Exercise 8.16 begins with *ord* voice sustaining the vowel /u/ on any pitch, then at temporal intervals of their own choosing the singer will add vocal fry using the vowel /I/ while continuing to sustain the ord pitch. The composite effect will be similar to the source characteristic of Tibetan chant (or the Kargyraa method of Tuvan throat singing) and most often will produce an 8ve subharmonic (Levin and Edgerton 1999).

Similar to Ex. 8.13, Ex. 8.17 is designed to combine voiced and unvoiced sounds with each retaining a separate identity. Here a voiced Latin text is joined by an air sound.

Exercise 8.18 adds a level of complexity. Here the cresc./decresc. of the air and voiced sounds are desynchronized from one another.

In Tibetan chant the mostly octave subharmonic is produced by: (1) an asymmetry of oscillation for both pitches or (2) the upper pitch of a subharmonic produced by the vocal folds and the lower pitch produced by the ventricular (or false) folds. Exercise 8.19 trains the ability to integrate the false folds and vocal fry with an *ord* vocal fold pitch (Edgerton 1999).

In addition to vocal fry, there are numerous methods for producing voiced multiphonics. There has been very little systematic research done in this area, though some

Adagio

Ex. 8.17 Voice with air sound

Ex. 8.18 Voice with air sound

Ex. 8.19 Ord. vocal pitch

Ex. 8.20 Asymmetry of oscillation

performers have consistently explored such methods over many years, including Phil Minton (2008) and Jaap Blonk (1998). Exercise 8.20 presents a fairly accessible two voiced biphonic sonority that seems to involve two separate modes in the male voice; a low tone that is somewhat stable combined with another tone that is similar to a

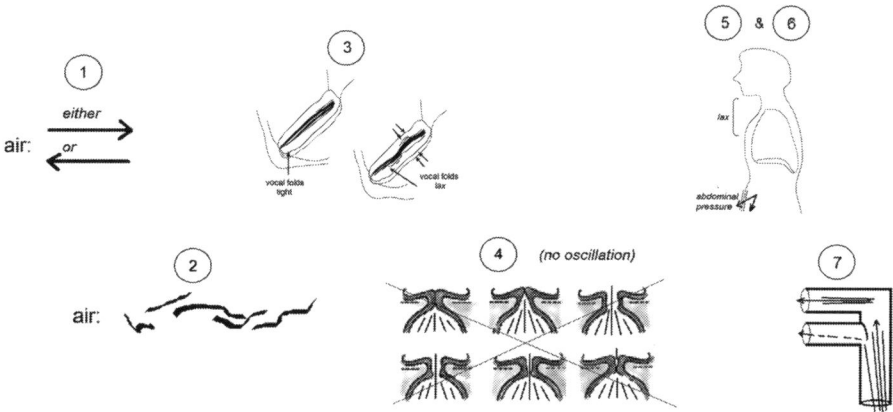

Ex. 8.21 Glottal whistle (M4)

whistle sonority. The steps to producing these tones may include: (1) producing ord voice, (2) shift tone to nasal cavity (increasing back pressure on vocal folds), (3) tighten the anterior portion of the vocal folds, (4) produce the so-called creaky voice (sing lowest tone, then go lower) keeping the vocal folds lax in one part, (5) broaden mouth opening, (6) imagine, then allow higher transient pitches (whistles) to be sustained.

The glottal whistle (M4) is a sound that occurs at the superior boundary of the glottis that feels and sounds like a whistle – potentially with no vocal fold oscillation. It has been presumed that the sound occurs as the result of a vortex produced at the upper edges of the glottis that may be produced on either an egressive or ingressive airflow. Generally airflow is low, though ingressive airflow seems to use higher flow volume than with egressive flow. A special property of the glottal whistle is to simultaneously produce two or more independent frequency contours over time which essentially provides the listener with a counterpoint of two or more tones. Singers tend to use either a lax or highly tensed glottis. Generally the nasal port is open, perhaps to effect feedback onto the supraglottal cavity.

Exercise 8.21 outlines a few tendencies for finding M4. Using airflow only, search for a high resonant tone by raising the palate, 'smelling a rose' and smiling like the joker. Then, almost like meditation, don't make the sound happen – rather, let it go and let the sound happen – the sensation is not of producing it but rather that it emanates from out of the top of the head. Always attempt to take emphasis away from the throat. For example, lay down on the floor – lift one or both legs and hold for 1 s, then repeat with longer intervals – the trick is to relax the torso and neck while keeping tension in belly. The steps outlined include: (1) airflow may be ingressive or egressive, (2) use only a little airflow, (3) there seem to be two methods of using laryngeal tension, one using a lax glottis and a second using a tightly constricted glottis with high subglottal air pressure, (4) no oscillation of the vocal folds, let the sound happen, don't produce it, (5 and 6) use lower torso and abdominal tension while relaxing upper torso and neck, (7) try nasal placement – often M4 uses the sense of nasal placement – this means that the velopharyngeal port is open and

Ex. 8.22 Oral, nasal and mixed resonances

mf

1. /u/ --
2. /o/ --
3. /a/ --
4. /e/ --
5. /i/ --

Non-Nasal   1/2 Nasal   Full Nasal

g. stp   g. stp   g. stp   g. stp   g. stp   g. stp

/i/ --

Ex. 8.23 Glottal stops with non-nasal, ½ nasal

non-nasal   *nasal*   *nasal*   *non-nasal*

g. stp   g. stp

/a ------------- u --------------- I ------------- i ------------- /

Ex. 8.24 Non-nasal to nasal with glottal stops at end

combined with the raised palate may contribute to the feedback loop necessary to set up the presumed supraglottal vortex (see Ex. 8.21).

8.2.3 Resonance

The resonator contributes to the extra-normal voice as a filter and an environment with varying pressures. Exercise 8.22 asks the singer to produce a sound that propagates through the oral cavity alone, then through the nasal cavity alone, then involving a mixture of both. This is produced using five vowels.

Exercise 8.23 asks the singer to produce glottal stops on the vowel /i/ using non-nasal, half-nasal and fully nasalized resonances.

Exercise 8.24 contributes a similar exercise in a slightly different formation.

Tuning/detuning resonator between two voices - listen for beating when slightly detuning vowels

non-nasal:
1. i --
2. i -- u ----

nasal:
1. i --
2. i -- u ----

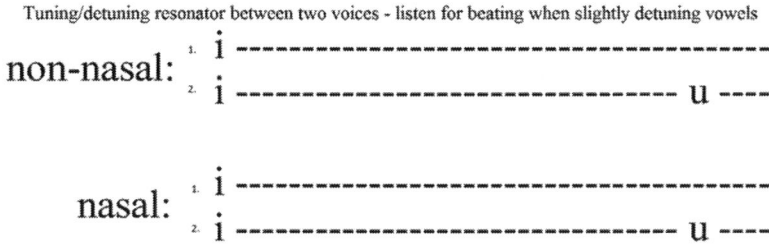

Ex. 8.25 Non-nasal vs. nasal tuning

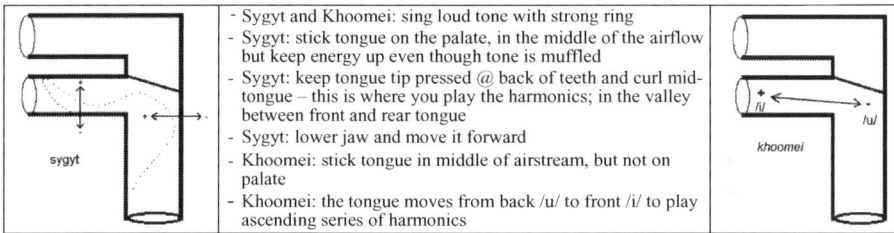

sygyt	- Sygyt and Khoomei: sing loud tone with strong ring - Sygyt: stick tongue on the palate, in the middle of the airflow but keep energy up even though tone is muffled - Sygyt: keep tongue tip pressed @ back of teeth and curl mid-tongue – this is where you play the harmonics; in the valley between front and rear tongue - Sygyt: lower jaw and move it forward - Khoomei: stick tongue in middle of airstream, but not on palate - Khoomei: the tongue moves from back /u/ to front /i/ to play ascending series of harmonics	khoomei

Ex. 8.26 Reinforced harmonics

Exercise 8.25 involves tuning resonant frequencies – this is similar to Ex. 8.14, which dealt with tuning source fundamental frequencies, but this time focused on the passive frequencies of the resonator. If listened to carefully in a highly resonant environment, it will be possible to hear beating between slightly detuned resonant frequencies.

The next exercise also involves tuning formant frequencies, but in this case tuning one harmonic directly in the center of a formant whose bandwidth has been considerably narrowed. In recent years there has been quite a lot written about the culture, performance and science of overtone singing. Therefore I will highlight only some of the most important concepts that a non-specialist can use in pedagogical settings. Exercise 8.26 presents two methods of articulation used in throat singing: (1) in *Khoomei* which uses tongue advancement to play successively higher harmonics as in the movement from /u/ to /i/ and, (2) in *Sygyt* which firmly places and retains the tongue tip on the alveolar ridge while the mid-tongue raises and the rear tongue moves away from the pharyngeal wall to play the successively higher harmonics (Levin and Edgerton 1999).

The velopharyngeal port offers not only the possibility of opening up the resonant properties of the nasal tract, but when the velum and uvula are engaged may also serve as an articulatory device. Exercise 8.27 is designed to emphasize both the resonant and articulatory aspects of this port (House and Stevens 1956, Feng and Castelli 1996, Chen 1997).

It is often claimed that operatic voice maintains a lower laryngeal position than popular voice, such as in country & western. Exercise 8.28 asks the singer to produce the vowel /u/ while changing laryngeal height from *ordinario* to high then low.

velopharyngeal port +/o - all nasal, all voiced at any pitch(es)

/ng/
/a/

Ex. 8.27 Velopharyngeal port (opening & closing)

Ex. 8.28 Laryngeal height

mf

laryngeal height
ord ------------hi -------------lo ----------------

/u/ ---

bilabial whistles

L
C
R

Ex. 8.29 Bilabial whistles

E¹ F¹ E¹ B¹ B² B³ B⁴ E¹ B² C³ F⁴ B² B¹ C³ F¹ E¹

1. place manner: fricative
2. place manner: whistle-like

Ex. 8.30 Frications and whistles using comprehensive mapping of vocal tract

8.2.4 Articulation

Humans articulate speech and song (segment the syntactical code) with many of the moveable parts about the glottis. Here are a few exercises that seem relevant to the production of the extra-normal voice. Exercise 8.29 presents an unvoiced, yet pitched production that often features multiphonics in the form of bilabial whistles. In this excerpt the lip will produce these whistle-like sonorities at the left, right and center. Bilabial pressure seems to vary from moderate to high and may bifurcate from single tones (limit cycle) to uncontrolled time-variant multiphonics.

Exercise 8.30 uses the mapping of articulation presented in Fig. 8.1. In this excerpt all sounds are sustained: during the first verse these articulations are

Ex. 8.31 Tongue trills (front, mid, rear)

/ng/ ------------------ uvula ---------------- /ng/ ---------------- gl -----------------------*(repeat as desired)*
　　　　　　　　　　tr　　　　　　　　　　　　　　　　stp

Ex. 8.32 Uvula trill, glottal stops, nasal vowels

voiced, glottal stops - choose any pitch

g　　g　　g　　g　　　g g g g *//.*
　　　　　　　　　　　　　　　　　　1. 5-tuplets
　　　　　　　　　　　　　　　　　　2. 6-tuplets
　　　　　　　　　　　　　　　　　　3. 7-tuplets

g = glottal stop(s)

Ex. 8.33 Glottal stops

Ex. 8.34 Uvula trill

uvula - ord　uvula - ord　uvula - ord　uvula - ord
　trill　　　　trill　　　　trill　　　　trill

Sol-vet sae-clum in　fa-----vil-------------la

produced as frications while in the second verse produced as whistle-like sonorities. The notation indicates the place in the oral cavity to which the tongue will produce stop, frication, whistle or approximation. In this exercise all the notated points are to be produced with the tongue tip.

Most people are able to produce either a front or rear tongue trill. Exercise 8.31 expands upon this by asking the singer to produce trills in the front, mid or rear lingual regions. Note that with all of these extra-normal behaviors, any sort of difference from *ord* production must produce a corresponding difference in the sound output (though not necessarily using a linear relationship), otherwise what's the purpose. The idea in Exercise 8.31 is to emphasize the potential differences between the front, mid and rear trills.

Exercise 8.32 alternates between sustained nasal sounds (ng), a sustained uvula trill and rapidly repeating glottal stops – repeat as desired.

Exercise 8.33 trains the proficiency of the glottal stop, which when produced quickly and as part of a sustained gesture may play a role in the production of classical music from North India such as that used by Parween Sultana (Sultana 1984), or alternatively by the high oscillatory behavior (see Fig. 8.4) that nearly resembles a turkey as exemplified by Sainkho Namtchylak (1999).

Exercise 8.34 returns to the uvula trill – here being produced with voice.

Ex. 8.35 Towards the turkey (high-pitched, rapid oscillation)

Ex. 8.36 Towards the turkey II

8.2.5 Heightened Potentials

This category refers to sonorities that are either built upon combinatorial principles or those that result in multiphonics (see Table 8.1) (Edgerton 2005). Exercise 8.35 combines (a) voiced sounds with (b) partial or fully nasal resonances with (c) glottal stops. These lead the singer towards an oscillation between two pitches (see Fig. 8.4) – potentially with wide spacing of an octave or more.

Exercise 8.36 continues the previous idea with the addition of a time-variant pitch contour and somewhat irregular ratios of nasalized onset & offset relative to glottal stops.

In Ex. 8.37 the singer is asked to produce a strong tone with much energy between ca. 3,000 and 6,000 Hz. At the vowel /u/, the tongue tip is placed on the alveolar ridge and sharply released as an accented grace note on the lingual /l/. Three different resonances are used that include non-nasal, nasal and nasal with a broad /i/ vowel. The lips should be relatively tight and rounded for the first two resonant postures.

The lip buzz may be produced as a brass lip buzz featuring clearly defined pitch contours or as bilabial whistles (Ex. 8.29). In Ex. 8.38 the singer is asked to produce a lip buzz combined with voice in oblique motion.

u   l-u   l-u   l-u -----   u --- l-u --------   1-u   1-u ---------------- 1-u

E^1 (at/u/ = tongue touching alveolar ridge; at /l/ = quick and harsh release)

non-nasal ------------------------- nasal ----------------------------------- nasal ---------------------------------
                                                                              /i/ bright + wide ("big grin")

Ex. 8.37 Towards the loo-ululation

Ex. 8.38 Voice and buzz,
in oblique motion

lip buzz
voice

Ex. 8.39 Higher voice
(falsetto for males) than lip
buzz, in oblique motion

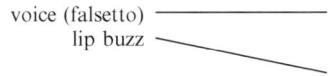

voice (falsetto)
lip buzz

Ex. 8.40 Lip buzz and voice,
in similar motion

lip buzz
voice

Ex. 8.41 Higher voice
(falsetto for males) than lip
buzz, in contrary motion

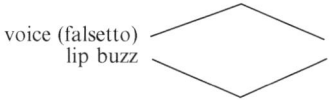

voice (falsetto)
lip buzz

voice   voice   voice   voice   voice   voice
w/ fry   w/ fry   w/ fry   w/ fry   w/ fry   w/ fry

lips (aperture):   /u/ ---
inner oral cavity: /u ---- l ----- u ----- e ------- u ------- i ------ u -----------,   u ---- l ------ u ----- e ------- u ------ i ------ u ----------

Ex. 8.42 [Imitated Tibetan] chant – combination of ord pitch with vocal fry (see Ex. 8.19 for use of ventricular folds with vocal folds)

In Ex. 8.39 the singer is asked to produce voice at a higher pitch than the lip buzz, which for males may mean producing a robust tone in the falsetto register.

In Ex. 8.40 the singer is asked to move the voice and lip buzz in similar motion, with the voice at a lower plateau than the lip buzz.

In Ex. 8.41 the singer is asked to move voice and lip buzz in contrary motion – this time with voice higher than lip buzz.

Exercise 8.42 leads towards the production of the source characteristics found in [imitated Tibetan-] Chant. However, in this sequence the singer is asked to combine voice with vocal fry, not with ventricular fold vibration (although naturally this may be substituted). Note that the lips are stable in a rounded position while the inner oral cavity will feature lingual movement – this will contribute to the perceptual movement of harmonics if the singer will have found the connection between tongue placement and the dominant resonance.

References

Blonk, J. (1998). *Vocalor* [CD]. Amsterdam: Staalplaat STCD 112.
Chen, M. Y. (1997). Acoustic correlates of English and French nasalized vowels. *The Journal of the Acoustical Society of America, 102*, 2360–2370.
Edgerton, M. (1999). Multiple sound sources of the vocal tract. *National Center for Voice and Speech, Status and Progress Report, 13*, 131–140.
Edgerton, M. (2005). *The 21st century voice*. Lanham: Scarecrow Press.
Edgerton, M., Neubauer, J., & Herzel, H. (2003). Nonlinear phenomena in contemporary vocal musical composition and performance. *Perspectives of New Music, 41*, 30–65.
Feng, G., & Castelli, E. (1996). Some acoustic features of nasal and nasalized vowels: A target for vowel nasalization. *The Journal of the Acoustical Society of America, 99*, 3694–3706.
Hall, D. (2002). *Musical acoustics*. Pacific Grove: Brooks/Cole.
House, A., & Stevens, K. (1956). Analog studies of the nasalization of vowels. *The Journal of Speech and Hearing Disorders, 21*(2), 218–232.
Kim, S. H. (1988). Scene from Heung Boo-Ga. On *P'ansori: Korea's epic vocal art & instrumental music* [CD]. New York: Nonesuch.
Levin, T., & Edgerton, M. (1999). The throat singers of Tuva. *Scientific American, 281*(3), 70–77.
McCoy, S. (2004). *Your voice: An inside view*. Princeton: Inside View Press.
Miller, R. (1986). *The structure of singing: System and art in vocal technique*. New York: Schirmer Books.
Minton, P. (2008). *No doughnuts in hand* [CD]. UK: Emanem.
Miranda, F. (1992). La Voz Cantante. On *Las Voces De La Voz* [CD]. Spain: Unió Músics.
Mongush, M. (1990). Sigit. On *Tuva: Voices from the center of Asia* [CD]. Washington, DC: Smithsonian Folkways Recordings.
Namtchylak, S. (1999). Night birds. On *Lost rivers* [CD]. Borken: FMP.
Neubauer, J., Edgerton, M., & Herzel, H. (2004). Nonlinear phenomena in contemporary vocal music. *Journal of Voice, 18*, 1–12.
Roederer, J. (1979). *Introduction to the physics and psychophysics of music*. New York: Springer.
Roubeau, B., Chevrie-Muller, C., & Arabia-Guidet, C. (1987). Electroglottographic study of the changes of voice registers. *Folia Phoniatrica, 39*(6), 280–289.
Sataloff, R. T. (1992). The human voice. *Scientific American, 267*(6), 108–115.
Schutte, H. K., & Miller, D. G. (1993). Belting and pop, nonclassical approaches to the female middle voice: Some preliminary conclusions. *Journal of Voice, 7*, 142–150.
Stratos, D. (1978). Passagi. On *Cantare la Voce* [CD]. Altavilla Vicentina: Cramps Records, 520.6119–VI.
Sultana, P. (1984). *An hour of ecstasy with Parween Sultana* [CD]. Dum Dum: EMI/Gramophone Company of India, Ltd.
Sundberg, J. (1977). The acoustics of the singing voice. *Scientific American, 236*(3), 82–84.
Sundberg, J. (1987). *The science of the singing voice*. DeKalb: Northern Illinois University Press.
Titze, I. R. (1994). *Principles of voice production*. Englewood Cliffs: Prentice Hall.
Titze, I. R. (2008). The human instrument. *Scientific American, 298*(1), 94–101.
Ward, P. H., Sanders, J. W., Goldman, R., & Moore, G. P. (1969). Diplophonia. *The Annals of Otology, Rhinology, and Laryngology, 78*, 771–777.
Ward, P. H., Goldman, R., Sanders, J. W., & Moore, G. P. (1970). Diplophonia [Film]. Nashville: Vanderbilt University School of Medicine.
Wingerath, A. (2004, July). Untitled. Private recording, Berlin.

Chapter 9
Registers Defined Through Visual Feedback

Donald Gray Miller

Abstract The concept of registers, designating distinct segments of the total frequency range of a singing voice, has engaged the attention of voice pedagogues for more than four centuries. Modern non-invasive technologies of spectrum analysis and electroglottography have opened the way to objective description and explanation of the mechanisms at the basis of the phenomena. In this article the essential features of the major registers of male and female voices, together with their transitions (*passaggi*), are described, distinguishing between those produced by changes in the vibration pattern of the vocal folds and those that result from shifts in the use of resonances (formants) of the vocal tract. The focus is largely on the operatic tradition whose beginnings date back to seventeenth-century Italy. The male and female differences revealed in the objective description of registers have important implications for pedagogy. Visual feedback from available technology enhances our understanding of these differences, as well as those between the operatic tradition and more contemporary genres such as belting and pop.

Keywords Registers • Electroglottograph (EGG) • Open/closed quotient • Formant tuning • Voice pedagogy • Passaggio • Singing voice • Chest • Falsetto • Whistle register

9.1 Introduction

Teaching singing is a practice that typically centers on modeling and imitation, rather than description and theory. The explanation for why this is naturally the case lies in the very limited power of language to describe sound, combined with the

D.G. Miller (✉)
Groningen Voice Research, Wasaweg 9, 9723 JC Groningen, The Netherlands
e-mail: d.g.miller@vocevista.com

S.D. Harrison and J. O'Bryan (eds.), *Teaching Singing in the 21st Century*,
Landscapes: the Arts, Aesthetics, and Education 14, DOI 10.1007/978-94-017-8851-9_9,
© Springer Science+Business Media Dordrecht 2014

hidden nature of the instrument. Thus the theoretical aspects of voice pedagogy can easily seem far removed from practical singing lessons.

As if that were not challenge enough, the concept of registers is particularly resistant to the generalizing that is characteristic of theory. Much of what can be said about other basic categories of voice pedagogy, such as breath management, phonation, resonation, and articulation, applies in a general way to all voices. Registers, however, are not only harder to describe, but they also vary more among individual singers than do the more general categories. Nonetheless, the great majority of singers and singing teachers acknowledge the problem of registers, which typically comes up in classical singing, where a commonly accepted goal is a unified voice, as in a 'seamless' or 'even' scale. This goal is challenged when different segments of the large frequency range threaten to sound like different voices.

Thus the problem arises–or sometimes does not–in the experience of attempting to unify the voice over an extended range of pitches, levels of loudness, and expression. The task of the teacher is to understand what causes an undesirable discontinuity in voice quality and to guide the pupil through remedies that are satisfactory with respect to both aesthetics and vocal hygiene. The task for theory and pedagogy–addressed here–is to identify and state some general truths that are helpful to singers and teachers in dealing with the problem as it arises.

The observations presented in this chapter take advantage of something new in the twenty-first century: affordable technology that can give the practitioners of singing–singers, and especially singing teachers–vital information that was not available to previous generations: (1) objective and detailed descriptions of the sounds and physiological processes behind them, and (2) immediate feedback on how well they are realizing in practice the tasks that they aim to accomplish. The feedback concerning the problem of registers comes primarily from two non-invasive signals: those of spectrum analysis and the electroglottograph (EGG). From these we can follow, respectively, the detailed adjustments of the formants in the vocal tract and the changes in the pattern of vocal-fold vibration at the voice source.

Having the signals available is one thing, and interpreting them effectively is another. The great majority of current singers and their teachers, including many who are exemplary in practice, have acquired their enviable skills without having the benefit of the signals, or even a thorough knowledge of the theory that the signals implement. The background theory will not be elaborated further in this chapter on registers, but it is hoped that the practical insights that the signals provide for the understanding of registers will encourage further reading (see McCoy 2012) in the theory itself. At this point in history the failure to include the theoretical explanation and the practical application of the signals in serious pedagogy courses unnecessarily deprives future singing teachers of what will later be recognized as common knowledge.

9.2 The Chest/Falsetto Dichotomy: Mechanical Registers

The first order of business is to establish what is properly identified as a register. In this it is helpful to consider the contrasting mechanisms that are often referred to as 'natural registers': those at opposite ends of a yodel, often called chest and falsetto (see Fig. 9.1).

The left panels show a spectrogram of 4s of a yodel. The right panels show 10 ms details at the cursors on the spectrogram, with audio (above) in time-corrected alignment with electroglottograph (EGG, below). The EGG signal gives a value of the closed quotient (CQ), reading the intersections of the EGG with the horizontal cursor as (ascending) glottal closing and (descending) opening. Apparent in the yodel is the rapid alternation between the 'natural registers,' with the contrasting closed quotients of 'chest' and 'falsetto,' here respectively 64 % and 38 % of their glottal cycles. Above and parallel to the spectrogram is a reading of the closed quotient history.

One can identify distinct vibratory mechanisms of the vocal folds that characterize the two modes, and it is generally established that the 'heavier' mode (chest):

- has shorter and thicker vocal folds;
- has deeper contact between the vocal folds in the vertical dimension;
- is characterized by a larger closed quotient;
- is characterized by dominance of the thyroarytenoid (TA) muscles over the cricothyroids (CT);
- produces a lower fundamental frequency at a given level of effort;
- tends to produce a spectrum in which the fall-off of amplitude in the higher harmonics is less steep.

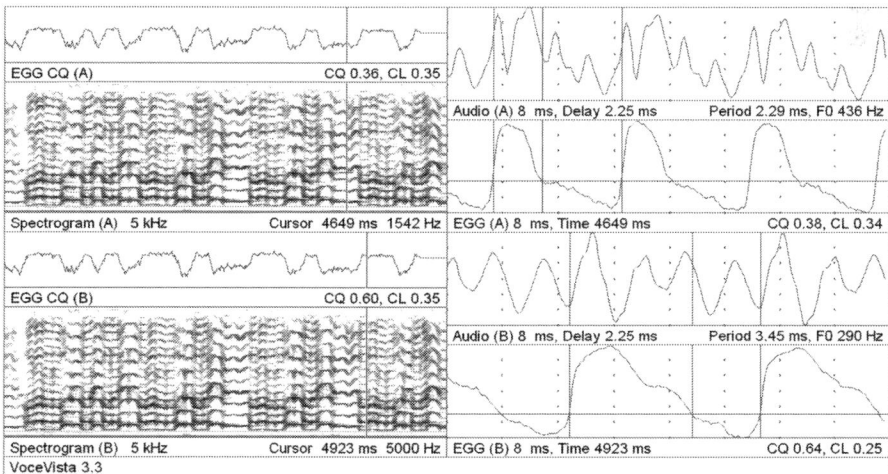

Fig. 9.1 Female yodel, with waveforms of EGG and audio at *D4* and *A4* displayed

While the above characteristics are generally accepted, the names of the two natural registers are not: for example, there is resistance to calling the 'lighter' mechanism in female voices 'falsetto'; a French preference is to avoid the choice by calling them M1 and M2; and so on. In what follows I shall use 'chest' and 'falsetto' (in quotation marks) to refer to the contrasting modes of vibration of the glottal voice *source*.

The transition between 'chest' and 'falsetto' in an ascending or descending scale can be regarded as the quintessential registration event. In many voices, but not all, it presents a great challenge to the ideal of the even scale. Most male voices, at least in the classical tradition, avoid the transition by generally not employing the 'falsetto' mechanism: in the higher frequency range where 'falsetto' would be the natural easy choice they make other adjustments, as we shall see. Something similar can be said about so-called 'belters,' both male and female. On the other hand, many female classical singers avoid using the 'chest' mechanism, extending use of the 'falsetto' mechanism to unusually low pitches. Because this primary register transition (PRT) naturally tends to happen at around 300–400 Hz (*D4-G4*) in both men and women, it is practicable for both genders to avoid it by making adjustments to extend the familiar mechanism for a limited range beyond where it occurs naturally and easily.

The 'chest' 'falsetto' contrast is simultaneously the original model for registers and a major obstacle to be overcome in classical voice training. From the earliest treatises on voice training one sees efforts to join the two registers seamlessly, and a good percentage of today's teachers strive explicitly for a sort of 'mix' that would combine the two registers. Because historically it has been difficult to see and document the movements of the vocal folds, much of the controversy revolves around the *terms* that are used to describe what is presumed to occur in the varied solutions offered for the problem of registers. In this article I shall attempt to restrict generalizations to what is observable and most commonly occurs.

For the majority of classical singers (including countertenors) who use primarily the 'falsetto' mechanism, as well as for female singers of other genres, both 'chest' and 'falsetto' mechanisms are part of their working arsenal. Many also speak of a 'mix,' although it is questionable to what extent, and even whether, the two mechanisms can be combined. In any case, a relatively even scale through the PRT is generally desired, and often achieved, whether or not the change of mechanism shows up clearly in the EGG signal. Figure 9.2 shows an octave scale beginning in 'chest' and ending in 'falsetto,' with EGG details at the transition pitches.

The figure shows the spectrogram (left) of a mezzo-soprano singing an octave scale from *A3* to *A4* on the vowel [a]. Above the spectrogram, which is duplicated below, is the closed quotient history. The cursors mark the moments in the spectrogram where time details of 10 ms are extracted and displayed in the right panels, which show time-aligned microphone and EGG signals. These come from adjacent tones in the scale, *C4-sharp* and *D4*, between which the glottal vibratory pattern shifts from 'chest' to 'falsetto,' with the closed quotient falling from 60 to 43 %.

EGG CQ (A)   CQ 0.60, CL 0.27

Audio (A) 10 ms, Delay 1.45 ms   Period 3.77 ms, F0 265 Hz

Spectrogram (A) 5 kHz   Cursor 2694 ms 1462 Hz   EGG (A) 10 ms, Time 2694 ms   CQ 0.60, CL 0.27

EGG CQ (B)   CQ 0.43, CL 0.27

Audio (B) 10 ms, Delay 1.45 ms   Period 3.61 ms, F0 277 Hz

Spectrogram (B) 5 kHz   Cursor 3819 ms 1250 Hz   EGG (B) 10 ms, Time 3819 ms   CQ 0.43, CL 0.27
VoceVista 3.3

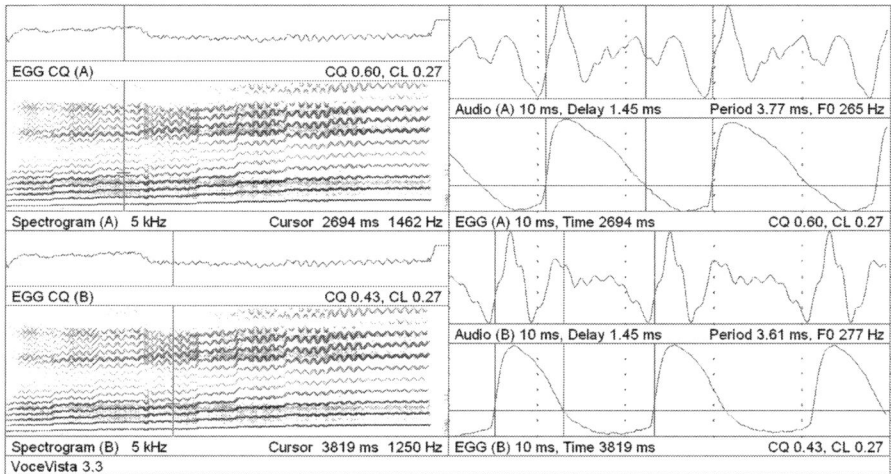

Fig. 9.2 Mezzo scale through the primary register transition

9.3   Acoustic Registers: Male and Female Second Passaggio

Singers often use the term register for other discontinuities besides the 'chest'/'falsetto' contrast discussed thus far. Some important registration events that occur as one goes through the whole compass are essentially changes in resonance, rather than in vibratory mechanism. In describing these it is best to deal separately with male and female voices. As a general rule, I have selected the transitions that get the most attention in voice training. They are described in terms of the changes that occur in the dominant resonance at the transition points.

Of these, let us consider first the registration event that occurs in the male 'secondo passaggio,' enabling the proper execution of the upper extension, which can some-times add as many as seven semitones to the range that can be easily achieved with open vowels.

When singing an open (high first formant) vowel in the 'chest' mechanism, male voices typically encounter a natural barrier where the F0 reaches the point where $2 \times F0$ – thus the second harmonic (H2) – arrives at the frequency of the first formant (F1). This point is usually reached in the range 300–400 Hz (D4-G4). In order to continue higher with the resonance tuning of F1/H2, there is a natural tendency to raise F1 by allowing the larynx to rise. This reduces the length of the vocal tract, which is a prime determinant of F1. In classical singing instruction this natural tendency is resisted. A correct execution of passaggio entails allowing F1 to fall below H2 as the fundamental frequency continues to rise. The consequent loss of the powerful F1/H2 resonance is then compensated, in the ideal case, by tuning the second formant (F2) to a harmonic higher than H2. (For the open back vowels [a] and [O], F2 is tuned to H3; for open front vowels [ae] and [E], F2 falls on H4.)

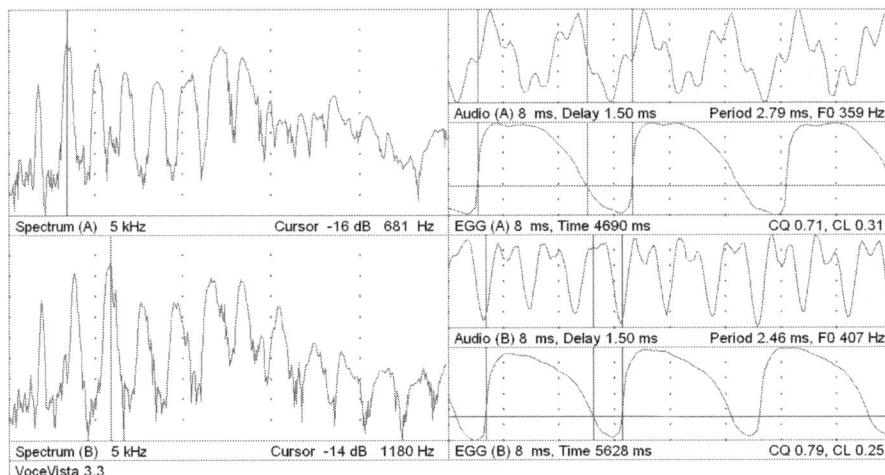

Fig. 9.3 Tenor passaggio, F4 and G4

On further scale steps beyond this passaggio point, skilled singers can adjust the F2 frequency to follow H3 or H4 on front vowels.

The essential element of the adjustment occurring at the passaggio point is the shift in the dominant resonance, rather than in the mechanism of the glottal voice source (see Miller 2008, Chapter 8). Naming the higher register 'head' can create confusion, since the move from 'chest to head' suggests what I have designated as the primary register transition, with its characteristic *reduction* of the closed quotient. On the contrary, in a typical robust operatic voice, the closed quotient tends to *increase* when the dominant harmonic shifts from H2 to H3 or H4. This can be seen in Fig. 9.3.

The figure shows power spectra (left) and microphone and EGG waveforms (right) of two pitches: *F4* (above) and *G4* (below). The moments displayed are taken from an octave scale from *A3-flat* to *A4-flat* sung by a robust tenor on the vowel [a]. The spectra show clearly how the dominant resonance passes from F1/H2 to F2/H3. This is reflected as well in the microphone signals, where the *F4* has a basic two-part form and the *G4* a three-part form within each glottal cycle. Note the increase in the closed quotient, measured here as 71 % and 79 %, respectively, with the move into the upper extension of the range. The basic pattern of the EGG signal, however, is maintained across the register change.

There is a generally recognized second passaggio for the female voice as well, where the registration event takes place approximately one octave above the male second passaggio. The most salient feature of this transition into the range of the upper extension is the full resonance that occurs when the fundamental frequency reaches the level of an open-vowel first formant at about 700–800 Hz (*F5-G5*). This gives a marked boost to the level of the first harmonic, which then retains its dominance on succeeding pitches until at least *B5-flat* or *C6* ('high C'), with F1 tracking H1 as it rises to its upper limit. This rise in the level of H1 can be seen in Fig. 9.4. As in the passaggio to the male upper extension, the major change is in resonance, rather than at the glottal source (see Miller 2008, Chapter 9).

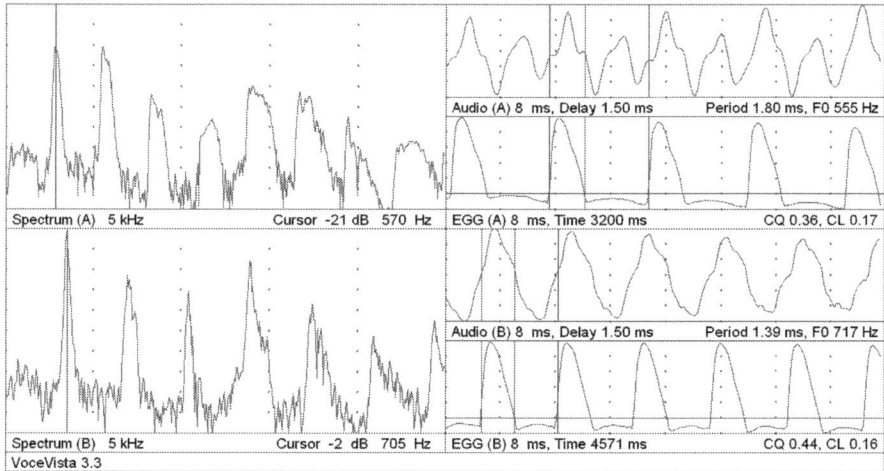

The figure contains labels:

Audio (A) 8 ms, Delay 1.50 ms   Period 1.80 ms, F0 555 Hz

Spectrum (A) 5 kHz   Cursor -21 dB 570 Hz   EGG (A) 8 ms, Time 3200 ms   CQ 0.36, CL 0.17

Audio (B) 8 ms, Delay 1.50 ms   Period 1.39 ms, F0 717 Hz

Spectrum (B) 5 kHz   Cursor -2 dB 705 Hz   EGG (B) 8 ms, Time 4571 ms   CQ 0.44, CL 0.16

VoceVista 3.3

Fig. 9.4 Soprano second passaggio, D5-flat and F5

The tones displayed are taken from an octave scale from *A4-flat* to *A5-flat* on the vowel [a]. Power spectra (left) and microphone and EGG waveforms (right) show the changes that occur in the transition from high middle register to the upper extension. Note the marked increase (here measured as 19 dB) in the level of the first harmonic as this reaches the frequency of the first formant. The level of H2 falls as it moves beyond F2, and on the higher note H1 is clearly dominant. This dominance remains for the pitches above *F5*, as F1 tracks H1. The modest increase in the closed quotient results from the shortening of the period, while the glottal closed phase of the two tones remains approximately the same.

An important consequence of the fact that F1 tracks H1 in this register is a relative homogenization of vowels in this range. Acoustic phonetics teaches us that the vowels we perceive are determined principally by the frequencies of the first two formants. Since F1 follows F0 in this register regardless of vowel, differentiation among sustained vowels is restricted to limited adjustments that are possible in F2 frequency, resulting in a sort of generalized front or back vowel, depending on whether F2 is moved higher or lower. Skilled singers also manage to suggest vowels in the brief transitions where they approach or leave a sustained vowel.

9.4 Whistle Register

A further female register that is typically recognized as 'whistle' or 'flageolet' is located above the pitches of the upper register just described. While it has received less scientific documentation than other registers mentioned here, the evidence indicates that its essential discontinuity from its lower neighbor is a result of F0 rising beyond the point where F1 can follow. The vocal tract can continue to provide resonance for the (dominant) first harmonic, however, by forming a cluster with the

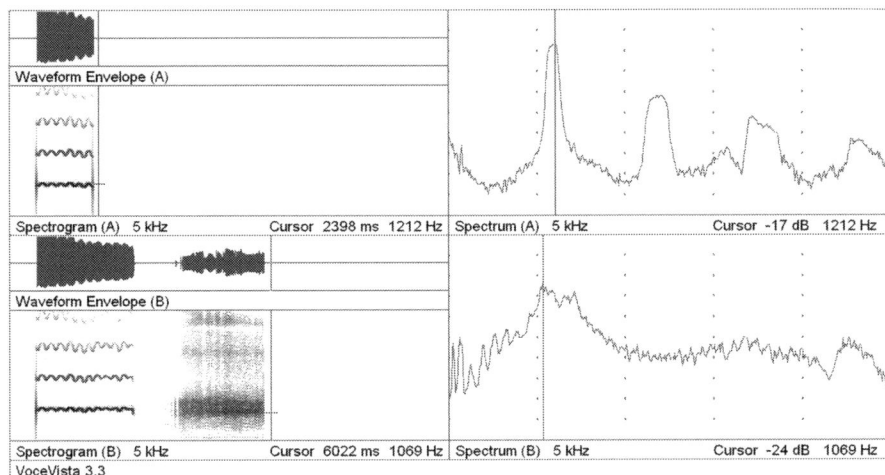

Fig. 9.5 High soprano, whistle register: sustained *E6-flat*, followed by vocal fry

proximate F2 (see Miller 2000, Chapter 2). Figure 9.5 shows an *E6-flat* with the vocal tract configured with F1 and F2 at approximately 1,100 and 1,400 Hz, respectively. The 1,400 Hz F2 suggests an explanation why operatic compositions for such sopranos rarely go beyond the *F6* (1,400 Hz) reached by the Queen of the Night in Mozart's *Zauberflöte*. Resonance beyond that which is provided by the F1-F2 cluster becomes much weaker, even if the vocal folds can vibrate at higher F0s.

The spectrograms in the left panels show a sustained *E6-flat*, followed by vocal fry, while maintaining the vocal tract articulation of the sung note. The power spectra in the right panels are averages of the last 400 ms before the sound stops, showing the sung sound (above) and the fry (below). The cursors in the power spectra show the fundamental frequency of the sung sound (above) and the first formant of the vocal fry (below). The second formant (not marked) is approximately 1,400 Hz. The two formants form a cluster with a width of about 300 Hz that resonates the first harmonic, located higher than F1 but still within the resonant cluster.

9.5 Lesser Transitions

In addition to the major transitions described thus far, singers also notice subtler 'lifts' at a few predictable points in their ranges. The Italian school tends to recognize a 'primo passaggio' in the male range that is a fourth or fifth below the more significant secondo passaggio described above. The explanation for this is found in the loss of the dominant resonance of F1/H3 at around *A3* to *B3* on the vowel [a]. An analogous loss in the female middle register typically occurs between *G4* and *A4*, where what can be a dominant F2/H3 is relinquished.

9.6   Voice Type and Register Transitions

In all the transitions described above the frequencies of the formants have an essential role in determining the pitches at which the registration events occur. Formant frequencies are determined by bodily vocal tract dimensions, as well as by articulations of tongue, mouth opening, larynx level, and of course vowel. Male vocal tract dimensions tend to be marginally greater than female, and those of basses are generally larger than those of tenors. These differences will be reflected in the pitches at which registration events occur. This is all well known, and the points at which the transitions occur are perhaps the most favored guide to voice classification in traditional singing pedagogy. It goes without saying that the transitions described here are also subject to adjustment according to voice type and individual build.

References

McCoy, S. J. (2012). *Your voice: An inside view* (2nd ed.). Columbus: Inside View Press.

Miller, D. G. (2000). *Registers in singing: Empirical and systematic studies in the theory of the singing voice*. Dissertation, Groningen.

Miller, D. G. (2008). *Resonance in singing: Voice building through acoustic feedback*. Princeton: Inside View Press.

Chapter 10
Body Mapping: Enhancing Voice Performance Through Somatic Pedagogy

Heather J. Buchanan

The singer uses his body both to sustain life and to cultivate his art.
He can never escape from himself,
for his physical life either furthers or hinders his artistic life.

(Wilhelm Ehmann 1968)

Abstract Body Mapping is a somatic (mind-body) education technique designed to teach musicians skills of self-evaluation and change for performing with sensory-motor integrity. It is one of the most recent disciplines to enter the somatic field and the only one currently with a primary focus on the movement needs of musicians. A self-inquiry method, the underlying premise of Body Mapping is the importance of understanding the neurophysiological connections in the human body that lead to freedom of movement. In addition to cultivating accurate and adequate body maps, the integration of kinesthesia into sensory awareness and the development of inclusive awareness provide musicians with the skills for embodied performing.

Quality of movement is critical for singers because it underlies all forms of musical communication and expression. This chapter presents vital information about the importance of movement for singers at every stage of their development. Beginning with accurate mind-body awareness, this chapter explains specific information clarifying a range of mapping errors and movement misunderstandings that plague singers and contribute to technical problems, musical frustrations, and music performance related injuries. The positive impact of BMG is illustrated through research case studies of college-level music students whose experiences revealed enhanced ability for and personal confidence with musical expression and

H.J. Buchanan (✉)
John J. Cali School of Music, Montclair State University, Upper Montclair, NJ, USA
e-mail: heather@bodymapping.net

S.D. Harrison and J. O'Bryan (eds.), *Teaching Singing in the 21st Century,*
Landscapes: the Arts, Aesthetics, and Education 14, DOI 10.1007/978-94-017-8851-9_10,
© Springer Science+Business Media Dordrecht 2014

heightened development of self-awareness. Body Mapping techniques may be readily integrated with vocal pedagogy to assist in evaluating the effectiveness of performance skills and for teaching singers to perform with ease.

Keywords Body mapping • Somatic education • Kinesthetic • Sensory awareness • Embodied performing • Self-awareness • Neurophysiological connections • Sensory-motor integrity • Self-evaluation

10.1   Introduction

10.1.1   Victoria's Story

Victoria is a voice performance major completing the final semester of her baccalaureate degree. She has studied voice privately since high school and has been active as a singer in numerous opera productions, choral ensembles, and solo engagements. She is working hard toward a career in opera and is preparing to audition for graduate studies at a range of prestigious music schools including Juilliard, Indiana University, and Peabody. However, in the final days before her senior recital she is plagued a variety of symptoms that are causing her concern. There is nagging neck tension that she cannot escape and her teacher is still reminding her about jaw tension too. In the more difficult passages of her repertoire she worries about having enough breath to make it through the long, high phrases. And as much as she tries to keep her ribs out during exhalation, she just finds this exhausting and she thinks her sound is no better for it anyway. Finally, in her practice today, her accompanist commented on her lack of expression and character, which is completely baffling because she loves performing and is trying very hard to communicate with the audience. At night when she's trying to go to sleep, there's a little voice inside Victoria's head that is very discouraging. It seems that no matter how hard she concentrates she just doesn't get better – even though she is one of the best students in the school. Being honest with herself Victoria is left with feelings of frustration and uncertainty about her prospects for the future.

10.1.2   Understanding Victoria's Story

While this story is an illustration of a composite of problems that frequently manifest in singers, there is a common thread underlying Victoria's problems. Movement. Movement that is tense, movement that is inaccurate, and movement that is not embodied and consequently made without full awareness. In addressing Victoria's technique there is also the need to question the paradigm within which she views herself as a singer, i.e. 'are you a mover?' For until Victoria fully comprehends that to sing is to move, and that the quality of her movements directly affects her capacity to sing effectively and efficiently – she will likely be overwhelmed with more information adding to the already complex volume of technique she is try to assimilate. The results will be variable at best.

Musical performance is demanding, and musicians who fail to honor the mind-body relationship underpinning their art place themselves at risk for some degree of suffering, be it technical frustrations or performance-related injury. By addressing movement quality, sensory engagement, and training awareness in our singers, we have the opportunity to empower them with knowledge and skills for mindful music-making. This is the work of Body Mapping.[1] For singers such as Victoria, Body Mapping, a form of somatic education, provides answers to movement-related problems and paves the way for artistic freedom.

10.2   Somatic Education

10.2.1   Evolution of Somatics

Somatic educators study and teach the practical relationship of the mind and body in action. The term 'somatic' derives from the Greek root 'soma' which literally translates as 'the study of the body' (Johnson 2009). In the field of education, somatics refers to 'the study of the body in movement' and 'the subjective experience of movement' (Caplan 2009). In the context of this chapter, somatics refers to 'any practical study of how the body operates in *movement*' (Johnson 2009).

There are several names historically associated with the evolution of somatics. F.M. Alexander, whose work began around a century ago, is regarded as the first authority. Other prominent names include Moshe Feldenkrais, Rudolph Laban, Irmgard Bartinieff, Joseph Pilates, Alexander Lowen, and Mabel Elsworth Todd. Each of these people made important discoveries about physiological functioning although their reasons for doing so varied. Moreover, their discoveries have also paved the way for more recent developments. For example, Eric Franklin's *Franklin Methode* is based on ideokinesis as defined by Mabel Todd in her book *The Thinking Body* (Franklin 2002). Body Mapping was discovered by William Conable (cellist and Alexander Technique teacher) and has been further developed by Barbara Conable (also an Alexander Technique teacher) and now Andover Educators (www.bodymap.org), a network of musicians trained to teach Body Mapping. Other medically based and therapeutic approaches to body work and movement education have also evolved. For example, testimonials about The Trager Approach, Rolfing

---

[1] The information in this chapter is based on Barbara Conable's (2000a) book *What Every Musicians Needs to Know About the Body*, my own study of Body Mapping to receive certification as a Licensed Andover Educator, my PhD research, and firsthand experience of the power of this information for over a decade through my work with the numerous musicians who have allowed me the privilege of sharing and working with them.

Structural Integration, and Hellerwork Structural Integration have all reported benefits to people seeking relief from bodily tensions. While musicians as a population are not specifically targeted by these approaches, testimonials reporting benefits for musicians exist on their websites.

For musicians seeking information about the body and the means to secure freedom of movement while performing, there are a variety of methodologies and therapies currently available. It should be noted that the highly specialized movement requirements of musicians, either generally or in particular performance areas, are not specifically addressed by all disciplines. Rather, it is incumbent on individuals to assimilate movement principles and reconcile them with the demands of their performance technique. The exceptions to this are The Alexander Technique, the Feldenkrais Method, and Body Mapping – disciplines with documented connections to the needs of musicians.

10.2.2   History of Body Mapping

Body Mapping has been in existence since the 1970s and is a comparatively new discipline in the field of somatic education. William Conable's discovery of the practical applications of the body map date back to 1973, and by 1975 both he and Barbara Conable were developing and using Body Mapping principles in their teaching of musicians and dancers at The Ohio State University. At the time of his discovery Conable was Professor of Cello at The Ohio State University. He was also a certified teacher of The Alexander Technique, having studied with two preeminent teachers of the technique, Marjorie Barstow and Frank Pierce Jones.

A revelatory teaching situation initiated Conable's (1995) thinking about the body map. It involved observation of a violin student experiencing difficulties with her bow arm, i.e. she was unable to bend 'her bow arm at the elbow'. He realized that her movement problem was the result of mis-mapping the location of her elbow joint. Conable stated the underlying principle thus:

> ... if there is a conflict between the way the body is mapped and the way it actually is, people will behave as if the map were true... the map is the interface between conscious awareness and the bodily mechanism: it is literally how we know ourselves.

Conable's (1995) development of Body Mapping was based on practical investigations that informed his understanding of body maps. He comprehended they were 'something constructed in consciousness' and further proposed 'the function of creating these maps may be in some way innate, but their contents are not.' Resulting from the experience of rapid change in the violin student with whom he consulted, he also surmised that because body maps were 'able to be changed, they must be learned' and the means by which they are created resulted from a variety of sensory stimuli, including 'the experience of movement, of touching and being touched...'.

Conable concluded that one of the most important aspects of the process of change was the evidence that it is possible to learn to change the map with ease and with surprisingly powerful results. This fact predisposed Body Mapping as an activity well suited to the needs of musicians who are routinely engaged in learning processes requiring development of specific motor coordination skills. Barbara Conable (2003) describes 'the wonderful synchrony' that occurred with Bill Conable's practical discovery and the scientific work that was being conducted simultaneously in the 1970s saying:

> Bill Conable and I did not know when he discovered the body map practically… that it was also being named and explored by neuroscientists. I learned about the scientists' work fairly recently. It would have helped us very much during our years of exploration to know about the scientists' work, but we didn't.

The discovery of the practical application of the body map was made through the needs of a musician's movement. The information was subsequently developed by William and Barbara into the self-inquiry method known as Body Mapping.

In 1997 Barbara Conable founded Andover Educators for the specific purpose of further developing the Body Mapping agenda. This included the training of musicians to teach the technique and deepen the understanding of it through professional exchanges and research. It was also her intention that Body Mapping textbooks with a specific pedagogical focus would also be published by musicians in Andover Educators.

10.3   The Scientific Basis of Body Mapping

10.3.1   Neuroscience – Establishing the Mind-Body Relationship via Body Maps

A musician's greatest asset is their brain – specifically the multipolar neurons that create elaborate neural networks called body maps. When musicians move, which they must do in order to sing or play, the quality of their movement and thus the quality of their musical performance is governed by the body maps developed in their brain. The work of neuroscientists confirms the existence and importance of the body map as described by William Conable (in Nichols 2004). Blakeslee and Blakeslee (2007) define body maps as neuronal representations of our physical being, i.e. aspects of 'the body's anatomy' that are 'systematically mapped onto brain tissue'. They further describe the structure and function of body maps as an organic network:

> … your brain maps your body, the space around your body, and the social world… Every point on your body, each internal organ and every point in space out to the end of your fingertips, is mapped inside your brain. Your ability to sense, move, and act in the physical world arises from a rich network of flexible body maps distributed throughout your brain – maps that grow, shrink, and morph to suit your needs.

While the practice of Body Mapping is relatively new, the idea of the body map is not. According to Conable, the concept of body map first appeared in scientific research about 100 years ago. This is supported by the neuroscientist Pellegrino (2001) who writes in his 2001 study that the concept on an 'internal representation

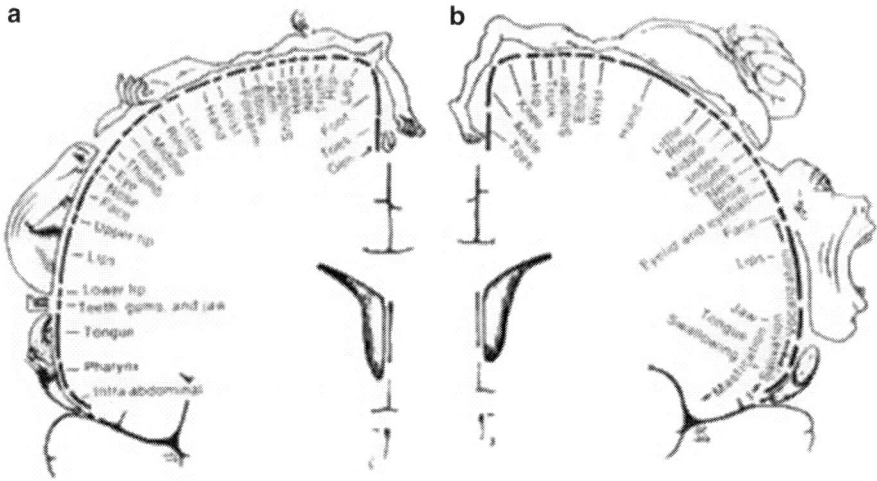

Fig. 10.1 Penfield's Homunculi (Split Martini n.d.)

of the body' based on the 'synthesis of visual and somatosensory sensations' is almost a century old. Nichols (2004) suggests that the concept of a body map first occurs significantly earlier, in the work of the nineteenth century British neurologist John Hughlings Jackson, who was a proponent of the view that 'the body is represented on the cortical surface in the appropriate spatial relationship based on experimental work by Fritsch and Hitzig (1870)'. Blakeslee and Blakeslee (2007) cite the work of British neurologists, Sir Henry Head and Gordon Holmes, who suggested the idea of the 'body schema' in 1911. Their research resulted in the understanding of the neural maps of the musculoskeletal system.

> Head and Holmes figured out that… signals from your body's musculoskeletal system are carried into your brain to determine your posture and the position of your limbs. According to Head, we build up internal postural models of ourselves in conjunction with models of the surface of our bodies. He dubbed this the body schemata (now just called body schema), defined as 'organized models of ourselves'.

In the 1930s and 1940s, research by Wilder Penfield, a surgeon at the Montreal Neurological Institute, laid the foundation of understandings about cortical representations and their relationships to touch and movement. His publication *The Cerebral Cortex of Man* (1950) contained data on approximately 520 human brains and detailed information about the brain's maps of the body's surface. Penfield's research was illustrated with a diagrammatic picture he nicknamed the homunculus (refer Fig. 10.1 Penfield's Homunculi). The homunculi as illustrated show the body maps for touch and voluntary movement in the right hemisphere of the brain. These maps are also duplicated in the left hemisphere of the brain. The primary somatosensory area (the darker shaded strip in Fig. 10.1) – called the primary touch cortex, contains body maps based on touch. The primary motor cortex (lighter shaded strip in Fig. 10.1) contains body maps for voluntary movements of the represented body parts.

The amount of cortical space allocated to specific body parts in the homunculi is notable. For example, in the primary motor cortex the muscles for the hands and mouth 'receive far richer projections from your motor cortex than do less dexterous muscle groups like those in your back, knees, and hips'. This is due to the 'fast-changing, highly coordinated ways' that hands and mouths are used by comparison to the large muscle groups in the legs, for example. Similar proportions are found in the primary somatosensory area as explained by Blakeslee and Blakeslee (2007).

> The sensory receptors in your body are distributed unevenly. They are densely concentrated in the body parts where you need high acuity and dexterity, and sparse in parts where superior sensory resolution isn't paramount.

The implications of this information should be obvious for musicians – upper body athletes – whose movements are highly repetitive and focused in the upper body. The regions of the body requiring the most dexterous coordination are naturally accommodated by the body maps in our brains. For example, the cortical surface for fingers, hands, lips and tongues is significantly richer than for the legs. In singers, fine motor coordination in the lower body is not utilized to the same extent as the upper body structures. Consider the complex use of the mouth and articulators – teeth, tongue and lips – for the formation of vowels and consonants in the execution of languages.

Neuroscience also confirms 'the maps in the executive areas of the cortex that represent the anatomy of the body are clearly dependent upon the motor and sensory experiences of the individual' (Nichols 2004). Or stated another way: 'the brain's representations of the body, of movements, and of sounds are all shaped by experience' (Schwartz and Begley 2002). Our neural patterns (body maps) are created by unique interactions with sensory stimuli (e.g. signals from the skin or the muscles or the retina) that are 'picked up and assembled' by the neurons and circuits in the brain (Damasio 1999). Nichols (2004) explains that our physical functioning is particularly influenced by 'conscious representations of the musculoskeletal system':

> Conscious representations of the musculoskeletal system will influence motor learning and planning, and will have downstream defects on the cortical maps in the executive areas of primary motor cortex. Therefore, the details of the body map can influence cortical representation along the entire chain of information flow, from planning through execution.

The accuracy of the information contained in the body map therefore corresponds with the accuracy of the movement generated by this information. Nichols (2004) confirms that 'if movement is based on an inaccurate knowledge or perception about the anatomy of the body, then pathologic changes can result.' Tendonitis and carpal tunnel syndrome are two examples of pathological changes in the musculoskeletal system resulting from poor quality motor behaviors (Nichols 2004). Nichols further states that 'over-training of one specific motor pattern can also lead to pathologic changes, such as focal dystonias, in the central nervous system.' In 2000 Nancy Byl reported on experiments on focal hand dystonia in three musicians. Her finding of an '85 to 98 percent improvement in fine motor skills…after they [musicians] took part in her sensorimotor retraining program' has lead to the conclusion that 'in at least some patients with focal hand dystonia, the degraded cortical representation can be repaired' (Schwartz and Begley 2002). However, Nichols (2010, October 10, personal communication) further cautions:

> It cannot be assumed that the "incorrect" usage of a musical instrument, or any other tool, or any part of the body is due to some distortion of the map on the motor cortex. The distortion of the map may develop in parallel with the disorder, but may be as much a result of the disease process or faulty motor practice…map distortions that develop may exacerbate and prolong the condition, however.

Neuroplasticity is also important to body maps and their implications for movement. Neuroplasticity is the brain's ability to change the content of neural networks and it is an ability that remains for the duration of one's life (Beringer 2010). Schwartz and Begley (2002) describe neuroplasticity as 'the ability of neurons to forge new connections, to blaze new paths through the cortex, even to assume new roles.' Blakeslee and Blakeslee (2007) explain that 'body-centered maps are profoundly plastic – capable of significant reorganization in response to damage, experience, or practice.' While Damasio (2003) states that 'it does take time to change the body and map the consequent changes' the fact of neural plasticity resulting on brain-body interactions is confirmed and of great significance to performing artists desirous of making changes in the way they play. Moreover, the fact that 'plasticity persists into adulthood' also supports the potential for musicians of all ages to change the information contained within their body maps (Schwartz and Begley 2002).

Another asset in our neurological functioning is the existence of mirror neurons. Neurophysiological research by Giacomo Rizzolatti in the early 1990s at Parma University, Italy, with Macaque monkeys established a set of preliminary understandings about coordination of motor events (Pellegrino et al 1992). However, it was not until 1996 that Rizzolatti first published research confirming mirror neurons and 'multiple mirror neuron systems that specialize in carrying out and understanding not just the actions of others but their intentions, the social meaning of their behavior and their emotions' was first published (Blakeslee 2006). As the name implies, mirror neurons explain 'the modeling/mimicking process that is central to much human learning' Sylwester (2002). The relationship between planned actions and mirror neurons is still under investigation, but a range of applications have already been confirmed. For example, mirror neurons allow us to read intentions, simulate actions, and empathize with others (Blakeslee 2006). While research into mirror neurons continues, to date it is believed that they 'facilitate the preliminary motor neuron simulation, priming, programming, and rehearsing that occurs in children', a process that 'obviously enhances our eventual mastery of complex motor behaviors' (Sylwester 2002).

Neural circuits also contribute to brain function. Damasio (1999) describes the brain as a 'system of systems' with 'the action of neurons depend[ing] on the nearby assembly of neurons' to which they belong. 'Mirror neurons represent one stage in information processing that integrates sensory information with information based on memory and associations' (Nichols 2010, October 10, personal communication).

The dynamic nature of brain circuits and their activities accounts for ongoing changes or brain plasticity. They also serve to connect different maps together (e.g. topographical and/or functional) (Damasio 1999; Nichols 2010, October 10, personal communication). Nichols acknowledges that we have limited understanding of how these circuits operate, but he believes that the 'manner in which focal dystonias and other neurological disorders arise will depend on a deep understanding of the operation of these circuits' (Nichols 2010, October 10, personal communication).

Questions about the ability of neuroscience to help musicians and other high level performers continue to be asked. For example, at the 2009 International Symposium on Performance Science, Altenmüller and Jabusch (2009) declared 'most neuroscientists consider music as an excellent paradigm to study brain mechanisms related to sensorimotor or perceptive learning,' furthermore:

> Many neuroscientists are interested in musicians and in the neurobiology of music perception and performance. This interest is usually motivated by the attractiveness of the topic (music as an art) and by the enormous effects of music on brain networks and brain morphology, demonstrating the powerful mechanisms of brain plasticity in the short- and long-term range.

Neuroscience can be considered an area rich in opportunity for collaborative studies with musicians, but the degree to which musicians' can be helped is still a matter of debate.

In short, scientific support for the body map is firmly established and research establishes that 'your brain is teeming with body maps' (Blakeslee and Blakeslee 2007). While significant progress has been made in understanding mind-body connections in the last century, Blakeslee and Blakeslee (2007) also recognize 'the science of body maps…is a widely underappreciated piece of the puzzle'. Nichols (2010, October 10, personal communication) confirms that 'brain maps are not only simple representations of anatomy' but also have 'functional representations as well' because movements as well as muscles are represented. However, current knowledge about brain functioning and sensory and motor coordination is sufficient to confirm the validity of the body map in relation to musical movement. This further underscores the importance of cultivating effective movement while developing musical technique. Nichols (2004) concurs with the need to emphasize 'the importance of educating musicians in anatomy and physiology of the motor system so that practices that can lead to pathology in the musculoskeletal system can be avoided'.

10.3.2   Accurate Body Map – Effective Movement

Neuroscience confirms that the integrity of a movement is determined by the integrity of the body map that governs it. Nichols (2004) clearly explains that 'the maps in the executive areas of the cortex that represent the anatomy of the body are clearly dependent upon the motor and sensory experiences of the individual'. Stated another way: 'the brain's representations of the body, of movements, and of sounds, are all shaped by experience' (Schwartz and Begley 2002). Our neural patterns – aka body maps – are therefore created by unique interactions with sensory stimuli, e.g. signals from the skin or the muscles or the retina, that are picked up and assembled by the neurons and circuits in the brain. Nichols (2004) further explains that body maps particularly influence our physical functioning:

> Conscious representations of the musculoskeletal system will influence motor learning and planning, and will have downstream effects on the cortical maps in the executive areas of primary motor cortex. Therefore, the details of the body map can influence cortical representation along the entire chain of information flow, from planning through execution.

The accuracy of the information contained in the body map therefore corresponds with the accuracy of the movement generated by this information. Nichols (2004) confirms that 'if movement is based on an inaccurate knowledge or perception about the anatomy of the body, then pathologic changes can result.' Tendonitis and carpal tunnel syndrome are two examples of pathological changes in the musculoskeletal system resulting from poor quality motor behaviors due to faulty body maps.

10.3.3   Other Neurological Assets – Brain Plasticity and Mirror Neurons

Neuroplasticity is also important to body maps and their implications for movement. Neuroplasticity is the brain's ability to change the content of neural networks and it is an ability that remains for the duration of one's life. Schwartz and Begley (2002) describe neuroplasticity as 'the ability of neurons to forge new connections, to blaze new paths through the cortex, even to assume new roles.' Blakeslee and Blakeslee (2007) explain that 'body-centered maps are profoundly plastic – capable of significant reorganization in response to damage, experience, or practice.' While Damasio (2003) states that 'it does take time to change the body and map the consequent changes', the fact of neural plasticity resulting on brain-body interactions is confirmed and of great significance to performing artists desirous of making changes in the way they move. Moreover, the fact that 'plasticity persist into adulthood' also supports the potential for musicians of all ages to change the information contained within their body maps. For singers who need to re-map specific movement patterns that have been well ingrained in their technique, this is good news. The brain is amenable to change which is made possible through the conscious re-mapping techniques taught in Body Mapping. In short – you can teach an old dog new tricks!

Another asset in our neurological functioning is the existence of mirror neurons. Neurophysiological research by Giacomo Rizzolatti in the early 1990s at Parma University, Italy, with Macaque monkeys established a set of preliminary understandings about coordination of motor events. However, it was not until 1996 that Rizzolatti first published research confirming mirror neurons and the multiple mirror neuron systems that specialize in carrying out and understanding the actions of others, their intentions, the social meaning of their behavior, and their emotions. As the name implies, mirror neurons explain 'the modeling/mimicking process that is central to much human learning' (Sylwester 2002). The relationship between planned actions and mirror neurons is still under investigation, but a range of applications have already been confirmed. For example, mirror neurons allow us to read intentions, simulate actions, and empathize with others. For singers this has two important implications. First, as teachers we can and should mirror movement for our students to help them understand the difference between effective and ineffective movement patterns. Secondly, dynamic and expressive singing is crucial if singers (and indeed singing ensembles) are to effectively communicate with audiences, because audiences mirror the performers' emotions via the singers' body language.

While the degree to which musicians can be helped by neuroscience is still a matter of debate, current knowledge about brain functioning and sensory and motor coordination is sufficient to confirm the validity of the body map in relation to musical movement. This further underscores the importance of cultivating effective movement patterns when developing vocal technique. Moreover, while attending to the technical needs of musicians is crucial, a secure somatic foundation also prevents performing-related pain and injuries resulting from faulty patterns of movement, tension, and poor posture.

10.4   Body Mapping

10.4.1   Why Body Mapping Is Important for Musicians

Movement is the means by which the singer sings, the instrumentalist plays, and the conductor evokes musical responses from the choir and orchestra. Movement is the basis for all forms and styles of musical expression and as a result it can be said that musicians literally move for a living. Body Mapping is the most recent education technique to enter the field of somatics and the only one currently with a primary focus on the movement needs of musicians. While its roots lie in the somatic practices established by F.M. Alexander, the underlying premise of Body Mapping is the importance of understanding the neurophysiological connections in the human body that lead to freedom of movement. In addition to cultivating accurate and adequate body maps, the integration of kinesthesia into sensory awareness and the development of inclusive awareness into musicians' habits of mind provide them with the skills required for embodied performing.

Body Mapping is a self-inquiry somatic education technique defined as 'the conscious correcting and refining of one's body map to produce efficient, graceful, coordinated, and effective movement' (Conable 2000a, b). The underlying principle is that 'the integrity of any movement depends upon the integrity of the body map that governs it' (Conable, in Vining 2008). Hence, if the body map is accurate the resulting movement is effective and free. If the body map is inaccurate or inadequate, movement is inefficient and potentially injury-producing.

10.4.2   Body Mapping Principles

Body Mapping is based on four main principles identified as (1) cultivating an accurate and adequate body map, (2) training movement, (3) training the relevant senses, and (4) training attention. Body Mapping helps musicians correct and refine their body map as it relates to their movement in music-making. Clarity about the three elements comprising the body map – structure, function, and size – is crucial in the process of attaining an accurate and adequate body map. Structure refers to human anatomy, predominantly the musculoskeletal system, although the nervous system is also important; function refers to physiology, the way anatomical structures interact to create movement; and size refers to the specific dimensions of the various muscle and bones involved in the mapping process.

10.4.3   Body Map Errors

There are various types of common mapping errors resulting in a detrimental effect on physical coordination and in movement that is either awkward or potentially injury-producing. **Errors in the size** of body map elements are among the most widespread mapping inaccuracies. For example, a singer who understands the true size of their spine and is able to deliver weight through the structure will experience an increased sense of strength and stability in their core. Another common size mis-mapping is evident in people who habitually stoop or compress their bodies to fit their psychological self-concept of a smaller height and size than their actual physiological dimensions.

   Structural mis-mapping includes the inaccurate map of location of joints. For example, a singer who has incorrectly mapped the location of the temporo-mandibular joints (TMJs) may experience tension resulting from forced or incorrect jaw movement or even pain and injury in the TMJs. When the TMJs (two joints) are correctly mapped on either side of the head slightly in front of the ears, the resulting movement is easier and more efficient and is unlikely to result in pain or injury.

   Functional misconceptions in the body map are also prevalent. Rib movement in breathing is a good example for singers because it is such a crucial part of the movement required for effective breath management. Rib movement must be correctly mapped – front, back and sides – at the breathing joints that allow rib movement. This requires mapping the joints of our ribs at the transverse thoracic process of our spines in back, and at the costal cartilage in front. Furthermore, fuller (deeper and wider) and freer breathing results when singers also understand the actual movement of the ribs, i.e. swinging up and out on inhalation and down and in on inhalation.

   Vagueness, blankness, or absence of a part of the body in the body map is the last type of mapping error identified by William Conable. He asserts these gaps in the body map information may be the result of any of the following four situations: ignorance of body information; imitation of poor habits of movement; withdrawing from an injury and never reestablishing contact with the injured part; and physical or psychological abuse, which leads the sufferer to disown or distort part of the body. Suppression of traumatic experiences, also referred to as 'freeze' in the 'fight – flight – freeze' reaction, is responsible for mental, physical and emotional paralysis in human beings. In some people, the frozen energy builds up over time and paralyzes or inhibits their ability to absorb and learn. In cases such as this, appropriate emotional support and treatment outside of the Body Mapping field is a fitting adjunct to the somatic work.

10.4.4 Training Movement

The importance of training movement as movement as opposed to training movement abstractly, with confusing images, or by inference, is crucial in Body Mapping. Courtesy of our brain structure and its effect on our physical functioning, the easiest way to retrain a tense of inefficient movement is to correct and refine the body map governing it. This is analogous to correcting the score from which the musician reads rather than constantly fixing the wrong note they are playing. Modeling good movement is also powerful for singers – an important reminder for studio teachers and choral conductors who are valuable visual role models.

10.4.5 Training the Senses

Training musicians in the relevant senses is also important. Students of Body Mapping are trained to understand kinesthesia (the sense of 'movement') and its relationship to the traditionally taught five senses (sight, sound, touch, taste and smell). The lack of recognition for kinesthesia as a sense is explained and corrected. Information from the kinesthetic sense is constantly available to us along with information from our other senses. With the exception of taste and smell, musicians must be trained to connect sound, kinesthesia, sight and touch in their awareness. The absence of kinesthesia in the training of the senses accounts for much of the ignorance of the relationship of this sense to the others, in particular the kinesthetic-aural connection. In many cases, the complete absence of kinesthetic awareness requires significant re-training. Musicians who have accurately mapped the function of their sense receptors for the relevant senses (ears, muscles and connective tissue, eyes, and skin) are able to access complete sensory awareness in their playing.

10.4.6 Training Attention

Training attention incorporates the ability to be more sensitive, discerning and responsible to body movement in the musical context. Barbara Conable (2003) uses the analogy of playing in tune to teach musicians how to apply the

Table 10.1 Comparison of auditory and kinesthetic sensory awareness

Sense	Sensitivity	Discernment	Responsiveness
Auditory	I hear the note I'm singing/playing	I sense the note is sharp	I bring the note back in tune
Kinesthetic	I feel my body as I sing/play	I sense I'm off balance	I bring myself back to balance

sensitivity-discernment-responsiveness cycle to their movement and body awareness. In Table 10.1 the key elements (sensory awareness, sensitivity, discernment, and responsiveness) are initially presented in the auditory context which is familiar and readily understood by musicians. The introduction of the kinesthetic sense and its relationship to musical movement is paralleled in the language and experience of musicians, thereby enhancing their comprehension of these concepts and how they are experienced.

On the recommendation of T. Richard Nichols, science advisor for Andover Educators and neurophysiologist at the Georgia Institute of Technology, USA, Andover Educators use the scientific term 'attention' to describe the completeness of sensory information and experience necessary for musicians. Synonymous with 'attention' are the terms 'awareness', 'consciousness', and 'mindfulness.' *Inclusive Awareness* is taught by teachers of Body Mapping. It is described as 'the skill of perceiving self and the world simultaneously' (Malde et al. 2009). Inclusion of the kinesthetic sense in this form of awareness is also required.

10.4.7 Constructive Rest

Cultivating inclusive awareness is achieved through various means, however use of a technique called *Constructive Rest* is regarded as the most effective way to begin training attention because 'constructive rest cultivates awareness, and awareness is the only means to change' (Vining 2008). Practice of constructive rest is recommended on a daily basis and typically involves lying down in a semi-supine position. To date there are two comprehensive sources of information on constructive rest in the Body Mapping literature. The first is an entire chapter devoted to it by David Vining (2008) who distinguishes constructive rest from regular resting with five goals:

1. to cultivate a whole and integrated body awareness. This is the most important step because the other four steps depend upon on;
2. to come to the greatest degree of muscular freedom you can find in the moment;
3. to work on the integrity of your breathing;
4. to develop an accurate and adequate body map;
5. to put yourself in a right relationship with space.

The second source of information is an audio guide for constructive rest by David Nesmith (2011). It is a multi-volume resource enhancing the practice of the five goals mentioned above. Key principles of The Alexander Technique and relevant Body Mapping information are woven throughout the guided constructive rest sessions.

10.5 Mapping Core Balance

Physical alignment that facilitates mechanical advantage results from core balance. Unfortunately for many singers, traditional definitions or concepts of 'good posture' elicit physiological responses resulting in tense and restricted movement. Examples of these well-intentioned instructions for 'good posture' include: 'stand or sit tall with your head pulled up by a string'; 'stand (or sit) up straight'; 'align your back with the wall'; 'shoulders back and chest up (high)'; 'bottom tucked under'; and 'keep your abdominals firm'. Unfortunately, these instructions often have a negative effect and yield examples of 'poor posture' because freedom of movement is inhibited in numerous ways. These include: decreased support for the body; creation of tension and rigidity; creation of extra work; restricted breathing capacity and support; tight jaw; restricted leg movement; limited arm and finger movement; chronically off-balance weight distribution (too far back). The ability to improve the kinesthetic sense is also limited and so too the capacity for musical and tonal variety. The alternative is to teach core balance.

10.5.1 The Core of the Body

The human body is built around the spine, which functions as the core structure for our balance. Whenever we sing we should perform with our entire body, which is supported and organized centrally around our spinal core. Visualize the core of a well-formed apple that provides the central structure for the surround flesh of the fruit. This metaphor translates to the location of the weight-bearing (forward) part of the human spine. Core balance begins by accurately mapping the structure, function and size of the spine. (Refer Fig. 10.2 to view the spine in context.) Experience has shown that people who accurately map their curvy vertebral column and understand its true size experience an increased sense of strength and stability in their spine. In turn, this facilitates effective weight bearing and weight delivery functions throughout the body, which translates into free movement.

10.5.2 Mapping the Spine for Structure, Function and Size

Structure: The spine comprises five divisions – seven cervical (neck) vertebrae, twelve thoracic vertebrae, five lumbar vertebrae, the sacrum and the coccyx. The size and shape of the vertebrae vary according to their function, and they also create

Fig. 10.2 Side view of spine outlining curves (Gorman 2013, 45, Reprinted with permission)

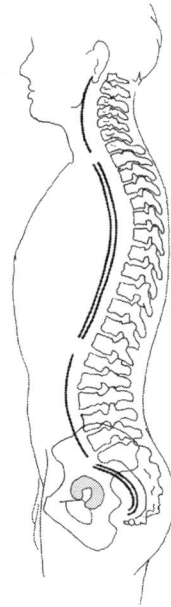

From The Body Moveable, (6th ed. vol.1, p 45) by D. Gorman, 2013, Toronto, Canada, Learning Methods Publications, Copyright 2002, Reprinted with Permission

space to accommodate the spinal cord. The spine is segmented and has four natural curvatures – cervical, thoracic, lumbar, and sacral.

Function: The spine is our massive internal support. The four curvatures help to maintain balance, absorb shocks, increase strength, and protect from fracture during movement. Two important functions of the spine are: (1) weight bearing of structures above and weight delivery into structure below via the front half of the spine; and (2) protection of the nerves of the spinal cord via the back half of the spine (refer Fig. 10.3). Look again at a picture or a model of the spine, and you will clearly see how this is possible. The spine's flexibility is due to its ingenious structure, which allows singers to be very mobile – bending and twisting the torso as needed to gesture. Most important is the gathering and lengthening movement that occurs during breathing. (This function is explained later in this chapter in the breathing section).

10.5.3 The Places of Balance

Body Mapping teaches singers how to stand and sit with ease (remember that many singers are seated during choir rehearsals), by mapping the six places of balance: (1) the atlanto-occipital (A-O) joint; (2) lumbar spine; (3) hip joints; (4) knees; (5) ankles; and (6) arm structure (see Fig. 10.4). These specific locations are taught first because they are the places where balance can be discerned most easily,

Fig. 10.3 Spine function
(Conable 2003, reprinted
with permission). Size:
The spine is a massive
internal structure providing
support for the body and all
its movement. The shape
and size of the vertebrae
correspond to the function
and amount of weight they
bear. Each vertebra is bigger
than the one above because
it has to bear and deliver
more weight

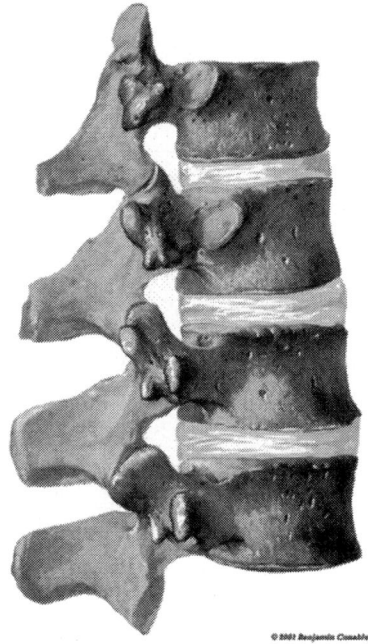

Fig. 10.4 The places of
balance (*1*. A-O Joint,
2. Lumbar Spine, *3*. Hip
Joints, *4*. Knees, *5*. Ankles,
6. Arm Structure)

although we ultimately use almost all structures in our body (except for organs) to find balance. Achieving balance when standing or seated is thwarted by the twin evils of 'posture' or 'relaxing'. For example, instructions to 'pull your shoulders back' or 'elevate the chest' typically result in an unnatural posture with misaligned arm structure and/or ribs, with tension detrimental to effective singing. By contrast, attempts to coax singers out of a 'stiff' or 'wooden' posture with instructions to 'relax' often yields some kind of slumping or drooping in the body alignment. Both of these problems result from mis-mapping the core of the body. Teaching our singers to find balance or poise around their core, and to discern the place of balance in relation to the core, frees them to develop dynamic and poised body usage.

The effects of misalignment and tension on vocal sound will vary according to the degree of distortion in the balance. As you read through the descriptions of each of the six places of balance, experiment with the effects of going in and out of balance on your voice. You will know when you have found balance – there is a rightness about it that is analogous to knowing when you are singing in tune. When you sing in tune correctly you hear it and some singers feel it too. An important note: when you initially find balance it is wise to use a mirror so you can see the accuracy of your alignment. Relying on how it feels frequently does not work (at first), because balance may be so far from the feeling of 'normal' for an individual. Learning to overcome this sensory confusion is helped by incorporating visual information and reconciling it with the kinesthetic as well as the auditory and tactile senses. Balance is the place where your body is at greatest ease and initiating movement in any direction is effortless. From balance you develop the capacity to just be in place without undue muscular effort because there is an absence of holding or tension.

The places of balance are not fixed positions because balance is a dynamic state. The importance of the places of balance is their role in organizing our body movement. Balance should be our orientation when we sing because it allows us to move easily in any direction required. When performing we continually move in and out of balance, but always returning to balance for orientation. Because it requires minimal work and effort, balance naturally facilitates the cultivation of muscle recovery required when the body is working, and this contributes to the overall ease of movement required to sing. The following six sections are deeper explanations of the places labeled in Fig. 10.4.

1. A-O Joint

The atlanto-occipital (A-O) joint is the place where the skull balances on the spine, i.e. the top vertebra (atlas) meets the base of the skull (occiput). You can locate the A-O joint by finding the intersection of an imaginary line from right between the base of the ears at the sides, the base of your nose at front, and the base of the occipital bone at the back/base of your skull. You can only locate the A-O joint by using your kinesthesia. Figure 10.5a, b illustrate the balance of the skull, with equal distance between front and back and the ears at the side. We free the A-O joint by intention, in the same way we think and sing a pitch. Learn to free the A-O joint so your head balances beautifully at its center on the spine.

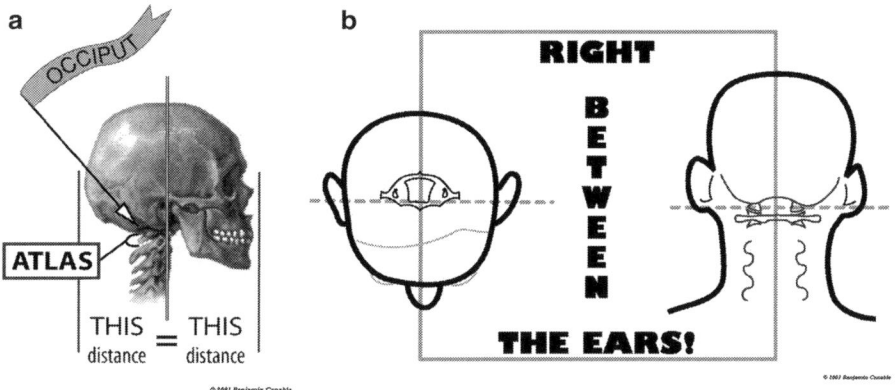

Fig. 10.5 (**a**) The A-O joint from side (Conable 2003, reprinted with permission). (**b**) A-O joint 'Right Between the Ears' (Conable 2003, reprinted with permission)

Fig. 10.6 (**a**) Lumbar spine (Conable 2003, reprinted with permission). (**b**) Lumbar spine in context (Gorman 2013, 45, reprinted with permission)

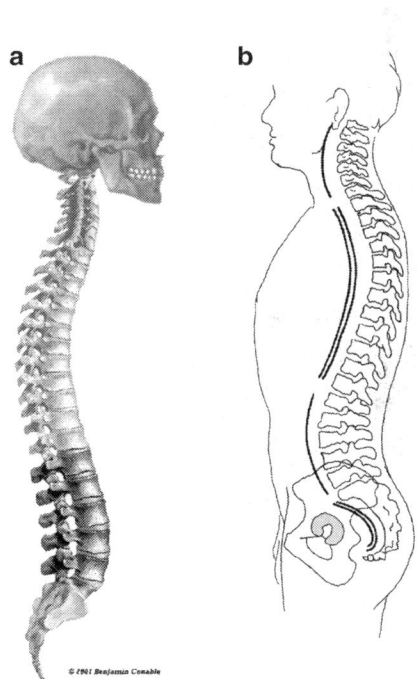

2. Lumbar Spine

The lumbar spine is the place where we balance our thorax on our lumbar vertebrae (refer Fig. 10.6a, b). The five lumbar vertebrae are the largest vertebrae in the spine and are designed to bear the weight of the structures above, i.e. the thoracic area, arms, neck and head. Explore the effects of balancing your thorax, along with your

Fig. 10.7 Hip joints and
pelvis (Conable 2003,
reprinted with permission)

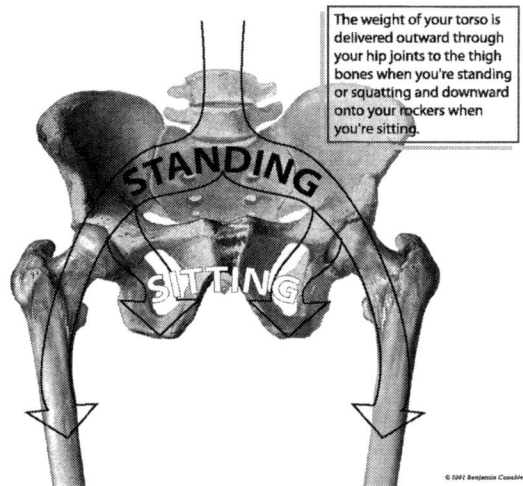

The weight of your torso is
delivered outward through
your hip joints to the thigh
bones when you're standing
or squatting and downward
onto your rockers when
you're sitting.

head, neck and arm structures, on your lumbar vertebrae. You can locate the lumbar
core via the sides of your body where you feel the pelvic (iliac) crest. This places
you in the vicinity of L3 (lumbar vertebra number 3), the middle of the five lumbar
vertebrae and the center of your lumbar spine. It is also the center of your lumbar
vertebrae from body front to back. Study Fig. 10.6a, b to see the central location of
the lumbar vertebrae.

3. Hip Joints

Our hip joints are the halfway point – top to bottom – in human beings. Mapping the
waist as our middle is a common mapping error. When standing weight is delivered
in an arch – down the spine, through the sacroiliac joints, and through the hip
joints out to the center of the thigh bone (femur) downward to the knees and feet
(refer Fig. 10.7). The pelvic rockers (sit bones) are located at the base of the pelvis.
These beautifully designed structures constitute our base when sitting, i.e. upper
body weight is transferred through the lumbar spine into the pelvic rockers. Study
Figs. 10.7 and 10.8 closely so you are clear that the hip joints are located higher than
the sit bones. You can also approximate the location of your hip joint by lifting your
leg and feeling where it moves in relation to your torso.

Experiment with the balance of the pelvis when standing and notice the effect this
has on other places in your body, including your knees and neck. Also experiment
with the balance of the pelvis when seated and note how this affects the delivery
of weight into the pelvic rockers. Observe that when you are seated with core
balance you do not sit on your legs, because your legs are outside of your pelvis.
Figure 10.8 illustrates the ideal weight distribution when seated, i.e. over the hip
joints and pelvic rockers, not thrown onto the back and pressuring the coccyx. Note
the external location of the hip-joints again in Fig. 10.7 and map them in relation to
your sit bones.

Fig. 10.8 Seated balance
(Conable 2003, reprinted
with permission)

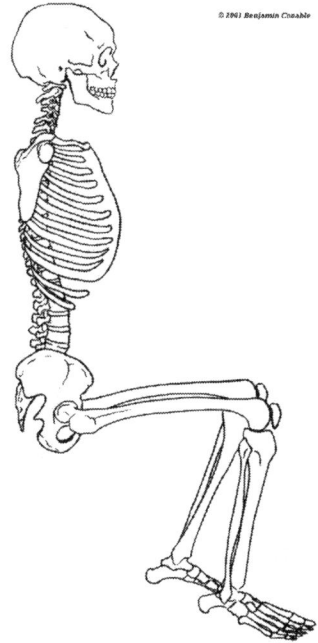

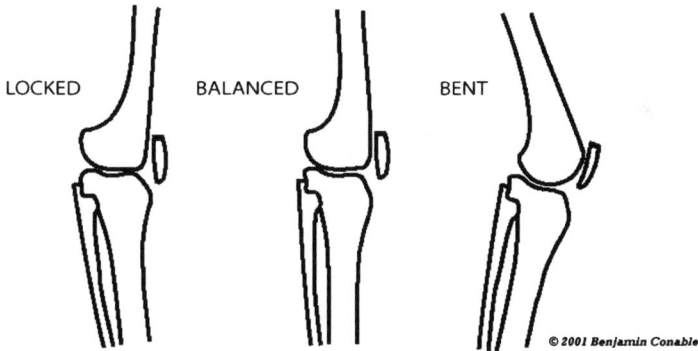

LOCKED   BALANCED   BENT

© 2001 Benjamin Conable

Fig. 10.9 Three positions of the knees (Conable 2003, reprinted with permission)

4. Knees

When standing, our upper body weight distributes downward through the knees to the ankles. There are three positions or conditions of the knees: locked, balance, and bent (refer Fig. 10.9).

Knees balanced (or sometimes described as 'soft') is the preferred state for core alignment. However, the knees will need to be locked as compensation to stabilize the body and protect the lumbar spine when the weight of your body is thrown back onto the lower back. This is nature's protective mechanism for the

Fig. 10.10 The ankle
and arch of the foot
(Conable 2003, reprinted
with permission)

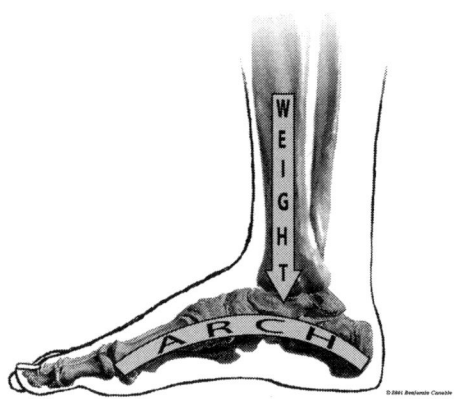

lumbar disks and it is dangerous to artificially unlock your knees when your weight is not balanced over your core.

5. Ankles

Body weight is delivered down the front of the lower leg through the ankle and into the arch of the foot when standing (refer Fig. 10.10). The arch of the foot is formed from the heel at the back to the ball of the foot at the front and excludes the toes. Toes are not included in the arch for core balance. Experiment with weight delivery in this fifth place of balance and observe how imbalance in your feet generates tension elsewhere in your body, such as your legs, back, and neck. Also notice what is happening to your breathing. The effects of misalignment and tension are profound because of the interconnectivity of the body structures. This is also a good time to talk to students about the shoes they wear when they sing, specifically the effects of heel size and height on their balance and capacity for weight delivery.

6. Arm Structure

Singers should not underestimate the importance of mapping their arm structure. As shown in Fig. 10.11, a complete arm structure includes the collarbone (front), shoulder blade (back), humerus (upper arm), radius and ulna (lower arm), carpal bones (wrist), and metacarpals and phalanges (hand). There are four joints in the arm structure: sterno-clavicular (where the sternum/breastbone meets the clavicle/collarbone), humero-scapula[2] (where the humerus/upper arm meets the scapula/shoulder blade), elbow, and wrist.

---

[2] The term 'humero-scapula' is used to describe the shoulder joint relationship between the humerus and scapula (shoulder blade). It is not an official anatomical designation. Author Thomas Mark (2003) identifies the shoulder joint as the glenohumeral joint due to the articulation of the ball ends of the humerus with the glenoid fossa on the shoulder blade, the small, basin-shaped surface that forms the outer end of the shoulder blade. Humeroscapular rhythm is an official

Fig. 10.11 Arm structure (Conable 2003, reprinted with permission). Note this is a front view of the right arm with the hand supine (palm facing upward)

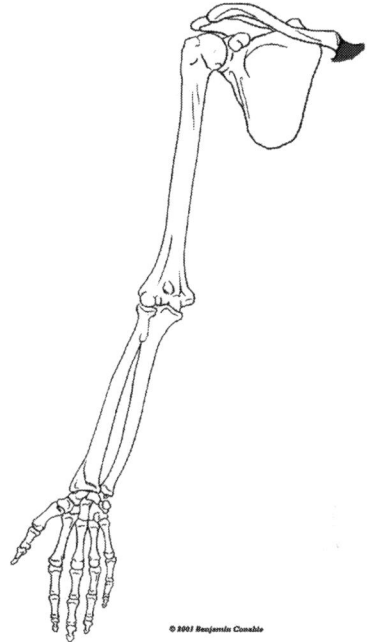

© 2003 Benjamin Conable

Fig. 10.12 Balance of collarbones and shoulder blades over ribs (Conable 2003, reprinted with permission)

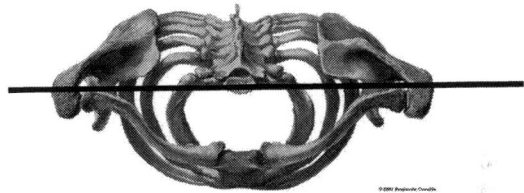

© 2003 Benjamin Conable

Figure 10.12 illustrates the balance of the arms in relation to the weight-bearing part of the spine. To find the balance of arms, the collarbones and shoulder blades should be elegantly suspended over the ribs –not pulled up or pulled back (military style), pulled down, or dropped forward into a slump. For singers it is crucial to find the balance of arms so that the structures for breathing are not impeded.

By now it should be clear that everything in your body is connected. Tension in one area will cause tension in other areas, impeding quality of movement and resultant musical sound. As you re-map the areas of your body that are inaccurately or inadequately mapped and, as a result, find core balance, you will notice how much you can also recover ease of movement, and reduce tension and distortion in your body and voice. This should also be evidence in your everyday living as well as in your musical performance, because the body in which you live is the body with which you perform.

anatomical designation used by anatomists and neurophysiologists to designate the phenomenon of correct, whole-arm movement.

10.6 Breathing

A chapter on Body Mapping for singers would not be complete without some discussion about breathing. In this chapter I will present an overview of *balanced breathing* as it is taught in Body Mapping (Conable 2000b). For more detailed discussion and explanations please refer to *What Every Singer needs to Know About the Body* (Malde et al. 2009) and *The Structures and Movement of Breathing: A primer for choirs and choruses* (Conable 2000b).

When I ask my students the question, 'how accurately and clearly can you describe the process of breathing?' their responses are invariably a mixture of half-truths, myths, distorted images, confusing descriptions, and sometimes information that is simply incorrect. What is clear is that in a room full of singers (sometimes as many as 160 which is the population of my largest choir), nobody agrees. After further discussion, however, we generally do agree that the difference between active breathing (singing) and passive breathing (sitting in class) is simply the result of how we're thinking about it (breathing) and trying to manipulate the process for singing. In other words, we try to move the breathing structures according to the mental constructs we have accumulated over time. Because much of the movement of breathing is concealed from our eyes and is experience internally, an accurate and clear understanding of the structures and movement of breathing is the most effective way to correct breathing problems and improve vocal technique, particularly in group settings such as choral ensembles. In Body Mapping we teach balanced breathing which is the way the body naturally functions in respiration. As singers our goal is to internalize this information and capitalize on it in ways that best suit our body and technique.

Balanced breathing produces a wavelike motion – sequential and coordinated – from top to bottom on inhalation and exhalation. The numerous structures utilized in breathing to the spine hold a close relationship or proximity. Once you have accurately mapped the nose and mouth, nasal pharynx, oral pharynx, laryngeal pharynx, larynx, trachea, bronchi, lungs, ribs, diaphragm, abdominal wall (front, sides, and back), inner pelvic muscles, pelvic floor, and spine, seek clarity about the way these structures function to produce tension-free breathing that is sequential and coordinated.

The breathing process is summarized in Table 10.2. Note that while the stages of the sequence are listed in numerical order, when the movement of breathing is tension-free and well-coordinated it may feel like a single movement or several simultaneous movements. Also note that the movement of the ribs and diaphragm on inhalation is coordinated simultaneously, i.e. one cannot occur without the other, but they are compromised in a body that is imbalanced. It is also crucial to accurately map the diaphragm which is the principal muscle of inspiration. The diaphragm is a thin, dome-shaped muscle dividing the thoracic cavity from the abdominal cavity. It arches up inside the ribs, changing from a highly-domed to a less-domed shape during inhalation, and returning to its highly-domed shape on exhalation (Malde et al. 2009).

Table 10.2 Balanced breathing (Malde et al. 2009)

Inhalation

 1. **Ribs** swing up and out while the
 2. **Diaphragm** contracts (descends)
 3. **Abdominal and pelvic viscera** moved outward and downward by powerful descending diaphragm
 4. **Pelvic floor** pushed downward by pressure of displaced viscera

Exhalation

 1. **Ribs** swing down and in
 2. **Diaphragm** ascends
 3. **Abdominal and pelvic viscera** flow inward and upward as diaphragm ascends and cylinder of abdominal musculature springs back inward as pressure from viscera is gradually reduced
 4. **Pelvic floor** muscles likewise spring back to neutral

Fig. 10.13 Gathering and lengthening of the spine (Conable 2003, reprinted with permission)

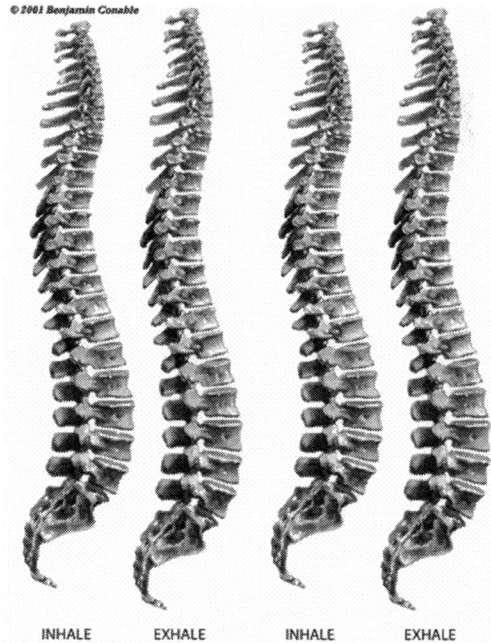

© 2001 Benjamin Conable

INHALE   EXHALE   INHALE   EXHALE

10.6.1 Gathering and Lengthening

As you work on your breathing you may also notice the gathering and lengthening movement of the spine, illustrated in Fig. 10.13. If we are balanced, on inhalation the spine gathers as the ribs swing up and out and the diaphragm contracts to its less domed position, partly as a result of our becoming bigger around the abdomen. The curves of the spine deepen, and the vertebrae move closer together, but only if we are sufficiently free. On exhalation, the spine lengthens reflexively as the ribs swing down and in, and the diaphragm returns to its highly domed position.

The lengthening phase is led by the famous up-and-over movement of the head that singing teachers have taught for hundreds of years, and which F.M. Alexander called 'forward and up' because of the slight but significant rocking of the head on the top vertebra in very free singing.

Gathering and lengthening are involuntary movements of the spine, and the lengthening is a marvelous primary source of support for the vocal sound for singers who cooperate with it. Remember, the spine is the core of all body movement – including breathing, singing, playing, and conducting. You will regain the spine's natural gathering and lengthening movement by avoiding conditions that inhibit freedom of movement, e.g. tightening your neck muscles, chronically shortening yourself, and mistakenly seeking a straight spine. To cultivate excellent breathing, there must be freedom from tension throughout the body, lively, ongoing body awareness, and an accurate body map of the structures and movement of breathing.

10.6.2   Breath Support

Broaching the subject of breath support is contentious. What do we really mean by the word 'support'? Can you clearly explain it? Do your students understand what you mean? Chances are it's a term often used but shrouded in confusion, particularly for those of you working with choral singers who have received most of their 'technique' via instructions from the podium. Explaining the concept of breath support is done more easily and effectively when singers begin with an accurate understanding of the structures and movement of breathing. Once this is clear, teaching them how to regulate the air pressure from the lungs that sets the closed vocal folds into vibration is the essence of breath support.

Singer, voice pedagogue and Licensed Andover Educator Melissa Malde (Malde et al. 2009) explains it thus:

> Assuming proper alignment, support in singing is the act of maintaining dynamic equilibrium between the expiratory breath flow, which originates with elastic recoil in the abdominals and pelvic floor and the resistance to that breath flow from the diaphragm, external intercostals, and vocal folds.

'Dynamic equilibrium' in this context is defined as opposing muscles working in tandem, i.e. one releases as the other contracts. Support may also be defined as 'the dynamic equilibrium between the muscles of expiration and inspiration.' A simpler way to express this, especially to choral singers, is: 'support is the balance between breath flow and resistance'[3] You need to choose the definition that makes the most sense to your students. What is certain is that your singers will be relieved to have a definition that makes sense to them and allows them to effectively develop their skills.

---

[3] Melissa Malde, DAM, associate professor of voice and vocal pedagogy, University of Northern Colorado, Friday, September 15, 2006, Andover Educators list-serve discussion.

10.7   Body Mapping Research Outcomes

Within the range of somatic education methods currently available, Body Mapping is the only technique predominantly focused on and developed around the movement needs of musicians. The importance of accurate biomechanical movement education in the training of musicians at all levels, and the compatibility of Body Mapping instruction in musical settings was confirmed in the qualitative research study *Body Mapping: Self-reflective Views of Student Musicians* (Buchanan 2010). The primary study participants were 12 undergraduate-level university student musicians from a range of performance areas (voice, piano, flute, violin, bassoon, organ, euphonium, and conducting) who studied Body Mapping as part of a performance-enhancement course for one semester.

   A number of important outcomes were evident for the students who successfully integrated Body Mapping techniques with their performing. First, the majority of study participants believe Body Mapping enhanced their ability to be musically expressive, citing specific examples such as dynamic control, sensitivity to phrasing, and improved emotional communication. Secondly, BMG improved understanding of specific technical elements as they applied to their performance area. These included richer tone quality, even vibrato, improved breath support, clearer articulation, and enhanced ability to handle faster tempi and louder dynamics, and improved intonation. Across all study performance areas, breathing technique was more clearly understood as a result of engagement with Body Mapping information.

   Thirdly, as performers, 9 of the 12 participants described themselves as more confident, grounded, and more focused during the intensity of performance. Fourthly, irrespective of their personal performance outcomes, all of the students in the study gained an appreciation for the importance and relevance of Body Mapping technique for musicians. This derived from their understanding of the relationship between movement and sound. Further, many of them experienced increased ease of motion in their general physical body use at some stage in the semester. The following sections briefly describe the successful student experiences with Body Mapping.

10.8   Enhancing Musical Expression

A person's ability to be musically expressive is dependent on a number of elements. These include technical skills, musical imagination and ideas, and the ability to convey the conventions of expression through phrasing, changes of dynamics, tempi, and timbre (tone color). Students who strongly believed Body Mapping had enhanced their ability for musical expression commonly described greater ease of movement that facilitated expressive outcomes (e.g. dynamics, phrasing, emotional information), and the ability to focus more easily on elements contributing to musical expression. Also notable was a greater sense of confidence with the ability to be musically expressive.

10.9   Technical Development and Training

A musician's technical development is achieved over a long period of time and is influenced by a range of elements. This has been documented in research by Ericsson et al. (1993), which places the acquisition of professional-level musical performance mastery at 8,000–10,500 h of practice. A person's age will also determine physical maturity, which has consequences for strength and coordination on an instrument (e.g. piano and cello), or their physiological development, which is crucial in the case of singers. During their lifetime, the majority of musicians will spend more hours developing and refining their technique and musicianship than actually performing in public. For students, the ability to understand the connections between technique and performance skills is paramount.

The most common element evident with student research participants (Buchanan 2010) was a better understanding of breathing. This insight was cited across a range of performance areas including singing, violin, piano, bassoon, and conducting. It underscored the students' belief in the consequences of effective breathing within performance areas where breathing was not previously considered to be of technical importance (e.g. violin, piano and conducting). Body Mapping also contributed to better coordination, flexibility, enhanced arm movement, and improved articulation.

10.10   Musical Performance Ability

The quality of a musical performance is dependent on the result of a person's technical facility, musical imagination, and emotional engagement. Whereas technical development is process, performance is product. The majority of students confirmed that Body Mapping changed their approach to performance. Throughout the Body Mapping literature, performers such as Caplan (2009), Johnson (2009), Malde et al. (2009), and Vining (2008) also describe improvements in their performing resulting from the integration of Body Mapping skills. Examples include the ability to be poised and responsive in performance, fluid movement, and confidence with the ability to engage musical ideas due to physiological ease. Data in Buchanan's (2010) study shows that student experiences often mirrored these improvements although not to the same degree of sophistication. This is due to the fact that these musicians are all experienced professionals who have spent many years integrating and refining Body Mapping with their musical technique. It is therefore reasonable to conclude that the students' experiences in this study were more modest by comparison.

Greater confidence was a frequent element of student experience; so too the ability to retain focus during the pressure of performance. There were also indications of feeling more centered or grounded, which led to more artistic freedom. A number of students also stated that Body Mapping changed the way they prepared prior to going onstage.

10.11 Self-Awareness

A gradual evolution of self-awareness in the students' experience was also experienced. It was fostered through self-reflection, a process that required students to analyze and evaluate their observations during the re-mapping process. Increased positive self-awareness was illustrated in a variety of ways, including students' journal entries, in-class interactions (e.g. questions, comments, final performance-presentations) and their *Agenda Helper* responses. This was also evident in interview comments they made regarding their technical development and practical situations e.g. rehearsals, master classes, and performances.

Cultivating self-awareness skills allowed students to make sensory connections (kinesthesia, sight, touch and sound) with cognitive information, which produced more efficient movement. At the beginning of their Body Mapping studies, students were often surprised that their physical habits required such careful and repeated attention. However, once they understood how mindfulness benefited them, they turned their attention to the challenge of cultivating awareness. A range of issues were identified by the students with regard to developing self-awareness, including: (1) finding solutions to technical challenges; (2) understanding how tension inhibited movement; (3) greater awareness of the consequences of movement patterns on symptoms of pain; and (4) understanding what they were actually doing physically in a range of musical and every-day activities.

Within the Body Mapping literature the term *inclusive awareness* is synonymous with *attention* and *mindfulness* and is defined by Conable (2000a) as 'the ability to be simultaneously self and world-perceiving'. Teachers of Body Mapping specifically advise students against concentrating because it directs attention to a single object or activity and consequently limits the broader field of awareness that is crucial for effective musical performance. Instead, students of Body Mapping are taught to *focus* attention, which results in more flexible mental functioning.

10.12 In Conclusion

Body Mapping is not a substitute for music lessons. It is an educational technique providing pedagogical tools that can be used as an adjunct to vocal instruction in studios and ensembles. Body Mapping can assist in the instructional process if one remembers that the easiest way to train free, efficient, effective, and beautiful movement is to help students to cultivate an absolutely adequate and accurate body map. Body Mapping also teaches musicians to connect their senses to movement, and cultivate inclusive attention as they systematically explore the relevant anatomical structures and physiological information of the body.

In my experience, the rate of change and an individual's capacity to manage it are major issues for students of Body Mapping. Those who address the learning process with consistent, systematic practice have yielded the greatest benefits. Through my own personal journey with Body Mapping and in the teaching of many music students, I have come to understand that the value of the Body Mapping information taught is not necessarily about results in that moment, but is best viewed as the foundation of an ongoing process. I have found that my practice is most fruitfully considered over the long term, in some cases as contributions to students' life-long journeys in self-awareness. In sum, over the course of a lifetime of artistic process, Body Mapping has the potential to transform the way performers refine technique, develop musically, and evolve as artists. This quote from Susan,[4] made after taking a course, conveys the power of Body Mapping through a student's experience (Buchanan 2010):

> I know how my body wants to function, and I can let it do that now – and everything is easier. I am a better singer. A great singer, who sings much more in tune ☺

If you are curious about the possibilities that Body Mapping presents for you (or your students) then ponder the following. Consider the ease and grace of your musical movements. Can you find balance? Are you poised when you sing? Is your body a dynamic, responsive instrument that readily serves the demands of vocal performance? Do you experience freedom in your music-making? If the answer to these questions in an unequivocal 'yes' – congratulations! You are safe from pain and injury and will know no physical limitations in your technique. However, if the answer to any of these questions is 'no', 'maybe' or 'sometimes', then consider how Body Mapping can help you enhance your musical performance ability as a singer.

References

Ackermann, B. (2010). Therapeutic management of the injured musician. In R. Sataloff, A. Brandfonbrener, & R. Lederman (Eds.), *Performing arts medicine* (3rd ed.). Naberth: Science and Medicine.

Altenmüller, E., & Jabusch, H. (2009, December 16). *How can neuroscience help performers?* Paper presented at the International Symposium on Performance Science, Auckland, New Zealand.

Beringer, E. (Ed.). (2010). *Embodied wisdom: The collected articles of Dr. Moshe Feldenkrais.* Berkeley: Somatic Resources and North Atlantic Press.

Blakeslee, S. (2006, January 10). Cells that read minds. *New York Times,* p. 10.

Blakeslee, S., & Blakeslee, M. (2007). *The body has a mind of its own: How body maps in your brain help you do (almost) everything better.* New York: Random House.

Brandfonbrener, A. (2010). Etiologies of medical problems in performing artists. In R. Sataloff, A. Brandfonbrener, & R. Lederman (Eds.), *Performing arts medicine* (3rd ed.). Naberth: Science and Medicine.

Buchanan, H. (2007). Enhancing music performance through somatic pedagogy: An introduction to Body Mapping for choral conductors. In H. Buchanan & M. Mehaffey (Eds.), *Teaching music through performance in choir. Vol. 2.* Chicago: GIA.

Buchanan, H. (2010). *Body Mapping: Self-reflective views of student musicians.* Armidale: University of New England.

---

[4] Excerpt from journal entry by Susan (identity changed) as presented in the Chapter Four case studies in *Body Mapping: Self-reflective Views of Student Musicians* by Heather J. Buchanan (2010).

Caplan, S. (2009). *Oboemotions*. Chicago: GIA.

Conable, B. (1995). *How to learn the Alexander Technique: A manual for students* (3rd ed.). Columbus: Andover Press.

Conable, B. (2000a). *What every musician needs to know about the body: The practical application of Body Mapping and the Alexander Technique to making music* (Revised ed.). Columbus: Andover Press.

Conable, B. (2000b). *The structures and movement of breathing: A primer for choirs and choruses*. Chicago: GIA.

Conable, B. (2003). *Hour one training manual*. Portland: Andover Educators.

Damasio, A. (1999). *The feeling of what happens: Body and emotion in the making of consciousness*. San Diego: Harcourt.

Damasio, A. (2003). *Looking for Spinoza: Joy, sorrow, and the feeling brain*. Orlando: Harcourt.

Ehmann, W. (1968). *Choral directing* (G. D. Weibe, Trans.). Minneapolis: Augsburg Publishing House.

Ericsson, K., Krampe, R., & Tesch-Roemer, C. (1993). The role of deliberate practice in the acquisition of expert performance. *Psychological Review, 100*, 363–406.

Franklin, E. (2002). *Relax your neck, liberate your shoulders: The ultimate exercise program for tension relief*. Hightstown: Elysian Editions.

Gilmore, R. (2005). *What every dancer needs to know about the body: A workbook of Body Mapping and the Alexander Technique*. Portland: Andover Press.

Gorman, D. (2013). *The body moveable. Vol. 2* (6th ed.). Guelph: Ampersand Press.

Harscher, J. (2010). Body Mapping for better playing. *Berklee Today*, pp. 31–33.

Johnson, J. (2009). *What every violinist needs to know about the body*. Chicago: GIA.

Lehmann, A., & Davidson, J. (2002). Taking an acquired skills perspective on music performance. In R. Colwell & C. Richardson (Eds.), *The new handbook of research on music teaching and learning* (2nd ed., pp. 542–560). New York: Oxford University Press.

Likar, A. (2003). *Amy Likar – Body Mapping*. http://www.amylikar.com/bodymap.html. Accessed 24 Aug 2003.

Malde, M., Allen, M., & Zeller, K. (2009). *What every singer needs to know about the body*. San Diego: Plural.

Mark, T. (2003). *What every pianist needs to know about the body*. Chicago: GIA.

Marxhausen, P. (2003). *Musicians and injuries*. http://eeshop.unl.edu/music.html. Accessed 24 Aug 2005.

Mills, K. (2003). Cellist strikes chord against pain: personal plight spurs research. *Telegram and Gazette*, C5. Retrieved 17 July 2003.

Nelson, S., & Blades-Zeller, E. (2002). *Singing with your whole self: The Feldenkrais Method and voice*. Lanham: Scarecrow Press, Inc.

Nesmith, D. (1999). What every musician needs to know about the body. *The Horn Call, 29*(4), 71–74.

Nesmith, D. (2001). How Body Mapping and the Alexander Technique will improve your playing. *International Musician, 99*(6), 11–12.

Nesmith, D. (2011). *Constructive rest: The audio guide series*. Columbus: SmartPoise Productions, LLC.

Nichols, R. (2004). *The scientific basis of Body Mapping*. http://www.bodymap.org/main?p=213. Accessed 9 June 2009.

Pearson, L. (2006). *Body Mapping for flutists: What every flute teacher needs to know about the body*. Chicago: GIA.

Pellegrino, G. (2001). Vision and touch in parietal area 5. *Trends in Cognitive Sciences, 5*(2), 50.

Pellegrino, G., Facliga, L., Fogassi, L., Gallse, V., & Rizzolatti, G. (1992). Understanding motor events: A neurophysiological study. *Experimental Brain Research, 91*(5), 176–180.

Sataloff, R., Brandfonbrener, A., & Lederman, R. (Eds.). (2010). *Performing arts medicine*. Naberth: Science and Medicine.

Schwartz, J., & Begley, S. (2002). *The mind and the brain: Neuroplasticity and the power of mental force*. New York: HarperCollins.

Shur, F. (2000). *Fight, flight, freeze*. http://www.growthinmotion.org. Accessed 24 Apr 2004.

Smith, B., & Sataloff, R. (2000). *Choral pedagogy*. San Diego: Singular Publishing Group.

Split Martini. (n.d.). Website. http://spiltmartini.com/2010/09/07/ms-bike-tour/. Accessed 18 Jan 2014.

Sylwester, R. (2002). *Mirror neurons*. http://www.brainconnection.com/content181_1. Accessed 9 June 2009.

Vineyard, M. (2007). *How you stand, how you move, how you live: Learning the Alexander Technique to explore your mind-body connection and achieve self-mastery*. Cambridge, MA: Da Capo Press.

Vining, D. (2008). *What every trombonist needs to know about the body*. Denton: Kagarice Brass Editions.

Chapter 11
Vocal Pedagogy and the Feldenkrais Method

Stephen J. Grant

Abstract This chapter explores how a vocal pedagogy based on the development of kinaesthetic awareness and movement can enhance the learning experience of vocal students. It will examine how an approach to vocal pedagogy based on the Feldenkrais Method can lead to learning that is more deeply understood in a physical or embodied sense. In doing this, it will look at how the method is taught and how it can form a vital part of an integrated educational approach. It will also attempt to clarify the thinking behind the method and to see how it may offer insights into questions currently being asked about motor learning and its implications for vocal teaching and learning.

The chapter will consider how this method may be a useful tool in support of the many different styles of vocal teaching that currently exist, from the most intuitive and traditional to the most scientifically informed. This may be due to the sensory specific nature of the learning undertaken and the context in which it can be understood. The Feldenkrais Method can be used to link traditional and scientific vocal pedagogical approaches to the sensory experiences of singers learning their craft. A basic question the Feldenkrais Method poses is: 'How do I bring my intentions into action'? This question is essential in understanding the perspective that the method provides, and also goes a long way towards answering a question posed by Harding (2007), which asks about how we make the link between vocal technical concepts and physical coordination. Or, more specifically, can we help vocal students to place instructions received in the vocal studio into a sensory context that is meaningful for them?.

Keywords Vocal Pedagogy • Feldenkrais Method • Posture • Embodied Learning • Somatic Learning • Vocal Health • Motor Learning • Attention

---

S.J. Grant (✉)
Vocal Department, Melbourne Conservatorium of Music,
University of Melbourne, Melbourne, VIC, Australia
e-mail: sjgrant@unimelb.edu.au

S.D. Harrison and J. O'Bryan (eds.), *Teaching Singing in the 21st Century*,
Landscapes: the Arts, Aesthetics, and Education 14, DOI 10.1007/978-94-017-8851-9_11,
© Springer Science+Business Media Dordrecht 2014

11.1 Feldenkrais – A Brief Introduction

The Feldenkrais Method is a learning approach that is used in a wide range of contexts, perhaps the best known of these in the area of rehabilitation and pain management. Moshe Feldenkrais (1904–1984), the method's founder, devoted much time to working with people in an effort to help them re-gain or improve functions that may have been compromised due to congenital conditions, or after stroke or accident. Of those trained in the method worldwide, a significant number are physiotherapists – their work has helped to bring the method more fully into the medical arena. Feldenkrais, however, also worked extensively with performers and artists and saw his work as being a way of helping them to establish more efficient postural and movement patterns and of finding ways to further realise their potential. The use of this method in the area of performance education is established, even though in the musical domain it is still less known than the Alexander Technique, for the founder F.M. Alexander (1869–1955) was part of an earlier generation. In spite of the breadth of applications that may be applied with the Feldenkrais Method, it is often thought of in the context of postural improvement.

The Feldenkrais Method is delivered in two ways: Functional Integration, which is hands-on work with individuals and *Awareness Through Movement*, which are classes using verbally guided movement, usually taught to groups. In a typical Feldenkrais *Awareness Through Movement (ATM)* lesson, a series of movements is explored, following functional themes. Care is taken in the lesson to establish the state of the nervous system and musculature before, during and after the movements. An important element is the shifting of attention between the performance of the movements, the quality of their execution and the sensory information that accompanies them. The intended result may include a change in the state of the musculature, a shift in kinaesthetic perception; changes in balance, breathing and posture often follow. The use of the movements and muscles subject to voluntary control are utilised in this method in a learning context that also seeks to develop a more refined kinesthetic sense, thereby revealing unconscious musculoskeletal patterns that are usually unconscious and that may inhibit free and healthy functioning. A difference between this method and others that aim to direct consciously the 'correct' movement, is its reliance on the self-organising abilities of the nervous system and its ability to respond spontaneously to the availability of more functional and more differentiated movement patterns. It does not depend on a particular technical approach, but rather emphasises the learning itself: 'The accent is on the learning process, rather than on the teaching technique' (Feldenkrais 1981). This process can be applied in many areas of human endeavour and improvement. Indeed, there are a number of strategies used in the Feldenkrais Method that seem particularly well suited to enhance the teaching and learning of music instrumental teaching, especially vocal teaching, where the student cannot see the vocal mechanism in operation and so must be taught through attention to sensation, overall physical awareness and acoustical feedback.

11.2 Posture

In the mainstream vocal pedagogical literature on classical singing there is general agreement about the elements that make up a properly produced sound – freedom of function (Miller 1986), a resonant, well-supported tone, rich in timbre and able to convey a wide range of human emotion with linguistic clarity. Posture is seen as having a key influence on vocal freedom, and many of the oft-quoted books on vocal production and vocal training have sections devoted to it (Bunch 1982, Doscher 1994, Brown 1996, Chapman 2006, Miller 2003). Chapman includes a thorough description of the influence of posture on sound, and elucidates in considerable detail the many functional relationships that exist between the body and the voice. However, even with the most basic approaches to posture, as in Richard Miller's well-known concept of 'noble posture' (1986), there is an acknowledgement of the importance of posture to singing.

Research on the improvement of posture and the musculoskeletal system has begun to look more closely at how these elements impact the voice. Rubin, Mathieson et al. (2004) explore the postural mechanics affecting the voice and advocates therapeutic solutions to achieve optimal goals, as do Wilson Arboleda and Frederick (2008), who include suggestions for targeted exercise programs. Shewell's 'Voice Skills Approach' has a range of solutions for the vocal studio (2008).

Teachers of singing are often aware of the postural problems or challenges that beset singing students. A quick fix approach may be to correct what can be observed in the moment, in the hopes of establishing something 'better' or more functional. But a difficulty frequently encountered is the obstacle that students may very well be unaware of what is influencing their postural organisation.

Taking the idea of posture more broadly, one might arrive at the idea of 'self-use', a term coined by F.M. Alexander in his book, *The Use of the Self* (1932). This technique began with Alexander investigating and ultimately improving difficulties he was having with his own voice. The Alexander Technique (AT) has been written about as the basis for both teaching and learning about instrumental playing (de Alcantara 1997) and singing (Heirich 2005). In writing on the applications of the Alexander Technique to music performance and on research done in this area, Elizabeth Valentine has contributed to a text that examines other aspects of mental and physical fitness for musicians (2004). Both Feldenkrais and Alexander saw postural improvement as a by-product, albeit an important one, of their work on neuromuscular re-education.

Coming after the work begun by Alexander, but working in another direction, was Feldenkrais, whose first publication was entitled *Body and Mature Behaviour* (Feldenkrais 1949). His focus is to use movement to gain kinaesthetic awareness and to improve human functioning.

Differing from the conscious re-directing advocated by Alexander, Feldenkrais uses the voluntary muscular system as a tool for developing a more refined kinaesthetic sense and sees any attempt to control posture consciously as *inappropriate*: 'This means that in the upright position there must be no muscular effort deriving from voluntary control, regardless of whether this effort is known and deliberate or concealed from the consciousness by habit' (Feldenkrais 1972). Feldenkrais begins immediately to re-train the kinaesthetic sense through movement, to gain awareness of what one has been unconsciously doing. Changes that come as a result of work within the method are then more clearly felt and more easily and spontaneously adopted.

11.3   Motor Learning and Attention

With the broad aim of finding ways to enhance the effectiveness of vocal pedagogy, it is worth taking a moment to refer to other recent writings in this area. In her chapter *Motor Skills and Attentional Focus in Studio Voice Teaching*, Adele Nisbet traces some of the current thought on the learning of motor skills, including a description of some things that can influence, positively or negatively, learning in the voice studio (2010). She cites a number of authors whose work on motor learning helps to clarify how some types of explicit knowledge (for instance, information detailing the functioning of the singing voice) may not actually be the most efficacious way of directing learning for singers. Drawing on the work of Gabriele Wulf, Nisbet writes of the possible need to shift the attentional focus away from the biomechanics of singing and to focus the attention elsewhere (Nisbet 2010). Perhaps it is true that a narrow focus on aspects of vocal performance that ultimately need to function without conscious interference can get in the way, but that is dependent on the way the focus or attention is directed and the pedagogical intention behind it. In a Feldenkrais lesson, one's attention may very well be drawn into observing some small aspect of movement, but that is only a step in the process of shifting attention to larger and more complete patterns of movement. Since the intention is to develop ever more functional patterns of movement, the small focus needs to find its way back into the whole. Nisbet also cites the work of Verdolini, who examines motor learning issues in the context of singing training. This author describes our reliance on 'implicit memory', which is critical to the kind of learning required for singing, and is, according to Verdolini (2000), directed by *perceptual* processes. Her idea of attending 'in the moment' has strong similarities to the kind of sensory awareness that is typical of a Feldenkrais ATM lesson.

In *Mindfulness*, psychologist Ellen Langer writes in a chapter about 'sideways learning,' which is also striking in its similarity to the process explored in a Feldenkrais lesson and also echoes elements of Verdolini's 5-step 'skill acquisition package.' Langer writes:

> the concept of mindfulness revolves around certain psychological states that are really different versions of the same thing: (1) openness to novelty; (2) alertness to distinction; (3) sensitivity to different contexts; (4) implicit, if not explicit, awareness of multiple perspectives; and (5) orientation in the present. (Langer 1997, 23)

It is important to be aware of the precise use of language that, particularly in the case of Verdolini, is chosen to describe different states. Verdolini makes a clear distinction between awareness (conscious thought about things) and attention (perception of sensory information). Feldenkrais uses these same terms, but with different meanings. His broader definition of awareness would include Verdolini's idea of attention, although it would encompasses other cognitive processes as well. Feldenkrais' interest in this instance, though, was not to set up the distinct categories that might be required for a formal experiment, but to shed light on and help improve the unified cognitive experience that makes up human action. He does, however (as will be discussed below), draw distinctions between 'learning' and 'performance' that can reveal some key points in the discussion.

11.4 Perception as a Guide to Action

When trying to understand the challenges people face when engaging in learning a set of new movements or actions, as singing students are often asked to do, Feldenkrais made the point that undifferentiated movement is linked to undifferentiated perception (Goldfarb 1994). This is something that can be recognised in the teaching studio, for example, as when a student is asked to sense their breathing, or to notice tongue or jaw tension. Their efforts often show a lack of awareness of a behaviour that may be very obvious to a trained observer/listener, and is an indication that habitual patterns of posture or movement generally lie below conscious awareness. It is in this context then that work with something like the Feldenkrais Method, which works towards making finer distinctions in movement *and* perception, can offer guidance. A prominent American Feldenkrais trainer, Lawrence Goldfarb, writes: 'A lesson is not about learning a particular movement; rather a lesson is about learning the distinctions necessary to perform a movement' (1994). The exploratory nature of the lessons allows the students to try out many new combinations of movements and to see which ones work the best. In order for this to happen, it is important for the student to sense what they are already doing – from there, further explorations can lead more easily to new perceptions.

11.5 Whole vs. Part Learning

In participating in this type of process, there is interplay between complex movements and their components. This could be seen to be analogous to what might normally occur in a singing lesson, with a focus on something quite specific, such as the movement or position of the soft palate. While one might have to address the specifics of such a movement, how it might feel, and how it might affect timbre, one would naturally relate it back to the bigger picture, in this case, the sung sound. This moving back and forth between the part and the whole is a constant feature of Feldenkrais lessons. As a strategy, it can help students to develop an understanding of this learning process. The 'part' can be an object of attention that is observed 'in the moment', but it an also be moved consciously into the background as a feature of the integrated whole.

Christine Bergan has written about a number of motor learning strategies and how they might be applied in the voice studio (2010). In a wide-ranging article, she includes a discussion on 'whole vs. part' learning. She suggests that teaching is an holistic task, and indeed a 'whole' approach might be more appropriate, at least for novice learners. Most singing teachers would no doubt use both small and large focus approaches in their teaching, but what appears critical is to be able to contextualize the detail back into the larger whole in a way that allows the student to retrace the steps for themselves – it is a process of integrating the learning back into the whole act of singing. If students can be led through such a process of moving attention back and forth (as applied in an ATM lesson), then perhaps there should be less hesitation in providing details that can shed light on what constitutes the proper functioning of the vocal mechanism. This also grounds the learning in the experience of the singer and helps them to find a safe and a more self-directed learning style.

If the Feldenkrais Method brings with it a particular type of learning process, it is also important to distinguish that process from our daily actions. It is a great thing if the new learning results in better posture or a freer sung sound, but the goal is not to maintain a constant consciousness of these things, nor to exercise conscious control (see Feldenkrais 1972). To further elaborate what takes place in the lessons, Goldfarb (1994) clearly makes the distinction between the two domains of learning and performance.

11.6   Exploratory vs. Performative Movement

Feldenkrais ATM lessons make use of this distinction, that movements carried out in the learning context can be exploratory in nature, without necessarily striving towards a particular goal. In a typical ATM lesson, a series of movements are performed that might be components of larger functional movement patterns, and the focus may be directed towards other aspects of movement that reflect healthy functioning, such as the breath becoming deeper or easier. The quality of attention given to the movements allows participants to notice habitual holding, or a lack of fluidity, and they are encouraged to slow the movements down and to stay well within a range of comfort. It is in fact this easy quality of the movements, coupled with a sense of how one's own movements are organized, may help when linking this process to other activities. A singer might then approach a new aspect of vocal technique with this same level of curiosity and investigation, paying attention to how something is being done, rather than launching straight into an attempt to do the 'correct' thing.

This is a key point, well worth emphasizing. There is not only an intention in ATM to teach a new or 'better' movement or action, but to train the student's kinaesthetic system to recognize what it is already doing and to move from that into the new pattern. It is not that we don't want our students to find the 'right' movement, but, it is often the case that students have no idea how they do what they are already doing, so simply demonstrating, or instructing them to do it a particular way, without helping them to sense what they are already doing, can become quite 'hit or miss'. It can also lead to feelings of inferiority, should they not be able to 'get it' (Goldfarb 1990).

The experiencing of such a process over time may lead to the ability to shift attention back and forth between a monitoring mode, wherein one is aware of aspects of one's performance, and a more performative phase, where a conscious monitoring takes a back seat to the performance itself. It may be that this process of developing awareness through movement could offer further perspectives on models of skill acquisition, described as having cognitive, associative and autonomous stages (Fitts and Posner 1967). While the movements performed in a Feldenkrais ATM lesson may correspond principally to the first two stages, the intention is also to develop skill in kinaesthetic awareness and switching levels of attention, which would allow someone whose skill level had progressed to the autonomous stage to have easier access to the associative or monitoring level, without interrupting the flow of performance.

11.7   Reversibility

This is a term used in a quite specific way within the Feldenkrais Method and is applied consistently in many ATM lessons. An easily visualized movement such as reaching forward with the arm may be the first movement in a series – as one explores the movement, attention will also be drawn to the return of the movement to its starting point, or its un-doing, in a sense. As movements become more subtle and differentiated throughout a lesson, accompanied by the gradual lessening of muscle tone that often happens an ATM, the idea of reversing the movement may even apply to the very start of the movement. By repeated trials of starting the movement and returning one senses how the voluntary muscles contract and then relax. This process can then be used to sense how we initiate even more complex movements, as in the preparation for and onset of singing. It is quite common that the postural and movement difficulties that singers show are already present at the start of sound. If one can get students to go carefully into and out of these patterns it can reveal to them how they enact what may be quite dysfunctional movements – as in shortening the back of the neck, or tucking in the chin at the onset of sound.

11.8   Embodied Learning

How often does one find that a student has been brought to a new level of performance only to find the next week or the next month that the learning has not been retained? Aside from instances where lack of practice is an issue, this seems a common enough occurrence. It may even account for what appears to be the 'magic' that is created in some voice studios. Students come away from a lesson feeling fantastic but struggle to retain the new information even a few hours or days afterwards. Part of the integrative work done in a Feldenkrais lesson, often coming at the end of a session or lesson when new patterns have emerged, is to get participants to go back and re-create the old pattern, consciously moving from it to the new one. When the current author revisits his own vocal training, there was no attempt on the part of any teacher to guide this sort of process. If and when he happened upon the 'right' pattern or sound, that was 'it'. The new sound was celebrated for what it was, but there was no attempt to re-create the old pattern or to compare the feeling of it to the new one. This conscious re-tracing of the steps leading in and out of a new pattern is a further step towards learning that is more clearly embodied.

In vocal training, breathing is one of the areas of teaching where the literature shows a wide range of differing opinions, but the topic always takes a central place in writings on the subject. In the teaching studio, students are often puzzled about what is it they are supposed to do with regard to breathing, and few of them seem aware of what they are actually doing. A number of different vocal pedagogical approaches, including ones that emphasise the abdominal muscles (either in or out), the ribs (ideas of rib retention or release) or the attempt at conscious control of the diaphragm, are seen as critical to the production of an ideal sound (Miller 1996). The evaluation of which of these techniques is functionally sound lies outside the scope of this chapter, but attention to the details of breathing and how it is affected both by observation and by other physical activities is a central concern of the Feldenkrais Method. As the majority of the muscles utilised for breathing also serve postural functions, improvements in postural organisation often have a liberating affect on breathing. A challenge faced by teachers of singing is to convey in an accurate and safe way to students how their breathing should proceed (Doscher 1994). This becomes not only a question of procedure, however, but is something that demands sensitivity or awareness on the part of the student. Neither posture nor breathing typically forms part of most persons' everyday awareness and so it may be seen that involvement in a process that develops, among other things, kinaesthetic awareness, might be seen to provide advantages that can enhance deeper learning. Feldenkrais devised a number of lessons that focused on specific aspects of breathing. It could also be said that most Feldenkrais lessons draw attention to the participant's state of breathing, to the connection between movement and breath, and seek to give a more complete kinaesthetic image of the movements, which take place as a result of either exhalation or inhalation. If a greater awareness of breath follows, and if the ability to observe one's own breathing patterns become more conscious, then it could prove a useful tool in the vocal studio.

A brief example of how the sensory awareness developed with the Feldenkrais Method demonstrates how both teachers and students can make sense of breath control. One example of a Feldenkrais ATM lesson explores, through many variations, the movements of the abdomen and chest and their changing volumes, in a variety of body orientations (supine, prone, side-lying, kneeling, etc.). In this lesson, one experiences the different effects gravity has on the way we organize such movements and how, through the course of the lesson, one comes to make ever finer sensory distinctions. One of the clear consequences of such a movement exploration is to sense quite clearly the relationships that exist within the body – for instance, what pushing the belly out does to the volume of the chest, decreasing its volume and increasing the tendency to close the glottis. Or, conversely, how a drawing in of the abdomen also affects the volume of the ribcage. In an ATM lesson none of these movements are prescribed as 'the way one should breathe', but they go a long way towards supporting instructions that may follow in the vocal studio, as well as giving students a clearer sense of what is taking place.

Following this description of select elements of the Feldenkrais Method and how the thinking behind it might be added to or applied in the vocal studio (and to vocal pedagogy in general), an instance of its specific application in an Australian tertiary institution will be now be mentioned.

11.9   Feldenkrais in the Curriculum

An integrated program was initiated in 2004 at the Victorian College of the Arts in Melbourne, Australia (now part of the Melbourne Conservatorium of Music, University of Melbourne). Classical singing students, as part of their undergraduate degree, received weekly Feldenkrais ATM lessons, alongside classes in applied vocal anatomy and, of course, voice lessons and performance workshops. This meant that as students learned about the functioning and care of their instruments, they also had the opportunity to embed the learning in the structured sensory context of a Feldenkrais class. The many functional relationships that exist between the voice and its support mechanism were explored in these movement classes. Students were then given the opportunity to experience how these new insights could be integrated into a performance workshop situation. In some cases, movement sequences that were explored in ATM lessons would be revisited in the performance workshops, with the result that the student performing, as well as those observing and listening, could experience firsthand the changes in sound brought about by these postural adjustments. This encouraged the students to further experiment with the lessons on their own and to begin to embody the changes more fully. As Feldenkrais argued, the focus of experience in postural work has to be on the process itself. It was this process of experimentation and discovery that helped students to make both clearer distinctions for themselves and to get an immediate sense of the embodied nature of this style of learning. But, not all of the lessons were equally popular. As each student's postural organization is unique, some lessons would create significant benefits for some students and negligible ones for others, owing to varying degrees of engagement, motivation to participate and understanding, as well as the degree of challenge in the lesson.

It is useful to note that the reason that movements in a Feldenkrais ATM lesson are verbally guided and not demonstrated is to be able help students to develop a self-generated learning process and a refined sensory discrimination, with themselves at the centre. The developments or changes that may take place are in relation to their own development, not measured against an ideal which is external to them. So, although an ATM lesson may have very clear instructions on how to proceed, there is, within that structure, no 'right' or 'wrong' movement.

Many students, in writing their journals for this course, wrote of how judgmental they were of their own singing, and how they valued the suspension of their critical faculties as they were doing these lessons. Some of them commented on how they could then apply this to their singing practice, allowing themselves to be more exploratory and open-minded in their approach. One student wrote: 'Instead of making criticisms and judgments about aspects of my technique that are not as developed as others', it is far more useful to observe why this may be happening' (data collected by the author).

There is no suggestion that, as singing teachers, judgments on how our students sing are unimportant, but it is worth considering that technical judgments can be based on evaluations that have more to do with the quality of the way sounds are produced, with more or less efficiency or effort, for example, than on a simple good/ bad, right/wrong bi-polar assessments. These tend to only encourage or discourage the student to see themselves and their technique in more polarized ways. By making of fine sensory distinctions through a safe, non-judgmental process, students strengthen their own individual nature as self-directed learners, even as they gain ease in movement and a reduced sense of effort.

11.10   A Way Forward

There is a burgeoning literature on which today's vocal teacher can draw. This includes the valuable research that is being conducted in the areas of motor learning, neuroscience, education and other related fields. It is vital, though, to find ways of working with students that encourage a more self-directed learning process and enhance the organic abilities that we possess as learners. The kinaesthetic sensory dimension is only one in our impressive repertoire of inherent capabilities, but it can be a very valuable one to develop. For that to occur, we need methods that demonstrate an understanding of the way we learn, and can facilitate, in a safe and enjoyable way, the further expansion of our capacities. As learners and teachers of singing, we can utilize the Feldenkrais Method, either directly, by taking part in classes or hands on work, or, we can also take from it some of the principles that are consistent with current thinking in motor learning and educational research. Little has been published to date connecting the Feldenkrais Method to singing. The most important written contribution to date is *Singing with your whole self: the Feldenkrais Method and voice*, which takes functional themes relating to voice and gives a brief series of Feldenkrais ATM lessons (Nelson and Blades-Zeller 2002). The authors look at some of the questions posed above, in particular the need to take instructions from vocal studio, which have often gone through a process leading from observation to prescriptive advice, and put them into a sensory context.

The Feldenkrais Method provides a methodology that is highly compatible with the teaching of singing, supporting a range of vocal pedagogical approaches. Its style of self-directed learning empowers singers to come to trust their own sensory feedback. This has implications for the fostering of pedagogies that enhance wellbeing, healthy vocal function and the further development of metacognitive skills.

References

Alexander, F. M. (1932). *The use of the self, its conscious direction in relation to diagnosis, functioning and the control of reaction.* New York: E.P. Hutton & Co.

Bergan, C. (2010). Motor learning principles and voice pedagogy: Theory and practice. *Journal of Singing, 66*(4), 457–468.

Brown, O. (1996). *Discover your voice: How to develop healthy voice habits.* San Diego: Singular Publishing Group.

Bunch, M. (1982). *Dynamics of the singing voice.* Wien: Springer.

Chapman, J. L. (2006). *Singing and teaching singing: A holistic approach to classical voice.* San Diego: Plural.

de Alcantara, P. (1997). *Indirect procedures: A musician's guide to the Alexander technique.* Oxford: Clarendon Press.

Doscher, B. M. (1994). *The functional unity of the singing voice.* Metuchen: Scarecrow Press.

Feldenkrais, M. (1949). *Body and mature behaviour: A study of anxiety, sex, gravitation & learning.* New York: International Universities Press.

Feldenkrais, M. (1972). *Awareness through movement: Health exercises for personal growth.* New York: Harper & Row.

Feldenkrais, M. (1981). *The elusive obvious.* Cupertino: Meta Publications.

Fitts, P. M., & Posner, M. I. (1967). *Human performance.* Belmont: Brooks Cole.

Goldfarb, L. W. (1990). *Articulating changes.* Retrieved from ProQuest Dissertations and Theses database (Document ID: 747624991).

Goldfarb, L. W. (1994). *Understanding standing.* Retrieved from ProQuest Dissertations and Theses database (Document ID: 742767421).

Harding, L. (2007). Voice science and vocal art, part one: In search of common ground. *Journal of Singing, 64*(2), 141–150.

Heirich, J. R. (2005). *Voice and the Alexander technique: Active explorations for speaking and singing.* Berkeley: Mornum Time Press.

Langer, E. J. (1997). *The power of mindful learning.* Reading: Addison-Wesley.

Miller, R. (1986). *The structure of singing: System and art in vocal technique.* New York: Schirmer Books.

Miller, R. (1996). *On the art of singing.* New York: Oxford University Press.

Miller, R. (2003). *Solutions for singers: Tools for every performer and teacher.* Oxford: Oxford University Press.

Nelson, S. H., & Blades-Zeller, E. (2002). *Singing with your whole self: The Feldenkrais method and voice.* Lanham: Scarecrow Press.

Nisbet, A. (2010). You want me to think about what?! A discussion about motor skills and the role of attentional focus in studio voice teaching. In S. Harrison (Ed.), *Perspectives on teaching singing: Australian vocal pedagogues sing their stories* (pp. 101–121). Bowen Hills: Australian Academic Press.

Rubin, J. S., Mathieson, L., et al. (2004). Posture and voice. *Journal of Singing, 60,* 271–275.

Shewell, C. (2008). *Voice work: Art and science in changing voices.* Chichester: Wiley.

Valentine, E. R. (2004). Alexander technique. In A. Williamon (Ed.), *Musical excellence: Strategies and techniques to enhance performance* (pp. 179–195). Oxford: Oxford University Press.

Verdolini, K. (2000). Principles of skill acquisition applied to voice training. In M. Hampton & B. Acker (Eds.), *The vocal vision: Views on voice by 24 leading teachers, coaches and director* (pp. 65–80). New York: Applause Books.

Wilson Arboleda, B. M., & Frederick, A. L. (2008). Considerations for maintenance of postural alignment for voice production. *Journal of Voice, 22,* 90–99.

Chapter 12
Perception, Evaluation and Communication of Singing Voices

Helen F. Mitchell

Abstract Listening to singing voices is an everyday occurrence for performers and pedagogues, and indeed for every music listener. Expert listeners make rapid judgments about singers' vocal quality and performance ability based on a single performance and use their perception of the overall quality to determine the vocal and technical processes involved in the production of the sound. In the singing studio, pedagogues monitor incremental and subtle changes in vocal quality throughout the training process and this enables them to tailor an appropriate technical and aesthetic program to each student.

Listeners' expertise is vital to music performance research and perceptual studies of the singing voice have drawn on expert listeners' aural acuity to corroborate and provide a framework for empirical studies of the singing voice and are vital to their ongoing integrity. Listeners possess tacit knowledge about performers' sound, yet little is known about how listeners process sensory information from a singer to conceptualise, recognise and verbalise the sound they hear. In describing sound, listeners focus on the more easily articulated technical and visual aspects of the performance, which are more easily articulated and generally avoid describing the overall sound of the singer.

This chapter will trace the development of three perceptual singing projects which examine the way in which listeners hear singing voices and the means by which they communicate them. It will reflect on recent empirical studies which aim to harness this expertise to evaluate singing and understand the limitations of language to communicate sound. Finally, it will propose future directions for perceptual studies to ensure they are relevant, accessible and applicable to singing pedagogy.

Keywords Music performance • Music perception • Singing voice • Singing training • Verbalisation • Verbal overshadowing

H.F. Mitchell (✉)
Sydney Conservatorium of Music, University of Sydney, Sydney, NSW, Australia
e-mail: helen.mitchell@sydney.edu.au

S.D. Harrison and J. O'Bryan (eds.), *Teaching Singing in the 21st Century*,
Landscapes: the Arts, Aesthetics, and Education 14, DOI 10.1007/978-94-017-8851-9_12,
© Springer Science+Business Media Dordrecht 2014

12.1 Experts' Perceptions of Singing Voices

Listeners' perception of sound quality is central to music performance research. We take for granted the phenomenal processing skills at work when we hear a singing voice, in performance, in assessment and in training. Experts are regularly charged with assessing singers' performances, both in comparison to other singers' performances (norm based, e.g. ranking in competitions) and against predetermined criteria (criterion based, e.g. scoring in examinations) (McPherson and Schubert 2004). In reality, examiners have reported that they form a holistic impression of the performance before returning to complete criteria, rather than complete criteria to form their overall judgment of the performance (Stanley et al. 2002). Listeners instinctively make an immediate judgment about each performer's sound quality and performance ability by automatically combining the available perceptual cues to determine the vocal and technical processes involved in the production of the sound (Ward 2004). While expert listeners make global assessments of vocal quality they are not always required to verbalise or justify the reasons that motivated their ratings. Indeed, they often avoid describing the overall sound when expressing the reasons for their judgments and focus on the more easily articulated technical and performance components by the performer and avoid describing the overall sound (Davidson and Coimbra 2001).

Perceptual studies in singing enable singing voice researchers to harness this instinctive processing to both validate and contextualise acoustic studies of the singing voice and to provide the means by which to report these findings in real world terms. Listeners' perceptions of voices are also fascinating in their own right, and it is essential we better understand the way in which listeners process singing sound. This chapter will report and consider a number of perceptual singing studies and how they utilise listeners' intuitive skill to assess and describe singing voices in training. It will also consider more recent work in singing voice, which aims to discover more about how listeners' hear individual singers, and how they recognise and describe individual voices.

12.2 Terminology for the Perception of Vocal Qualities

Two key perceptual studies inspired my interest in perceptual evaluation of singing voices as they sought to understand expert listeners' judgments of overall vocal quality and determine what elements or vocal qualities influence their judgments. Wapnick and Ekholm (1997) interviewed singing pedagogues to identify and generate discreet criteria on which to assess singing voices. Their interviews established 12 generally accepted perceptual criteria for the assessment of voice quality in classical singing (appropriate vibrato, color/warmth, diction, dynamic range, efficient breath management, evenness of registration, flexibility, freedom throughout vocal range, intensity, intonation accuracy, legato line, and resonance/ring). Pedagogues then listened to vocal performances and were asked to rate them on each of the 12 criteria, and for overall quality. The most reliable scores among judges were overall score and intonation accuracy and it was generally difficult to reach consensus in pedagogues' interpretations of individual criteria in the singing samples. Ekholm et al. (1998) simplified the spread of criteria to four (to resonance/ring, clarity/focus, colour/warmth and appropriate vibrato) as well as the overall quality of the voice, and matched these to possible measurable acoustic features. In fact, prompting listeners to isolate particular features of vocal quality showed once again, that individual criteria were strongly correlated with listeners' judgments of overall quality, rendering individual assessments on each criterion at least partially redundant. Categorising individual vocal qualities could not conclusively explain which, if any, key factors which motivated listeners' decisions in judging overall quality. It would appear that listeners' primary evaluation is indeed based on their appraisal of the whole performance, rather than the sum of its parts.

These results prompted further empirical perceptual studies, which sought to elicit more detailed, and perhaps less structured, information in order to achieve consensus and then to codify and demystify ratings of overall vocal quality. The first explored the way in which a perceptual study could assist our understanding of vocal technique, training and improvement.

12.3 Attributing Sound Transformation to Vocal Instruction

In the singing studio, pedagogues observe the incremental and subtle changes in vocal quality throughout the training process and this enables them to tailor an appropriate technical and aesthetic program to each student (Ward 2004). Singing pedagogy texts play an important role in the communication of singing techniques, but the lack of 'sound' transmission means it is not always clear how specific techniques are interpreted and heard in the act of singing, and whether all singing pedagogues construe them in the same way. In assessment, it is apparent that listeners do hear technical flaws as they prescribe technical solutions in auditions and examinations (Davidson and Coimbra 2001; Stanley et al 2002). It is therefore vital to draw on pedagogues' tacit knowledge about vocal quality through the terminology used in the modern singing studio and objectively verify listeners' perceptions of vocal instructions.

My PhD research defined and examined a major pedagogic singing technique, the 'open throat' in the twenty-first century singing studio. In the existing singing literature, open throat is recognised as a complex process, which is both a pedagogical instruction and a perceived sensation or action that results in a specific sound quality. Renowned pedagogue Richard Miller commented that 'it would be hard to find a voice teacher who recommended singing with a closed throat' (Miller 1996, 58) and leading voice scientist William Vennard suggested it was the 'condition agreed upon by most voice teachers as desirable for resonance' (Vennard 1968, 252). The first step was to investigate its use and prevalence in the twenty-first century singing studio. In an interview study, current singing pedagogues spontaneously identified open throat as an important and widely used pedagogic technique, and critical to achieving a good classical vocal quality (Mitchell et al. 2003). These pedagogues used instructions like 'laugh', 'cry/sob' or 'pre-yawn' to achieve an open throat, and reported that it elicits a sound quality which is perceived as 'balanced and coordinated', 'free', 'open', 'even/consistent', 'warm', and 'healthy'.

Mitchell and Kenny (2006) then aimed to assess the perceptual validity of the open throat technique by singing pedagogues, to determine whether this pedagogic technique could reliably produce perceptual changes to singing voices, and match sound quality to vocal instruction. Fifteen expert singing pedagogues assessed forty-eight *messe di voce* and twenty-four song samples (including six repeats to test reliability) of six advanced singing students under two conditions: 'optimal' (O), representing use of maximal open throat technique and 'suboptimal' (SO), representing reduced open throat. Pedagogues were asked to identify each sample as O/SO. The majority of pedagogues correctly identified 84 % of *messe di voce* and 82.7 % of song samples as O, which indicated that listeners were consistent in making a dichotomous choice in identifying a singing technique through perceptual evaluation. We confirmed that pedagogues could reliably hear a consistent sound quality associated with the use of open throat technique and that it was an important element of a perceptually superior classical vocal quality.

These results confirmed that there is a sound quality associated with the use of open throat technique, and that it is a perceptual reality to singing pedagogues and singers. Few studies document singing pedagogy through systematic perceptual research. Here, it was possible to link pedagogic instructions used in singing teaching to a reliable perceptual consensus to expand our understanding of vocal quality.

12.4 Monitoring the Sound of Progress

Having established that expert pedagogues can reliably identify the application of a single technique (Mitchell and Kenny 2006), the goal of subsequent studies was to discover if listeners could perceive singers' progress during and as a result of tertiary vocal training (Mitchell et al. 2010). Perceptual evaluation by expert listeners is critical at all stages of training to monitor and assess singers' progress. In the studio, pedagogues apply numerous techniques over a period of time, rather than single techniques in isolation, to enable singers to achieve their optimal vocal quality. There is a fundamental expectation that students will advance methodically over the course of their singing training (Cain 2001) and this is reflected in both curriculum design and examination procedures in tertiary training. Accordingly, vocal performances throughout training will reflect the singer's stage of vocal development (Reid 2001).

Comparing samples by the same performer has been an effective means to identify transformations in timbre using the open throat technique (Mitchell and Kenny 2006), and similarly in 'forward' and 'backward' placement (Vurma and Ross 2003). In each case, listeners were forced to make a dichotomous choice between the singing samples by the same singers and their comparisons confirmed that there were audible differences in singers' sound quality achieved by the application of different techniques. They confirmed that it was possible to match figurative expressions used in singing teaching to perceptual responses and expand our understanding of acoustic measures as applied to pedagogical instructions and vocal quality. In perceptual testing terms, focussing listeners to attend to adjacent vocal samples by the same singer enabled them to concentrate on the differences achieved by each individual singer, and ensured the application of the techniques was universal in a real world setting. Singers and pedagogues rarely apply a single technique in isolation, so the next obvious step was to understand changes in vocal quality through the deliberate instruction during advanced training (Mitchell et al. 2010).

Prior to this study, there was only one perceptual study of singers in tertiary training. Vurma and Ross (2000) recorded student singers before and after tertiary training and invited expert listeners to evaluate 'tone quality' in each student's performances. These singers' performances were presented independently, rather than in pairs of pre/post training, and they correlated listeners' scores with singers' total length of singing training (1–10 years). Results proved to be controversial, and listeners' rating scores could not conclusively demonstrate an increase in rating score after longer periods of training. Singers pre and post samples were not presented in pairs, so listeners were not forced to make dichotomous choices between their performances. Rather, listeners judged all singing performances as if in the same year's cohort. Vurma and Ross' study presented interesting experimental design challenges for subsequent studies investigating the sounds of progress in tertiary singing training.

Mitchell et al. (2010) conducted a perceptual study investigating listeners' perceptual evaluation of the 'sound of progress' in singing students over two complete years of tertiary vocal training and acquisition of vocal technical mastery, to see if listeners hear systematic progress by students in training. Fifteen singers sang Caccini's *Amarilli, mia bella* each year at the start of each academic year of vocal training (Y1, Y2, Y3) and ten expert pedagogues assessed a set of each singer's three performances, with performance years presented in randomised order. We asked listeners to first rank each singer's three performances from best to worst and then to rate each of the three performances from 1 to 10 out of 10. We anticipated that ratings out of 10 might indicate the extent of the differences between the three performances.

Listeners could clearly discriminate between performances by the same singers at key stages of training and reached agreement in their assessments. Y3 performances were awarded the top rank significantly more often than Y1 performances, but not significantly more than Y2 performances. That is, Y3 performances showed a consistent improvement from Y1 performances. Listeners were consistent in their ratings of each singer's three performances and the score for Y3 performances was significantly higher than Y2 or Y1 performances, but Y2 scores were not significantly different from Y1 scores. Overall, the majority of singers' performances in the final year were considered the best, and scored the highest. While there was individual variability in singers' systematic stages of improvement during 3 years of professional training the overall results indicated that most singers demonstrated a perceptible improvement by Y3.

This study deliberately employed both a 'norm based' ranking and 'criterion based' scoring assessment procedure (McPherson and Schubert 2004) to measure singers' level of attainment at a particular stage of training (Y1–Y3) by requiring listeners to discriminate between performances by the same singer. Comparison between two samples by the same performer is regarded as the most effective means by which to identify subtle transformations in timbre (Handel 2006), but in this case, listeners heard three annual performances by each singer and were asked to chart the amount of difference and improvement they heard across the three samples. Ranks and scores were then correlated to the chronological years of training.

As pedagogues' perceptual judgments are usually confined to evaluating a single performance at a time, which may be influenced by the memory of a previous performance by the same singer or performances by other singers in training, it was important to introduce an element of comparison between a singer's performances in this study. Here listeners identified Y3 as a pivotal point in singers' development, through their sound quality, but also showed that progress was not a linear progression in every case. We supplemented the puzzling data presented by Vurma and Ross (2000), and confirmed that individual singers' vocal progress does not necessarily follow a single dimension en route to vocal mastery.

12.5   Perceptual Consensus Defies Verbal Description

So far, we have considered comparative analyses of singing voices, first to identify singers' use of a single singing technique, and then to identify the application of multiple techniques in pursuit of vocal mastery during training. In a real world setting, singers strive for a complete vocal sound, and expert listeners assess the fully formed singing sound. This section will explore listeners' evaluations of singing performance in both authentic and experimental settings, to better understand how listeners rate and rank singing voices.

12.5.1   The Authentic Singing Audition

Authentic assessment settings provide an ideal opportunity to observe experts' judgment processes in action. The singing audition is essential across the arts to both identify talent and in this case, to determine access to music training courses. Judges must make immediate decisions regarding candidates' vocal ability and training potential, however, there is limited understanding about the tacit knowledge of listeners, their decisional processes and criteria they apply to form their judgments. This following study observed the singing auditions for singers to gain entry to a BMus degree at a leading conservatorium of music over a 2.5-day period (Mitchell and Kenny 2008). We recorded these singing auditions, and examined the way in which the panel achieved consensus to admit candidates to the degree (as voice major, minor or not accepted). We also captured the panel's comments and descriptors about each singer (with a view to matching these to acoustic measures, discussed in detail in Mitchell and Kenny 2008). Here, our focus is on the adjudication process, and the descriptors used by the panel to describe the singers they heard.

Listeners could clearly discriminate between performers in this audition, and reached agreement within the panel on each of their assessments and allocations to major, minor or to not accept. In terms of consistency, there was no effect of time or day on the audition outcomes, that is, decisions were made consistently across the 2.5 days of auditions. Audition reports contained the singer's allocation (major, minor, not accepted) and a written account of the singer.

The panel's comments were primarily focused on the candidates' overall vocal quality, with supplementary comments on overall presentation, musicality, and personality of the singers. Appropriate terms were applied consistently to each category, with majors deemed to have a 'high' vocal quality and a superior 'instrument'. Majors were described to have the potential or talent for a career in the singing profession. Minors were more likely to have a 'pleasing' vocal quality, and would attract technical comments or criticisms, if the voice itself was deemed to have potential for further study. Candidates not admitted to the degree received fewer comments, and most focused on a 'sweet' voice, which was not vocally or technically equipped for the rigours of the degree. Detailed examination of the panel's audition reports did not identify explicit features or descriptors that would explain their decision making process. Mostly, the comments were repetitive and simple descriptors were used to explain the overall quality of the voice, and in the pursuit of understanding the decision making process, lacking in tangible information.

12.5.2 The Experimental Setting

While expert pedagogues have been unable to conclusively corroborate elements or features of overall vocal quality (Ekholm et al. 1998; Wapnick and Ekholm 1997), they were able to reliably and consistently identify the use of singing techniques (Callinan-Robertson et al. 2006; Mitchell and Kenny 2006; Vurma and Ross 2003). Most perceptual studies of the singing voice depend on expert listeners' aural perceptions to substantiate empirical studies of the singing voice (which may involve corresponding acoustic analysis). To facilitate this, listeners are often asked to assess multiple singing performances by cross-sections of singers, as if in authentic performance evaluations or 'norm-based' assessments, as in a competition or audition. Listeners' average scores for each singer are used to rank order the voices or performances by overall preference (from best to worst). These types of studies enable us to rank the vocal quality of each singer within a cohort.

In the study of open throat technique, we also sought listeners' overall assessment of vocal quality in independently presented samples (Kenny and Mitchell 2004, 2006). Fifteen expert judges rated twenty-four samples with six repeats of six advanced singing students under two conditions: 'optimal' (O), which represented the application of the maximal open throat technique; and 'suboptimal' (SO), which represented the application of the reduced open throat technique and were required to identify the use of open throat technique and then to rate each performance on a scale from 1 to 10 and to verbalise the reasons for their responses. Our primary purpose for this study was to link these scores to acoustic measures taken on each performance.

Our attention is now focused on listeners' overall rankings and comments. In authentic settings, listeners are not required to verbalise or justify the reasons that motivated their scores, and it is often difficult to discern the reasons for their choices. In experimental setting, we can include structured experimental measures to ensure that listeners are, in fact, making consistent decisions. Here, we included repeated samples, to test listeners' reliability in scoring vocal samples. Listeners were consistent in their ratings of overall quality, producing exactly the same score, on average, for five of the six repeated samples. As expected overall, the singing samples association with the application of open throat technique (O) were rated higher than the samples associated with reduced open throat technique (SO).

Interestingly, these listeners demonstrated an overall preference for certain singers, and listeners ranked their favourite three singers consistently higher than others. When judges identified an overall good vocal quality with faulty technique, they were most likely to comment on technical flaws and recommend necessary vocal technique. For the singers ranked most highly, singers attracted few comments, and it would seem that the more beautiful the voice is perceived, the more difficult it is to describe.

12.5.3   What Does This Mean for Future Perceptual Studies?

These studies identified two critical issues that demand further investigation. First, it would appear that listeners' primary evaluation of singing is indeed based on their appraisal of the whole performance. Next, it would appear that listeners are more able to describe less appealing singing voices through a series of technical instructions for improvement and are less able to articulate the sound quality of their preferred voices.

The lack of descriptors for vocal quality presents an intriguing perspective on how listeners assess the sound quality of singers. Both the authentic and experimental studies here confirm the existing published studies of vocal assessment and description, where assessments focus on the overall quality of the performance/performer (Stanley et al. 2002) and vocal quality is difficult to articulate or itemise (Davidson and Coimbra 2001). In singing examinations, Davidson and Coimbra reported that examiners' own reports (not transmitted to students), rather than describe sound quality, resorted to noting features of candidates' visual appearance, dress or demeanour, possibly to facilitate recall of the sound of the performance. They suggested that their examination panel did not describe the vocal quality as the singers, having been admitted to the degree, would have an adequate or suitable overall vocal quality and that this was a 'stable element' of their vocal sound.

It may be that putting a sound into words (verbal encoding) is an inappropriate means of depicting a holistic vocal quality. More importantly, verbalising voice quality may reduce the ability to discriminate between voices and even hinder the memory of the performance/performer. Verbal overshadowing, where quite literally, the 'words get in the way' has been extensively investigated in visual and taste domains but has to date, received little attention in the auditory domain.

12.6   Do the Words Get in the Way?

The following studies stemmed from these unexpected findings, that listeners did not describe vocal quality (Kenny and Mitchell 2006; Mitchell and Kenny 2008). Listeners may not have adequate or suitable words to categorise or itemise particular vocal qualities to discriminate between singers (Ekholm et al. 1998), but further, that the act of verbalising the sensory experience or perception of listening to a singing voice may affect and indeed, distort, listeners' memory of that experience.

12.6.1   The Value of Words

So far, we have considered that verbalising the sound quality of singing voices as a complex task for listeners. In examinations, auditions and in experimental settings, listeners are consistent in their judgments of overall quality, both with themselves, and in agreement with other judges. Yet, listeners regularly avoid explaining the sound information that generated their decision.

Sensory experiences, such as seeing a face, tasting a wine or hearing a voice are potentially susceptible to the phenomenon of *verbal overshadowing*. While viewers, tasters and listeners rely on verbalisation to communicate their perceptions of the sensory experiences, the modality of the stimulus (in this case, auditory) does not match the task for communication (verbalisation). However, to date, we have relied on verbalisation to communicate perceptions of performances and performers. It could be that verbalisation is an inadequate representation of the auditory experience. Quite simply, words may not capture the voice we heard.

Verbal overshadowing (VO) is well documented as a negative contributor to the memory of sensory experiences. It has been most evident in face recognition, when witnesses to a crime have to describe the perpetrator to police, and then identify him from a line-up of similar faces (Schooler et al. 1997). First, the witnesses do not have adequate terms to discern the individual differences (in simplistic terms, we have few terms beyond eyes, nose, mouth), and then the act of verbal description distorts the visual (or aural/taste) memory. Studies in laboratory settings have confirmed the VO effect by comparing the responses of viewers who describe the faces, with viewers who simply remember the face (Dodson et al. 1997). Beyond face recognition, the verbal overshadowing phenomenon affects taste (Parr et al. 2006) and speaking voice recognition (Perfect et al. 2002; Vanags et al. 2005). It has also negatively influenced listeners' recognition of musical pieces (Margulis 2010).

Studies in speaking voice demonstrated the same VO effect in the auditory domain (Perfect et al. 2002; Vanags et al. 2005). As in the face/robber studies, listeners heard a single speaking voice, then were assigned to a verbal description group or a no-description control group. When listeners heard the same sentence in the line-up, neither group (verbal or control) was particularly good at identifying the target voice (21.4 % of verbal group vs. 50 % of control group). Vanags et al. (2005) first used the same sentence, then altered the line-up sentence, so it was different to the original speaker sentence, and found that listeners were more susceptible to VO when the line-up test stimulus were different from the original spoken phrase used at encoding (18 % of verbal group vs. 53 % of control group). As in Perfect et al.'s study (2002), neither verbal description nor control group was proficient in identifying the target voice (24 % of verbal group vs. 48 % of control group).

The available evidence from auditions, examinations and experimental settings suggests listeners may susceptible to the effect of VO in their perception of individual singing voices. Accordingly, two studies investigated the effect of VO on singing voice recognition, to understand how listeners form auditory impressions of a singer. The main objective was to examine the impact of verbal description on the recall of classical singers' voices, what terms listeners have to describe singers, and if putting a sound 'into words' distorts listeners' memory of the singer.

In the first study (Mitchell and MacDonald 2011), six singers were recorded singing an Italian aria *Caro mio ben* and German lied *Seligkeit*. Fifty listeners heard a single voice singing *Caro mio ben* and were assigned to either a verbal description group or a control group. As in the visual studies, the verbal group wrote a detailed description of the target voice and the control group did not. All listeners heard a voice line-up of *Seligkeit* and were asked to identify the original target voice and to rate their confidence in their decision.

There was a reliable VO effect and listeners in the verbal group were less likely to recognise the target than listeners in the control group (24 % verbal group vs. 48 % control group). Providing a verbal description reduced listeners' identification accuracy of target voice, but it did not reduce listeners' confidence ratings of their decision. Overall, only 18 of 50 listeners correctly identified their target voice from the line-up (37 %).

In the second study (Mitchell and MacDonald 2012), we sought to simplify the test and rather than changing the line-up song, it remained the same as the initial target voice song. Again, 50 listeners heard a single voice singing *Caro mio ben* and were assigned to either a verbal description group or a control group. This time, there was again a reliable VO effect and listeners in the verbal group were again less likely to recognise the target than listeners in the control group (20 % verbal group vs. 48 % control group). There was no difference in confidence scores between the verbal and control groups. In this test, only 17 of 50 listeners correctly identified their target voice from the line-up (34 %).

Despite the simplification of the experimental design, the VO effect was robust, and regardless of stimuli, listeners were susceptible to VO. Describing the voices impaired listeners ability to recognise them, although listeners were unaware of the impact of verbalisation on their responses, demonstrated through equal confidence ratings.

Verbalisation of singing voices was an inadequate representation of listeners' auditory experience and limited listeners' ability to recall and identify singers' sound quality. These results have profound implications for the way in which we consider musical performance and how music listeners recognise, process and describe a performer's sound.

12.6.2   The Words That 'Got in the Way'

Most listeners identified that the singer was a soprano, or at the very least, that she was female. Some listeners debated whether their target singer might be a mezzo-soprano. Listeners variously debated the singer's age from a 'young singer in her 20s' to a 'mature female' or 'a woman over the age of 40 as the voice sounded 'mature''. Other comments were concerned with vibrato, diction or articulation, and emotional content. A few listeners mentioned words traditionally associated with the singing sound, such as 'rich and warm', 'breathy', 'clear and pure' and 'bright'. Finally, for a small number of listeners the sound they heard evoked a mental picture of the target voice singing, for example, 'brown hair, short', 'anglosaxon' to 'mannish' or a 'bigger woman'.

Overall, results confirmed that the act of verbal description, or putting a sound 'into words', was not only essentially uninformative, but actually distorted listeners' memory and subsequent recall of the original performer. The poor overall recognition scores also indicated that listeners (regardless of task) are surprising unreliable at recognising performers by sound alone.

Verbal description may be an imperfect means to communicate the perception of sound, but it is the tool that is used by musicians and pedagogues, particularly in the context of teaching and learning. Our challenge is to recognise the potential disparity between sound and verbalisation and to develop ways to address this in the studio.

12.7   Implications and New Directions for the Singing Studio

Listeners' conceptualisation of a singer's vocal quality is a complex feat, as the sound contains multiple acoustic properties as well as musical, technical and aesthetic cues, all of which contribute to the overall performance (Handel 2006).

12.7.1   Sharing Sound Usurps Words

In the studio, singers cannot hear their own voices in the same way as their teacher, yet teacher and student need to communicate about vocal quality to enable them to work to improve the vocal sound. Southcott and Mitchell (2013) explored the use of recordings as a tool to assist the communication and feedback process in the singing studio. Singers were recorded in the studio and listened to their performance through high quality headphones and asked to rate their performance, before attempting to improve their performance. While singers did not increase their scores for their second performances, they reported that hearing themselves sing was 'helpful, empowering, and confidence-building'. The more experienced singers were better equipped to improve their overall sound following playback, in comparison to novice singers. These experienced singers were better attuned to subtle features of their vocal quality and their training enabled them to not only identify, but also to correct perceived vocal flaws.

12.7.2   Longitudinal Tracking

Memories of vocal sound, whether recent or long-term, have the potential to be misremembered. Recording annual (or more frequent) performances has the potential to provide a unique and stable record of singers' development during training. It offers a novel addition to tracking individuals' progress and a new way in which to remember and describe sound quality. By providing fixed perceptual reference points or aide memoires of singers' vocal transformations, we can ensure they are not limited by memory or insufficient verbal descriptions of singers' vocal quality.

12.8   Conclusions and Future Directions

Listeners possess tacit knowledge about singers' sound, yet little is known about how listeners process sensory information from a singer to conceptualise, recognise and verbalise the sound they hear. In describing sound, listeners focus on the more easily articulated technical and visual aspects of the performance, which are more easily articulated and generally avoid describing the overall sound of the singer.

Perceptual studies of the singing voice rely on expert listeners' aural expertise to align empirical studies of the singing voice with real world training and are critical to their ongoing integrity. There may not be any fixed cues that determine listeners' judgments of vocal quality, but by applying established empirical research methods, we are able to reflect on and to understand more about listeners' expert judgments so empirical studies are both meaningful and useful to those who can use and practise them.

References

Cain, T. (2001). Continuity and progression in music education. In C. Philpott & C. Plummeridge (Eds.), *Issues in music teaching* (pp. 105–117). London: Routledge Falmer.

Callinan-Robertson, J., Mitchell, H. F., & Kenny, D. T. (2006). Effect of pedagogical imagery of 'halo' on vocal quality in young classical female singers. *Australian Voice, 12*, 39–52.

Davidson, J. W., & Coimbra, D. (2001). Investigating performance evaluation by assessors of singers in a music college setting. *Musicae Scientiae, 5*(1), 33–53.

Dodson, C. S., Johnson, M. K., & Schooler, J. W. (1997). The verbal overshadowing effect: Why descriptions impair face recognition. *Memory & Cognition, 25*(2), 129–139.

Ekholm, E., Papagiannis, G. C., & Chagnon, F. P. (1998). Relating objective measurements to expert evaluation of voice quality in Western classical singing: Critical perceptual parameters. *Journal of Voice, 12*(2), 182–196.

Handel, S. (2006). *Perceptual coherence: Hearing and seeing.* New York: Oxford University Press.

Kenny, D. T., & Mitchell, H. F. (2004). Visual and auditory perception of vocal beauty: Conflict or concurrence? In S. D. Lipscomb, R. Ashley, R. O. Gjerdingen, & P. Webster (Eds.), *8th international conference on music perception & cognition (ICMPC8)*. Evanston: Causal Productions.

Kenny, D. T., & Mitchell, H. F. (2006). Acoustic and perceptual appraisal of vocal gestures in the female classical voice. *Journal of Voice, 20*(1), 55–70.

Margulis, E. H. (2010). When program notes don't help: Music descriptions and enjoyment. *Psychology of Music, 38*(3), 285–302. doi:10.1177/0305735609351921.

McPherson, G. E., & Schubert, E. (2004). Measuring performance enhancement in music. In A. Williamon (Ed.), *Musical excellence: Strategies and techniques to enhance performance* (pp. 61–82). Oxford: Oxford University Press.

Miller, R. (1996). *The structure of singing: System and art in vocal technique.* New York: Schirmer Books.

Mitchell, H. F., & Kenny, D. T. (2006). Can experts identify 'open throat' technique as a perceptual phenomenon? *Musicae Scientiae, 10*(1), 33–58.

Mitchell, H. F., & Kenny, D. T. (2008). The tertiary singing audition: Perceptual and acoustic differences between successful and unsuccessful candidates. *Journal of Interdisciplinary Music Studies, 2*(1&2), 95–110.

Mitchell, H. F., & MacDonald, R. A. R. (2011). Remembering, recognising and describing singers' sound identities. *Journal of New Music Research, 40*(1), 75–80.

Mitchell, H. F., & MacDonald, R. A. R. (2012). Recognition and description of singing voices: The impact of verbal overshadowing. *Musicae Scientiae, 16*(3), 307–316.

Mitchell, H. F., Kenny, D. T., Ryan, M., & Davis, P. J. (2003). Defining open throat through content analysis of experts' pedagogical practices. *Logopedics Phoniatrics Vocology, 28*(4), 167–180.

Mitchell, H. F., Kenny, D. T., & Ryan, M. (2010). Perceived improvement in vocal performance following tertiary-level classical vocal training: Do listeners hear systematic progress? *Musicae Scientiae, XIV*(1), 73–93.

Parr, W. V., Green, J. A., & Geoffrey White, K. (2006). Wine judging, context and New Zealand Sauvignon Blanc. *Revue Européenne de Psychologie Appliquée/European Review of Applied Psychology, 56*(4), 231–238.

Perfect, T. J., Hunt, L. J., & Harris, C. M. (2002). Verbal overshadowing in voice recognition. *Applied Cognitive Psychology, 16*(8), 973–980.

Reid, A. (2001). Variation in the ways that instrumental and vocal students experience learning music. *Music Education Research, 3*, 25–40.

Schooler, J. W., Fiore, S. M., & Brandimonte, M. A. (1997). At a loss from words: Verbal overshadowing of perceptual memories. In D. L. Medin (Ed.), *The psychology of learning and motivation: Advances in research and theory* (pp. 291–340). San Diego: Academic.

Southcott, I. E., & Mitchell, H. F. (2013). How singers hear themselves: Using recordings in the singing studio. Australian Voice, 15, 20–28.

Stanley, M., Brooker, R., & Gilbert, R. (2002). Examiner perceptions of using criteria in music performance assessment. *Research Studies in Music Education, 18*, 43–52.

Vanags, T., Carroll, M., & Perfect, T. J. (2005). Verbal overshadowing: A sound theory in voice recognition? *Applied Cognitive Psychology, 19*(9), 1127–1144. doi:http://dx.doi.org/10.1002/acp.1160.

Vennard, W. (1968). *Singing: The mechanism and the technic* (5th Aufl.). New York: Fischer.

Vurma, A., & Ross, J. (2000). Priorities in voice training: Carrying power or tone quality. *Musicae Scientiae, 4*(1), 75–93.

Vurma, A., & Ross, J. (2003). The perception of 'forward' and 'backward placement' of the singing voice. *Logopedics Phonatrics Vocology, 28*(1), 19–28.

Wapnick, J., & Ekholm, E. (1997). Expert consensus in solo voice performance evaluation. *Journal of Voice, 11*(4), 429–436.

Ward, V. (2004). The performance teacher as music analyst: A case study. *International Journal of Music Education, 22*(3), 248–265. doi: 10.1177/0255761404047406.

Chapter 13
The Teacher-Student Relationship in One-to-One Singing Lessons: An Investigation of Personality and Adult Attachment

Sofia Serra-Dawa

Abstract The characteristic isolation of one-to-one singing lessons based on two elements confined to work together over time implies strong adaptation in order for the ultimate goal of teaching artistic individuality, maturity and independence to be achieved. In a functional relationship there is space for all attributes to be developed whereas in relationships without solid compatibility, the student's development might be compromised.

This chapter presents the singing setting in a multidirectional perspective giving voice to both teachers and students. The teacher-student dyads were video recorded in their lessons during one academic year. The behaviours were analysed and complemented with the psychological questionnaires NEO PI-R (Costa and McCrae 1992) and Adult Attachment Scale (Collins and Read 1990) to evaluate personality and attachment respectively. This approach was developed in order to: contextualize the singing teacher-student relationship; profile personality and adult attachment characteristics in singing teachers and students; report stable characteristics of the relationships; distinguish functional from dysfunctional singing teacher-student relationships; indicate the usefulness of using personality and adult attachment instruments for understanding the singing relationships.

This study contributes to the clarification of teacher-students' relationship. The combination of observational studies with the data from psychological instruments provided a more accurate indication that singing teachers and students tend to behave according to their personal and psychological characterisation, which takes the understanding of singing lessons into a more objective setting. These findings are of relevance for heads of vocal departments, singing teachers and students by providing means of predicting, interpreting and supporting relational quality.

S. Serra-Dawa (✉)
Escola das Artes, Research Center for Science and Technology in Art,
Portuguese Catholic University, Porto, Portugal
e-mail: sofiaserradawa@gmail.com

S.D. Harrison and J. O'Bryan (eds.), *Teaching Singing in the 21st Century*,
Landscapes: the Arts, Aesthetics, and Education 14, DOI 10.1007/978-94-017-8851-9_13,
© Springer Science+Business Media Dordrecht 2014

Keywords Singing lessons • Teacher-student relationship • Personality • Adult attachment

The impact of relationships in the wellbeing of each individual is an important matter studied through social psychology theories. Finding satisfaction in work places, family and love life depends greatly on how we relate to other people (Dwyer 2000, 1). Likewise, a successful relationship between teacher and student in a one-to-one instrumental/singing setting may impact the performing outcome of the student in a sense that by developing a healthy relationship the learning processes may benefit (Kennell 2002, 244).

Singing, possibly more than any other instrument, seems to have clear personal approaches that indicate a necessity to regard the relationship in different ways: being body oriented, the use of lyrics, and the interpretation of character. In this type of lesson, the otherwise normal barrier of the instrument is not applicable and singing teacher and student are 'confronted' directly in a face-to-face interaction (both having the instrument incorporated). For all these reasons, the voice seems to be an instrument that demands a closer observation and a different approach in pedagogical terms.

The relationship between teacher and student, which in most cases extends over several years, should ideally be a source not only of musical knowledge but also inspiration, motivation and psychological growth. In a 'healthy' relationship there is space for all attributes to be developed and grown; whereas in relationships without solid compatibility, the student's development might be compromised. So the choices of matching singing teachers and students should be considered with accuracy. Heads of department, teachers and students seem to establish combinations that are in most cases based on pure intuition. Research using psychological background instruments (such as personality and adult attachment), which may contribute towards providing relational quality for students and teachers, is of great importance and yet such work is scarce.

13.1 Literature Review

13.1.1 The Personality of Singing Teachers and Students

Of all types of psychological measures, personality has strong relevance in profiling both the sense self and of group belonging (Kemp 2004, vii). In music, personality has been studied in regard to skill identification, talent prediction, musical preferences, and musical sub-grouping identification (according to different instruments).

Several studies identified common characteristics of instrumentalists according to their instrument, suggesting that there may be a personality grouping factor (Bell and Cresswell 1984, 91; Kemp 2004). The same personality correspondence, of different patterns of variations according to the instrument and repertoire played, was confirmed by Kemp (2004) in orchestral instrumentalists. These instrumentalists were identified as having common characteristics, whereas singers, performance pianists, organists and conductors who were non-orchestral had higher levels of individualism, imagination and low levels of conservatism (166).

Various factors may contribute to differences being identified between singers and orchestral instrumentalists. The instrument itself may be a provider of information because whereas instrumentalists may have a more protected posture towards an audience, the solo singers face their performances frontwards without other elements between. This may constitute a contribution towards developing extroversion in higher levels than orchestral players, for instance (Kemp 2004, 173). Kemp also suggests that singers are more extroverted (associated to the capacity for performing solo) since they do not spend as many hours isolated (which potentiates introversion) as instrumentalists do, due to the natural limitations of vocal overuse. Singers are also shown to have higher adjustment, sensibility and independence as they work in different settings where those characteristics are more likely to be developed than other instrumental players: 'Viewed in its total ... the musician without an instrument appears to attract a very different type of person' (Kemp 2004, 175).

Singers are also portrayed as being more anxious and sensitive than other instrumentalists reflecting the less tangible teaching approach to their instrument: identifying sensations to match the teachers' requests may be more demanding than other visible and touchable instruments and more likely to produce effect by visual means (Howard 1982 in Kemp 2004, 174). Another characteristic identified by Howard (ibid.) is that singers tend to depend strongly more on their teachers. That dependency was justified by the fact that singers do not hear the sound of their instrument as other instrumentalists do and that the instrument requires added sensation search in order to produce the appropriate sound.

In regard to music teaching feedback, Schmidt (1989, 118–119) concluded that personality might influence the delivery of feedback, for extroversion and introversion are variables that may determine the interaction with the students and the amount of explanatory behaviour of teachers towards students. The teaching itself, as well as the relationship between teacher and students, may be influenced by the personalities of teacher and student.

The discussion around personality variables and music teaching is extensive but does not seem to have reached a consensus. Several authors consider personality as the most important element of teaching effectiveness (Pembrook and Craig 2002; Schechtman 1989; Wink 1970; Young 1990) whereas other authors defend a weak relation between successful teaching and personality (Davidson et al. 1998; DeNovellis and Lawrence 1983; Goodstein 1987; Wubbenhorst 1991).

The present study may contribute to the research on teaching and personality by using personality as a means through which the relationship between teacher and student may be better described, examined and therefore contribute towards its better comprehension.

13.2   Research Tools and Theories

In order to evaluate personality on both singing teachers and students in the present research, the personality test NEO PI-R (Costa and McCrae 1992) was chosen. The NEO PI-R is an instrument that has strong and well-established roots in psychological assessment and within music research (Chamorro-Premuzic et al 2009; Jäncke and Sandmann 2010; Kemp 2004; Moss et al. 2006). This instrument provides a dimension and trait description of each individual meant to allow a comparative analysis between individuals. The evaluation of personality, unlike attachment (presented later) does not provide a classification of style. Rather, the results presented are in scales from where participants (teacher or student) may be compared as being more or less characterized by a certain characteristic of their personality. The NEO PI-R is constituted by five domains and six traits (for each of the domains) as presented in Fig. 13.1. The dimensions provide a resume of underlining traits, which are subgroups of more specific elements of personality describing 'emotional, interpersonal, experimental, attitudinal, and motivational styles' (Costa and McCrae 1992, 14). The under layers of characteristics (traits) within the major factors that can help interpret behaviors in singing lessons.

The personality measurement may be used for pathological reasons, but it also is applied on 'normal' individuals within non-medical and non-psychological research, and with vocational applications.

The comparative analysis of dyads' personality (presented later) was made based on existing literature on marital relationships. This choice was made in order to base the present study on principles of personality combination existing in psychology (Shiota and Levenson 2007). The existing studies present different perspectives that mostly are associated with examining the existence of a direct impact of similar/contrasting type of personality identified through domains and traits. A simpler way

N: NEUROTICISM					
n1 Anxiety	n2 Angry hostility	n3 Depression	n4 Self-Consciousness	n5 Impulsiveness	n6 Vulnerability
E: EXTROVERSION					
e1 Warmth	e2 Gregariousness	e3 Assertiveness	e4 Activity	e5 Excitement-Seeking	e6 Positive Emotions
O: OPENNESS					
o1 Fantasy	o2 Aesthetics	o3 Feelings	o4 Actions	o5 Ideas	o6 Values
A: AGREEABLENESS					
a1 Trust	a2 Straightforwardness	a3 Altruism	a4 Compliance	a5 Modesty	a6 Tender-Mindedness
C: CONSCIENTIOUSNESS					
c1 Competence	c2 Order	c3 Dutifulness	c4 Achievement Striving	c5 Self-Discipline	c6 Deliberation

Fig. 13.1 Domains and traits in NEO PI-R (Costa and McCrae 1992)

of expressing this comparative analysis would be the popular belief in 'opposites attract'. Indeed, psychological studies identifying contrasting personality traits between couples, confirm a tendency to have longer and more satisfying relationships by partners with contrasting personalities in comparison to similar personalities (Dryer and Horowitz 1997; Shiota and Levenson 2007).

13.2.1   The Adult Attachment of Singing Teachers and Students

The other instrument used to evaluate the teacher-student relationship was the psychological test *adult attachment scale* (Collins and Read 1990), which is based on adult attachment theory. This theory, though explored in fields other than pure psychology and psychiatry, does not seem to yet have raised points of interception with music research. The choice of including attachment theory in the study of singing teacher-student relationships, beyond the fact that it had not been previously used, had a complementary purpose. By using the personality tests the observation of participants had a comparative but rather individualistic approach whereas the attachment theory had the potential to identify the participants' style of relation with another person. Adult attachment, within psychology theories, defines best elements of a relationship: dependency/independency, proximity/avoidance, security/fear of rejection, all measured in regard to self-esteem and sociability (Bartholomew 1990).

The research on Adult Attachment was initiated by John Bowlby (1969), who outlined the theory that attachment, or the 'lasting psychological connectedness between human beings' (Bowlby 1969, 194), had a survival character as a basic component of human nature. The attachment was initially characterized as having four components: 'proximity maintenance', defined as the desire to be close to the person of attachment; 'safe haven', seeking comfort and safety in the attachment figure when faced with threat of fear; 'secure base', exploration of surrounding environment with the attachment figure working as a safe base; and 'separation distress', anxiety experienced when the attachment figure is absent (Bowlby 1988). The initial attachment theory was related to children and their attachment figure (in most cases, the mother).

Following the expansion of attachment theory, Mary Main developed tools for evaluation of attachment in adults that lead into the *Adult Attachment Interview* (*AAI*; George et al. 1984). This allowed new perspectives for attachment comprehension through mental and behavioural patterns of organization (Soares 2007).

The growing interest in attachment applied to adult romantic relationships resulted in the development of instruments reporting romantic attachment. Hazan and Shaver (1987) made a transposition of Mary Ainsworth studies of infant-mother attachment in 1987 with particular interest on the styles of attachment (Canavarro 1999, 122).

Fig. 13.2 Model of attachment styles distributed according to score tendencies (Bartholomew 1990, adapted from Shaver and Fraley 2004)

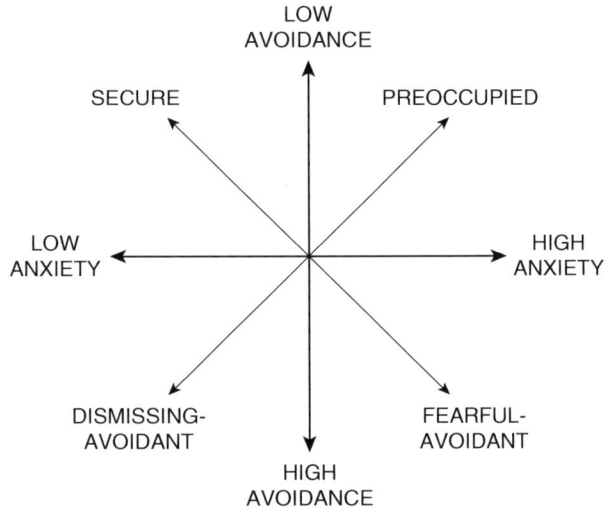

Built over the two dimensions of attachment (anxiety and avoidance), the four styles dependent on the score tendencies of respondents were characterised as secure or insecure (anxious-preoccupied, dismissive-avoidant, fearful-avoidant). The dimensions were defined as: *Anxiety*: Reflects the level of worry about being rejected or not loved by partners; *Avoidance*: Reports the level of intimacy limitation and independence from the person of attachment (See Fig. 13.2).

The development of attachment instruments built from observation, structured interviews and self-report questionnaires enabled a wider attachment evaluation to be considered.

The development of new instruments favoured the comprehension of several questions raised initially by Bowlby. For instance, several studies were developed in order to connect the experiences of attachment from early infancy to adulthood and its development in intimate relationships (Berman et al. 1994; Feeney 1999; Hazan and Shaver 1987; Shaver et al. 1988), psychological problems (Atkinson 1997; Dozier et al. 1999; Greenberg 1999; Sroufe et al. 1999), and therapeutic relationships (Dozier and Tyrell 1998; Mallinckrodt et al. 1995; Slade 1999; Sperling and Lyons 1994; West and Sheldon-Keller 1994). Other studies have associated attachment to relational violence (Holtzworth-Munroe et al. 1997; Lions-Ruth and Jacobvitz 1999), sexual orientation (Kurdek 2002; Kurdek and Schmitt 1986; Mohr 1999), religion (Kirkpatrick 1999), twins and singletons (Torgersen et al. 2007), and health and strong personal relationships (Bayley 2006).

The adult attachment research had become well established as the means of understanding close relationships, but had not yet been widely applied in education until Robert Pianta implemented the attachment theory in the teacher-child relationship through observation and measurement on teachers, parents and children in kinder gardens and primary schools (Pianta 1997).

The attachment appropriateness for the study of instrumental teacher/student relationships lays its focus on the therapist-patient relationship and some friendship relationships where Weiss (1991) defends the existence of attachment bonds.

Adding to Ainsworth's (Ainsworth et al. 1978) research, Weiss (1991) concluded that relationships do not need to be parental or sexual in order to create attachment. Taking that, the teacher-student relationship was considered within an appropriate group through the observation of preliminary lessons where it was also visible the levels of personal involvement between teacher and student (informal conversations, personal advice and confidential exchanges).

Regarding couples' 'pairing', literature reported an association between the quality of relationships and styles of attachment. The secure style in opposition to both avoidant and anxious-ambivalent (insecure) attachment characterized people with behaviours of trust, satisfaction and independence (Feeney et al. 1994; Kirkpatrick and Davis 1994; Simpson 1990).

Collins and Read (1990) implemented scale measures on a revised version of attachment: adult attachment scale-R (Collins and Read 1990). The revised version is constituted by 18 items scored on a 5 point *Likert*-type scale by applying the scales and identifying the individuals' styles.

Within the adult attachment instruments the AAS-R (Collins and Read 1990) seemed to be the less invasive, with fewer intimate matters, which were not relevant for the direct purpose of this study. It presents a clear characterisation of individual attachment style in order to compare with the other participant (teacher or student).

The two psychological instruments used in the present research (personality and attachment) were believed inseparable and the personality always implicit on a certain degree in attachment (Vaughn and Bost 1999). Several studies compared, analysed and reinforced the existing relations between the measures of personality and adult attachment (Bäckström 2001; Carver 1997; Shaver and Brennan 1992; Shiota et al. 2006).

13.3 The Study

In a 1-year observation, the participants were 11 singing teachers and 54 students. The study had three stages where participants were video recorded during their one-to-one singing lesson. The observations of recorded lessons were complemented with the psychological questionnaires NEO PI- R (Costa and McCrae 1992) and Adult Attachment Scale (Collins and Read 1990) to evaluate personality and attachment respectively.

Considering the possibilities of qualitative analysis as defended by Livingston (1987), the use of video recordings would be the most appropriate way to follow, organize and structure people's behaviour in situ. In this study, the use of recordings of lessons seemed of great importance to register, repeat and re-evaluate the behaviours in more detail.

The required conditions for selection of participants for this research were: (i). teaching/studying in a higher education institution; (ii). having singing as the main instrument of study for each student; and (iii). regular singing lessons with the teacher being observed.

13.3.1 Methods

The qualitative analysis of this research (videos, annotations, reports) was under-taken from a multilateral point of view in order to provide a wide perspective of observation and cover the relational setting not only from the observations (videos) but also including the perspective of participants involved in the relationship itself (questionnaires and interviews). This qualitative analysis was then complemented with the psychological reports (personality and attachment) that provided an identi-fication of scale and styles ideal in combination with this qualitative research. So, it was expected that the relationships identified (what happened), included possible reasons of that behaviour (why) and the consequences of that behaviour (effect) which was provided through the questionnaires.

13.3.2 Aims

The use of all the above approach was developed in order to: contextualize the singing teacher-student relationship; profile personality and adult attachment characteristics in singing teachers and students; report long-term characteristics of the relationships; distinguish functional from dysfunctional singing teacher-student relationships; indicate the usefulness of using personality and adult attachment instruments for understanding the singing relationships.

13.3.3 Procedure

Based on personality, adult attachment and behavioural description, the information was conveyed in order to profile dyads and evaluate their relational functioning. In order to accomplish this task, all characterization of personality (domains and traits) was based on Costa and McCrae (1992, 14–18) and Costa and McCrae (2000, 73–74) and attachment descriptions based on Bartholomew (1990). An integral analysis to the videos was made as well as a qualitative description. For each lesson an individual report was made. The data was organized into larger and comparative analysis between teacher-student dyad. The descriptions of personality and attach-ment were then evaluated in specific behaviours found consistently in the singing lessons between singing teachers and students. The traits and style characterization were analyzed through observing repeated behaviours rather than single-event behaviours that were discarded.

Taking that a negative relationship might influence the musical development of students (Hallam 1998, 230), the present research also hypothesizes the combinations of teachers and students where the relationship may be more functional or dysfunc-tional: dysfunctional (in the present chapter's context) being considered as low relationship quality, rather than necessarily the precursor of relational breakup.

13.4   Results: The Confluence of Measures

The results regarding the participants' domains of personality presented an exclusively high score for neuroticism, which follows existing literature, where the same tendency is presented in musicians (Dews and Williams 1989, 45; Roe 1958) and particularly in singers (Kemp 2004, 93–94). It was evident that the singers' group in itself had characteristics that were common for all dyads regarding the combination of neurotic traits, for instance. Taking the assumption that at least some dyads (within all participants) had functional relationships and that within the singers' group identified in previous literature the same characteristics were found, the present analysis prioritized dyads where elements had different characteristics (particularly those with extreme values) in order to evaluate the effects of the difference having a positive impact on the relationship, as in 'opposites attract', presented earlier. The observations of relational behaviours were therefore considered in comparison to contrasting elements located within the personality traits of teacher and student, summarized in Table 13.1.

In most cases the contrasting trait scores reported positive influence for the singing lessons, however, the appropriate traits should be considered and a generalized application of contrasting score is not recommended.

A list of contrasting personality traits proved to have bigger impact on the quality of singing teacher-student relationship: (n1) *anxiety,* providing balanced rhythms of speech and interaction; (e2) *gregariousness,* raising the mood of the lessons and therefore approximating the dyad; (e4) *activity,* potentiating higher involvement of the other element; (e5) *excitement-seeking,* bringing energetic stimulation to the lesson; (o4) *actions,* allowing the necessary tools to be implemented; (o5) *ideas,* intellectually challenging behaviours; (a4) *compliance,* prudent behaviour helping to accept better the other person; and (a6) *values,* not presenting an impact on relationships.

Another personality trait proved to be innocuous, as it did not seem to affect the relationship: (e3) *assertiveness,* singers developing appropriate skills in order to face audiences. Additionally, one trait was identified as avoidable in contrasting scores between singing teacher and student: (n6) *vulnerability* as one element did not seem to compensate the other but rather affect negatively. For instance, for teachers scoring high in vulnerability the questioning of students often resulted in behaviours of insecurity. In order to establish the hierarchical order of contribution towards the singing teacher relationship Fig. 13.3 illustrates the different levels found.

Most contrasting traits were identifiable through teacher-student's behaviour, having most contributed towards representing the quality of the relationship. However, several traits did not provide any conclusive behavioural information. Within the identifiable behaviours most traits contributed towards the relationship's quality and one trait proved to be innocuous for the relationship. Most contrasting traits interfered positively with the relationship by providing higher levels of quality whereas other traits contributed towards its dysfunctionality. For the traits contributing for dysfunctional relationships it was also possible to observe that one trait clearly should not be combined contrastingly (n6, vulnerability) and three other traits could benefit from working together if the conditionality is followed.

Table 13.1 Recommended scoring in accordance to recurrent behaviours for each personality trait with High Score (HS) and Low Score (LS)

Personality trait	Behaviours	Recommended scoring
N: NEUROTICISM		
n1: Anxiety	Students (HS) presented accelerated rhythm of speech, tense and worried approach to singing with teacher (LS) bringing the rhythm of the student to a more stable state. Teachers (HS) tended to speak fast, change unjustifiably between teaching approaches with a student (LS) patient and focused	Having one of the elements (regardless of being the teacher or student) balancing the other element's anxious state might be positive for the relationship
n6: Vulnerability	Teachers (HS) fear the evaluation by students when demonstrating through singing in contrast to students (LS) managing situations by inverting roles with teacher and delivering feedback	Contrasting scores for vulnerability is not recommended
E: EXTROVERSION		
e2: Gregariousness	Student (LS) had reserved and isolated behaviours (such as remaining in silent) when stimulated by the humorous side of teacher (HS)	High score for teachers in contrast to the students' low score may provide positive encouragement for a singer student
e3: Assertiveness	–	Assertiveness did not constitute a valid measure as participants scoring low, typically avoid public speaking. This sample did not show that, perhaps through the developed skills required for singers to face public
e4: Activity	Teacher (HS) induced the student (LS) to be more vigorous. On the opposite, students (HS) tended to use more gestures against the contained behaviour of teacher (LS)	Contrasting scores (from either teacher or student) may be beneficial to the relationship
e5: Excitement-seeking	Both teacher and student (HS) in contrast to the other (LS) resulted in highly energetic, excited behaviour particularly by willing to risk more in technical terms	High scoring for this trait resulted positively in both teacher and student
e6: Positive emotions	One element (HS) tended to explore external factors to influence vocal quality: 'let the Sun inspire your singing'	High scoring for this trait in contrast to the other element (either teacher or student) reflects positively

(continued)

Table 13.1 (continued)

Personality trait	Behaviours	Recommended scoring
O: OPENNESS		
o4: Actions	Choices of unusual types of repertoire. Students (HS) with teachers (LS) saw requests unattended. Comparatively with the opposite scoring, students (LS) got more 'exotic' choices of repertoire	High scoring for teachers may be positive
o5: Ideas	Teachers' (LS) narrow variety of methods. On the other hand, when faced with a student (HS), demonstrated highly analytic and intellectual curiosity that seemed to challenge positively the teacher's opposite personality tendency	Contrasting score is recommended
A: AGREEABLENESS		
a1: Trust	Students (LS) translated in suspicious response to teachers' directions: 'Why are you asking me this exercise', 'this is not working on my voice' with teachers (HS) responses: 'I don't believe you, be honest with it… It's not that bad, it feels worse than it sounds'. On the other hand, teacher (LS) resulted in feeling threatened from questions of student (HS)	Low score of teacher with high score for student seems preferable in opposition to high scoring teacher and low student scoring
	So students' (HS) teachers (LS) may benefit the development of the student by following most of the teachers' directions	
a2: Straightforwardness	Teachers (LS) presented a more 'manipulative' side by switching between different approaches, moving from repertoire to technique and back without letting the student consciously understand what and why it is happening	Contrasting score may be beneficial
	Students' (HS) behaviour was shown for instance with: 'You have been promising me this reference for some time: Now it's urgent' (student to teacher)	
a4: Compliance	Teacher (HS) identified by tolerance and patience in exploring the same method as many times as necessary and student (LS) by becoming aggressive with his/herself	Contrast scores may benefit the relationship in particular if the teacher's score high in opposition to student low

(continued)

Table 13.1 (continued)

Personality trait	Behaviours	Recommended scoring
	On the opposite teachers' (LS) behaviours were associated with contesting and impatience regarding the students' requests: 'To me that's better, but what do I know?'	
a6: Tender-mindedness	Teachers (HS) tended to understand the physical conditionings of voice and adapting the lessons. Teachers (LS) insisted on working on voice despite the students (HS) requests	Contrasting scores may help balance the relationship. Preferably, teachers should score high
C: CONSCIENTIOUSNESS		
c1: Competence	Students (LS) feeling frustrated although singing seemed to be going well and facing in a defeated way the technical challenges. Teachers (HS) responded through adding sensibility to approach the student ('dear', 'darling')	The teachers' high score is recommended although students low score in opposition may not be beneficial
	On the other hand, teachers (LS) were more defensive and blaming student for lack of preparation. The students (HS) responded with persistence	
c2: Order	The students (HS) bring questions regarding repertoire, auditions and career advisement. Students (LS) were characterized through often not knowing where scores were, not preparing presentations, displaying all belongings in different places of the room, forgetting scores and having to leave the room. On the teachers (LS) most disorganized behaviours concerned their agenda and career appointments arrangements, which interfered with the lessons dates and times	Contrasting scores might benefit the relationship The ideal setting for this trait would be both elements scoring high. However, the contrasting dyads may benefit from more balanced organization
c3: Dutifulness	Teachers (HS) was visible through for instance: 'I don't want surprises… I must hear all pieces you'll sing on exam'	Contrasting scores may be beneficial in either teacher or student as one element may balance the other
	In opposition to that, for teachers (LS) was characterized through texting on mobile phone while students sing or the students (HS) trying to divert the lesson from general conversations into singing	

(continued)

Table 13.1 (continued)

Personality trait	Behaviours	Recommended scoring
c5: Self-discipline	Teachers (HS) revealed following a consistent drive of the students' voice. The students' (LS) behaviour was mostly related with feeling frequently discouraged. Neither participants scored in the opposite direction (teacher LS or student HS)	High scoring on teachers may benefit the relationships
c6: Deliberation	Teacher (LS) demonstrated spontaneity in interpretation of songs by laughing, dancing or crying. The student (HS) observed and when confronted with the teacher crying got closer and offered help This behaviour indicated how close a singing teacher student relationship might be and how the use of lyrics might raise emotion	Low score for deliberation on teachers does not seem recommended

Note: Only traits with opposite scoring within the singers' sample were considered for this Table

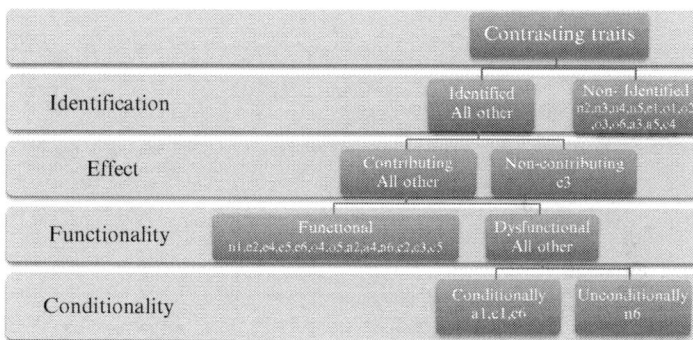

Fig. 13.3 Hierarchical representation of traits' contribution for the singing teacher-student relationship. Letters represent personality traits as presented in Fig. 13.1

The characterization made through personality testing, as shown above, allows a perception of potential expected behaviours between singing teachers and students that can provide the means for distinguishing functional from dysfunctional relationships. This instrument may be particularly important when used previously to the relationship in order to profile dyads and highlight characteristics that ultimately will raise the quality of relationship.

The other instrument used for the evaluation of singing teacher-student relationship was the adult attachment scale. For the participants' analysis it was considered the combination of attachment styles as suggested earlier. With this instrument it was possible to group the dyads in correspondence to their styles, as shown in Fig. 13.4.

Fig. 13.4 Distribution of
participants (teachers and
students) according to styles
of adult attachment (Collins
and Read 1990)

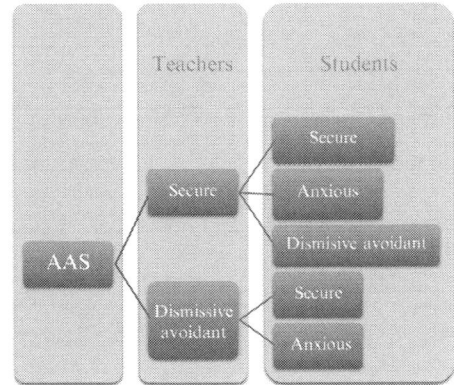

Figure 13.4 illustrates all combinations of participants' styles of attachment, which presents five combinations between teachers and students. Other eight combinations of attachment style would be possible but did not appear within the present sample. The repetition of combinations, however, seemed important as it allowed a comparative analysis between dyads.

As a starting point the teachers' styles were comparatively observed. Clearly different behaviours were noticed between teachers with secure and dismissive-avoidant styles in terms of availability towards their students, stability of the lessons, teaching adaptability and personal involvement. The dismissive avoidant had lower levels of proximity with their students, translated in fewer personal conversations, using little adaptation towards the singing needs of the students and by keeping the same methods persistently being used. In both cases, teachers tended to give too much information to their students as if compensating for their lack of adaptability. So, it was not felt an expected 'avoidance' in the teaching itself but rather in the relational and adaptive behaviours towards the students.

The behaviours presented in Table 13.2 characterized the main differences identified in the relationships of teachers with secure attachment in comparison to dismissive avoidant attachment.

The major contribution of this instrument for the evaluation of a relationship seemed to be at the levels of proximity in comparison to the levels of availability found in the other element of the dyad.

Availability is a particularly important element in the teacher-student relationship. Without meaning that the teacher has to be available for all moments of the students' career life, when lessons were regularly planned, and students had access to exchange occasional information with teachers (through phone, email or by office planned time), this seemed to give great comfort to students and reinforces the importance of availability. For the secure teachers, availability was also translated in letting the students communicate more during the lessons than dismissive avoidant teachers.

Table 13.2 Comparative analysis of behaviours in teachers with secure and dismissive avoidant attachment

Teachers' style of attachment	
Secure	Dismissive-avoidant
Care for students: always asking how students are at beginning of lesson or how the students spent the previous week	**Little personal involvement:** less involvement with the students' external life
Teaching adjustment: switch between strategies for the benefit of student's development	**Stick to same approach:** although the approach often seems to take longer to result, the approaches are insisted
Adaptation to physical conditions: lessons are more adapted to the physical condition of the students by engaging in conversation when the voice becomes tired or students' voice is not responding	**Same methods of vocal use:** the same methods are used in order to solve additional complications and more continuous singing activities
Balanced justification of teaching strategies: intercalate singing with explanations; give indications when intended needed	**Over justification the teaching options or no justifications:** teachers tended to used one extreme of behaviour or the other
Balanced availability: regular lessons and possible contact between lessons if necessary	**Little availability:** lessons are hard to schedule, part of lessons are spent trying to find space on agenda; teacher-student distance makes it hard to communicate between lessons

Table 13.3 Comparative analysis of behaviours in students with secure in comparison to other styles of attachment

Students' style of attachment	
Secure	Anxious, dismissive-avoidant, fearful avoidant
Questioning: question teachers more than other styles	**Fears rejection:** do not question teachers' choices or indications
More independent taking own decision and depend less on the teacher	**More dependent**: count with teacher for most decisions, particularly concerning their career
Less problematic: Rarely reported being involved in problems with other individuals of the educational institution	**More problematic**: students brought to lessons relational problems and arguments with other people from the institution
Confident: without seeming arrogant take singing with more confidence	**Worried**: fear failure more often

On the students' characterization, a wider range of attachment styles were demonstrated. A comparative analysis of behaviour differentiation between secure and insecure styles of attachment is presented in Table 13.3.

The behaviours between secure and insecure styles were clearly identified as presented in Table 13.3, however, between the insecure there was not a clear differentiation to allow a consistent classification. A contributing factor might be as expressed in the literature, that secure styles are clearly identifiable in comparison with all other styles but not between the other dismissive avoidant, anxious and fearful-avoidant styles within mixed couples (Feeney et al. 1994; Kirkpatrick and Davis 1994; Simpson 1990).

Regarding the behavioural observation of dyads according to the styles of adult attachment of the other participant it was noticed that secure matched with secure elements projected a more functional relationship than mixed dyads. In the secure-secure dyads the relationships in most cases seemed to provide the necessary elements for the singing activities to progress smoothly, whereas in mixed dyads the relationship tended to interfere more often with the working activities.

Furthermore, an analysis was performed to evaluate whether teachers' secure style matched with insecure student projected a different type of dysfunctional relationship from insecure teachers with secure student. Taking that the teachers seem to have most interference in the lessons outcome, it seemed that preferably dyads with secure teachers performed better lessons than the opposite. Further research (with larger number of participants) is believed to bring clearer elements to the evaluation of singing teacher-student attachment.

13.5   Conclusion

The combination of observational studies with the data from psychological instruments provided a more accurate and valuable indication that singing teachers and students tend to behave according to their personal and psychological characterisation, which takes the understanding of singing lessons into a more objective setting. Furthermore, the application of psychological instruments into music studies and specifically in singing was enriched by the combined use of personality and adult attachment in observations. Its findings are of relevance for heads of vocal departments, singing teachers and students by providing means of predicting, interpreting and supporting relational quality.

The studied lessons revealed similar characteristics in terms of most teacher domination observed in instrumental lessons indicating that between vocal and instrumental lessons this characteristic is generally maintained. Adding to that result, this study contextualized the interactions occurring in singing lessons and concluded that teacher dominance is based on two essential factors: the personal characteristics, whenever teachers' traits are characterised by dominant behaviours; and by professional conditionings, which imposed an attitude of being 'in charge'. The first factor indicated that most teachers follow a personality characterisation of high scoring assertiveness (e3) translated in being more decisive and confident. However, in a few dyads an inversion of roles was observed, in which the student was effectively in charge of the lesson: driving conversations or diverting between matters of lessons. For these dyads, the characterisation clearly presented students with more dominant characteristics or teachers with insecure style of attachment. Nevertheless, this research confirms the previous characterisation of instrumental setting by Daniel (2006), Hepler (1986) and Persson (1996) but adds to previous literature the fact that occasionally, rare dyads present inverted roles of lessons' dominance.

The consistency of teachers' behaviour in response to different students was tested and an adaptive behaviour was felt from most of the teachers towards the different characteristics of students in terms of teaching approach, types of feedback and communication means. These elements of interactive adaptability are in conformity to the previous study by Presland (2005) where teachers adapt to students as the variable element; but it contrasts with Reid's (2001) perception that teaching adaptability is not yet implemented in instrumental teaching. The present study adds to Presland (2005) and Reid (2001) by identifying the element of the students' personality and adult attachment that is responsible, if not for all, for most variations of behaviour.

The observation indicated that the relationships developed into becoming more personal and often included elements from the personal lives of both teacher and student. The relational development between teacher and student includes a wide list of variables, such as means of accurate communication: the further the relationship developed the fewer complementary tools became needed, single gestures or vocalizations being sufficient for students to understand the teacher's intentions, suggesting that the relationship with the student could have major impact on other aspects of singing.

The personality and attachment tests provided an identification of potential behaviours that ultimately influence the teacher student relationship. The use of such elements consists in a complementary validated psychological element that increases the potential of teacher-student relationships working in higher levels of quality and previously to the relationship, measuring the personal potentialities of both teacher and student.

Currently there are few effective tools available to provide heads of department, teachers and singing students with clear prediction of relational success. In higher education, where a graduate course might last for 3 or 4 years, a student who spends half that time in a dysfunctional relationship may ultimately see his/her professional potential being affected and perhaps limiting a future career. The identification of predictive relationship matching is therefore of great importance and this study contributes towards the quality of those relationships.

The present chapter has demonstrated which traits of personality and attachment styles might be crucial for the quality of relationships between singing teachers and students and concluded, like Mason (2000), that there are as many ways to teach singing as there are singing teachers. However, each teacher and student is equipped with a group of characteristics that allow a behavioural prediction and there is benefit for teachers and students in being more aware of the effects and effectiveness of these pairings.

References

Ainsworth, M., Blehar, M., Waters, E., & Wall, S. (1978). *Patterns of attachment: A psychological study of the strange situation*. Hillsdale: Erlbaum.

Atkinson, L. (1997). Attachment and psychopathology: From laboratory to clinic. In L. Atkinson & K. J. Zucker (Eds.), *Attachment and psychopathology* (pp. 3–16). New York: Guildford Press.

Bäckström, M. (2001). Measuring adult attachment: A construct validation of two self–report instruments. *Scandinavian Journal of Psychology, 42*, 79–86.

Bartholomew, R. (1990). Avoidance of intimacy: An attachment perspective. *Journal of Social and Personal Relationships, 7*, 147–178.

Bayley, T. M. (2006). *The relationship between adult attachment and physical health, with a specific focus on the adjustment to infertility*. Unpublished doctoral thesis, University of Sheffield.

Bell, C. R., & Cresswell, A. (1984). Personality differences among musical instrumentalists. *Psychology of Music, 12*, 83–93.

Berman, W. H., Marcus, L., & Berman, E. R. (1994). Attachment in marital relations. In M. B. Sperling & W. H. Berman (Eds.), *Attachment in adults: Clinical and developmental perspectives* (pp. 204–231). New York: Guilford Press.

Bowlby, J. (1969). *Attachment and loss*. New York: Basic Books.

Bowlby, J. (1988). *A secure base*. New York: Basic Books.

Canavarro, M. C. (1999). Inventário de sintomas psicopatológicos – BSI. In M. R. Simões, M. Gonçalves, & L. S. Almeida (Eds.), *Testes e Provas Psicológicas em Portugal* (Vol. II). Braga: APPORT/SHO.

Carver, C. S. (1997). Adult attachment and personality: Converging evidence and a new measure. *Bulletin of Personality and Social Psychology, 23*, 865–883.

Chamorro-Premuzic, T., Swami, V., Furnham, A., & Maakip, I. (2009). The big five personality traits and uses of music: A replication in Malaysia using structural equation modeling. *Journal of Individual Differences, 30*, 20–27.

Collins, N. L., & Read, S. J. (1990). Adult attachment relationships, working models and relationship quality in dating couples. *Journal of Personality and Social Psychology, 58*, 644–683.

Costa, P. T., Jr., & McCrae, R. P. (1992). *Revised NEO Personality Inventory (NEO-PI-R) and NEO Five-Factor Inventory (NEO-FFI) professional manual*. Odessa: Psychological Assessment Resources.

Costa, P. T., Jr., & McCrae, R. R. (2000). *NEO PI-R Manual Professional (NEO PI-R), Inventário de Personalidade NEO Revisto*. Lisboa: CEGOG-TEA.

Daniel, R. (2006). Exploring music instrument teaching and learning environments: Video analysis as a means of elucidating process and learning outcomes. *Music Education Research, 8*, 191–215.

Davidson, J. W., Moore, D. G., Sloboda, J. A., & Howe, M. J. (1998). Characteristics of music teachers and the progress of young instrumentalists. *Journal of Research in Music Education, 46*, 141–160.

DeNovellis, R., & Lawrence, G. (1983). Correlations of teacher personality variables (Myers-Briggs) and classroom observation data. *Research in Psychological Type, 6*, 37–46.

Dews, B., & Williams, M. S. (1989). Student musicians' personality styles, stresses, and coping patterns. *Psychology of Music, 17*, 37–47.

Dozier, M., & Tyrell, C. (1998). The role of attachment in therapeutic relationships. In J. A. Simpson & W. S. Rhodes (Eds.), *Attachment theory and close relationships* (pp. 221–248). New York: Guilford Press.

Dozier, M., Stovall, K. C., & Albus, K. E. (1999). Attachment and psychopathology in adulthood. In J. Cassidy & P. R. Shaver (Eds.), *Handbook of attachment: Theory, research and clinical applications* (pp. 497–519). New York: Guildford Press.

Dryer, D. C., & Horowitz, L. M. (1997). When do opposites attract? Interpersonal complementarity versus similarity. *Journal of Personality and Social Psychology, 72*, 592–603.

Dwyer, D. (2000). *Interpersonal relationships*. London: Routledge.

Feeney, J. (1999). Adult romantic attachment and couple relationships. In J. Cassidy & P. R. Shaver (Eds.), *Handbook of attachment: Theory, research and clinical applications* (pp. 355–377). New York: Guildford Press.

Feeney, J. A., Noller, P., & Callan, V. J. (1994). Attachment style, communication and satisfaction in the early years of marriage. In K. Bartholomew & D. Perlman (Eds.), *Advances in personal relationships* (Vol. 5, pp. 269–308). London: Jessica Kingsley.

George, C., Kaplan, N., & Main, M. (1984). *Attachment interview for adults*. Unpublished manuscript, University of California.

Goodstein, R. E. (1987). An investigation into leadership behaviours and descriptive characteristics of high school band directors in the United States. *Journal of Research in Music Education, 35*, 13–25.

Greenberg, M. T. (1999). Attachment and psychopathology in childhood. In J. Cassidy & P. R. Shaver (Eds.), *Handbook of attachment: Theory, research and clinical applications* (pp. 469–496). New York: Guildford Press.

Hallam, S. (1998). *Instrumental teaching: A practical guide to better teaching and learning.* Oxford: Heinemann.

Hazan, C., & Shaver, P. (1987). Romantic love conceptualized as an attachment process. *Journal of Personality and Social Psychology, 52*, 511–524.

Hepler, L. E. (1986). *The measurement of teacher-student interaction in private music lessons and its relationship to the field dependence/field independence.* Unpublished doctoral dissertation, Case Western Reserve University.

Holtzworth-Munroe, A., Stuart, G. L., & Hutchinson, G. (1997). Violent versus nonviolent husbands: Differences in attachment patterns, dependency, and jealousy. *Journal of Family Psychology, 11*, 314–331.

Howard, V. A. (1982). *Artistry: The work of artists.* Indianápolis: Hackett.

Jäncke, L., & Sandmann, P. (2010). Music listening while you learn: No influence of background music on verbal learning. *Behavioral and Brain Functions.* doi:10.1186/1744-9081-6-3.

Kemp, A. E. (2004). *The musical temperament: Psychology and personality of musicians.* Oxford: Oxford University Press.

Kennell, R. (2002). Systematic research in studio instruction in music. In R. Colwell & C. Richardson (Eds.), *The new handbook of research on music teaching and learning* (pp. 243–256). New York: Oxford University Press.

Kirkpatrick, L. A. (1999). Attachment and religious representations and behavior. In J. Cassidy & P. R. Shaver (Eds.), *Handbook of attachment: Theory, research and clinical applications* (pp. 803–822). New York: Guildford Press.

Kirkpatrick, L. A., & Davis, K. E. (1994). Attachment style, gender, and relationship stability: A longitudinal analysis. *Journal of Personality and Social Psychology, 66*, 502–512.

Kurdek, L. A. (2002). On being insecure about the assessment of attachment styles. *Journal of Social and Personal Relationships, 19*, 811–834.

Kurdek, L. A., & Schmitt, J. P. (1986). Relationship quality of partners in heterosexual married, heterosexual cohabiting, and gay and lesbian relationships. *Journal of Personality and Social Psychology, 51*, 711–720.

Lions-Ruth, K., & Jacobvitz, D. (1999). Attachment disorganization: unresolved loss, relational violence, and lapses in behavioural and attachment strategies. In J. Cassidy & P. R. Shaver (Eds.), *Handbook of attachment: Theory, research and clinical applications* (pp. 520–554). New York: Guildford Press.

Livingston, E. (1987). *Making sense of ethnomethodology.* London: Routledge.

Mallinckrodt, B., Cocle, H. M., & Gantt, D. L. (1995). Working alliance, attachment memories, and social competencies of woman in brief therapy. *Journal of Counselling Psychology, 42*, 79–84.

Mason, D. (2000). The teaching (and learning) of singing. In J. Potter (Ed.), *The Cambridge companion to singing* (pp. 204–220). Cambridge: Cambridge University Press.

Mohr, J. J. (1999). Same-sex romantic attachment. In J. Cassidy & P. R. Shaver (Eds.), *Handbook of attachment: Theory, research and clinical applications* (pp. 378–394). New York: Guildford Press.

Moss, S., Garivaldis, F. J., & Toukhsati, S. R. (2006). The perceived similarity of other individuals: The contaminating effects of familiarity and neuroticism. *Personality and Individual Differences, 43*, 401–412.

Pembrook, R., & Craig, C. (2002). Teaching as profession: Two variations on a theme. In R. Colwell & C. Richardson (Eds.), *The new handbook of research on music teaching and learning* (pp. 786–817). New York: Oxford University Press.

Persson, R. (1996). Brilliant performers as teachers: A case study of commonsense teaching in a conservatoire setting. *International Journal of Music Education, 28*, 25–36.

Pianta, R. C. (1997). Adult-child relationship processes and early schooling. *Early Education and Development, 8*, 11–26.

Presland, C. (2005). Conservatoire student and instrumental professor: The student perspective on a complex relationship. *British Journal of Music Education, 22*, 237–248.

Reid, A. (2001). Variations in the ways that instrumental and vocal students experience learning music. *Music Education Research, 3*, 25–40.

Roe, A. (1958). *The psychology of occupations*. New York: Wiley.

Schechtman, Z. (1989). The contribution of interpersonal behaviour to the prediction of initial teaching success: A research note. *Teaching and Teachers Education, 5*, 243–248.

Schmidt, C. P. (1989). Individual differences in perception of applied feedback. *Psychology of Music, 17*, 110–122.

Shaver, P. R., & Brennan, K. A. (1992). Attachment styles and the 'big five' personality traits: Their connections with each other and with romantic relationship outcomes. *Personality and Social Psychology Bulletin, 18*, 536–545.

Shaver, P. R., & Fraley, R. C. (2004). *Self-report measures of adult attachment*. University of Illinois. Available online at. http://www.psych.uiuc.edu/~rcfraley/measures/measures.html. Accessed 22 Jan 2009.

Shaver, P. R., Hazan, C., & Bradshaw, D. (1988). Love as attachment: The integration of three behavioral systems. In J. Sternberg & M. L. Barnes (Eds.), *The psychology of love* (pp. 68–99). New Haven: Yale University Press.

Shiota, M., & Levenson, R. (2007). Birds of a feather don't always fly farthest: Similarity in big five personality predicts more negative marital satisfaction trajectories in long-term marriages. *Psychology and Aging, 22*, 666–675.

Shiota, M. N., Keltner, D., & John, O. P. (2006). Positive emotion disposition differentially associated with big five personality and attachment style. *Journal of Positive Psychology, 1*, 61–71.

Simpson, J. A. (1990). Influence of attachment styles on romantic relationships. *Journal of Personality and Social Psychology, 59*, 971–980.

Slade, A. (1999). Attachment theory and research: Implications for the theory and practice on individual psychotherapy with adults. In J. Cassidy & P. R. Shaver (Eds.), *Handbook of attachment: Theory, research and clinical applications* (pp. 575–594). New York: Guildford Press.

Soares, I. (2007). Desenvolvimento da teoria e da investigação da vinculação. In I. Soares (Ed.), *Relações de Vinculação ao Longo do Desenvolvimento: Teoria e Avaliação* (pp. 13–46). Braga: Psiquilibrios.

Sperling, M., & Lyons, L. (1994). Representations of attachment and psychotherapeutic change. In M. B. Sperling & W. H. Berman (Eds.), *Attachment in adults: Clinical and developmental perspectives* (pp. 331–348). New York: Guildford Press.

Sroufe, L. A., Carlson, E., Levy, A., & Egelang, B. (1999). Implications of attachment theory for developmental psychopathology. *Development and Psychopathology, 11*, 1–14.

Torgersen, A. M., Grova, B. K., & Sommerstad, R. (2007). A pilot study of attachment patterns in adult twins. *Attachment and Human Development, 9*, 127–138.

Vaughn, B. E., & Bost, K. K. (1999). Attachment and temperament: Redundant, independent, or interacting influences on interpersonal adaptation and personality development? In J. Cassidy & P. Shaver (Eds.), *Handbook of attachment* (pp. 198–225). New York: Guilford Press.

Weiss, R. S. (1991). The attachment bond in childhood and adulthood. In C. M. Parkes, J. Stevenson-Hinde, & P. Harris (Eds.), *Attachment across the life cycle* (pp. 66–67). London: Routledge.

West, M., & Sheldon-Keller, A. E. (1994). Psychotherapy strategies for insecure attachment in personality disorders. In M. B. Sperling & W. H. Berman (Eds.), *Attachment in adults: Clinical and developmental perspectives* (pp. 313–330). New York: Guildford Press.

Wink, R. L. (1970). The relationship of self-concept and selected personality variables to achievement in music student teaching. *Journal of Research in Music Education, 18*, 234–241.

Wubbenhorst, T. M. (1991). Music educators' personality types as measured by the Myers-Briggs type indicator. *Contributions to Music Education, 18*, 7–19.

Young, M. (1990). Characteristics of high potential and at risk teachers. *Action in Teacher Education, 11*, 33–40.

Chapter 14
Negotiating an 'Opera Singer Identity'

Jane Oakland

Abstract Forming an identity as a musician has become a vibrant topic for music research, not least because of the changing landscape of the music industry and the need continually to evaluate what it means to be a musician. In this chapter I explore the concept of an 'Opera Singer Identity' and how an understanding of this construction can help teachers support their students both in preparing for, and maintaining, a professional career. The empirical data used in this chapter is derived from a larger study which investigated the effects of redundancy on opera choristers. Using the framework of a professional identity, which describes what a person does, and a subjective identity, which is what a person feels they are, I propose that the 'Opera Singer Identity' is a professional identity because it is endorsed by paid work and the social and cultural status given to the job title and I highlight the fragility of an identity that is based primarily on external validation. Instead, I suggest that singers and their teachers could give more attention to subjective identities, such as being a 'singer', a 'performer' or a 'musician' in order to encourage continuity of self in a diverse employment market.

Keywords Opera singers • Musical identity • Career transitions

14.1   What Is Identity and Why Is It Important?

Identity is: 'knowing who we are, who others are, them knowing who we are, us knowing who they think we are' (Jenkins 2008, 5).

The concept of self and identity is well documented in a wide variety of academic contexts and 'has been one of the unifying themes of social sciences for the last twenty

J. Oakland (✉)
Psychology Department, Glasgow Caledonian University, Glasgow, Scotland, UK
e-mail: jane.oakland@btinternet.com

S.D. Harrison and J. O'Bryan (eds.), *Teaching Singing in the 21st Century*,   221
Landscapes: the Arts, Aesthetics, and Education 14, DOI 10.1007/978-94-017-8851-9_14,
© Springer Science+Business Media Dordrecht 2014

years' (Jenkins 2008, 28). Although the term has been criticised for its ambiguity (Brubaker and Cooper 2000) it is still as Jenkins (2008, 13) points out, 'the basic cognitive mechanism that humans use to sort out themselves and their fellows, individually and collectively'. In other words, identity can be thought of as a process of self-knowledge, developed in part through interactions between the self and the society we live in. Language is considered to be one of the main symbolic systems for negotiating such social interactions and Hargreaves et al. (2002) believe that music acts in a similar way to spoken language, as a medium through which people construct identities and change existing ones.

14.1.1 Continuity of Self

If identity is seen as a continually evolving, dynamic process, dependent on life events, thought should also be given to the way individuals maintain a stable sense of self. Markus and Nurius (1986) introduced the concept of 'possible selves', which refers to an individual perception of the future-orientated components of self. This future-orientated self is closely connected with a past and present self-concept, thereby creating a continuity of self during life transitions. Change or transition forms part of natural development and musicians undergo many transitions during their musical development, such as becoming a music student (Burland and Pitts 2007), moving from student to professional musician (Creech et al. 2008), or career termination (Oakland et al. 2012). The concept of 'possible selves' implies that a musician who has high self-esteem as a student is likely to enter the profession with high expectations of success, whereas a student who has struggled may find it difficult to imagine professional opportunities. Looking for stability through adverse change can be a more complicated process requiring an individual to re-evaluate elements of a 'past self' in order to imagine a 'future self' (Oakland et al. 2012).

Bennett (2007) found that most performance-based musicians defined themselves according to their instrumental speciality, which implies a self-definition that is reliant on professional performing opportunities. However, Hargreaves et al. (2002) point out that it is the way in which humans view themselves in relation to these culturally defined roles that is central to our concept of identities in music. Because a musician's career is increasingly based on a portfolio of activities (performance and non-performance), a broader meaning given to such labels such as musician, singer or violinist could give greater stability to the self in a changing work environment.

14.1.2 The Professional and the Subjective Identity

When Mills (2004, 2006) investigated the careers of music college graduates she based her work on the concepts of a professional identity and a subjective identity.

The former refers to what a person actually does in terms of employment, and Mills cited the examples of doctors and lawyers who take their identity from the work they do and subsequently the time spent doing that work. The subjective identity is what people feel they are, regardless of employment. This is particularly relevant to performing artists who may spend more time working in an office than performing, where the meaning given to being a violinist or a singer may need to rely on a subjective view of identity rather than paid musical employment. Mills (2004) gives the example of 'performer teachers' who see themselves more as musicians than teachers, even though the majority of their employment comes from teaching.

The opera singer label could be thought of as a professional identity because it describes the type of work that certain singers undertake. However, differing perceptions of this title by individual singers and the general public mean that the expectations associated with this identity can vary. For example, professional opera singers commonly view the label as validation of their skill level because it implies that they are in employment (although the same may not be true for students or freelance opera singers), but the term is often used by the wider public to describe any singer who has classical training. The criteria of what constitutes an opera singer is also changing as many well-known artists now engage in what has become known as 'cross-over' activities. Expectations of labelling are also likely to influence the behaviour and thought processes of a singer's identity construction. For example, Pascale (2002, cited in Welch 2005) describes the case of a woman born in Barbados but living in the USA. She considered herself to be a non-singer in the USA because in that society, singing meant being able to perform to others and therefore be subjected to critical evaluation. However, in Barbados, she felt able to call herself a singer because in that culture a singer was someone who sang along with other people in a more informal way without being judged on technical abilities. Welch (2005) attributes this to different internal representations of what it is to be a singer. This example also shows how the appropriateness of a particular identity is influenced by the environment or context within which it is perceived. An issue addressed in this chapter is the relationship between a singer's internal or subjective view of being singer and the external context in which it is perceived.

14.2 The Profession of 'Opera Singer'

> The opera business is very selective: you've got to be attractive, you've got to have a good personality but above all you've got to be fit, and I don't think they underline any of those in the job description.

These comments were made by a singer who has recently been forced to give up an operatic career. No reference is made to the voice in this 'job description'. Instead emphasis is given to the physicality of the work. This singer was unable to work, not due to loss of vocal ability but the onset of physical disabilities. The extract shows that vocal ability alone is no longer sufficient to make a career as an opera singer.

The work of an opera singer has seen many changes since opera first emerged as an art form, around 1600. According to Rosselli (1992) there was initially no such recognised profession as 'opera singer'. Even the term 'singer' was not a clearly defined trade, with many singers accompanying themselves on instruments, composing their own songs, or alternating between singing and playing instruments. These performers were totally dependent on patrons from a higher social standing to provide them not only with a living but also a position in society. Musicians employed by the nobility were expected to give regular performances, and additionally, to serve in other non-musical ways such as gardening or embroidery (Rosselli 1992, 9). Early opera choristers of nineteenth Century were generally regarded as being the 'working class' of the opera world. Rosselli (1992, 202) also notes that most Italian chorus singers were ordinary working people who sang in their spare time, many of them not even able to read music.

'Being an opera singer' has grown considerably in status since these early beginnings. Opera is still a medium that provides the most employment for classically trained singers but the demands of contemporary opera production require singers to be proficient in much more than just singing. Technological advances mean that video and cinema screening is normal practice but this places enormous pressure on singers to be all-round, glamorous performers. Technology has also paved the way for greater investment in lighting and set design in the quest for ever greater visual spectacles which, some may say, detracts from the core musical quality of opera. Bennett (2008) feels that technological change can, in general, create exciting new opportunities for performing artists, but at the same time she notes that many performers are forced to supplement performing with teaching, administrative or non-musical work – a situation not unlike the early beginnings of opera profession. Economically, it is likely that greater investment in technology may ultimately reduce the number of singers employed on a production. The number of live opera performances may also decrease as the popularity of live relays and cinema screening increases. These current trends in the opera industry mean that singers need to be multi-skilled and flexible in their approach to making a living.

This chapter continues by reporting one part of an extensive study that explored the effects of redundancy and identity formation for opera choristers (Oakland et al. 2013). Examination of the loss of identity can shed greater light on how that identity is constructed. Findings of this study showed that occupational crisis caused the professional 'opera singer identity' to fragment revealing several subjective identities: being a musician, being a performer and being a singer. The singers who were most successful in adapting to change were those who were able to renew their allegiance to these subjective identities and thereby re-evaluate the meaning of 'being an opera singer'. The findings of this study also highlighted the individual differences in adapting to change which are explained by models such as those by Schlossberg (1981). She states that it is not the transition itself that is important but how the transition fits with an individual's circumstances at the time and their perception of the change. Therefore, the following section takes a personal approach to the presentation of data in order to emphasise the importance of individuality in perception of self. All names used are fictitious.

14.3 Methods

14.3.1 The Participants

I conducted in-depth semi-structured interviews with seven UK-based opera choristers who had recently been made redundant from full-time employment. The singers had all been full-time opera choristers for a minimum of 10 years and a maximum of 26 years. This meant that self-labelling as an opera singer had become synonymous with professional employment. Table 14.1 outlines the career history of the participants. With one exception (Joe), the redundancies occurred as part of corporate re-structuring plans. All participants were given a choice of opting for early redundancy or waiting until it was inevitable. Seven singers chose early redundancy because they felt this gave them some degree of control over their future.

14.3.2 Data Analysis

The data I collected were analysed using Interpretative Phenomenological Analysis (IPA). This qualitative method of analysis provides an in-depth, subjective account of individual experiences of a phenomenon (see Smith et al. 2009). IPA acknowledges the active role of the researcher in accessing these experiences. At the time of the study I was myself a professional opera singer and I believe this was a contributing factor to the richness of data obtained. IPA analysis follows a series of stages that systematically identify themes and patterns, first across individual transcripts and then the whole data set. Following the detailed analysis of one transcript, the process

Table 14.1 Participant information

Participant	Age	Marital status	Career history	Current employment
Helen	49	Married, two children	20 years with one company. Chose redundancy 2004	Working fulltime in property business
Moira	49	Single parent, one child	11 years with one company. Chose redundancy 2004	Combines freelance work with gardening
Hugh	47	Single	20 years with one company. Made redundant 2004	Freelance chorister
Fiona	50	Married, two children	28 years with two companies. Chose redundancy 2001	Teaches singing and does concert work
Andy	50	Married, two children	10 years freelance singer. 10 years fulltime singer. Chose redundancy 2001	Freelance teacher and conductor
Beth	52	Married	23 years with two companies. Asked to be made redundant 2001	Paints and runs an art gallery
Joe	50	Single	25 years with two companies. Made redundant 2000	Teaches singing

is repeated with every transcript, carefully considering each case in its own right, in addition to exploring shared commonalities across the transcripts (i.e. what is recurrent). The latter are then transformed into a narrative account that combines textual evidence with researcher interpretation. Three elements of identity formation were found to be influential in making sense of occupational change, namely the singers' relationship with work, the stage, and singing.

14.4 The Opera Singer Identity

14.4.1 'Me' and the Job

The theory of role identity salience views the self as a construction of roles, defined in part by social structure and in part by the individual (Tajfel 1978). Critical to this perspective is the assumption that some roles or allegiances are more salient than others. Self-definition that is associated with a salient role is likely to be more important because it influences and overall concept of self. Therefore positive self-esteem relies on successful performance of salient roles (Callero 1985). Because work occupies a large percentage of our lives it is therefore likely that for a professional musician, an occupational role will have a high degree of salience. A successful career will therefore influence an overall concept of self. The extracts below demonstrate how special the participants felt to be able to call themselves opera singers:

> When somebody asks me what I do for a living and I say I'm an opera singer, it's immense and I don't want to let that go. I don't want to say I used to be an opera singer. (Moira)

> I definitely rode on the fact that I was an opera singer, nothing to do with singing but the name of the job and the level of the job. I had this great pride that actually I sing with a national company. I got a lot of my identity from that. (Fiona)

> A job like a singer, my feeling for that is you're a very gifted very special person to be allowed to do a job like that, there are so few of us around. (Helen)

For these singers the job title has more influence on identity formation than their talent as singers. In addition, like Fiona, all the singers placed great value on belonging to a high-ranking opera company because it validated their level of professional standing. The fear expressed by Moira of being an 'ex-opera singer' was shared by all the female participants because they felt it would reflect on the level of their abilities both within the musical community and in the eyes of the wider public. Theoretically, all the singers could look for freelance employment, but some were limited by family commitments, and Joe by his physical incapacities. At the time of the interviews, Hugh was the only singer working as a freelance chorister but comments from Helen highlight the difference in status perceived between permanent and freelance choristers:

> Towards the end when I made the decision to go early, I was officially part-time and it was awful, it felt like you were nothing on the stage. You were automatically looked on

differently, even by colleagues. I was then classed as a part-time chorister and that was the start of the loss of status if you like, it was the beginning of realising that I wasn't going to be the same person.

Helen opted for early redundancy 1 year before the final notices were issued. The extract highlights an identity that is dependent on validation not only from an audience but also from colleagues. Hugh adapted to this situation by decreasing his loyalty to the job:

As a free-lancer you can often be stuck at the back of the stage as just being an extra body, and now I just stand back and let the full-timers get to the front of the stage if they want. As a full-time chorister I think I cared more about the work than I do as an extra chorister.

A commonality between Hugh and Helen is that they both experienced a psychological lack of presence on stage when they were no longer on a permanent contract. Although they were functioning physically on the stage in the way they always had, there was no sense of belonging. Because opera choristers work in close proximity with each other there can be a sense of family attached to being a member of a company. For example, Joe talked of 'feeling safe' and 'returning home' when he worked with his favourite opera house. Loss of employment is therefore a loss of community, which Helen interpreted as rejection. Other singers avoided long-term feelings of rejection by reappraising the work that had once given them status and security. Andy said he didn't think he had ever called himself an opera singer, which allowed him to follow other musical pursuits such as conducting. Others focussed on the negative aspects of the work. For example Beth commented that her working life was 'like being in prison' while Fiona described her life as an opera chorister as 'living in a wee bubble', metaphors which suggest containment and constraint. Devaluing the profession in this way reduced the salience of a professional identity and these singers were in a better position to explore other avenues of self.

To say 'I'm an opera singer' has been a way for the singers to feel special and different within the wider community. The singers relied on the title for individual and group status as well as endorsement of professional abilities. They also used the prestige of the company they worked for to support their identity in music. Without that support they were just singers with no external validation of their abilities. This may be symptomatic of a profession where artists are constantly under evaluation by the general public as well as their colleagues. Bennett (2009) notes that future of music work is more likely to follow the protean career model which is shaped by the individual rather than the organisation (Hall 1976), and where the employee will have less employer support and need to be more self-reliant (Weick 1996). This requires a strong sense of identity that is not solely linked to one company or a specific job title.

14.4.2 'Me' and the Stage

The nature of operatic work creates another dimension to 'self-forming' due to the addition of the stage and acting requirements. Davidson (2005) suggests that a singer is constantly creating a tension between the 'character' on stage and the 'real person' on stage. Living and working in a theatrical environment is a major contributor to the opera singer identity. When the participants were no longer able to work on the stage, the delicate balance between stage and real-life was also disrupted. Andy and Hugh felt that the stage was something to be left behind at the end of a working day but there were others who felt the stage was an integral part of the self. For Beth and Moira, this element of self helped provide continuity during career disruption. Beth talked of how she had to 'learn to be an ex-opera singer' as if learning a new role and thereby reinforced her performer identity. Davidson (2002) examined the qualities and personality traits that constituted being a performer. She concluded that one of the characteristics of a performing personality is being able to 'show off' in a number of different ways. This is clearly seen in Moira's perception of what it means to be a singer:

> I'm not a shy little wallflower when I'm away from the stage. Being a singer is attention seeking. I don't want to sit back and let someone else take centre stage.

Moira seems to focus more on her need to be the centre of attention rather than her loss of professional singing work. When she was made redundant Moira enlisted on a gardening course, which provided her with a different stage:

> I went in as an opera singer and I think I was accepted in the first week and when the principal of the college found out that I had been an opera singer, he brought the local newspaper in and I have a photo of myself – the singing gardener or something like that.

Because Moira's view of 'being a singer' is 'being centre stage' she still feels able to describe herself as an opera singer in a non-musical world. The acceptance she refers to appears to be for herself, as a celebrity in the wider community, rather than fitting in as a potential gardener. Helen and Joe appeared less able to function outside of a theatrical environment:

> You can be someone else not just the person you are. When you work on a stage you go through life being so many different people. I don't feel comfortable with this person who doesn't do what I do.

Without a theatrical environment Helen experienced a self with which she was unfamiliar and appears to have limited resources to adapt to real-life or discover the 'real Helen'. In the extract she talks about herself in the third person as if she is observing a physical body which functions in daily life, but one with which she is unable to engage psychologically. Joe talks more specifically about his loss by referring specifically to the opera, Peter Grimes. In this opera the chorus represent a powerful village community that turn against the misfit Peter Grimes with disastrous results:

> There's something about being in the company of like-minded individuals. Like Grimes. When you get a real community, work as a community together, and you're all really acting your character, living your character, and to have experienced that and then not to have it anymore is difficult.

Joe used this opera as a metaphor several times during the interview. His comments show confusion between what is acted and what is lived and highlight what it means to lose a professional community where relationships are built on and off stage. Joe wants to feel included as part of a community but seems to identify with the character of Peter Grimes in order to help him make sense of his loss.

There is a danger of creating an ideology about stage life that cannot be truly replicated in real life and for Helen loss of the theatre equates with a loss of self. However, Beth and Moira have found ways to bring elements of performance into daily life and Joe appears to make sense of his personal crisis through theatrical metaphor. For opera singers the relationship between self and stage appears to be more complex than what Davidson (2002, 108) describes as 'the cultural expectations of the operatic Diva' or that 'loud' personalities are drawn to becoming opera singers'. This is an area ripe for further investigation.

14.4.3 Music, Singing and 'Me'

Relatively little has been documented that makes specific reference to identity and the voice, in the context of a professional singing career. Any understanding of what constitutes a sense of self for a singer must also take into account the embodiment of the vocal instrument. As Welch (2005, 245) points out, the voice is 'an essential aspect of our human identity: of who we are, how we feel, how we communicate and how other people experience us'. A singer communicates entirely through their own body and unlike an external musical instrument, the voice grows with the body and dies with the body. Therefore the voice is likely to play a major role in establishing and maintaining an identity through any life transition. At the time of the interviews, differences emerged between those participants who still viewed themselves and their voice as an inseparable unit and those who took a more objective view of their voice. This comment by Moira shows a feeling of total unity with her voice:

> You can't separate your voice from who you are. I don't believe you can talk about your singing as a separate thing, it's not like a violin or a pianist, it's you, it's human.

Moira sees her voice as a living entity unable to be separated from the physical person and in her mind, this sets her apart from instrumentalists. For Beth, the physical sensations of singing appeared to be an essential experience in order to maintain this sense of self:

> I need an avenue that I can give energy into, it's part of who I am, it's like a fix, there's nothing like it, it's like sex.

Comparisons with sex and drugs imply a fundamental need for the addictive 'high' that singing can induce. More than just a term of identification, singing becomes an essential activity for personal well-being. However, after many years of professional work, comments by Fiona show how easy it is to lose this physical awareness:

> Singing means energy, expression, not identity now, it was identity for years, it isn't identity now.

These comments clearly indicate the differences between a professional and subjective identity. Energy and expression represent the internal, embodied elements of singing, but Fiona doesn't equate these elements with an identity that she based primarily on a job title. It is possible that after many years of professional work, these fundamental elements of singing may have retreated into the background as priority is given to the professional self. Fiona even felt that her professional self dictated the type of clothes she wore which were scruffy rehearsal leggings, stage costume or evening dress. She had no clothes she felt she could call her own. It was a self that, on reflection, Fiona said she was never comfortable with. The close physical and psychological relationship between self and voice has been beneficial to Fiona in renegotiating her sense of self but it can also have a negative effect on wellbeing in a crisis situation. For example, Helen has not been able to make any sung sound since being made redundant and the comments below from Joe show the psychological impact that loss of work can have on vocal self perception:

> I think a singer is somebody who earns a living at it, and, I don't. I earn my living teaching you see so I can't really say I am (a singer). I'm not sure that I get a great thrill out of the physical process of singing any more. I make a noise with my voice.

For Joe the professional and subjective identities are still inseparable. Loss of professional status means that not only has he lost his identity as a singer but also the physical enjoyment of the act of singing. Andy and Hugh cope with the loss of a professional identity by devaluing the role played by singing in their careers:

> Singing isn't the be all and end all for me, I've always been a general musician, it was a way of making a living, satisfying my musical desires, so it wasn't that I was mad keen on opera, I was mad keen on music. (Andy)

> It hasn't been a total obsession but it's basically been a way of earning a living. But you know, the whole colour of music, it kind of nourishes the soul in a way that sitting in an office could never do. (Hugh)

Andy and Hugh both see the voice as a tool to access other areas of musical experience. Andy prefers the broader title of musician rather than singer. Hugh places music on a par with basic physical needs similar to the 'fix' described by Moira. Singing was the means to access this sustenance. Andy and Hugh raised the profile of music in their lives in a way that allowed them to develop a positive self-concept as a musician rather than rejection as a singer. This process can be likened to what is commonly known as 'positive appraisal', which Folkman and Moskowitz (2000) define as changing the meaning of a situation in such a way that a person is able to experience positive emotions from changing events. If life events prevent singers from using the voice as a means of communication there is likely to be a major disruption to a sense of self. The singers who coped best with the loss of professional status were those who could separate the subjective vocal identity, which can be influenced by self-perception, and the professional vocal identity, which is dependent on external factors and the critical acclaim of others.

Summarising these findings, the singers who were most successful in adapting to change – Fiona, Andy, Beth, Moira and Hugh decreased the importance of the opera singer title and focussed more on the subjective elements of the work to maintain continuity of self. These subjective elements were individually prioritised but underlying each was the quest to retain an outlet for physical and emotional expression. Because the voice will always be a biological part of a person it can be therefore seen as a stable point of reference from which to monitor change. Not every singer gave the act of singing equal salience, but in different ways, all the participants used the voice as a resource to make sense of a changing self.

14.5 Implications for Teachers

It is obviously not in the interests of teachers or their students to consider the consequences of career crisis as part of a training schedule. However this chapter raises certain dilemmas for the teaching profession. As singing teachers do we train singers for the profession or for technical excellence? The obvious answer is 'both', but if a singer is totally focussed on technical prowess it is easy to lose sight of the fundamental reasons for entering the profession in the first place, which hopefully are a love of music and a love of singing. It is easy for these criteria to become lost amidst the pressures of professional life. In a business that is dominated by the critical acclaim of others, this chapter has shown the fragility of relying solely on a professional identity for self-esteem. It was the individual subjective perceptions of self in relation to music, voice and performing that determined stability and continuity during career disruption.

Bennett (2009) proposed that the conservatoire curriculum should do more to address current developments in the profession by encouraging performing arts students be flexible in the way they label themselves. She notes that the term 'dance artist' has been adopted to help dancers cope with the realities of making a living in the contemporary profession. Giving a broader definition to the meaning of being a dancer means that professional success need not be judged on performance alone. The term 'dancer' then becomes a subjective identity which can form the basis for the development of additional skills in order to sustain a professional career. It is possible that encouraging singers to define themselves in broader terms such as a 'vocal artist' could help maintain a sense of continuity through professional change. However, the status given to the 'opera singer' title by the female singers suggests that the social and cultural perceptions of this title may be difficult to change in the short term.

Questions also need to be asked as to whether the broadening of a singer's self-concept may detract from artistic excellence which requires focus and commitment to one particular role. Research into sport career transition has shown that there are positive advantages for athletic performance in athletes who derive their identity solely from the athletic role (Werthner and Orlick 1996) but that greater levels of emotional distress are experienced when an athlete disengages from sport (Miller and Kerr 2002). There are no straightforward answers to these questions. Teachers play a vital role in a singer's development and should encourage students to continually reflect on their musical and vocal sense of self at the same time as honing technical skills. It is also important for young students to have realistic role models, not just of successful singers but those who have had experience of carving out a portfolio career. In addition, teachers who work with established professional singers should also be vigilant for signs of an over reliance on a professional identity (i.e. reliance on external validation of self) which can leave a singer vulnerable in a time of crisis.

14.6   Conclusions

The opera singer identity has been shown to be a complex structure that for the singers in this study was primarily endorsed by paid employment. However, during a working life, the professional opera singer identity may overshadow core constituents of that identity such as being a singer or a musician. The pressures imposed on (opera) singers by directors, conductors and managements mean that sometimes a singer's only source of support is their personal teacher or coach. Retaining a love of music and the voice can help establish a secure, durable but flexible sense of self and thereby encourage career longevity.

References

Bennett, D. (2007). Utopia for music performance graduates. Is it achievable and how should it be defined? *British Journal of Music Education, 24*, 179–189.

Bennett, D. (2008). *Understanding the classical music profession. The past, the present and strategies for the future.* Aldergate: Ashforth.

Bennett, D. (2009). Academy and the Real World: Developing realistic notions of career in the performing arts. *Arts and Humanities in Higher Education, 8*(3), 309–327.

Brubaker, R., & Cooper, F. (2000). Beyond identity. *Theory and Society, 29*(1), 1–47.

Burland, K., & Pitts, S. (2007). Becoming a music student: Investigating the skills and attitudes of students beginning a music degree. *Arts and Humanities in Higher Education, 6*(3), 289–308.

Callero, P. M. (1985). Role identity salience. *Social Psychology Quarterly, 48*(3), 203–215.

Creech, A., Papageorgi, I., Duffy, C., Morton, F., Haddon, E., Potter, J., De Bezenac, C., Whyton, T., Himonides, E., & Welch, G. (2008). From music student to professional: The process of transition. *British Journal of Music Education, 25*, 315–331.

Davidson, J. W. (2002). The solo performer's identity. In R. A. R. MacDonald, D. J. Hargreaves, & D. Miell (Eds.), *Musical identities* (pp. 97–113). Oxford: Oxford University Press.

Davidson, J. W. (2005). Bodily communication in musical performance. In D. Miell, R. MacDonald, & D. J. Hargreaves (Eds.), *Musical communication* (pp. 215–238). New York: Oxford University Press.

Folkman, S., & Moskowitz, J. T. (2000). Stress, positive emotion and coping. *Current Directions in Psychological Science, 9*(4), 115–118.

Hall, D. T. (1976). *Careers in organisations.* Glenview: Scott Foresman.

Hargreaves, D. J., Miell, D. E., & Macdonald, R. A. R. (2002). What are musical identities and why are they important. In R. A. R. MacDonald, D. J. Hargreaves, & D. Miell (Eds.), *Musical identities* (pp. 1–20). Oxford: Oxford University Press.

Jenkins, R. (2008). *Social identity.* Abingdon: Routledge.

Markus, H., & Nurius, P. (1986). Possible selves. *American Psychologist, 41*, 954–959.

Miller, P. S., & Kerr, G. (2002). Conceptualising excellence: Past present and future. *Journal of Applied Sport Psychology, 14*, 140–153.

Mills, J. (2004). Working in music: Becoming a performer-teacher. *Music Education Research, 6*(3), 245–261.

Mills, J. (2006). Working in music: The pianist. *Music Education Research, 8*(2), 1–15.

Oakland, J., MacDonald, R. A., & Flowers, P. (2012). Re-defining 'Me': Exploring career transition and the experience of loss in the context of redundancy for professional opera choristers. *Musicae Scientae, 16*(2), 135–147.

Oakland, J., MacDonald, R. A., & Flowers, P. (2013). Identity in crisis: The role of work in the formation and renegotiation of a musical identity. *British Journal of Music Education, 30*(2), 261–276.

Rosselli, J. (1992). *Singers of Italian opera: The history of a profession.* Cambridge: Cambridge University Press.

Schlossberg, N. K. (1981). A model for analysing human adaptation to transition. *The Counselling Psychologist, 9*(2), 2–17.

Smith, J. A., Flowers, P., & Larkin, M. (2009). *Interpretative phenomenological analysis theory, method and research.* London: Sage.

Tajfel, H. (1978). *Differentiation between social groups: Studies in the social psychology of intergroup relations.* London: Academic.

Weick, K. (1996). Enactment and the boundaryless career: Organizing as we work. In M. B. Arthur & D. M. Rousseau (Eds.), *The boundaryless career: A new employment principle for a new organisational era* (pp. 40–57). New York: Oxford University Press.

Welch, G. F. (2005). Singing as communication. In D. Miell, R. MacDonald, & D. J. Hargreaves (Eds.), *Musical communication* (pp. 239–259). Oxford: Oxford University Press.

Werthner, P., & Orlick, T. (1996). Retirement experiences of successful Olympic athletes. *International Journal of Sport Psychology, 17*, 337–363.

Part III
Approaches to Style

Chapter 15
Style and Ornamentation in Classical and Bel Canto Arias

Martha Elliott

Abstract This chapter will focus on ornamentation in Classical and Bel Canto arias. I will first give a short overview of ornamentation in Italian arias from the seventeenth and early eighteenth century, including a basic discussion of the use of small graces, trills, turns, appoggiaturas and grace notes. I will also look at the development of the cadenza and improvised variations in da capo arias. I will provide references from treatises of the period and musical examples to show students the origins of the Italian florid style. I will then spend the major part of the chapter exploring how these approaches changed and developed in the later eighteenth and early nineteenth centuries, and how students can apply the tools learned in the earlier Baroque style to Classical and Bel Canto repertoire. I will again provide references and instructions from period treatises, as well as musical examples. I will try to show students how to identify and choose stylistically appropriate gestures for different composers and periods, including Mozart, Rossini, Bellini and Donizetti. I will also talk about choosing an appropriate approach to vibrato and articulation for this repertoire.

Using my experience in the studio with my Princeton undergraduate students, I will share how I help them layer the stylistic and performance practice decisions onto their developing technical mastery. I usually want a student to feel comfortable and confident with basic vocal technique first, before delving into more subtle issues of style and ornamentation. Yet in some cases, finding an appropriate approach to style can help to solve technical issues. It is always fascinating to me how the two areas complement each other.

Keywords Ornamentation • Performance practice • Vocal style • Bel Canto • Classical • Florid style • Italian arias

M. Elliott (✉)
Department of Music, Princeton University, Princeton, NJ, USA
e-mail: melliott@princeton.edu

S.D. Harrison and J. O'Bryan (eds.), *Teaching Singing in the 21st Century*,
Landscapes: the Arts, Aesthetics, and Education 14, DOI 10.1007/978-94-017-8851-9_15,
© Springer Science+Business Media Dordrecht 2014

When my Princeton undergraduate students bring in a Classical or Bel Canto aria or song to sing in their voice lesson, they have most likely not taken a vocal literature class which exposed them to the development of period style and ornamentation since the early Baroque. As liberal arts students, they are very smart and motivated, and quite accomplished in many areas, but it is my job to teach them what they need to know about style and performance practice as well as vocal technique. Perhaps they have already worked on some seventeenth and early eighteenth-century pieces in the *24 Italian Songs and Arias* collection. Perhaps they have used the John Glen Patton edition of *26 Italian Songs and Arias* and know about the restored original versions of the well-known Schirmer edition pieces. Perhaps they have tried adding some small ornaments of their own, or even composed a cadenza or variations for the da capo of a Handel aria. When they come to work on late eighteenth or early nineteenth century Italian repertoire, I want them to have a sense of continuity in the approach to ornamentation and know where certain gestures and practices come from. I want them to understand the origins of the Italian florid style and see its culmination in the music of Rossini, Donizetti and Bellini. In this chapter, I will give a brief overview of some of these origins, and explore how approaches to ornamentation, articulation, and vibrato changed and developed in the late eighteenth and early nineteenth centuries. I will try to show students how to identify and choose stylistically appropriate musical gestures for Classical and Bel Canto repertoire as well as how to use the tools of performance practice and style to complement and support their developing vocal technique.

15.1 Early Baroque Origins

In the early seventeenth century, writers on music cautioned singers to take care with their approach to ornamentation. 'The singer will always be praised who with a few ornaments makes them at the right moment,' said Lodovico Zacconi in his singing treatise of 1596 (Zacconi 1979, 70). Vocal music of the sixteenth century had become so contrapuntal and ornate that the text was difficult to understand. Composers of the Florentine Camerata School, or *seconda praticca* as the style was also known, decided to take a new approach and write solo songs in which the text was simply set and clearly intelligible. For his 1602 collection of songs called *Le nuove musiche* or 'the new music', Giulio Caccini wrote an introduction in which he explained how the songs should be performed. The overall message was that most of the ornaments were already written into the music and the singer need only add a few things here and there (Caccini 1970). This sounds similar to Zacconi's recommendation from 5 years earlier. The big challenge is to figure out what those few ornaments are and where to put them.

Most writers of the early Baroque distinguish between two basic kinds of ornaments: graces and diminutions. Graces, or *accenti*, are small gestures that don't significantly alter the contours of the melody, but rather adorn it with trills and appoggiaturas. Diminutions are more florid decorations in which the singer divides

Trill, or plain shake

Gruppo, or double relish

Ex. 15.1   Caccini: from *Le nuove musiche* (1602) (Strunk 1950, 24)

a larger note value into smaller portions by adding more rapid notes. This was also known as 'coloring the notes' or *coloratura*, because a white note of longer duration became a series of black notes of shorter duration. The most popular place to add diminutions was at a cadence. Depending on the situation, singers could also add diminutions in the middle of an aria by recomposing the melody to a greater or lesser degree. Voices that moved with dazzling speed and accuracy were highly praised. While it was understood that different voices had differing natural ability with diminutions – also known as *passaggi*, or *dispositione*, it was always important to keep the divisions even and in time. If a singer had less flexibility and difficulty moving with clarity and precision, he or she would be told to avoid divisions altogether. It was always important to keep *passaggi* from overwhelming the music. 'The diminutions would become tiresome when the ear is saturated with them' cautioned Giovanni Camillo Maffei (1979, 52).

The trill was considered the most important small grace. In the seventeenth century, it could be an ornament on one note, called a *trillo*, or an alternation of two adjacent notes, known as a *gruppo*. Scholars disagree about the intended meaning of Caccini's instruction for the *trillo*, from the introduction to *Le nuove musiche* (see Ex. 15.1). It is not clear if the accelerating rhythm notated in Ex. 15.1 is the recommendation for practice or performance. In the latter part of the seventeenth century, the one note *trillo* fell out of use, replaced by the more popular two-note *gruppo* which became known as the plain shake or trill. The trill could be added at the singer's discretion on a long note, or, more commonly, at a cadence. It could be used wherever a grace was needed, but not so often as to become tiresome. The two notes should be clearly differentiated and well articulated. To achieve a quick, clean shake, singers were to practice slowly and increase speed gradually.

Singers were encouraged to use a crisp, detached kind of articulation in order to execute fast, clean trills and divisions. This also helped to make the text clear and intelligible by promoting an articulation based on the rhythms of natural speech. Monteverdi advised 'it would also be necessary to have a single guiding precept; that is, that they should tend to speak in singing and not, like this one, sing in speaking' (Monteverdi 1995, 111). Along the same lines, vibrato that interfered with the clarity of divisions, trills or text, was discouraged. When I teach undergraduates who have not sung much nineteenth-century or operatic repertoire, I feel like I am working with 'original instruments'. An 18 or 19 year old voice is usually still light and flexible and able to learn to differentiate ornaments and text clearly before too much weight or a too wide vibrato get in the way. Of course I want to teach my students to sing a legato line with consistent tone and breath connection. But for earlier repertory, a feeling of speaking on pitch is stylistically appropriate, and helps develop an easy, natural vocal production.

15.2   Late Baroque Origins

Throughout the history of the Italian florid style, from the early Baroque through the early nineteenth century, a push and pull existed between composers and singers over who was responsible for ornamentation, how much should be added and where. Even though Caccini tried to dictate and control the use of ornamentation in his *Le nuove musiche*, singers of the time went ahead and added their own, sometimes quite extensive ornamental touches anyway. One of the most famous songs from that collection is 'Amarilli mia bella.' An ornamented version of the song seen in a contemporary source, Egerton Manuscript 2971, includes so many added divisions and decorations that the well-known melody is almost unrecognizable.[1] By the beginning of the eighteenth century, it seemed the situation had not changed much. Pier Francesco Tosi, a famous singer and teacher, disapproved of the current state of ornamentation in his 1723 treatise *Observations on the Florid Song*. He chastised his students 'to avoid that torrent of passages and divisions so much in the mode… [my opinions] condemn the abuses of the modern cadences' (Tosi 1987, 52). From his perspective at the end of his long career, he thought the then current fashion of decorating cadences was extremely overdone. Yet as the eighteenth century progressed, ornamentation became even more elaborate and virtuosic. Writing in 1789, music critic and historian Charles Burney exclaimed 'which excited such astonishment in 1734, would be hardly thought sufficiently brilliant in 1788 for a third rate singer at the opera' (Burney 1789, 814). So you can see that there was an ongoing difference of opinion about how much added ornamentation was acceptable or desirable.

The late Baroque period produced a large number of treatises about singing and performing music. The most important and useful works were Leopold Mozart's treatise on playing the violin (Mozart 1985), C.P.E. Bach's treatise on keyboard playing (Bach 1949), a guide to playing the flute by Johann Quantz (1985), and a translation of Tosi (with additions) into German by Johann Friedrich Agricola (1995). Rules about ornamentation were often complex and even contradictory from one source to another. Ornaments were still discussed in terms of two basic types: graces and divisions. Of the graces, in vocal music, the trill and the appoggiatura continued to be most

---

[1] You can hear a recording of both versions on *Songs of Love and War: Italian Dramatic Songs of the 17th and 18th centuries*, with Julianne Baird, soprano, Colin Tilney, harpsichord, and Myron Lutzke, cello; Dorian 90104, 1990.

important. The trill in the late Baroque was always understood to be the figure with two pitches alternating. It was most common to start the trill on the upper note, but scholars argue that some situations demanded a main note start. The trill was sometimes notated, sometimes not, but it was always expected at major cadences. It could also be added at other less prominent cadences, or to decorate an internal melody. It could be combined with appoggiaturas and other preceding and concluding figures.

Appoggiaturas were sometimes notated, but more often not. If they were written into the music, the notation was often inconsistent. They could be notated as regular sized notes, thus as part of a melody, or as smaller ornamental notes with a variety of lengths and values. Singers were expected to know where and how to add appropriate appoggiaturas if they were not notated. Most commonly, an appoggiatura could add expressive dissonance to a strong beat. In this case it was usually played or sung on the beat, receiving more emphasis, volume and length. It could take half the value of the main note, two-thirds the value in a triple meter, or the total value of the main note before a rest. Appoggiaturas could also add decoration by filling in thirds or other larger intervals. In these situations, they could be played or sung with less emphasis and volume than the surrounding notes. They could also be shorter and come before the beat. Certain cadential formulas were expected in recitatives including repeating the penultimate note of a falling fourth, and filling in descending thirds.

Divisions and variations were used to add interest and variety to da capo arias. A singer could fill in slower rhythms with faster ones, recompose a sequence of faster notes to vary patterns and contours, and generally show off his or her technical and compositional abilities. Of course, all ornamental additions had to follow correct voice leading and counterpoint rules, which every singer was expected to know. The most common place to add divisions was still at a cadence. Some divisions and other smaller ornaments could be added in the first statement of the A section of an aria, perhaps a bit more in the B section. But more variety was expected in the return of the A section, with the most excitement and interest coming at the final cadence. Earlier in the eighteenth century, a singer might just slow down a bit to fit in something extra as the aria came to a close. As the century progressed, however, this stretching became longer and longer, until the orchestra had to come to a full stop and wait for the singer to complete the final flourish. As extensive and elaborate as these cadenzas became, they were still supposed to be completed all in one breath, on the penultimate syllable, before the final trill. Yet singers found ways to sneak extra breaths to prolong their moment of glory.

The 'usual' approach to articulation in the late Baroque was still considered separate and detached, though instrumentalists were often encouraged to emulate a singer's more legato *cantabile* style. It was important to distinguish between notes that needed more stress and emphasis and those that needed less. As Quantz put it in his treatise on playing the flute:

> Musical ideas that belong together must not be separated; on the other hand, you must separate those ideas in which on musical thought ends and a new idea begins…You must know how to make a distinction in execution between the *principal* notes, ordinarily called *accented* or in the Italian manner, *good* notes, and those that pass, which some foreigners

call *bad* notes. Where it is possible, the principal notes always must be emphasized more
than the passing. (1985, 122–23)

Vibrato was still discouraged as an obvious or ongoing presence. It could be used
for special dramatic or ornamental effect, but in general, voices that shimmered
with a small, fast vibration were preferred over voices with a slower, wider vibrato.
For the most part, in order to make sure the ornaments and text were clearly differentiated and clearly understood, it was important for singers to use a natural,
flexible, yet unobtrusive quality of vocal vibrato, as well as a variety of smooth and
detached articulations.

15.3   Classical Era Practices (Late Eighteenth Century)

Many of the ornaments and notational conventions from the Baroque period continued into the Classical Era, changing slightly to adapt to new trends and tastes. Of the
essential small graces, appoggiaturas and trills were still most important, with the
turn figure becoming increasingly popular. Trills were notated more often, usually
with a simple '*tr*,' but could also be added where not indicated. Most Classical era
trills started on the upper note, but more situations demanded or suggested a main
note start. Trills combined with preceding and concluding figures, as well as different
kinds of appoggiaturas, became more elaborate and complex. In the ornaments he
composed for an aria by J.C. Bach, Mozart adds a variety of trill figures to the end
of the opening flourish (See Ex. 15.2). A trill was always expected at a final cadence
whether it was notated or not.

Appoggiaturas were also notated and executed with more variety as well in the
Classical era. Like late Baroque appoggiaturas, they could be written as a regular
sized note as part of the melody, as a small ornamental note with a long or short
value, or occasionally as a small ornamental note with a slash though the stem.
An example of a written out appoggiatura can be found in Illia's first aria from
Idomeneo: the E♭ upper neighbor on 'cagion tu sei' is an eighth note appoggiatura
notated as a regular sized note (Ex. 15.3a). Similarly in 'Vedrai carino,' the quarter
note B on 'ti voglio dar' is a long, lower neighbor appoggiatura written into the
melody with a regular sized note (Ex. 15.3b). This gesture also appears in many
familiar places: 'Batti batti, bel Massetto,' 'non so piu cosa son, cosa faccio,' 'Porge
amor,' and 'e di piacer' from 'Dove sono,' (Ex. 15.3c) to name just a few. When you
come upon this kind of appoggiatura, you can perform it with the added emphasis
that this figure requires.

Classical appoggiaturas were also sometimes written as small ornamental notes
with a variety of note values. In Dorabella's aria 'Smanie implacabile,' the appoggiaturas are written as small quarter notes, and should be performed stressed and on
the beat, lasting for a quarter note (Ex. 15.4b). In Illia's third aria from *Idomeneo* we
see three types of small ornamental notes: a sixteenth note before an eighth note in
m. 18, a sixteenth note before a half note in m. 22, and an eighth note before a dotted
half note in m. 22 (Ex. 15.4a). In m. 18, the appoggiatura could either be performed

Ex. 15.2 J.C. Bach: 'Cara la dolce fiamma' with embellishments by Mozart (Brown and Sadie 1989, 305)

stressed and on the third beat, effectively becoming two sixteenths and an eighth note, or alternatively, it could be shorter and slightly before the beat. In m. 22, the appoggiatura should definitely be stressed and on the beat, though, since the aria is in a triple meter, its length could be anywhere from an eighth note to a quarter note. In m. 24, one might want to make the appoggiatura match the length of the one in m. 18, or, for added expression and variety, make the first one shorter and the second one longer.

Some nineteenth and twentieth-century piano vocal scores of Classical era music have made editorial decisions about the notation of appoggiaturas. For example, in the Kalmus piano vocal score of *The Marriage of Figaro*, the appoggiatura at the end of the *colla parte* section in Susanna and Figaro's second duet is written as a small eighth note with a slash through it (Ex. 15.5a). In the Peters orchestra score, as well as the *Neue Mozart Ausgabe* critical edition, it is written as a small sixteenth note without a slash. In this situation, the appoggiatura could be performed stressed and on the beat as two sixteenth notes, or short and slightly before the beat, depending on the desired characterization. In the 6/8 Allegretto section of Despina's first aria, the ornamental notes in the accompaniment are written as small eighth notes with slashes through them in the Schirmer piano vocal score (Ex. 15.5b), and small sixteenth notes in the NMA. These would probably be better performed as grace notes, short and before the beat. It is always useful to consult a scholarly edition

Ex. 15.3 (**a**) Mozart 'Padre, germani,' mm. 16–18, from *Idomeneo* (1781). (**b**) Mozart 'Vedrai carino,' mm. 15–16, from *Don Giovanni* (1787). (**c**) Mozart 'Dove sono,' mm. 7–8, from *The Marriage of Figaro* (1786)

when considering issues of appoggiatura notation. However, it is also helpful to be aware of the different performance gestures possible, and make choices that are appropriate for the dramatic expression.

Appoggiaturas can also be added when not notated, to strengthen the expressive dissonance on a strong beat, to fill in passing tones, or to enrich a cadence or in combination with a trill. In Illia's first aria, the opening phrase could take an F appoggiatura to fill in from the G to the E♭ on 'foste' (Ex. 15.6a). In Susanna's 'Deh vieni' some of the phrases end with appoggiaturas written in, for example 'notturna face,' (Ex. 15.6c) while others do not, like the opening 'bella' (Ex. 15.6b). In m. 29, Mozart writes an exquisitely expressive long G# lower neighbor appoggiatura on

Ex. 15.4 (**a**) Mozart 'Zeffiretti lusinghieri,' mm. 18–24, from *Idomeneo* (1781). (**b**) Mozart 'Smanie implacabile,' mm. 17–19, from *Cosi fan tutte* (1790)

Ex. 15.5 (**a**) Mozart 'Se a caso madama,' mm. 94–96, from *Marriage of Figaro* (1786). (**b**) Mozart 'In uomini,' mm. 24–25, from *Cosi fan tutte* (1790)

'fresca' (Ex. 15.6d) to decorate the A. At the conclusion of the following phrase, you could decorate the F of 'adesca' at the end of the next phrase with a lower neighbor E or jump up to the upper neighbor G (Ex. 15.6e). In fact, you could decorate all the phrase endings that don't have appoggiaturas written in already, or, for variety, choose to leave some plain. The best way to learn how to add appoggiaturas, is to

Ex. 15.6 (a) Mozart 'Padre, germani,' mm. 6–8, from *Idomeneo* (1781). (b) Mozart 'Deh vieni, non tardar,' mm. 8–9, from *Figaro* (1786). (c) Mozart 'Deh vieni, non tardar,' mm. 14–15, from *Figaro* (1786). (d) Mozart 'Deh vieni, non tardar,' mm. 28–29, from *Figaro* (1786). (e) Mozart 'Deh vieni, non tardar,' mm. 31–32, from *Figaro* (1786)

notice where and how they are written in by the composer, and then imitate that usage in similar, non-notated situations.

In Classical recitatives, certain standard practices carried over from the Baroque period. These include filling in descending thirds with passing tones and repeating the penultimate note at cadences that are approached by a falling fourth. Scholars disagree about the rules for adding appoggiaturas to blunt endings of feminine syllables in recitatives. Some believe that a word ending in an unstressed syllable should always take an appoggiatura, and that a 'blunt ending,' or two of the same pitches in a row, should always be avoided. Other scholars argue that period sources allow optional appoggiaturas for feminine endings depending on the specific text and dramatic situation. For example, the opening declaration in the recitative before 'Deh vieni,' has three blunt endings in a row (Ex. 15.7). The second two should definitely take appoggiaturas: a repeated C on 'affanno' and an F to fill in the third on

Ex. 15.7 Mozart: 'Giunse alfin il momento,' mm. 5–7, from *Figaro*

'mio.' The opening phrase could take a repeated lower neighbor B on 'mo<u>men</u>to' for a quality of longing, or a jump to the upper neighbor D for a more hopeful expression- or, leave the opening phrase plain for a simple, straightforward effect. Of course, these kinds of situations occur throughout Classical recitatives, and it is important to add appoggiaturas to shape characterization and inform the dramatic action. You must be careful not to use too many of the same kind of appoggiatura in a row, which might evoke a sea-sick kind of monotony. Rather, be imaginative and use appoggiaturas to add variety and expression. Also remember to include a spoken quality of articulation, still favored from Baroque usage.

The controversy surrounding blunt endings extends into music in arias and ensembles as well. Some scholars argue that a feminine ending with two of the same pitches always requires an appoggiatura. Others are more flexible in their approach. Take the trio in Act One of *Figaro* as an example: in the Count's opening line, blunt endings on 'sento' 'an<u>date</u>' and 'sca<u>cciate</u>' could express his fury and power (Ex. 15.8a). If Basillio were to copy that same rhythm, with blunt endings on 'punto' 'giunto' and 'perdo<u>nato</u>' he would then show his manipulative deference to the Count (Ex. 15.8b). Another option would be for the Count to add appoggiaturas and in contrast, let Bassilio highlight his irritating buffo quality by keeping the blunt endings as they are. And there are always more choices to explore. Rather than simply following rules in a period treatise, or executing the literal notation in the score, a singer should make choices that enliven the dramatic action and enrich the characterization.

The turn figure appeared more frequently in Classical era music, sometimes written out in large notes, or as small ornamental notes, or even notated as a turn sign. The specific pattern of the turn was also quite variable in, rhythm, speed, shape and direction (Ex. 15.9; also Ex. 15.2).

Diminutions, improvised variations and cadenzas became more and more elaborate as the eighteenth century drew to a close. Two contrasting styles of music demanded slightly different approaches to ornamentation: the Adagio style, characterized by a slower tempo and more cantabile melody, could take added trills, turns, appoggiaturas, and some modest diminutions. The Allegro, or Bravura style, required more extensive coloratura, more recomposition of the melody, and generally more exciting

Ex. 15.8 (**a**) Mozart: 'Cosa sento' from *Figaro*, mm. 4–9. (**b**) Mozart: 'Cosa sento' from *Figaro*, mm. 16–23

rhythms and showy vocalism. Examples 15.10 and 15.11, which highlight both styles, are from an aria by Luigi Cherubini with prepared embellishments by the famous castrati Luigi Marchesi, who was greatly admired in his day.

In arias, cadenzas were expected at the final cadence, but could also be added at a pause, or before the reprise of a Rondo form main theme. Writing in 1773, Burney complained about over-done cadenzas at cadences:

> …such long winded licentiousness prevails in the cadences of every singer, as it is always tiresome, and often disgusting; even those great performers need compression…a few select notes with a great deal of meaning and expression given to them, is the only expedient that can render a cadence desirable. (Burney 1969, 377)

This sounds similar to the sentiments expressed by Zacconi almost 200 years before! Even Mozart was concerned that his singers would take too many liberties with his music. In a letter of January 14, 1775, regarding *La finta giardiniera* he wrote: 'Next Friday my opera is being performed again and it is most essential that I should be present. Otherwise my work would be quite unrecognizable (Anderson 1985, 259).

Singers of the day would most likely improvise their flights of fancy on the spot, creating a unique display for every performance. I advise my students to try out different ideas in the studio or practice room, either recording their attempts, or writing them down. Once they have decided on something they like that feels comfortable, they can write it into their music, or into a notebook, and practice it so they know what they are doing. Often, I will jot down some suggestions on a piece of staff paper, or in their music. And as a matter of fact, historians have found

Ex. 15.9 (**a**) Mozart 'Ah guarda sorella' mm. 86–91 from *Cosi*. (**b**) Mozart 'Non mi dir' m. 33 from *Don Giovanni*. (**c**) Mozart 'Non mi dir' mm. 90–92 from *Don Giovanni*. (**d**) Mozart 'Ch'io mi scordi di te' K. 505, m. 81. (**e**) Mozart 'Ch'io mi scordi di te' K. 505, mm. 166–67. (**f**) Mozart 'Ch'io mi scordi di te' K. 505, mm. 213–14

Ex. 15.10 Marchesi: Cherubini variations on opening adagio measures (Haas 1931, 225)

countless numbers of just such scribbling from singers or perhaps voice teachers of the period, or even from the composers themselves. For example, Mozart customized ornaments for one of his favorite singers in his aria 'Ah se a morir mi chiama.' The embellishments he wrote down for Aloysia Weber show turns, trills, appoggiaturas and longer divisions and cadenzas (See Ex. 15.12.).

For other examples of Classical era ornamentation, I suggest Will Crutchfield's article 'Voices' in the Classical section of Brown and Sadie's *Performance Practice: Music after 1600*, and for more of Mozart's ornamentation, Neumans's *Ornamentation*

Ex. 15.11 Marchesi: Cherubini variations on rondo theme (Haas 1931, 225)

and Improvisation. Examples of Haydn's ornaments for his own works can be seen in the tenor aria 'Quando mi dona un cenno' from the oratorio *Il ritorno di Tobia* in the Henle critical edition of the complete works, and in A. Peter Brown's *Performing Haydn's 'The Creation.'* By studying surviving ornamentation suggestions from period sources, we can find inspiration for our own inventions. Students can also listen to recordings by performers who specialize in ornamentation, and should also

Ex. 15.12 Mozart: 'Ah se a morir mi chiama' from *Lucio Silla* (1772), embellishments added for Alloysia Weber, 1778 (Neumann 1986, 231; reprinted with permission) look at instrumental music. Mozart's piano concertos contain many wonderful examples of Rondo variations and cadenzas that, while not specifically vocal, still demonstrate stylistically appropriate gestures.

While the legato or *cantabile* style became more popular at the end of the eighteenth century, Classical era treatises continued to recommend a detached and separate articulation and modest use of vibrato for most situations. In discussing a bass singer, Mozart expressed his preference in a letter of June 12, 1778: 'Meisner, as you know, has the habit of making his voice tremble at times, turning a note that should be sustained into distinct crotchets, or even quavers – and this I never could endure in him…The human voice trembles naturally – but in its own way – and only to such a degree that the effect is beautiful' (Anderson 1985, 552). Domenico Corri, in his singing treatise of 1810, reflects a common Baroque approach to articulation: 'Every note ought to have, as it were, a different degree of light and shade according to its position' (Corri 1968, 52). So when I am teaching my students how to approach Classical era repertoire, I want them to use a variety of detached and smooth articulations as the situation demands. I want them to give individual notes different weights, lengths and stresses according to the rhythm of the phrase or amount of dissonance present. I want their trills and divisions to be clean and clear, not muddied by a too wide or omnipresent vibrato.

In working with two students on the second duet in *Figaro*, I noticed that my corrections depended on where they were in their technical development. The baritone brought an even legato to the piece and needed to sing with more detached articulation, vary the lengths and stresses he gave each note and pay more attention to the rests and short phrases. The soprano, in contrast, needed to elongate her vowels and not close down too much on her consonants. In the alternating detached and smooth phrases at the end of the duet, each helped balance the other, and each learned a new tool of articulation. When coaching a student on 'Vedrai carino,' of course I encouraged her to sing with a beautiful legato, but also wanted to fine-tune her ornamentation. For example, the forschlage ornament that leads to the first E on 'carino' must be a distinct gesture, sung with clarity and energy, whether it starts on the beat or slightly before the beat. At the end of the first phrase (see Ex. 15.3b), the lower neighbor on 'dar' and the upper neighbors on 'naturale' and 'disgusto' need extra emphasis to highlight the dissonant appoggiatura feeling. I even recommended adding small cadenzas at the fermata at the final 'dove mi sta' and final 'qua.'

15.4 Bel Canto Practices

In the nineteenth century, the legato style gained favor over the detached approach, and vibrato became accepted for more expressive situations, though it was still considered a defect if too much tremolo disturbed the flow of a pure and steady tone. The use of portamento and rubato also increased, mostly in the service of dramatic expression and 'beautiful singing' or *bel canto*. Ornamentation

Ex. 15.13 (a) Donizetti: 'Regnava nel silenzio,' mm. 6–9, from *Lucia di Lammermoore* (1835). (b) Donizetti: 'Una furtive lagrima,' mm. 31–34, from *Elixer of Love* (1832)

of vocal music became most elaborate as the florid style reached its peak. At the same time, composers began writing more and more performance instructions and ornamentation into their scores, and became more precise with the rhythmic notation of small graces. Appoggiaturas now were more likely to be composed into a melody, with the precise length of the appoggiatura indicated by the specific value of a regular sized note. This can be seen in Ex. 15.13 from Donizetti. In 'Regnava nel silenzio' (Ex. 15.13a) notice the stressed dissonant C on 'silenzio' followed by the stressed dissonant A on 'alta' and G on 'note.' In 'Una furtive lagrima' from *Elixer of Love*, Donizetti writes a dissonant lower neighbor on 'confondere' in m. 32, and two descending appoggiaturas on 'poco' and 'suoi' in m. 33 (Ex. 15.13b).

Composers also wrote appoggiaturas as small ornamental notes, perhaps to indicate a slightly different type of stress, or possibly merely as an inconsistency of notation. Plenty of situations in arias, songs and recitatives from this period still needed added appoggiaturas, perhaps for words ending in unstressed syllables, or to add expressive dissonance to a strong beat. 'Una voce poco fa' contains examples of all these situations: for the first 'lo giurai' (Ex. 15.14a), Rossini writes a small ornamental note E as an appoggiatura before the two eighth notes on D. Some scores print this as a sixteenth note, some as an eighth note with a slash through the tail. This is usually performed stressed and on the beat, taking the entire value of the first eighth note. For the second 'lo giurai' (Ex. 15.14b), he embellishes the triplet with a descending scale and leaves the two D's on the downbeat plain. You could certainly add an E appoggiatura here as well, even though it is not written. Later on, in the Moderato section of the aria, Rossini writes a long, juicy lower neighbor note on 'obbediente' (Ex. 15.14c) that feels very much like a written out

a

b

c

Ex. 15.14 (a) Rossini: 'Una voce poco fa,' mm. 23–24, from *Barber of Seville* (1816). (b) Rossini: 'Una voce poco fa,' mm. 27–28, from *Barber of Seville* (1816). (c) Rossini: 'Una voce poco fa,' mm. 59–60, from *Barber of Seville* (1816)

a

b

Ex. 15.15 (a) Donizetti: 'Belle siccome un angelo,' m. 33, from *Don Pasquale* (1843). (b) Donizetti: 'Belle siccome un angelo,' mm. 46–47, from *Don Pasquale* (1843)

appoggiatura, similar to what we saw in 'Una furtive lagrima.' As shown in these examples, many eighteenth-century rules governing the length of appoggiaturas, notated or added, still applied well into the following century, but more flexibility became the norm for a number of new kinds of situations.

By the third decade of the nineteenth century, a small ornamental note with a slash across its tail was understood to be a grace note, which would most likely be performed short and before the beat (See Ex. 15.15; see also Ex. 15.14c above).

However, sometimes, for dramatic effect, you may want to add expressive dissonance to a strong beat, or emphasis to an unaccented syllable. In these cases I would suggest performing the ornamental notes as appoggiaturas (see Ex. 15.15b). Knowing the earlier practices and conventions of notation and how they have developed and changed will help you make choices about performing appoggiaturas in later music.

The early nineteenth century saw the rising popularity of the main note start for trills and turns. Composers wrote out turns more frequently, using both large and small sized notes. However, a variety of patterns were possible, and singers could change what was written and substitute the ones they preferred. Examples 15.16a–d are from chamber pieces and songs. Rossini's 'Ecco ridente' also has wonderful examples of written out trills, turns and flourishes (see Ex. 15.17). Once you become familiar with the compositional patterns of the music of this period, you will begin to feel confident about adding and substituting appropriate shapes and gestures.

In the early nineteenth century, more and more sources make recommendations for cadenzas and coda variations. Domenico Corri's treatise from 1810 lists generic cadenzas in every key with longer and shorter possibilities (Corri 1968) (See Ex. 15.18). Manuel Garcia in his famous treatise *Traité complet du l'art du chant* (Garcia 1975), offers several pages of cadenza suggestions for known opera arias, which could be transposed and/or substituted into other arias. Garcia also gives several pages of coda variations that could either be added to specific bravura arias or adapted and transferred into other arias (See Ex. 15.19). It is fascinating to look through this dazzling wealth of material, first to see what was commonly practiced at the time, and then to get ideas for your own inventions. Many example of period ornamentation can be seen in the *New Grove* articles on 'Rossini' and 'Improvisation: Nineteenth Century' as well as the *New Grove Dictionary of Opera* 'Ornamentation' article. I also recommend both Austin Caswell's collection 'Embellished Opera Arias,' published by A-R Editions (Caswell 1989), and Will Crutchfield's article 'Voices' in the nineteenth century section of *Performance Practice: Music after 1600* (Brown and Sadie 1989). The famous soprano Laure-Cinthe Damoreau, who sang at the Paris Opera from 1825 to 1849 and premiered more than 20 leading roles, shared many of her cadenzas and improvised ornaments with her students at the Paris Conservatoire. She encouraged her students to study these and, rather than perform them verbatim, use them as models for composing their own. Her treatise, *Classic Bel Canto Technique*, with extensive examples of ornamentation, is easily accessible in a Dover score (Damoreau 1997) (See Ex. 15.20).

Of course there are many stories involving Rossini and his preferences for ornamentation of his music. In one anecdote, a singer supposedly added so much ornamentation to one of his early arias, that Rossini vowed to write all ornamentation into his scores from then on, thus avoiding such vain displays from disfiguring his music (Pleasants 1966, 91–93). Yet he is also quoted as saying 'the repeat is made expressly that each singer may vary it, so as best to display his or her peculiar capacities' (Crutchfield 2001, 121). In another story, a young Adelina Patti sang such a florid rendition of 'Una voce poco fa' for the older composer that he remarked: 'Very nice, my dear, and who wrote the piece you have just performed?' (Osborne 2004).

Ex. 15.16 (**a**) Bellini: 'Quando incise su quell marmo,' mm. 26–27, from *Composizione da camera* (1829, 1835). (**b**) Donizetti: 'La ninna nanna' (1839) mm. 121–22, reprinted in *Composizione da camera*. (**c**) Rossini: 'Anzoleta avanti la regatta,' mm. 40–41, from *La regatta veneziana* (1835) (Elliott 2006, 148). (**d**) Rossini: 'Anzoleta avanti la regatta,' mm. 44–45, from *La regatta veneziana* (1835) (Elliott 2006, 148)

Ex. 15.17 Rossini: 'Ecco ridente,' mm. 15–24 from *Barber of Seville* (1815)

Ex. 15.18   Corri: cadenza suggestions from *The Singer's Preceptor* (1810) (Corri 1968, 75–6)

Surely a compromise can be found. Most of the thousands of performances of 'Una voce poco fa' now available on YouTube, use the same set of now 'standard' variations and cadenzas that you can hear in recordings from the early twentieth century. Most singers who perform 'Ecco ridente,' or 'Bella siccome un angelo,' dutifully perform the cadenzas and flourishes written into the score by Rossini and Donizetti. Yet evidence from the period suggests that while composers were notating their music more precisely, and exerting more control over the improvised additions of singers, they still expected singers to embellish the music in their own way. I try to encourage my students to be a little bit adventurous and come up with some new ideas of their own, based on ideas and patterns that were common in the period. Rather than just singing the notes on the page, I urge students to recognize ornamental notes and perform them as decorations. Rather than simply performing

Ex. 15.19 Garcia: coda variants from *Traité complet de l'art du chant: Part II* (1847, facs. Geneva, 1985, 72)

Ex. 15.20 Damoreau: cadenza suggestions from *Methode de chant* (1849) (Damoreau 1997, 93)

cadenzas that have become 'traditional,' I recommend that students learn about improvised variations and then, as Burney suggested, try to devise those 'few select notes with a great deal of meaning and expression.'

References

Agricola, J. F. (1995). *Anleitung zur Singkunst.* A translation [with additions] of Pier Francesco Tosi's *Opinioni de'cantori antichi e moderni.* Berlin, 1757. *Introduction to the art of singing* (J. Baird, Trans.). Cambridge: Cambridge University Press.

Anderson, E. (1985). *The letters of Mozart and his family* (3rd ed.). London: Macmillan.

Bach, C. P. E. (1949). *Versuch über die wahre Art des Clavier zu spielen*. Berlin, 1753; part 2, 1762. *Essay on the true art of playing keyboard instruments* (W. J. Mitchell, Trans.). New York: Norton.

Brown, H. M., & Sadie, S. (Eds.). (1989). *Performance practice: Music after 1600*. New York: Norton.

Burney, C. (1789). *A general history of music*. London: Harcourt, Brace and Company.

Burney, C. (1969). *The present state of music in France and Italy*. Facsimile of the 1773 London ed. New York: Broude Brothers.

Caccini, G. (1970). *Le nuove musiche*. Florence 1601. Modern edition edited by H. Wiley Hitchcock in *Recent researches in the music of the Baroque era* (Vol. 9). Madison: A-R Editions. Preface translated into English in John Playford, *An introduction to the skill of musick*. London 1654.

Caswell, A. (Ed.). (1989). *Embellished opera arias* (Recent researches in the music of the nineteenth and early twentieth centuries, Vol. 7 and 8). Madison: A-R Editions.

Corri, D. (1968). *The singer's preceptor*. London, 1810. In E. Foreman (Ed.), *The Porpora tradition*. New York: Pro Musica Press.

Crutchfield, W. (2001). Improvisation – II, 5, ii. Nineteenth-century vocal music. In S. Sadie (Ed.), *The new Grove dictionary of music and musicians* (Vol. 12). New York: Grove's Dictionaries.

Damoreau, L.-C. (1997). *Classic Bel Canto technique* (V. Rangel-Ribeiro, Trans.). New York: Dover.

Elliott, M. (2006). *Singing in style: A guide to vocal performance practices*. New Haven: Yale University Press.

Garcia, M. (1894). *Hints on singing*. New York: Edward Schuberth.

Garcia, M. (1975). *Traité complet de l'art du chant*. Paris, 1874, facs. Geneva, 1985. *A complete treatise on the art of singing: Part two*. New York: Da Capo Press, 1975, and *A complete treatise on the art of singing: Part one* (D. V. Pasche, Trans.). New York: Da Capa Press, 1984.

Haas, R. (1931). *Aufführungspraxis der Musik: Handbuch der Musikwissenschaft*. Potsdam: Akademische Verlagsgesellschaft Athenaion.

Maffei, G. C. (1979). *Letter on singing*. Naples, 1562. In C. MacClintock (Ed.), *Readings in the history of music in performance*. Bloomington: Indiana University Press.

Monteverdi, C. (1995). In S. Denis (Ed.), *The letters of Claudio Monteverdi*. Oxford: Clarendon Press.

Mozart, L. (1985). *Versuch einer gründlichen Violinschule*. Augsburg, 1756. *A treatise on the fundamental principles of violin playing* (2nd ed., E. Knocker, Trans.). Oxford: Oxford University Press.

Neumann, F. (1986). *Ornamentation and improvisation in Mozart*. Princeton: Princeton University Press.

Osborne, R. (2004). *Il Barbiere di Seviglia* (ii). In L. Macy (Ed.), *Grove music online*. http://www.grovemusic.com. Accessed 25 Mar 2012.

Pleasants, H. (1966). *The great singers*. New York: Simon and Schuster.

Quantz, J. (1985). *Versuch einer Anweisung die Flöte traversiere zu spielen*. Berlin, 1752. *On playing the flute* (2nd ed., E. R. Reilly, Trans.). New York: Schirmer.

Strunk, O. (Ed.). (1950). *Source readings in music history: The Baroque era*. New York: W.W. Norton.

Tosi, P. F. (1987). *Opinioni de' cantori antichi e moderni*. Bologna, 1723. Reprint, Bologna: Forni, 1968. *Observations on the Florid song* (2nd ed., J. E. Gaillard, Trans.). London 1743. Reprint ed. Michael Pilkington. London: Stainer and Bell.

Zacconi, L. (1979). *Prattica di musica utile et necessaria si al compositore...si anco al cantore*. Venice 1596. Excerpted in C. MacClintock (Ed.), *Readings in the history of music in performance*. Bloomington: Indiana University Press.

Chapter 16
Handel and the Voice Practitioner: Perspectives on Performance Practice and Higher Education Pedagogy

Paul McMahon

Abstract This chapter addresses Baroque performance practice through the perspectives of higher education pedagogy and practical applications in the music of a seminal composer of the Baroque period, George Frideric Handel (1685–1759). The account of the data is motivated by the author's dual role as a vocal pedagogue in tertiary education and professional singer regularly performing the solo tenor repertoire of the Baroque period.

The literature indicates structured pedagogy in historical performance practice within conservatoires and universities in the United Kingdom lags behind the academic methodology of institutional equivalents in North America. The empirical data within the current research supports this phenomenon, suggesting performers emerging from conservatoires and university music departments in the United Kingdom and Australia experience limited formalised academic training in the theoretical and practical constituents of Baroque performance practice.

Following a qualitative research paradigm, the research reports on findings from semi-structured interviews with a range of professional singers. The methodology also employs reflexive practice and draws upon related literature, offering a critical narrative grounded within dominant topics from the data.

The research findings present themes critical to higher education pedagogy. These matters include comparative analysis and discourse upon primary and secondary sources, and tuition in oratorical vocal practices inherent in the affective performance of Baroque vocal music. The study also suggests the function of the performer-teacher fulfils a significant pedagogic role in student: instructor dialogue, while evaluative listening in the context of recordings and experiential scenarios in choral singing present vigorous academic applications.

P. McMahon (✉)
School of Music, Research School of Humanities and the Arts, College of Arts and Social Sciences, Australian National University, Canberra, ACT, Australia
e-mail: paul.mcmahon@anu.edu.au

S.D. Harrison and J. O'Bryan (eds.), *Teaching Singing in the 21st Century*,
Landscapes: the Arts, Aesthetics, and Education 14, DOI 10.1007/978-94-017-8851-9_16,
© Springer Science+Business Media Dordrecht 2014

Keywords Baroque vocal music • Eighteenth-century performance practice • Handel • Higher education pedagogy

16.1 Introduction

Drawing upon a larger study investigating the theoretical and applied aspects of performance practice (McMahon 2012), this chapter examines pedagogic perspectives upon Baroque performance practice within higher music education. It reflects upon the experiences of professional singers actively engaging the presentation of Baroque music, and comments on performance practice pedagogy in repertoire for the tenor voice by a seminal composer of the Baroque period, George Frideric Handel[1] (1685–1759).

In assessing the comprehensive perspectives offered by a gender-diverse sample of vocalists, basso continuo players and other instrumentalists, conductors, vocal coaches and singing teachers, McMahon (2013) establishes the broad vocal, musical, artistic and educative implications of research pertaining to period performance practice teaching. Contextualising a research sample encompassing all voice-types, the publication's scope of enquiry presents an illuminative backdrop to the current chapter. Furthermore, it permits the reader to move beyond the exemplar of the tenor voice within the study and pedagogical approaches in Baroque performance practice discussed below.

16.1.1 Rationale and Motivation for the Study

The popularity of vocal music written in the Baroque period, c. 1600–1760 remains unabated with audiences and performers of the twenty-first century (Jones 2006). Compositions by masters of the Italian, French and German Baroque are frequently performed in concert halls and opera theatres throughout the world. Ready access to digital technology makes the vast oeuvre of recorded music of the Baroque period instantly available to a mass consumer market. Through individual lessons, coaching, recitals, ensemble rehearsals and performances, the operatic, oratorio and solo vocal literatures of the Baroque period forms a core component of studies for singing students in conservatoires and universities (Wright and Kauders 1992).

The mid-twentieth-century saw the rise of scholarly research in the role of period instruments and historically informed, period-specific performing practices. Under the leadership of erudite directors influenced by this intellectual pursuit, period

---

[1] Baptised Georg Friederich Händel, the spelling of Handel's name that he adopted upon settling in England is applied throughout this chapter (Dean 1982; Hicks 2007).

performing ensembles emerging in Europe and the United Kingdom flourished, supplementing the burgeoning demand for historically informed recordings of Baroque music.

16.1.2 Performance Practice in Baroque Vocal Music, the Research Problem and the Aims of This Study

In respect of the chapter's title, it is pertinent to delineate the term *performance practice* as it pertains to vocal music of the Baroque period. Encompassing a range of components, performance practice comprises interaction between nuances of dynamics, rhythm and tempo, and the articulation of text. It addresses the delivery of *affekt*, or implicit emotive feeling within the music and text. Performance practice also embraces distinctions in the ornamentation and interpretation of repertoire (Cyr 1992; Donington 1973, 1982 et al.). It encompasses the declamation of recitative through the oratorical, speech-like inflections discussed within the vocal treatises of the eighteenth-century, such as Tosi (1723), Agricola (1757), Mancini (1774) and Hiller (1780). Baroque performance practice also encompasses study of other primary sources, including instrumental treatises, historical documents and compositional manuscripts.

Composers of the Baroque period commonly gave sparse written indication of their intentions regarding performance practices, as these conventions were considered requisite knowledge for performers of the time (Cyr 1992). Therefore, elements of phrasing, articulation and syllabic inflection, dynamics, vocal character and tempo were frequently left to the performers' discretion. As a skeletal outline of the score, the extensive extant collection of Handel's autograph manuscripts bear testament to this phenomenon (Burrows and Ronisch 1994; Dean 1976).

The author's dual occupational roles contextualise this research and establish the professional practitioner of solo tenor repertoire as the central phenomenon of the study. As a tenor soloist singing a broad range of Baroque repertory, interpretive discussions concerning performance practice are frequently encountered within the rehearsal process.

Duties as a singing teacher in higher education also necessitate regular dialogue with students grappling the interpretation of Baroque repertoire. With minimal access to structured, theoretical teaching in the components of performance practice, some pupils are baffled by the variance of editorial rigor in vocal scores. Others discover hurdles in the ornamentation of *da capo* arias, or struggle to master the speech-like declamation of recitative. Students may also comment on their perceptions of performance practice applied by singers within recordings produced under the banner of 'historically informed' performance.

The paucity of indications within composers' manuscripts regarding aspects of performance practice is one of the motivating factors of this research. The existing vocal treatises of the eighteenth-century offer some guidance regarding the inter-pretation of performance practice. These sources suggest the primary purpose of

Baroque music was to move the passions or emotions of the listener. Tosi (1723) advises that it was the singers' obligation to transport the audiences' emotions through the conventions of affective delivery. In addition, Mancini (1774) counsels the singer to perform recitative in imitation of an orator's rhetorical delivery. That is, matching the rhythm of the text to declamatory speech, emphasising the affective meaning of the words through faster or slower tempos, ascending and descending graduations of dynamics and subtle variations of vocal tone. Tarling defines rhetoric as:

> a particular way of speaking by an orator whose main aim is to persuade the listener. Persuasive speaking uses various techniques that influence the emotional response of the listener in order to bring him round to the speaker's opinion. (2004, i)

Furthermore, Tarling suggests:

> the principal skill of the rhetorical performer lies in the identification of the emotional content represented by the musical text, and the communication of this to the audience. (2004, 104)

In some part, Tarling's commentary upon rhetorical presentation sums up the educator's task in relation to Baroque performance practice, as comprehensive pedagogy within higher education accepts a substantial role in the pre-professional development of both theoretical and practical skills. The literature evidences far-reaching musicological studies in Baroque performing practices (Cyr 1992; Donington 1973, 1982; Neumann 1993 et al.) and extensive advancements in vocal pedagogy research (Chapman 2006; Miller 1986, 1993; Sell 2005 et al.). Through emergent high-profile ensembles, the critical and commercial success of historically informed performance of Baroque music is also well documented.

However, some European conservatoires, including the Schola Cantorum in Basel (http://www.scb-basel.ch/index/117099) and the Royal Conservatoire in The Hague (http://www.koncon.nl/en) offer comprehensive, specialised pedagogy in period performance practices. The literature also implies structured pedagogy in performance practice within higher education in the United Kingdom lags behind the pedagogic approach of institutional counterparts in North America (Butt 2002; Taruskin 1982). Reinforcing this phenomenon, the empirical data analysed in this study indicates performers emerging from higher education institutions in the United Kingdom and Australia experience limited academic grounding in Baroque performance practice (Gilchrist 2010; Massingham 2007; Padmore 2010 et al.).

Despite the sustained investment in the presentation of operatic, oratorio and choral music of the Baroque period within the confines of higher education, empirical data in this research suggests systematised pedagogy combining theoretical and practical aspects of performance practice is scant (Gilchrist 2010 et al.). Where it exists, Baroque performance practice teaching is commonly devolved, in part, to the musicologist, or perhaps the choral director or specialist vocal coach (Tucker 2008). However, choral conductors may be ill equipped in terms of the requisite theoretical and practical knowledge of Baroque performance conventions (Partridge 2010). As government funding for higher education in Australia and England diminishes, the resultant contraction of labour resources places on tenuous footing the ongoing role of the specialist Baroque vocal coach (Evans et al. 2011; Langlands et al. 2011; Lomax-Smith et al. 2011).

Given these contexts, students develop limited capacity to balance the technical skills absorbed in the singing teacher's studio with the declamatory vocal practices and theoretical deliberations espoused within the eighteenth-century treatises (Tosi 1723; Mancini 1774; Agricola 1757; Hiller 1780). These phenomena confirm the primary status of the literature and more significantly, the stimuli for this research.

This chapter addresses aspects of pedagogy and applied performance practice in the repertoire for tenor voice by Handel as a means of informing teaching methodologies in tertiary music education and identifying avenues of further research.

16.1.3   Ethics

The human research conducted within this project has research ethics approval under Griffith University Ethics Protocol QCM 2107HREC.

16.2   George Frideric Handel

The following paragraphs briefly introduce George Frideric Handel, one of the foremost composers of vocal music in the Baroque period. Setting in context the tenor voice as a fundamental element of this research, the discussion also considers several distinguished German, Italian and English tenors who performed under the composer's direction.

Handel's principal vocal genres include the *opera seria*, Italian cantata, English oratorio and English ode. These works serve as conduits for the transmission of affective elements of text and music, declamatory vocal practices and ornamentation comprising the gamut of performance practice. Handel's life is the subject of many biographers' studies, including the comprehensive publications by Burrows (1994, 1997), Burrows and Dunhill (2002), Hogwood (1984, revised 2007), Hicks (2007) and the documentary biography by Deutsch (1955). Grounded within the scholarship of these academics, the chronology in Table 16.1 briefly outlines some of the significant events in Handel's life pertaining to the current research. (For the sake of brevity, Handel's surname is abbreviated to 'H' within Table 16.1).

16.2.1   Handel's Tenors

Although the castrato and *prima donna* soprano voices frequently took significant roles in Handel's Italian *opera seria*, the composer featured roles for the tenor voice in 27 of his 42 Italian operas. The famous Italian tenor Francesco Borosini

Table 16.1 A brief timeline of Handel's life and some of his works for the tenor voice

Date	Biographical annotation
1685	H born in Halle on 23 February
1692	H begins music study with Zachow in Halle
1702	H enrols as a law student at Halle University
1703	H moves to Hamburg; meets tenor Mattheson and joins the Hamburg opera orchestra
1704	H composes *Almira*, his first *opera seria*[a]
1705	Mattheson sings tenor roles in Handel's *Almira* and *Nero* in Hamburg[a]
1706	H leaves Hamburg, destined for Italy
1707	Opera *Rodrigo* premieres in Florence[a]
1708	Oratorio *La Resurrezione* premieres in Rome[a]
1710	H appointed Kapellmeister to the Elector of Hanover; makes his first visit to London
1711	*Rinaldo* presented at Queen's Theatre, Haymarket; H returns to Hanover
1712	H journeys to London; premieres several operas
1713	Queen Anne endows H an annual pension
1719–28	H appointed Music Director of the Royal Academy of Music. Operas staged by the Academy include *Radamisto*, *Flavio*, *Giulio Cesare* (revival), *Tamerlano*, *Rodelinda*, *Scipione*, *Alessandro*, *Admeto* (revival)[a]
1729	Royal Academy of Music closes; H journeys abroad to engage Italian singers for a new opera company
1729–34	H presents operas including *Lotario*, *Partenope*, *Poro*, *Tolomeo* (revival) at the King's Theatre, in partnership with John Heidegger[a]
1732	Performances in London include *Ezio*, *Sosarme* and the English oratorio *Esther*[a]
1733	H directs *Acis and Galatea* and *Esther* in Oxford[a]
1734	Operas in the Covent Garden season include *Arianna* (revival) and *Ariodante*[a]
1735	H includes oratorios in his opera subscriptions; *Alcina* premieres[a]
1736	*Alexander's Feast* and *Cecilia, volgi un sguardo* premiere[a]
1737	H presents *Arminio*, *Giustino* and *Berenice* at Covent Garden[a]. H's company subsequently closes in June
1739	H presents *Saul* and *Israel in Egypt* at Lincoln's Inn Fields Theatre, London. [a]Significant tenor roles in most of the oratorios composed 1739–52
1741	H presents his final season of *opera seria* in London; composes *Messiah*[a]
1742	*Messiah* premieres in Dublin[a]
1743	*Samson* premieres at Covent Garden[b]. *Messiah* first performed in London[a]
1751	Deteriorating eyesight interferes with the composition of *Jephtha*[b]
1753	Last newspaper report of H playing in a public performance
1759	14 April: H dies at his London home; 20 April: funeral at Westminster Abbey

Key: [a]contains significant tenor role; [b]tenor voice assigned title role

(c. 1690–after 1747) sang the dominant role of Bajazet in the 1724 premiere of Handel's *Tamerlano* (HWV 18). The English tenor John Beard (c. 1717–91) also created substantial operatic roles as Lurcanio in *Ariodante* (HWV 33), Oronte in *Alcina* (HWV 34) and Fabio in *Berenice* (HWV 38).

With the demise in popularity of *opera seria* in London, and the advent of the English oratorio form, the tenor voice began to take prominence in Handel's output. Beard sang the title roles in Handel's *Belshazzar* (HWV 61), *Samson* (HWV 57) *Judas*

Maccabaeus (HWV 63) and *Jephtha* (HWV 70), and took principal roles in every oratorio and ode by Handel, excluding *The Choice of Hercules* (HWV 69), which contains no music for the solo tenor voice (Dean 2007a). Consideration of the noteworthy tenors who performed under the composer's direction helps place the tenor voice in the context of pedagogic dialogue upon performance practice. The appendix contains biographical summaries of Beard, Borosini and other significant tenor soloists:

German

• Johann Mattheson (1681–1764)

Italian

• Carlo Arrigoni (c. 1697–1744)
• Francesco Borosini
• Annibale Pio Fabri (1697–1760)
• Giovanni Battista Pinacci (1694/5–1750)

British

• John Beard
• Alexander Gordon (c. 1692–1754/55)
• Thomas Lowe (d. 1783)

16.3   Methodology

16.3.1   Data Collection Procedures

Through use of qualitative research procedures (Creswell 2003, 2007; Denzin and Lincoln 2000), this chapter examines pedagogic methodologies and resources in the context of the professional practitioner. Accessing the insights of performers and reporting upon the tenor voice as a single phenomenon, this chapter contributes diverse perceptions of these singers' integration of theoretical and practical components of Baroque performance practice. By so doing, the chapter aims to identify effective processes for advanced pedagogy in higher music education.

The practitioner study combines elements of the biographical and the expert interview in a semi-structured format (Flick 2006; Robson 2002; Seidman 1991; Wengraf 2001). The practitioner interviews were designed to gather coherent data for coding, analysis and reporting within the study. The interviews with Gilchrist, Padmore, Partridge and Robson took place during a field trip to the United Kingdom in 2010. Langridge and Tucker were interviewed during visits to Australia, and Massingham was interviewed in Brisbane, Queensland.

The establishment of reflexive practices supplements the triangulation of data collection methods (Creswell 2003; Mertens 2003). Reflexivity, the researcher's 'reflection on their own data making role' (Richards 2005, 42), recognises the collaborative role of researcher and respondent in producing data, and acknowledges the investigator as being themselves part of the data field.

Reflexivity within this type of research adds rigour and depth to the study, as the researcher subjects their role in the enquiry to the same degree of scrutiny as the rest of the data (Mason 1996). The researcher's 'introspection and acknowledgement of biases, values, and interests' (Creswell 2003, 182) has assisted the integration of data within this analysis (Adler and Adler 1998). This type of reflexivity includes reflection upon the researcher's own university and conservatoire music training, his role as a teacher of singing and lecturer in music, and his experiences as a professional performer in the field of Baroque music. The manner of reflexivity acknowledges 'that the researcher is part and parcel of the setting, context, and culture they are trying to understand and analyse' (Liamputtong and Ezzy 2005, 43).

16.3.2 Analytical Process

Following the principles of qualitative research procedures, the audio recordings of the research interviews were transcribed, and the transcripts subsequently prepared for preliminary coding (Creswell 2003; Richards 2005). Critical reading and the generation of data codes produced generalised themes, which further assisted the analytical process (Creswell 2003; Strauss and Corbin 1990).

Coding of the interview transcripts, together with the researcher's reflection upon them developed concepts within the data (Creswell 2003; Richards 2005). The grouping of concepts into categories allowed the researcher to move up from the data through reflection and analytical questioning, forming the basis of an interpretation of the themes and the divergent perspectives which became apparent (Richards 2005). The analytical narrative that has been constructed offers rich descriptions of the data, and includes quotes from the practitioners and thematic categories couched in the language of the participants. These 'in vivo' terms (Creswell 2003, 192) further add to the depth and rigor of the analysis.

16.3.3 Research Sample

The eight British and Australian tenors involved in this study are a representative cross-section of practitioners who are generally considered eminent in their field. In accordance with well-established research methodology, this process is a purposive sampling that 'aims to select information-rich cases for an in-depth study' (Liamputtong and Ezzy 2005, 46).

	Years of higher education	
Practitioner	Conservatoire	University
Partridge	1956–60	n/a
Langridge	1958–62	n/a
Robson	1973–75; 75–77	1970–73
Massingham	1972–74; 1975–77	n/a
Tucker	1980–82	1976–79
Padmore	n/a	1979–82
Gilchrist	n/a	1985–90
McMahon	1992; 2003–2005	1987–89; 91

Table 16.2 Presentation of the research sample practitioners and a timeline in higher music education

These accomplished professional performers (see Table 16.2) evince diverse experiences in the pedagogical process of music training, although collectively they share a recognised expertise in the vocal music of Handel. All participants have agreed to their being identified in the research findings contained within this chapter. The age group of the sample ranges from 43 to 73, and significantly includes the late English tenor Philip Langridge (1939–2010). The researcher also reflects upon his own training and experience in Baroque performance practice, again according to well-established methodologies (Ellis 2004; Ellis and Bochner 2000; Spry 2001). The appendix includes brief biographical notes on these performers.

16.3.4 Limitations of the Study

In expressing a desire for reflection upon the verbal exchanges between investigator and participant within face-to-face interviews, one acknowledges the limitations of this study. Some prospective European and North-American performers withdrew, as logistical hurdles in co-ordinating freelance performers' schedules to coincide with a field trip from Australia proved insurmountable. Other factors, including the structure of the overriding study as an investigation of the tenor voice, means this research is non-representative of gender balance.

16.3.5 Research Question

Addressing academic and professional experiences, this chapter investigates pedagogical resources and techniques informing performance practice within Handel's output for solo tenor voice. The chapter outlines the researcher's perception of the concepts and themes within the data arising from the research question:

Were there specific pedagogy techniques employed during your tertiary training or resources encountered in your professional life that have contributed to your knowledge of performance practice in Handel's vocal music?

16.4 Findings

The research findings incorporate five principle themes, outlined below.

16.4.1 Choral Tradition

Handel's English oratorios and odes offer a wealth of suitable material for choral presentations. The interview data confirms that the tradition of choral singing is a significant influence upon the development of appropriate performance practice skills in this repertoire.

Padmore (2010) portrays the impact of the English choral tradition upon his first singing teacher's instructive approach to Handel, conventions 'that informed me, in some ways' (Padmore 2010). Langridge (2008), Partridge (2010) and Tucker (2008) describe the dominant force that the English choral tradition exerts upon singers' approach to Handelian repertory. In the absence of specialised classes in Baroque performance practice in their conservatoire training, Massingham (2007) and Robson (2010) explain participation in choirs as a decisive introductory component to performance protocols within Handel's vocal music.

Self-Reflection upon Choral Tradition

Singing in choirs during conservatoire and university training provided an introductory overview to Handel's English oratorios and odes. This activity also provided insights into the interpretative foundations of ornamentation and declamatory practices presented by solo singers in works such as *Messiah*, *Alexander's Feast* and *Samson*. The inspirational and motivational elements of choral participation proved to be an essential experiential stepping stone in the progression towards a solo singing career.

Analytical Reflection and Theoretical Conception of Choral Tradition

The sheer number and popular appeal of English oratorios and odes by Handel offer choral directors an extensive selection of works for concert presentation (Dean 1990). Through interaction with the music director within the rehearsal process, choral concerts offer singers experiential scenarios, particularly in the application of performance practice. Opportunities to learn, rehearse and present the solos within these works may also arise for undergraduate and postgraduate singers in the conservatoire and university environment (Padmore 2010; Robson 2010; Tucker 2008). Such opportunities allow students to engage in the application of performance practice, both on a theoretical and practical level (Robson 2010). Reflection upon such events also presents valuable learning experiences for singers (Massingham 2007; Robson 2010).

The interview data confirms the role of choral singing as a pedagogical resource (Grant and Norris 1998) and also its function as an introductory apparatus to performance practices (Massingham 2007; Padmore 2010). As interviewees confirmed, participation in choral singing has long formed an active component of higher music education courses (Ellis 2005; Harker 2008; White 1982). Reflection upon the interview data confirms the educational value of such institutional ensembles as a vehicle of pedagogy in Handelian performance practice. This research recognises the instructional role of choral conductors and the desirability of ongoing professional development for conductors, given their prime role in the training of Baroque performance practice and in vocal pedagogy.

16.4.2   Recordings

The practitioner survey produced useful commentary upon the multifarious application of recordings. Recordings act as devices assisting professional singers formulate the interpretive foundations of Baroque performance practice within teaching and performing environs.

In reflecting upon his university music education, Padmore (2010) identifies recordings as a significant informative resource concerning Handelian performance. He posits the listener's reaction to singers is a meaningful phenomenon in this context, such as the reference to his own impressions regarding the singing of the late English tenor Anthony Rolfe-Johnson (1940–2010), who:

> ...made so much sense to me, ...he was such a naturally gifted singer, particularly in Bach and Handel, just the right quality of sound and interpretation... recordings make a huge difference to us now...you do respond to singers that you hear on disc and you respond to ways that they interpret performance practice, ornamentation, declamation.... (Padmore 2010)

In similar vein, Robson (2010) cites the impact of recordings throughout his university studies. He suggests the accumulative refinement of performance practice within recordings of Handel's music confirms the pedagogical significance of these media. The influence of historically informed research became apparent in recordings during the late 1960s and the 1970s, indicating the respect for performance practice engendered by certain ensembles. An earlier tradition of Handel recordings:

> ...which [Robson's teacher] Alexander Young [1920–2000] typified...that tradition came from a pre-war idea of Handel, but certainly after the war, there was a great change in the way people were looking at Handel...Alexander Young would say, 'well, we've moved on a bit from there. I wouldn't do that in that way anymore'. But that's the same as me having recorded Tamerlano...then 20 years later looking at it again in a new light and from a different perspective. (Robson 2010)

Self-Reflection upon Performance Practice and Handel Recordings

My undergraduate music degree during the late 1980s coincided with the production of a wealth of recordings emerging from the United Kingdom and Europe under the banner of historically informed performance (Butt 2002). Scholarship casts many recordings of Handel's music released during this time under the cloudy spectre of 'authenticity' within performance (Butt 2002; Dreyfus 1983; Taruskin 1982, 1995 et al.) However, the quality of musicianship, the technical standards, the use of copies of instruments of the period and gut strings, the lower performing pitch and the featuring of singers who generally employed a flexible, declamatory singing style made many of these recordings an enticing combination of attributes.

While not implying that they hold to the term 'authentic' or should be labelled as definitive, the Handel recordings by the late English tenor Anthony Rolfe-Johnson were influential during my tertiary education. When combined with a cross-section of other secondary and primary sources, recordings remain valuable devices in the preparation of Baroque performance practice.

**Analytical and Theoretical Reflection upon Performance Practice
and Handel Recordings**

Practitioners' commentary upon recordings as key experiences and assets in the context of education and the professional career confirm the far-reaching role of such resources. The function of recordings is such that it places listening practices within a dialogue. Furthermore, the research literature endorses listening as a vital module of communication, scholarship and musical expression (Bogdan 2001; Cavner and Gould 2003; Duker 1964).

The literature also points to the role of music recordings in the process of collaboration and assessment that occurs within learning protocols (Abril 2006; Bogdan 2001). Within the perspective of education, recordings assist in stimulation of the imagination (Cobbs 2005). The practitioner responses in the data reinforce the phenomenon of recordings as an integral aspect of instruction, in terms of how they cultivate a sense of performance practice associated with Handel.

Theoretical conceptions also incorporate recordings as a vital aspect of a vibrant conservatoire and university pedagogy. Instruction promoting evaluative listening links academic concepts and the practical application of Baroque performance practice in various phases of musical preparation. Scholarly guidance within higher education also promotes a discourse whereby recordings and practical music making are both employed as a means of instruction and research.

16.4.3   Text-Music Interaction

Relationships between the intrinsic functions of text and music contribute to one's understanding of performance practice. Besides his experience singing Handel's

English oratorios, Tucker (2008) describes his preparatory procedures and working relationship with the tenor roles in Handel's *opera seria* oeuvre:

> ...through the traditional Italian operatic angle...there were aspects of declamation and recitative in Italian which were very helpful to me concerning the performance of Handel... the logic of the phrasing and the building of the aria as an extension of the recitative and an awareness of Italian metric structure. (Tucker 2008)

Massingham (2007) alludes to declamatory vocal practices as a constituent element of performance practice. In discussing the philosophy of his teacher, Sir Peter Pears (1910–1986), Massingham suggests that a deep-seated connection with the emotive content of the text lies at the heart of successful interpretive practice. Driven by the affective sentiment of the musical and dramatic language, Pears' sense of character informed his interpretation of Handel's music, and indeed, all his performing. When he was singing:

> ...he was totally in character, and to me, it's that sense of character, which actually informs the way it is performed. He would emphasise accented syllables in the text, usually with an appoggiatura, and then release the stress by giving less weight to the following syllable... Those types of linguistic choices are important, especially in recitatives, as they reflect the declamatory principles at the heart of Baroque performance practice. (Massingham 2007)

Analytical Reflection and Theoretical Conception of Text-Music Interaction

Considering the central concepts within the statements by Tucker (2008) and Massingham (2007), the following characteristics align as unifying principles: declamation, phrasing, metric structure, emotive content, *affekt* and character. When presented in a complementary manner, these features give the interpretation of Baroque vocal music a sense of cohesion and accord.

While it might be inferred that the components indicated by the practitioners exist as individual entities, the data as a whole suggests that a well-rounded and informed interpretation of Handel's vocal music brings these foundations into accord. The role of declamation is closely tied to a well-defined concept of the musical phrasing (Ransome 1978). Declamatory singing intensifies an oratorical delivery, as the singer heightens the speech rhythm and accentuation of the text through melodic and rhythmic inflection (Tosi 1723; Mancini 1774 et al.). From this grounding in text-music structures grows the emotive connection with affective meaning (Powers 1980). Such practices enable the development of character as a through-line within a work, the portrayal of affective words and phrases and the dramatic representation of recitatives and arias (Webb 1983).

Further analytical reflection confirms the significance of various pedagogical elements in higher education, including the interpretive principles of text and music as equal partners. Educating singers in the art of foreign languages enhances the appreciation of textual nuance and meaning, while enriching an affective and expressive portrayal of the words (Parr 2006). Analysis of the survey data also supports the pedagogical role of the specialist vocal coach. On both a theoretical and practical level, these practitioners ideally assist the singing student to refine the elements of declamation, affective representation and characterisation of the text and music.

16.4.4   Discourse Between Performer-Teacher and Student

Several practitioners interviewed discussed the function of a constructive dialogue with their teacher in relation to aspects of Handelian performance practice. Partridge (2010) and Robson (2010) refer to dialogue in their study of Handel's tenor repertoire with the English tenor Alexander Young; likewise Massingham (2007) with his teacher, Peter Pears.

Self-Reflection upon Discourse Between Performer-Teacher and Student

The occasion of my first professional engagement to perform the tenor solos in Handel's *Messiah* coincided with a period of postgraduate study. As an experienced oratorio soloist well versed in Handelian performance practice, my then teacher offered suggestions on the many aspects of performance practice in *Messiah*. His instruction in the declamatory presentation of recitatives and the expression of affective text was particularly enlightening. The erudite perspective of an adept performer was a prominent and effective component of his teaching practice. This mode of instruction establishes the significant role that informed vocal teachers play in the pedagogy of Baroque performance practice, and it accentuates the benefit of complementary skill sets and proficiencies among conservatoire and university academic staff (Kreber 2003).

Analytical Reflection and Theoretical Conception of Performer-Teacher: Student Discourse

The literature deliberates upon the phenomenon of dialogue within related aspects of teaching and learning, and in professional practice. Further consideration of this literature suggests that a perceptible interchange of viewpoints within dialogue develops understandings between the parties in the learning environment (Tacelosky 2008). Waghid (2006) also suggests dialogue within teaching and learning practices incites creativeness, through analytical consideration of existing conventions and paradigms.

Listening underpins musical expression; it is a formal component of dialogue and a fundamental module of interaction and scholarship (Bogdan 2001; Cavner and Gould 2003; Duker 1964). Developing core listening skills and an underlying sense of trust between the performer-teacher and student, dialogue is a fundamental principle in the pedagogic and musical process that develops singers' interpretive skills in performance practice.

The interview data in this study also highlights the significance and diversity of the performer-teachers' role in higher education. Analysis of the data suggests that singers' skills in listening and constructive discourse develop within the educational environment. Generalisations emerging from the data also suggest the fostering of mutual respect and the promotion of constructive dialogue in scholarly educational contexts assists learning constructs within performance practice. It can also be inferred that professional development for academic staff is desirable in maintaining resilient links between the realms of professional performance and educational institutions.

16.4.5   Sources and Editions

The assemblage of extant primary source material pertaining to Handel's works offers editors a tangible basis for the preparation of editions (Burrows 1983; Burrows and Ronisch 1994; Dean 1976). However, the extensive variation of editorial interpretation in relation to performance practice questions the validity of some publications. This portent is also one of the problems motivating the current research.

Self-Reflection upon Editions of Handel's Works as Sources in Performance Practice

Reflecting upon the training and resources I have experienced in relation to performance practice in Handel's music, exposure to the great diversity of editions has been a constant feature. As an undergraduate student, I studied the recitative 'Comfort Ye' and aria 'Ev'ry Valley' from Handel's *Messiah*. The only locally available edition was by Ebenezer Prout (1902). My initial conception of performance practice was based upon this romanticised nineteenth-century edition. My then teacher possessed a more recent edition of *Messiah* (Watkins Shaw 1959). Although Burrows' (1987) edition emerged around that time, Watkins Shaw's publication was promoted as one of the most reliable editions of *Messiah*.

Perceptions of Baroque performance practice during my university training were coloured by editions, such as the *Messiah* scores edited by Prout and Watkins Shaw. Through these two distinct secondary sources, I began to question, at least superficially, the different ornamentation practices indicated by each editor. At that stage of my education, the enquiry went only as far as stimulating dialogue with my singing teacher. In turn reflecting upon his own experiences of performing *Messiah*, these discussions included some brief comments on editorial practice regarding *appoggiaturas*.

I soon purchased the Watkins Shaw edition; principally as the typeface was more legible than the Prout edition. In the teaching context, some fleeting references were made to several 1950s LP recordings of *Messiah* and a recording conducted by Sir Charles Mackerras (1925–2010) (Handel 1967). These resources formed the principal sources of interpretive assistance on performance practice in Handel's music during my undergraduate training.

Reflecting upon that phase, it is evident that my interpretive process involved a rigid, sometimes unquestioning approach to issues of performance practice. This viewpoint was formulated partly by inexperience and a paucity of resources, and perhaps more fundamentally, the instructed belief that the indications within a published edition were above reproach. With the benefit of further education, dialogue with professional performing colleagues and perusal of primary sources including treatises and composers' manuscripts, this scenario changed. Furthermore, critical analysis of recordings and access to recent scholarly editions of *Messiah* by Burrows (1987) and Bartlett (1998) now provide a more broadly informed palette, which assists the interpretation of performance practice.

Analytical Reflection and Theoretical Conception of Editions as Informative Resources in Handel Performance Practice

Interrogation of the survey data underscores the impact that editorial decisions can have upon inexperienced singers. While editorial practice plays a role in the comparative and analytic process within pedagogy, editions themselves usually offer a singular viewpoint in terms of performance practice. It is suggested that editions are most effective when viewed in conjunction with a variety of materials. These complementary sources may include critical analyses of recordings, perusal of autograph and conducting manuscripts and aspects of person-to-person dialogue.

Handel's works as edited by third parties offer avenues in performance practice training in higher education. Building perspectives upon performance practice, systematised instruction in this environment offers a means of engagement with the interpretive issues confronting the editor; not the least of which is the chaotic, and at times illegible state of Handel's autograph manuscripts (Burrows and Ronisch 1994).

Examined in conjunction with primary source materials, including composers' manuscripts, conducting scores, instrumental parts and wordbooks, comparative analysis and discourse regarding edited scores builds a robust and informative strand in academic procedures. Such practices allow students to construct informed interpretations of performance practice through erudite perspectives upon editorial sources. These scholarly methods promote a consultative environment that assists students to contend with the complexities of performance practice.

16.5   Summary and Conclusions

Assessment of the data reveals five conceptual resources encountered within practitioners' educative and professional experience contributing to expertise in the performance practice of Handel's vocal music. Practitioners describe experiential aspects of choral singing as an introduction to concepts within performance practice and the pedagogical influence of choral singing in Handel's music. Institutional ensembles have a key role to play in the ongoing development of these skills.

Practitioners refer to recordings and the influential role that singers and recorded music play in forming students' perceptions of performance practice in Handel's music. Recordings are associated with the development of listening, collaborative and dialogic techniques within pedagogy, and potentially assist students to link theoretical concepts in performance practice.

A balance between declamatory vocal practices, textual nuance and musical interpretation emerge as complementary elements in Handel's vocal music. Oratorical delivery intensifies the musical phrasing, and allows vivid characterisation through the portrayal of affective text. In turn, these procedures underline the importance of foreign language training in higher education.

Constructive dialogue between the performer-teacher and the student emerges as a strong element of performance practice pedagogy. Instruction in declamatory practices and the expression of affective text, and the interaction between performer-teacher and student reinforces listening as a scholarly pursuit in performance practice pedagogy. Comparison of Handel's autograph manuscripts with secondary sources underlines the interpretive range and variance of editorial quality in respect of performance practices. The phenomenon of editorial variation forms a contextual motivation for comparative and analytical pedagogy in higher education. Furthermore, this resource suggests that critical, scholarly editions of Baroque music contribute to a rich selection of secondary sources in performance practice pedagogy.

Considered in light of the broad literature (McMahon 2012) and gender-diverse studies (McMahon 2013), the research processes and genesis of this chapter suggest the findings are applicable to all voice-types, as practitioners incorporate the emergent pedagogic principles and cross-genre perspectives in music by Handel and other composers of the Baroque period. While the outcomes of this research guide educational methods, consideration of the research sample and the emergent empirical data suggests paradigms exploring pedagogical practices in European and North American institutions of higher education will effectively serve ongoing enquiry. Exploration of performance practice pedagogy in such organisations may offer additional insights to the performance of Handel's vocal music, while enriching institutional teaching methodologies in Baroque performance practice.

Appendices

Biographical Summaries of Handel's Principal Tenors

German

Johann Mattheson
Mattheson became acquainted with Handel in 1703 and is one of the first tenors whose work with the composer is documented (Dean and Knapp 1995). As his voice matured, Mattheson began to take principal tenor roles with the Hamburg Opera, among them Fernando in Handel's *Almira* (HWV 1) and the title role in *Nero* (HWV 2) (Buelow 2007).

At the Hamburg Opera, Handel conducted Mattheson's opera *Cleopatra*, with the composer singing the role of Antonius. Mattheson became director of music at Hamburg Cathedral between 1715 and 1728, eventually being appointed secretary and diplomatic assistant to the English ambassador to Hamburg (Buelow 2007).

Mattheson's skills encompassed the composition of philosophical and critical reports on many aspects of music. His treatise *Der vollkommene Capellmeister* (Harriss 1981) is a theoretical and philosophical epistle written for musicians employed by the church, or those engaged by secular establishments, such as the court or town council. It includes a comprehensive discussion of the relationships between music and *affekt* (Buelow 2007).

Italian

Carlo Arrigoni

A Florentine lutenist, singer and composer, Arrigoni was active in London between 1731 and 1736 (Hill 2007). Burney documents some of the Italian's activity with Handel's rival opera company, the Opera of the Nobility, which staged Arrigoni's opera *Fernando* in 1734 (Mercer 1957). Arrigoni played the lute in the premiere of Handel's *Alexander's Feast* at Covent Garden in 1736. In the same concert series, he performed as lutenist in Handel's concerto, Opus 4, Number 6 (HWV 294). Ever the practical composer, Handel took advantage of Arrigoni's native tongue and his evidently fine voice, engaging the Italian to perform as tenor soloist in the cantata *Cecilia, volgi un sguardo* (HWV 89) (Dean 1977).

Francesco Borosini

The Italian tenor Borosini came to prominence during his tenure at the Viennese imperial court from 1712 to 31 in operas and oratorios by Caldara and Fux. He appeared in various operatic roles throughout Italy and debuted in London as Bajazet in Handel's *Tamerlano* in 1724. Other operatic roles for Handel included Grimoaldo in *Rodelinda* (1725) and Sesto in a revival of *Giulio Cesare* (Dean 2007a).

Handel dated the completed *Tamerlano* manuscript on 23 July 1724. The pivotal role of Bajazet was extensively revised upon Borosini's arrival in London, with the *tessitura* lowered in several of the arias. Dean and Knapp (1995) suggest that Handel may have had an intermediate working score that is no longer extant, as the autograph manuscript does not contain all the significant changes that occurred before and after the copyist completed the performing score (Hamburg MA/1056). A notable example is Bajazet's aria 'Ciel e terra', composed in E major in the autograph, yet adjusted in the performing score to D major.

Borosini was also responsible for more significant structural change within Handel's conception of *Tamerlano*. Best (2001) suggests Borosini brought with him the libretto and score of Gasparini's *Il Bajazet, Dramma per musica*. These documents inspired Handel to incorporate an extensive onstage death scene for Bajazet, serving to concentrate the drama within the opera's conclusion (Dean and Knapp 1995).

Annibale Pio Fabri

A prominent Italian tenor and composer, Fabri's debut at Modena in 1714 launched a singing career that saw him sing principal roles in all major Italian operatic centres, with performances also in Vienna, Madrid and Lisbon. Accademia Filharmonica, the music education institution established in Bologna in 1666, commissioned Fabri to compose several oratorios in 1719–20 (Dean 2007b).

Burney notes Handel's journey to Italy in 1728 to audition singers for his forthcoming London season. Recording the singers who returned to London with Handel, Burney reports 'Signor Annibale Pio Fabri, a most excellent tenor' (Mercer 1957, 760). Fabri created Berengario in *Lotario*, Emilio in *Partenope* and Alessandro in *Poro*, and he sang in revivals of several other works by Handel.

Giovanni Battista Pinacci

Florentine tenor Pinacci appeared in the principal centres of Italian operatic activity throughout his career. He performed in operas by noted composers, including Bononcini (1670–1747), Hasse (1699–1783) and Pergolesi (1710–36). Handel engaged Pinacci for the London seasons in 1731–2, in which the Italian created Massimo in *Ezio* and Haliate in *Sosarme* (Dean 2007d). In describing the aria 'La turba' from Handel's *Sosarme*, Burney noted:

> ...the tenor singer, Pinacci, is excellent in the present theatrical style;...the agitation and passion of the singer is painted by the instruments in iterated notes, which neither incommode the performer, nor distract the attention of the hearer by complication (Mercer 1957, 773).

British

John Beard

English tenor Beard began his vocal training as a treble in the choir of the Chapel Royal. His Covent Garden debut in 1734 as Silvio in *Il pastor fido* (HWV 8) marked the dawn of a distinguished singing career and an intensive association with Handel's music. Beard took principal roles in every oratorio and ode by Handel, excluding *The Choice of Hercules* (HWV 69, 1751), which contains no music for the solo tenor voice (Dean 2007c).

Beard created the operatic roles as Lurcanio in *Ariodante* (HWV 33), Oronte in *Alcina* (HWV 34) and Fabio in *Berenice* (HWV 38). He therefore gave more premiere performances of Handel's work under the composer's direction than any other male singer (Dean 2007c).

Alexander Gordon

Following his valediction from the University of Aberdeen, the Scottish tenor Gordon began his career teaching languages and music. He lived in Italy for some years, where documentary evidence suggests he performed in Messina in 1716 and in Naples in 1717–18 (Dean 2007e).

Returning to Britain in 1719, Gordon became a member of the Royal Academy in 1720, where he sang Tiridate in Handel's *Radamisto*. After performing Ugone in Handel's *Flavio*, Gordon retired from the stage to commence a career researching the Roman artefacts unearthed in Scotland and northern England (Dean 2007e).

Gordon became secretary for the Society of Antiquities (1736–41). Emigrating to the American colonies where he lived for the remainder of his life, Gordon became secretary to the Governor of South Carolina (Dean and Knapp 1995; Dean 2007e).

Thomas Lowe

An English tenor and actor, Lowe became well known at Vauxhall Pleasure Gardens as a singer in light entertainments and ballads. He frequently interchanged with John Beard as Macheath in *The Beggar's Opera* and performed many of the vocal works of his friend Thomas Arne (1710–78). Lowe appeared at Covent Garden in oratorios by Handel in 1743 and 1748–51 (Dean 2007f).

Between 1763 and 1769, Lowe leased Marylebone Gardens, mounting concerts and light entertainments. In comparing Lowe with John Beard, Burney described Lowe's voice as:

> ...the finest tenor voice I ever heard in my life, for want of diligence and cultivation, he never could safely be trusted with anything better than a ballad, which he constantly learned by his ear; whereas Mr Beard, with an inferior voice, constantly possessed the favour of the public by his superior conduct, knowledge of Music, and intelligence as an actor. (Mercer 1957, 1010)

Biographical Summaries of Tenor Voice Practitioners Interviewed Within the Research

James Gilchrist

Gilchrist read medicine as a choral scholar at King's College, Cambridge and practised in the medical profession before turning to a fulltime career in music in the mid-1990s. He appears regularly as a soloist in Baroque repertoire with many major European early music ensembles. His recent performances include Damon in Handel's *Acis and Galatea* with the Academy of Ancient Music; the title role in Handel's *Judas Maccabeus* with The King's Consort; Handel's *Messiah* with The Sixteen directed by Harry Christophers; the Bach cantata pilgrimage with Sir John Eliot Gardiner and the English Baroque Soloists and regular engagements as the Evangelist in the Bach *Passions* with the Orchestra of the Age of Enlightenment, the Gabrieli Consort and the English Baroque Soloists. (http://www.jamesgilchrist.co.uk)

Philip Langridge, CBE (1939–2010)

Langridge studied the violin at the Royal Academy of Music, commencing his working life as an orchestral violinist before singing began to dominate his career in his 20s. Noted for his consummate performances of English opera and oratorio, his vast repertoire spanned the music of major Baroque composers including Handel, Monteverdi and Purcell to music of the twentieth-century, particularly the vocal works of Benjamin Britten (Loppert 2007).

Gregory Massingham

The Australian tenor Gregory Massingham is Head of Opera and Senior Lecturer in Voice at the Queensland Conservatorium Griffith University. Massingham combines his academic commitments with a busy performing schedule in Australia and New Zealand. He is a regular guest artist with orchestras and choral groups including Sydney Philharmonia Choirs, for whom he has appeared as soloist in Handel's *Samson*, *Solomon* and *Israel in Egypt*, as well as the Evangelist role in Bach's St Matthew and St John Passion. (http://www.griffith.edu.au)

Mark Padmore

Padmore studied music as a choral scholar at King's College, Cambridge before undertaking major collaborations with prominent European early music practitioners, including leading roles in the French Baroque repertoire of Charpentier and Rameau with William Christie and Les Arts Florissants. Padmore also developed a lasting association with Philippe Herreweghe and the Collegium Vocale, Ghent, with whom he regularly performs the music of Bach, particularly the Evangelist in the *Passions*. His performances and recordings of the music of Handel in partnership with the English Concert, directed by Andrew Manze, the English Baroque Soloists under Sir John Eliot Gardiner and the Gabrieli Consort with Paul McCreesh are critically acclaimed. (http://www.markpadmore.com)

Ian Partridge CBE

One of England's most versatile lyric tenors, Ian Partridge studied at the Royal College of Music and the Guildhall School of Music and Drama. He is highly respected for his interpretations of the works of Monteverdi, Schütz, Handel and Bach, as well as Schoenberg, Weill and Britten. A broad discography discloses his proficiency in the vocal works of Handel, with recordings of *Alexander's Feast*, *Chandos Anthems*, *Dixit Dominus* and *Nisi Dominus* under Christophers, *Esther* and *La Resurrezione* under Hogwood and *Israel in Egypt* and the *Ode for St Cecilia's Day* under Willcocks. A Professor at the Royal Academy of Music, Partridge regularly gives master classes in song and early music performance throughout the United Kingdom and abroad and was awarded a CBE in 1992 for his services to music. (http://www.ianpartridge.pwp.blueyonder.co.uk)

Nigel Robson

One of Great Britain's leading lyric tenors, Robson studied music at the University of York and the Royal Northern College of Music. His performance repertory ranges from the music of Monteverdi and Handel to acclaimed performances of the operatic and concerted music of Benjamin Britten. Robson's performances and recordings of Handel's music include *Alexander's Feast*, *Jephtha* and *Tamerlano* under Sir John Eliot Gardiner with the English Baroque Soloists. (http://www.ingpen.co.uk)

Mark Tucker

Internationally recognised as an exponent of Baroque music, Mark Tucker is a graduate of the University of Cambridge and the Guildhall School of Music and Drama, London. His career includes operatic and concert performances and recordings with some of the world's leading interpreters of Baroque music, including Sir John Eliot Gardiner, Nikolaus Harnoncourt, Rene Jacobs, Emmanuelle Haïm, Ton Koopman and Sir Roger Norrington. (http://www.harrisonparrott.com/artist/mark-tucker)

References

Abril, C. R. (2006). Music that represents culture: Selecting music with integrity. *Music Educators Journal, 93*(1), 38–45.

Adler, P. A., & Adler, P. (1998). Observational techniques. In N. Denzin & Y. S. Lincoln (Eds.), *Collecting and interpreting qualitative materials* (pp. 79–110). London: Sage.

Agricola, J. F. (1757). *Anleitung zur Singekunst*. Berlin: G. L. Winter.

Bartlett, C. (Ed.). (1998). *Messiah*. Oxford: Oxford University Press.

Best, T. (2001). *Tamerlano*. Halle: Arthaus.

Bogdan, D. (2001). Musical listening and performance as embodied dialogism. *Philosophy of Music Education Review, 9*(1), 3–22.

Buelow, G. J. (2007). Mattheson, Johann, *Grove Music Online*: Oxford Music Online.

Burrows, D. (1983). The composition and first performance of Handel's 'Alexander's Feast'. *Music and Letters, 64*(3/4), 206–211.

Burrows, D. (Ed.). (1987). *Messiah*. London: Peters.

Burrows, D. (1994). *Handel*. Oxford: Oxford University Press.

Burrows, D. (Ed.). (1997). *The Cambridge companion to Handel*. Cambridge: Cambridge University Press.

Burrows, D., & Dunhill, R. (2002). *Music and theatre in Handel's world*. Oxford: Oxford University Press.

Burrows, D., & Ronisch, M. J. (1994). *A catalogue of Handel's musical autographs*. Oxford: Clarendon Press.

Butt, J. (2002). *Playing with history: The historical approach to musical performance*. New York: Cambridge University Press.

Cavner, D., & Gould, E. (2003). Whole language and music-listening instruction: Part 2 of 2. *Music Educators Journal, 89*(5), 19–25.

Chapman, J. L. (2006). *Singing and singing teaching: A holistic approach to classical voice*. San Diego: Plural.

Cobbs, L. (2005). Learning to listen, listening to learn: Teaching poetry as a sensory medium. *English Journal, 94*(4), 28–32.

Creswell, J. W. (2003). *Research design: Qualitative, quantitative and mixed methods approaches* (2nd ed.). Thousand Oaks: Sage.

Creswell, J. W. (2007). *Qualitative enquiry and research design: Choosing among five approaches*. Thousand Oaks: Sage.

Cyr, M. (1992). *Performing baroque music*. Portland: Amadeus Press.

Dean, W. (Ed.). (1976). *G. F. Handel: Three ornamented arias*. London: Oxford University Press.

Dean, W. (1977). An unrecognized Handel singer: Carlo Arrigoni. *Musical Times, 118*(1613), 556–558.

Dean, W. (1982). *The new Grove Handel*. London: Macmillan.

Dean, W. (1990). *Handel's dramatic oratorios and masques*. Oxford: Clarendon Press.

Dean, W. (2007a). Borosini, Francesco, *Grove Music Online*: Oxford Music Online.

Dean, W. (2007b). Fabri, Annibale Pio, *Grove Music Online*: Oxford Music Online.

Dean, W. (2007c). Beard, John, *Grove Music Online*: Oxford Music Online.

Dean, W. (2007d). Pinacci, Giovanni Battista, *Grove Music Online*: Oxford Music Online.

Dean, W. (2007e). Gordon, Alexander, *Grove Music Online*: Oxford Music Online.

Dean, W. (2007f). Lowe, Thomas, *Grove Music Online*: Oxford Music Online.

Dean, W., & Knapp, J. M. (1995). *Handel's operas, 1704–1726*. Woodbridge: Boydell Press.

Denzin, N. K., & Lincoln, Y. S. (Eds.). (2000). *Handbook of qualitative research* (2nd ed.). Thousand Oaks: Sage.

Deutsch, O. E. (1955). *Handel: A documentary biography*. New York: Da Capo Press.

Donington, R. (1973). *A performer's guide to baroque music*. London: Faber and Faber.

Donington, R. (1982). *Baroque music: Style and performance*. New York: W.W. Norton.

Dreyfus, L. (1983). Early music defended against its devotees: A theory of historical performance in the twentieth century. *Musical Quarterly, 69*(3), 297–322.

Duker, S. (1964). Listening. *Review of Educational Research, 34*(2), 156–163.

Ellis, C. (2004). *The ethnographic I: A methodological novel about autoethnography*. Walnut Creek: AltaMira Press.

Ellis, K. (2005). Vocal training at the Paris Conservatoire and the choir schools of Alexandre-Étienne Choron: Debates, rivalries and consequences. In M. Fend & M. Noiray (Eds.), *Musical education in Europe (1770–1914): Compositional, institutional, and political challenges* (pp. 125–144). Berlin: Berliner Wissenschafts-Verlag.

Ellis, C., & Bochner, A. (2000). Autoethnography, personal narrative, reflexivity: Researcher as subject. In N. Denzin & Y. Lincoln (Eds.), *The handbook of qualitative research* (pp. 733–768). Thousand Oaks: Sage.

Evans, R., Conyngham, B., Cornwell, R., et al. (2011). *20 years after the Dawkins review: Tertiary music education in Australia task force report*. Accessed 15 Jan 2012, from http://sydney.edu.au/music/docs/DOC_LT_Tertiary_Music_Education_Task_Force_Report_Sept_2011.pdf

Flick, U. (2006). *An introduction to qualitative research* (3rd ed.). London: Sage.

Gilchrist, J. (2010). *Baroque performance practice pedagogy and the twenty-first century practitioner: Handel's tenor repertoire*. Cheltenham: Research Interview.

Grant, J. W., & Norris, C. (1998). Choral music education: A survey of research 1982–1995. *Bulletin of the Council for Research in Music Education, 135*(Winter), 21–59.

Handel, G. F. (1967). *Messiah [CD]*. Hayes: EMI Records.

Harker, B. (2008). Milton Babbitt encounters academia (and vice versa). *American Music, 26*(3), 336–377.

Harriss, E. C. (Ed.). (1981). *Johann Mattheson's Der vollkommene capellmeister*. Ann Arbor: UMI Research Press.

Hicks, A. (2007). Handel, George Frideric, *Grove Music Online*: Oxford Music Online.

Hill, J. W. (2007). Arrigoni, Carlo, *Grove Music Online*: Oxford Music Online.

Hiller, J. A. (1780). *Anweisung zum musikalish-zierlichen Gesange*. Leipzig: J. F. Junius.

Hogwood, C. (1984, 2007). *Handel*. London: Thames and Hudson.

Jones, A. V. (2006). Staging a Handel opera. *Early Music, 34*(2), 277–287.

Kreber, C. (2003). The scholarship of teaching: A comparison of conceptions held by experts and regular academic staff. *Higher Education, 46*(1), 93–121.

Langlands, A., et al. (2011). *Funding for universities and colleges for 2010–11 and 2011–12*. Accessed 15 Jan 2012, from http://www.hefce.ac.uk/pubs/circlets/2011/cl05_11/

Langridge, P. (2008). *Baroque performance practice and the twenty-first century practitioner: Handel's tenor repertoire*. Sydney: Research Interview.

Liamputtong, P., & Ezzy, D. (2005). *Qualitative research methods* (2nd ed.). South Melbourne: Oxford University Press.

Lomax-Smith, J., Watson, L., & Webster, B. (2011). *Higher education base funding review final report*. Accessed 15 Jan 2012, from http://www.deewr.gov.au/HigherEducation/Policy/BaseReview/Documents/HigherEd_FundingReviewReport.pdf

Loppert, M. (2007). Langridge, Philip, *Grove Music Online:* Oxford Musc Online.

Mancini, G. (1774, 1777). *Pensieri e riflessioni pratiche sopra il canto figurato*. Vienna: Stamparia di Ghelen.

Mason, J. (1996). *Qualitative researching*. London: Sage.

Massingham, G. (2007). *Baroque performance practice pedagogy and the twenty-first century practitioner: Handel's tenor repertoire*. Brisbane: Research Interview.

McMahon, P. (2012). *Baroque performance practice pedagogy and the twenty-first century practitioner: The tenor repertoire of George Frideric Handel*. Unpublished Ph.D. dissertation, Queensland Conservatorium Griffith University, Brisbane.

McMahon, P. (2013). Practitioner reflections on higher education pedagogy: Performance practice and the music of Handel. In *Proceedings of the 8th International Congress of Voice Teachers* (pp. 147–156). Brisbane.

Mercer, F. (Ed.). (1957). *A general history of music: From the earliest ages to the present period by Charles Burney* (Vol. 2). New York: Dover.

Mertens, D. M. (2003). Mixed methods and the politics of human research: The transformative-emancipatory perspective. In A. Tashakkori & C. Teddlie (Eds.), *Handbook of mixed methods in social & behavioral research* (pp. 135–164). Thousand Oaks: Sage.

Miller, R. (1986). *The structure of singing: System and art in vocal technique*. New York: Schirmer.

Miller, R. (1993). *Training tenor voices*. New York: Schirmer Books.

Neumann, F. (1993). *Performance practices of the seventeenth and eighteenth centuries*. New York: Schirmer Books.

Padmore, M. (2010). *Baroque performance practice pedagogy and the twenty-first century practitioner: Handel's tenor repertoire*. London: Research Interview.

Parr, C. (2006). Eight simple rules for singing multicultural music. *Music Educators Journal, 93*(1), 34–37.

Partridge, I. (2010). *Baroque performance practice and the twenty-first century practitioner: Handel's tenor repertoire*. London: Research Interview.

Powers, H. S. (1980). Language models and musical analysis. *Ethnomusicology, 24*(1), 1–60.

Prout, E. (Ed.). (1902). *Messiah*. Sevenoaks: Novello.

Ransome, A. (1978). Towards an authentic vocal style and technique in late baroque performance. *Early Music, 6*(3), 417–419.

Richards, L. (2005). *Handling qualitative data: A practical guide*. London: Sage.

Robson, C. (2002). *Real world research: A resource for social scientists and practitioner-researchers*. Oxford: Blackwell.

Robson, N. (2010). *Baroque performance practice pedagogy and the twenty-first century practitioner: Handel's tenor repertoire*. London: Research Interview.

Seidman, I. (1991). *Interviewing as qualitative research*. New York: Teachers College Press.

Sell, K. (2005). *The disciplines of vocal pedagogy: Towards an holistic approach*. Aldershot: Ashgate.

Spry, T. (2001). Performing autoethnography: An embodied methodological praxis. *Journal of Contemporary Ethnography, 7*(6), 706–732.

Strauss, A. L., & Corbin, J. (1990). *Basics of qualitative research: Grounded theory procedures and techniques*. Newbury Park: Sage.

Tacelosky, K. (2008). Service-learning as a way to authentic dialogue. *Hispania, 91*(4), 877–886.

Tarling, J. (2004). *The weapons of rhetoric*. St Albans: Corda Music.

Taruskin, R. (1982). On letting the music speak for itself: Some reflections on musicology and performance. *Journal of Musicology, 1*(3), 338–349.

Taruskin, R. (1995). *Text and act: Essays on music and performance*. New York: Oxford University Press.

Tosi, P. (1723). *Opinioni de' cantori antichi, e moderni o sieno osservazioni sopra il canto figurato*. Bologna: Lelio dalla Volpe.

Tucker, M. (2008). *Baroque performance practice and the twenty-first century practitioner: Handel's tenor repertoire*. Sydney: Research Interview.

Waghid, Y. (2006). University education and deliberation: In defence of practical reasoning. *Higher Education, 51*(3), 315–328.

Watkins Shaw, H. (Ed.). (1959). *Messiah*. Sevenoaks: Novello.

Webb, R. T. (1983). Handel's oratorios as drama. *College Music Symposium, 23*(2), 122–144.

Wengraf, T. (2001). *Qualitative research interviewing: Biographic narrative and semi-structured methods*. London: Sage.

White, J. P. (1982). Significant developments in choral music education in higher education between 1950–1980. *Journal of Research in Music Education, 30*(2), 121–128.

Wright, D., & Kauders, B. (1992). Individually enterprising. Within the 'UK City of Music, 1992' is the Birmingham Conservatoire, four music schools in one. *Musical Times, 133*(1790), 162–165.

Chapter 17
Contemporary Vocal Artistry in Popular Culture Musics: Perceptions, Observations and Lived Experiences

Diane Hughes

Abstract Contemporary vocal artistry is often discussed in somewhat veiled contexts. The term 'artist' is commonly used to describe a singer in popular culture musics (PCM) and, although inherent artistry is implied, what specifically constitutes artistry is largely undetermined in PCM. The qualitative research discussed in this chapter addresses the concept of artistry through the perspectives of artists and of potential influencers on artistry. The participants' perceptions, observations and lived experiences provide rich data in which artistic parameters are clearly identified. The research identifies that artistry in PCM, its features and its influencers, simultaneously pose opportunities and distinct challenges for contemporary singers. Consideration of the embodied voice alone, devoid of its influencers, processing and treatments, is perceived as limiting potential artistry. While 'true' artistry is defined and celebrated, it is through discussion of individuality and its intrinsic creative, expressive and technological components that participants reveal strategies for developing and maintaining artistic integrity.

Keywords Singing • Artistry • Popular culture • Music • Technology • Individuality • Originality • Creativity

17.1 Introduction

In an interview on his own creative process, Bob Dylan refers to the dedication required in true artistic pursuits. Preferring not to represent popular culture that is short lived, Dylan describes his artistic intention that was 'to do something that

D. Hughes (✉)
Media, Music, Communication and Cultural Studies, Macquarie University,
Sydney, NSW, Australia
e-mail: diane.hughes@mq.edu.au

S.D. Harrison and J. O'Bryan (eds.), *Teaching Singing in the 21st Century*,   287
Landscapes: the Arts, Aesthetics, and Education 14, DOI 10.1007/978-94-017-8851-9_17,
© Springer Science+Business Media Dordrecht 2014

stood alongside Rembrandt's paintings' (Hilburn 2004). Dylan's analogy to art is reminiscent of the commonplace use in the singing profession of the term artist and its implied inherent artistry; traditional vocal pedagogy often entails instruction in the art of singing. Renowned classical pedagogue, Richard Miller, asserts that artistry requires 'the technical means … and that vocal technique and artistic expression are inseparable' (Miller 1996, xvi). When discussing expressive singing, Sell (2005) suggests that artistry involves interpreting rather than following a composer's instructions (156). How do these traditional artistic concepts and traits translate to vocal artistry in popular culture musics[1] (PCM) in which an aural tradition is more prevalent than interpreting a score and when a naturalness of vocal production is prized?

The methods or processes that enable or underpin artistic endeavours are often less perceptible than the resultant artistic manifestations. This is further complicated when the physical artistic medium is the actual artist and particularly when the artistic instrument, the singing voice, is physically embodied. Often inherent artist traits are intangible and difficult to define, and consequently are even more difficult to address pedagogically. Barthes (1977) discusses the complexity of embodied performance when he writes, 'the 'grain' is the body in the voice as it sings, the hand as it writes, the limb as it performs' (188). This complexity deepens when considering a 'para-linguistic dimension' (Middleton 2000, 29) of sound, emotion and song lyrics, or when a 'hook'[2] (Kronengold 2005) is effectively determined 'by bundling together the meaning, resonances and sound-shapes of the words together with the melodic, rhythmic, timbral and articulatory dimensions of their sung performance' (Middleton 2000, 29). There are also song moments in PCM that are encountered and recalled and 'depend on the ability of performers to instil a dynamic, shifting instant with a sense of the fantastic' (McKinney 2005, 314). PCM singers also need to display emotive expression through the physicality executed in performance and associated gestures (Schneider 1994). Additional general performance characteristics and nuances, specifically related to musical styles, are evident in PCM (Stephens 2008; Soto-Morettini 2006). Add the use of technology to the complexity of singing in PCM and you begin to explore 'the way technology allows the voice to be radically separated from the body' (Neumark et al. 2010, 93). This chapter details the physical and non-physical artistic attributes that are identified in a study of artist and influencer perspectives on contemporary artistry in PCM.

---

[1] Popular culture musics (PCM) is a term used to describe musical styles within popular culture (Hughes 2010). When considering this term it is noteworthy that in Dylan's interview with Hilburn (2004), Dylan also discusses the songwriting process in relation to popular culture. Songwriting is widespread in PCM.

[2] A hook is considered to be a memorable musical phrase that is typically easily repeated. Kronengold (2005) discusses the hook as 'the most determinate aspect of a song' (386).

17.2 The Contemporary Music Industries

PCM includes a range of genres that typically evolve with their own intrinsic cultural, social and musical signifiers. In a broad context, genre relates to a category of artistic endeavour that is 'characterized by a particular style, form, or content' (Genre 2012). Frith (1996) defines genre in relation to the market appeal that a specific genre generates (76) within the recording industry. Historically, major record labels have dominated professional popular music practices and yet, given that the Internet and other platforms now enable a range of music accessibility and intent, it is timely to recognize the plurality of these music industries (Williamson and Cloonan 2007). It is also timely to recognize that not all artists within PCM are commercially motivated and that, within any contemporary music genre, there exist subgroupings of musical styles bound by distinct modes of expression (Style 2012) or stylistic nuances.

17.3 Research Aim, Methods and Rationale

The qualitative research discussed in this chapter provides an in-depth analysis of artistry in PCM from multiple standpoints. The aim of this research was to investigate the concept of contemporary vocal artistry through the perspectives of artists and of potential influencers on artistry. Ethics approval for this study incorporated the de-identification of participants who were purposively sampled to account for the diversity of personnel involved in artistry in PCM. Participants. included professional singers (PS), early career singers (ECS), contemporary singing teachers (CST) with experience in contemporary in performance, professional musicians (PM) with experience in accompanying and/or working collaboratively with contemporary singers, sound technicians (ST), recording engineers (RE), and record producers (RP). Professional singers are those who are employed in the music industries and have substantial performance and/or recording experience; early career singers are those with less than 3 years professional performance and/or recording experience. Several participants have multifaceted careers, and, as such, the professional experience of some participants is relevant to more than participant one category. The participant category that appears in brackets after a direct quotation in the following discussion is therefore in relation to the context of the specific response cited. The primary research method utilised in-depth, semi-structured interviews of eighteen participants. An inductive constant comparative analysis method (Merriam 1998, 159) was used to determine similarities and differences in participant responses, through which concepts and themes emerged. The participants' perceptions, observations and lived experiences provide rich data in which artistic parameters are clearly identified. The findings therefore have implications for developing and maintaining artistic integrity in PCM.

17.4   Findings and Emergent Themes

17.4.1   Theme 1: Individual Expression

The findings identify contemporary vocal artistry as singing in a specific genre or musical style with individual expression and musical skill (musicality). Artistry is viewed as combining the technical and aesthetics of singing, in which singers learn to 'paint' (CST) with their vocal strengths rather than portray vocal weaknesses. The analogy to painting is seen in relation to an artist's capability to use vocal colours or tones during singing:

> The way that their voice paints the picture that they want to paint. So I see it as a really artistic, creative thing. I see vocal artistry as, um, the most personal of all instruments. And it's like, the musical signature of a person (PM).

Participants were consistent in the view that artistry is vocal expression, through which lyrical interpretation, musical elements, emotion, originality, creativity and passion are communicated. While individual expression was a common theme, several singer participants also expressed the concept of 'authenticity' in artistry that enables the individual self to be portrayed through vocal expression:

> So it's finding your own voice, and your own interpretation of a song, and I guess that comes with the honesty of it (PS).

While individual expression was seen to involve a high level of 'authenticity' in expressive and creative elements, individuality also equates to the believability in performance:

> …there are some people that will go onstage and become this completely different thing, which is entertaining and fantastic but, I still think that through your vocal artistry there will always be an element of that truth of who you are (ECS).

The individuality of voices, or 'individual sound' (ECS), is identified as a recurring concept. A participant response that related individuality to personality affirms another aspect of individual sound:

> …some people's voices have a lot of personality, but don't necessarily have a lot of quality. And other voices have a really pure and beautiful [tone] (PS).

More simply, and as another professional singer stated, individual expression equates to originality and the ability to 'stand out' from others within the profession.

17.4.2   Theme 2: Technical and Musical Ability

The ways in which lyrics and musical elements are interpreted and performed were viewed as affecting singing, particularly in relation to dynamics, phrasing and nuances, and vocal timbre. While the ability to replicate and maintain pitch was consistently viewed by participants as essential in true artistry, the notion that vibrato camouflages inaccurate pitch (PS) was raised by a participant who was also highly experienced in recording and producing professional singers. The ability for singers to sing in key and with straight tone was therefore identified as an essential skill. An inability to control pitch also brings into question whether there is 'the ability to control other aspects of artistry' (CST). Although conceding that artistry is not always about perfect notes, another singing teacher viewed the ability to sing in key as facilitating 'the communication with much more clarity'. Contrastingly, the appeal of vocal perfection that includes pitch was viewed by some participants as undermining an artist's ability to convey emotion:

> So sometimes it's those little, um, scratches in your voice, or the way your voice falters on an emotional line that connects with the audience and that has more artistry, than somebody who sings it perfectly (PS).
> ... there's a lot of bending and modulation that happens in contemporary music. And I think if the bends and modulations were done tastefully, and in time, and in good rhythm, then it sounds OK (CST).

Another singer, experienced in performing and recording, alluded to the difference in pitch accuracy and musical ability in the context of live and recorded performances:

> I think in a live scene there's that huge adrenaline rush of performing to a crowd and sometimes I think the delivery is often not so much pitch perfect or not even in the tone or timbre of the sound but often in the emotion of the song. You don't even notice the imperfections of it. Whereas in a recording studio you can go over it, you can perfect it. You're hearing it back as well (ECS).

While not advocating for artists to mimic the vocal sound of others *per se*, actively listening to self and others was consistently viewed as a way of acquiring and developing skills:

> I can't tell you the feeling of satisfaction when you hear something, and you're...something that you've sung, you hear it ... deep down, every note, everything, phrasing, dynamic variation, breathing, all of it, you're like, 'Awesome, that's great'. Like, that's really good, I'm really happy with that. But more often than not, I watch it back and there's, you know, there are things that you, you learn from (PS).
> So vocal artistry has a lot to do with your influences ... little characteristics of singing that you'll pick up through listening to other artists (RE).

Learning how to listen in different contexts also aids the development of artistry. Participants described how effective hearing can be situation dependent. For example, inadequate volume monitor levels in performance often translate to over-singing[3] to compensate; professional singers, experienced in recording, noted the ways in which hearing in this environment (through headphones) can affect aural perception and pitch integrity.

Musical knowledge in contemporary artistry is not typically acquired in a traditional context. In some instances musical ability was referred to as a somewhat

---

[3] In this context over-singing relates to overloading the singing voice by singing too loudly, or through pushing or forcing the voice to be heard.

osmotic process that is acquired through listening, singing or engaging with a musical instrument. Few participants viewed the ability to read music as essential in contemporary artistry:

> I don't think any of them read music, or…I mean, I think formal training can sometimes get in the way of emotional expression (PM).

Although not essential, the ability to read music particularly for some types of professional work, such as session singing or in musical theatre where interpretation of the score is paramount, was regarded as desirable.

17.4.3   Theme 3: Stylistic Integrity

Understanding specific musical styles, and the ability to display the nuances of any given style or musical integrity, was a recurring participant concept in relation to true artistry. Understanding the traditions of any given style, and being able to communicate those traditions, is viewed as underpinning stylistic integrity:

> I think it's important that whatever style people are singing in, that … they're grounded in the traditions of that style (PM).

Inherent within the link between artistry and stylistic integrity is that the artistry and traditions displayed in one specific style may not be equally relevant or easily transferable to another musical style. The level of artistic intensity also varies in different performance contexts and musical styles. This in turn was seen to dictate the load[4] or the demands that artistry and stylistic integrity places on the voice at any given time. Participants were specifically asked to comment on artistry in relation to various genres and/or musical styles. While specific genres were seen to have their 'own difficulty and challenges' (CST), the artistry of some genres, such as musical theatre, was viewed as requiring more technical ability than others. In contrast, and in the context of singer-songwriter artistry, the inference to limitations in technical capability was linked to individuality of style, self-perception and/or musical intent:

> The singer-songwriter is often, I reckon, at the bottom end because they often just write for what they can do, whereas singers tend to have to apply what they do to other people's writing, which means they're often going beyond themselves (PS).
> … when I'm teaching a singer-songwriter, often we'll have the discussion … 'Do you perceive yourself to be a guitarist who sings? Or do you perceive yourself to be a singer who self-accompanies? 'And I think it's often in the orientation of the student's perception of [himself or herself] that the answer to that question comes about (CST).

---

[4] Vocal load typically refers to the physical demands or phonatory effort (Chang and Karnell 2004) placed on the voice; this can be the vocal intensity, as a result of an extended time spent singing or through repeatedly singing for extended periods of time. It is noteworthy that participants also discussed artistic and stylistic demands that require a high level of phonatory effort.

> With a songwriter and not so much a performer, I would think artistry is more in their lyrics and how they present that or in the music that they write (ECS).

17.4.4   Theme 4: Technological Applications

Technology, amplification, software applications and effects were cited as technological examples that can affect the resultant sound of the singing voice and influence artistry, expand artistry, enable artistic manipulation or even create artistry (Hughes 2012a, b). Technological applications are therefore seen to offer creative opportunities while also posing distinct challenges. Participants identified that at times various types of technology, including applications that involve pitch correction, can be applied to the singing voice even without an artist's knowledge. Participant responses indicate that the greater an artist's understanding of technological applications, then the greater the artistic control. To possess limited technological understanding was viewed as restricting artistry and some forms of technological applications, such as sound reinforcement, were identified as being essential to contemporary vocal artistry. Additional essential understanding of technology and the singing voice includes microphone type and use, and applied effects such as reverb. Comprehensive understanding of technological applications was viewed as aiding the ability of artists to communicate their individual requirements:

> Learning that the quality of the technical equipment they're using and the people that may be or may not be operating it for them is also important. And the way that they interact with, for example, the microphone, and using foldback, whether it be full monitors or ear monitors ... if worked with well, they actually have more opportunity to be an effective reinforcement of their vocal artistry (CST).
> I think that sound guys listen to you a lot more seriously. I've learnt that the hard way. Just that, they listen to you a lot more seriously if you know your stuff (CST).

Technology was also discussed more generally with the suggestion that artistry involves the manipulation of an artist's surroundings that includes technology:

> ... surroundings include stage, perhaps screen, audience, PA system, microphones. Uh, and a band (ST).

17.4.5   Theme 5: Artistic Image

While the sonic and musical qualities of artistry were viewed as being essential components, the visual aspects of artistry were also discussed as manifestations of individual expression and communication:

> Artistry flows from the individual. I mean, art flows from the individual. So, out of that individual ... art is ultimately an expression of that person. So out of that same expression will often come a sense of image (CST).

Artistic image was seen to develop over time and to typically develop along with musical intention. Image that emerged through individual expression of a musical style was seen to have a level of authentic representation, whereas a constructed image was negatively viewed:

> I think that if you try to make or try to create an image, then you stop being creative. I think that you've really got to present who you really are (CST).
>
> I'd like to think that still, cream kind of rises in a way. People with unique abilities and unique talents, or really good people, good singers, um…kind of get there. We'll always have the kind of bubblegum stuff, and the manufactured stuff, and the created stuff, and the produced stuff. I mean, that's not going to go away. But it only lasts a little bit of time. But the classic artists, I'd like to think, remain with us (PS).

While it appears that an image can be constructed to far outweigh vocal ability, participants acknowledged that the music industries are now 'image-driven' (PS). Examples were proffered where artistry that did not involve a visual image or an appropriate look negatively impacted on an artist's ability to gain professional recognition and success. However visual expressions of artistry were seen to encompass more than the physicality of appearance:

> So for an artist, their artistry is not only their music these days, but is also how they present themselves, how they present their clips, how they perform on stage, how they interact with their fans (ECS).

Discussion of image also incorporates the ideology on which the artistry is based and the ways in which artistic identity is shaped and conveyed. In this context, image traits were seen to facilitate interest and to draw an audience:

> …like, someone like Eva Cassidy. Brilliant, brilliant singer. Could never really find her place, because she didn't have anything that made people stop and go 'Wow, who is she? What does she stand for? How do I identify with her?' (PS).
>
> Watching someone perform is probably just as important as the sound that's coming out of their voice. You've probably got a few exceptions that maybe don't fit the product image that they might want (RE).

17.4.6   Theme 6: Confidence and Presence

Artistry was also viewed as the totality of being that includes lived experiences. In this context, confidence and presence, although distinct, are central to constructive experiences and artistry. Confidence was thought to develop through preparation and experience, whereas presence equated to performed artistry:

> Confidence is based on preparation. So the more prepared you are, the more confident you are … being familiar with the material, being familiar with the people you're working with … and confidence does contribute to presence, in the level in which the presence is received. So someone can have, I think, a low amount of presence, like they don't command as much of the stage or attention … but I've seen a lot of young performers that do, no matter where you put them, they're always gonna stand out. They command … the stage (PS).
>
> … an audience will often feed off a person's presence onstage, and that presence, the strength of that presence will often be informed by the level of the artist's confidence (CST).

17.5   Artistic Parameters: Influencers and Influences

The themes identified in this research aid in understanding the factors and issues inherent in contemporary vocal artistry. This section summarises the principle influences and influencers[5] identified within the themes that impact on contemporary artistry. Figure 17.1 lists the influencers and influences identified specifically in relation to developing artistry. Influencers on artistry prominently feature in participant responses. From family and friends and their ability to aid or diminish confidence, to the impact of those engineering, producing and/or managing resultant sound were identified:

> … the person who's in control of the technical side of things is working with the vocalist and doesn't understand the vocalist's style and market, and all that kind of stuff, then…it will change the way that they produce the — the sound, for the artist (PS).

The potential impact of the commerciality or commercial intent on artistry, and in particular on those artists signed to record labels, was evident when a producer discussed the expectations of the record label and/or producer and their resultant influence on artistry. This influence was also seen in the commercial interest and desire to meet the expectations of a potential audience. Further discussion on the influences on artistry included access to resources, particularly in relation to the type and quality of sound equipment. Several participants also discussed the influence of an effective soundcheck on artistry in live performances. Cultural and social influences

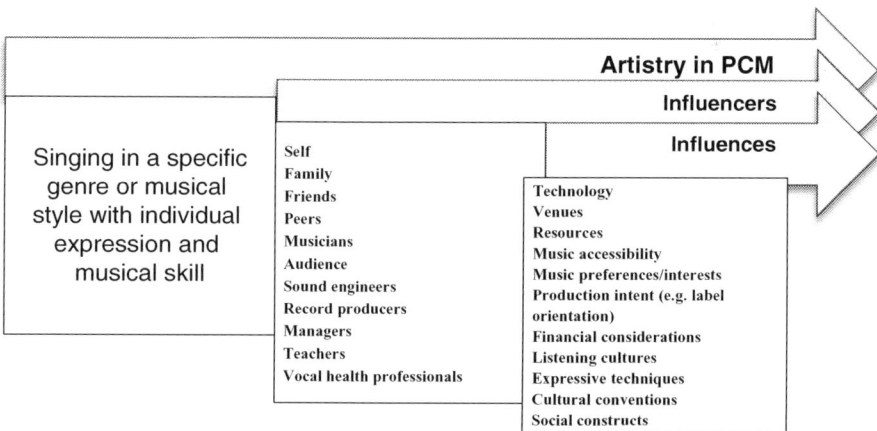

Fig. 17.1 Influencers and influences in developing artistry

[5] The term 'influencer' is specifically used to focus the people that may impact on artistry separately to potential influences.

were also noted, and the sexualisation in commercial music and video production was viewed as significantly impacting on vocal artistry:

> The sexualisation of culture, you know, when you think of pop videos and the visual side of the way we now sell music and sell songs, or perform music and perform songs. The influence on that I think, on even the sounds we make, the sounds that…when we listen to Beyoncé or Lady Gaga, are they being influenced by the kind of, the way they know that they're going to visually sell a song? Even what songs are written about these days, the kind of, the topics, the subjects. And if we go on, and if you're going to perform and sing themes that are [what] we might describe as raunchy or aggressive or violent, it's going to obviously affect the way we are vocally (PS).

17.6 Pedagogical Relevance and Implications

The relevance and function of contemporary vocal pedagogy is discussed in this section in light of the research findings. Figure 17.2 represents identified pedagogical artistic relevance mapped to the study's emergent themes. Individual expression appears first in the developmental chain as it is the most prominent theme in the research findings and needs to be recognised when designing appropriate pedagogy suited to the individual student. However, consideration of the embodied voice alone, devoid of its influencers and treatments, is perceived as limiting potential artistry. The developmental chain concludes with the more performative constructs. While 'true' artistry is defined and celebrated in the research findings, it is through discussion of individuality and its intrinsic creative, expressive (musicality, intent and image) and technological components, that participants revealed strategies for developing and maintaining artistic integrity.

17.6.1 Vocal, Expressive and Stylistic Techniques

The relevance to 'understanding your voice, understanding your style' (PS) for effective learning and teaching in PCM, entails a broad spectrum of pedagogical

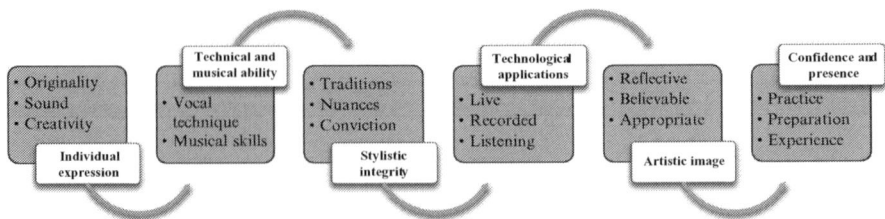

Fig. 17.2 Pedagogical development to underpin artistry

strategies. However, the distinction was made that contemporary vocal pedagogy should not shape the sound of a voice to suit specific repertoire or voice type:

> You've got to learn a lot about your voice, enough so that you're able to know what the rules are, and then also know how to break the rules … so that you can interpret [a song] your way, rather than trying to stick yourself into a mould (CST).

A foundational approach to teaching vocal technique that recognises the individuality in vocal sound, while embedding healthy vocal production,[6] is crucial. The naturalness of vocal production, typical in much PCM, does not negate the relevance of healthy vocal technique. Participants viewed vocal health as aiding vocal expression and career aspirations. Learning about the voice, about healthy vocal production in the context of the individuality of the voice, enables further skill development as participants suggest:

> I think you can learn, I don't think you just 'are'… your voice is the most personal of all instruments. You need to learn how to use it. How to expand it, how to manipulate it, how to hone your skill at singing … and [be] encouraged to develop the next step (PM).
>
> And being educated on what my voice does, and what my voice is capable of. And when you understand that, you have more of a perspective on where you fit (PS).

A singer's artistry may be hampered or compromised, without a foundation in vocal technique that includes appropriate posture, breath management, articulation and free vocal production. There are however, differences between traditional classical technique and singing technique for PCM particularly in relation to the latter involving a more unaffected sound and artistic choices that may at times include breathy tone or even a spoken quality. Often artistic choices relate to integrity of musical style and so another crucial pedagogical strategy is to engage in the exploration of vocal nuances that enable musicality and stylistic integrity. This presents challenges to singing teachers who do not often have a score to interpret, but who rely on an aural appreciation and implementation of appropriate musical and stylistic elements. While there is a prolific use of backing tracks in contemporary singing teaching, the experience of working with musicians should not be overlooked in developing ability as one participant warned:

> … especially now that backing tracks are so easy to come by, you're gonna get kids that are growing up just only ever performing with backing tracks, and having no idea of how to work with a band or a musician, and it's completely different. And it makes you… not lazy, but it's easy to perform to something that sounds the same every time you've performed to it, but it is harder to put that artistry into it, because you can't breathe life into it, and you can't feel it and hold little bits out longer when it calls for it, and things like that. But I think that takes quite a lot of time to learn how to do that with a band. Or just even a pianist. And I think that's a very important thing to learn how to do. And I think that's been also one of the biggest growth experiences for me, is working with good musicians (PS).

---

[6] There have been recent high profile professional singers whose vocal health issues have impacted on career commitments (McKinley 2011). Learning to embody healthy vocal production is crucial to developing and sustaining career aspirations.

17.6.2   Technological Treatments and Processing

The technological treatment of the singing voice occurs in live performance and during the recording process. It is therefore important to distinguish between the acoustic singing voice or the inputted sound, and the processed singing voice known as resultant sound (Hughes 2010). As the latter suggests, the resultant sound of the voice is that typically heard as the result of technological application (Hughes 2012a, b). Technology can also be utilized to enhance the teaching praxis in several resultant sound contexts. Recording and subsequent playback of singing can augment understanding of the individual sound:

> I think it's … sort of like an out-of-body experience moment, when you hear your voice played back or on a microphone … from a young age I was exposed to that … and I don't really recall being thrown by it. But … I've seen a lot of people being thrown by how they sound, and it really puts them off when they sing (PS).

As participants continually expressed ways in which they are affected by what and how they hear their voice, providing opportunities for critical or active listening also aids in expressive techniques. Similarly, providing opportunities for visual playback is also important, particularly in relation to the physicality of performance and the correlation between the visual and aural selves.

The moment the singing voice progresses from the embodied instrument to being technologically treated, either in live performance via amplification or during the recording processes through technological 'enhancement', the singing voice is typically beyond the control of the singer. The type of application, the level of processing and those responsible for the sound engineering, can impact on the resultant vocal sound. Pedagogical strategies must therefore include the singing voice in the context of technological treatment. This means more than using rudimentary microphone and amp equipment in studio teaching. It means engaging with sound engineers and technicians, and developing understanding of the sound frequency spectrum. Teaching about vocal processing and treatment includes effects such as graphic equalization, compression, and reverb. It also involves microphone technique, monitoring sound, an appreciation of room acoustics and knowledge of the equipment being used. An understanding of recording processes and techniques is vital to those singers engaging in recording. Learning about technological treatment and vocal processing should not have to be through an on the job 'trial and error' (CTS) method. In the new music industries where so many music clips are uploaded to various Internet platforms, and are therefore easily accessible, contemporary artists have too much at stake to impede optimum resultant performances and sound.

17.6.3   Performance Constructs

Pedagogical strategies also need to include ways in which performance skills may be developed. This includes discussion of the visual image, and its correlation to musical style, that will be seen in performance. Strategies to ensure effective practice and preparation aid the development of positive performance experience that in turn will benefit the student's confidence.

17.7 Conclusion

The findings identify that contemporary vocal artistry is expressivity, individuality and stylistic integrity. While popular culture is sometimes criticized for the mass production of artefacts that have seemingly little or no intrinsic artistic value, the concept of high art verses low art is beyond the scope of this chapter. Instead this discussion has focused on the artistry and artistic traits identified in specific research on vocal artistry in PCM. The findings identify that a singer in PCM may be grounded in a specific musical style or may be versatile in singing across genres. However, artistry in PCM is not about moulding the voice for a particular sound or to suit particular repertoire. Rather, artistry celebrates uniqueness, musicality and originality. Typically a singer in PCM creates, communicates and evokes emotion or response. An artist also interprets and/or comments on experiences and issues, and uses skills, technologies and procedures in artistic endeavours. Although artistry is sometimes influenced by opportunity, as pedagogues we need to recognise that not all artistry is commercially motivated:

> I think there's two types of artists, there's the ones that want to go the commercial side, and they want to record, and they want to make money and money and money, and be really on the Top 40 … And then there's the other artist, who just want to sing their songs. And who don't want to compromise the words of their songs, or the melody of their songs, or whatever. And are quite happy to do their own gigs, and not have that (PM).

Irrespective of the motivation, there are many expectations and demands on contemporary vocalists. Adequate preparation goes a long way in meeting these expectations and demands. Dave Grohl, Foo Fighters, summarised this in his 2012 GRAMMY acceptance speech saying that '… singing into a microphone and learning to play an instrument and learning to do your craft – that's the most important thing for people to do'[7] (The Recording Academy GRAMMY Awards 2012). Singing teachers have a responsibility to provide opportunities for the development of artistic skills and to acknowledge that contemporary artistry encompasses many features associated with singing in popular culture musics (PCM). Often these features relate to the physicality of singing, to audible vocal traits and to implemented technologies. Students therefore need to be committed to the process of comprehensive learning and development.

The findings reveal that contemporary artistry is heavily influenced by technology both in live performance and in recordings. It must be remembered too that as PCM

---

[7] This acceptance speech was at the 54th Grammy Awards ceremony, February 2 2012, when Foo Fighters were awarded 'Best Rock Performance' for 'Walk', a track from *Wasting Light* [RCA Records/Roswell Records]. http://www.grammy.com/nominees. Accessed 20 May 2012.

are continually evolving, and as new musical technologies are contemporaneously being developed and implemented, contemporary artistry should not be considered as requiring a finite skill set. While healthy vocal production should always be paramount in developing foundational technique, the encompassing skill set should accommodate the individual voice, and the related features of musical and stylistic integrity. Learning strategies should include experiences that enable students to strive artistically:

> To be artistic, sometimes the brushstrokes aren't always going to be right. But it's the end painting that you get, after you've painted over it a number of times (CST).

Most importantly singing teachers need to provide strategies for singers to own and develop their artistry in ways that do not impose artistry, but ensure that other influencers or influences do not negate artistic intent:

> … because if you don't know what it is that you want, people can perceive it in a different way, and take it somewhere else … if you're clear on your artistry, and know exactly what it is that you want from a recording, or from a look, an image of some sort, or … what it is that you want to portray … then it's anyone's for the taking … and that's why I think it's so important to know these kinds of things before you…you know, jump (ECS).

References

Barthes, R. (1977). The grain of the voice. *Image, Music, Text* (trans: Stephen Heath) (pp. 179–189). New York: Hill and Wang.

Chang, A., & Karnell, M. P. (2004). Perceived phonatory effort and phonation threshold pressure across a prolonged voice loading task: A study of vocal fatigue. *Journal of Voice, 18*(4), 454–466.

Frith, S. (1996). *Performing rites: Evaluating popular music.* Oxford: Oxford University Press.

Genre. (2012). In *Merriam-Webster.com.* http://www.merriam-webster.com/dictionary/genre. Accessed 16 May 2012.

Hilburn, R. (2004). Rock's enigmatic poet opens a long-private door. *Los Angeles Times* April 4 2004. http://articles.latimes.com/2004/apr/04/entertainment/ca-dylan04. Accessed 15 May 2012.

Hughes, D. (2010). Developing vocal artistry in popular culture musics. In S. Harrison (Ed.), *Perspectives on teaching singing: Australian vocal pedagogues sing their stories* (pp. 244–258). Bowen Hills: Australian Academic Press.

Hughes, D. (2012a). Mediocrity to artistry: Technology and the singing voice. In J. Weller (Ed.), *Educating professional musicians in a global context* (pp. 60–64). Proceedings of the 19th International Seminar of the Commission for the Education of the Professional Musician (CEPROM) International Society for Music Education, Philippos Nakas Conservatory, Athens. 10–13 July 2012.

Hughes, D. (2012b). My sound, our sound: Constructing the aesthetic in contemporary vocal production. In L. Giuffre & P. Spirou (Eds.), *Routes, roots and routines: Selected papers from the 2011 Australia/New Zealand IASPM Conference* (pp. 58–71). IASPM-ANZ Annual Conference, Victoria University of Wellington, New Zealand. 23–25 November 2011. http://search.informit.com.au/browsePublication;isbn=9780975774755;res=IELHSS. Accessed 25 Mar 2014.

Kronengold, C. (2005). Accidents, hooks and theory. *Popular Music, 24*(3), 381–397.

McKinley, J. [*New York Times*]. (2011). Surgery, cancellations as singers opt to protect their assets. In *Sydney morning herald,* 24 Nov 2011. http://www.smh.com.au/entertainment/music/surgery-cancellations-as-singers-opt-to-protect-their-assets-20111123-1nuyp.html. Accessed 14 May 2012.

McKinney, D. (2005). Cruising a road to nowhere: Mechanics and mysteries of the pop moment. *Popular Music, 24*(3), 311–321.

Merriam, S. B. (1998). *Qualitative research and case study applications in education.* San Francisco: Jossey-Bass.

Middleton, R. (2000). Rock singing. In J. Potter (Ed.), *The Cambridge companion to singing* (pp. 28–41). Cambridge: Cambridge University Press.

Miller, R. (1996). *The structure of singing.* New York: Schirmer Books.

Neumark, N., Gibson, R., & van Leeuwen, T. (2010). *Voice: Vocal aesthetics in arts and media.* Cambridge: Massachusetts Institute of Technology.

Schneider, S. (1994). Closing words: Gesture in song. In *Concert song as seen: Kinesthetic aspects of musical interpretation* (pp. 71–78). Stuyvesant: Pendragon Press.

Sell, K. (2005). *The disciplines of vocal pedagogy: Towards an holistic approach.* Aldershot: Ashgate.

Soto-Morettini, D. (2006). *Popular singing. A practical guide to: pop, jazz, blues, rock, country and gospel.* London: A & C Black Publishers Limited.

Stephens, V. (2008). Crooning the fault lines: Theorizing jazz and pop vocal singing discourse in the rock era 1955–1978. *American Music, 26*(2), 156–195.

Style. (2012). In *Merriam-Webster.com.* http://www.merriam-webster.com/dictionary/style. Accessed 16 May 2012.

The Recording Academy GRAMMY Awards. (2012). Foo fighters win best rock performance. In *54th GRAMMY awards ceremony,* 2 Feb 2012. http://www.grammy.com/videos/foo-fighters-win-best-rock-performance. Accessed 20 May 2012.

Williamson, J., & Cloonan, M. (2007). Rethinking the music industry. *Popular Music, 26*(2), 305–322.

Chapter 18
Pathways for Teaching
Vocal Jazz Improvisation

Wendy Hargreaves

Abstract This chapter will present three common educational pathways used by teachers of vocal jazz improvisation. In the first approach, teachers immerse students in the sounds of jazz. Like a child learning to speak, students subconsciously absorb musical language, then progress to imitating masters and producing spontaneous creations of their own. The second method, in contrast, focuses on a conscious learning of the musical building blocks of jazz. Utilising theoretical analysis, students are guided through a sequenced curriculum that encompasses elements of melody, harmony and rhythm. From this, they attain a base knowledge that serves as a springboard for creation. The third pathway teaches vocalists to improvise on an instrument. This approach is often employed to avoid the difficulty singers experience with applying theoretical concepts without a fixed point of reference for pitch. Overall, this chapter will explore the strengths and weaknesses of the three pathways for teaching vocal jazz improvisation. The discussion makes conscious the options for twenty-first century music educators, and alerts them to the relevant environmental considerations when selecting a method.

Keywords Improvisation • Jazz • Education • Vocalists • Instrumentalists • Pedagogy

18.1 Introduction

Over the past decade, pedagogical pathways for teaching vocal improvising have been a focus of jazz research (e.g., Bock 2000; Heil 2005; Wadsworth-Walker 2005). A debate over which method is superior may have diverted attention from how context affects application. This chapter seeks to examine the pathways and reconceptualise their attributes as compatibilities or challenges for vocalists in

W. Hargreaves (✉)
Queensland Conservatorium, Griffith University, Brisbane, QLD, Australia
e-mail: orac@bigpond.net.au

S.D. Harrison and J. O'Bryan (eds.), *Teaching Singing in the 21st Century*,
Landscapes: the Arts, Aesthetics, and Education 14, DOI 10.1007/978-94-017-8851-9_18,
© Springer Science+Business Media Dordrecht 2014

the context of the classroom setting. Once situated, pedagogues may assess the suitability of methods from a grounded perspective. As this chapter will show, the debate can then be shifted from which pathway is universally superior to which method is better suited to a given setting. It offers educators the opportunity to select and refine their approach for a more effective application.

The chapter begins by briefly defining improvisation and considering why vocalists are being taught to improvise. The discussion presents three pathways for teaching. The central directive of each pathway is illuminated, then followed by an appraisal of its compatibility and challenges for vocalists, and a discussion of the teacher's role. The chapter references jazz literature and datum from two studies of Australian jazz musicians conducted by the author as part of doctoral research. The first study (Hargreaves 2010) is an online survey of 209 Australian jazz performers. The second study (Hargreaves 2011) consists of 22 interviews with professional Australian jazz singers and jazz educators working in Australian tertiary institutions. The chapter then considers pathways in the context of the tertiary institution, the private studio setting, and combined instrumental and vocal classrooms. It concludes by recommending that the question of a superior pathway for teaching vocal improvisation be reconceptualised. Instead, teachers can ask which pathway is best suited to the classroom setting where it will be applied.

18.2 Defining Improvising

Defining improvising is a complex task and a source of disagreement (Benson 2003, 1–3; Whiteoak 1999, 215–216). The contention centres on how far a rendition must deviate from the original referent to shift the credit for creation from the composer to the performer. Rather than enter the debate, this chapter will adopt a definition nominated by jazz musicians themselves. In the Hargreaves (2010) survey, Australian adult jazz performers (n = 204) were asked to label 'the act of making changes to the rhythm or melody of a jazz song during a live performance but keeping the composer's original tune recognisable to an audience'. Eighty-three percent preferred the label 'interpretation' to 'improvisation'.

In practical terms, the result shows 'interpretation' to be favoured by jazz musicians when describing the first rendition of the chorus in a traditional jazz performance. The finding is congruent with references in literature to jazz musicians reserving the use of 'improvisation' for describing the solo where more radical alterations occur (e.g., Berliner 1994). Hence, in this chapter, vocal improvisation will refer to vocal solos occurring after the first chorus where scat syllables are used in place of lyrics.

18.3 Consideration of Why Vocalists Are Being Taught to Improvise

Jazz education curriculum includes improvisation typically under the justification that it is integral to the identity of jazz (e.g., Baker 1989, 13–14; Coker 1990, 4–5). This argument stands up well for instrumentalists who are expected to improvise

Fig. 18.1 Role expectations
of jazz musicians (Hargreaves
2010)

Should jazz musicians be able to improvise a
solo?

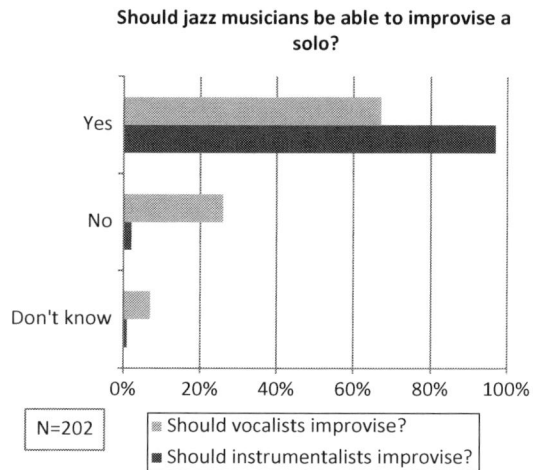

on 'virtually every tune at every performance' (Wadsworth-Walker 2005, 195). However, when the argument is transferred to vocalists, it becomes clouded by differing role expectations.

When Hargreaves (2010) asked Australian jazz musicians (n = 202) whether jazz instrumentalists should be able to improvise a solo on request, 97 % said 'yes' (see Fig. 18.1). In contrast, when the same respondents were asked if vocalists should be able to improvise a solo, agreement dropped to 67 %. The results show a lower expectation for vocalists to improvise.

This perception intrudes on the justification that vocalists should be taught to improvise. If the role of improviser is already fulfilled by instrumentalists, the singer may not experience the same need to learn improvising to participate in jazz. History shows some renowned singers of jazz did not improvise (e.g., Frank Sinatra and Billie Holiday). Perhaps the fundamental question vocal jazz pedagogues should ask is why should these particular students be taught to scat? There may be many reasons ranging from the students' desire to learn it to it being a requirement of a degree. Each answer is as legitimate as the option not to teach singers to scat at all.

If, for whatever reason, vocal improvisation is taught, it would seem prudent to guard against any negative impact that role expectation may produce. For example, the assumption that vocalists can leave the improvising to instrumentalists may reduce opportunities for vocalists to develop their skills. One student at a Melbourne university shared his experience that, although he was studying improvisation alongside instrumentalists, 'I still have ensemble teachers who will never ask if I'm taking a solo' (T. Barton, personal communication, July 22, 2009).

In all, the pathways for teaching vocal improvisation can be successfully trodden if desired. A teacher can act as a facilitator and guide, offering singers the chance to be included in the joy of improvising. In the words of singer Kurt Elling, 'What am I going to do, sing one chorus of *All of Me* and then sit out for 20 min while all these guys have all this fun?' (Nemeyer 2008, 158).

18.4 The Aural Pathway

18.4.1 What Is the Aural Pathway?

The first of the three pathways for teaching vocal improvisation to be examined is the aural pathway. This method, also used for acquiring speech, is a familiar human experience. The pathway centres on students hearing and absorbing patterns of sounds, imitating what is heard and then reproducing ideas based on their acquired storehouse of musical elements and procedures. It does not require a theoretical understanding of music to be successful. One example of a famous vocalist who learnt by this pathway is Jon Hendricks. In an interview with Reid (2002), Hendricks recounted how in his youth he used to learn by heart all the instrumental solos on the jukebox at the local cafe (100–103). Hendricks later replicated the aural pathway with his students at the University of Toledo, where he instructed them to set aside the notated music in order to concentrate on listening and letting the music 'enter through your ear into your mind' (Hendricks in Pellegrinelli 2005, 411).

A central concept that arises in discussions of the aural pathway is audiation. This term, as coined by Gordon (2007), describes the process of mentally hearing music even if sound is not physically present. The potential for the mind to spontaneously generate internal melodies provides a fertile source of ideas that help meet the constant compositional demand of improvising. Jazz literature offers many references to musicians drawing on musical ideas that they 'pre-hear' (Berliner 1994). It is considered a desirable experience (Berliner 1994).

While instrumentalists and vocalists can both draw upon audiated ideas for improvising, audiation also contributes to developing motor programs for the prephonatory tuning necessary for singing (Sundberg 1987, 60–62). Prephonatory tuning is the positioning of the vocal musculature for an intended pitch prior to producing sound. The significance of audiation to this process is recognised by Wadsworth-Walker (2005) when she notes vocalists must audiate sounds prior to accurate phonation (162). As Spradling (2007, 67) writes, 'Singers can only sing what they hear.'

Overall, the central directive of the aural pathway is to absorb the musical elements used in improvisation by listening. Once inputted into the auditory storehouse, patterns and procedures may remerge as audiated ideas (Hargreaves 2012). Exactly how the initial absorption is successfully achieved requires further exploration, however, on the surface it appears repetition is a salient factor (e.g., Berliner 1994, 95–102), while the conscious understanding of music theory is not considered to be essential (e.g., Niemack 2004, 6).

18.4.2 The Compatibility of the Aural Pathway with Vocalists

As already discussed, audiation is used by vocalists in prephonatory tuning to accurately phonate notes. It seems understandable therefore that vocalists would favour the aural pathway as a method of learning improvising, given that it incorporates

Fig. 18.2 How jazz musicians began to improvise (Hargreaves 2010)

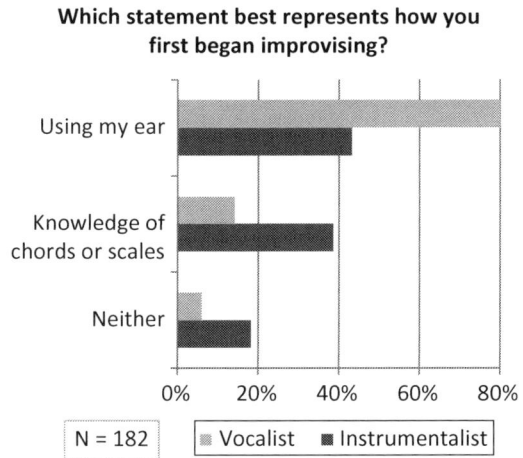

Which statement best represents how you first began improvising?

N = 182   ▨ Vocalist   ■ Instrumentalist

audiation. The survey (Hargreaves 2010) supported this conjecture. Jazz musicians (n = 182; vocalists, n = 50; instrumentalists, n = 132) were asked to indicate which statement best represented how they first began improvising (see Fig. 18.2). The response options were: (1) using my ear to pick notes that sounded good, (2) selecting notes because they were known to be in the chord or scale, (3) neither statement.

Chi square analysis of the survey results revealed a very highly significant association between whether the respondents were instrumentalists or vocalists and how they began improvising (χ^2 (2) = 19.758, $p < .000$). It showed vocalists were nearly twice as likely as instrumentalists to begin improvising by ear. These findings support the supposition that vocalists may prefer the aural pathway because it is compatible with their dependence on audiation for prephonatory tuning.

Another compatibility of the aural pathway with singing is that the approach does not require the conscious identification of pitch. Vocalists can proceed from an audiated idea directly to performance whereas beginner instrumentalists must consciously convert the audiated idea to absolute pitch in order to press the correct button (Hargreaves 2012). Singers' reduced motor feedback creates a natural difficulty for identifying pitch because they have no visual or tactile clues. Consequently, the option to bypass thinking in absolute pitch may hold appeal.

The vocalist's difficulty in pitch identification is reflected in a general lack of awareness of the absolute pitch being sung during improvisation. Hargreaves' (2010) survey shows only 2 % of vocalists (n = 1) reported having a constant awareness of absolute pitch while improvising, compared to 49 % of instrumentalists (n = 65). Chi square analysis reveals the frequency of awareness of absolute pitch while improvising is a very highly significant difference between singers and instrumentalists (χ^2 (4) = 70.382, $p < .000$). Singers are less likely to be aware of absolute pitch. The finding supports the possibility that singers may also favour the aural pathway because it is compatible with bypassing the identification of pitch.

18.4.3   The Challenges of the Aural Pathway for Vocalists

One challenge of the aural pathway is that it relies on the vast inputting of jazz elements into the auditory memory in a genre that is no longer popular music. Jon Hendricks' successful aural immersion may have been due partially to him being a product of his time and environment. A modern day Hendricks is less likely to find an in-house music system of a public café playing recordings of Charlie Parker. Jazz educator Dan Quigley made this point on the subject during an interview:

> …[T]he biggest issue in general with jazz today is that it's not the popular music on the radio and it's not in our face all the time. I remember one of my teachers saying to me that because we are not in that situation where we're saturated by jazz, to be good at it you have to saturate yourself in that scenario. (Dan Quigley in Hargreaves 2011)

The reduced exposure to jazz in social settings, however, does not necessarily correspond to reduced access. The technology explosion of the twenty-first century provides students with fast access to a wealth of recordings if desired. This ready access and easy acquisition may have also affected inadvertently the listening habits of students, as singer and educator Kristin Berardi observed:

> What I'm finding now with not just singers but instrumentalists too in the jazz schools at the moment, because we can acquire so much music now, you can chuck it on your Ipod and people have a lot of stuff, but they don't deeply listen… (Kristin Berardi in Hargreaves 2011)

Another challenge of the aural pathway is the negative side-effects produced by omitting the theoretical understanding of music. Without this knowledge, singers may be alienated from other musicians, and unable to communicate in a common vocabulary. For example, Australian bass player and jazz educator Craig Scott observed the inability of some vocalists to tell instrumentalists their preferred key for a song (Hargreaves 2011). The lack of knowledge may also inhibit the singer's development as an independent musician (Alt 2004).

18.4.4   The Teacher's Role in the Aural Pathway

An important pedagogical distinction of the aural pathway is that time is spent listening rather than identifying or analysing what is heard. The teacher's role therefore is to facilitate opportunities to aurally absorb jazz elements. Some methods include giving call and response exercises, encouraging the imitation of a solo and repetition of patterns, providing ear training classes, and instigating a listening program. The teacher can utilise these opportunities to direct students to appropriate jazz models so that listening time is spent effectively (e.g., Coker 1990; Reeves 2001; Weir 2001). Each of these methods also enables the development of a subconscious aural familiarity which is necessary for accurate prephonatory tuning.

18.5   The Theory Pathway

18.5.1   What Is the Theory Pathway?

A second approach to teaching vocal improvisation is the theory pathway. This pathway seeks to train students with a fundamental, conscious awareness of the elements of jazz, incorporating music theory and music literacy. It operates on the premise that by understanding the nature and function of isolated components, teachers can equip students with compositional strategies for their improvisation toolkit. The theory pathway, known by many names such as the chord-scale approach, is identified by Kenny and Gellrich (2002, 126) as the most widely practiced method of teaching improvisation in western education. It is also the foundation of many improvisation instructional books (e.g., Aebersold 1992; Coker and Baker 1981; Crook 1999; Reeves 2001).

A prerequisite of working and thinking in the theory pathway is conceptualising pitch. Levitin (2008, 15–22) describes pitch as a psychological construct used to mentally represent and distinguish audio frequencies. Whether pitch is conceived as relative or absolute, it allows students to perceive a measured relationship between tones, which they can later consciously replicate when they apply music theory to practice.

18.5.2   The Compatibility of the Theory Pathway with Vocalists

One attribute of the theory pathway which may account for its popular selection by jazz educators is that the curriculum content can be easily compartmentalised and transferred from teacher to student. Unlike the aural pathway, jazz elements can be consciously identified, analysed and practiced then measured in isolated exercises. Australian jazz singer and pianist Sharny Russell sees music analysis as providing vocalists such as herself with 'something to hang my hat on' (Hargreaves 2011). Sudnow (2001, 22–32), in his autoethnographic study of learning to improvise on piano, described his excitement at being furnished with scales he could strategically apply to chords. Evidently, the theory pathway provides somewhere to direct conscious focus in the otherwise allusive processes of improvisation.

Aside from the advantages of a sense of direction and a measurable curriculum, the theory pathway also offers vocalists a language for communicating with jazz musicians in ensembles. Knowledge of music theory provides a common vocabulary for discussing music elements and can empower singers for verbalising their preferences for keys, harmony, tempo, style and rhythmic feel.

18.5.3   The Challenges with the Theory Pathway for Vocalists

The theory pathway generates some specific challenges for vocalists. The approach relies on building a theoretical understanding of music elements, yet instructional texts may not begin at a foundational level. Instead, a prerequisite base knowledge is often expected (e.g., Aebersold 1992; Crook 1991, 9; Weir 2001, 16). A difference between students' entry level of understanding theory in improvising classes may become an issue when applying the pathway in group settings. As Alt (2004, 391) observes, 'Students who play band and orchestral instruments are required to read rhythms and pitches form the first day they pick up the instrument.' He notes that the same is not required of singers, who are instead called on to imitate a line played on piano. Vocalists may generally have a lower base knowledge of music theory than instrumentalists and consequently, in a mixed class of instrumentalists and singers, vocalists may lag in the theory pathway.

A second requirement for students of the theory pathway is to think and work in pitch. Instrumentalists can meet this need by using aural, visual, tactile or kinaesthetic feedback to monitor the notes they are performing. Without the same quantity or quality of feedback (Pressing 1988, 135), singers face additional challenges. First, singers need to be equipped with a system for conceptualising pitch, such as note names, solfa or scale degree numbers. Once students master such a system, they require an identified aural reference point to allow them to connect the note they hear with where it is positioned in a pitch system. From this reference point, they can calculate a desired note. For example, if asked to perform F#, the singer needs to be able identify conceptually the note in relation to others using a pitch system, hear and identify one fixed aural reference point, then calculate the note's position relative to the reference point. In contrast, the instrumentalist simply presses the F# button or key.

Another difficulty in the pathway is created by the need for vocalists to audiate a note prior to performance, a step that instrumentalists may bypass. Australian jazz educator and pianist Louise Denson explained the difference like this:

> [I]f you study theory and you're an instrumentalist, to some extent you can put your fingers in the right place and if you know that this arpeggio goes with this chord, even if your ear isn't really up to understanding why… you can play notes that are going to work. Whereas I think with vocalists you have to hear what's happening because otherwise you can't physically make your voice go to the right notes. (Louise Denson in Hargreaves 2011)

Visible here is a discrepancy in the ease in which the theory pathway is travelled by instrumentalists and vocalists. A lack of familiarity with the sound will interfere with singers' ability to perform given exercises. In contrast, instrumentalists can apply a theoretical concept to a given scenario by mechanically placing their fingers on the corresponding buttons of an instrument without aurally predicting the result. The omission is beneficial for beginners who are as yet unfamiliar with how each concept will sound. Vocalists, however, must insert the step of audiation or risk 'fumbling around trying to find out where that pitch is' (Dan Quigley in Hargreaves 2011).

18.5.4   The Teacher's Role in the Theoretical Pathway

The role of the teacher in the theory pathway is to impart knowledge by disseminating information about jazz elements such as melody, rhythm and harmony. The aim of the approach is to equip students with the basic tools of jazz, and raise understanding of how they are applied in improvisation. It follows the premise that, with this understanding, students will apply these principles to appropriate scenarios when improvising.

The theory pathway incorporates methods in the classroom such as teaching scales and chord progressions, supervising the practice of patterns through 12 keys, musically analysing patterns and solos and setting transcription assignments. Unlike the aural pathway, theory methods utilise an awareness of pitch coupled with an explanation of musical function. Teachers require students to move away from mimicry to a conscious understanding of components. For vocalists, the need to conceptualise pitch and audiate prior to accurate phonation are ever-present complications which require specialised assistance from the teacher to navigate the theory pathway effectively.

18.6   The Instrument Pathway

18.6.1   What Is the Instrument Pathway?

The instrument pathway has received less direct attention in jazz literature than the previous two methods. The benefits of learning instruments while learning to improvise on voice are referenced frequently (e.g., Berkman 2009, 1–2; Coker and Baker 1981, 131–132; Weir 2001, 16) yet the genuine instrument pathway is not commonly offered as a viable option. When instruments are used to *supplement* vocal studies, they are credited with supplying the missing motor feedback and assisting harmonic conceptualisation. In contrast, a genuine instrument pathway is where improvisation is learnt *primarily* on an instrument. The transference to singing does not occur until after improvisation is mastered instrumentally.

History shows several renowned musicians who travelled the instrument pathway, beginning as instrumentalists but later achieving recognition as singers. They include Louis Armstrong, Chet Baker, Darmon Meader, Jennifer Shelton and Kevin Mahogany. Wadsworth-Walker's (2005) research of pedagogical practices also contains examples. Of the seven 'master-pedagogues' of vocal improvisation interviewed by Wadsworth-Walker, six trained originally as instrumentalists, not singers.

The reason why advanced instrumentalists make good vocal improvisers is curious. A popular assumption in literature is that it is brought about by the instrumentalist's greater knowledge of music theory (e.g., Coker and Baker 1981, 4; Weir 2001, 13). There is, however, another possible explanation, which centres on the development of skills in audiation. The instrumentalist's habit of utilising repetitive practice to master fingering (Berliner 1994) and the capacity to bypass audiation during the developmental phase of the theory pathway (Hargreaves 2012), may subject the player to the necessary quantity of aural input to advance the audiation of jazz elements ahead of the pace of the typical singer. For example, practising the locrian scale through all 12 keys in order to master fingering means that the instrumentalist is inadvertently hearing the pattern at least 12 times. Vocalists, however, may not persist in practising beyond one key centre because, without buttons to push, the repetition is deemed unnecessary (Weir 2001, 180). As a result, the instrumentalist becomes more familiar with the sound of the scale than the singer. This in turn increases the instrumentalist's storehouse of audiated ideas for use in improvising. When they later switch to singing, the audiation bedrock is already in place.

Whatever the reasons for its success, the instrument pathway is a third avenue for teaching vocalists to improvise. The key to this approach is not using instruments to temporarily supplement development, but instead teaching improvising on an instrument to an advanced level, comparable to other players, prior to switching to vocal improvisation.

The instrument pathway sits rather uncomfortably in jazz voice education. Tertiary institutions are unlikely to adopt the approach because students enrolled as vocalists are expected to be assessed as singers not as players. Vocalists may learn an instrument as a minor study, or experience a limited term under the instruction of an instrumentalist. However, mastering an instrument is not deemed their primary goal. Thus the instrument pathway is more likely to occur inadvertently when musicians switch streams from instrument to voice, or when students personally seek out instrumental training at a private studio.

18.6.2   The Compatibility of the Instrument Pathway with Vocalists

One strength of vocalists following the instrument pathway is that it equalises their learning experience with other students of improvisation. The benefits of being able to see and touch an instrument produces a stronger awareness of pitch identity. In this mode, theory becomes a more compatible approach. Teachers can now instigate a curriculum universally without obstacles to comprehension or complications in application.

The instrument pathway also provides vocalists with the opportunity to bypass the need to audiate prior to producing sound. This means students can gradually develop an auditory familiarity with jazz elements like instrumentalists by performing them repetitively without 'pre-hearing' them. In effect, the instrument pathway acts as a developmental stepping stone in the process of singers learning to audiate jazz elements.

18.6.3 The Challenges with the Instrument Pathway for Vocalists

The instrument pathway presents some challenges for vocalists. First, it requires students to invest a significant effort in studying an instrument. This may not pose a problem for students who begin as instrumentalists and decide later to change to singing. However, for students who begin as singers, the lengthy diversion needed to master improvisation on an instrument to an advanced level can be time consuming. It is the equivalent of a tertiary student completing two degrees.

A second challenge in the instrument pathway is student motivation. The pathway requires a commitment and perseverance to reach a high standard on an instrument, which may be difficult to maintain if playing does not enthuse vocal students as much as singing. This possibility becomes an important pedagogical consideration given Eisenberg and Thompson's (2003) finding that student motivation is a contributor to achievement in improvisation.

A third difficulty vocalists may experience is the instrument pathway does not address the challenges that are uniquely vocal. For example, the acquisition and execution of a suitable scat vocabulary is not covered in instrumental lessons. Likewise, the large variation of vocal timbre available to singers and the mechanical issues of registers are left untouched. Improvising instrumentalists may switch successfully to scat singing; however, the new challenges of the vocal apparatus still lie ahead.

18.6.4 The Teacher's Role in the Instrument Pathway

A teacher utilising the instrument pathway with singers can initially enjoy the simplicity of teaching vocal students as they would instrumentalists. With visual and tactile feedback now available, singers can travel a pseudo-theory pathway without any special adaptations. No accommodation in curriculum is necessary beyond ascertaining an appropriate entry level, monitoring student motivation and encouraging a practice routine comparable to instrumentalists.

The most important teaching consideration is likely to be negotiating when the transition from instrument to voice will occur and how the change can be assisted. Teachers can provide support for the new obstacles the student encounters with scat vocabulary and the mechanics of the vocal apparatus. Advanced instrumental students who pursue scat singing may find the experience liberating as they no longer need to convert audiated ideas to absolute pitch in order to press the correct buttons (Hargreaves 2012).

18.7 Teaching Considerations for Applying Pathways in Classroom Settings

As already discussed, the three teaching pathways for improvisation produce natural compatibilities and challenges for vocalists due to singers' lack of visual and tactile motor feedback. Consideration of the educational environment illuminates two variables that further affect the efficacy of teaching methods. The first variable to consider is whether vocal improvisation is being taught in a studio setting or at a tertiary institution.

The need for periodic assessment and universal benchmarks by tertiary institutions may influence the choice of pathway. The more concrete goals found in theory pathway allow the subdivision of the curriculum into timetabled components which can be isolated and tested for understanding. In contrast, the somewhat nebulous process of subconscious absorption used in the aural pathway is less compatible with periodic measurement. Imitation may be tested to some extent; however, ascertaining whether a concept is stored in the auditory memory is not feasible, nor can outcomes be reproduced on demand. Consequently, the aural pathway is likely to be more amenable to private studios where pace, curriculum and progress are more flexible.

A second reason why the aural pathway may suit the private studio is that musical literacy is not required. As already discussed, music literacy and theoretical understanding are of lower importance to the pathway than inputting into the auditory storehouse. The private studio teacher is at liberty to work solely with imitative methods if desired, without references to the written page or to the conscious identification of music elements. Such an approach is less likely to be acceptable in a tertiary setting where a base level of literacy is required and even tested prior to admission into a course. If the aural pathway is to be adopted at tertiary institution, teachers may need approval for theory to be marginalised in favour of directing more time to listening, or teachers may need to ensure that the desirable literacy skills are being attained through other subjects.

Tertiary institutions are also probably less suitable for vocalists to travel the instrument pathway. Philosophically, students enrolled as vocalists are expected to sing. Unless students physically change enrolment part way through a course from an instrument to singing, the university is unlikely to accept vocalists diverting their principal study time and assessment to an instrument. Unfortunately this is the magnitude of the diversion necessary for the instrument pathway to be successful. The private studio may accommodate the pathway more readily. Vocalists approaching improvisation through the instrument pathway can be directed to an instrumental teacher. Once improvisation has been mastered on the instrument, a private studio voice teacher can assist with the transition to the vocal apparatus.

The theory pathway can be instigated in either the tertiary institution or the private studio. In either setting, the teacher can accommodate the singer's needs by teaching a system for conceptualising pitch, providing an aural reference point and supplying sufficient listening opportunities to input the audiation bedrock, thus enabling accurate prephonatory tuning. The teacher plays an important role in assessing the vocal student's knowledge of music theory, and coaching in the compensatory skills necessary to progress along the theory pathway. On the whole, the approach can be successful in either classroom setting; however, when the class mixes vocal with instrumental students, another variable is introduced.

The second variable affecting the efficacy of pathways for teaching vocal improvisation is whether the improvisation classroom is reserved for vocalists or if it functions as a combined class of vocalists and instrumentalists. In the singers-only classroom, the teacher can tailor each pathway to accommodate the compatibilities and challenges vocalists face. For example, if voice students have little familiarity with music theory, the teacher can commence theory lessons at a more foundational level.

Tertiary institutions, however, appear more inclined to run improvisation classes that combine instrumentalists and singers. Six of the seven Australian jazz educators interviewed reported that improvisation training takes place in combined classes at their tertiary institution (Hargreaves 2011). Educator Craig Scott made this observation, which may account for the practice:

> Universities all around Australia, all around the world at the moment, are looking at conservatoria and music departments with a very jaundiced eye because it costs the same to give one to one lessons as it does to give a chemistry lecture to 500 people. We are unfashionably expensive... (Craig Scott in Hargreaves 2011)

The financial pressure for larger classes may explain the preference for universities to combine instrumental and vocal classes whenever possible. Hence, the integration may be motivated financially rather than pedagogically.

In selecting which pathway to instigate in the combined classroom, it is unsurprising that educators lean towards theory. The need for measurable goals and periodic assessment, and the greater ratio of instrumentalists to vocalists in classes suggests a method that is compatible with players is most appropriate. Unfortunately, these factors conspire against the singer's tendency to lean towards the aural pathway.

The natural differences between vocalists and instrumentalists become evident particularly when teaching the theory pathway to a combined class. Vocalists are likely to begin with a lower foundational knowledge of theory, as already discussed. Any efforts to apply theoretical knowledge to examples will always be complicated for singers by their dual need to audiate prior to phonation and the challenge of thinking in pitch. Tertiary educator Jamie Oehlers gave an example of asking his students to 'play a minor 6 pentatonic off the flat 2 on a dominant chord' (Hargreaves 2011). He observed 'a saxophone player can press a button and produce a tone that's pretty close to the note that's intended' whereas vocalists 'don't have the ability to hit and miss like that' (Hargreaves 2011). Teachers who undertake the theory pathway in a combined class consequently must ensure vocalists are equipped with a method for thinking and operating in pitch, as well as receiving sufficient aural input to implant any jazz exercises they are expected to phonate.

An alternative approach for teaching improvising to a combined class is the aural pathway, where the vast and repetitive inputting of jazz elements by sound is prioritised over theoretical analysis. Vocalists may function well without the need to think in pitch. Conversely, instrumentalists face the obstacle of converting audiated ideas into absolute pitch in order to know which buttons to press, creating other teaching challenges.

The third option for the combined classroom, the instrument pathway, causes no difficulties in application because in essence it operates as if the class is solely for instrumentalists. However, as already discussed, students enrolled as vocalists in a tertiary institution are unlikely to be permitted to pursue this option to the necessary depth without changing their enrolment from vocalist to instrumentalist.

18.8   Conclusion

Recent research and literature has debated which is the superior pathway for teaching vocal improvising. However, by considering the nature of singing and the environment in which pathways are applied, variables impacting on method effectiveness are illuminated. This chapter has examined the aural, theory and instrument pathways and presented their attributes as compatibilities and challenges for singers. The discussion explored the application of the pathways in the settings of private studios, tertiary institutions, and the combined vocal and instrumental classroom. It becomes evident that trying to answer the question of which single pathway is superior for all circumstances is not of much practical benefit for teachers. It ignores the impact of classroom setting and the resultant teaching considerations. It seems more helpful therefore to reconceptualise it as two questions: Which pathway, with its inherent compatibilities and challenges for vocalists, is best suited to the setting where teaching improvising will occur? And, What teaching considerations will assist its application?

References

Aebersold, J. (1992). *How to play jazz and improvise*. New Albany: Jamey Aebersold Jazz.
Alt, D. (2004). Triple threat training program's weakest area: Reading music: Reinforcing sight reading in voice the voice studio for singer/actors. *Journal of Singing, 60*, 389–393.
Baker, D. (1989). *Jazz pedagogy: A comprehensive method of jazz education for teacher and student*. Van Nuys: Alfred Publishing.
Benson, B. (2003). *The improvisation of musical dialogue*. Cambridge: Cambridge University Press.
Berkman, D. (2009). *The jazz singer's guidebook*. Petaluma: Sher Music.
Berliner, P. (1994). *Thinking in jazz*. Chicago: The University of Chicago Press.
Bock, D. (2000). Pedagogies for scat singing. *Masters Abstracts International, 38*(06), 1407.
Coker, J. (1990). *How to listen to jazz*. New Albany: Jamey Aebersold.
Coker, P., & Baker, D. (1981). *Vocal improvisation: An instrumental approach*. Lebanon: Studio P/R.
Crook, H. (1991). *How to improvise: An approach to practicing improvisation*. Rottenburg: Advance Music.

Crook, H. (1999). *Ready, aim, improvise*. Rottenburg: Advance Music.

Eisenberg, J., & Thompson, W. (2003). A matter of taste: Evaluating improvised music. *Creativity Research Journal, 15*, 287–296.

Gordon, E. (2007). *Learning sequences in music*. Chicago: GIA Publications.

Hargreaves, W. (2010). [National survey of jazz instrumentalists and vocalists]. Unpublished raw data.

Hargreaves, W. (2011). [Interviews with Australian jazz singers and tertiary jazz educators]. Unpublished raw data.

Hargreaves, W. (2012). Generating ideas in jazz improvisation: Where theory meets practice. *International Journal of Music Education: Practice, 30*, 354–367.

Heil, L. (2005). The effects of two vocal jazz improvisation methods on high school choir students' attitudes and performance achievement. *Dissertation Abstracts International, 67*(09), 3341.

Kenny, B., & Gellrich, M. (2002). Improvisation. In R. Parncutt & G. McPherson (Eds.), *The science and psychology of music performance* (pp. 117–134). Oxford: Oxford University Press.

Levitin, D. (2008). *This is your brain on music: Understanding a human obsession*. London: Atlantic Books.

Nemeyer, E. (2008). Interview: Kurt Elling. *Jazz Improv, 8*, 156–159.

Niemack, J. (2004). *Hear it and sing it!* New York: Second Floor Music.

Pellegrinelli, L. (2005). The song is who? Locating singers on the jazz scene. *Dissertation Abstracts International, 66*(05), 1555A.

Pressing, J. (1988). Improvisation: Methods and models. In J. A. Sloboda (Ed.), *Generative processes in music* (pp. 129–179). Oxford: Oxford University Press.

Reeves, S. (2001). *Creative jazz improvisation*. Upper Saddle River: Prentice Hall.

Reid, K. (2002). An exploration of the lineage of jazz vocal improvisation through the analysis of representative solos by Louis Armstrong, Ella Fitzgerald, Jon Hendricks, Mark Murphy, Kevin Mahogany and Kurt Elling. *Dissertation Abstracts International, 63*(11), 3786A.

Spradling, D. (2007). *Jazz singing: Developing artistry and authenticity*. Edmonds: Sound Music Publications.

Sudnow, D. (2001). *Ways of the hand: A rewritten account*. Cambridge, MA: MIT Press.

Sundberg, J. (1987). *The science of the singing voice*. Dekalb: Northern Illinois University Press.

Wadsworth-Walker, C. (2005). Pedagogical practices in vocal jazz improvisation. *Dissertation Abstracts International, 65*(12), 4504A.

Weir, M. (2001). *Vocal improvisation*. Rottenburg: Advance Music.

Whiteoak, J. (1999). *Playing ad lib: Improvisatory music in Australia 1836–1970*. Sydney: Currency Press.

Chapter 19
Voice in Worship: The Contemporary Worship Singer

Daniel K. Robinson

Abstract Who is the Contemporary Worship Singer? In the past church singers have either been thought of as choristers or as a soloists but recent developments in Christian worship have seen vocal leadership of congregational singing evolve. Historically founded in the emotive hymnody of the Holiness movement (c.a. 19th Century) as well as the impassioned delivery of black gospel (c.a. 19th–20th Century), the worship setting of the Contemporary Worship Singer is not a simple 'subset' of either (or both), but an idiom that now, at the commencement of the twenty-first century, forms the umbrella under which both hymnody and gospel find their place among a range of Christian worship expressions. This chapter will seek to develop a map by which singing teachers might understand the multiplicity of today's worship constructs. With five distinct worship settings using three worship forms, the vocal task of the Contemporary Worship Singer in the twenty-first century has taken on a variety of expressions. This multiplicity of construct challenges today's singing teacher to step beyond the 'one-size-fits-all' application of vocal technique to the 'task specific' tuition that today's church singer requires; classical or contemporary. The chapter then informs vocal pedagogues to be mindful of specific cultural influences, environmental considerations and unique vocal challenges facing the Contemporary Worship Singer and their 'Voice in Worship'. The chapter commences with a defining overview of worship constructs.

Keywords Contemporary worship singer • Worship • Liturgical worship • Traditional worship • Contemporary worship • Blended worship • Emerging worship

How has music and singing become synonymous with Christian worship given the apparent disconnect between the subjective experience and the objective activity? To the uninitiated this might seem like an inconsequential consideration, but it

D.K. Robinson (✉)
Academic Department, Djarts Contemporary Voice Studio, Brisbane, QLD, Australia
e-mail: daniel@djarts.com.au

S.D. Harrison and J. O'Bryan (eds.), *Teaching Singing in the 21st Century*,
Landscapes: the Arts, Aesthetics, and Education 14, DOI 10.1007/978-94-017-8851-9_19,
© Springer Science+Business Media Dordrecht 2014

Fig. 19.1 Layers of
contextual terminology
(Robinson 2011)

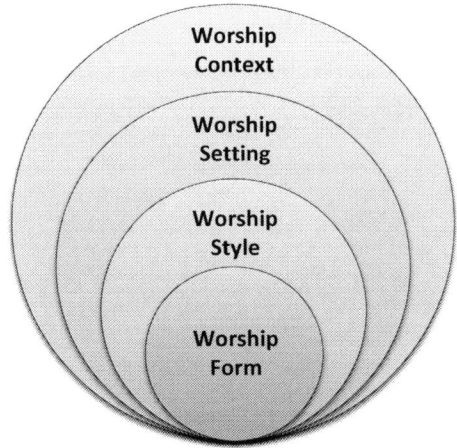

actually strikes at the very core of the Contemporary Worship Singer's psyche; directing their orientation to the task of vocal leadership and the view of their voice in that task. That is, what place does music, and in this case the expression and importance of the music through singing, hold in the cultural activity of worship? To highlight this point further, listen to the voice of Sharon[1] who states, 'When I do sing words I want to know that I believe them, that they come from my heart; that if I'm singing to God then I'm believing that they're going to God's ears' (Robinson 2011). Notice that in this statement Sharon's orientation is not attentive to her voice or the manner in which it is used; moreover the positioning of her theological and practical understanding is revealed in the first and foremost focus of her revere: God. The voice, at best, is secondary.

Of course, Sharon's personal views, albeit prevalent among many, do not speak on behalf of the predicted 1.9 billion Christians globally (Brierley 1997); and herein lies the difficulty in working with the Christian worship singer. The multiplicity of views and opinions is as varied as it is diverse. This being said there are some major groupings under which the modern Christian worshipper can be assembled, whereby informed and 'task-specific' vocal pedagogy can be designed and applied in a useful manner. Figuratively, a layered view of modern Christian worship constructs can be illustrated as in Fig. 19.1.

19.1 Worship Context

The outer, all encompassing, layer of worship context is that which unites all Christian worshippers. A correct theological understanding of music acknowledges that 'Music has been the art form elected from among all others to give voice

---

[1] Sharon was one of nine interviewees whose views were recorded during my recent doctoral research into the Australian Contemporary Worship Singer (Robinson 2011). Sharon worshipped in a contemporary Pentecostal church (Brisbane, Queensland).

to Christian worship…, and to be used by the church to teach and correct the saints' (Elwell 2001). Music, in most worship constructs, is used to deliver doctrine while uniting congregants in a singular activity: singing. In a recent article titled 'Why we sing' (2011) Bob Kauflin writes, 'Singing allows us to seamlessly combine doctrine with devotion, intellect with emotion, and objective truth with our subjective response to it'.

Contextually, singing's importance is found in its inclusivity, which conjoins participants around doctrinal truths in a manner that is aesthetically derived from the surrounding culture. The use of singing as a universal pillar has led Tony Payne (2001) to state, 'Christians may have argued how to sing or what to sing, but few have ever disputed that singing was the natural response of the creature to the Creator'.

19.2 Worship Setting

The radical impact of the sixteenth century's reformation segmented the church, paving the way for today's hybrid worship expressions. Robert Greer (2003) has aptly suggested: 'With the Protestant Reformation the notion of a singular infallible dogma within Catholic tradition was replaced by thousands of infallible dogma within the statements of faith of the many ecclesial bodies that make up Protestantism'. Simply, the modern Christian church is no longer governed by a single set of doctrines. Recently, scholars (Kropf 2005; Begbie 2008; Evans 2006; Davis 2010) have suggested that one of the key aspects that distinguishes today's various worship constructs is music and the manner in which it is employed during worship. Mark Evans (2006) writes, 'For Christians, the experience of congregational music is often crucial to their worship, to their response to God's character'. The experiential orientation of believers in worship is often characterised as either observing God's transcendent nature or as seeking God's immanent presence. Warren Wiersbe (2000) acknowledges it is difficult to achieve a balance between these two points of focus. Wiersbe writes that the difficulty is found in the '…conflict between the objective and the subjective in worship. We're too prone to judge a worship experience by our feelings rather than by the fact that we have obeyed God and tried to please and glorify Him'.

Simply, understanding the innumerable hybrids that form according to regulative (transcendent) and normative (immanent) theological approaches, along with generational and personal musical (stylistic) preferences, can present as a confusing landscape to the unversed.

19.3 Worship Styles

The various western worship expressions can be presented under five headings. The five worship styles are: (1) Liturgical, (2) Traditional, (3) Contemporary, (4) Blended and (5) Emerging (Robinson 2011; Pinson 2009; Cherry 2010).

19.3.1   Liturgical Worship

The oldest worship style, *Liturgical Worship*, has developed from the Roman Catholic service design of the Middle Ages (500–1500 AD). The label 'Liturgical' should not be confused with the term 'liturgy'. Dawn (1995) explains that 'the term *leitourgia* [liturgy], composed of the Greek words *ergon* ('work') and *laos* ('people'), actually means 'the work of the people' and thus designates every action of the laity'. While every worship style employs a liturgy, Liturgical Worship is distinguished by its predominant use of classic hymns and prescriptive rites. An example of this style is the High Anglican Church, which typically accompanies the congregational singing with an organ while directing its progression through the service using the Book of Common Prayer (Wainwright and Tucker 2006). This worship style might also be observed in the post Vatican II Roman Catholic Mass as well as many of today's Lutheran services.

19.3.2   Traditional Worship

The *Traditional Worship* style developed as a reaction to the prescriptive form of Liturgical worship. J. Ligon Duncan (2009) states that 'the preached word is the central feature of Reformed [Traditional] worship' which is different to its predecessor (Liturgical Worship) that holds the celebration of the Eucharist as central. Evolving from the Pietist and Methodist renewal (ca. 18th Century), Traditional Worship employs hymns which are 'written to accommodate untrained voices and thus to permit the maximum participation of the masses in the worship service. Typically, hymns are short, strophic, and rhythmically simple, and they usually do not modulate to remote keys' (Russell 1997). Stereotypically observed in Presbyterian, Wesleyan and Salvation Army churches, Traditional Worship's hymns may be written for the unskilled voice but as Evans (2006) contends, 'The evangelical hymn writers greatly increased the vocabulary of their congregations and their ability to cope with complex theological language and thought'.

19.3.3   Contemporary Worship

The twentieth century observed the development of three new movements of worship expression. The first, Pentecostal worship began with the Azusa Street revival (1906) in Los Angeles. The second new movement of the twentieth century, the Charismatic Renewal, often referred to as 'neo-Pentecostalism' (Williams 2001) developed 'within historic churches' during the 1950s. Most recently,

> In the last decades of the twentieth century, charismatic worship has exerted a great influence on worship of all faiths. The charismatic model of free-flowing praise, Old Testament worship pattern, accommodation of contemporary culture, use of popular sounding music, embrace of technology, and emotional appeal has altered worship practice in many

congregations around the globe. Particular to this phenomenon is the music usually referred to as 'praise and worship' music. (Segler and Bradley 2006)

The third new movement was predominantly a musical one. Known as the 'Praise and Worship' movement the reformation of hymnody, saw the development of the modern chorus. Leon Neto (2010) asserts that in 'the same way traditional hymns were the sound image of the Great Awakening [Traditional Worship] and tent revivals, Praise and Worship songs are the face of the new millennium Christian church'.

Collectively Pentecostalism, the Charismatic, and Praise and Worship movements are grouped under the label *Contemporary Worship*. The Contemporary style can be observed in Pentecostal churches like the Assemblies of God and the denomination that birthed the Praise and Worship movement: John Wimber's Vineyard. Importantly though, the Contemporary worship style is not restricted to Pentecostal and Charismatic churches alone; with many main-line churches embracing the Contemporary style's capacity to 'engage culture on the levels of language, music, intimacy, emotion, simplicity, and story' (Wilt 2009).

19.3.4 Blended Worship

It is this same infiltration of contemporary styled worship into mainline churches that led to a widely utilised hybrid: *Blended Worship*. Michael Lawrence and Mark Dever (2009) define Blended worship as 'corporate worship that consists of its biblical elements (prayer, singing, reading and preaching God's Word, the ordinances of baptism and the Lord's Supper) but in a variety of styles or forms'. Essentially Blended worship style combines, or blends, the strengths of the Liturgical or Traditional style with the employment of the Contemporary style and more importantly, music. Sometimes referred to as 'Convergence Worship', this style is often observed as a specially designed service held by churches conventionally given to Liturgical or Traditional style services. 'Some Anglican churches, for example may hold a Sunday night church service which will also employ the stylistic features of a Contemporary worship style while holding to the narration of [the] Anglican liturgy' (Robinson 2010). The Blended worship style uses a combination of old and new hymns as well as recently written choruses.

19.3.5 Emerging Worship

The most recent development in worship service design has been the *Emerging Worship* style. Emerging worship seeks to move away from the linear employment of the worship service elements. Emerging worship advocate Dan Kimball (2004) suggests 'there is no model of an emerging worship gathering because each one is unique to its local church context, community, people, and specific leaders of the church'. In seeking to restructure the linear progression of the worship service the design of Emerging worship is reliant on enabling the worship participant to freely move between worship stations at their own discretion.[2] Emerging worship seeks to utilise music in much the same way as the Blended style, with both hymns and choruses employed. In describing his own Emerging church's use of music, Kimball (2009) writes, 'we generally start off with about ten minutes of musical worship… the band leads in pop-worship songs that are usually upbeat and mainly celebratory. The musical worship leader selects both modern pop-worship songs and hymns'. Again, similar to the Blended worship style, Emerging worship is often found (though not exclusively so) as a specifically designed service, created as an adjunct to established churches of various denominational persuasions.

19.3.6   Worship Form

The final contextual layer, *Worship Forms*, further defines individual worship contexts. The three worship forms, which are not always mutually exclusive (you can have a thematic-modular hybrid, for example), are used to order modern Christian worship: Modular, Thematic and Flow (Robinson 2011).

The *modular* worship form is defined as moving 'through distinct modules of worship with no one module regarded more highly than another, though the Eucharist (communion) is often seen as a climatic point' (Robinson 2010). The worship settings most likely to employ the modular form are Liturgical and Traditional.

Thematic is based on a central theme. For instance, if the theme is 'God's Love', then all the service components (including songs, sermon and bible readings) will be governed by the overarching theme of God's love. Often the climatic point of this worship form is found in the sermon. The Thematic form is most often observed in Traditional, Blended and Emerging worship settings.

Flow derives its name from the flowing nature of the service components. Typically found in the Contemporary and Blended worship settings, a service using the Flow form will often have two distinct points of climax: one during a set of songs (typically known as the 'Worship Set') and a second during the sermon. It is important to note that these two points of climax can be independent occurrences: that is, there needn't be a theme connecting the two climax events.

Because each worship form uses the same building blocks (music, sermon, communion etc.) it is important to recall Liesch's (1996) clarification which suggests that the three worship forms 'are not mutually exclusive; they can be blended'. Figure 19.2 therefore presents the correlation of worship style with worship form.

Figure 19.2 will form the basis of the Contemporary Worship Singer's Assessment tool, which will be presented at the end of the chapter.

---

[2] Kimball (2004) describes the variety of worship stations as including 'water basins, clay tables, or other scripturally-based stations for people to worship God through creative expression'.

Fig. 19.2 Worship style
and worship form
(Robinson 2011)

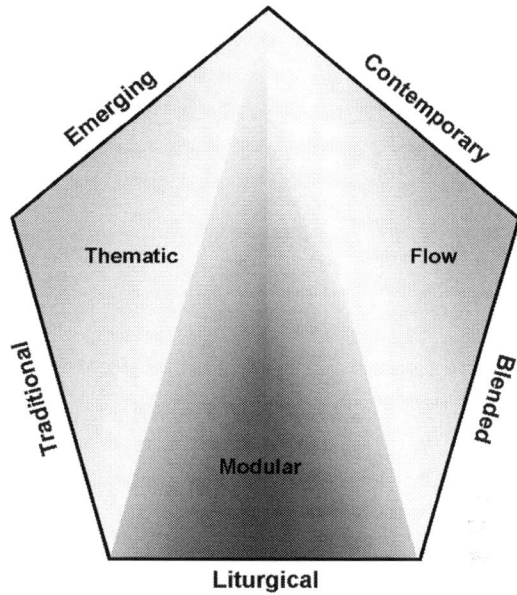

19.4 Culture

As shown above, the twenty-first century constructs and multiplicity thereof is striking and they set the Contemporary Worship Singer apart from their peers in the wider singing community. Another facet of the Contemporary Worship Singer's role that distinguishes their vocal leadership task from other singers' is the unique culture in which they exist. Three topics of cultural significance are worthy of note: Excellence, Performance and Celebrity.

19.4.1 Excellence

Within western Christian culture the word 'excellence' is often coined in the adage 'Giving God your best!' Marva Dawn (1995) holds the importance of excellence in worship in the highest regard when she comments, 'The Church should be among the social institutions that set the highest artistic standards, especially because we need excellence and greatness to worship God'. The challenge to set the 'highest artistic standards' presents some difficulties for the Contemporary Worship Singer and the responsibilities it infers. Analysis of recent data[3] (Robinson 2011) would

---

[3] Unless otherwise stated all research data is taken from my recently completed study into the Contemporary Worship Singer (Robinson 2011).

suggest that the standards adhered to by many Contemporary Worship Singers fall short of best practice as outlined in the literature. With 42 % of research participants having received no singing lessons, it is difficult to ascertain how a standard of vocal excellence can be achieved. Furthermore, less than 25 % of survey respondents received any formal instruction for their role as a Contemporary Worship Singer. One practical implication of the low levels of training is observed in the poorly practiced discipline of vocal warm-ups. Seventy eight percent of survey respondents indicated that they do not warm-up their voices, either prior to the church services or before a worship team practice.

Arguably, excellence is (or should be) the goal of every artist, Christian and non-Christian alike. It is not the attainment of excellence (product) that differentiates the sacred task from the secular. It is the manner in which excellence is achieved (process) that truly sets Contemporary Worship Singers apart. The culturally celebrated notion of 'process over product' is exemplified in Bryan Chapell's (2009) encouragement for authentic praise over and above excellent performance. He writes, 'Concerns for both adequate performance and grateful praise will make us strive for excellence in worship expression, but only the latter truly honours God alone'.

19.4.2 Performance

In seeking to achieve the right balance of authentically derived excellence in the preparation and display of their vocal leadership, Contemporary Worship Singers are confronted with a second challenge: performance that does not draw attention to the performer.

The term 'Performance' received a mixed reception among recent research participants, with respondents polarised as to whether the term was positive or negative. According to most participants the Contemporary Worship Singer should not draw attention to themselves, but instead direct attention to God. Superficially this seems to be a legitimate position to hold in the context of Christian worship: *God should be the focus of the worship event*. But this same position becomes a cultural tripwire, hidden to the most observant of Contemporary Worship Singers with a number of the tasks fundamental to the Contemporary Worship Singer's role inadvertently reinforcing the prominence of the Contemporary Worship Singer.

The performance of the vocal task is often presented in front of hundreds (sometimes thousands[4]) of people. The challenge facing the individual singer is one of balance. When the singer presents a covert performance they run the risk of rendering the vocal presentation void of charisma which can suppress the involvement

---

[4] It is estimated that there are 193 churches with a regular attendance of over 2,000 worshippers in the wider Los Angeles (California, US) area alone (McGrath 2012).

Fig. 19.3 Covert and
overt performance
(Robinson 2011)

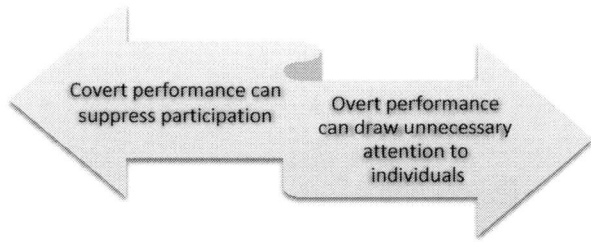

of worship participants. If the presentation is overt in its performance (beyond that which is appropriate to the worship setting) the singer might draw undue attention to themselves (see Fig. 19.3).

This tension of opposing ideals can leave the singer confused and disordered in their presentation.

19.4.3 Celebrity

The third cultural challenge facing the Contemporary Worship Singer is the culturally disagreeable status of 'celebrity'. Again, any suggestion that the worship singer might draw attention to themselves above and beyond directing attention to God is generally seen as problematic.

Despite the often contextually prominent nature of the role, the synonymous application of the word 'celebrity' with the word 'fame' appears to conjure an avoidance of such labels lest the terms position the singer as one who seeks to rob God of the glory that is His due. The attention generated by the celebrity status of the Contemporary Worship Singer results in a responsibility they carry beyond singing. For example, eight of the nine interviewees acknowledged significance in the term 'worship lifestyle'. Contemporary Worship Singers carry an awareness of their leadership responsibility into their everyday lives. This is a unique attribute of the role. The Contemporary Worship Singer is encouraged to lead an exemplary Christian life both in and out of the church setting.

Succinctly, the cultural challenge facing the Contemporary Worship Singer is presenting vocal leadership to the congregation with excellence, but not so much excellence that it would subvert authentic praise; perform in a manner that strikes the perfect balance of not too little and not too much; and despite undertaking the task on a stage in front of an audience of admiring worship participants, the concept of celebrity should be shunned. In an age that celebrates perfection (i.e. air brushing and auto-tune), engaging and overt performance, as well as cultivating the 'cult of celebrity' the Contemporary Worship Singer is confronted with a perplexing assignment.

Fig. 19.4 Acoustic space
balance (Robinson 2011)

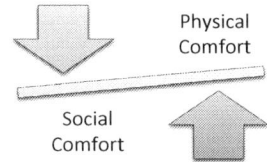

19.4.4 Environment

Today's Christian worship is conducted in buildings (of various architectural designs) supported by modern amplification and audiovisual presentation; which is no different to every other modern public performance space. What differentiates the Christian worship space from secular performance space is the activity that takes place inside. Chapell (2009) outlines some of the activities housed within today's churches, writing, 'Despite having great architectural variety, Christian churches still have common denominators: a place to proclaim the Word; a place to gather for prayer, praise, and receiving the Word; a place to administer and receive the sacraments; and others.' Each of these goings-on is considered sacred and seeks to develop a reverential response from worshippers. My recent research (Robinson 2011) revealed that while most Contemporary Worship Singers are not consciously aware of the worship space's effect on their worship the impact is nonetheless apparent. Two significant aspects, acoustics and equipment, are worthy of note here.

19.4.5 Acoustical Space

One of the issues pertaining to the acoustic space of the modern church environment is the soft surfaces found in many modern auditoriums: carpeted floors and walls, along with cushioned seating, combine to absorb live acoustics. Soft surfaces quell the live acoustic created by the human voice, dampening the auditory feedback necessary for good singing. Consequently, both the congregant and the Contemporary Worship Singer are challenged to lift their vocal output to a point of discomfort and at times, vocal distress. McCoy (2004) explains that our 'speech [and singing] must be at least 20 dB louder than the ambient noise for easy intelligibility. This helps explain why voices become easily fatigued in noisy environments such as a party or dance'. Therefore, one aim of the Contemporary Worship Singer is to monitor the acoustic space for levels that mitigate healthy and sustainable involvement. Seemingly juxtaposed to this aim is the leadership role of the Contemporary Worship Singer, which instinctively seeks to embolden the congregant to give voice to their collective praise. The difficulty is that people sing when they are confident that their own voice will join with the voices around them in a way that does not overly expose their own singing. Balance must be obtained (see Fig. 19.4). Too much volume and the worship participant will cease participating due to physical discomfort. Too little volume and the worship participant will cease participating due to social discomfort.

19.4.6 Equipment

Today's worship spaces have been enhanced by technologies designed to assist the audiovisual experience of the worship participant. My research revealed that regardless of the worship setting, the Contemporary Worship Singer will find themselves using these technologies in their role. Two technical tools are prominently used by the Contemporary Worship Singer: microphones and foldback monitors.

Almost all (98 %) research participants used a microphone when they perform their duties as a Contemporary Worship Singer. The Contemporary Worship Singer is confronted therefore with the challenge of *how* to use the microphone. Secondly, only two survey respondents used their own microphone at church. This raises the concern of general physical health for the Contemporary Worship Singer. The close proximity of the microphone to the mouth allows transmission of virus and bacteria from one vocalist to the next as they share the church's microphones.

The Contemporary Worship Singer should be instructed on how to request a good monitor mix. Most (88 %) of the survey respondents enjoyed the facility of foldback through either floor monitors or in-ear monitors. The majority of survey participants indicated that they could generally hear themselves through the monitor system. The 30 % of survey respondents who are unable to hear themselves clearly through the foldback system might benefit from instruction in what to request in the monitor mix. Further enhancement of foldback might also be gained with an upgrade in the church's audio system to include multiple foldback sends and pre-fader auxiliary sends with equalisation.

It is important to note here that no delineation between classical and contemporary singing styles can be derived from the data set according to environment. That is, both classical and contemporary vocalists are using microphones (and foldback) in all modern worship settings; requiring classical and contemporary singing teachers to teach microphone technique and how to work with foldback monitors.

19.5 Voice

Fundamentally, the main tool of the Contemporary Worship Singer is their voice. We are fortunate to have many excellent texts available in the twenty-first century that advocate for rigorous and robust vocal technique in both the classical and contemporary disciplines; so I will not add to or unwittingly challenge established preferences here. This being said, there are a number of key points that affect every Contemporary Worship Singer[5] and the use of their voice.

19.5.1   Classical or Contemporary

The question of *'Which is best?'* is raised often for the Contemporary Worship Singer. Without wanting to abdicate the responsibility of the pedagogue, the singer is best placed to decide which vocal discipline will serve the development of their voice and the vocal activities to which they wish to apply it. The research (Robinson 2011) revealed that most churches are still using a mix of hymns (classical) and choruses (contemporary), and many of the research respondents (72 %) do not sing outside their church context. Interestingly, Sweetman (2012), while observing the Australian worship landscape, has suggested that 'the Hillsong contemporary worship model appears to be growing in influence and acceptance…the contemporary music "tide" is still on the way in.' It may be that the modern chorus will come to dominate the twenty-first century worship context, but at this stage it is merely conjecture. It is therefore advisable for singing teachers to intentionally discuss their student's worship setting, identifying both style and form (as well as the predominance of repertoire; hymn or chorus), in order to ascertain which technique will be most beneficial for the singer. The Contemporary Worship Singer's Assessment Tool, presented at the end of this chapter, will assist teachers and their students in identifying the most appropriate technical discipline for their individual worship setting.

19.5.2   Vocal Demands

There is a spectrum of vocal load according to worship style. For instance, in the Contemporary worship style, the flowing design of the worship set can require a singer to be constantly singing for 30–40 min. Length of worship set is not the only point to be considered when assessing vocal load. For example, a singer involved with the Emerging worship setting may need to sing through a 30-min vocal set; however the worship set design in the Emerging style will intentionally minimalize any single voice dominating the congregational singing. This in turn lowers the vocal load experienced by the Contemporary Worship Singer in the Emerging worship style. The vocal load, when considered alongside the inadequate training of

---

[5] It is necessary to address the use of the term 'Contemporary' to name today's worship singer (Contemporary Worship Singer). I have chosen to employ the label 'Contemporary' due to its capacity to evolve with the times. Interchangeable terms such as 'Today's Worship Singer' or 'Modern Worship Singer' could also be used, but I have preferred the label 'Contemporary Worship Singer' for the sake of continuity throughout the chapter.

many Contemporary Worship Singers, exposes many singers to vocal wear and tear, which in turn can lead to vocal damage.

19.5.3   Harmonies

One skill that a few research participants indicated they use to mitigate vocal fatigue due to unfavourable tessitura and set lengths was the employment of harmonies. The low use of harmonies, as exhibited by the research cohort, is partly due to the low levels of musicianship also apparent in the group; that is many Contemporary Worship Singers do not read music. Musical literacy is only part of the 'chicken and egg' puzzle when addressing the use of harmonies. While full transcriptions of four-part harmony (SATB) do exist for worship repertoire the shorthand 'lead sheet' (melody, lyrics and chords) is generally preferred. Without transcribed vocal parts many Contemporary Worship Singers are required to develop harmony parts by ear.

The practice of singing harmonies by ear can be cumbersome and inaccurate. Firstly, even simple block chord compositions (modern worship choruses) can receive an infinite array of harmonic interpretations. Problems may arise where two singers, assigned to the alto harmony for example, sing conflicting but equally valid harmonic lines. The second issue of inaccuracy arises when underdeveloped singers seek to develop a harmonic line by ear. The 'hit and miss' nature of harmonic exploration can be a distraction to fellow singers and the congregation. Conclusively, the Contemporary Worship Singer is benefitted by the ability to sing harmonies by ear and should therefore seek assistance in the development of this skill.

19.6   Contemporary Worship Singer's Assessment Tool

Determining the best pedagogical approach for individual Contemporary Worship Singers is obviously challenged by the multiplicity of the construct, cultural persuasions and various environmental and vocal demands. I have developed the Contemporary worship singer's assessment tool (Fig. 19.5) in order to enable the teacher and student to quickly assess the student's worship setting, by which task-specific vocal pedagogy might be designed and applied.[6]

After a brief explanation of the worship styles and forms by the teacher (presented earlier in the chapter), the singer is asked to choose one of the 'indicator tabs' (see Fig. 19.6) to place on the *Contemporary Worship Singer's Assessment Tool* indicating their perception of the worship setting that they typically sing in.

---

[6] Please note that the worship forms (Modular/Thematic/Flow) are not labelled on Fig. 19.5, but are simply represented by the shading. Refer to Fig. 19.2 for clarification.

Fig. 19.5 Contemporary worship singer's assessment tool (Robinson 2011)

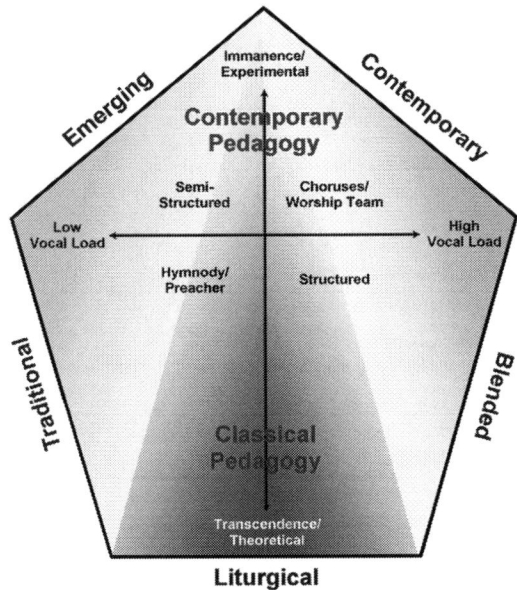

Fig. 19.6 Contemporary worship singer assessment tool indicator tabs (Robinson 2011)

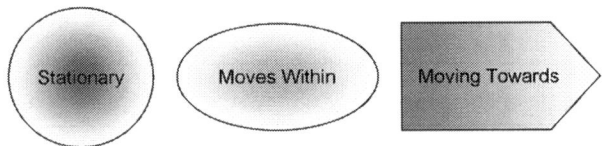

The selection of the tabs and the corresponding placement will inform and direct both student and teacher regarding specific style, form and vocal loads. Specifically, the tool suggests which pedagogical discipline might best serve the singer in the demonstration of their vocal task. Explicitly, students who place their indicator tabs on the upper region of the assessment tool may be best served with contemporary techniques, whereas those singers whose tabs are placed in the lower regions might benefit from a predominance of classical instruction.

19.7   Conclusion

The Contemporary Worship Singer is a unique vocalist within the wider community of singers. Much of the distinction is found in the context of their role: the multiplicity of constructs and the unique cultural requirements. Singing teachers of all pedagogical persuasions are encouraged to acquaint themselves with the context of each Contemporary Worship Singer while seeking to design and employ task-specific tuition. Beyond open discussion with each Christian student, every pedagogue's knowledge base will be enhanced by 'field trips' to student's churches in order to form a deeper understanding of 'Voice in Worship'.

References

Begbie, J. (2008). *Resounding truth: Christian wisdom in the world of music.* London: Society for Promoting Christian Knowledge.

Brierley, P. (1997). *World churches handbook.* London: STL, Christian Research, Hunt & Thorpe.

Chapell, B. (2009). *Christ-centered worship: Letting the gospel shape our practice.* Grand Rapids: Baker Academic.

Cherry, C. M. (2010). *The worship architect: A blueprint for designing culturally relevant and biblically faithful services.* Grand Rapids: Baker Academic.

Davis, J. J. (2010). *Worship and the reality of God: An evangelical theology of real presence.* Downers Grove: IVP Academic.

Dawn, M. J. (1995). *Reaching out without dumbing down: A theology for worship for this urgent time.* Grand Rapids: William B. Eerdmans.

Duncan, J. L. (2009). Traditional evangelical worship. In J. M. Pinson (Ed.), *Perspectives on Christian worship: 5 views* (pp. 99–123). Perspectives. Nashville: Broadman & Holman.

Elwell, W. A. (2001). Evangelical dictionary of theology. In W. A. Elwell (Ed.), *Evangelical dictionary of theology.* Grand Rapids: Baker Academic.

Evans, M. (2006). *Open up the doors: Music in the modern church* (Studies in popular music). London: Equinox.

Greer, R. C. (2003). *Mapping postmodernism: A survey of Christian options.* Downers Grove: InterVarsity Press.

Kauflin, B. (2011). Why we sing. *Worship Leader* (pp. 28–31). November/December.

Kimball, D. (2004). *Emerging worship: Creating worship gatherings for new generations.* Grand Rapids: Zondervan.

Kimball, D. (2009). Emerging worship. In J. M. Pinson (Ed.), *Perspectives on Christian worship: 5 views* (pp. 288–333). Perspectives. Nashville: Broadman & Holman.

Kropf, M. (2005). How do we know when it's good worship? *Vision* (pp. 36–44). September/October/November.

Lawrence, M., & Dever, M. (2009). Blended worship. In J. M. Pinson (Ed.), *Perspectives on Christian worship: 5 views* (pp. 218–268). Perspectives. Nashville: Broadman & Holman.

Liesch, B. (1996). *The new worship: Straight talk on music and the church.* Grand Rapids: Baker Books.

McCoy, S. (2004). *Your voice: An inside view* (2 Aufl). Princeton: Inside View Press.

McGrath, A. (2012). *The future is not so 'bright' for atheism.* Retrieved April 18, 2012, from ABC: http://www.abc.net.au/religion/articles/2012/04/13/3476271.htm

Neto, L. (2010). Contemporary Christian music and the praise and worship style. *Journal of Singing, 67*(2), 195–200.

Payne, T. L. (2001). Music in the evangelical tradition. In W. A. Elwell (Ed.), *Evangelical dictionary of theology* (pp. 800–803). Grand Rapids: Baker Academic.

Pinson, J. M. (2009). Perspectives on Christian worship: 5 views. In L. G. Goss (Ed.), *Perspectives.* Nashville: Broadman & Holman.

Robinson, D. K. (2010). Teaching the contemporary worship singer. In S. D. Harrison (Ed.), *Perspectives on teaching singing: Australian vocal pedagogues sing their stories* (pp. 276–292). Brisbane: Australian Academic Press.

Robinson, D. K. (2011). *Contemporary worship singers: Construct, culture, environment and voice.* Dissertation, Griffith University, Brisbane.

Russell, J. (1997). A 'place' for every voice: The role of culture in the development of singing expertise. *Journal of Aesthetic Education, 31*(4), 95–109.

Segler, F. M., & Bradley, R. (2006). *Christian worship: Its theology and practice* (3rd ed. Aufl). Nashville: B&H Publishing Group.

Sweetman, J. (2012). Defining corporate worship: Module 9. In *Christian worship*. Brisbane: Malyon College.

Wainwright, G., & Tucker, K. B. W. (2006). *The Oxford history of Christian worship*. New York: Oxford University Press.

Wiersbe, W. W. (2000). *Real worship: Playground, battle ground, or holy ground?* (2 Aufl). Grand Rapids: Baker Books.

Williams, J. R. (2001). Charismatic movement. In W. A. Elwell (Ed.), *Evangelical dictionary of theology* (pp. 220–224). Grand Rapids: Baker Academic.

Wilt, D. (2009). Contemporary worship. In J. M. Pinson (Ed.), *Perspectives on Christian worship: 5 views* (pp. 143–217). Perspectives. Nashville: Broadman & Holman.

Chapter 20
Take My Hand: Teaching the Gospel Singer in the Applied Voice Studio

Trineice Robinson-Martin

Abstract Vocal pedagogy for gospel music is relatively new to the field of vocal pedagogy and voice science. Even within the genre, information on how to address the musical and technical development of the gospel singer is not readily available. This chapter is intended to provide preliminary information on the various aspects of teaching gospel singing. First a brief background of the cultural perspective from which the performance of the genre stems will be presented. It is intended to help the voice teacher understand some of the cultural sensitivities that accompany this style of music. Next, general information regarding pedagogy for gospel singing will be briefly discussed. This information includes the role of the instructor and other aspects of teaching the gospel singer that should be considered or recognized.

In specifically addressing the pedagogy of the gospel style, some of the basic vocal (Sound) and musical (Style) components associated with gospel singing will be presented. The characteristics discussed in these sections are not intended to be a definitive source for 'How to sing gospel music!' Rather these sections should serve as preliminary information on how to address some of the musical components of a gospel music performance in the voice studio. For pedagogic simplicity, these components will be organized in terms of the 'gospel sound' and 'gospel style.' The gospel 'sound' will refer to the vocal characteristics and parameters used by gospel singers, and the gospel 'style' will refer to musical stylistic components used during performance. Although each component will be discussed in isolation, it should be understood that their execution is combined in a variety of ways to display a variety of interpretations. The chapter will conclude with general comments.

Keywords Black • Gospel • Voice • Singing • Pedagogy • Training • Somatic Voicework • Religious • Music • African-American • Belting • Chest Voice • Style • Soul

T. Robinson-Martin (✉)
Academic/Education Division, Soul Ingredients® Voice Studio, Lawrenceville, NJ, USA
e-mail: info@DrTrineice.com

S.D. Harrison and J. O'Bryan (eds.), *Teaching Singing in the 21st Century*,   335
Landscapes: the Arts, Aesthetics, and Education 14, DOI 10.1007/978-94-017-8851-9_20,
© Springer Science+Business Media Dordrecht 2014

20.1 Background: What Is Black Gospel Music?

There are five sacred music genres in the Black sacred music tradition (Wise 2002; Robinson-Martin 2010). These are Lined or Metered Hymns (established in the 1700s), Spirituals (various styles established between the 1700s and 1950s), Gospel Hymns (established in 1900), Gospel Songs (established 1940), and Standard Sacred Classical Forms in which African Americans compose (established 1937). Gospel music represents a certain musical and cultural aesthetic used in the performance and composition practices of Black sacred music (Burnim 1985; Wise 2002; Robinson-Martin 2010). It is a genre whose performance encompasses elements of work songs, Negro spirituals, blues, jazz, rhythm and blues, and hip-hop. It is a musical tradition that celebrates the contemporary Black religious experience, a musical expression of Black liberation of Black theology, and a musical experience that is deeply rooted in Black life and culture (Burnim 1988; Robinson-Martin 2010).

More than just a musical genre to the culture it represents, Gospel music tends to reflect the emotional, spiritual, physical, and historical journey of those who participate, and testifies to the contribution religion has made towards that journey (Burnim 1985; Williams-Jones 1975; Robinson-Martin 2010). The culture of gospel music is made up of a belief system that consists of a variety of Christian denominations that comprise the Black Church. They include Baptist, African Methodist Episcopal, Holiness, Pentecostal, and the derivatives of such.

Within its culture of origin, the religious component of gospel singing (i.e. the Spirit-driven aspect of gospel music) is considered *the* most important aspect of a gospel music performance. It is this dynamic that separates the concept of gospel music as being ministry from that of merely entertainment. Gospel performers who sing gospel music as part of their ministry do so with the purposeful intent of ministry—to minister the Word of God to all who listen, including themselves—not simply to entertain. When these artists perform, there is a commitment to stretch beyond entertainment and emotions, and minister to the listener's spirit (Robinson-Martin 2010).

Within the context of ministry, gospel music serves as a platform for emotional expression for all who participate. While technique in terms of vocal skills is not a perquisite of such expression, the production of gospel music is not 'as many in the past have contended, the mere feeble attempt by the 'untrained' and 'unlearned' to express themselves by whatever haphazard means possible' (Burnim 1985, 165; Robinson-Martin 2010). There is a particular structure that exists for musical expression within gospel music. It is determined and bound by the gospel cultural aesthetics and practices that define its musical language (Robinson-Martin 2010).

Many gospel scholars have noted that technique, as valued in the gospel community, is demonstrated by the manner in which the singer uses different aspects of the gospel aesthetic to articulate the emotion behind a given message. The cultural aesthetics of gospel music can be defined as those musical and nonmusical components of a gospel performance that are deemed beautiful, of value, and ultimately contribute to a culturally-viable performance of gospel music.

20.2   Considerations/Issues for Teaching Gospel Singing

The primary and traditional way to learn gospel music is by singing in the church. It is through imitation, participation, and constant exposure to gospel music and culture, singers learn the musical vocabulary, interpretation, and learn how to execute other aesthetics associated with gospel music (Burnim 1985; Wise 2002; Robinson-Martin 2010). For the gospel singer, the vocal studio serves as secondary yet necessary platform for musical and technical development. In the vocal studio, singers can (Robinson-Martin 2010):

1. develop, strengthen, and learn strategies to preserve their instrument;
2. learn how to execute the various musical components found in gospel music in a manner that is culturally viable and is both compatible with, and maximizes the capabilities of, their vocal instrument;
3. learn to channel the singer's own emotional interpretation of the music through the execution of gospel music aesthetics.

However to effectively accomplish these tasks, there are certain sensitivities and considerations the voice teacher must acknowledge when working with a gospel singer. The two most important of these considerations is choosing an appropriate vocal technique and recognizing the contribution of the Holy Spirit from both a spiritual and cultural standpoint (Robinson-Martin 2010).

20.2.1   The Technique

There are many vocal techniques and strategies that exist and have been very successful in developing and preserving the voice. Some techniques are based on aural and kinesthetic perception, some on voice science, and some are based on both. When choosing the appropriate technique for gospel singing, the teacher should use a vocal technique that is appropriate for gospel singing styles. The chosen technique should be based on both aural and kinesthetic perception and voice science, from which the resulting sound product most closely resembles that of a cultural-viable gospel 'sound.' The gospel 'sound' is more closely related to normal speech or even sounds that occur in vernacular speech, than it is to formal speech or resonant sound products. Thus the chosen technique should prepare the vocal instrument to produce these sounds in manner that will strengthen and preserve the voice (Robinson-Martin 2010).

In specifically training the vocal instrument, the singer should kinesthetically and aurally learn to first identify, and then develop, his or her vocal registers while maintaining the most neutral, least manipulated position of the vocal tract. In other words, the singer should be able to aurally identify and kinesthetically produce chest register (thyroarytenoid dominant registration), head register (cricothyroid dominant registration), and a mix or blended register, with the least amount of manipulation to the vocal tract to produce the resulting sound. Once the registers are developed and this kinesthetic and aural awareness is in place, then specific pharyngeal landscapes (i.e. positioning of the vocal tract) that directly correlate with particular vocal qualities found in gospel singing can be introduced and further developed (Robinson-Martin 2010).

This approach to vocal training is represented in voice training methodologies like Somatic Voicework™ the Lovetri Method, and perhaps a few others. In Somatic Voicework™ the Lovetri Method specifically, the goal of the methodology is functional freedom for the vocal instrument (LoVetri 2006). Functional freedom implies that the voice can be or has been conditioned to phonate freely on any sound, in any registration, and on any pitch within a singer's (potentially expandable) range, abstract of any pre-established parameters that cater to a specific genre. This means that if a singer is functionally free, when a female singer, for example, is asked to sing A4 (A above middle C), not only is the registration interchangeable, but the registration is not determined nor depended upon the pharyngeal landscape produced. In other words a female should be able to, if they so choose, comfortably sing a A4 with a brassy belt vocal quality, light chest-mix, bright head voice, rounded traditional classical sound or whatever they choose. To execute these tasks efficiently, however the chest register has to be developed and conditioned to do so (LoVetri 2006). Generally speaking, voice techniques that stem from the standard classical-based voice technique conditions students to only produce vocal sounds that are expectable in the European Classical Art music tradition. Even when these techniques are taught to singers of genres other than classical art music, many of the parameters that constitute a trained voice in the classical art tradition are still valued and remain the learning objectives for these singers (i.e. pure and consistent vowel sounds, continuous vibrato, clarity in the sound, distinct articulation of pitch, etc.). The problem with accepting these types of parameters is that it can potentially limit the singer's ability to execute the sounds and performance practices commonly found in gospel singing. The outcome potentially results in a sound that lay people would refer to as 'trained' or 'proper,' and thus would immediately set them apart from those they would consider 'real' or 'authentic' gospel singers.

A trained singer in any genre of music is defined by: a singer that has full and free command of his or her instrument yet has the ability to comfortably and effectively execute the sound and stylistic parameters established by the community the genre represents. Therefore when developing a singer, an ideal approach would be to 'train' the vocal instrument from a functional standpoint (i.e. abstract from any genre based parameters, but focused solely on the person and his or her instrument in itself) and 'nurture' the development of the style.

Gospel music is a style of singing that promotes individuality instead of imitation. Therefore using a functional approach to vocal training, like Somatic Voicework™ the LoVetri Method, will allow and even encourage the singer's natural, unmanipulated voice or sometimes speaking voice to be the building block for vocal development. This approach also acknowledges the sound and stylistic parameters of gospel music, and creates functional goals that support the desired stylistic output. For example if a singer wants to create a brassy belt quality on a C5, this methodology advocates gently coaxing the chest register up in the singers range until the singer can conformatably sing the note at varying dynamic and intensity levels (LoVetri 2006). The use of aural and kinesthetic awareness (i.e. the 'somatic' aspect of this approach) is also what allows the singer to be in tune with their body, their instrument, and become aware of its capabilities and limitations in terms of vocal qualities, vocal intensity, and stamina. It is this level of awareness and vocal strength training that can directly contribute to the preservation of the singer's instrument, for when the singer then chooses to exceed their capabilities and limitations for expressive purposes, is just that, a choice, not a demand.

20.2.2   Spiritual Considerations

Depending on the teacher and/or singer, teaching religious music in the vocal studio can be quite different from teaching secular music because of the spiritual element that must, at minimum be acknowledged during the performance. In gospel music ministry, the teacher should recognize that the power of the Holy Spirit (also referred to as 'The Anointing') is an element of gospel singing that can take precedent over and often supersede 'proper' technique during performance (Robinson-Martin 2010). The Holy Spirit is the power of God that resides in the believer, and empowers the believer to function in ministry assignment. Under the control and power of the Holy Spirit, the person is believed to have powers and abilities that supersede one's natural ability in the flesh. This is exemplified in the ability of injured singers to maintain prominent careers in gospel music ministry (e.g. Pastor Donnie McClurkin's ability to sing with paralyzed vocal folds), and also in other gospel singers' ability to sing with vocal qualities that are perceived as harmful (e.g. vocal qualities called mid-voice[1]). Understanding this dynamic, the instructor can further assist the singer by providing a solid technical foundation for which The Anointing can enhance (Robinson-Martin 2010).

20.2.3   Teaching Gospel Aesthetics

Gospel singing styles are highly prized for the individuality the gospel singer can bring to the music (Williams-Jones 1975; Robinson-Martin 2010). The acceptance of, and more important the expectation of, individual interpretation or personalization of the performance is at the heart of the Black aesthetic (Burnim 1985; Robinson-Martin

---

[1] Mid-voice vocal quality will be described later in the chapter.

2010). Gospel music is not like classical art music, musical theater, or other genres in which the singer must learn to interpret his or her own emotions through the emotional intent of a given composer or character. Gospel music is a medium for the *personal* expression of one's *own* emotions, experiences, and convictions. The musical and stylistic choices a singer makes when interpreting a song should thus directly correlate to the emotional context of their story or emotional perspective (Robinson-Martin 2010). The more the vocal instructor understands about the musical and nonmusical aspects associated with a gospel performance, and understands how to incorporate these aspects into the vocal instrument in a manner that preserves the voice, the more effective the teacher will be in developing the gospel singer.

20.3   Gospel Sound: Vocal Parameters for Gospel Singing

Vocal pedagogy aims to determine the most efficient and effective vocal technique for the performance of a given style of music. A typical structure for vocal pedagogy is usually determined by specific vocal parameters a singer should display when executing a culturally-viable performance of that genre. Vocal pedagogy for gospel singing is new to the field and thus a definitive list of vocal parameters for gospel singing does not exist to date. However through my own doctoral research, I recognized that there are some perceptual characteristics whose executions are either generally expected of gospel singers, revered in gospel singers, and/or are specifically beneficial to obtain for the effective execution of the stylistic tools used in gospel music performance. These perceptual characteristics can be categorized into the following parameters[2]: *tone quality, color, and timbre; vocal range; vocal agility; vibrato; efficient breath management; emotional intensity;* and *variations of dynamic* (Robinson-Martin 2010).

20.3.1   Tone Quality, Color, and Timbre

Tone quality, color, and timbre are terms that describe the aural characteristics or qualities associated with a particular voice or instrument. In the voice, a singer's tone quality can be affected by a combination of: the singer's use of registration and degree of vocal fold closure; tongue and jaw position; and the use of the constrictor muscles in the throat and back of tongue (Robinson-Martin 2010).

Due to the individualistic nature of the genre, there are many tone qualities used in gospel singing. Depending on the singer, the vocal timbres and colors can

---

[2] While some of the parameters listed share the same title as parameters used in classical vocal pedagogy, the definition and/or intent of execution are often different.

range from a raspy, brassy belt, or 'heavy chest' sounding voice, to a light, breathy head/falsetto voice. However in terms of registration, the registers primarily used are chest register, and/or Mix register. When head voice or falsetto is used, it is typically used with incomplete closure to produce a breathy sound (or the 'sweet' sound referred to by some of the contemporary gospel choir directors), or it is produced with a very firm closure with intensity (Robinson-Martin 2010).

The variations of vocal qualities used in gospel singing usually correspond to the style of gospel music performed. Traditional gospel has certain vocal tendencies that are slightly different from more Inspirational gospel, which are slightly from more contemporary gospel styles like Rhythm and Praise (i.e. the gospel music version of Hip-hop and Rhythm and Blues). Generally speaking most gospel styles have vocal qualities that tend to be more warm and full sounding rather than thin and bright sounding qualities. The darkest vocal qualities found in gospel singing still maintains a certain level of brightness, particularly in comparison to the classical sound. The level of brightness tends to increase specifically for the female as she ascends above the pitch A4, maintaining the most brassy, bright quality at D5 and above. This level of brightness or fullness in the sound has just as much to do with the vocal registration used as it does with the shape of the mouth and throat (or pharyngeal landscape) used when tones are being produced. As with other Contemporary Commercial Music (CCM) styles, there tend to be a smaller space to the back of the mouth and throat, and a wider space to the front of the mouth when producing sound. When combined with chest register, this results in a brighter sound in comparison to the dark and full classical sound that results from a larger space in the back of the mouth and throat. The fullness heard in the gospel sound, particularly in the mid- to lower vocal ranges, typically results from space to the back *and* front of the mouth with the larynx in a speech or neutral position. While these vocal qualities are the most common, in the past 10 years a very bright, brassy, almost nasal sound is becoming increasingly popular and/or accepted. This sound is particularly popular with male and female gospel recording artists that have higher voice types and perform the gospel music style of 'Rhythm and Praise.'

Another vocal quality heard in the gospel genre is a quality gospel scholars refer to as 'Mid-voice.' Mid-voice is a full chest or chest mix quality sung with a gravel or rasp in the sound of which is maintained over a succession of pitches. To date, this specific vocal quality has not been formally studied as to how it is physiologically produced. However it can be described as maintaining contraction in the upper/superior constrictor muscles (or squeezing the back of the throat between the uvula and the base of the tongue), while maintaining the CCM pharyngeal landscape described above. Some gospel singers suggest that this vocal quality should only be executed under the Anointing, otherwise vocal damage may occur. One could argue that perhaps there is a subconscious level of relaxation that occurs within that constricted sound under the Anointing that doesn't naturally happen. Thus a possible technique for producing that sound quality without vocal damage would be to take the pressure out of the throat and concentrate the contraction to the back of the mouth instead of squeezing the throat. A technique similar to that used for teaching screaming in rock music styles.

Vocal range requiring the most development/stamina

Tenor/Baritone   Alto   Soprano

Fig. 20.1 Vocal ranges (Robinson-Martin 2010)

20.3.2   Vocal Range and Tessitura

There is a great affinity towards displaying a wide vocal range when singing gospel music, particularly within a song. Using melodic improvisation as a tool of musical expression, a singer is expected to demonstrate a vocal range of at least one octave, and potentially an octave and a half to two octaves, in one song. Within a given range, the ability to maintain a high tessitura using a belt quality, or some form of mix (i.e. chest mix or head mix) is typically expected during climactic portions of a song. This is also prominent for singers that sing as part of a gospel choir or vocal ensemble. As it is typically only three part harmony (i.e. soprano, alto, tenor), tenors are expected to sustain ranges of C4-G4, altos ranges Eb4-B5, and soprano ranges G4-D5, all plus or minus a major second (see Fig. 20.1). Basses and Baritones generally sing tenor parts, or a soprano or alto parts an octave lower, as determined by the singer's capability and/or the music director. Therefore a crucial part to vocal training for the gospel singer is to develop, strengthen, and build endurance in the use of chest, mixed, head registrations and belt qualities, particularly in these ranges (Robinson-Martin 2010).

20.3.3   Vocal Agility

Flexibility in the voice is an attribute that is often found in the gospel singer. The ability to properly execute many of the stylistic nuances found in gospel singing (i.e. melismas, glissandos, bends, etc.) requires some level of agility in the voice. The importance of obtaining this attribute has increased greatly with the popularity of melismatic singing (i.e. vocal 'runs') in contemporary gospel music styles (Robinson-Martin 2010).

Generally speaking, lighter voice types tend to be more agile than heavier voice types. Thus from a technical standpoint, vocal agility can be taught by choosing exercises that either employs a lighter mechanism (i.e. head voice/falsetto, light chest or mix), or moves towards a lighter intensity with use of decrescendos. To develop this technique, students can start with general sighing as a means of being aware of what releasing the 'pressure' or 'weight' in the sound feels like. As the student becomes more aware of this physical sensation, the student can begin sighing and purposefully landing on specific pitches. Finally the student can sigh while singing a descending pentatonic scale (as shown in Fig. 20.2). Other aspects

Fig. 20.2 Descending
pentatonic scale (Robinson-
Martin 2010)

Descending Pentatonic

of agility that should be nurtured include flipping in and out of different registers, and maintaining general mobility in the sound (Robinson-Martin 2010).

20.3.4 Vibrato

Vibrato is a vocal characteristic widely used, accepted, and expected in a gospel music performance. Acquiring the ability to control one's vibrato is a good skill to have as a gospel singer because vibrato can also be used as a stylistics tool for emotional expression. Whether used on open vowels, long notes, or at the end of phrases (i.e. terminal vibrato), vibrato can be added or omitted to stress a certain word or phrase at a climactic moments of a song (Robinson-Martin 2010).

20.3.5 Efficient Breath Management

Stamina, vocal and emotional intensity, emotional dynamics, and the ability to sustain long notes or phrases are both necessary and highly regarded skills to the gospel music community. To efficiently execute all five of these components in the context of performance, the singer will have to establish an effective breath pattern. Pending the situation, gospel performance practices yield themselves to numerous body movements and gestures that may not always be the most efficient for breathing (Robinson-Martin 2010). In addition to this, there is a natural tendency in gospel's high-energy movements to resort to a quick and shallow breath when replenishing the body's air supply. Therefore in addition to advocating a low breath, it may also benefit for the singer to learn to stabilize the rib cage in a lifted and opened position during movement (LoVetri 2006). This may decrease the potential for added pressure and constriction in the clavicle area and neck, which can result from high (clavicular breathing), shallow breathing (Robinson-Martin 2010).

20.3.6 Emotional Intensity and Dynamics

Emotional intensity and dynamics are very closely related in a gospel music performance. The ability to sing with emotional intensity is an important component in the gospel sound. While the concept of maintaining emotional intensity is often mistaken for vocal intensity or singing loudly or with excessive tension in the body, emotional intensity is not solely dependent upon volume. One can be loud and intense, as when yelling at someone, or soft and intense as when scolding someone in a public setting. In both examples there are dynamic variations in the expression (some words are louder or punctuated more than others), yet the dynamic variations are not dependent upon the overall volume of the speech. Emotional intensity can be defined as the characteristic/quality in a person's tone of voice that directly relates to the listener's aural perception of the speaker's level of conviction (Robinson-Martin 2010). Thus the emotional intensity and variation in dynamic level that occurs in the interpretation of song, should directly relate to the singer's conviction and should correspond the changes in the dynamic level that occurs in their natural speech.

Since gospel music is not traditionally performed to entertain but to minister to the congregation about the Word of God, emotional intensity is typically used to effectively relay the message of the Gospel. It is *the* vocal component that could potentially convince a congregation that the spoken/sung words are true, and a component that requires a level of focus and sincerity on the part of the singer. Establishing a certain level of conviction in a singer is not the responsibility of the vocal instructor. That's something that must be acquired by singer during his or her spiritual journey. The vocal instructor should, however, encourage the singer to obtain a level of conviction if the singer's intent is to minister through music (Robinson-Martin 2010).

20.4   Gospel Style: Soul Components

Gospel scholar Dr. Raymond Wise defines the 'style' of gospel music as the execution of those musical components of gospel music performance that distinguish gospel music from other musical genres (Wise 2002; Robinson-Martin 2010). For example, most styles of African American music contain some form of improvisation as part of their performance practices. However, the manner in which improvisation is executed in jazz will be different from the manner in which it is executed in gospel. A jazz vocalist might improvise by scat-singing using a variety of nonsense syllables, while a gospel singer might only use one or two different syllables. In addition to scat singing there are other aspects of melodic improvisation that not only differ between various genres of African American music, but also within the gospel genre and subgenres.

According to gospel scholar Dr. Mellonee Burnim (1985; Robinson-Martin 2010), it is through emersion of the Black music culture that a performer learns how to determine which structural, rhythm, textual, and/or melodic units are potentially expandable. The performer then demonstrates this knowledge in a personal way during the performance. In efforts to describe these expandable units in the most abstract/broad sense, they will be categorized into three major aspects of improvisations in the following section. These three aspects include melodic improvisation, rhythmic improvisation, and textual improvisation (Robinson-Martin 2010). While in practice the execution of these elements are intertwined, for simplicity they will be discussed separately.

Fig. 20.3 Composed melody of 'Amazing Grace'

Fig. 20.4 Possible interpretation of melody of 'Amazing Grace'

Fig. 20.5 More complex interpretation of melody of 'Amazing Grace'

20.4.1 Melodic Improvisation

There are two prominent types of melodic improvisation. They are alterations to the melody (*simple* and *complex*), and melodic interpolations. The first type, alterations to melody, refers to the manner of which notes are added to a preexisting melody. These alterations can be *simple* in terms of only adding a few notes to an existing melody, or *complex* by adding many notes to the melody. *Simple melodic alterations* include, but are not limited to, the addition of passing notes and/or escape tones, and other slight changes to the melody (Robinson-Martin 2010). For example, the composed melody of 'Amazing Grace' is written as in Fig. 20.3.

When *simple alterations* are added for expressive purposes, the musical phrase can be interpreted as in Fig. 20.4.

This type of alteration is often used in the beginning of a song. As the song develops and moves towards a climax, the singer may integrate more *complex melodic alterations* to the melody. *Complex alterations* consist of adding and/or changing several notes to an existing melody in effort to enhance its melodic structure (Robinson-Martin 2010). An example of a slightly more complex alteration to the minor alteration melody of 'Amazing Grace' (shown in Fig. 20.4) would be as shown in Fig. 20.5.

Alterations to the melody can become even more complex with the insertion of melodic interpolations. *Melodic interpolations* include but are not limited to: melodic ornamentation like 'melismas' (i.e., singing many notes in one syllable within a phrase—also known as 'runs'), and 'tails' or 'grupettos' (i.e., adding one

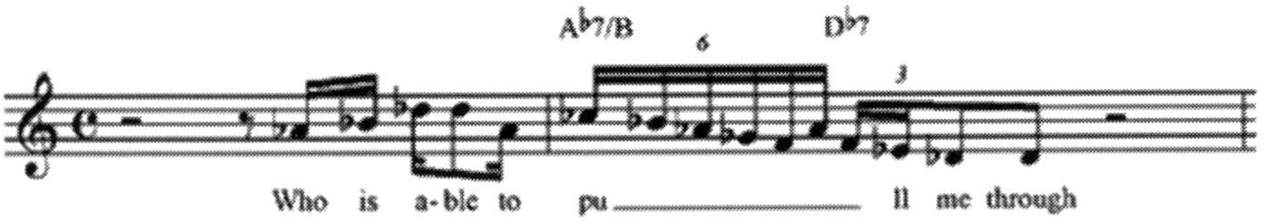

Fig. 20.6 Excerpt from 'Open My Heart' as performed by Yolanda Adams (Robinson-Martin 2010)

or more notes at the end of a sustained tone), in addition to other vocal nuances such as note bending, slides, slurs, portamentos, and word distortion (Robinson-Martin 2010). The complexity of the melodic interpolations, in terms of the melodic scales used and rhythmic executions, ultimately determine the overall complexity of the musical interpretation.

Strategies for developing this type of melodic improvisation mainly stem from paying attention to the natural speech inflections when speaking a phrase from an emotional perspective (Robinson-Martin 2010). For example, take the phrase 'I just want to thank you for all that you have done.' First, say the phrase as emotionally flat as possible. Listen to pitch inflections that correspond to the speech pattern. Then with the most appreciative, exaggerated, yet sincere deposition, say the phrase again and listen to if, how, and when the pitch changes. Did the pitch go up on certain words? Was there a slur within the phrase? Try saying the phrase again, but this time with more of a reflective, positive, content disposition. Was there a difference in the pitch inflections? If so, how? Once the ear becomes trained to be attentive to these inflections, then those inflections can be set to music. If the spoken inflection yields a slur that ascends in pitch, so should the improvised melody. If the spoken inflection yields a descending pitch pattern, so should the melody. As instructors know more about the different forms of melodic improvisation and the pedagogy that supports it, they can better assist their student in setting his or her expressions to music.

In terms of specifically teaching melodic ornamentations, particularly 'runs' and 'tails,' this may be the most complex and the most difficult stylistic tool to teach. These ornamentations not only require a certain level of flexibility in the voice, rhythmic phrasing, and harmonic understanding, but there is a certain 'feel' that goes along with their execution. This 'feel' is one of those stylistic aspects that must be acquired through the submersion of a specific style of gospel singing in order for its execution to be perceived as culturally viable (Robinson-Martin 2010).

Once the feel is acquired, the execution of melodic ornamentations can be further developed and nurtured in the vocal studio with vocal exercises and by assisting the student with aural transcriptions of melodic ornamentations. Depending on the complexity of the run or tail, it is important to note that an accurate transcription on staff paper may not be possible (particularly since even the best trained musicians have difficulty accurately notating 'soulful' rhythmic phrases). Therefore, use simple note heads without the stem to notate a rhythmic approximation of where and when the ornamentation begins, and to provide an overall idea of the notes to be performed (Robinson-Martin 2010). Figures 20.6 and 20.7 are two examples of

Fig. 20.7 Excerpt from 'Still I Say Thank You' as performed by Smokie Norful (Robinson-Martin 2010)

Fig. 20.8 Example of rhythmic improvisation exercise (Robinson-Martin 2010)

how melodic runs can be notated for teaching purposes. Again as this is not a composition exercise, one would not be concerned with the proper key or time signatures, rather that it provides enough information to serve as a starting point (Robinson-Martin 2010).

20.4.2   Rhythmic Improvisation

Rhythm is another stylistic element that must be acquired through submersion of the gospel style. Oftentimes, gospel performers will rhythmically alter the melody of a selection by using some form of syncopation based on 'feel.' The singer will either elongate or shorten the rhythmic patterns of the original composition, while keeping the notes of the melody in accord with the original melody. Particularly in relation to portraying the emotional intent of the singers, variations of rhythmic patterns, along with melodic improvisation, can be a very effective tool for emphasizing important words, phrases or concepts (Robinson-Martin 2010).

Similar to the development of melodic improvisation, a singer can develop rhythmic improvisation by simply paying attention to rhythm of the singer's natural speech. The hesitation that occurs when one is trying to find the right words to say, or the running of words together at the height of excitement are just a few of the natural rhythmic grouping or phrasing that occurs in everyday speech.

Other ways rhythmic improvisation can be further developed in vocal studio is by adding twists to regular vocal warm-ups and encouraging students to play with the rhythm while singing a particular vocalise. For example, once the student is comfortable with a given five note scale pattern, the student can then practice the technique of elongating and abbreviating the rhythm by changing the rhythmic pattern of the exercise as they modulate (Robinson-Martin 2010). (See Fig. 20.8.)

Having the student create a short set of lyrics that can be set to different rhythmic patterns consisting of five or six notes is another exercise that can be used in the vocal studio to develop rhythmic improvisation. The only requirement of this phrase is

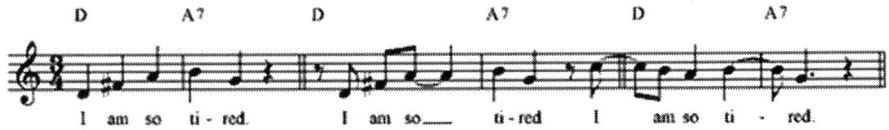

Fig. 20.9 Five-note melodic patterns (Robinson-Martin 2010)

that it be meaningful to the student at the time of the lesson. For example, 'I-am-so-ti-red' can be set to the melodic patterns in Fig. 20.9 that consist of five notes (Robinson-Martin 2010).

20.4.3 Textual Improvisation

The last major aspect of improvisation discussed focuses on improvising using the text of song. Textual improvisation in gospel music is very similar to the textual phrasing techniques used in African American blues and jazz, and other folk-based music styles in that the grouping and execution of the lyrics are closely related to the grouping and execution of passionate, vernacular speech. It is through the text, and the manipulation of such, that the performer can plainly articulate their level of conviction and emotional perspective in a manner that is uniquely personal to the performer. When the singer has a clear perspective from which the song stems, developing ways in which the lyrics can be manipulated becomes easier and the execution becomes more natural. The most general types of textual improvisation used in gospel music are *textual interpolations, textual phrasing, testimony*, and *ad libbing* (Robinson-Martin 2010).

Textual interpolations, as described by gospel scholar Dr. Horace Boyer (1979; Robinson-Martin 2010), are the adding of extra words to the original text. For example, the phrase 'Lord, I'm tired' can be executed as 'Lord (*you know*) I'm (*so*) tired' when textual interpolation is used (Boyer 1979, 27; Robinson-Martin 2010). As the singer becomes comfortable with the execution of the story, inserting extra words into the lyrics should become natural, as it is very personal as to how one expresses him or herself.

Textual phrasing is a technique, used by storytellers, in which words are grouped together within a phrase or strategically emphasized in order to portray an emotion or a perspective. For example, the phrase 'God has been good to me' can be sung/read as '**God** (pause) has been **good** to me' or 'God has been (pause) **so good** to me.' The manner in which the words are grouped, emphasized, and executed depends upon the emotional perspective of the storyteller (Robinson-Martin 2010).

In addition to these types of textual phrasing, lyrical and rhythmic repetition is also used as a stylistic tool. For example, 'Lord, you've been good to me' could be performed 'Looooord…Lord, Lord, Lord, you've been good to me.' Textual phrasing is used in all styles of gospel singing. However, the extent of the use of repetition as a stylistic tool varies between performers and sub-styles within the gospel music genre (Robinson-Martin 2010).

A *testimony* is a short, personal story, spoken or sung that a performer shares with the congregation to provide an example of how they believe God has worked in their life. Spoken testimony can be executed in the beginning of a song as a way of introducing or transitioning to the next song. Testimony may also be used in the middle of a song as a way of transitioning to a different section and building excitement and empathy amongst the listeners (Robinson-Martin 2010).

Ad libbing is a type of textual improvisation that consists of generating short improvised phrases over a chorus or over a vamp (a repeated section that extends the end of a song). The text used during an ad lib section can be a direct extension of the lyrics being sung by a choir, or it can be a sung testimony with text that is different from that of the choir. For example, if the choir is singing 'Thank You,' the lead singer could then provide short testimonial phrases that display his or her gratitude for who God is and what he has done (Robinson-Martin 2010).

In terms of teaching, the most commonly asked question by novice students, particularly as it relates to textual improvisation, is how does one know what to say. My first response is usually, 'Tell me how you would respond in the context of this situation,' since the text created usually stems from the singer's conviction on the subject matter. To articulate the singer's conviction, there are many different sources from which text for improvisation can be derived. Text can come from testimony or personal experiences or circumstances, from related biblical scriptures or stories, or even from an expansion/extension of the composed lyrics (Robinson-Martin 2010).

Just as in all other music genres, there are certain reoccurring themes from which most gospel lyrics are based. They are love, faith/trust, encouragement, submission, gratitude, and the role of Christ (e.g., Savior, Provider, Redeemer, etc.) (Robinson-Martin 2010). Dr. Horace Boyer (1985; Robinson-Martin 2010) describes the lyrics of gospel music as consisting of the following three variations:

> (a) scriptural quotes or paraphrases of the scriptures, such as songs 'You Must Be Born Again,' 'Peace, Be Still,' and 'He'll Understand and Say, Well Done'; (b) praise/adoration of the Savior, represented by such songs as 'He's the Joy of My Salvation, Yes He is,' 'God Can Do Anything But Fail,' and 'You Can't Beat God Giving'; and (c) supplication, as in 'Touch ME, Lord Jesus,' 'Give Me a Clean Heart,' and 'Precious Lord, Take My Hand'. (131)

Developing an understanding of these major themes will allow the singer to more freely and confidently execute the different types of textual improvisation throughout the different styles (Robinson-Martin 2010).

In addition, many 'stock phrases' are used during the execution of textual improvisation in gospel music. Stock phrases are general phrases or references that are commonly used within the gospel community. They include personal references like: 'He woke me up this morning and started me on my way'; 'He put food on my table and clothes on my back'; etc. Some stock phrases also reference bible stories (Robinson-Martin 2010). With continued exposure to gospel music and its culture, these phrases will become more familiar to the singer, and with practice and experience, the singer will learn to integrate them into his or her own lyrical vocabulary (Robinson-Martin 2010).

While various types of textual improvisation are executed differently depending on the style of gospel music that is being sung, all textual improvisation requires a deep understanding of, and connection to, the message of the song. Using the basic themes found in gospel music mentioned above (i.e., love, faith/trust, encouragement, submission, gratitude, and the role of Christ), the teacher can ask the students to journal specific, personal examples of how these themes relate to their personal relationship with God (Robinson-Martin 2010).

20.5   Summary

When teaching the gospel singer, one must first identify and understand the musical and cultural aesthetics associated with the music, and then address the student's musical development from those aspects specifically valued within the gospel community. This chapter was intended to serve as a basic introduction to these aesthetic components. Readers should understand that the mere execution of the components/characteristics listed in this chapter do not constitute a singer as a gospel singer. In other words, instructors should not expect their students to master any one component as if it were to be *the* validating feature of what constitutes a singer as a culturally-viable gospel performer. However all parameters and components discussed should be addressed in the vocal studio, and integrated in a manner that is most conducive to the singer's natural voice, speech pattern, and emotional expression.

References

Boyer, H. (1979). Contemporary gospel music. *The Black Perspective in Music, 7*(1), 5–58.

Boyer, H. (1985). A comparative analysis of traditional and contemporary gospel music. In I. Jackson (Ed.), *More than dancing: Essays on Afro-American music and musicians* (pp. 127–145). Westport: Greenwood.

Burnim, M. (1985). The black gospel music tradition: A complex of ideology, aesthetic, and behavior. In I. Jackson (Ed.), *More than dancing: Essays on Afro-American music and musicians* (pp. 147–167). Westport: Greenwood.

Burnim, M. (1988). Functional dimensions of gospel music performance. *Western Journal of Black Studies, 12*(2), 112–121.

LoVetri, J. (2006). *Somatic voicework™: The LoVetri method instructor text*. Contemporary Commercial Music Vocal Pedagogy Institute at Shenandoah University.

Robinson-Martin, T. (2010). *Developing a pedagogy for gospel singing: Understanding the cultural aesthetics and performance components of a vocal performance of gospel music*. Doctoral dissertation, Teachers College Columbia University.

Williams-Jones, P. (1975). Afro-American gospel music: A crystallization of the Black aesthetic. *Ethnomusicology, 19*(3), 373–385.

Wise, R. (2002). *Defining African American gospel music by tracing its historical and musical development from 1900 to 2000*. Doctoral dissertation, Ohio State University. *Dissertation Abstracts International.*

Part IV
The Training Ground

Chapter 21
The Conservatorium Environment: Reflections on the Tertiary Vocal Setting Past and Present

Margaret Schindler

Abstract The change in governance, which came about in Australian institutions of higher education in the early 1990s and gradually throughout much of the world, led to the amalgamation of a majority of independent conservatoires with universities. This change to institutional culture impacted key characteristics of tertiary music education particularly in the training of performers. This chapter will reflect on institutional culture prior to amalgamation and the factors which shaped the learning experience of today's tertiary classical vocal students, within the context of the Queensland Conservatorium Griffith University. It will identify the challenges for staff and arts education institutions as a whole, in responding to pressure from the wider university sector to produce students who are 'industry ready' in the face of steady contraction of program offerings and staff resources. The structuring of vocal study within a wider context of undergraduate, postgraduate and higher research degree models will be identified. Additionally, the role of trainee principal programs and other initiatives such as summer schools, in advancing the standard of singing and performance craft in this country will also be discussed.

Keywords Tertiary classical voice • Conservatoires • Vocal pedagogy • Classical singing

21.1 Introduction

Voice teachers recognise that the study of the vocal arts is a holistic undertaking. Development is an incremental process, often not linear and quite slow, as aspects of vocal technique are fundamentally motor- learned. 'The concepts and ideas that

M. Schindler (✉)
Queensland Conservatorium, Griffith University, Brisbane, QLD, Australia
e-mail: m.schindler@griffith.edu.au

S.D. Harrison and J. O'Bryan (eds.), *Teaching Singing in the 21st Century*,   353
Landscapes: the Arts, Aesthetics, and Education 14, DOI 10.1007/978-94-017-8851-9_21,
© Springer Science+Business Media Dordrecht 2014

are used to teach singing are planted like seeds that grow' (Chapman 2012, 167). The objective then of any music institution is to create an environment that nurtures and facilitates this development, not only of the singer but of the artistic whole, 'a combination of mind, body, imagination and spirit – all of which work together – no one without the other' (Bunch 1998, 1).

In this chapter, I will discuss some of the issues in the context of my own experience and practice at Queensland Conservatorium Griffith University (QCGU), a music institution which has enjoyed a reputation as one of the centres for producing excellent singers in the Southern hemisphere. Throughout its history of over 50 years, it has produced some of Australia's finest classical singers, many of whom have forged substantial musical careers both within Australia and abroad. Its alumni are well represented in tertiary voice faculties throughout Australia. There is national recognition of its fine reputation and a tacit affection for those founding staff that shaped its ethos as an institution fostering performance excellence and deep learning (Roennfeldt 2012).

The change in institutional governance, which came about in Australian institutions of higher education in the early 1990s and gradually throughout much of the world, led to the amalgamation of formerly independent conservatoires with universities. This change to institutional culture impacted key characteristics of tertiary music education particularly in the training of performers.

This chapter will reflect on institutional culture prior and post amalgamation and the learning experience of tertiary classical vocal students. It will identify the challenges for staff and arts education institutions as a whole, in responding to pressure from the wider university sector to produce students who are 'industry ready' in the face of steady contraction of program offerings and reduced funding for staffing resources and productions. The structuring of vocal study within a wider context of undergraduate, postgraduate and higher research degree models as a way of consolidating musical training will be discussed. Additionally, new and existing trainee principal programs in state and national companies and summer schools, as well as the role they play in advancing the standard of singing and performance craft in this country will be identified. Implications for tertiary level vocal study within a domestic and international context will also be discussed.

In creating a context for today's learning and teaching environment at Queensland Conservatorium, it is necessary to reflect on four major factors which impacted the development of voice teaching at Queensland Conservatorium since its establishment in 1957.

21.1.1 The Musical and Cultural Environment

Queensland Conservatorium was opened in 1957 at a time when arts organisations were becoming more professionalised. Opera Australia, formerly known as the Elizabethan Trust Opera company, toured Brisbane commencing in the late 1950s and throughout the 1960s, its performances often augmented by local singers for whom the Conservatorium served as a training ground. The formation of the

Queensland Opera Company in the late 1960s and the multiple levels of professional companies that emerged through the 1970s saw a symbiotic relationship between the growth in performing arts and the growth of the institution. The professionalization of music making gradually became a more active focus of Conservatorium training. Retiring performers began moving into the teaching domain, sparking the development of the Conservatorium Opera School. In the 1980s, a growing investment in the arts in Queensland produced the Commonwealth Games, the Queensland Performing Arts Complex and Expo88, each of which had a strong cultural component. This state-based infrastructure heralded the significant expansion of the arts in Queensland, becoming more outward looking. The legacy of Expo was to have flow on benefits for the arts, for years to come. When the Labor government took office in 1989, Premier Wayne Goss established the Biennial Music Festival, a precursor for Queensland Music Festival, which together with the Brisbane Festival are now highlights in the calendar of artistic events. Out of these initiatives came the opportunity for Queensland Conservatorium to showcase its own work through the expanded resources of a festival environment. Over the years, these alliances have encouraged the institution to produce pedagogically sound yet exploratory operatic productions and other performance initiatives, providing opportunities for students that are somewhat unique.

While Brisbane has always had an active pro-amateur arts scene, there was considerable expansion through the 1980s in terms of choral societies and musical theatre. Expectations of audiences also changed throughout this period leading to the demand for greater professionalization of performance presentation, a trend reflected in expectations of music institutions. Throughout the 2000s, the growth in performance activity in small and unusual venues, paid small ensemble work such as vocal quartets and freelance professional musicians in the form of street entertainment have complemented the diversity of Brisbane's musical activity and influenced the professional context of tertiary music study today.

21.1.2   Higher Education Environment

The Conservatorium remained an independent tertiary music institution until the Dawkins Reforms of the late 1980s, when many music institutions throughout Australia (and elsewhere in the world) were forced to amalgamate with universities. Over time, the academic year shortened from 33 weeks to 28. By the mid 1990s, semesters contracted further to 13 weeks. At Queensland Conservatorium, second practical studies were cut, except for a limited number in the education strand. Rationalisation of course weightings effectively resulted in a halving of course contact time, many ensembles were reduced or discontinued. A large number of part time teachers, some of whom had quite specialist expertise, were no longer engaged, as they had only a small number of students. The growth in diversity of course offerings however, did see the introduction of specialty strands in jazz, music technology, popular music and in 2011, musical theatre.

Following amalgamation, Conservatorium courses were aligned with the wider university to become 'semesterised', although performance studies did not formally adopt this model until 2006. When it was finally implemented, it met with considerable resistance from performance study teachers who recognised the needs for some type of constraints in terms of retaining student focus but who also saw the potential for stifling the developmental process in needing to fulfil short term goals. 'The constant need for students to prepare new and finessed repertoire for exams detracts from vocal progress' (Chapman 2012). Peter Roennfeldt sees it as an institutional conundrum, saying, 'It goes against the grain of what we know as practitioners. I think there has to be a way to assess developmental success rather than end point success' (personal interview, April 26, 2012).

The introduction of the Higher Education Contribution Scheme (HECS) coincided with amalgamation and initiated a change in student culture. Suddenly students were paying, albeit in on a deferred basis, for their education costs (or part thereof). The need to maintain part time employment as a result of HECS led to a tendency by some to negotiate the increasing offering of elective-based course structures within the curriculum, with students often 'choosing a pathway least disruptive to their overall lifestyle.' (personal interview, Roennfeldt, April 26, 2012).

21.1.3   The Institution and Its Growth

When the Queensland Conservatorium opened its doors in 1957, it had five fulltime vocal students. The department slowly grew in response to factors both internal and external, the most significant growth occurring in the 1970s with the massification of higher education and the Conservatorium's move from South Brisbane to the Gardens Point campus in 1975. The move to the new campus with its performance infrastructure and new staff signalled a key development of the institution and the vocal department. In 1971, the Conservatorium became a College of Advanced Education: the numbers of fulltime students in proportion to part time began equalising. This created a critical mass that allowed for the building of classes and practical activities that could offer a range of training. It also engendered collegiality through productions and the development of choirs, promoting the ensemble experience as well as the solo vocal arts. The Conservatorium increased its student numbers from approximately 300 at the time of amalgamation to around 500 by the time it moved to South Bank in 1996. Current student numbers are close to 800 including those students of the Bachelor of Popular Music delivered on the Gold Coast campus of QCGU.

This has changed some previous characteristics of the learning environment; however it has also brought with it a vibrant diversity in course offerings and in creative activity. The facility at South Bank comprises several large performance spaces and a state of the art concert hall, and is located in close proximity to key arts organisations and strategic partners such as Queensland Performing Arts Centre, Opera Queensland, the Queensland Symphony Orchestra and the ABC.

21.1.4   People

The vocal department was established by South Australian tenor Peter Martin, who was subsequently joined by James Christensen. Both of these teachers were pupils of Clement Q. Williams of Adelaide and the strong link with the Elder Conservatorium was reflected in the profiles of early lecturers and students of the Queensland Conservatorium. These included Janet Delpratt, Janice Hearne (Chapman), Janice Larking, Henry Howell and Neville Wilkie. The institution was characterised by performance activity: staff student collaborations of operas, oratorios and the works of local composers. Individual staff maintained noteworthy profiles as soloists with ABC orchestras, in oratorio, lieder recitals and small vocal ensembles.

Edward Talbot taught at the Conservatorium from the late 1960s and slowly a community of learning began to evolve through the 1970s, led by Janet Delpratt. Early teachers embedded a strong culture of performance activity and the importance of exposing students to the pivotal repertoire including oratorio and art song. A new appointment in stagecraft and theatre practices in 1976 saw Giuseppe Sorbello establish the Conservatorium Opera School, which has continued to flourish. He was successful in harnessing the existing energy in the community music scene and integrating it with the Conservatorium program to provide showcase opportunities for its students. Voice teacher Margaret Nickson also made a valuable contribution to the faculty, joining the staff during the 1970s.

The next generation of teachers including Gregory Massingham and Adele Nisbet emphasised the perspective of the more recent scientific developments in vocal pedagogy. In the 1980s two of Australia's most eminent opera singers Donald Smith and Margreta Elkins joined the staff, enhancing teaching and learning with their vast experience on the international stage. They brought a perspective that both inspired and shaped the next stage in the development of the department. The collective contribution of these key individuals contributed to a seemingly endless run of national competition winners of the ABC Competition, the Australian Singing Competition and the Metropolitan Opera Auditions. Appointments in the 1990s, including Joseph Ward OBE, Anthea Moller, Andrew Dalton, and Movement teacher Anna Sweeny under the directorship of the late Anthony Camden, enriched the pedagogical perspective by virtue of their disparate and rich backgrounds. This convergence of leading operatic figures and teachers fostered a vibrant vocal culture resulting in a number of student successes and several iconic Conservatorium Opera School productions.

The present day voice faculty comprises mostly alumni of the institution, several of who teach and perform concurrently, maintaining the profile and learning culture which has traditionally characterised the department. The most recent appointments to the staff include the current head of voice Margaret Schindler, Movement specialist Anna Sweeny, and Lisa Gasteen OAM, Practice Professor in Opera. Within this rich spectrum of experience, the strong influences of many and various world authorities continue to inform and challenge pedagogical practices.

21.2   The Study Experience of Singers
         Prior to Amalgamation

Prior to amalgamation, courses centred on the Bachelor of Music and Diploma of Music, with the option of a 1 year Preparatory Course (initiated for singers who frequently lacked musical literacy skills sufficient for entry to the Bachelor of Music). Postgraduate Diplomas were also offered. The course structure comprised four major elements. There was a strong emphasis on the acquisition and consolidation of fundamental musical skills, focused primarily on the study and performance of Western Art Music. The number of electives was significantly smaller than today's curriculum. Subjects such as Ethnomusicology and Electronic Studio served as precursors to World Music and Music Technology respectively, both of which have a vibrant presence in today's curriculum. Course content is detailed below.

21.2.1   Principle Study (Voice)

- one to one study of classical voice for 1 h per week
- Chief Practical Study Workshop for 1.5 h per week
- Modern Languages (French, German and Italian) for 1.5 h per week in first and second semester, increasing to 2 h per week for the remaining six semesters of study
- Studio Teaching Methods (now known as Vocal Pedagogy) for 1 h per week throughout second year and 2 h per week throughout third year
- Second Practical Study (piano), 30-min lesson each week for eight semesters
- Vocal repertoire, 1-h class, semesters 1 and 2, fourth year.
- Seminars and masterclasses as directed

21.2.2   Core Subjects

- History and Literature of Music, 2 h per week for six semesters of study
- Research Project, a substantial scholarly study undertaken with academic supervision, in the fourth year of the Bachelor of Music
- Writing Techniques, a study of twentieth-century compositional styles – 2 h of lecture contact continuously throughout 4 years of study
- Musicianship (Aural) for 1.5 h per week for six semesters of study
- Musicianship (Practical) for 1.5 h per week for six semesters of study

21.2.3   Group Activities

- Directed Group Activities, 4 h per week. This includes choral ensembles and opera ensemble

21.2.4   Electives

- (academic or practical), 1 h per week, commencing year 2 for six continuous semesters.

21.3   Today's Learning Experience for Conservatorium Classical Singers

The majority of students who audition for study of classical voice at Queensland Conservatorium aspire to be performers. As young singers, their vocal instrument and their musical background can be limited. The ethos of the department is to foster deep learning in all aspects of the vocal arts and to nurture the individual attributes of each student towards a professional life in music. Similarly to previous times, present-day Conservatorium students are enrolled in performance study, a core set of music literature and music literacy courses, a professional skills course and ensemble activities as well as electives. There is a set of co-requisites for the study of classical voice as well as other courses more specific to vocal training.

The principal focus in the formative years of vocal study is technique, acquired primarily through the one to one lesson and including the study of vocal physiology, anatomy, vocal health as well as physical awareness and function in the study of Movement and Stagecraft. Language study comprises comprehension and lyric diction, preceded by the study of phonetics. The first 2 years of undergraduate study focus on Italian, followed by French and German in later years of the degree program. Other support subjects serve to enhance professional skills and industry expectations.

In 2010, QCGU underwent a review of its undergraduate degree programs that resulted in the abolition of some courses and the expansion of others. For voice, this meant an expansion of language study and the provision of a fulltime lecturer in Movement and Stagecraft, Ms Anna Sweeny, a former staff member who returned after a lengthy period of freelance engagement. The appointment of Lisa Gasteen OAM to Practice Professor in Opera enhanced performance activities through weekly masterclasses and forums. Within this revised framework, vocal study has been reshaped according to the following structure. For ease of presentation, I have clustered these under the following headings: Technical skills; Performance Skills; Musical Skills; and Ongoing Learning. While some of the courses listed cross a number of boundaries, it is possible to categorise them in this way.

21.3.1   Technical Skills

The **one to one lesson** remains central to the practical study of voice and is the primary focus for students in performance programs. Students receive individual lessons of 30 and 60 min duration at undergraduate level, according to course of study, and 90 min at postgraduate level for 13 weeks per semester. Performance examinations are held at the end of each semester where consistently high achievement is required in order to remain in a performance-oriented course of study. The one to one lesson, which includes piano accompaniment, is the primary focus of performance study students of classical voice. Students in postgraduate courses receive 45 min of individual vocal coaching each week to support the work of the one to one lesson.

Accent Method Breathing is taught as a component of Movement and Stagecraft. This is a structured, incremental breathing course of one semester, which forms part of the vocal curriculum and is taught in a group setting to first year vocal students.

Undergraduate and postgraduate students engage in **Movement and Stagecraft** for 2–4 h each week depending on individual student needs and level of study. Taught in a class setting, this activity comprises elements of physical function and alignment essential to strength and ease of stage movement, which form the foundation for the development of vocal craft and theatre skills including national and historic dance as sourced in opera, and mask work.

Language studies in phonetics, Italian, French and German are offered throughout the undergraduate and postgraduate courses. A significant proportion of weekly lectures is devoted to the performance of repertoire and text analysis. Language study is delivered for 4 h per week throughout each semester, with an intensive course offering at postgraduate level.

21.3.2   Musical Skills

Music Craft is an activity designed to enhance musical skills in postgraduate students. It is conducted in a one to one setting with a vocal coach, with a view to improving singers' skills in sight-reading, repertoire acquisition and score preparation.

Keyboard studies is a one semester course in the Bachelor of Music, delivered in a class setting with specific aims on basic orientation and keyboard harmony. Prior to amalgamation, Conservatorium singing students studied piano as a second instrument. This proved beneficial in consolidating musical literacy and providing a valuable support for teaching activity later in their careers.

Individual vocal coaching is offered within the postgraduate vocal programs. In weekly sessions of 45 min to an hour, students explore vocal repertoire, its style and interpretation, as well as considerations of lyric diction.

21.3.3   Performance Skills

QCGU has an established **opera ensemble** and the institution is renowned for the quality and diversity of its productions. Archival photographs of esteemed vocal alumni appear throughout the corridors: Lisa Gasteen, Jeffrey Black, Miriam

Gormley, Claire Gormley, Adrian McEniery, Rosario La Spina, Leanne Keneally, Louise Callinan, Jason Barry Smith, Amy Wilkinson and many more. The opera program presents one fully staged opera each year and a program of operatic excerpts, directed and conducted either in house or with guests. This activity assumes a 10-h commitment within the academic timetable.

Postgraduate opera class is a weekly activity of 3 h' duration that comprises units of study exploring and performing operatic repertoire from the Baroque period to the present day. Students are instructed by specialist staff on the use of stylistic devices, and characterisation in performance.

Classical vocal students engage in weekly **performance classes**. These classes frequently feature guest artists, teachers, coaches or conductors, however they are mostly tutored by departmental staff, where students have the opportunity to perform and to receive feedback from staff and peers. Classes are held in large performance spaces at the Conservatorium and occasionally in neighbouring performance venues within the Southbank cultural precinct.

Queensland Conservatorium students will complete four semesters of **choral activity** as part of the degree program delivered in chamber settings and large choral ensembles. This is a significant contraction from previously when choral studies maintained a presence in the program for the duration of the degree. This change to course requirements combined with greater flexibility in choice of electives has led to a reduction in the number of larger works able to be performed and to a general diminution of choral activity within the institution. Furthermore, the de-socialisation of study has seen some large group activities become less viable owing to lack of student availability.

Chamber Music is compulsory for all third year Conservatorium students including classical voice, and forms a key component of assessment activities for this year of study. Tutored by fulltime staff, it encourages greater musical collaboration and knowledge of repertoire.

21.3.4 Ongoing Learning

My Life as a Musician was introduced into the curriculum in 2011 and focuses on building knowledge and a skills base for a professional life in music. This type of course is widely represented in Australia and abroad.

This course focuses on musicians' health and well-being including playing-related injuries; students engage in Improvisation and Movement, journalise aspects of their learning and reflect critically on music in performance. Established industry professionals provide insight into musical funding organisations within Australia, and the range of career paths in music. Students learn about copyright issues, recording rights, as well as performance practice, presentation, networking and self-promotion through social media. In terms of its relevance to singers, this course has significant benefits even if some learning activities are not entirely commensurate with their stage of development.

Course electives in the third and fourth years of the Bachelor of Music enable a number of students to 'curate' their degrees by selecting those courses which will enhance their strengths in achieving professional goals. Vocal students generally utilise this flexibility in their course design to increase language study either at the Conservatorium or cross-institutionally or to broaden their skill base through vocal pedagogy, choral ensemble, choral conducting and so forth.

Vocal Pedagogy, previously known as Studio Teaching Methods and offered in various forms since establishment, has developed to become the most comprehensive program of its kind in Australia. Pedagogy 1, a component of one semester covering fundamentals such as vocal physiology and anatomy, acoustics and articulation, is compulsory for all third year singing students. Vocal pedagogy is team-taught delivering classical and contemporary voice perspectives as well as incorporating the expertise of other voice professionals.

21.4   Integrating Vocal Studies

The integration of various aspects of vocal study into a cogent artistic whole takes place primarily through the one to one lesson. Here the voice teacher will utilise their knowledge and experience to reference course content in assisting the student to synthesise the various components of their craft. Performance activities such as workshops, public concerts, opera projects and special events also serve as a means to consolidate student learning.

Another way in which course components are integrated and synthesized is through use of the multi-disciplinary team. Voice teachers routinely work in tandem with a speech therapist, Movement teacher, or physiotherapist studio, targeting specific technical issues. For students, cross-disciplinary instruction increases the sense of coherence in assimilating a growing body of knowledge. Motor learning, experienced in activities like Accent Method Breathing, is vital to ensure the efficient use of techniques promoted within the studio. Significant amounts of repetition, once the desired vocal behaviour has been facilitated, encourage motor learning and the foundation of kinaesthetic feedback. For teachers, the expertise of other voice professionals can help to inform perceptions and to dispel myths surrounding poor vocal habits.

21.5   Changes in Teaching and Learning in Response to External Factors

Changes in the structure and length of the academic year, and also the increased demands of the profession, have highlighted a need for greater 'efficiency' in the way voice is taught at tertiary level. Voice teachers have the opportunity to utilise the growing body of scientific information to refine their pedagogical strategies, a view supported by Janice Chapman:

> In the past, singing teaching was transmitted through intuitive, experiential, and experimental methodology based on subjective sensations, often using unrealistic imagery. But prior to the development of fibreoptics and endoscopy, this was all that was available. Now, when reality-based imagery is used, it changes and enhances the singers' learning potential and the haphazardness is reduced.' (2012, 329)

Ongoing professional development of tertiary voice teachers is recommended if we are to keep abreast with the information readily available to students via the internet: 'It should be pointed out that students have access to current information via the Internet, are doing their own research and demanding more from teachers. Student-led education is the modern paradigm and teachers need to catch up and keep up' (Chapman 2012, 329).

21.6   Changes to Staff Expectations

In the years following amalgamation, conservatoires and other specialist schools struggled to fully integrate with some wider university practices and expectations. Prior to amalgamation 'staff were expected to just do the thing they were good at and be otherwise left alone' (Roennfeldt, personal interview, April 2012). The change in institutional culture which followed amalgamation brought with it greater diversity of course curriculum, hence some staff were required to fill managerial roles. Some appointments of new academic staff members in the late 1990s carried with them employment conditions that included the holding of a higher research degree or the expectation that one would be acquired if appropriate. This proved confronting for a number of staff; however others have taken up the challenge of research and have flourished. Interdisciplinary activity has served to interface neatly with the research component that forms part of the tertiary teacher's professional profile. In the case of staff that have predominantly performance-oriented profiles, the university's research outcomes, which recognise artistic practice as research, have resulted in greater recognition for the value of creative activity.

21.7   Challenges for the Institution

At a conference held by the NTEU in Feb 2012, entitled 'Future of Higher Education – Australian Universities Today and Tomorrow', a formal debate was held on whether the concept of the university, as it was known previously, was 'dead'. A discussion ensued comparing the freedom of the Whitlam era, which saw 'the abolition of tuition fees, introduction of a means tested living allowance and the rapid expansion of places. Since then, successive Australian governments, education thinkers and managers have sought to improve access to universities whilst trying to contain the costs' (Rea 2012, 17). In the case of the Conservatorium, salary proportion has become a larger part of the budget, meaning that discretionary funds have shrunk. Creating an additional pressure is the public expectation that when conservatoires or specialist schools stage an event, it will reflect a commercial or professional standard.

21.8 National Perspectives and Trends on Voice Training

The historical model for Conservatorium voice training was established in the *bel canto* era, and continued until the nineteenth century. It was characterised by daily singing lessons and supervised practice. Chapman writes: 'I think that this method in effect involved the training of the singer's ear to recognize and accept those sounds that the teacher preferred rather than the ones that the singers themselves would find aurally acceptable' (2012, xvi). The model that exists in today's Conservatoires is that of the weekly singing lesson with unsupervised practice, something which Chapman believes can hinder vocal development as 'students do not have the opportunity and time to develop an understanding and acceptance of their own aural mismatch' (2012, xvii).

It is widely documented that the training model for classical singers in the *bel canto* era comprised 7 years of vocal study with a master teacher (Miller 1996). While today's tertiary singing students do not receive daily lessons as did their eighteenth century counterparts, nor do they live with their voice teachers as some students did, there is still widespread recognition of the time frame which motor learned aspects of singing require, as well as the physical, psychological, and emotional developmental processes which accompany the study of voice. This is reflected in the way higher education courses are structured in Australia and throughout the world. Traditionally students undertake a 4-year undergraduate course (sometimes preceded by an enabling program of 6–12 months), followed by 2 years of postgraduate study. An increase in operational costs has led to some music institutions exploring other modes of transmission to reduce the costs of one to one teaching. Increasingly, the focus is on postgraduate training not just for higher degree qualifications but to consolidate vocal study.

The role of bridging programs has gained greater importance within the context of a contracting professional singing environment Young Artists Programs continue to play a key role in providing advanced performance training and professional experience for singers post tertiary study. A range of Australian performance organisations, including state opera companies, Opera Australia, Pacific Opera, Melbourne Symphony Orchestra, and others deliver vibrant programs and educational initiatives. Alongside this activity is a growing interface between higher research degrees and trainee principal programs in Australia. In 2012, Opera Victoria introduced a Young Artists Program which combines professional employment as a trainee principal artist with Opera Victoria, while simultaneously fulfilling the requirements of a 2-year Masters in Music at the University of

Melbourne. The Dame Nellie Melba Opera Trusts offers development programs that mentor and support post tertiary singers as a bridging to professional life. The Australian National Academy of Music also introduced a Master of Music program in 2011, to interface with both Melbourne University and Griffith University in providing students the opportunity to attain a Masters qualification while undergoing intensive performance training. While not yet available to students of singing, this trend is testament to the increased value being placed on higher degree qualifications while recognising the rise in portfolio careers. A dynamic working model between Queensland Conservatorium and Opera Queensland has proved fruitful in building a focused interaction between student training and professional engagement.

21.9 Summer Schools

Throughout the world, summer schools, winter schools, performance intensive courses and so forth abound, offering singers the opportunity to work with renowned performers, teachers, coaches, directors and other allied staff in enhancing their craft and developing contacts for further study or professional engagement. While Australia has relatively few established programs of this kind, the recent Lisa Gasteen National Opera School has emerged as a way of bringing some of the world's finest voice professionals to mentor and instruct approximately 25 singers over a period of several weeks. Such initiatives have the potential to act as critical links in determining the professional pathways of young Australian singers through ensuring they make appropriate choices in terms of teachers, coaches, trainee principal programs and in the art of auditioning.

21.10 Conclusion

The changes that have evolved slowly within Australian arts education institutions and throughout the world have impacted the training environment for classical singers and their learning experience as a whole. Recent commentary in The Australian highlighted the impact of MOOCs (massive open online courses) on the fundamental nature of higher education and the environment in which it will be delivered, predicting a dramatic alteration over the next 10–15 years (Ferrari 2012). While this may or may not be directly relevant to the training of musicians at tertiary level, it points towards a trend that threatens the fundamental nature of higher education and its perceived value within society.

Many of the current changes to arts education are mirrored in the challenges that the professional environment faces. State and national opera companies and other major performance organisations have been compelled to reduce operational costs and re-shape artistic objectives to remain competitive in a leaner, meaner funding environment where commercial gain is paramount to survival. This has decreased opportunities for both emerging and established professional artists. Competition for government funding, state and federal has seen the refocusing of arts organisations on versatility and adaptability, with a stronger emphasis on regional outreach and educational incentives to shore up support. It is incumbent on the tertiary vocal environment to respond to these trends by being adaptable while adhering to the basic tenets of the vocal arts.

While recognising the importance of the bel canto style of vocal training, today's arts education institutions cannot provide 7 years of daily individual tuition. Pedagogical practices can, however, be adapted to better utilise the substantial and increasing body of knowledge and research in voice and voice -related disciplines and variations on modes of delivery. Universities are well positioned to implement an interdisciplinary approach with incentives for research through collaboration with allied areas such as speech pathology, medicine, and sports psychology. Tertiary voice teachers can ensure that course content instils deep learning and first principles as well as a sense of alignment with long-term goals and professional pathways, and we can continue to serve as models of good professional practice to our students. Over time, understanding of voice and voice training has improved radically, which feeds back into pedagogical practice at the same time as resources are heavily constrained. The great challenge for voice training over the next decades is to optimise the effects of the former and minimise the limitations caused by the latter.

References

Bunch, M. (1998). *A handbook of the singing voice*. London: Bunch.

Chapman, J. L. (2012). *Singing and teaching singing. A holistic approach to classical voice*. San Diego/Oxford/Brisbane: Plural.

Ferrari, J. (2012, June 27). Teachers' credibility test as kids log in, tune out. *The Australian*, 7.

Miller, R. (1996). *On the art of singing*. New York/Oxford: Oxford University Press.

Rea, J. (2012, March). Australian universities today and tomorrow. *NTEU Advocate, 19*, 1.

Roennfeldt, P. Interview with Margaret Schindler, April 26, 2012.

Roennfeldt, P. (2012). *Northern Lyrebird: The contribution to Queensland's music by its conservatorium 1957–2007*. Brisbane: Australian Academic Press.

Chapter 22
More than Just Style: A Profile of Professional Contemporary Gig Singers

Irene Bartlett

Abstract Professional contemporary gig singers (PCGS) – you've heard their voices and watched their performances in restaurants, at corporate events and conference dinners; at social functions such as weddings and parties; in bars and pubs; at outdoor food and music festivals and as 'support' acts for 'star' performers at stadium and theatre concerts. They are the backbone of the entertainment industry 'gigging' wherever music is used for entertainment; yet we know very little about them empirically as a population of professional voice users.

The few existing studies that include contemporary commercial music (CCM) singers in their participant samples have been narrow in scope with focused laboratory-based testing of small samples, investigations with homogenized groups of singers, or clinic-based studies of singers seeking treatment for voice disorders. With the latter group there appears to be a presupposition of inevitable, *style-driven* vocal damage linked to a belief that CCM singers are for the most part 'untrained'. These views may be attributed to authors' backgrounds in classical singing and their aesthetic preferences for a tone and quality based on an implicit stylistic hierarchy favouring classical voice; the emic (insider) viewpoint suggests that the picture is really quite different.

Keywords Singing research • Professional contemporary gig singers • Contemporary commercial music (CCM) • CCM singing styles • Registration • Vocal pedagogy • Vocal health • Voice symptoms

I. Bartlett (✉)
Queensland Conservatorium, Griffith University, Brisbane, QLD, Australia
e-mail: i.bartlett@griffith.edu.au

S.D. Harrison and J. O'Bryan (eds.), *Teaching Singing in the 21st Century*, 367
Landscapes: the Arts, Aesthetics, and Education 14, DOI 10.1007/978-94-017-8851-9_22,
© Springer Science+Business Media Dordrecht 2014

22.1 Background

Since the 1930s, rapid advances in the development of audio-visual technology and the proliferation of electronic media have enabled world audiences to listen to, watch and read about the 'popular music' phenomenon. More than at any time in the past, the music industry and supporting media are dominated by the singing voice where 'Star' performers create, or are created by an ever-evolving range of music styles. The majority of these performers do not sing classical repertoire; they belong to the genre 'contemporary commercial music' (CCM) which encompasses a wide range of non-classical vocal styles (for example: pop, rock, country, R&B, dance, rap, jazz and numerous associated sub-styles) (LoVetri 2002).

Supporting this view, Meyer (2013) offered the following market summary of the economic realities of today's style based music industry (Fig. 22.1).

'Excluding record sales and looking only at live performance, we find that 4.5 % of the live performance market place appears to be comprised of classical singers [Opera in Fig. 22.1] while the remaining 95.5 % is comprised of contemporary commercial music styles' (Meyer 2013). Meyer's 'Broadway', 'Broadway tours' and 'Top 5 musicals of 2012' (Fig. 22.1) represent 'current' Broadway shows where again CCM styles dominate the marketplace: that is, 6 % Legit/classical (e.g. Phantom of the Opera), 22 % Traditional (Annie, Chicago, Cinderella Nice Work If You Can Get it), 33 % Contemporary (Book of Mormon, Lion King, Wicked, Newsies, Pippin, Matilda), 39 % Pop/Rock (Jersey Boys, Kinky Boots, Mamma Mia, Rock of Ages, Motown, Once, Spiderman).

In addition to the upsurge in CCM styles for music theatre productions, Masnick and Ho (2012) highlight a bigger revenue growth area for CCM singers: 'From 1999 to 2009, concert ticket sales in the US tripled from $1.5 billion in 1999 to $4.6 billion in 2009; a 300 % growth in 10 years'. Professional CCM performers create an audience 'fan' base through 'live' performances where their specific stage personae, vocal individuality and style innovation determines career success. To ensure career longevity these 'star' singers establish high marketability and public appeal through

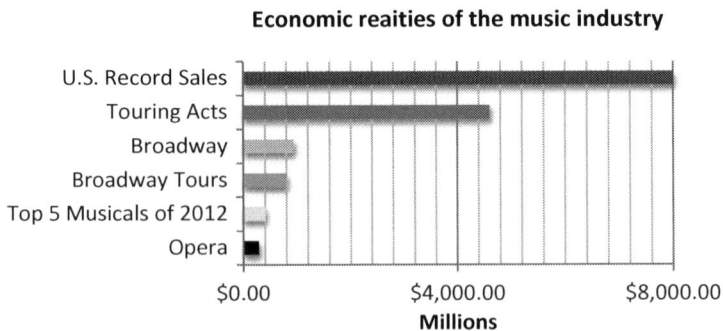

Fig. 22.1 Market summary (Meyer 2013)

concert performances, recordings, public appearances and product endorsements (Bartlett 2011; LoVetri 2008). Media coverage ensures their continued high public profile with reports centred most typically on their 'onstage', 'offstage' lifestyles. Sensational reports of catastrophic vocal events, such as the vocal fold haemorrhage suffered by pop diva Adele, attract wide media coverage most often due to concert and/or tour cancellations. Without systematic research of the incidence of voice problems for singers of all styles and genres (including classical), such reports serve to reinforce a suspect yet prevailing view that voice damage is an inevitable consequence of a CCM singing career.

22.2 Research and the CCM Genre

Other than some ethnographic reports (for example: Fiske 1989; Shuker 2001), researchers have not yet afforded CCM singer/performers the same attention as has been given to their counterparts in the classical music field. Given their significant number and high public visibility, it is surprising that published research on CCM singer/performers remains sparse and under-theorised (Bartlett 2010; Wilson 2003; Thalen and Sundberg 2001), and their pedagogical needs seemingly neglected by those pedagogues who have dominated the singing voice literature (Lobdell 2006; Williams 2003).

The knowledge that some authors (for example: Chapman 2006; Bunch 1997; Reid 1992; Miller 1986) have brought to the field is invaluable. They have exerted a positive influence on the singing voice community generally; however, their views of CCM performance typically are outsiders' or 'etic' views (Pike 1990) that have been focused by their experience and knowledge of the classical tradition of singing and not grounded in either extensive study or personal experience of CCM singing performance. In the absence of alternative commentary from authors with 'emic' or insider (Pike 1990) knowledge and conceptualization of the CCM field, outsider views continue to risk missing the nuances of PCGS experience – thereby effectively negatively impacting and hindering the development of an appropriate pedagogy for singers of CCM styles.

There is a building research literature in the area of music theatre where the phenomenon of 'belt' voice production has attracted considerable interest from researchers in the fields of voice science and vocal pedagogy (for example: Barlow and LoVetri 2010; Bourne et al. 2010; Stone et al. 2003; Björkner 2008; Bjorkner et al. 2006; Estill 1989, 1988; Schutte and Miller 1993; Lawrence 1979; Edwin 2010, 2007, 2005; Lebon 1986; Miles and Hollien 1990; Melton 2007; Spivey 2008; Popeil 2007; Wells 2006; Saunders 2001). Saunders (2001) described 'Belting' as a dynamic theatre sound produced from a mixed speaking voice and belt sound as, 'the apex of a spoken crescendo'. She went on to suggest that Belt singing includes, 'all the colors and mobility of a well- trained speaking voice'. Within the list of authors (see above) all have agreed that this speech based voice quality is very different to that produced by classical singers and that, in the past, classically back-grounded pedagogues have construed these differences in sound production, tonal quality and technique as potentially vocally damaging.

In a recent study, Ferrone et al. (2010) tested the view of a group of 'professional listeners' on the extensive use of 'La MaMa' vocal technique (a belted speech production used by actors). The general consensus of the listener group was that this technique would lead to symptoms of vocal abuse. However, contrary to this consensus, the researchers (Ferrone et al. 2010) reported a marked improvement in the vocal strength and resilience of the actors who were trained in this method over a 6-week period:

> The majority of professional listeners (11/12) judged that this technique would result in symptoms of vocal abuse; however, acoustic data revealed statistically stable or improved measurements for all subjects in most dependent acoustic variables when compared with both post-training and post-performance trials. (14)

Although the participants in this study were actors, this finding has important implications for professional CCM singers as it speaks to the relevance of training programs where the discipline and application of *specific* exercise can work to build and strengthen the vocal instrument regardless of style or particular style elements (e.g. Belt). Such research is important for the wider community of CCM singers, and most necessary for professionals in the field where some degree of belt singing is integral to their performance practice.

The 'professional listeners' in the Ferrone et al. (2010) study were not identified, however their opinions resound with similar views of CCM singing voice production from etic commentators in the literature of the field; that is, that 'belt' singing styles can induce vocal damage in singer exponents. My research findings (Bartlett 2011) indicate that the traditional perception of CCM styles as 'inevitably damaging' lacks empirical support. Most importantly, this research highlights the need for a developed pedagogy which addresses belt voice production within a range of style-relevant CCM techniques while recognizing, understanding and valuing the differences in vocal production that distinguish CCM from traditional western classical singing.

22.3   Out of the Darkness and into the Light

In addition to the specific interest in music theatre singing, there is evidence of developing research activity in other areas of CCM; for example, research of mainstream CCM singing styles such as rock, pop, dance (Zangger Borch and Sundberg 2002, 2011; Zangger Borch et al. 2003), and country music (Burns 1986; Cleveland and Stone 1997; Cleveland et al. 1999, 2001; Hoit et al. 1996). However, all of the above mentioned studies were limited to laboratory-based observations of specific elements of CCM style production such as sound source, acoustic properties and breath measurement and most involved only small numbers of participants (commonly only one participant). None were inclusive of the complex interactions of 'live' CCM performance.

Other reports of mainstream CCM performance styles (Pop, Rock, Jazz, R&B, Country and the associated sub-styles) have been, for the most part, informed commentary and pedagogical opinion rather than empirical report. Nonetheless, these expositions have been invaluable for progressing consideration and debate in the CCM field and the authors have been strong advocates for the development of a pedagogy that supports CCM singers by addressing the specific style demands of CCM performance. For example, Robert Edwin (through his regular discourse in 'the Bach to Rock Connection' in the *Journal of Singing* 1985–2011) continues to report his teaching practice with both classical and CCM students, documenting his commitment to breaking down barriers of aesthetic bias as he highlights CCM singing styles as undeniably 'mainstream' and artistically valuable (Edwin 2010, 2002, 1997).

22.4 Identifying PCGS as a Population of Professional Voice Users

There continues to be a dearth of research in the field of 'live' CCM performance. PCGS are the face of the modern music industry; whether as lead singers in band settings (e.g., duo, trio, quartet or big band), or as *one-out* solo performers, professional contemporary gig singers (PCGS) are the backbone of the 'live' music industry. They are professional voice users acting as the conduit between the audience and fellow band members/instrumentalists.

The descriptive term 'professional' has many definitions and these definitions have been interpreted and applied in different ways. Phyland (1998) found variations in the literature where some authors used 'professional' when referring to a single genre of singing, excluding all but 'classically-trained singers', while others (Greene and Mathieson 1989) applied the metric of intensity and length of training, and proficiency of singing technique. Teachey et al. (1991) included yearly income earned from performance regardless of style of singing; while Sataloff (1984) suggested that the professional status of a singer is measured by the length of time spent in performance and on a performer's reliance on voice for occupational purposes. Noting these differences in definition, researcher and classical voice pedagogue Richard Miller (2006) cautioned against the broad-brush application of the term 'professional' in research papers:

> … to make such information useful, various schools and techniques of singing should be identified in research reports. Participants should not all be indiscriminately lumped together as 'professional singers' nor should students even at graduate level be designated professional opera singers in published reports (201).

Although specifically referring to singers in the classical genre, Miller's advice for a careful attribution and systematic deconstruction of the term 'professional' is sound suggestion for writers of any occupational study. Without such specification, the status 'professional' as it has been applied in the past (Perkner et al. 1999) may be misleading for the reader with the reported outcomes of research rendered unreliable.

A review of the literature revealed only two studies that reported the 'lived' experiences of PCGS (Bartlett 2011; Lobdell 2006). Lobdell interviewed nine 'professional' band singers in 'live performance' environments in Louisiana (U.S.A.) representing a range of style groups 'other than opera/classical' (e.g., pop, rock and roll, country, folk, Creole and fusion music such as Cajon/roots/folk/pop). Her singers qualified as 'professional' in that they performed music for pay; she was able to report that while some of her participants made their living 'solely as musicians', others supplemented their performance income with 'day jobs' (Lobdell 2006, 8).

Similarly, the 102 participants in my study (Bartlett 2011) performed music for pay and had self-identified against a criterion of '6 h or more' of gig performances per week. Participants said that they earned 'all' or 'part of' their weekly income through regular performance in local, national and sometimes international contexts where they were called upon to sing across a broad range of CCM styles. Thirty-seven participants reported singing performance as their 'sole income' while the rest (65 participants) earned a significant income from singing but were employed also in 'other work'. In addition to their 'professional' status these singers were further defined as belonging to a particular group of professionals known in the CCM industry as 'gig' singers.

22.5   Gig Singers

'Gig' is a descriptive term used in the everyday language of musicians globally. In recent times the word has common parlance and is used by both performers and their audiences to describe participation in any type of commercial performance, (i.e.) 'I have a gig tonight', 'I am going to a gig tonight'. What follows is an insider's view of what it is to be a professional contemporary 'gig' singer (PCGS).

Until the advent of digital backing tracks those in the industry used 'gig singer' to describe a singer who worked within a 'band' environment; that is, as one of a collective group of musicians. This traditional model continues, but ongoing advances in music technology (for example, midi, wave, MP3) and the resultant proliferation of pre-recorded, instrumental backing tracks has allowed CCM singers to work independently of supporting 'live' instrumentalists. Currently a 'gig' can be any type of paid performance in a commercial venue, whether the singer is 'one out' (a solo performer playing an instrument and singing, or a singer performing with backing tracks only), a band singer accompanied by a full rhythm section (piano or keyboard, electric or acoustic bass, electric or acoustic drums, and possibly guitar) or, a session singer (singer employed in a recording studio for advertising jingles or as a 'back-up' harmony singer on a recording) – she/he will describe themselves commonly as 'a gig singer'.

22.6   PCGS in the Australian Context

Participants in my research (Bartlett 2011) were representative of all the aforementioned 'gig' possibilities. They were *insiders,* able to speak to their experience of a range of issues that impacted their *real world* performance lives including; training histories, performance styles, performance environments, vocal health issues and the prevalence and the impact of these, if any, on their professional performances.

To ensure that all participants qualified as PCGS they were measured against an Australian industry standard for 'a gig': that is, a 3–4 h performance 'call' (the duration of a performance). Prospective participants met this criterion if they were performing at one to two gigs per week minimally ('6 or more hours per week'), for 3–4 h per performance call calculated as an annual average. The number of hours per call could vary for studio (session) singers, but still needed to meet the criterion of '6 or more hours per week' on average. This minimum standard for inclusion effectively excluded amateur or 'occasional' singers from the study.

In summary, my participants said that they worked regularly within the CCM industry; all reported that they were expected to sing across a wide range of CCM styles, in a range of 'live music' commercial venues including pubs, clubs, hotel function rooms and recording studios. They worked as solo performers or band singers (lead or back-up) and/or session singers typically in band environments (either in 'covers' bands emulating 'star' recording artists or performing their original music, or some with some combination of both). Results from the study produced a demographic of PCGS participants' ages and gender, their background training and performance experience, performance styles and performance environments. In addition, this population of PCGS voiced their beliefs about the relationships between voice symptoms and voice problems in their performance histories, describing both their performance practices and their management strategies for problems if and when these occurred.

22.7   Style and Vocal Health

As reported earlier, in the literature of the field, the contention of an inevitable relationship between style and voice damage appears to rely heavily on investigations of treatment-seeking samples and/or the opinions of commentators applying a classical-style aesthetic. PCGS participants in my study (Bartlett 2011) stood outside both sets of constraints; in comparison to reports in the literature the information they gave is grounded in their personal realities with some interesting parallels with the outsider (*etic*) views, and much that is different.

For example, PCGS *did* believe that singers were more susceptible to vocal damage than other groups of professional voice users. They attributed this susceptibility to the duration and high-energy voice production necessary in their 'live' performances, and at one point some participants' contributions appeared to support

Table 22.1 Participants' views of styles that are potentially 'damaging'

Style	Frequency
Rock	28
Heavy Rock (inclusive of metal, death metal and associated scream styles)	32
Pop	14
Fusion	11
Dance/funk	5
Belting	8
R&B	3
Country/yodeling	3

NB. 44 participants nominated one specific style as 'damaging', while 28 others nominated multiple styles

the view of commentators in the literature that 'some' contemporary styles have potential to be vocally damaging. However, they *did not* agree that all CCM styles are inherently damaging. Some PCGS suggested that 'Rock' related styles and some particular CCM style elements potentially were more damaging than others. Where they held this belief participants were asked to list the style or styles they considered as particularly problematic. Within this group, 28 participants nominated Rock specifically and 32 others volunteered further qualification, nominating sub-styles such as *Heavy Rock* and a range of rock-related 'scream' styles including: Metal, Death Metal, New Metal, Punk, Scar, Thrash and Grunge (Table 22.1).

For example: the following comments from two long career PCGS identify 'Heavy Rock' as potentially damaging: 'Any forced or unnatural use of the voice as in heavy metal, rock singing' (#1); 'Shouting or screaming rock style must be damaging over time' (#2).

Participant #1 was 41 years of age. He sang *Rock* and *Country* styles *all the time*, managing 4 h calls for five gigs per week in pubs and clubs *all the time* and restaurants and hotel function rooms *sometimes*. Similarly, Participant #2 was an experienced PCGS. He was 50 years of age; he was singing 'pop', 'rock', 'country', and 'old time' *all the time* at three gigs per week with an average of 4 h for each performance call. His gigs were in clubs *often* and restaurant and hotel function rooms *sometimes*.

These participants were typical of male PCGS in the study. Both reported singing 'rock' styles *all the time* in their gig performances, but differentiated between the 'rock' styles that they sang and the scream styles represented in Table 22.1 as *Heavy Rock*. This differentiation may be a reflection of a repertoire preference within the same basic performance style group or may represent the participants' perception of dangers in the style-driven vocal production of singers in the Heavy Rock category. It is interesting to note that although many participants ranked 'rock' as their *least preferred* style and the *most likely* to be damaging to their vocal health, the majority of the PCGS in the study reported singing 'rock' or associated sub-styles *sometimes* in their gig performances. This seeming incongruence could be an outcome of commercial necessity; that is, the available performance/employment opportunities fuelled by a venue and audience demand for 'rock' styles.

22.8 Style and Training

Extensive *insider* experience led me to conclude that inappropriate or poor technique rather than style in itself is most likely to induce voice damage in singers of CCM styles (Bartlett 2010). The documented longevity of PCGS participants in my doctoral study (Bartlett 2011) supports the view that CCM style elements can be managed in the long term if employed as *vocal effects* within a healthy, balanced vocal production and practiced within a regime of effective training. These findings reflect those of Ferrone et al. (2010) and indicate that style-related vocal productions perceived as vocally abusive may not be necessarily so. Further indications are that, in fact, non-traditional focused voice training systems might lead to improved vocal strength and flexibility for CCM singers.

In terms of training backgrounds there appears to be a prevailing view that CCM singers are, for the most part, 'untrained'. All 102 participants in my research responded to a set of questions regarding duration and type of training both currently and in the past (Bartlett 2011). While twenty-eight said they had no training at all and 16 reported training for less than 12 months, the majority reported some level of training. Distribution of the length of training is shown in Table 22.2.

More than half of those who participated in the study (n=58) had substantial training histories. Forty-four had been training for 1–8 years. Ten participants had done so for 10–14 years, and four each had 15 years of training.

Table 22.2 Participants' training

Years during which training occurred	Participants
0	28
Less than 1 year	16
1	9
2	6
3	6
4	7
5	6
6	2
7	7
8	1
10	3
11	5
12	1
13	1
15	4
Total	74

Participants reported this training as either classical or contemporary, or a combination of both. Interestingly, many participants were unclear as to the training and/or performance backgrounds of their teachers. LoVetri and Weekly (2003) found that many singing voice teachers claimed to teach contemporary style and technique but had no specific pedagogical training in the field. Further research might investigate linkages between CCM singers' development of vocal health issues and the lack of specific CCM techniques and/or style experience on the part of teachers. Such research would add empirical data to recent expert opinion that the application of classical style technique to CCM vocal production is inefficient if not detrimental to singers' vocal health (Edwin 2000; LoVetri 2002; Wells 2006).

22.9   PCGS and Vocal Health Issues – More than Just Style?

Rather than attributing their vocal health issues to style alone, PCGS participants in my study (Bartlett 2011) offered complex attributions of causative factors for their voice problems when they occurred. In contrast to reports in the literature, the majority of participants believed that poor performance environments, inappropriate technique, pressures to perform regardless of vocal health issues and their speech related 'on the gig' and 'after the gig' behaviours had a greater impact on their vocal health than did style.

In terms of environment PCGS reported that their work-life reality was characterized by performance venues where high levels of background noise and poor acoustics were commonplace. Some linked these 'less than perfect' environments to a range of "other" health-risk factors; for example, "having to perform while sick, smoky environments" (#6). This response points to possible contractual responsibilities or expectation of fellow band members/audiences (It should be noted that since the data collection phase of this study was finalized, Australian Government legislation has banned smoking in all public places so the issue of smoky atmospheres is no longer a concern for PCGS unless their performances take place in private residences).

Some participants were aware of the possible vocal health implications of singing repertoire in keys inappropriate to their tessitura (the comfort range for an individual singer where the voice has depth of tone and timbre and the resulting sound is open and free of tension). Regardless of style, the choice of performance keys may have a significant impact on singers' vocal health. Inappropriate key choice is particularly problematic for female CCM singers where style relevant vocal production demands speech quality (a thyroarytenoid dominant muscular action) taken past the 2nd passaggio (register transition). This speech related voice production has to be maintained to Bb4 (all mainstream styles such as pop, rock, country and R&B) and, for some repertoire as high as Eb5 (especially in music theatre repertoire).

In addition to poor performance environments their singing voice loads, many PCGS participants reported an awareness of potential relationships between vocal health problems and their speaking voice use 'on the gig' and 'after the gig'. Male singers especially reported that they stayed in the gig room and socialized with audience and fellow band members between 'sets' where commonly, they would need to raise their speaking voice production above the din of background noise. Further, many reported socializing 'after the gig' where excessive speaking would add to the heavy voice load of their long duration gig performances.

22.10   PCGS Experience of Voice Problems

Interestingly, PCGS participants reported few voice problems, but where these occurred they managed them, seeking little help from voice specialists (Bartlett 2011). They described an awareness of and vigilance in monitoring voice symptoms and they spoke to a range of factors they believed impacted performances. They said that they knew when they were in a situation that could be vocally damaging and that they used coping strategies to successfully 'manage' problems that did occur. These strategies included preventative measures such as: modifying their 'on the gig' and 'after the gig' behaviours, controlling their performance conditions through appropriate application of live sound reinforcement, and practicing a range of vocal health supports such as vocal exercises and vocal rest.

This population of singers experienced the gamut of symptoms that typically signify voice problems (see Table 22.3) and indeed, most reported some occurrence of voice problems during their careers.

The low response to the high end of the rating scale (*always or nearly always* and *often*) suggests that the symptoms experienced by PCGS were superficial rather than durable and the experience seemed to be typically short-lived and inconsequential in relation to their ability to maintain and continue their singing performances. Moreover, in stark contrast to the earlier literature's assertion that CCM styles and vocal damage are synonymous, overall participants reported few voice problems. When problems did occur these were usually superficial rather than durable with effects on performance occurring at below-normal distributions. That is, PCGS' voice symptoms were likely to be problematic only in the short term and typically when these occurred they were successfully managed.

Rather than style PCGS participants pointed to a broader range of environmental and performance-based issues that impacted their performance lives with voice symptoms occurring as a result.

Table 22.3 Experience of voice symptoms over the past 12 months and frequency of effect on performance

Symptoms	1 Always or nearly always	2 Often	3 Sometimes	4 Not very often	5 Hardly ever, or never	Total
Hoarseness or roughness of the voice	5	18	33	19	25	100
Lost your voice		1	5	23	68	97
Severe dry throat	1	4	21	27	46	99
Very sore throat	2	4	–	–	–	98
Laryngitis following a cold	1	2	9	13	73	98
Strained voice	2	11	30	32	25	100
Tired or weak voice	2	17	26	33	20	98
Breathy-sounding voice		7	24	25	42	98
Inability to get high notes	1	9	36	26	18	100
Inability to achieve enough loudness or volume of the voice	–	3	15	27	54	99
Inability to control vocal tone or quality of the voice	–	2	18	36	43	99
Inability to control vocal pitch	–	2	11	23	63	99
Excessive mucus, phlegm	3	16	19	22	39	99
Physical tension – e.g., neck, shoulders – that has affected your voice	5	8	25	19	41	97
Emotional or mental stress that has affected your voice	2	12	21	27	36	98

22.11 Summary

The literature of singing voice lacks empirical evidence to support the view that singers of CCM styles develop voice problems in greater number than do singers of classical styles. The few existing studies that include contemporary commercial music (CCM) singers in their participant samples have been narrow in scope with focused laboratory-based testing of small samples, investigations with homogenized groups of singers, or clinic-based studies of singers seeking treatment for voice disorders. Given these limitations, it may be that writers in the singing voice field have taken prevalence as an indicator of inevitable vocal damage for singers of CCM styles without contextualizing CCM singing practice beyond style choice.

Much research exists in the area of occupational voice health risk and singers are reported consistently as the occupation at greatest risk (Fritzell 1996; Titze et al. 1997; Verdolini and Ramig 2001; Williams 2003). However, there is little discussion of the prevalence of voice problems or problematic symptoms for the professional functioning of singers. If, as Russell (1999) suggests, voice symptoms are precursors to voice problems, it is noteworthy that a majority of PCGS participants (Bartlett 2011) reported that symptoms had not been enduring or impairing. On these singers' data, if prevalence as it relates to voice damage is a quality involving persistence and impairment as well as sporadic and passing onset then the reports of lower rates of incidence suggest that problems are not nearly as significant in PCGS' experience as might have been predicted from the literature. For this population of CCM singers voice problems were acute rather than chronic, reflecting a strong indication toward high prevalence but low incidence rates. These reports of low incidence suggest that symptoms and problems that do occur are passing rather than sustained with no permanent impact on the singers' performance abilities.

The self-reports of the participants in my study (Bartlett 2011) and those interviewed in Lobdell's (2006) report offer important insights into what it is to be a 'professional contemporary gig singer'. A key finding in Lobdell's (2006) research suggested that her PCGS participants were more focused on their interactions and associations with audience and fellow band members than they were with their own vocal health. Similarly, participants in my study reported that they sang across a range of CCM styles, in a wide range of venues with variable acoustic environments where the music was incidental to the business of food and drink delivery and audience socializing. They believed that some CCM styles could be damaging to their vocal health but suggested that performance environments, performance conditions and, variables of speaking voice use and on and off gig behaviours had a greater impact.

These accounts offer a rare, 'insider' perspective into the issues that confront PCGS' vocal health, and describe PCGS' management of voice problems if and when these do occur. Most importantly, many participants reported long and continuous performance careers and afforded the view that vocal damage is neither an inevitable nor impossible consequence for their CCM performance styles. Rather than style PCGS (Bartlett 2011) suggested that 'unavoidable' factors such as the physical demands of pre- and post- performance activities, pre- and post- stresses of social interactions, the rigors of travel and the expectations of audiences and fellow band members were some of many aspects of their work-lives that might adversely affect their vocal health.

We now know more about CCM singers than we did in the past. Most importantly, we know that their performance environments and singing voice production are very different to that of their classical counterparts. That is, their singing is characterized by the text (lyric) delivered in speech quality with conversational phrasing, ornate melodic embellishments, accented rhythmic articulation and beat anticipations, syncopated passing notes and idiosyncratic tone and timbre and that the resulting vocal individuality and style innovation are strong determinants for a CCM singer's career success.

Given the significant numbers of singers in the CCM industry and the reality and globality of the phenomenon, the PCGS participants in my research (Bartlett 2011) and those in Lobdell's (2006) study have provided important generic contextual information for singing teachers and voice care specialists who manage CCM singers in the course of their studio and clinical work. Their stories contrast much of the existing knowledge from etic reports in the literature and highlight the importance of including source knowledge from the singers themselves as the field progresses its understanding and support for this significant population of professional voice users.

References

Barlow, C., & LoVetri, J. (2010). Closed quotient and spectral measures of female adolescent singers in different singing styles. *Journal of Voice, 24*(3), 314–318.

Bartlett, I. (2010). One size doesn't fit all: Tailored training for contemporary commercial singers. In S. D. Harrison (Ed.), *Perspectives on teaching singing: Australian vocal pedagogues sing their stories* (pp. 227–243). Brisbane: Australian Academic Press.

Bartlett, I. (2011). *Sing out loud, sing out long – A profile of professional contemporary singers in the Australian context.* Published doctoral thesis, LAP Lambert, Saarbrücken.

Bjorkner, E., Sundberg, J., Cleveland, T., & Stone, E. (2006). Voice source differences between registers in female musical theatre singers. *Journal of Voice, 20*(2), 187–197.

Björkner, E. (2008). Musical theater and opera singing: Why so different? A study of subglottal pressure, voice source, and formant frequency characteristics. *Journal of Voice, 22*(5), 533–540.

Bourne, T., Garnier, M., & Kenny, D. (2010). Music theatre voice: Production, physiology and pedagogy. In S. D. Harrison (Ed.), *Perspectives on teaching singing: Australian vocal pedagogues sing their stories.* Brisbane: Australian Academic Press.

Bunch, M. (1997). *Dynamics of the singing voice* (4th ed.). New York: Springer.

Burns, P. (1986). Acoustical analysis of the underlying voice differences between two groups of professional singers: Opera and country and western. *The Laryngoscope, 96*(5), 549–554.

Chapman, J. (2006). *Singing and teaching singing: A holistic approach to classical voice.* San Diego: Plural.

Cleveland, T. F., & Stone, R. E. (1997). Estimated subglottal pressure in six professional country singers. *Journal of Voice, 11*(4), 403–409.

Cleveland, T. F., Stone, R. E., & Iwarsson, J. (1999). Voice source characteristics in six premier country singers. *Journal of Voice, 13*(2), 168–183.

Cleveland, T. F., Sundberg, J., & Stone, R. E. (2001). Long-term-average spectrum characteristics of country singers during speaking and singing. *Journal of Voice, 15*(1), 54–60.

Edwin, R. (1997). Renting La Boheme. *Journal of Singing, 54*(1), 59–60.

Edwin, R. (2000). Apples and oranges: Belting revisited. *Journal of Singing, 57*(2), 43–44.

Edwin, R. (2002). Belting: Bel canto or brutto canto? *Journal of Singing, 59*(1), 67–68.

Edwin, R. (2005). Contemporary music theatre: Louder than words. *Journal of Singing, 61*(3), 291–292.

Edwin, R. (2007). Popular song and music theater: Belt is legit. *Journal of Singing, 64*(2), 213–215.

Edwin, R. (2010). Popular song and music theater: Personal and pedagogic aesthetics. *Journal of Singing, 66*(5), 575–577.

Estill, J. (1988). Belting and classic voice quality: Some physiological differences. *Medical Problems of Performing Artists, 3*(1), 37–43.

Estill, J. (1989). Analysis and synthesis of six voice qualities. *Journal of Acoustical Society of America, 86*(1), 36.

Ferrone, C., Galgano, J., & Ramig, L. O. (2010). The impact of extended voice use on the acoustic characteristics of phonation after training and performance of actors from the La MaMa experimental theater club. *Journal of Voice.*

Fiske, J. (1989). *Understanding popular culture.* London: Routledge.

Fritzell, B. R. (1996). Voice disorders and occupations. *Logopedics Phonatrics Vocology, 21*(1), 7–12.

Greene, M. C. L., & Mathieson, L. (1989). *The voice and its disorders* (2nd ed.). London: Whurr.

Hoit, J. D., Jenks, C. L., Watson, P. J., & Cleveland, T. F. (1996). Respiratory function during speaking and singing in professional country singers. *Journal of Voice, 10*(1), 39–49.

Lawrence, V. (1979). Laryngological observations on 'Belting'. *Journal of Research in Singing, 2*(1), 26–28.

Lebon, R. L. (1986). *The effects of a pedagogical approach incorporating videotaped demonstrations on the development of female vocalists 'belted' vocal technique.* Unpublished doctoral thesis, University of Miami, Miami.

Lobdell, M. (2006). *An investigation of the voice in live performance: A qualitative analysis of voice use by bands.* Unpublished doctoral thesis, University of Louisiana, Lafayette.

LoVetri, J. (2002). Contemporary commercial music: More than one way to use the vocal tract. *Journal of Singing, 58*(3), 249–252.

LoVetri, J. (2008). Contemporary commercial music. *Journal of Voice, 22*(3), 260–262.

LoVetri, J., & Weekly, E. M. (2003). Contemporary commercial music (CCM) survey: Who's teaching what in nonclassical music. *Journal of Voice, 17*(2), 207–215.

Masnick, M., & Ho, M. (2012). World wide entertainment report. TechDirt.com. Retrieved from *TechDirt.com/skyisrising.*

Melton, J. (2007). *Singing in music theatre: The training of singers and actors.* New York: Allworth Press.

Meyer, D. (2013). *The future of collegiate voice pedagogy. SWOT analysis of current practice – Implications for the next generation of singers and teachers of singing.* Unpublished Paper presentation, 8th international congress of voice teachers.

Miles, B., & Hollien, H. (1990). Whither belting? *Journal of Voice, 4*(1), 64–70.

Miller, R. (1986). *The structure of singing: System and art in vocal technique.* New York/London: Schirmer Books/Collier Macmillan.

Miller, R. (2006). Voice pedagogy: Registration. *Journal of Singing, 62*(5), 537–539.

Perkner, J. J., Fennelly, K. P., & Balkisson, R. (1999). Self-reported voice problems among three groups of professional singers. *Journal of Voice, 13*, 602–611.

Phyland, D. J. (1998). *Self-reported voice problems among professional singers.* Unpublished master's dissertation, La Trobe University, Bundoora.

Pike, K. L. (1990). On the emics and etics of Pike and Harris. In T. N. Headland, K. L. Pike, & M. Harris (Eds.), *Emics and etics: The insider/outsider debate* (Vol. 226). Newbury Park: Sage.

Popeil, L. (2007). The multiplicity of belting. *Journal of Singing, 64*, 77–80.

Reid, C. L. (1992). *Essays on the nature of singing.* Huntsville: Recital Publications.

Russell, A. (1999). *Voice problems in teachers: Prevalence and prediction.* Unpublished Doctoral dissertation, La Trobe University, Bundoora, Australia.

Sataloff, R. T. (1984). 'How i do it' – Head and neck and plastic surgery. A targeted problem and its solution: Efficient history taking in professional singers. *Laryngoscope, 94*(8), 1111–1114.

Saunders, M. (2001, January 3). 'Definitions and thoughts on 'Belt,'' handout from *music theatre and the belt voice – II.* National Association of Teachers of Singing winter workshop, New York.

Schutte, H. K., & Miller, D. G. (1993). Belting and pop, nonclassical approaches to the female middle voice: Some preliminary considerations. *Journal of Voice, 7*(2), 142–150.

Shuker, R. (2001). *Understanding popular music* (2nd ed.). London: Routledge.

Spivey, N. (2008). Music theater singing. Let's talk. Part 2: Examining the debate on belting. *Journal of Singing, 64*(5), 607–614.

Stone, R. E., Cleveland, T. F., Sundberg, J., & Prokop, J. (2003). Aerodynamic and acoustical measures of speech, operatic, and broadway vocal styles in a professional female singer. *Journal of Voice, 17*(3), 283–297.

Teachey, J. C., Kahane, J. C., & Beckford, N. S. (1991). Vocal mechanics in untrained professional singers. *Journal of Voice, 5*(1), 51–56.

Thalen, M., & Sundberg, J. (2001). Describing different styles of singing: A comparison of a female singer's voice source in 'Classical', 'Pop', 'Jazz' and 'Blues'. *Logopedics Phoniatrics Vocology, 26*(2), 82–93.

Titze, I., Lemke, J., & Montequin, D. (1997). Populations in the U.S. workforce who rely on voice as a primary tool of trade: A preliminary report. *Journal of Voice, 11*(3), 254–259.

Verdolini, K., & Ramig, L. O. (2001). Review: Occupational risks for voice problems. *Logopedics Phonatrics Vocology, 26*(1), 37–46.

Wells, B. (2006). On the voice – Belt technique: Research, acoustics and possible world applications. *Choral Journal, 46*(9), 65–77.

Williams, N. R. (2003). Occupational groups at risk of voice disorders: A review of the literature. *Occupational Medicine, 53*(7), 456–460.

Wilson, P. (2003). Sinful modern music: Science and the contemporary commercial singer. *Australian Voice, 9*, 12–16.

Zangger Borch, D., & Sundberg, J. (2002). Spectral distribution of solo voice and accompaniment in pop music. *Logopedics Phoniatrics Vocology, 27*(1), 37–41.

Zangger Borch, D., & Sundberg, J. (2011). Some phonatory and resonatory characteristics of the Rock, Pop, Soul, and Swedish dance band styles of singing. *Journal of Voice, 25*(5), 532–553.

Zangger Borch, D., Sundberg, J., Lindestad, P., & Thalen, M. (2003). Vocal fold vibration and voice source aperiodicity in phonatorily distorted singing. *TMH-QPSR Journal, 45*(1), 87–91.

Chapter 23
Developing a Tertiary Course in Music Theatre

Paul Sabey

Abstract So you want to develop a tertiary course in Music Theatre? There is a common misconception that by offering some singing, dancing and acting classes you have provided all it takes to produce a successful performer in Music Theatre. It takes a lot more. My experience over some 26 years of delivering a high quality musical theatre program is the basis for this chapter on developing a tertiary course in Music Theatre. The chapter will explain the requirements to set up a program that will provide the best possible learning experience for your tertiary Music Theatre students.

Keywords Music theatre • Act • sing • Dance • Perform • Show • Agent • Audience

23.1 My Story

I started at Mountview Academy at the age of 22 as a singing teacher. Mountview was at that time primarily an acting school, with a couple of dance and singing classes that were in no way fully integrated within the acting course. At that time the musical theatre industry was demanding a performer with a range of skills. The performer who was a triple-threat talent became necessary for employment in Music Theatre, yet there were limited opportunities for students in the UK to learn all three skills in acting, singing and dance in one course.

Following discussion with leading industry professionals about what the business wanted and what casting agents required, I put together a proposal of a new practical form of study. I was a young upstart, and when I think about this now, it astounds me to think I was younger than many of the students in the music theatre

P. Sabey (✉)
Queensland Conservatorium, Griffith University, Brisbane, QLD, Australia
e-mail: p.sabey@griffith.edu.au

S.D. Harrison and J. O'Bryan (eds.), *Teaching Singing in the 21st Century*, 383
Landscapes: the Arts, Aesthetics, and Education 14, DOI 10.1007/978-94-017-8851-9_23,
© Springer Science+Business Media Dordrecht 2014

course I now lead. The then Principal became excited by the idea and supported the implementation of a new form of training, one that equally incorporated singing, dancing and acting. The Principal also supported the employment of new staff and upgraded the facilities.

All Musical Theatre and Acting students in the first year of this new regime took part in a foundation course in Year 1, with a heavy emphasis on the acting. All students then specialized thereafter, however, as the third year was a performance year, this allowed only 1 year for specialization. It soon became clear that this specialization needed to start from day one. Over a period the course design evolved. There was constant tweaking of the course, working out how to best meet the needs of students heading into a demanding and competitive industry. This included intense consultation determining hours between subjects, the allocation of time given to subjects, the course content and student demand. Over the next 20 years Mountview became one of the leading schools in music theatre. One particularly exciting aspect of learning and teaching music theatre in London was the opportunity for students to take advantage of ongoing visits by heavyweight industry professionals. Students were given access to a range of famous performers, attended West End performances, and had great casting opportunities. As a result of Mountview's success, I was asked to contribute to many other course developments across the world, assisting in music theatre course design, reviewing current course designs in places like New Zealand, and giving Master classes around the world in musical theatre.

After 23 years of continuing innovation and success at Mountview, an exciting invitation came from the Queensland Conservatorium, Griffith University to write a new music theatre program, with an accompanying request to be Head of the Program. A sea change was imminent.

Now, in a new country and overseeing a new program with different requirements, constraints and opportunities, the Bachelor of Musical Theatre program at Queensland Conservatorium, Griffith University presents another set of challenges. While the country and environment is different, the passion held by all the students is as powerful as that of their British counterparts. This chapter is an examination of how I have set up a successful tertiary music theatre program, based on experiences honed over a quarter of a century.

23.2   Course Structure

Let us assume that the course content and structure are the primary elements in achieving the goal to train a performer. For the purpose of this chapter, I have made the premise that the course will be 3 years in duration, delivered over six semesters (two per year). The 3 years should be divided into 3 year-long blocks of study with the learning outcome of each year being:

Year 1, or Level 1	Acquisition of techniques
Year 2, or Level 2	Application and development of the techniques
Year 3, or Level 3	Performance, using the techniques

Using this as a rough overview of the training structure will help the focus on course and subject content and for the students to understand what is expected of them over the study period.

If the course you are planning has a maximum duration of 2 years, the answer is not to omit a complete Level, rather, deliver Level 1 in the first year (over two semesters), Level 2 in the first semester of the second year and Level 3 in the final semester of the course. Alternatively, all six semesters can be delivered through the addition of a summer semester to the academic timetable, enabling the students to have a complete 3-year degree delivered in two.

23.3 Acquisition of Techniques

Technical development in performance takes time. Jumping straight to performance with no foundation of performance technique in singing, dancing or acting has shortcomings. For example, in singing, there is no point having 64 songs in your portfolio if you don't have the technique to sing one of them well. So, in setting up your new course, there is no point in moving straight to performance and performance values if the students have not learned and secured techniques in singing, dancing and acting first.

On many occasions I have seen students performing to a paying audience too early in their studies. There is a problem with this. People choose to study because they want to learn, and in the performing arts it's essential to gain solid performance techniques before trying to break into the business. Students usually enter a course with their own bag of bad habits, poor or non-existent performance techniques and interesting ideas of 'how to perform'. That's why they want to study: to lose poor habits and gain correct knowledge. If, after only a short period of them being introduced to new and correct techniques, they are put under the 'spotlight' to a paying audience, they will invariably revert back to where they feel safe, which makes the last series of weeks somewhat redundant. Is the premature exposure to the paying audience more of a financial one for the institution rather than what is actually best for the student?

The same can be said for students in the early stages of their study wanting to go to 'open' auditions. It is worth asking them why they want to reveal themselves only half prepared? Audition panels will readily remember that first impression, which is very hard to shift. On many occasions I have heard casting directors say... 'No, I don't want to see that person again, I've seen them before and I don't think they are good enough'. This is an appropriate comment if the original audition was of a recent graduate but if the audition was before studying or in the early months of a 3-year course it makes all the subsequent hard work and development pointless.

My advice to students is: do not reveal yourself too soon and with only part of a technique. Wait and make sure that the 'first impression' is the best it can possibly be. If you are not successful at getting the part after all your learning and preparation, it is not because you didn't have the skills to do it: you most probably didn't match what they were looking for. But, having given your best possible performance, will certainly lead to your details being kept on file and your performance being remembered.

23.4 Course Content

Assuming the course is being delivered over 3 years, firstly deliver the core subjects over Level 1 and Level 2 in addition to some specialised, focused, small-scale performances and then deliver the larger productions at Level 3.

Each week, over four semesters at Levels 1 and 2, the students should be taught the following core music theatre subjects:

1. Acting

    (a) Voice and Speech

2. Singing, music and musicianship

    (a) Ensemble
    (b) Solo
    (c) Music Theory

3. Dance

    (a) Jazz
    (b) Tap
    (c) Ballet
    (d) Movement

In addition to these subjects, there needs to be the opportunity for the students to apply the content of class work to performance. One of the most successful ways of bringing the techniques taught in class into their performance is to provide 'Performance Workshops', such as the following:

Semester 1	Song and Dance
Semester 2	Modern Text Play
Semester 3	The Classical Musical
Semester 4	The Modern Musical

As an ideal, the time percentage given to the core subjects and 'Performance Workshop' each week should be:

Acting	20 %
Voice and Speech	10 %
Singing, Music and Musicianship	20 %
Dance	20 %
Performance Workshop	30 %

The next section will look at the core subjects before explaining the performance workshops.

23.5   Core Subjects in Levels 1 and 2

The core subjects should ideally be delivered each week throughout Level 1 and Level 2. The aim of these subjects is to progress the student to an advanced technical standard, equip them with a wide repertoire, give them a strong level of fitness and physical agility, and provide the student with the tools to be able to communicate both text and song to an audience through a believable performance.

In looking at the core subjects, I will focus on each of the areas for a moment, mainly to give you points to consider when planning a structured course of lessons and what ideally should be the learning outcomes.

23.5.1   Acting

Crucially, the music theatre performer needs to be a strong actor. If you as the course creator know that acting is not your area of expertise, find someone with the requisite skills to take these courses. It is not important at all for the tutor to know about Musical Theatre; they are there to teach the students to act. The sequence of acting classes should explore, develop and produce a believable, emotionally rich dramatic character. Over 2 years of classes, the students should be challenged with a variety of demanding texts, characters and situations. These classes are normally taken in groups, once a week throughout the semester.

23.5.2   Voice and Speech

Students should explore, develop and realize their individual speaking voices. They should have a practical understanding of how to use the breath and body correctly, the tools to produce sounds and pronunciation within text and the ability to apply the skills to accent and character demands. Again, these lessons are taken in groups with an experienced voice and speech teacher once a week throughout the semester, but may be contracted to the weeks prior to a presenting a performance workshop.

23.5.3   Singing, Music and Musicianship

Through both ensemble and solo singing classes, students should develop practical knowledge of how to use the voice safely and manage its ongoing care. They should, through exercise and song, begin to apply correct vocal techniques to their singing and build on this throughout the course.

One-to-one lessons are recommended in recognition that each student requires individualized development on their instrument for at least the first 2 years of the degree, as each voice is unique. Each student will present with different vocal faults, which require an individual approach in diagnosis and pedagogical strategies. Singing teachers experienced in teaching crossover classical and popular music techniques are best suited to teaching musical theatre. By third year, lessons may diminish in length or number and instead support the development of roles or songs for the student.

Through the ensemble classes, students will develop their singing and musicianship skills in harmony, unison, dynamics, blend, style, diction and energy. They will learn how to conserve their voices, to develop voice care strategies and to sing a range of repertoire that will challenge and develop their musicianship skills.

Music Theory. Think what the students will need to be able to do both throughout the course and after graduating. They will need to be able to learn new repertoire, practice and memorize work covered in a music rehearsal, be able to communicate with the Musical Director using 'musical' language and be able to understand and mark their scores with note changes and music instructions. Possible areas of instruction might include basic keyboard skills, sight-reading music, the acquisition of scales, modes and key signatures, rhythm and meter, and aural skills. Obviously these subjects can be expanded on if time permits. However, basic musicianship should be the bare minimum of their theory knowledge, with perhaps the opportunity to develop skills in key transposition and modulation, song-writing and part-writing for voice and keyboard.

23.5.4   Dance and Movement

This should be a practical development of the technical skills and performance required in Jazz, Tap and Ballet. The outcome should be a performer who has the technical and expressive ability to dance to a musical theatre standard. They should have acquired knowledge of how the body and muscles work and their safe use. There needs to be classes in all three, delivered in a vertical stream, so that first year students who are admitted with a high degree of skill in dance can dance in the top class while those who have been admitted with few dance skills can develop at a gentler pace. It is recommended that a team of experienced dance teachers with specific skills in each area take the classes.

Movement classes may either be delivered weekly or in regular blocks (say 1 or 2 days each semester). Whilst these classes will, at times, be script related, they should also encourage and develop the actor's freedom to role-play using both the study of children and animals. They should explore the energy needed to fill an empty space and gain the confidence to do so whilst being both physically still and energised motion. Movement classes may include Introduction to Clowning and Circus techniques. Guest tutors are often ideal for these types of classes.

Fig. 23.1 Black box theatre
at the Musical Theatre
department, Queensland
Conservatorium, Griffith
University, copyright 2014.
(Used with permission)

As with all of the classes and Performance Workshops (with the possible exception of one-to-one singing lessons) students should develop a strong ability to work within and small group or large ensemble. They should also learn to give and receive constructive feedback to/from their colleagues. They must, at all times, be in an environment where they can 'play' – as training performers they need to let go of their inhibitions and not be judgmental of others in order that they can truly jump in and tackle what is being asked of them, with no reservation or hesitation. It is ultimately the responsibility of the Principal or Director to make this part of the course philosophy.

23.5.5 Performance Workshops

Firstly, these opportunities are not productions, but workshops. There is no reason for these to be large-scale events, costing considerable amounts of money. They should be shown in a small space with whatever set is available, such as a few chairs, a couple of rostra blocks, or a table. A black box theatre space is ideal but not mandatory. A black box is an unadorned theatre space with the walls painted black and a simple lighting and technical rig, with moveable sets and seating arrangements. Black boxes are commonly used in experimental theatre but are most commonly used in university settings because of the relative ease of staging student productions (Fig. 23.1).

The emphasis must be on the students' acting and performing skills and not on a highly polished, expensive production. Costumes should only be what the students can find themselves. The budget sheet should be not far from zero for production costs, because any money spent on lighting, set and costumes is money that could have been spent on teaching. This is not to advocate that these elements are not important: they are, but just not in Level 1 and Level 2 'Performance Workshops'. It must be about the students' development and not the end result.

Casting should be used to challenge the students at these levels. Do not play safe with typecasting. Audiences should be kept to a minimum, with perhaps fellow students at Level 1 and family and friends at Level 2, and any audience should be well briefed that the work they are about to view is a work in progress and not a finished product, hence the title Workshop.

So, with this in mind, let us now discuss four possible 'workshop' ideas.

23.5.6   Song and Dance

Working with a Musical Director and a Choreographer, this should be a practical exploration and development, culminating in a presentation of singing and dancing through various musical theatre styles and the introduction to understanding what is required from them to work as part of a company. As a suggestion, you might want to choose several full company numbers to work on. These could be: '*Who Will Buy?*' from the musical *Oliver*, the title song from '*Oklahoma*', '*One Day More*' from *Les Misérables* and '*Aquarius*' from the musical *Hair*, for example, and '*Luck Be A Lady*' from *Guys and Dolls* for the men and '*My Body*' from *The Life* for the women.

Although these are only possible suggestions, they are very good choices for the development of performance skills. In addition to company numbers, there should be opportunities for students to work on ensemble repertoire for two or three people (duets and trios), which will help them deliver a more exposed performance. Possible suggestions for repertoire include: '*Wheels of a Dream*' from the musical *Ragtime* (one man and one woman), '*Sun and Moon*' from the musical Miss Saigon (one man and one woman), '*My Friend*' from the musical *The Life* (two women), '*What Would I do?*' from the musical *Falsettoland* (two men) and '*Sue Me*' from the musical *Guys and Dolls* (one man and one woman).

By working as a member of an ensemble, students will learn the importance of arriving to each session ready to work with their homework memorized, and with an attitude of openness and willingness to learn. Colleagues and peers will soon notice if they are not achieving this and, as peers are wont to do, will help that person to develop a more professional attitude.

23.5.7   Modern Text Play

Working with a director, this play should have been written post-1945 and may be in any accent. As with Song and Dance, it must involve the whole group of students and be worked on, over the semester, towards a performance. Finding a play to fit exact student numbers is often very difficult, therefore it is usual for students to share parts at this stage. For example, two women may play the same part.

One starts and then around half way through she hands over the apron to the next woman and so on.

For music theatre one of the most important things to remember is that the students need to develop as actors. So, by picking a good script and having the very best director will encourage them to really develop in this area of performance. In my experience, prior to studying, the only text many students have been exposed to has been within a musical. By removing the tunes, some find this quite a challenging project at first. Suitable plays include: '*Blackrock*' (Nick Enright 1992), '*Road*' (Jim Cartwright 1986), '*Angels in America*' (Tony Kushner 1993) and '*How to disappear completely and never be found*' (Fin Kennedy 2005).

23.5.8   The Classical Musical

Working with a Director, Musical Director and Choreographer, this is the first time the students are required to draw together all their skills through a full length musical. During Level 1, they worked on bringing the techniques needed for singing and dancing together, and then the play allowed them to develop their acting skills. Now, in Level 2, they should be ready to apply all three skills to their work. This is where the term 'triple threat' comes from – the performer who can act, sing and dance. As with the previous 'Workshops', it is intended students will study, rehearse and present the musical to a small audience. The Classical Musical should be chosen to be suitably challenging for the students and, as with the play, may require a double cast or role sharing. The term Classical Musical refers to musicals written roughly prior to 1955. Possible choices could include: '*Babes in Arms*' (1937), '*Anything Goes*' (1934), '*My Fair Lady*' (1956), or '*Oklahoma*' (1943), for example. This 'Workshop' will require them all to focus on the legit (legitimate) singing work covered in their singing lessons during Level 1 along with stylized dancing.

23.5.9   The Modern Musical

Working with a Director, Musical Director and Choreographer, students further explore the skills required to act, sing and dance through a modern piece of musical theatre. Over semester four they study, rehearse and prepare for presentation to an audience a workshop version of a musical. The term Modern Musical refers to musicals written roughly after 1955. Depending on the student's level of dance, possible pieces could include: '*West Side Story*' (1957), '*Little Shop of Horrors*' (1982), '*Fame*' (1988). '*Rags*' (1986), '*Personals*' (1985), for example. This workshop should, as with the previous ones, challenge their boundaries in acting, singing and dancing. Double casting may also be required here to give all students an equal opportunity to perform.

23.6 Equal Opportunity

It is essential that all students be provided an equal opportunity to perform in their 'Performance Workshops'. It could be argued that Student A is not good enough so they should only be in the chorus, but they were accepted into the course by audition and are paying the same fees as the other students, and therefore deserve an equal chance to perform a major role. People develop performance skills at different speeds. If they have been shown to be weak at acting during the Modern Text Play it does not mean they should not further develop this skill in the Classical Musical. Having said that, casting should not be setting the student up to fail by putting them in unrealistically challenging roles. Casting should be based on a benchmark that the student can reasonably reach by the end of the rehearsal period.

The easy option would be to hide them away at the back, reducing their performance opportunities. As an educator, my preference is to pull them to the front and help them work through their difficulties, and support them to success. Having said this, there may be the occasional student who, for whatever reason, does not reach the mark or take the course seriously. After all options have been exhausted, the best approach in dealing with these students who have failed to improve is to remove them from the course, hopefully by helping them find other areas in theatre where they are more suitable, if they so wish.

23.7 Level 3 – Performance Using the Techniques

At this level the focus should be on performance. Exposing the students to how it is in the business will assist them in the transition from student to working performer. If the timetable allows, an ideal model is for them to rehearse, full time, with a Director, Musical Director and Choreographer towards a performance to the paying public in a fully equipped venue. Subject to finance, my suggestion would be to do a minimum of three productions over the year (roughly equating to 8 weeks rehearsal and 2 weeks in the theatre for each production). Possible productions might include:

Production 1	Full-scale musical
Production 2	Smaller-scale musical or play
Production 3	Showcase

The order of productions 1 and 2 may be reversed.

Level 3 is the stage where students should hopefully be ready to make the jump from a more forgiving studio audience to an unforgiving paying public, including industry professionals. The option to start with a full-scale musical or a smaller production is entirely down to your own preference, schedule, theatre availability, however, the showcase should be the last event and used, by the students, as the springboard into the business.

The showcase should primarily be intended for industry professionals such as agents, casting directors, producers, and writers, to introduce the student cohort.

The content of this production should be a mixture of monologues and small group scenes, solos and duets and company musical (song & dance) numbers. These should be seamlessly linked together to create an equal opportunity for the students to showcase their skills. It must not show what the students cannot do (or have difficulty doing) but show them at their absolute best.

This production is NOT the time to challenge the students but to celebrate their unique skill sets. Keep the show short. A length of between 60 and 80 min is best because industry professionals are there to look at the students, their performance ability both as a soloist and within an ensemble, and to decide if they fit into their portfolio of clients. Industry professionals want performers to be good, as they will be future employers of your students. In the case of the showcase, they are often willing the students to do well. Don't allow this individual audience to become a confidence stumbling block for your students.

The showcase should have at least two different audiences. It is not advisable to mix them up. A midday performance is ideal for industry professionals to attend during their working day, and should not be too full of over-excitable family and friends. Well-meaning family and friends can get in the way of why the professional audience is there. Leave that for another performance opportunity. Do all that you can to make the showcase as productive and enjoyable for the industry professionals–offer them some food before the show, choose a performance space that is easily accessible for them and that is quick to get to. They are viewing this during the working day, and time out of the office for an agent is time away from them finding work for their clients. Most of all, with the Showcase, use it as the main tool to proudly display all the amazing work you, your staff and students have done over the 3 years.

Throughout Level 3 (Semesters five and six), core subjects should be offered as support for the productions when required, for example: singing lessons/coaching may be required to assist the Musical Director with the score, or the voice and speech teacher may be required to assist with any accents required.

It is also advisable that, during Level 3, possibly between productions, students receive lectures on marketing, audition techniques, Curriculum Vitae preparation, career development, taxation and other requirements of being self-employed, guest lectures with agents and talks with working performers about the business.

23.8   Assessment

Assessing performance students can at times prove troublesome because it is subjective. For the core subjects taught over Levels 1 and 2 it is important for you to agree, with your staff, what the students are expected to achieve through the semesters in each of the subjects and make sure this is clearly identified to the students. A mark given at the end of the semester for continuous development is usual, however, continuous assessment throughout the semester may be an alternative assessment to the summative mark. This marking process leads to a detailed report of each student's development.

Music Theory is not marked using this assessment method because it is, and should be, marked by results in regular tests/examinations.

Performance Workshops should be marked by both the creative team working on the showing, and personnel not connected to the production who only mark the performance, producing two sets of marks (process and performance). These two sets of marks should be weighted according to the position of the showing in relation to where it is within the course structure. For example, the marks for Level 1 Song and Dance should be weighted more towards process and less on the end result (performance) and the Showcase (in Level 3) should have a weighting on performance.

In addition to the continuous assessment of core subjects, and the process/performance method used to mark Performance Workshops, there should be further opportunities for students to show their skills during Levels 1 and 2 and have them marked. These could include singing concerts, with each student presenting a solo song to the panel/small audience; dance showings, with students working towards a presentation of a Jazz, Tap and Ballet routine; speech presentations where students perform a rehearsed speech to a panel/small audience. Be creative in what you show and when in the year you show it. However, be careful of two things. First, do not overload the students so that they feel they are unable to fully reach the level they want to achieve because they have too many balls in the air to juggle at one time. Second, observe the golden rule of not showing too much, too soon. Keep it small, keep it safe and allow them to grow using their newfound techniques.

23.9   Discipline

One thing not discussed yet is discipline! Music theatre is a disciplined art form. If the curtain goes up at 7.30 then, the curtain goes up at 7.30. It is essential that discipline be instilled in all members of the course, staff and students equally. Any student or staff arriving late to a class means the curtain has gone up, their understudy is on and they will not be allowed to perform. You can transfer this into the day to day running of the course by insisting on punctuality from the entire team. If a class is due to start at 10.30 for example, then it really must start at 10.30 and anyone arriving late should not be allowed to join in but made to sit and watch.

In dance, it is potentially physically damaging to a student if they arrive late, miss part of the warm-up and go straight into the routine, as it would be for a singer to jump straight into a song having missed the warm-up. Set this expectation from day one so that professional behaviours and dispositions become another aspect of the course deliverables. The purpose of a course is not just to give techniques and performance opportunities but to produce 'good' company members; that is, someone who is punctual, prepared, hard-working, committed, supportive, and enjoyable to be with. In fact, as a guide, ask yourself would YOU want to employ them? If the answer is no, then do something about it.

When it comes to attendance, I have always used the phrase 'Each day you miss, everyone else gets a day better'. So, using this as a question, the students ask themselves if they do not feel like getting out of bed, usually works better than an alarm clock or a bucket of water! Obviously, there are times when there is no option but to stay away and that is fine; just make sure the students know that it is their responsibility to catch up on any work missed.

23.10   Performance Opportunities Outside the Course

Students sometimes ask if they can perform outside of their course during their study, for example: being involved in an amateur production; singing with a band; or auditioning for a professional show. My usual response is no. Not during Levels 1 or 2. The reason for this is that they should not show themselves off and be judged too soon before their technique has become engrained and secure. Also, old techniques may be perpetuated at these times, and starting a busy week with an exhausted body and voice is not recommended for students.

During Level 3, and especially towards the latter end of the year, students are permitted to audition for professional work and, if they are successful in gaining a part, which results in them having to leave the course early, then the course has succeeded. Remember, treat ALL the students equally and with the same rules, and you should not come up against too many problems.

We now have the course shape; the course content, the Performance Workshops, the assessment of work and the professional behaviours expected of the students so let us look at staffing the course.

23.11   The Teaching Team

The thing I have found most difficult in all my years of setting up and running courses is finding the right team to deliver it. A course is only as good as the staff teaching it, likewise a lengthy and detailed course document is worthless if the interpretation is not done by passionate and skilled teachers.

Invest in getting the right team: it's not easy, but will certainly be one of the best investments you make. A healthy balance between permanent and visiting staff is essential to ensure the students have continuity for continuous development of technique and the flexibility to be able to work with and interpret a variety of approaches.

As a basic minimum requirement, the regular staff should deliver the core subjects and visiting staff should deliver the Performance Workshops and the productions at Level 3. Having said this, teaching staff frequently enjoy the opportunity to get out of the classroom and be creative through a Performance Workshop: this is perfectly acceptable. However, if the teacher of Jazz Dance choreographed all the musical showings, then the students would miss out on learning from other choreographers and will only have one contact for their 'little black book'. So, use the Jazz teacher for the Jazz core subject teaching and maybe one or possibly two Performance Workshops only.

The advantage of having a constant flow of visiting people is that there is new energy, ideas, skills and contacts breathing life into the course, students and regular staff.

23.12 Little Black Book

The student's 'little black book' is basic information about professional industry people they have worked with or met who they may consider to be of possible use in the future. Throughout their studies and into their careers, the students should keep details of:

Names of who they meet
Circumstances of where they met them
Contact details if possible
Student opinions on the professional
What the professional likes/dislikes regarding performance (e.g.: likes a lot of physicality or hates eye contact being made)

This 'book' can then be used to remind themselves of a person they have worked with previously if they are due to meet or audition for them again in the future. This is an important and frequently overlooked tool. If a student can go into an audition and the person says, 'haven't I seen you before?' and the student can recall where they met, this goes a long way in rekindling a former working relationship, which may help them in securing their next role.

So, the course is now prepared and ready to go, but we have no students yet.

23.13 Auditioning

Remember, do not expect perfection – perfection possibly does not need to study! Be clear about what you are looking for. Look for a strong level of ability or potential in two out of the three core areas of acting, singing and dancing. Take your time when holding auditions and get to know as much as you can about each person you see. Allow enough time in the schedule to work with them as sometimes it takes auditionees a while to control their nerves. Be supportive and inform them that you want them to be good, for without students, you do not have a course.

Having been at the cutting edge of musical theatre training for over 26 years, and seeing (on average) over 1,600 applicants each year, I have developed a format to audition a large number of applicants, which allows the time to individually work with the ones in which I am interested.

The two-part audition works well for the purpose of auditioning potential students. During the first part, applicants start their audition in a group dance workshop where they warm-up, take part in technical exercises, then learn and perform a short routine. Following dance, each student presents to the panel a prepared song of their own choice from the musical theatre repertoire. The song should allow them the opportunity to act through the text as they perform it.

On average, as a guide, you could see 50 applicants in a morning (group dance and solo song). At the end of Part 1, the panel will have seen each student dance, heard them sing and watched them act through the presentation of the song, which makes it easy for them to create a shortlist of applicants to invite into Part 2. For the applicants not invited into Part 2, the audition ends.

During Part 2, the much smaller group of applicants present two prepared monologues and perform their second solo song. It is at this point that you can work and chat with them to find out if they will be suitable for the course and whether the course will give them what they are looking for. As previously mentioned, create a safe and friendly environment for people to work in. Ask yourself, would you want to audition for this panel?

23.14 Facilities

We now have a complete course and a cohort of students but nowhere to house them. The cost of setting up appropriate facilities can be high. Keep the health and safety of your students and staff at the forefront of any plans or developments, including soundproofing and sprung floors for the dance classes. One of the most important and often skimmed over facility for the training of music theatre is suitable flooring for dancing–bad floors can lead to all sorts of injuries for the students and staff. For 100 students there needs to be several singing teaching studios all containing good quality electronic keyboards, a mirror, a desk and chairs; at least 3 large dance studios with sprung floors, barres, working sound systems, mirrors and curtains; at least 2 black boxes in high rotation and each with quality pianos; one dedicated room with AV equipment for lectures and music theory classes; a staff room; a private meeting room; a student lunch room and study space; toilet and shower facilities; internet and phone connectivity; and an attractive foyer for those companies who will be utilising the black boxes as performance spaces.

Remember, amazing facilities do not make a course. Dedicated, passionate staff and committed, enthusiastic students make a good course.

23.15 Conclusion

I started this chapter by stating 'There is a common misconception that by offering some singing, dancing and acting classes you have provided all it takes to produce a successful performer in music theatre'. It really does take a lot more!

Reference

Griffith University. (2014). *Queensland Conservatorium black box theatre*. Brisbane: Griffith University.

Chapter 24
Training the Singing Researcher

Scott D. Harrison

Abstract The post-graduate vocal pedagogy space in has enjoyed a gradual resurgence in the past decade. Pedagogues and practitioners with a desire to reflect, improve their credentials and contribute to the body of knowledge and practice have undertaken formal studies to enhance the standing of the profession. This chapter examines this development, focussing on the types of study available, the contributions made and the implications for further development in the future. Study options range from short courses dedicated to furthering the understanding of science, through to full-length doctoral programs that focus on deep reflection on repertoire, technique, genre, sociology and psychology. Drawing on several case studies, the purpose of the chapter is to expose the options available and open up the dialogue as to what the future might hold for enhancing pedagogical practices through post-graduate study.

Keywords Singing researchers • Case study • Research skills • Career aspirations • Research training

24.1 Introduction

The study of singing in tertiary institutions is largely focussed on performance outcomes, particularly in the undergraduate years. As students progress through to the final stages of their undergraduate studies, many are confronted with the reality of the need for further options post-graduation. For some, this comes in the form of on-the-job training in the workplace (indeed, many students undertake singing and teaching work throughout the course of the their degree), for others the option of

S.D. Harrison (✉)
Queensland Conservatorium, Griffith University, 140 Grey St,
South Brisbane, 4101 QLD, Australia
e-mail: scott.harrison@griffith.edu.au

S.D. Harrison and J. O'Bryan (eds.), *Teaching Singing in the 21st Century*,   399
Landscapes: the Arts, Aesthetics, and Education 14, DOI 10.1007/978-94-017-8851-9_24,
© Springer Science+Business Media Dordrecht 2014

postgraduate study looms large. This advanced study typically falls into training in performance, pedagogical training and research pathways. The former tends to extend the undergraduate experience described in the Schindler chapter above: intense training in singing, coaching, stagecraft and languages. The area of pedagogy is broader in scope, though a surprisingly limited number of offerings are available for students wanting to undertake this pathway; similarly there are a small number of research programs that give opportunities for deep reflection on aspects of performance and pedagogy.

This chapter largely focuses on research programs and the preparation of singing researchers.

24.2   Background

While acknowledging that some singers have no formal tertiary training in singing, the literature to date suggests that undergraduate degrees do little to prepare musicians for life beyond the tertiary music school. Lanskey (2001), writing about approaches to addressing this at the Guildhall School of Music and Drama notes that 'it was demonstrated to students that learning to teach is not just peripheral to a performer's development, but can grow from one's instrumental development and be central to it. Then as students start to think like teachers they are be better equipped to answer issues emerging in future performance situations, and those related to teaching' (9). At a similar time, Royal Conservatoire The Hague instigated the research project *The Teacher of the 21st Century*. This project began by envisaging the artist's needs and societal role by the year 2015 taking into account social trends of the time (Smit 2003, 2–5). Burt and Mills (2006) found that Conservatoire students '... are often assumed to spend their days in solitary practice undertaking what might appear a highly 'restrictive' approach to their learning.' Students at the Royal College of Music commented that they would probably do some instrumental teaching when they graduate and that they would most like to teach in a conservatoire (see Mills 2006). Similarly, students at Queensland Conservatorium Griffith University ranked performing or composing as their main career choice, followed by producing, then teaching in a university or college (Lebler et al. 2008), as represented in Fig. 24.1.

More recently Bridgstock (2011, 21) suggests that

> Students can enter creative courses with only the vaguest of notions regarding what they will do afterwards, influenced by unrealistic or romantic ideas about the world of work in their fields, or with an overly rigid, foreclosed and unrealistic career identity. These career identity issues influence their engagement with learning during the course, and also their career-related behaviours afterwards.

The desire for conservatoire students who see teaching as a second string career option (after artistic pursuits), and the stated preference for that teaching to take place in the tertiary setting creates an interesting conundrum for the training of singers. The days of are iconic performers automatically taking teaching posts in

Career aspirations

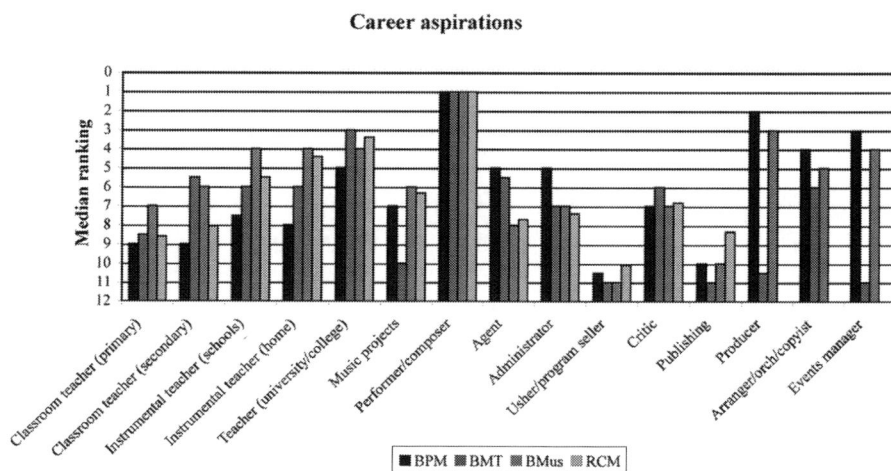

Fig. 24.1 Career aspirations of students at QCGU

conservatoires are not over, but the signs are there that it will not be long before the pendulum swings to permit only those with doctoral degrees to teach in music institutions. Graduates report that there is a lack of emphasis on research and its potential benefits during undergraduate years '… It was all about playing, and we were told that our four year BMus degree was equivalent to an Honours degree … this turned out not to be the case' (Draper and Harrison 2011). Furthermore, the participants in Draper and Harrison's 2011 study comment that despite having a masters degree, there was no background in formal, high level research … 'my research has also consisted of writing and playing music over the years rather than being involved in the world of academic writing about music … I was fully ignorant of the entire context and current philosophy in qualitative research' (89).

Even the doctoral degree, however, does not guarantee a post in a university. As Shaw (2011) found 'In 1973, 55 % of PhD recipients had tenure track positions within 6 years of earning their PhDs. In 2006, merely 15 % of recent graduates found themselves in this position'. Draper and Harrison (2011) concur:

> For the musician, however, jobs, salary and promotion are seemingly unrelated to motivation to undertake a doctoral program…there is little need for a research degree to play in an orchestra, or band or any music role outside academia. Inside academia, the reverse applies.

This presents an interesting conundrum. The motivation for students pursue further studies was pursued in a study reported by Harrison (2011) who found four major reasons student giving for undertaking research: love of learning; access to resources connection to the subject matter and altruism. Returning to the study of Burt et al., it seems clear that after 5 years graduates are still not interested in making money but few see the need for further study (see Fig. 24.2).

In sum, the performer who wants to enter the academy requires doctoral level qualifications that may or may not guarantee an academic post. Students who complete an

Hopes after five years

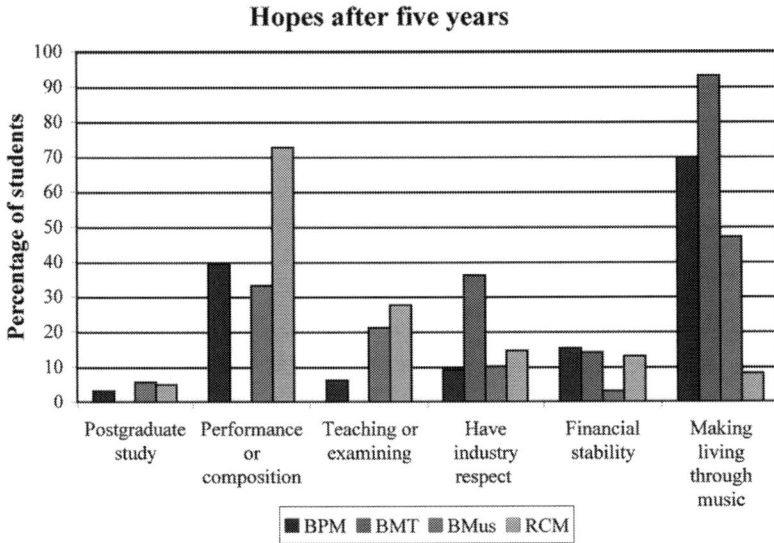

Fig. 24.2 Career hopes of students 5 years after graduating

undergraduate degree are ill equipped to begin the process of obtaining the requisite skills to enter a graduate program of study, or necessarily have interest in so doing.

24.3 Developing Researchers

It would appear that, in order for the academy to be maintained, and for the singing field to be progressed, a concerted effort is required to engage students in research prior to completing their undergraduate program. This approach, combined with developing research skills embedded in both traditional doctoral programs and practice-based programs forms the basis for the discussion below.

24.3.1 Generic Research Skills

A debate exists about how best to engage researchers in the early stages of their training. For many, the emphasis is on understanding the historical basis for research – learning the ologies: musicology, ethnomusicology, ontology and so on. For the pragmatists, the emphasis is on doing: have students undertake a project and learn on the job. This second approach appears to be more engaging for the beginning researcher but it implies that knowledge of conceptualising, reading, data gathering, analysing and writing will be taught along the way. In taught programs (honours,

Masters, DMA), this is possible but in 2–3 year supervised research programs (PhD and MPhil), the approach is more ad hoc and relies on the skills and attributes of the supervising team (Hamilton and Carson 2013). As with the teaching of singing, the research training process involves bringing out the best in the student, modelling behaviours and not necessarily structuring projects to a one-size fits all approach (Emmerson 2013). Towl and Senior (2010, 301) refer to this as the need for 'authentic training in the form of hands-on research experience.' In the process, they note that students are aware of the importance of the mentor/mentee relationship in becoming researchers post-graduation.

24.3.2 *Research Skills for Singing Researchers*

A range of idiosyncratic issues faces the beginning singing researcher. The first relates to the age-old problem of the voice being located within the body and related, the reliance on singing development being linked to physical development. Singers often present for undergraduate study with less developed musicianship and academic skills than instrumentalists. While this is not universally the case, singers can be strong in oral presentation but lack the writing skills required for traditional research.

A second related concern is that knowledge of physiology is often lacking, even though the instrument is primarily a physical one. The same could be said of instrumentalist, and their need to understand biomechanics, the interaction of their instrument with the body but for singers the need for understanding stance, breath, resonance and articulation, as well as musical style, is more acute.

Musical style, as evidenced by the preceding chapters, is diverse for the singer, singing teacher and singing researcher. There are a small number of singers of (and studies into) cross-over styles however the one instrument needs to be capable of either maintaining one style consistently or of quickly adapting between styles. This becomes a problem for the singing researcher who needs to both hone their field of work, yet make it palatable for the broader community.

One final concern relates to the plethora of pedagogical approaches and camps in the singing teaching community. From purely science-based to purely metaphor-based teaching, perhaps no other teaching fraternity has so many disparate approaches. If research is based on validity, reliability and generalizability, then each of these concerns raises issues for the training of singing researchers. What follows are a series of cases in which these four concerns are addressed and illuminated.

24.4 Cases

Use a case-study methodology (Stake 2005), the cases below are drawn from research students with whom the author has worked. In some instances the cases are made up of an amalgam of several students with similar needs and/or subject matter. All cases have been allocated a pseudonym, and the accounts are reconstructions based on real life experiences including supervision notes, emails and recollections.

24.4.1 Rick

Rick is primarily a speech pathologist who came to the university to study aspects of breathing. His ongoing practice as a consultant, teacher, opera singer and cathedral chorister meant that the project was deeply embedded in practice. Strictly speaking, Rick was originally attempting to document and justify his existing practices, and to gain the approval of the academy to continue. Rick chose to take a traditional PhD, rather than a practice-based Doctor of Musical Arts (DMA), in part because the status of the DMA in relation to the PhD was unknown at the time of his commencement. While his own practice definitely influenced the project, the core elements involved scientific measurement and teacher judgments on the efficacy of the breathing technique he was seeking to investigate.

Rick came to his studies with considerable experience in the workplace, and a solid undergraduate training in both his domain of knowledge and in articulating thoughts about his practice in oral and written forms. He was initially allocated supervision with expertise outside the area of his study, and without doctoral qualifications. This raises the issue, identified by Draper and Harrison (2011) and Hamilton and Carson (2013) of the lack of appropriate supervision in emerging areas in performing arts research. Research will, of course, always be in an emerging area but because of music's late entry to the academy in many western settings, this issue has been further exacerbated. In the mid 2000s, the conservatoire was largely staffed by performer/teachers (see Schindler 2010) and the number of staff qualified to supervise doctorates (i.e. doctoral qualifications and supervision of doctorates to completion) was minimal. Rick's study involved quantitative and qualitative measures, with a slightly stronger emphasis on the quantitative aspects. This created further complications for Rick as he attempted to analyse data without adequate expertise with this material. Eventually, a supervisor from outside the conservatoire (with little music knowledge) was engaged to assist in this analysis.

As a fulltime worker, another challenge was to find the time to work on his project, to meet with his supervisory team and to allocate adequate resources in the completion phase of the project. A busy practice, an ongoing performance schedule and international teaching commitments further slowed progress on the dissertation. A positive to emerge from the busyness and international connections was that examiners were relatively easy to find, and those that were nominated had a very secure understanding of the content of the final document. Rick proudly claims that he managed his doctoral studies with minimal supervision. His candidature involved no less than five supervisors, and while he never had more than two at any given time, the institution was fortunate that the skill set he brought into the degree was sufficient to carry him through the higher levels of study required and that he was able to negotiate through the supervision changes with relative ease.

Ultimately, Rick's project moved the field forward enormously, and the marrying of the disciplines of speech pathology and singing has enhanced understanding of studio practice of breathing and articulation. Rick has become the acknowledged international expert in this area. He undoubtedly would have achieved this without a doctorate, but the imprimatur of academy gives his work weight in both medical and musical environments. This was, of course, his stated original intent and, unlike most doctoral projects, he stayed true to this aim throughout the rather elongated course of his studies.

24.4.2 Sue

Sue is an experienced singer, with an interest in what many would describe as the heavier repertoire – Mahler, Wagner, Puccini and the like. The project centred on songs of death – not exactly light-hearted material – but importantly, assessment of the performance of the work featured strongly in the project design. This is not to diminish the written aspects of the project. A balance between the creative work and the written documentation was arrived at relatively early in the project through the engagement of three supervisors with complementary skills: an opera singer, a pianist/musicologist and a singer/researcher/academic manager. In addition, as this was located in a practice-based program (DMA), the responsibility for the overall management of the project rested with a program director who shared the oversight for this, and other similar projects across the 3 years of candidature.

This combination proved to work reasonably well. The opera singer brought an enormous wealth of experience from the international stage to the teaching of technique and style. The pianist was involved as both accompanist and mentor, bringing enormous musicological depth (partly as a result of his own training at one of the world's top universities). Both these supervisors empathised as performers, while the third brought an overarching and policy management perspective to the work. The use of three supervisors is not common practice in this particular practice-based program. An hour per week per supervisor is allocated; and this becomes an expensive operation – more so than teaching one-to-one undergraduates. This project was perhaps akin to the undergraduate training model for singers, with each area contributing to the overall finished product (see Harrison 2012; Harrison and O'Bryan 2012). At the doctoral level, however, the candidate is potentially preparing for an academic career – one that would require the teaching of singing, and other skills such as research methods, musicology, ensemble skills and the like. The investment of more than the standard two supervisors was considered worthwhile because of the potential of the candidate to take her place in academe post doctorate. In addition, the idiosyncrasies of the project demanded a range of expertises were committed to the project from the outset.

Furthermore, the normal requirement is that all assessment takes place at the end of the degree, and this was problematic for a candidate presenting three song cycles as a major aspect of the assessment. The solution was to present 'works-in-progress' so that there was a record of the process, and to present the three cycles again for summative assessment at the end of the degree, along with the research document. This idea was borrowed from the visual arts, where the final exhibition and exegesis come together for live examination by the same panel. The outcome saw the true marrying of formative and summative assessments, along with a genuine combination of performance and text-based work, not unlike that which is now expected in research evaluation exercises across the globe.

The challenges in the research training of this candidate are largely logistical. Resources for supervision are one consideration, and there are also the additional issues of staging performances to consider. Fortunately, having a team member in the supervisor/accompanist role mitigated many of the concerns somewhat, but venues, technology to record the performances and audience involvement all brought their own complications.

In the final analysis, the project was truly practice-centred: an almost perfect fusion of performance and high quality written documentation disseminated to relevant audiences in both a time-released formative fashion and a final summative assessment. The appointment of an appropriate supervisory and management team was the lynchpin to the success of the project overall.

24.4.3 Darren

Darren is working the contemporary field with emphases on pedagogy, theology and liturgy. The original intent of Darren's project was to provide a practice-based guide for his studio teaching, and for similar studios. Darren came into doctoral studies with a Masters degree, and though it was in a related subject area, it did not incorporate research methods and extended writing. Perhaps more importantly, he brought deep knowledge and experience of his domain, which covered studio teaching, theological training, liturgy and performance. These 'street-skills,' while not recognised by the university, proved to be invaluable aspects of his study as he negotiated his methods and design. The project design involved survey and interview. His unfettered access to the community, while acknowledged at times as ethically awkward, meant that he was able to gain insider knowledge that ultimately contributed to both his study and to the field at large. The main issue was the write-up and dissemination of his findings. His oral expression was generally adequate and his command of genre-specific language secure. Through his private studio, album recordings, seminars and church-based service, he had a strong local profile and was in the midst of developing a national profile at the time of his enrolment. The shaping of the project into a work that would be both acceptable in the academic setting and relevant to his audience was, at times, challenging. The supervisory team, one of whom had almost no knowledge of the content but brought vast experience as a supervisor would could 'finish' students, worked together on micro and macro aspects of the written document to bring it to fruition – ahead of the university-proscribed end-date. This was made possible, in part, by the use of a wiki for tracking the progress of the dissertation. Through the wiki, earlier iterations of each chapter, the conversations about the decisions made, and the tracking of progress on the project was possible. A distinct advantage of this tool was that it true blended learning was enabled. Darren lived locally, and the team met with him face-to-face quite frequently. However, when the inevitable periods of travel for either candidate or supervisors threatened to interrupt the flow of the project, the wiki provided a constant; grounding to which all members of the team could relate.

Another revelation in Darren's research training was the provision of teaching about web-based approaches to dissemination. Darren was reluctant to engage in this compulsory aspect of the course-work, but found it to be a revelation in improving the reach of his work to a wider audience. In the immediate post-doctoral phase, his work attracted international interest, both within his community of singers and in the broader research environment. The degree of success of this strategy could be put down to engagement with social networking site, and the writing of a blog throughout his candidature.

For Darren, the main concerns were ethical dilemmas dealing with cohorts of whom he had intimate knowledge in order to gather data, and in providing him with the most appropriate skill set in writing and structure. The team provided the latter through the micro/macro approach to the dissertation and through a combination of domain knowledge and research training knowledge, delivered in part through web-based technologies.

24.4.4 Peter

Peter is a distinguished performer of early music who came to the doctorate with a masters degree (including an extended dissertation later converted to a book) and a healthy discography of more than 30 commercial recordings over a 15 year period. Peter originally enrolled in the practice-based Doctor of Musical Arts (DMA), but later transferred to the PhD. This was made possible through outstanding results in the coursework for the DMA, and through his demonstrated ability to critically analyse and write up findings from the works he was performing.

Peter's case, like Sue's, demonstrates the constant dichotomy of the artist in the academy so eloquently highlighted by Schippers (2007) and Borgdorff (2010). The recognition of high-level performance as research is a major achievement for the conservatoire, however Peter still had to prove himself in academic terms in order to be admitted to the PhD. Unlike Sue, the doctorate itself did not involve perfor- mance per se, but it would not have been possible for the dissertation to be written without deep experiential knowledge of performing in diverse settings. His supervi- sory team included a musicologist with early music experience, and a singer with a similar career history to his own. As a distance candidate, Peter did not make use of the online facilities employed by Darren: supervision took place via telephone and email, with occasional face-to-face visits. Peter's course work gave him a good understanding of research method and design, and his prior degrees helped with the final writing stages. The training provided to Peter largely revolved around clarity of writing, and establishing the veracity of his claims for the analysis of his chosen works. He also undertook interviews as part of his data collection, and the project therefore provided him with access to the leading conductors and singers in his field. Peter was a highly motivated candidate, one who could see an end goal in academic life, while tempering that with the knowledge that his study was going to enhance his practice, and the practice of others in similar fields.

A number of presentations, papers and book chapters along the way helped to ensure that his standing was such that his full-time academic career commenced immediately after graduation. As Shaw (2011) and Draper and Harrison (2011) noted above, Peter is fortunate to find himself in the 15 % of graduates with work in academe, and he has demonstrated that it is possible for the marriage of art and the academy to blissfully co-exist. It should be noted, though, that Peter is in his early forties, and moved cities several times in order to achieve this goal. So, while the marriage may be blissful, the courtship was not straightforward.

The underlying message in Peter's case is that personal tenacity, a rare combination of academic ability and high performance skills shared with willingness to accept mobility as a consequence of progression can reap rewards. The research training aspects of Peter's situation were largely driven through a staged progression of activities beginning with a masters degree, undertaken simultaneously with high-level performance, entry to a professional doctorate and finally to a PhD and a position in one of the top universities in the country. It would appear a seem-less career to the outside observer, but the success was largely born of person graft and determination.

24.5   So What?

The illuminative cases described above reveal a number of responses to the issue of research training for singers. The primary revelation is that research training is largely contextual and relies on the research students and their supervisors to muddle their way through the agreed projects. The determination and motivation of the individuals involved play a major role in the timely completion and ultimate success or otherwise of the research degree. There are, however, a number of other take-home messages apparent in the cases.

Firstly, that online technologies can assist in developing the project while it is in progress, and in disseminating the outcomes. Darren's project was particularly strong in this area, and this approach resulted in an expeditious outcome with wide impact.

Secondly, that interdisciplinary components are a common feature of many research programs. Because of the broad nature of singing activities, the potential for research incorporating fields such physiology, anatomy, history, sociology, performance practice, musicology, theology and related area is enormous. This presents resourcing and methodological challenges that are mainly overcome through institutional interactions, and the appointment of appropriate supervisory teams.

Thirdly, that the marriage of art and academia is possible through the careful construction of programs of study that incorporate performance and other aspects of musical endeavour. While Sue's case is probably the most obvious example of this, each project relied on the tacit knowledge of researcher/performer to bring the final outcome to fruition.

Finally, that multi-exegetical formats are emerging as the norm. Doctoral studies can presented as DVDs, websites, performances and written work and the written component doesn't necessarily enjoy the predominance it once did. For musicians, this is right and proper – that the artwork is centrally located, examined and agreed to as being of doctoral level.

The research space in music, and in singing in particular, has much to offer the singing teaching community. This entire volume is comprised of those who have devoted their lives to enhancing the knowledge about singing, and developing the art of vocal pedagogy for future generations. The critical point in this process is how the training takes place in masters and doctoral programs, and this surely provides the profession with new ways of thinking about singing and teaching singing.

References

Borgdorff, H. (2010). The production of knowledge in artistic research. In M. Biggs & H. Karlsson (Eds.), *The routledge companion to research in the arts* (pp. 44–63). Abingdon: Routledge.

Bridgstock, R. (2011). Skills for creative industries graduate success. *Education & Training, 53*(1), 9–26.

Burt, R., & Mills, J. (2006). Taking the plunge: The hopes and fears of students as they begin music college. *British Journal of Music Education, 12*, 51–73.

Draper, P., & Harrison, S. D. (2011). Through the eye of a needle: The emergence of practice-led doctorates in music. *British Journal of Music Education, 28*(1), 87–102.

Emmerson, S. (2013). No two are the same. In S. Harrison (Ed.), *Research and research training in music and music education*. Dordrecht: Springer.

Hamilton, J., & Carson, S. (2013). *Supervision and scholarship*. Paper presented at effective supervision of creative arts research degrees symposium, Brisbane, 8 February 2013.

Harrison, S. D. (2011). There's a fine line between pleasure and pain: Why students enrol in higher degrees in music and music education. *Australian Journal of Music Education, 1*, 68–77.

Harrison, S. D. (2012). Letting go: An auto-ethnography of supervising the research higher degree in music. *International Journal of Music Education, 30*(2), 99–110.

Harrison, S., & O'Bryan, J. (2012). *One-to-one teaching: Parallels and paradoxes in approaches to studio teaching and supervision*. Paper presented at the reflective conservatoire conference, London, 19 March 2012.

Lanskey, B. (2001). *Minding the gaps: A synopsis of the processes involved in revamping the Guildhall's B.Mus. 4 year instrumental teaching curriculum*. Newsletter ½ Research Centre in Learning and Teaching Guildhall School of Music and Drama.

Lebler, D., Burt-Perkins, R., & Carey, G. (2008, July 20–25). *What the students bring: Examining the attributes of commencing conservatoire students*. Paper presented at the 28th world conference of the international society for music education, Bologna, Italy.

Mills, J. (2006). Performing and teaching: The beliefs and experience of music students as instrumental teachers. *Psychology of Music, 34*(3), 372–390.

Schindler, M. (2010). Performers as teachers: A tertiary perspective. In S. D. Harrison (Ed.), *Perspectives on teaching singing: Australian pedagogues sing their stories*. Brisbane: Australian Academic Press.

Schippers, H. (2007). The marriage of art and academia: Challenges and opportunities for music research in practice-based environments. *Dutch Journal of Music Theory, 12*(1), 34–40.

Shaw, K. (2011). The PhD problem: Are we giving out too many degrees? Accessed 19 May 2011 from http://arstechnica.com/science/news/2011/04/the-phdproblem-what-do-you-do-with-too-many-doctorates.ars

Smit, N. (2003). *The teacher of the 21st century*. The Hague: Royal Conservatoire.

Stake, R. (2005). *The art of case study research*. Thousand Oaks: Sage.

Towl, M., & Senior, C. (2010). Undergraduate research training and graduate recruitment. *Education and Training, 52*(4), 292–303.

Chapter 25
Postlude: The Future of Singing Pedagogy

Scott D. Harrison and Jessica O'Bryan

Abstract As we noted at the beginning of the volume, the vocal mechanism has not changed since the documentation of singing pedagogy began 500 years ago. The diversity in musical styles and the pace at which technology has advanced has certainly changed, but we remain relatively uninformed about the origins of singing and the ways in which environment, culture and society interact to influence vocal production and interpretation. In this volume, we have sought to provide an avenue through which practitioners, early career and experienced researchers have attempted to improve the knowledge, understanding and appreciation of diverse music styles. We have also sought to find ways to apply this new pedagogical knowledge for the benefit of our students in the future.

Keywords Teaching singing • Pedagogical diversity • Future perspectives

25.1   What Does the Future Hold?

25.1.1   Increased Diversity

Diversity, as we noted earlier, is a touchstone for the unfolding century. As a result, the scope of the book is necessarily vast, and we trust that you have read those aspects that are relevant to your own research, teaching and performance. In one sense, there is contrary information provided within the volume. This is because our singing practices are bound up in the peculiarity of each voice and the particular environments and cultures in which the learning takes place. For example, the gospel

S.D. Harrison (✉) • J. O'Bryan
Queensland Conservatorium, Griffith University, 140 Grey St,
South Brisbane, 4101 QLD, Australia
e-mail: scott.harrison@griffith.edu.au; jessica.obryan@gmail.com

S.D. Harrison and J. O'Bryan (eds.), *Teaching Singing in the 21st Century*,
Landscapes: the Arts, Aesthetics, and Education 14, DOI 10.1007/978-94-017-8851-9_25,
© Springer Science+Business Media Dordrecht 2014

setting is rather different from the classical singing studio or the music theatre training environment, with its emphasis on the triple threat performer. Each has its own heritage, its own set of expectations and its own expected outcomes. Within these settings, the individual voices have their own pathologies, unique timbres and personalities. There can be no one-size-fits-all approach, and this volume has sought to celebrate that diversity.

25.1.2   Interface Between Content and Pedagogy

Each voice is unique: age, gender, personal circumstances can mean that the sound can vary from day to day, week to week. This, along with the environment and culture, helps to drive the pedagogical approach. In some respects, the learning of music is unique because the content determines pedagogy. The content of the singing lesson – whether it be a group setting, a individual singing studio or a community choir – responds to and embraces these variables, and the technical work and repertoire help to create the learning activities. As in most learning settings, no two lessons will be the same. Because of the individual nature of each voice, this is perhaps more so in the singing environment.

25.1.3   The Role of Research

Until the last part of the twentieth century, music research has been perceived as an irrelevant pastime, relegated to those who have long since given up the idea of a performance career. The advent of practice-based research has meant that research is now interwoven with practice. It reflects on practice, informs practice and facilitates changes in practice. As Harrison and Draper (2013) note, a key issue in music research is that tacit knowledge and processes are articulated in an artistic setting. Furthermore, the dissemination of that knowledge is suited to the context and audience for which it is intended. For singing teachers, this may be contrary to the accepted position. Singing teachers typically have much tacit knowledge but would not consider this to be research. The documentation and dissemination of that knowledge is of utmost importance if our discipline is to advance. In the digital age dissemination can take many forms, of which some are approachable to both the singer and singing teacher. Examples include weblogs, videos, workshops and text-based outputs such as magazines and volumes such as this. In that sense, we trust that the volume has opened the door to singing teaching studios as a means to enhancing practice. This volume should not be viewed as a closed document: rather it is the beginning of dialogue about how singing might be taught in the future.

25.2   Where to from Here?

We have a responsibility to encourage unorthodoxy, welcome diversity and embrace openness to create the cultural and structural conditions to kindle (or re-kindle) learning. Music teaching has tended to focus on the one-to-one setting and while this has value, there is an opportunity to open studio doors to embrace the concept of 'tramping' (Price 2013). For singing teachers, this doesn't just mean expanding the learning of the individual. It mitigates against silos and allows students the 'right to roam.' Studio teaching is the cornerstone of music learning, and should remain so. However, there is much to be learned from the cross-fertilization that occurs when studio teachers delve into each other's practices and students share the experiences they have gained from such exchanges. On the role of research Edison (1999, n.p.) noted:

> I have not failed. I've just found 10,000 ways that won't work. When I have eliminated the ways that will not work, I will find the way that will work … If I just get to see you do it and be inspired, wonderful.

Frequently, this is the experience of the singing teacher. We attempt many different ways to unlock the potential in our students, and when we find it, the student and the teacher are both inspired and invigorated by that moment.

25.3   In Conclusion

While we may never know the origins of singing in all its complexity, we do know it to be part of the human condition. As folk singer Pete Seeger notes:

> Songs are funny things. They can slip across borders. Proliferate in prisons. Penetrate hard shells. I always believed that the right song at the right moment could change history. (1955)

The singing teacher in the twenty-first century is therefore charged with an awesome responsibility. We hope that this volume has helped teachers and singers to execute songs in such a way that change is possible – through all forms of song. This is, after all, what singing is all about.

References

Edison, T. (1999). *The papers of Thomas A. Edison: The wizard of Menlo Park, 1878*. Baltimore: Johns Hopkins University Press.
Harrison, S., & Draper, P. (2013). Evolving an artistic research culture in music: An analysis of an Australian study in an international context. In S. Harrison (Ed.), *Research and research education in music performance and pedagogy*. Dordrecht: Springer.
Price, D. (2013). *OPEN: How we'll work, live and learn in the future*. London: Crux.
Seeger, P. (1955). Testimony for the house of Un-American activities committee, August 15, 1955.

Manufactured by Amazon.ca
Bolton, ON